本书获外交学院"李嘉诚学术基金"资助

简明西方文化史

A Concise Textbook of Western Cultural Studies

张晓立　编著

图书在版编目(CIP)数据

简明西方文化史/张晓立编著. —北京:北京大学出版社,2013.4
(21世纪英语专业系列教材)
ISBN 978-7-301-22318-5

Ⅰ.①简… Ⅱ.①张… Ⅲ.①英语—高等学校—教材②文化史—西方国家 Ⅳ.①H31

中国版本图书馆 CIP 数据核字(2013)第 057687 号

书　　　名：简明西方文化史
著作责任者：张晓立　编著
责 任 编 辑：李　娜
标 准 书 号：ISBN 978-7-301-22318-5/H·3281
出 版 发 行：北京大学出版社
地　　　址：北京市海淀区成府路 205 号　100871
网　　　址：http://www.pup.cn　新浪官方微博:@北京大学出版社
电 子 信 箱：zbing@pup.pku.edu.cn
电　　　话：邮购部 62752015　发行部 62750672　编辑部 62759634　出版部 62754962
印　刷　者：北京虎彩文化传播有限公司
经　销　者：新华书店
　　　　　　650 毫米×980 毫米　16 开本　23.5 印张　760 千字
　　　　　　2013 年 4 月第 1 版　2019 年 5 月第 2 次印刷
定　　　价：58.00 元

未经许可,不得以任何方式复制或抄袭本书之部分或全部内容。
版权所有,侵权必究　举报电话:010－62752024
　　　　　　　　　　　电子信箱:fd@pup.pku.edu.cn

《21世纪英语专业系列教材》编写委员会

(以姓氏笔画排序)

王立非	王守仁	王克非
王俊菊	文秋芳	石　坚
申　丹	朱　刚	仲伟合
刘世生	刘意青	殷企平
孙有中	李　力	李正栓
张旭春	张庆宗	张绍杰
杨俊峰	陈法春	金　莉
封一函	胡壮麟	查明建
袁洪庚	桂诗春	黄国文
梅德明	董洪川	蒋洪新
程幼强	程朝翔	虞建华

Table of Contents

Two Prologue Poems ··· 1
Preface ·· 3
Introduction ·· 5

PART ONE
  Articles Selected for Specific Topics, Themes and Events ··············· 17
An Opening Article ·· 19
Unit One
  1. Cultural Theory and Cultural Studies ··· 24
  2. Culture, a Broad Humanistic Concept ··· 27
  3. History, a Riddle for Humans ·· 39
Unit Two
  1. West Is Not a Directional Concept Alone ······································ 45
  2. Western Culture and Its Deep Implications ··································· 47
Unit Three
  1. Religion, a Human Spiritual Pillar and Faith ·································· 53
  2. Judaism, a Mother Religion of Some Religions ····························· 57
  3. Christianity, a Spiritual Rock of the West ····································· 67
  4. Religious Reformation, a Milestone Event
     that Paved the Way for the Rise of
     Western Capitalism and Power ··· 80
Unit Four
  1. Roman Empire, the First Western Power ······································· 89
  2. Hellenistic Civilization, a Beauty of the West ······························ 104
  3. Greek Mythology, a Treasure of the West ···································· 110
Unit Five
  1. Colonialism, a Global Expansion Idea ·· 124
  2. Capitalism, a Crazy Devil for Angels ·· 130
Unit Six
  1. Renaissance: a Turning Point for the West ·································· 147
  2. The Enlightenment, an Age of Soul Liberation ···························· 157
  3. Post-Modernity (POMO), a Rebellious Movement ······················ 173
Unit Seven
  1. Commercial Revolution, in Hot Pursuit of Wealth ························ 179
  2. Industrial Revolution, a Driving Force for Society ······················· 186
  3. Scientific Revolution, a Miraculous Instrument for
     the Rise of the West and Its Leadership ······································ 208
  4. Science and Scientific Spirit ·· 218

5. Information Revolution or Explosion ··· 230
Unit Eight
   1. A History of Economic Ideas, a Key for Wealth ···················· 234
   2. A History of Political Philosophy of the West ····················· 256
Unit Nine
   1. The Culture of the United States ·· 261
   2. A Book Excerpt Illustrating Cultural Contradictions of Modern Capitalism ·········· 263
   3. Introduction to and Postscript of a Book Entitled
      American Culture since WW II by Paul Levine ················· 265
Unit Ten
   An Understanding of Western Culture ······································ 271
Unit Eleven
   The Millennium of the West, a Golden Age? ····························· 285
Unit Twelve
   An Introduction to the Clash of Civilizations ····························· 287
Postscript
   Western Culture: a Beast and a Beauty? ··································· 292

PART TWO
   Special Case Study ··· 295

PART THREE
   Exercises for the Textbook ·· 329

Appendix I ··· 351
Appendix II ·· 365
Postscript/Final Remarks for the Whole Textbook ··························· 367

Two Prologue Poems

Essay on Man

By Alexander Pope[①]

All nature is but art, unknown to thee;
All chance, direction, which thou canst not see;
All discord, harmony not understood;
All partial evil, universal good;
And spite of pride, in erring reason's spite,
One truth is clear,
Whatever is, is right.

A World in a Flower

By William Blake[②]

To see a world in a flower,
And a heaven in a sand;
Hold infinity in the palm of your hand,
And eternity in an hour.

[①] Alexander Pope (21 May 1688—30 May 1744) was an 18th-century English poet, best known for his satirical verse and for his translation of Homer. Famous for his use of the heroic couplet, he is the third-most frequently quoted writer in *The Oxford Dictionary of Quotations*, after Shakespeare and Tennyson. This poem is taken from his famous series poem entitled *The Essay on Man*. The *Essay on Man* is a philosophical poem, written in heroic couplets and published between 1732 and 1734. Pope intended this poem to be the centerpiece of a proposed system of ethics that was to be put forth in poetic form. It was a piece of work that Pope intended to make into a larger work; however, he did not live to complete it.

[②] William Blake (28 November 1757—12 August 1827) was an English poet, painter, and printmaker. Largely unrecognized during his lifetime, Blake is now considered a seminal figure in the history of both the poetry and visual arts of the Romantic Age. His prophetic poetry has been said to form "what is in proportion to its merits the least read body of poetry in the English language". His visual artistry has led one contemporary art critic to proclaim him "far and away the greatest artist Britain has ever produced". Although he lived in London his entire life except for three years spent in Felpham he produced a diverse and symbolically rich corpus, which embraced the imagination as "the body of God", or "Human existence itself".

Preface

I am honoured and delighted to have this opportunity to write a short Preface to *A Concise Textbook of western Cultural Studies*. This is Professor Zhang Xiaoli's first book published in English and its fame has been much enhanced for the fact that the book was published by such a prestigious publisher in China as Peking University Press, which definitely underscores its academic significance. Like all the best textbooks it has its origins in teaching and learning and was first conceived while Professor Zhang Xiaoli was teaching a course on the history of western culture at the China Foreign Affairs University.

Although the book's title refers to western Cultural Studies, it subject matter is much broader than this; offering, as it does, a fascinating survey of the development of key aspects of western culture. The range and significance of the material will be of immense interest and use to students and academics working in this area.

I think it is very important that books of this nature are published. Besides their academic value, they also have the essential function of increasing intellectual exchanges between China and the West. There can be little doubt that this book will make a valuable and important contribution to an increase in mutual understanding.

Professor John Storey
Director of the Centre for Research in Media and Cultural Studies
University of Sunderland
The United Kingdom of Great Britain and Northern Ireland

Introduction

This concise textbook of western cultural studies of introductory nature is prepared for the course of the same title in an attempt to provide the course participants and interested readers with a handbook simple and concise enough to present a learning guidance for this field so that they can read something very basic, yet essential to the topic under discussion. The history of western civilization is a huge and magnificent topic as the time period it covers is so long and the contents it includes are so rich and diverse. It is almost impossible even to browse such a huge topic within such a short period of time as is allowed by this course. Therefore, the conductor of this course has compiled the following brief textbook in the form of an anthology of the history of western civilization with an attempt to provide the learner with an effective and facilitating vehicle to learn something about western civilization with a clearer orientation. The history of western civilization can be summed up in a numerical order from one to ten as follows, which can provide a concise and panoramic picture of the outline of western civilization evolution. Moreover, some 30 odd articles are presented within this textbook so that the readers can read them to form a rough idea of the key concepts and vital issues concerning the history of western civilization and some of the current issues related to the West. It must be admitted that in terms of culture, the influence of the West chiefly represented by American pop culture is quite powerful nowadays with its cultural products extending to and even occupying much of the global market in many developing countries and has exerted tremendous impact upon younger generation of different countries. The West has occupied and firmly consolidated the commanding heights of culture with its economic power and military strength to promulgate an idea that the western culture represents the orientation of a global culture. The world is still very diverse culturally and it still remains to be seen if one culture of a region (the West) can replace cultures of other regions (the West versus the rest). For sure, it is human nature to see something diverse and colorful rather than something homogeneous and monotonous. No doubt, the western culture has made its remarkable contributions to the human civilization with scientific inventions, organizational ideas and institutional designs, which, however, does not qualify it fully as a flagship or beacon for global cultural development. Cultural diversity must be maintained and cultural dominance should be shunned. If tolerance is one of western cultural traditions, this tradition should be carried out in the cultural exchanges between the East and West to establish a harmonious and tolerant world in which strong cultures and weak ones, mainstream cultures and marginalized ones should co-exist in peace and in mutual respect.

The following part of this textbook is compiled in a way so as to provide a precise and concise account of the major themes, features, figures and events of the western culture as arranged in a numerical order from one to ten. The themes and events are not necessarily listed or arranged according to their chronological order therein mentioned or discussed.

ONE dominant and persistent tradition: Judeo-Christian Tradition that has sketched and highlighted the very core value and cultural feature of the West

It can be safely claimed that the whole development and evolution of history of western civilization is chiefly based upon the Judeo-Christian tradition, without which it definitely has lost its religious validity and spiritual buttress. Judeo-Christian tradition has exerted tremendous and unparalleled influence upon the metamorphosis of the western culture both at religious and secular levels. Almost every big historic event has something to do with this religious tradition.

In a sense, the history of the West as a whole is one of Christianity amplified, verified, modified and justified or even nullified. Many of the core values of the West can find their ancestral roots in the Bible. An in-depth and thorough analysis of western civilization would be impossible without some basic understanding of Judeo-Christian tradition in general.

TWO chief propelling and guiding ideological ISMs: Capitalism and Colonialism that have heralded and strengthened the global expansive basis of the West

The rise, expansion and flourishing of the West has been propelled and pushed by these two key ISMs to a great extent. What happened in 1492 (Columbus Ocean Voyage and Christian seize of Granada) heralded the beginning of the rise of the West by opening an age of colonialism which very much facilitated and consolidated the overseas expansion of the West, which in turn decisively guaranteed and secured its global hegemonic position it still has held up till now. Capitalism, rising hand in hand with colonialism, which defines and governs its political, social and economic structure, has replaced feudalism to become a dominant ideology of the West. As a fundamental and legitimate social system of a new ruling class, capitalism is in a sense an ideological and cultural symbol and synonym of the West. Although colonialism is already gone in form as one of the propelling forces, economic globalization is said to have appeared as a new type of colonialism for the western expansion or even occupation of the global market. In this process, capitalism remains a driving force of the West in maintaining its global dominance.

THREE milestone and historical movements: Renaissance Movement, the Reformation and Enlightenment Movement that have shaped or defined the nature and the course of the West

It is indisputably argued that three major movements have significantly and decisively shaped the developmental course of the West and their argument is largely true. These three movements have presented some milestone significance for the orientation of the western civilization. First of all, the significance of Renaissance signaled the departure from the Medieval Ages of the West, marking the beginning of a historic shift from theological rule and religious dominance over the society to a more humanistic approach in people's life attitude and way of thinking. By breaking down the hegemonic rule of the Church in people's daily behavior and acts, Renaissance did so much in freeing people from theological bondage to aspire for personal expression and individual liberation. Renaissance had dawn an age in which people began to be concerned with more of their life for today than after-world. It is with the age of Renaissance that equal, if not more attention, was given to people's secular happiness and dignity than to divine pursuit. Human power and glory were promoted and promulgated. It is an age in which giants were needed and produced. It is from the age of Renaissance that the idea that Man, instead of God, became a center of the universe began to prevail.

The Religious Reformation Movement, through coherent and concise logical rationalization of capitalist behavior in terms of religious explanations, provides divine justification for the secular progress of capitalistic spirit, once and for all removing the religious barrier and block for the rapid and massive development of capitalism and greatly enhancing its social and economic influence in the West. For the first time, the pursuit of material wealth, hereto despised and shunned for religious reasons, became a glorious goal of human beings. Furthermore, one's material status became a sign of divine grace and one's wealth, a symbol of faith. Material pursuit and religious piety have been perfectly and adeptly combined through Protestant Reformation of traditional Christianity. Capitalism, under the coat of religious belief, has embarked upon the world arena with full religious glorification and justification. Unlike traditional Christianity that greatly blocked the development of capitalism, Protestant

Reformation eased and smoothed the way for the world-wide expansion of capitalism under the holy name of God, spreading God's gospels and acquiring as much wealth as it is able to at the same time.

The Enlightenment Movement is by nature an intellectual and cultural movement aimed at expanding and promoting humanistic traditions initiated by Renaissance Movement and eliminating ignorance, intolerance and lack of scientific awareness. By and large, it is a continuation of the previous two movements in a way that it has held high the flag of rationalism, humanism and liberalism, providing the ideological and cultural framework for the budding capitalistic social structure and paving the way for the smooth and upward development of industrialization that served as an economic basis for the rise of capitalism as a new dominant class on a global stage. Enlightenment as a movement is historically significant in that strongly influenced by the rise of modern science and by the aftermath of the long religious conflict that followed the Reformation, the thinkers of the Enlightenment were faithfully devoted and fervently committed to secular views based on reason or human understanding only, which enlightenment representative figures hoped would provide a strong basis for beneficial changes affecting every area of life and thought. The enlightened understanding of human nature was one that emphasized the right to self-expression and human fulfillment, the right to think freely and express one's views publicly without censorship or fear of repression from any authority. The slogan of the Enlightenment Movement is to think freely and independently, regardless of any authority or institution, religious or secular alike. The Enlightenment Movement has created an intellectual and cultural tradition in the West that final judgment of truths lies in the hand of science and reason instead of mighty power of God alone as was the case before.

FOUR epoch-making revolutions: Commercial, Industrial, Scientific and Information Revolutions that have chartered the course of the western Civilization

It goes without saying that something that can rightly and justifiably be called a revolution must be revolutionary by nature or in essence, which can cause fundamental and structural change in the field it has affected. This definition of revolution applies to these four revolutions in the history of the West as each of these four revolutions not only heralded a new epoch, but also brought fundamentally structural changes to human society. The Commercial Revolution responded to the basic desires of human beings for material wealth through commercial activity made possible by free trade first within a region and then extended to global scale. The Commercial Revolution is on the one hand the pure manifestation of human material desires massively released and on the other prompted by the previous great geographical discovery that opened and chartered a new ocean trade and commercial route between the East and West, rapidly enhancing the global influence of capitalism and greatly facilitating material accumulation worldwide. The Commercial Revolution, according to historians, preceded or rather was succeeded by yet another epoch-making revolution, the Industrial Revolution. The process of the Industrial Revolution, which first began in England and culminated in the USA in the West, spanning about two century, is still going on nowadays worldwide. Many emerging economies today like China, India, etc. are being industrialized now. Industrialization is a revolution that has led human society to an industrial age in which driving force for productive progress is propelled by a new mode of production based on machinery, factory system, technology and economy of scale. The Industrial Revolution would have been impossible without scientific breakthroughs that have witnessed a revolution in science itself. Spirit of science is one of the outstanding features of western culture, which defies authority and verifies truth through experiments. The Scientific Revolution, represented by such scientific giants as Copernicus, Galileo, Newton, Darwin,

Kepler and Bohr, to name only a few, broadened horizon of humans about the nature and world around them. Scientists regard as their life purpose to explore and discover natural law and secrets to bring their benefits to human daily life. From religious superstition to scientific way of thinking, human beings experienced a great leap forward in their mental reasoning, thus opening another field for human beings to understand this world and beyond. The latest revolution that first occurred in the West and that is taking place in some other regions in the world is what is precisely labeled as Information Revolution prominently characterized by the breakthroughs and improvement of information technology based upon telecommunication and micro-electronic technology, which have led to the wide and massive use of computers and the Internet. The Information Revolution is thus called as it has brought revolutionary changes to the way people live and work. For the first time in human history, information can be transmitted instantly to almost every corner of the world and geographical distance has been made irrelevant. People's life and work have been arranged accurately and arbitrarily via digital control and computerized management. In sum, these four revolutions, which all occurred first in the West, have once and for all changed the way people think, work, live and entertain. Their significance can never be overestimated.

FIVE distinctive periods of human social evolution in the West: the Age of Antiquity, the Middle Ages, the Pre-modern Period, the Modern Period and the Post-modern Period

This division of social developmental stages into five distinctive periods are manifested by the outstanding characteristics each of them demonstrated. Until the end of Antiquity, human society was largely one by nature of nomads and agriculture with people relying on nature for basic subsistence in terms of material well-being. Due to backward means of production, people were subordinated to natural power and their life quality was at the mercy of nature. The mode of production during this period of time was primitive and low-efficient with people being unable to shake off the bonds of natural disasters and adverse climate elements. The advent of the Middle Ages witnessed the dominance of theological power governing human activities in the West. The Middle Ages, also called "the Dark Ages", was a period of time in the West in which ignorance, religious intolerance, prejudice and spiritual oppression were rampant, marking a pretty bleak chapter in the history of the western culture. The darkness of the Medieval Ages was cleared by the dawn of a new idea that human beings, instead of God, should occupy the central stage of human society, posing great challenge to the then theological authority represented by the Church with a strong inclination of admiration of the ancient Greco-Roman cultural heritages that glorified the creativity of human beings rather than the splendor of a divine power. A epoch-making movement called Renaissance ended the Middle Ages and brought the West into a new period hereto referred to as Pre-modern Age. It was during this period of time that many significant historic events took place that prompted a process in which the establishment of Europe as a center of political and economic influence for human civilization began. With capitalism and colonialism starting to develop in full swing around the end of 17th century, the Modern Age began, which lasted for about two centuries until the end of 19th century when capitalist class took hold over the society in the West. The modern era in the West was a period of time full of conflicts, changes, transitions and transformations, in which the West experienced the completion of industrialization and urbanization and in which the whole world suffered from the two world wars. The most significant historical change is the establishment and consolidation of western influence and to some extent hegemony on the development course of human beings with the rise and fall of British Empire to be finally replaced by the United States of America whose dominance over the global affairs has still continued. In the post modern age, the United

States of America has led the world by entering so-called the post-industrial age or information age based upon knowledge economy. In terms of cultural as well as social evolution, the present-day world is faced with different social types. Some countries, especially countries in the West are already in the post-modern age while some other countries like emerging economies are still in the process of industrialization and urbanization. Still some other countries like African countries in particular have not yet embarked upon the journey toward industrialization. The gap between the rich and poor countries, between so-called advanced and backward countries has highlighted the very diverse features of social and economic development in today's world. Development gap in economic growth and social structural transformation reflects the true reality of international community. The sense of superiority amplified by this gap is a clear manifestation of the West to a very large extent that economic globalization currently in full swing around the world implies cultural westernization that holds Americanization as its final and singular standard. The division of social development into these five periods is marked by a constant and continuous shift from nomadic civilization through agrarian civilization and industrial civilization to current information civilization with transformations taking place one after another in economic, social and cultural fields respectively.

SIX pillar and core concepts/themes: Representative Democracy, Market Economy, Rule of Law, Secularism (separation of church and state), Rationalism and Constitutionalism

Throughout the history of the West, some concepts or themes have stood out as being so influential and pervasive that they have governed the mentality and social behavior of the westerners. The early form of democracy can find its ancestral tradition in classical Hellenistic civilization in the political pattern of city-states. Although the connotation of democracy has changed over its evolution, its core idea remains unvaried and basic, which has been reaffirmed through famous remarks made Abraham Lincoln when he expressed his famous statement of establishing a government of the people, by the people and for the people. Market in the first place is product of commercial revolution and its functions go far beyond a marketplace where people engage in trading business. Market has become an economic mechanism that governs economic activities through some basic laws such as supply and demand, competition and valuation. An economic institution based on market principles has become a prevailing and dominant system that has been adopted by almost every country now in the world, albeit with different forms. As one of the three pillars in American political culture (and in some degree in western political culture), **rule of law** is an antithetical political ideal or idea to absolutism or autocracy featured by rule of man. Rule of law is both procedural and substantial through an iron principle and lofty ideal that all is equal before law regardless of one's social status or material wealth. Given the long history of ecclesiastical rule and dominance in the West, it is very significant that **secularism** as reflected by the separation of church and state has eventually prevailed in the West so that capitalism as an emerging ideology can get rid of the bondage of religion to advance without obstacles to become a propelling force for social and economic progress in the West. Secularism has made it possible for people in the West to pursue material wealth without abandoning their spiritual and religious beliefs. Secularism has also freed secular political entity or governance from intervention from any religious force, eliminating the possible appearance of a theocratic state in the West as a modern state institution. **Rationalism**, as opposes to empiricism, in western philosophical tradition, represents the view that regards and stresses reason as the chief source and final test of knowledge and truth. Strongly holding that reality itself has an inherently logical structure, the rationalist asserts that a class of truths exists that the intellect can grasp directly. There are, according to the rationalists, certain rational principles—especially in logic and mathematics, and even in ethics and metaphysics—that are so fundamental that to deny them is to fall into contradiction and confusion of thought. Rationalism is a pillar of scientific spirit which has led the West out of the Medieval ignorance toward an age of reason, which in turn boosted the liberation of productive force. The final result of the long evolutionary process of political system in the West is found in constitutionalism, which is also one of the three pillars in American political culture and of western political culture at large. As a major political form of government in the West, constitutionalism sets the pattern for political rule based upon the supremacy of constitution, which guarantees that governors can't execute their power. without the consent of the governed.

SEVEN pioneering and enduring ideas or ideals: Innovation, Competition, Efficiency, Equality, Justice, Freedom (Liberty) and Social Progress

The West has made its own political, economic and social advancement propelled by these seven pioneering ideas. **Innovation** has been a strong driving force for the West in its scientific, technological and organizational breakthroughs. The current West has found the source of strengths from innovation which is key part of its culture. **Competition** is key element in market economy, a dominant economic form of the West. It is through fair, free and open competition that the best of everything can be produced. In economics, competition can optimize the allocation of productive factors and natural and human resources. **Efficiency**, as one of the core values of capitalism, aims at acquiring maximum output or benefits with minimum input or costs. The most prominent merit of capitalistic mode of production is economy of scale based upon the idea of efficiency that highlights the advantage of capitalism over other types of social and economic system. **Equality** is a long-time ideal of the West given the long period of time of feudalistic rule in Europe with a strong hierarchical social and power order. As the Declaration of American Independence clearly expresses, equality is among the inalienable rights of human beings that can never be deprived or violated. Equality is also one of the three ideals expressed as the motto of French Revolution. **Justice** as part of natural rights of man is a product of modern age and has appeared as an antithetical ideal to some social ills and evils in the early stage of primitive capital accumulation of capitalism. Justice is inherent in natural law principle, which is the foundation of western legal ideas and system. Justice has been upheld as a core value as well as the holy goal of social reform and progress in the West, especially in modern time and it is a continuation of equality which, if strongly promoted through legal procedure, should produce social order and harmony as a logical result. No any social progress can be counted as real progress without element of justice strongly advocated and protected in a society through legal procedures. **Freedom** including personal freedom, political and economic freedom, is basic human nature that should be guaranteed by law. No government, nor any institution, nor any authority shall have any right to infringe upon personal freedom without any legal ground. Political and economic freedom has been written into Universal Declaration of Human Rights as basic conditions for a civilized society. The history of western Civilization is one filled with fierce struggle for individual liberty against totalitarian and autocratic regimes like feudalistic monarchies and arbitrary church authority. **Progress** has been a deeply-rooted idea in the West since early Greco-Roman culture. To every problem, there must be a solution. This is the basic tenet of social progress based upon optimism for human progress at large. The West has had a long tradition of looking to the future and of taking overall social progress as a final judgment of the validity of any human institution. The Progressive Movement in the United States in late 19th century and early 20th century demonstrated this spirit of the West in that it eradicated social ills and evils of any type through political, social and legal measures, paving the way for the coming of a civil society. The Civil Rights Movement in the United States in the 1960's is another clear manifestation of this progressive tradition, eliminating racial prejudice and discrimination and enhancing the holy principle that everyone is equal regardless of their races and ethnic backgrounds.

EIGHT unique history-making events: the Birth, Crucifixion and Resurrection of Jesus Christ; the Crusades; the East-West Schism; Constantine the Great and his Conversion to Christianity; Columbus Discovery of the New World; the Black Death; the Independence of the United States of America and the Explosion of A-Bomb

The birth, crucifixion and resurrection of Jesus Christ may be or should be viewed as the single most important series of events not only in the West, but also the whole world. Without Jesus Christ, there would have been no Christianity, of which there are about two billion adherents worldwide now although they are divided into different denominations. Most of the countries now in the world adopt the **Gregorian calendar**, also called the **western calendar** and the **Christian calendar**. The influence of Christianity upon the West is immense and immeasurable. No wonder some people claim that the western culture is in essence a Christian culture. Christian influence upon political structure, economic system and legal institution is pervasive, persistent and prevailing.

The **Crusades** were a series of religious expeditionary wars blessed by Pope Urban II and the Catholic Church, with the stated goal of restoring Christian access to the holy places in and near Jerusalem. Jerusalem was and is a sacred city and symbol of all three Abrahamic religious faiths, Jews, Christians and Muslims and it is still a contending point and hot spot in today's world. The aftermath of the Crusades sowed the seeds of religious confrontation between Christianity and Islam and a lot of clashes in the name of civilization are in reality religious conflicts that can trace back to the period of the Crusades.

Constantine the Great and his Conversion to Christianity demonstrates its significance by the fact that after his conversion to Christianity, Christianity became a dominant religion in the Mediterranean region, establishing its legal status in Roman Empire. Since this event, Christianity has become a para-official state religion in many countries in the West, consolidating theological control over secular affairs in Europe in general and in Roman Empire in particular. For a long time after that, Christianity remained in this status and its influence extended to almost every corner of a society. With Constantine's Conversion, Christianity completed its own transformation of status from a suppressed religion to a legally official religion in Roman Empire. It is not until the beginning of the Reformation that Christianity began to experience a radical and fundamental metamorphosis. With the Religious Reformation, Christianity as a dominant religion in the West became further divided into traditional Christianity and new protestant denomination that first appeared in Europe and then flourished in North America. Protestant Christianity began to influence some major countries in terms of political and economic development.

The East-West Schism, sometimes known as the **Great Schism**, is the medieval division of Chalcedonian Christianity into eastern (Greek) and western (Latin) branches, which later became known as the eastern Orthodox Church and the Roman Catholic Church respectively. Relations between East and West had long been embittered by political and ecclesiastical differences and theological disputes. Prominent among these were the issues of "filioque", whether leavened or unleavened bread should be used in the Eucharist, the Pope's claim to universal jurisdiction, and the place of Constantinople in relation to the Pentarchy. This Great Schism divided Christianity into two major parts, establishing the current religious pattern in Europe or in the West in general that are still valid today.

It can be safely said that the whole modern world history, not the history of the West alone, would have been totally re-written without **Columbus ocean voyages or expeditions**, under the auspice of the then Spanish Queen Isabelle, over the Atlantic Ocean which led to the accidental discovery of North American Continent. Between 1492 and 1503, Columbus completed four round-trip voyages between Spain and the Americas, all of them under the sponsorship of the Crown of Castile. These voyages marked the beginning of the European exploration and colonization of the American continents, and are thus of enormous significance in western history. It must be acknowledged that history is full of many accidental incidents that have made human history evolve this way than otherwise. Therefore, there is no **IF** assumption or subjunctive mood in history. What would be to happen must have been bound to happen sooner or later. Some people call it oracle while others call it law of universe. It is these accidental incidents that have made history unpredictable, thus challenging and interesting.

The **Black Death** was one of the most devastating pandemics in human history, peaking in Europe between 1348 and 1350. Although there were several competing theories as to the etiology of the Black Death, it has been conclusively proven via analysis of ancient DNA from victims in northern and southern Europe that the pathogen responsible is the *Yersinia pestis* bacterium. Some people say that the Black Death was the first punishment to human beings by early globalization. Like everything that has two sides of the same coin, the aftermath of the Black Death is not negative alone. At least, it purified racial quality and enhanced ethnic immunity via the elimination of the poor, sick and disabled. Evidence shows that European population quality improved through this devastating pandemics.

The Birth of the United State of America opened a new era of human history. Nobody would deny or argue against the significance and importance of the birth of the USA as an independent country in late 18th century, without which the history of modern world must have been totally different or rewritten. The whole world today is still strongly feeling the strong and lingering effect of this historic event as the USA is expanding its national influence globally. The USA presents to the whole world a unique way of social and economic development, which sets a global standard of what is the right way for a strong nation's rise. Even though many of the features of the rise of the USA are exceptional or inimitable due to some insurmountable limitations, the USA does provide the whole world with a possibility that a wonderful dream, no matter how fancy it may be, can come true through human efforts. It is unrealistic for any country to copy without any abridgment success story of American miracle. However, it is nihilistic to repudiate the heritages of the nation-building of the USA for its exceptionalism. A dialectical way of thinking in this regard should be adopted in a comprehensive analysis of the USA, of its successes and failures, of its inspirations and frustrations. In sum, a careful study of America as a relative young and dynamic nation is unavoidable in the exploration of western culture.

The Explosion of A-Bomb, the successive possession of weapons of mass destruction by a few countries in the world and possible proliferation of such weapons in the future are like the opening of Pandora's Box, which has led human beings to a death journey of no return. Human beings, with their intelligence and creativity, have sowed a seed of self-destruction in their efforts to construct a better world by conquering the nature and unfolding the secret of the nature. Atomic bombs, Hydrogen bombs and Neutrongen bombs are called weapons of massive destruction that are able to destroy the whole world a dozen times given their current storages on earth. Peaceful use of nuclear power used to be a nice wish for human beings aided by the scientific discovery of power of nuclear fission and fusion. Weapons of massive destruction are like the Sword of Damocles, forever being able to turn the possibility of human destruction into a potential reality. The creation of A-Bombs is a typical example of modern Frankenstein in which the creator is killed or destroyed by what is created.

NINE great documents/declarations: Law of the Twelve Tables, Magna Carta (also widely known as the Great Charter of the Liberties of England), the Declaration of American Independence, the Emancipation Proclamation, the Communist Manifesto, the Universal Declaration of Human Rights, Yalta Agreement, Schuman Declaration and United Nations Millennium Declaration (MDGs)

Ideas are powerful and they may be even more powerful than material power. Ideas expressed in documents can change the world. In human history, many important documents are so inspiring that they have caused magnificent revolutions. Listed here are nine great and magnificent documents/declarations, each of which has made historic impact upon human social evolution in the West and in the world as a whole. The significance of all these documents/declarations is to be explored through specific recount of the historical background and aftermaths of each of these documents /declarations. They all have something in common, which is that they all have exerted lasting and tremendous influence upon the social development of human beings at large. It should be pointed out that not all these documents/declarations are listed within the context of the study of western culture. Some of them have global significance such as the Communist Manifesto, Universal Declaration of Human Rights, Yalta Agreement, Schuman Declaration and United Nations Millennium Declaration. The reason to extend the significance of these documents /declarations to a global scale is that since 1492, the focus of global importance in terms of political, economic and social development has shifted to the West (European continent first and then to North America). The West has become a dominant force on global arena with its expansive power and influence felt throughout the world. Given the fact that American has become flagship of the West, in a sense, American influence means the western influence which equates global influence. A careful study or review of all these documents/declarations will facilitate a better understanding of the western culture in terms of ideas.

TEN giant figures: Jesus Christ, Socrates, Alexandra the Great, Columbus, Martin Luther, Sir Isaac Newton, Adam Smith, Karl Marx, Abraham Lincoln and Albert Einstein

There are numerous famous people who can be called ones who have influenced history. A rough check of any history book can provide a long list of names, about which well-educated people are supposed to know at least something. It is indeed hard, if not impossible, to single out only ten giant figures in the West. The selection of these ten figures is evidenced by hard facts about their unparalleled contributions to and exceptional influence on the course of the western civilization. There is no dispute to claim that without each of these ten figures, the world we see today would not have been the same. This statement may face a charge that history is made by heroes or gigantic figures. History is a continuous live record of what people think, write, act and vision. These people with their ideas and behaviors and the way they think did make a huge difference for human society in the West at least. Personal role in making history, in transforming society and in influencing common people's attitude can never be overestimated. These people are important as they all belong to a category of founders, initiators and pioneers of certain fields, of certain movements and of certain events that have left inscrutable marks on human history. It is true that this list may be expanded or altered with different preferences or emphasis of different people. It is also true that a longer list must include this short list and some people must always have been on the list no matter what kind of standard is adopted. Gigantic figures are giants because they have made huge influence in history, which is the logic behind the selection of these ten figures as being giant and great.

Double H (Hebraic and Hellenistic Traditions) Assumption in the Studies of Western Culture

In the study of western Civilization, there is a famous Double H assumption, which states that Hebraic and Hellenistic cultures are two cradles or genetic roots of western Civilization. Therefore, to enrich this short and concise anthology, two informative and introductory articles concerning this double H assumption are included to provide the reader with a starting point to search for the roots of western culture. The past 1,000 years or the second millennium from 1000 to 2000 witnessed a shift of focus of human civilization from the East to the West. The famous British magazine *Economist* published a millennium issue toward the end of the second millennium, listing the most important events that occurred during those 1,000 years, from which it can be seen how the West rose and the East declined. A summary of the abundant information about western Cultural History may be brief and far from being exhaustive, serving only as an introductory instrument for a further analysis of western civilization history. A statement as such thus made, it is highly recommended that people who wish to make some investigation of western culture shall begin their interesting and rewarding effort by choosing to read the following articles and information carefully at least once. It is believed that they can beneficially form a basis for the further study of the topic under discussion.

Sixteen Features Outlining Modern Civilization/Western Civilization

Among historians, sociologists, economists and anthropologists, a consensus exists that modern civilization era has begun since 1500, which also marked the beginning of the rise of the West, which in turn has fundamentally changed the way people live, work and entertain. The following sixteen features sum up the way modern civilization/Western civilization presents itself in different fields of human existence.

Sixteen outstanding Nizations or Lizations that have featured modern civilization:

1. Rationalization in people's way of thinking (Modernity and Enlightenment)
2. Humanization in people's way of behavior and their major concerns (Renaissance Spirit)
3. Secularization in people's faiths and beliefs (Religious Reformation)
4. Urbanization in people's way of residence (Industrialization and Mass Immigration)
5. Democratization in organizational structures (Bourgeois Revolution)
6. Legalization in institutional and daily affairs management (Prevalence of Rule of law based upon Natural Human Rights)
7. Industrialization in production of material wealth (technology and mass mode of production based upon the idea of efficiency and professionalism)
8. Commercialization in social activity (Commercial Revolution)
9. Marketization in exchanges of goods and services (Market Economy)
10. Equalization in social status and inter-personal relations (French Revolution)
11. Liberalization in people's pursuit of aims (American Revolution)
12. Segmentation in labor and employment (value of division of labor and law of comparative advantages and core competitiveness of a person and a state)
13. Diversification in ideology and cultural heritages (Principle of Tolerance)
14. Individualization in the expression of human demands (Sign of Individualism)
15. Globalization in people's mobility and scope of activity (Globalism manifested and demonstrated)
16. All is capitalized, which means that capital is King in a transformation of organization structure from a market economy to a market society. To crown them all, everything is

capitalized, which means everything can be measured or valued or priced in terms of capital or money or all can be purchased or consumed.

Four Guiding Principles of Modern Civilization/Western Civilization
1. Scientific Spirit (rationalism and experimentalism)
2. Political Democracy (liberalism and constitutionalism)
3. Market Economy (competition and efficiency)
4. Artistic Freedom (Innovation and Rebellion)

About This Textbook and a Brief Acknowledgment

The study of western Culture is a huge and comprehensive topic that requires a brain-raking effort. This concise textbook is designed and compiled with an attempt to facilitate the study of the subject in discussion. Structurally, the textbook as mentioned above is divided into three main parts followed by two appendix parts containing each a course outline and a short reading list for the subject. The first part contains some 30 articles outlining and illustrating some of the most important concepts and events of the western cultural studies. The second part is composed of a case study about Jewish people and their history and current status. The third part is devoted to a few sets of exercises concerning the learning of western culture. Most of the materials and information herein adopted and adapted are from the Internet and cyber channels and a small portions of them are based upon hard-copy book sources. For the Internet sources, they are chiefly from *Wikipedia* and some other useful websites. These materials have been simply and briefly edited and, for some, substantially revised to come up with a concise version to suit the use of students and learners who are interested in western Culture Study. It can be clearly seen from this fact that modern information technology is indeed useful and beneficial to human beings. I hold this truth to be self-evident that good and useful knowledge and information should be shared and disseminated among the public for a wider circulation and usage to bring more benefits to more people. In spite of this, here again, I would like to avail myself of this opportunity to express my heart-felt appreciation to those who have labored on-line diligently and honestly with a good will to spread and promote useful and beneficial information to those who are thirsty for knowledge with a firm belief that education can change one's fate and life path. Their generous efforts and good will should be appreciated deeply and thankfully. I am also deeply and immeasurably indebted to those who have provided their invaluable help and guidance in getting this concise textbook published. For their efforts and help, I express hereby my deep and sincere gratitude. Cooperation along with competition should be held as important values for human beings. Without competition, no progress of human society would be possible. Without cooperation, however, no peace would be imagined and constructed. We should always strike a judicious balance between these two equally important ideas and codes of conduct so that a world of more diverse cultural traditions can be established to the benefit of common people on earth.

PART ONE

Articles Selected for
Specific Topics, Themes and Events

An Opening Article

Editor's remarks: *this article is chosen as the opening one because it is intended to tell us something we always ignore or fail to think about, which is expressed in a question as follows: "what is the most important thing in life?" This question in fact defies any ready answer and different people of different ages and of different cultural backgrounds have different answers. It may also be an open question to which there may be no answer at all. Some people say wealth is the answer while others claim health is more important than wealth. Still some hold that wisdom is of the paramount importance as it can bring a happy life since happiness is the most important thing in one's life. Therefore, it follows naturally that wisdom seems to be the most important thing in life. Yet, the problem arises there as well. Wisdom is hard to define and some people say it can only be proved by some hard evidence. It is said that a happy life is evidence of wisdom, which poses a further question as for what happiness implies. Nothing is perfect including life itself. Buddhism insists that life is a bitter and sorrowful process and the best people can do is to diminish its bitterness and sorrowfulness. According to Buddhist doctrine, avoidance of bitterness and diminishing of sorrowfulness is a wise and sagacious way of life. Different people present different ways of avoiding pains and of seeking pleasures and which one is better than another is always subject to subjective judgment rather than objective standards. Therefore, don't keep asking why you do a thing for love or money, but just enjoy the process of doing a thing you choose to for the sake of loving it.*

Where Is Wisdom We Have Lost in Knowledge?[①]

Knowledge comes by taking things apart: analysis. But wisdom comes by putting things together.

—John A. Morrison

It is much better to have common sense without education, than to have education without common sense.

—Robert G. Ingersoll

People always ignore a very basic fact that common sense is not so common.

—François-marie Arouet (Voltaire)

If you travel northwest from Athens, on the road to Corinth, you will come to the ruins of the once great city of Delphi. Delphi is the place once thought by the Greeks to be the center of the world. Here, in the 6th century B.C., the Oracle in the Temple of Apollo, was at its busiest, as it was called upon to dispense wisdom and to give answers to some of the pressing questions of the day. But, the Oracle of the classical world was silent before the age old questions like Who am I? Why am I here? What should I be doing? and Where am I going? From the beginning of time man has been trying to make sense of himself and his world. He has been seeking understanding. But as time marches on, man isn't getting the understanding he seeks, he isn't happier, and he hasn't been able to conquer his own nature. What's wrong? With all

---

[①] This opening article of the textbook is taken from a website magazine called *Foundations Magazine*. One can visit its website at www.foundationmag.com for more detailed information. This article has been edited and adapted through the editor of this book for its own proper purpose.

the great minds and thinking that have gone before us, with all the lessons of history left for us to examine, it is difficult to imagine why we aren't further along than we are. Why are we asking the same questions in our search for meaning, the Greeks were asking 2,600 years ago. Do we not yet have enough information available to us?

We now live in a world where we are inundated with more information, on a daily basis, than we can possibly process. It is an over-communicated environment. There are so many unwanted messages bombarding us, that often the ones we want get lost in the noise. The average person can now communicate faster, with more people—without thinking—than ever before. Information has become disposable. It doesn't matter whether you are connected to the Internet or not. We get hit with it at every turn. At work. At home as we try to relax. And at all points in between. So what about it? What are we doing with this information? Is all this information really doing us any good? Are we living happier lives? Are we experiencing fewer problems? Are our decisions better? Are we any wiser? History tells us that we haven't learned much in spite of all we know. The situation changes, but the problems remain the same.

Clearly, we need to do something better with all of this information. T. S. Eliot posed the question: "Where is the wisdom we have lost in knowledge? Where is the knowledge we have lost in information?" In a day and age where the number one shows are sitcoms and we commonly find best sellers written by those on the fringe of society, we are clearly in need of better thinking. We need wisdom.

The Bible has a lot to say about wisdom. In Proverbs, a book devoted to wisdom, we are told that wisdom is the principle thing. Though it cost us all that we have, get wisdom. What is this elusive quality called wisdom? How do we get it? First, let's begin by taking a look at the four levels of thinking. The first level is data—simple facts and figures. Next we have information. Information is data that's been collected and organized. It is a reference tool. Something we turn to when trying to create something else. The third level is knowledge. This is information that we have digested and now understand. Organized as knowledge, the information we have collected is given a context. The fourth and final level is wisdom.

Today, wisdom has become for many, indistinguishable from knowledge. But they are two different things. Often, what we find touted as wisdom is simply opinion. Knowledge is not wisdom. There is a big difference. Wisdom is the proper use of knowledge. To be more precise, wisdom is knowledge that has been applied in a way that takes into account all its pertinent relationships and that is consistent with universal laws. A glut of information can be a kind of Catch-22. While it adds to our knowledge, it can be a block to our wisdom. We can be so busy trying to process more and more information, that we don't have the time for the quiet contemplation that is essential for the development of wisdom. Without contemplation, we lose perspective and can lose our grounding. Without our bearings we lose a sense of place. Confused, we are more easily swayed. It is essential then, that we learn to let the unwanted information we receive go in one ear and out the other and to get the knowledge we need, to stop somewhere in between. It is interesting that armed with mountains of information, we have turned arguing into a national pastime. It seems one can always provide more information to support a claim. We begin to think might makes right—more is better. In turn, relationships fracture as we go off with our own tangential, myopic views. We lose perspective. Knowledge too, is a funny thing. It can deceive us into thinking we are wise.

Knowledge alone is not wisdom. For example, have you ever known someone who is incredibly smart, maybe they get straight A's in school, or maybe they have several degrees, and yet their life is a complete mess? Perhaps you know someone who is sufficiently educated and yet they can't hold a job, can't act on basic instructions, and they seem to be constantly faced with a host of problems. What's wrong? These people aren't dumb. They don't seem to lack the necessary information to be a success in life. Yet for them, life is one struggle, one upset, after another. Sadly, they lack wisdom. Many people know a great deal but are all the more foolish because of it. They have not yet learned how to apply the knowledge they have. For the successful conduct of life, mere knowledge is not enough. Sometimes we say that someone has no *common sense*. Indeed, common sense is a part of wisdom. Common sense is applying knowledge to solve the everyday problems common to all people in a way that is better than that which might come naturally. As a society, in trying to create a law for every situation, we have lost the perspective of the principles common to a community of people. We too can become so tightly focused that we lose our ability to apply what we learn generally to our own lives specifically. And so we lack common sense. Knowledge that doesn't take shape in deeds—that doesn't apply itself to life—is trivia. If you can't apply it, it's just knowledge for knowledge sake; it's just something to get intellectual about. Knowledge alone leads to arrogance. This is not to undervalue knowledge, but there must be some thinking as to what are the ends of the knowledge being attained, of the relationship of the knowledge you are gaining to the conduct of your life and to the life of those around you. Why do you know what you know? And what are you doing about it? Knowledge alone does not result in clear vision, a proper perspective, meaning, and the right behavior. But when this transformation does occur, we call it wisdom. How do we get wisdom? How do we develop it and make it a part of our lives?

Fundamentally, it is important to understand that wisdom is grounded in reality in two ways. To connect with reality and develop wisdom, we need to learn to be aware. Aware of ourselves and aware of those around us. We can learn from other people's success and we can learn from their mistakes. From early on, we have all been told that we should learn from other people's mistakes. Yet we see people in trouble all the time, but we forget to learn from their mistakes. Every person you come into contact with, good or bad, is for you, a lesson in living if you will only be aware. You need to define where they are off or what they are doing right and then determine what that means for you. Everything that you observe is a chance for you to figure out what it means and what you are supposed to do about it. When you see a problem in life, yours or someone else's, something is wrong. What it is you are seeing? Figure it out. It is important that you know. Then, if you know something works and you don't do it, that's being disconnected from reality. We Human Beings are the only living things that can decide to disconnect ourselves from reality. We are inclined to do what we want and not what we know we should do. We can, and often do, choose to live according to what is unreasonable; what makes no sense. We can do things in the same old way and justify doing it. But, we are only kidding ourselves. Living with reality takes an effort on our part. But, it is essential that we do the things that we know must be done and stop doing those things we know we shouldn't be doing. Understand the law of Cause & Effect. Things happen to us for a reason. We are the sum total of the decisions we have made and the actions we have taken to this point.

When you make a mistake, don't gloss over it. Take a look at it. Seek to understand why you did it and why it doesn't work, why it doesn't get you the results you want. Articulate it. To learn something is to be able to put it into words. Then when you catch yourself doing something that is counter productive, something you know from observation doesn't work, stop. Make one little change in your life. Begin to practice what you learn in order to create habits. If it is right, keep at it whether you see immediate results or not. A successful life is made up of a series of course corrections. They all add up to create the substance of your life. Learn to step back from any situation and look at it objectively. It is helpful to take the personalities out. Take out all of the emotions and egos and determine the right thing to do regardless of who is involved.

Then put the personalities back in and proceed with what must be done. This is living by principle and wisdom. It will help you to not compromise what is right and to live consistent with universal law.

Be proactive. This does not mean to be more assertive. *Proactiveness* is not an attitude, but is instead a product of our thinking that comes from being connected to our own behavior; by seeing how we contribute to our own problems. It means to determine in advance your response to any situation that may come your way. Don't allow yourself to just react to the stimulus of your environment. Of course, it's hard to do this when you are in the middle of an action. Your emotions are in the way and your perspective is gone. It's hard to stop and ask yourself, What am I doing? This is why you must think through the events in your life and think through to the conclusion of the approach you are using. If then, you don't like the results, change your approach, before you're caught behaving in way you'll wish you hadn't. A wise person will think about situations he might become involved in so that he might know in advance how he will respond. Don't just get through a day. Absorb the day. Make it a part of your life. You can't afford to take an aimless approach to life. Take it seriously. If you don't, no one else will. Pick up on everything that is happening around you. By asking yourself, What am I supposed to be doing? How am I going to do it? and When am I going to do something about it? You avoid a lot of mistakes. When you start thinking about your life, many problems disappear. When you live perceptively, when you get in touch with reality, and start doing what you know is right, problems disappear.

In 1677, the Dutch philosopher Spinoza, suggested that wisdom is seeing things *sub specie eternitatis*, that is, in view of eternity. A foundational principle of wisdom is to have a long term perspective; to see the big picture; to look beyond the immediate situation. Of course, an all encompassing, total perspective is possessed only by God. Although it can only be approached by humans, it is an ideal we should seek. In this regard, it is helpful to study events and people throughout history. The past is the sum of all we are today. Understand it. Know why we are where we are today. Napoleon said, "May my son study history for it is the only true philosophy, the only true psychology." Take time each day with those who have left their lives for our example. In time, it will broaden your perspective and deepen your understanding. You will gain many lifetimes of experience in your own.

Walter Lippmann observed that "a boy can take you into the open at night and show you the stars; he might tell you no end of things about them, conceivably all that an astronomer could teach. But until and unless he feels the vast indifference of the universe to his own fate, and has placed himself in the perspective of cold and illimitable space, he has not looked maturely at the heavens. Until he has felt this, and unless he can endure this, he remains a child, and in his childishness, he will resent the heavens when they are not accommodating. He will demand sunshine when he wishes to play, and rain when the ground is dry, and he will look upon storms as anger directed at him, and the thunder as a personal threat." He may know knowledge but he doesn't have wisdom. Wisdom places us in our proper roles in relationship to everything else around us and in so doing helps us to develop emotional maturity. Wisdom requires humility. You must be teachable. If you are to put these things into practice, you must be willing to take a look at what you thought you knew about yourself and the ideas you hold. It requires an outward focus not a selfish one. Often people who know a lot can't get past that fact and as a result never gain insight into what they know.

A wise man never stops asking questions. He realizes that what he knows is but a drop in a sea of knowledge. As we examine the results of our behavior and learn from the experiences of others, and conform to the laws common to every living thing, we begin to create a yardstick to judge what we know and the knowledge we come into contact with. We can learn what is acceptable. You are the only one that can gain wisdom for yourself. No one can make you wise or make you not wise. It's up to you. Any time you see, hear, or experience a lesson for better living, it's up to you to do something about it. The job of living is to make this decision. Put what you have learned into practice or you will never be wise. A philosopher by definition, is a lover of wisdom. We all should be philosophers. You can talk beautiful ideas, but if you don't put it into action, it is as if you know nothing. Ask yourself, what did I learn today? How would I do it differently? and How do I transfer this lesson to my own life? Then, apply it. You then begin to live intelligently. To live with understanding. To live with meaning. To live with wisdom and to experience with sagacity should be a life motto for all.

Questions or Topics for Pondering and Further Discussion for the Opening Article:

1. How do you personally define wisdom?
2. Are there any differences between oriental wisdom and occidental wisdom?
3. *Wise are those who know bottom line does not always have to be their top priorities.* Please comment.
4. *Fear of God is the beginning of wisdom.* Please make some comment on it.
5. What is the relationship between accumulation of knowledge and acquisition of wisdom?
6. What are the features of a life of wisdom?
7. What is meant by Spinoza's suggestion that wisdom is seeing things in view of eternity.
8. What is your life motto that guides your way of life or of thinking?

Unit One

1. Cultural Theory and Cultural Studies

Editor's remarks: the following article is chosen in order to provide the reader/learner with a theoretical framework and basic concept concerning cultural theory and studies. After all, people need some basic understanding of culture at its theoretical level to understand its rich implication. It should be noted that cultural theory is so diverse and elusive sometimes and cultural studies, so comprehensive and inclusive that cultural studies as an interdisciplinary subject are unique cultural phenomenon. However, it is always better to know than to be ignorant about something that fundamentally concerns human material well-being and spiritual fulfilment. The significance of cultural studies in facilitating human understanding of complex and metaphysical confusions and existential dilemma cannot be overestimated. It is with this idea in mind that the editor of this textbook has chosen this article to begin the journey of exploration of western culture.

Culture Theory is the branch of comparative anthropology and semiotics (not to be confused with cultural sociology or cultural studies) that seeks to define the heuristic concept of culture in operational and/or scientific terms. In the 19th century, "culture" was used by some to refer to a wide array of human activities, and by others as a synonym for "civilization." In the 20th century, anthropologists began theorizing about culture as an object of scientific analysis. Some used it to distinguish human adaptive strategies from the largely instinctive adaptive strategies of animals, including the adaptive strategies of other primates and non-human hominids, whereas others used it to refer to symbolic representations and expressions of human experience, with no direct adaptive value. Both groups understood culture as being definitive of human nature.

According to many theories that have gained wide acceptance among anthropologists, culture exhibits the way that humans interpret their biology and their environment. According to this point of view, culture becomes such an integral part of human existence that it is the human environment, and most cultural change can be attributed to human adaptation to historical events. Moreover, given that culture is seen as the primary adaptive mechanism of humans and takes place much faster than human biological evolution, most cultural change can be viewed as culture adapting to itself. Although most anthropologists try to define culture in such a way that it separates human beings from other animals, many human traits are similar to those of other animals, particularly the traits of other primates. For example, chimpanzees have big brains, but human brains are bigger. Similarly, bonobos exhibit complex sexual behaviour, but human beings exhibit much more complex sexual behaviours. As such, anthropologists often debate whether human behaviour is different from animal behaviour in degree rather than in kind; they must also find ways to distinguish cultural behavior from sociological behavior and psychological behavior.

Acceleration and amplification of these various aspects of culture change have been explored by complexity economist, W. Brian Arthur. In his book, *The Nature of Technology*, Arthur attempts to articulate a theory of change that considers that existing technologies (or material culture) are combined in unique ways that lead to novel new technologies. Behind that novel combination is a purposeful effort arising in human motivation. This articulation would suggest that we are just beginning to understand what might be required for a more robust theory of culture and culture change, one that brings coherence across many disciplines and reflects an integrating elegance.

Cultural Studies is an academic field grounded in critical theory and literary criticism. Characteristically interdisciplinary, cultural studies provides a reflexive network of intellectuals attempting to situate the forces constructing our daily lives. It concerns the political dynamics of contemporary culture, as well as its historical foundations, conflicts and defining traits. It is distinguished from cultural anthropology and ethnic studies in both objective and methodology. Researchers concentrate on how a particular medium or message relates to ideology, social class, nationality, ethnicity, sexuality and/or gender, rather than investigating a particular culture or area of the world. Cultural studies approaches subjects holistically, combining feminist theory, social theory, political theory, history, philosophy, literary theory, media theory, film/video studies, communication studies, political economy, translation studies, museum studies and art history/criticism to study cultural phenomena in various societies. Thus, cultural studies seeks to understand the ways in which meaning is generated, disseminated, and produced through various practices, beliefs and institutions, also politically, economically and even social structures within a given culture.

History. The term was coined by Richard Hoggart in 1964 when he founded the Birmingham Centre for Contemporary Cultural Studies. It has since become strongly associated with Stuart Hall, who succeeded Hoggart as Director. From the 1970s onward, Stuart Hall's pioneering work, along with his colleagues Paul Willis, Dick Hebdige, Tony Jefferson, Michael Green and Angela McRobbie, created an international intellectual movement. Many cultural studies scholars employed Marxist methods of analysis, exploring the relationships between cultural forms (the superstructure) and that of the political economy (the base). By the 1970s, the politically formidable British working classes were in decline. Britain's manufacturing industries were fading and union rolls were shrinking. Yet millions of working class Britons backed the rise of Margaret Thatcher. For Stuart Hall and other Marxist theorists, this shift in loyalty from the Labour Party to the Conservative Party was antithetical to the interests of the working class and had to be explained in terms of cultural politics.

In order to understand the changing political circumstances of class, politics and culture in the United Kingdom, scholars at the CCCS turned to the work of Antonio Gramsci, an Italian thinker of the 1920s and 1930s. Gramsci had been concerned with similar issues: why would Italian laborers and peasants vote for fascists? In other words, why would working people vote to give more control to corporations and see their own rights and freedoms abrogated? Gramsci modified classical Marxism in seeing culture as a key instrument of political and social control. In this view, capitalists used not only brute force (police, prisons, repression, military) to maintain control, but also penetrated the everyday culture of working people. Thus, the key rubric for Gramsci and for cultural studies is that of cultural hegemony.

This line of thinking opened up fruitful work exploring agency, a theoretical outlook which reinserted the active, critical capacities of all people. Notions of agency have supplemented much scholarly emphasis on groups of people (e. g. the working class, primitives, colonized peoples, women) whose political consciousness and scope of action was generally limited to their position within certain economic and political structures. In other words, many economists, sociologists, political scientists and historians have traditionally failed to acknowledge that everyday people do indeed play a role in shaping their world or outlook. Although anthropologists since the 1960s have foregrounded the power of agents to contest structure, first in the work of transactionalists like Fredrik Barth and then in works inspired by resistance theory and post-colonial theory.

At times, cultural studies' romance with the notion of agency nearly excludes the possibility of oppression, overlooking the fact that the subaltern have their own politics, and romanticizes agency, exaggerating its potential and pervasiveness. Popular in the 1990s, many cultural studies scholars discovered in consumers ways of creatively using and subverting commodities and dominant ideologies. This orientation has come under fire for a variety of reasons. Cultural studies concerns itself with the meaning and practices of everyday life. Cultural practices comprise the ways people do particular things, such as watching television or eating out, in a given culture. In any given practice, people use various objects (such as iPods or crucifixes). Hence, this field studies the meanings and uses peoples attributes to various objects and practices. Recently, as capitalism has spread throughout the world (a process associated with globalization), cultural studies has begun to analyze local and global forms of resistance to western hegemony.

The movement toward globalization in our world serves as an important reason to examine Cultural Studies. According to Richard Longworth, author of "Caught in the Middle: America's Heartland in the Age of Globalism," it is just getting started. We are now in the stage of re-invention instead of industrialization. In the past 20 years, communication technology has made this possible and has moved very rapidly. Because we are increasing communication worldwide, globalization has a major effect on how we look at Cultural Studies because we are constantly being exposed to the ideologies of mass media. In addition, human culture itself is becoming more unified as a result of globalization. For example, Stuart Hall has striven to combine many topic areas of study, such as interpersonal relationships and the influence of the media. He believes we should be studying the unifying atmosphere in which they all occur and from which they emanate—human culture. This human culture is starting to become more and more unified itself because of globalization and therefore can be further examined through Cultural Studies.

Overview

In his book *Introducing Cultural Studies*, Ziauddin Sardar lists the following five main characteristics of cultural studies:

- Cultural studies aims to examine its subject matter in terms of cultural practices and their relation to power. For example, a study of a subculture (such as white working class youth in London) would consider the social practices of the youth as they relate to the dominant classes.
- It has the objective of understanding culture in all its complex forms and of analyzing the social and political context in which culture manifests itself.
- It is both the object of study and the location of political criticism and action. For example, not only would a cultural studies scholar study an object, but she/he would connect this study to a larger, progressive political project.
- It attempts to expose and reconcile the division of knowledge, to overcome the split between tacit cultural knowledge and objective (universal) forms of knowledge.
- It has a commitment to an ethical evaluation of modern society and to a radical line of political action.

Contemporary Cultural Studies

Sociologist Scott Lash has recently put forth the idea that Cultural Studies is entering a new phase. Arguing that the political and economic milieu has fundamentally altered from that of the 1970s. He writes, "I want to suggest that power now is largely *post-hegemonic*." Hegemony was the concept that de facto crystallized Cultural Studies as a discipline. Hegemony usually refers to the "preponderant influence or domination of one nation over another." It has meant domination through ideology or discourse... He writes that the flow of power is becoming more internalized, that there has been "a shift in power from the hegemonic mode of *'power over'* to an intensive notion of *power from within* (including domination from within) and power as a generative force." Resistance to power, in other words, becomes complicated when power and domination are increasingly (re)produced within oneself, within subaltern groups and within exploited people.

On the same subject, American feminist theorist and author of *Gender Trouble* Judith Butler wrote in the scholarly journal *Diacritics* an essay entitled *Further Reflections on the Conversions of Our Time*, in which she described the shift in these terms:

> *The move from as tructuralist account in which capital is understood to structure social relations in relatively homologous ways to a view of hegemony in which power relations are subject to repetition, convergence and re-articulation brought the question of temporality into the thinking of structure. It has marked a shift from a form of Althusserian theory that takes structural totalities as theoretical objects to one in which the insights into the contingent possibility of structure inaugurate a renewed conception of hegemony as bound up with the contingent sites and strategies of the re-articulation of power.*

Institutionally, the discipline has undergone major shifts. The Department of Cultural Studies at the University of Birmingham, which was descended from the Centre for Contemporary Cultural Studies, closed in 2002. Although by this time the intellectual center of gravity of the discipline had long since shifted to other universities throughout the world. Strong Cultural Studies programs can be found in the United Kingdom, North and South America, Europe, Australia, Asia and there are a host of journals and conferences where Cultural Studies research is published and presented.

2. Culture, a Broad Humanistic Concept[①]

Editor's remarks: culture as an elusive and inclusive academic term or concept can be defined narrowly and broadly, which alone poses some grave challenge to the study of it. However, elusive as it may turn out to be, culture as a concept is pervasive and tangible in people's daily life. What people do, think, choose and imagine has much to do with their cultural inclinations, which reflects their value orientations. An thorough and in-depth analysis of western culture would be totally impossible without first of all a basic understanding of culture as a key term in the process of this academic pursuit. First things first, to define culture in the most exact and explicit way possible may be a mission impossible. However, it is this mission that has brought great pleasure for human beings to keep exploring what is unknown about themselves and about the world around them. When a journey begins, the most important and pleasurable thing is what people can see and experience on the way rather than the final destination. The charm of culture lies not only in its diversity, but also its complexity, which alone provides much food for thought for those who care and concern terminal meaning of life of human beings.

When **Culture** (Latin: *cultura*, lit. "cultivation") first began to take its current usage by

---

[①] The main contents and central ideas of this material are chiefly based upon the entry of "culture" for its definition and implication from *Wikipedia*. The materials listed hereafter follow the same case unless otherwise directed or footnoted for their citation sources.

Europeans in eighteenth- and nineteenth-century (having had earlier antecedents elsewhere), it connoted a process of cultivation or improvement, as in agriculture or horticulture. In the nineteenth century, it came to refer first to the betterment or refinement of the individual, especially through education, and then to the fulfillment of national aspirations or ideals. In the mid-nineteenth century, some scientists used the term "culture" to refer to a universal human capacity. For the German nonpositivist sociologist Georg Simmel, a famous sociologist, culture referred to "the cultivation of individuals through the agency of external forms which have been objectified in the course of history". In the twentieth century, "culture" emerged as a concept central to anthropology, encompassing all human phenomena that are not purely results of human genetics. Specifically, the term "culture" in American anthropology had two meanings: (1) the evolved human capacity to classify and represent experiences with symbols, and to act imaginatively and creatively; and (2) the distinct ways that people living in different parts of the world classified and represented their experiences, and acted creatively. A distinction is current between the physical artifacts created by a society, its so-called material culture and everything else, the intangibles such as language, customs, etc. that are the main referent of the term "culture". The etymology of the modern term "culture" has a classical origin. In English, the word "culture" is based on a term used by Cicero in his *Tusculan Disputations*, where he wrote of a cultivation of the soul or *cultura animi*, thereby using an agricultural metaphor to describe the development of a philosophical soul, which was understood teleologically as the one natural highest possible ideal for human development. Samuel Pufendorf took over this metaphor in a modern context, meaning something similar, but no longer assuming that philosophy is man's natural perfection. His use, and that of many writers after him "refers to all the ways in which human beings overcome their original barbarism, and through artifice, become fully human".

The concept of "culture" is described by Velkley as follows:

The term "culture," which originally meant the cultivation of the soul or mind, acquires most of its later modern meanings in the writings of the eighteenth-century German thinkers, who on various levels developing Rousseau's criticism of modern liberalism and Enlightenment. Thus a contrast between "culture" and "civilization" is usually implied in these authors, even when not expressed as such. Two primary meanings of culture emerge from this period: culture as the folk-spirit having a unique identity, and culture as cultivation of inwardness or free individuality. The first meaning is predominant in our current use of the term "culture," although the second still plays a large role in what we think culture should achieve, namely the full "expression" of the unique of "authentic" self.

The German philosopher Immanuel Kant (1724—1804) formulated an individualist definition of "enlightenment" similar to the concept of *bildung*: "Enlightenment is man's emergence from his self-incurred immaturity." He argued that this immaturity comes not from a lack of understanding, but from a lack of courage to think independently. Against this intellectual cowardice, Kant urged: *Sapere aude*, "Dare to be wise!" In reaction to Kant, German scholars such as Johann Gottfried Herder (1744—1803) argued that human creativity, which necessarily takes unpredictable and highly diverse forms, is as important as human rationality. Moreover, Herder proposed a collective form of *bildung*: "For Herder, Bildung was the totality of experiences that provide a coherent identity, and sense of common destiny, to a people." In 1795, the great linguist and philosopher Wilhelm von Humboldt (1767—1835) called for an anthropology that would synthesize Kant's and Herder's interests. During the Romantic era, scholars in Germany, especially those concerned with nationalist movements—such as the nationalist struggle to create a "Germany" out of diverse principalities, and the nationalist struggles by ethnic minorities against the Austro-hungarian Empire—developed a more inclusive notion of culture as "worldview." According to this school of thought, each ethnic group has a distinct worldview that is incommensurable with the worldviews of other groups. Although more inclusive than earlier views, this approach to culture still allowed for distinctions between "civilized" and "primitive" or "tribal" cultures. In 1860, Adolf Bastian (1826—1905) argued for "the psychic unity of mankind". He proposed that a scientific comparison of all human societies would reveal that distinct worldviews consisted of the same basic elements. According to Bastian, all human societies share a set of "elementary ideas" (*Elementargedanken*); different cultures, or different "folk ideas" (*Völkergedanken*), are local modifications of the elementary ideas. This view paved the way for the modern understanding of culture. Franz Boas (1858—1942) was trained in this tradition, and he brought it with him when he left Germany for the United States.

In the nineteenth century, humanists such as English poet and essayist Matthew Arnold (1822—1888) used the word "culture" to refer to an ideal of individual human refinement, of "the best that has been thought and said in the world." This concept of culture is comparable to the German concept of *bildung* : "... culture being a pursuit of our total perfection by means of getting to know, on all the matters which most concern us, the best which has been thought and said in the world." In practice, *culture* referred to an élite ideal and was associated with such activities as art, classical music, and haute cuisine. As these forms were associated with urban life, "culture" was identified with "civilization" (from lat. *civitas*, city). Another facet of the Romantic movement was an interest in folklore, which led to identifying a "culture" among non-elites. This distinction is often characterized as that between "high culture", namely that of the ruling social group, and "low culture". In other words, the idea of "culture" that developed in Europe during the 18th and early 19th centuries reflected inequalities within European societies. British anthropologist Edward Tylor was one of the first English-speaking scholars to use the term "culture" in an inclusive and universal sense. Matthew Arnold contrasted "culture" with "anarchy"; other Europeans, following such philosophers as Thomas Hobbes and Jean-Jacques Rousseau, contrasted "culture" with "the state of nature". According to Hobbes and Rousseau, the native Americans who were being conquered by Europeans from the 16th centuries on were living in a state of nature; this opposition was expressed through the contrast between "civilized" and "uncivilized". According to this way of thinking, one could classify some countries and nations as more civilized than others and some people as more cultured than others. This contrast led to Herbert Spencer's theory of Social Darwinism and Lewis Henry Morgan's theory of cultural evolution. Just as some critics have argued that the distinction between high and low cultures is really an expression of the conflict between European elites and non-elites, some critics have argued that the distinction between civilized and uncivilized people is really an expression of the conflict between European colonial powers and their colonial subjects.

Other 19th century critics, following Rousseau, have accepted this differentiation between higher and lower culture, but have seen the refinement and sophistication of high culture as corrupting and unnatural developments that obscure and distort people's essential nature. These critics considered folk music (as produced by "the folk", i. e., rural, illiterate, peasants) to honestly express a natural way of life, while classical music seemed superficial and decadent. Equally, this view often portrayed indigenous peoples as "noble savages" living authentic and unblemished lives, uncomplicated and uncorrupted by the highly stratified capitalist systems of the West. In 1870 Edward Tylor (1832—1917) applied these ideas of higher versus lower culture to propose a theory of the evolution of religion. According to this theory, religion evolves from more polytheistic to more monotheistic forms. In the process, he redefined culture as a diverse set of activities characteristic of all human societies. This view paved the way for the modern understanding of culture.

Biological Anthropology: the Evolution of Culture

Discussion concerning culture among biological anthropologists centers around two debates. First, is culture uniquely human or shared by other species (most notably, other primates)? This is an important question, as the theory of evolution holds that humans are descended from (now extinct) non-human primates. Second, how did culture evolve among human beings? Gerald Weiss noted that although Tylor's classic definition of culture was restricted to humans, many anthropologists take this for granted and thus elide that important qualification from later definitions, merely equating culture with any learned behavior. This slippage is a problem because during the formative years of modern primatology, some primatologists were trained in anthropology (and understood that culture refers to learned behavior among humans), and others were not. Notable non-anthropologists, like Robert Yerkes and Jane Goodall thus argued that since chimpanzees have learned behaviors, they have culture. Today, anthropological primatologists are divided, several arguing that non-human primates have culture, others arguing that they do not. This scientific debate is complicated by ethical concerns. The subjects of primatology are non-human primates, and whatever culture these primates have is threatened by human activity. After reviewing the research on primate culture, W. C. McGrew concluded, "[a] discipline requires subjects, and most species of nonhuman primates are endangered by their human cousins. Ultimately, whatever its merit, cultural primatology must be committed to cultural survival [i. e. to the survival of primate cultures]."

McGrew suggests a definition of culture that he finds scientifically useful for studying primate culture. He points out that scientists do not have access to the subjective thoughts or knowledge of non-human primates. Thus, if culture is defined in terms of knowledge, then scientists are severely limited in their attempts to study primate culture. Instead of defining culture as a kind of knowledge, McGrew suggests that we view culture as a process. He lists six steps in the process:

1. A new pattern of behavior is invented, or an existing one is modified.
2. The innovator transmits this pattern to another.
3. The form of the pattern is consistent within and across performers, perhaps even in terms of recognizable stylistic features.
4. The one who acquires the pattern retains the ability to perform it long after having acquired it.
5. The pattern spreads across social units in a population. These social units may be families, clans, troops, or bands.
6. The pattern endures across generations.

McGrew admits that all six criteria may be strict, given the difficulties in observing primate behavior in the wild. But he also insists on the need to be as inclusive as possible, on the need for a definition of culture that "casts the net widely":

Culture is considered to be group-specific behavior that is acquired, at least in part, from social influences. Here, group is considered to be the species-typical unit, whether it be a troop, lineage, subgroup, or so on. Prima facie evidence of culture comes from within-species but across-Group variation in behavior, as when a pattern is persistent in one community of chimpanzees but is absent from another, or when different communities perform different versions of the same pattern. The suggestion of culture in action is stronger when the difference across the groups cannot be explained solely by ecological factors.

As Charles Frederick Voegelin pointed out, if "culture" is reduced to "learned behavior", then all animals have culture. Certainly all specialists agree that all primate species evidence common cognitive skills: knowledge of object-permanence, cognitive mapping, the ability to categorize objects, and creative problem solving. Moreover, all primate species show evidence of shared social skills: they recognize members of their social group; they form direct relationships based on degrees of kinship and rank; they recognize third-party social relationships; they predict future behavior; and they cooperate in problem-solving. Nevertheless, the term "culture" applies to non-human animals only if we define culture as any or all learned behavior. Within mainstream physical anthropology, scholars tend to think that a more restrictive definition is necessary. These researchers are concerned with how human beings evolved to be different from other species. A more precise definition of culture, which excludes non-human social behavior, would allow physical anthropologists to study how humans evolved their unique capacity for "culture". Chimpanzees are humans (*Homo sapiens*) closest living relative; both are descended from a common ancestor which lived around five or six million years ago. This is the same amount of time it took for horses and zebras, lions and tigers to diverge from their respective common ancestors. The evolution of modern humans is rapid: *Australopithicenes* evolved four million years ago and modern humans in past several hundred thousand years. During this time humanity evolved three distinctive features:

(a) the creation and use of conventional symbols, including linguistic symbols and their derivatives, such as written language and mathematical symbols and notations; (b) the creation and use of complex tools and other instrumental technologies; and (c) the creation and participation in complex social organization and institutions.

According to developmental psychologist Michael Tomasello, "where these complex and species-unique behavioral practices, and the cognitive skills that underlie them, came from" is a fundamental anthropological question. Given that contemporary humans and chimpanzees are far more different than horses and zebras, or rats and mice, and that the evolution of this great difference occurred in such a short period of time, "our search must be for some small difference that made a big difference—some adaptation, or small set of adaptations, that changed the process of primate cognitive evolution in fundamental ways." According to Tomasello, the answer to this question must form the basis of a scientific definition of "human culture". In a recent review of the major research on human and primate tool-use, communication, and learning strategies, Tomasello argues that the key human advances over primates (language, complex technologies, and complex social organization) are all the results of humans pooling cognitive resources. This is called "the ratchet effect": innovations spread and are shared by a group, and mastered "by youngsters, which enables them to remain in their new and improved form within the group until something better comes along." The key point is that children are born good at a particular kind of social learning; this creates a favored environment for social innovations, making them more likely to be maintained and transmitted to new generations than individual innovations. For Tomasello, human social learning—the kind of learning that distinguishes humans from other primates and that played a decisive role in human evolution—is based on two elements: first, what he calls "imitative learning", (as opposed to "emulative learning" characteristic of other primates) and second, the fact that humans represent their experiences symbolically (rather than iconically, as is characteristic of other primates). Together, these elements enable humans to be both inventive and innovative, and to preserve useful inventions. It is this combination that produces the ratchet effect.

What is uniquely characteristic about human societies is what required symbolic cognition, which consequently leads to the evolution of culture: "cooperative, mixed-sex social groups, with significant male care and provisioning of offspring, and relatively stable patterns of reproductive exclusion." This combination is relatively rare in other species because it is "highly susceptible to disintegration." Language and culture provide the glue that holds it together. Chimpanzees also, on occasion, hunt meat; in most cases, however, males consume the meat immediately, and only on occasion share with females who happen to be nearby. Among chimpanzees, hunting for meat increases when other sources of food become scarce, but under these conditions sharing decreases. The first forms of symbolic thinking made stone-tools possible, which in turn made hunting for meat a more dependable source of food for our nonhuman ancestors while making possible forms of social communication that make sharing—between males and females, but also among males, decreasing sexual competition:

So the socio-ecological problem posed by the transition to a meat-supplemented subsistence strategy is that it cannot be utilized without a social structure which guarantees unambiguous and exclusive mating and is sufficiently egalitarian to sustain cooperation via shared or parallel reproductive interests. This problem can be solved symbolically.

Symbols and symbolic thinking thus make possible a central feature of social relations in every human population: reciprocity. Evolutionary scientists have developed a model to explain reciprocal altruism among closely related individuals. Symbolic thought makes possible reciprocity between distantly related individuals.

Language and Culture and Their Mutual Relations

The connection between culture and language has been noted as far back as the classical period and probably long before. The ancient Greeks, for example, distinguished between civilized peoples and bárbaros "those who babble", i.e. those who speak unintelligible languages. The fact that different groups speak different, unintelligible languages is often considered more tangible evidence for cultural differences than other less obvious cultural traits. The German romanticists of the 19th century such as Johann Gottfried Herder and Wilhelm von Humboldt, often saw language not just as one cultural trait among many but rather as the direct expression of a people's national character, and as such as culture in a kind of condensed form. Herder for example suggests, "*Denn jedes Volk ist Volk; es hat seine National Bildung wie seine Sprache*" (Since every people is a People, it has its own national culture expressed through its own language). Franz Boas, founder of American anthropology, like his German forerunners, maintained that the shared language of a community is the most essential carrier of their common culture. Boas was the first anthropologist who considered it unimaginable to study the culture of a foreign people without also becoming acquainted with their language. For Boas, the fact that the intellectual culture of a people was largely constructed, shared and maintained through the use of language, meant that understanding the language of a cultural group was the key to understanding its culture. At the same time, though, Boas and his students were aware that culture and language are not directly dependent on one another. That is, groups with widely different cultures may share a common language, and speakers of completely unrelated languages may share the same fundamental cultural traits. Numerous other scholars have suggested that the form of language determines specific cultural traits. This is similar to the notion of Linguistic Determinism, which states that the form of language determines individual thought. While Boas himself rejected a causal link between language and culture, some of his intellectual heirs entertained the idea that habitual patterns of speaking and thinking in a particular language may influence the culture of the linguistic group. Such belief is related to the theory of Linguistic Relativity. Boas, like most modern anthropologists, however, was more inclined to relate the interconnectedness between language and culture to the fact that, as B. L. Whorf put it, "they have grown up together".

Indeed, the origin of language, understood as the human capacity of complex symbolic communication, and the origin of complex culture is often thought to stem from the same evolutionary process in early man. Evolutionary anthropologist Robin I. Dunbar has proposed that language evolved as early humans began to live in large communities which required the use of complex communication to maintain social coherence. Language and culture then both emerged as a means of using symbols to construct social identity and maintain coherence within a social group too large to rely exclusively on pre-human ways of building community such as grooming. Since language and culture are both in essence symbolic systems, twentieth century cultural theorists have applied the methods of analyzing language developed in the science of linguistics to also analyze culture. Particularly the structural theory of Ferdin and de Saussure which describes symbolic systems as consisting of signs (a pairing of a particular form with a particular meaning) has come to be applied widely in the study of culture. But also post-structuralist theories that nonetheless still rely on the parallel between language and culture as systems of symbolic communication, have been applied in the field of semiotics. The parallel between language and culture can then be understood as analog to the parallel between a linguistic sign, consisting for example of the sound [kau] and the meaning "cow", and a cultural sign, consisting for example of the cultural form of "wearing a crown" and the cultural meaning of "being king". In this way it can be argued that culture is itself a kind of language. Another parallel between cultural and linguistic systems is that they are both systems of practice that is they are a set of special ways of doing things that is constructed and perpetuated through social interactions. Children, for example, acquire language in the same way as they acquire the basic cultural norms of the society they grow up in—through interaction with older members of their cultural group.

However, languages, now understood as the particular set of speech norms of a particular community, are also a part of the larger culture of the community that speak them. Humans use language as a way of signaling identity with one cultural group and difference from others. Even among speakers of one language several different ways of using the language exist, and each is used to signal affiliation with particular subgroups within a larger culture. In linguistics such different ways of using the same language are called "varieties". For example, the English language is spoken differently in the USA, the UK and Australia, and even within English-speaking countries there are hundreds of dialects of English that each signals a belonging to a particular region and/or subculture. For example, in the UK the cockney dialect signals its speakers' belonging to the group of lower class workers of East London. Differences between varieties of the same language often consist in different pronunciations and vocabulary, but also sometimes of different grammatical systems and very often in using different styles (e. g. cockney rhyming slang or Lawyers' jargon). Linguists and anthropologists, particularly sociolinguists, ethnolinguists and linguistic anthropologists have specialized in studying how ways of speaking vary between speech communities. A community's ways of speaking or signing are a part of the community's culture, just as other shared practices are.

Language use is a way of establishing and displaying group identity. Ways of speaking function not only to facilitate communication, but also to identify the social position of the speaker. Linguists call different ways of speaking language varieties, a term that encompasses geographically or socioculturally defined dialects as well as the jargons or styles of subcultures. Linguistic anthropologists and sociologists of language define communicative style as the ways that language is used and understood within a particular culture. The difference between languages does not consist only in differences in pronunciation, vocabulary or grammar, but also in different "cultures of speaking". Some cultures for example have elaborate systems of "social deixis", systems of signaling social distance through linguistic means. In English, social deixis is shown mostly though distinguishing between addressing some people by first name and others by surname, but also in titles such as "Mrs.", "boy", "Doctor" or "Your Honor", but in other languages such systems may be highly complex and codified in the entire grammar and vocabulary of the language. In several languages of East Asia, for example Thai, Burmese and Javanese, different words are used according to whether a speaker is addressing someone of higher or lower rank than oneself in a ranking system with animals and children ranking the lowest and gods and members of royalty as the highest. Other languages may use different forms of address when speaking to speakers of the opposite gender or in-law relatives and many languages have special ways of speaking to infants and children. Among other groups, the culture of speaking may entail not speaking to particular people, for example many indigenous cultures of Australia have a taboo against talking to one's in-law relatives, and in some cultures speech is not addressed directly to children. Some languages also require different ways of speaking for different social classes of speakers, and often such a system is based on gender differences, as in Japanese and Koasati.

1946—1968: Symbolic versus Adaptive Theory

Parsons' students Clifford Geertz and David M. Schneider, and Schneider's student Roy Wagner, went on to important careers as cultural anthropologists and developed a school within American cultural anthropology called "symbolic anthropology", the study of the social construction and social effects of symbols. Since symbolic anthropology easily complemented social anthropologists' studies of social life and social structure, many British structural-functionalists (who rejected or were uninterested in Boasian cultural anthropology) accepted the Parsonian definition of "culture" and "cultural anthropology". British anthropologist Victor Turner (who eventually left the United Kingdom to teach in the United States) was an important bridge between American and British symbolic anthropology. Attention to symbols, the meaning of which depended almost entirely on their historical and social context, appealed to many Boasians. Leslie White asked of cultural things, "What sort of objects are they? Are they physical objects? Mental objects? Both? Metaphors? Symbols? Reifications?" In *Science of Culture* (1949), he concluded that they are objects *"sui generis"*; that is, of their own kind. In trying to define that kind, he hit upon a previously unrealized aspect of symbolization, which he called "the symbolate"—an object created by the act of symbolization. He thus defined culture as "symbolates understood in an extra-somatic context".

Nevertheless, by the 1930s White began turning away from the Boasian approach. He wrote:

> *In order to live, man like all other species, must come to terms with the external world... Man employs his sense organs, nerves, glands, and muscles in adjusting himself to the external world. But in addition to this he has another means of adjustment and control... This mechanism is culture.*

Although this view echoes that of Malinowski, the key concept for White was not "function" but "adaptation". Whereas the Boasians were interested in the history of specific traits, White was interested in the cultural history of the human species, which he felt should be studied from an evolutionary perspective. Thus, the task of anthropology is to study "not only how culture evolves, but why as well.... In the case of man ... the power to invent and to discover, the ability to select and use the better of two tools or ways of doing something—these are the factors of cultural evolution." Unlike 19th century evolutionists, who were concerned with how civilized societies rose above primitive societies, White was interested in documenting how, over time, humankind as a whole has through cultural means discovered more and more ways for capturing and harnessing energy from the environment, in the process of transforming culture. At the same time that White was developing his theory of cultural evolution, Kroeber's student Julian Steward was developing his theory of cultural ecology. In 1938 he published *Basin-Plateau Aboriginal Socio-political Groups* in which he argued that diverse societies—for example the indigenous Shoshone or White farmers on the Great Plains—were not less or more evolved; rather, they had adapted differently to different environments. Whereas Leslie White was interested in culture understood holistically as a property of the human species, Julian Steward was interested in culture as the property of distinct societies.

Like White he viewed culture as a means of adapting to the environment, but he criticized Whites "unilineal" (one direction) theory of cultural evolution and instead proposed a model of "multilineal" evolution in which (in the Boasian tradition) each society has its own cultural history. When Julian Steward left a teaching position at the University of Michigan to work in Utah in 1930, Leslie White took his place; in 1946 Julian Steward was made Chair of the Columbia University Anthropology Department. In the 1940s and 1950s their students, most notably Marvin Harris, Sidney Mintz, Robert Murphy, Roy Rappaport, Marshall Sahlins, Elman Service, Andrew P. Vayda and Eric Wolf dominated American anthropology. Most promoted materialist understandings of culture in opposition to the symbolic approaches of Geertz and Schneider. Harris, Rappaport, and Vayda were especially important for their contributions to cultural materialism and ecological anthropology, both of which argued that "culture" constituted an extra-somatic (or non-biological) means through which human beings could adapt to life in drastically differing physical environments.

The debate between symbolic and materialist approaches to culture dominated American anthropologists in the 1960s and 1970s. The Vietnam War and the publication of Dell Hymes' *Reinventing Anthropology*, however, marked a growing dissatisfaction with the then dominant approaches to culture. Hymes argued that fundamental elements of the Boasian project such as holism and an interest in diversity were still worth pursuing: "interest in other peoples and their ways of life, and concern to explain them within a frame of reference that includes ourselves." Moreover, he argued that cultural anthropologists are singularly well-equipped to lead this study (with an indirect rebuke to sociologists like Parsons who sought to subsume anthropology to their own project):

> *In the practice there is a traditional place for openness to phenomena in ways not predefined by theory or design—attentiveness to complex phenomena, to phenomena of interest, perhaps aesthetic, for their own sake, to the sensory as well as intellectual, aspects of the subject. These comparative and practical perspectives, though not unique to formal anthropology, are specially husbanded there, and might well be impaired, if the study of man were to be united under the guidance of others who lose touch with experience in concern for methodology, who forget the ends of social knowledge in elaborating its means, or who are unwittingly or unconcernedly culture-bound.*

It is these elements, Hymes argued, that justify a "general study of man," that is, "anthropology". During this time notable anthropologists such as Mintz, Murphy, Sahlins, and Wolf eventually broke away, experimenting with structuralist and Marxist approaches to culture, they continued to promote cultural anthropology against structural functionalism.

1940—Present: Local versus Global Perspective

Boas and Malinowski established ethnographic research as a highly localized method for studying culture. Yet Boas emphasized that culture is dynamic, moving from one group of people to another, and that specific cultural forms have to be analyzed in a larger context. This has led anthropologists to explore different ways of understanding the global dimensions of culture. In the 1940s and 1950s, several key studies focused on how trade between indigenous peoples and the Europeans who had conquered and colonized the Americas influenced indigenous culture, either through change in the organization of labor, or change in critical technologies. Bernard Mishkin studied the effect of the introduction of horses on Kiowa political organization and warfare. Oscar Lewis explored the influence of the fur trade on Blackfoot culture (relying heavily on historical sources). Joseph Jablow documented how Cheyenne social organization and subsistence strategy between 1795 and 1840 were determined by their position in trade networks linking Whites and other Indians. Frank Secoy argued that Great Plains Indians' social organization and military tactics changed as horses, introduced by the Spanish in the south, diffused north, and guns, introduced by the British and French in the East, diffused West. In the 1950s Robert Redfield and students of Julian Steward pioneered "community studies," namely, the study of distinct communities (whether identified by race, ethnicity, or economic class) in western or "westernized" societies, especially cities. They thus encountered the antagonisms 19th century critics described using the terms "high culture" and "low culture."

These 20th-century anthropologists struggled to describe people who were politically and economically inferior but not, they believed, culturally inferior. Oscar Lewis proposed the concept of a "culture of poverty" to describe the cultural mechanisms through which people adapted to a life of economic poverty. Other anthropologists and sociologists began using the term "sub-culture" to describe culturally distinct communities that were part of larger societies. One important kind of subculture is that formed by an immigrant community. In dealing with immigrant groups and their cultures, there are various approaches:

- Leitkultur (core culture): A model developed in Germany by Bassam Tibi. The idea is that minorities can have an identity of their own, but they should at least support the core concepts of the culture on which the society is based.
- Melting Pot: In the United States, the traditional view has been one of a melting pot where all the immigrant cultures are mixed and amalgamated without state intervention.
- Monoculturalism: In some European states, culture is very closely linked to nationalism, thus government policy is to assimilate immigrants, although recent increases in migration have led many European states to experiment with forms of multiculturalism.
- Multiculturalism: A policy that immigrants and others should preserve their cultures with the different cultures interacting peacefully within one nation.

The way nation states treat immigrant cultures rarely falls neatly into one or another of the above approaches. The degree of difference with the host culture (i.e., "foreignness"), the number of immigrants, attitudes of the resident population, the type of government policies that are enacted, and the effectiveness of those policies all make it difficult to generalize about the effects. Similarly with other subcultures within a society, attitudes of the mainstream population and communications between various cultural groups play a major role in determining outcomes. The study of cultures within a society is complex and research must take into account a myriad of variables.

Cultural Analysis and Its Significance

In the United Kingdom, sociologists and other scholars influenced by Marxism, such as Stuart Hall and Raymond Williams, developed Cultural Studies. Following nineteenth century Romantics, they identified "culture" with consumption goods and leisure activities (such as art, music, film, food, sports, and clothing). Nevertheless, they understood patterns of consumption and leisure to be determined by relations of production, which led them to focus on class relations and the organization of production. In the United States, "Cultural Studies" focuses largely on the study of popular culture, that is, the social meanings of mass-produced consumer and leisure goods. The term was coined by Richard Hoggart in 1964 when he founded the Birmingham Centre for Contemporary Cultural Studies or CCCS. It has since become strongly associated with Stuart Hall, who succeeded Hoggart as Director.

From the 1970s onward, Stuart Hall's pioneering work, along with his colleagues Paul Willis, Dick Hebdige, Tony Jefferson, and Angela McRobbie, created an international intellectual movement. As the field developed it began to combine political economy, communication, sociology, social theory, literary theory, media theory, film/video studies, cultural anthropology, philosophy, museum studies and art history to study cultural phenomena or cultural texts. In this field researchers often concentrate on how particular phenomena relate to matters of ideology, nationality, ethnicity, social class, and/or gender. Cultural studies is concerned with the meaning and practices of everyday life. These practices comprise the ways people do particular things (such as watching television, or eating out) in a given culture. This field studies the meanings and uses people attribute to various objects and practices. Recently, as capitalism has spread throughout the world (a process called globalization), cultural studies has begun to analyze local and global forms of resistance to western hegemony. In the context of cultural studies, the idea of a *text* not only includes written language, but also films, photographs, fashion or hairstyles: the texts of cultural studies comprise all the meaningful artifacts of culture. Similarly, the discipline widens the concept of "culture". "Culture" for a cultural studies researcher not only includes traditional high culture (the culture of ruling social groups) and popular culture, but also everyday meanings and practices. The last two, in fact, have become the main focus of cultural studies. A further and recent approach is comparative cultural studies, based on the discipline of comparative literature and cultural studies.

Scholars in the United Kingdom and the United States developed somewhat different versions of cultural studies after the field's inception in the late 1970s. The British version of cultural studies was developed in the 1950s and 1960s mainly under the influence first of Richard Hoggart, E. P. Thompson, and Raymond Williams, and later Stuart Hall and others at the Centre for Contemporary Cultural Studies at the University of Birmingham. This included overtly political, left-Wing views, and criticisms of popular culture as "capitalist" mass culture; it absorbed some of the ideas of the Frankfurt School critique of the "culture industry" (i.e. mass culture). This emerges in the writings of early British cultural-studies scholars and their influences: see the work of Raymond Williams, Stuart Hall, Paul Willis, and Paul Gilroy. Whereas in the United States Lindlof & Taylor said, "Cultural studies [were] grounded in a pragmatic, liberal-pluralist tradition". The American version of cultural studies initially concerned itself more with understanding the subjective and appropriative side of audience reactions to, and uses of, mass culture; for example, American cultural-studies advocates wrote about the liberatory aspects of fandom.

The distinction between American and British strands, however, has faded. Some researchers, especially in early British cultural studies, apply a Marxist model to the field. This strain of thinking has some influence from the Frankfurt School, but especially from the structuralist Marxism of Louis Althusser and others. The main focus of an orthodox Marxist approach concentrates on the *production* of meaning. This model assumes a mass production of culture and identifies power as residing with those producing cultural artifacts. In a Marxist view, those who control the means of production (the economic *base*) essentially control a culture. Other approaches to cultural studies, such as feminist cultural studies and later American developments of the field, distance themselves from this view. They criticize the Marxist assumption of a single, dominant meaning, shared by all, for any cultural product. The non-marxist approaches suggest that different ways of consuming cultural artifacts affect the meaning of the product. This view is best exemplified by the book *Doing Cultural Studies: The Case of the Sony Walkman* (by Paul du Gay et al.), which seeks to challenge the notion that those who produce commodities control the meanings that people attribute to them. Feminist cultural analyst, theorist and art historian Griselda Pollock contributed to cultural studies from viewpoints of art history and psychoanalysis. The writer Julia Kristeva is influential voices in the turn of the century, contributing to cultural studies from the field of art and psychoanalytical French feminism.

Cultural Change: Aftermath of Social Change or Its Igniter?

Cultural invention has come to mean any innovation that is new and found to be useful to a group of people and expressed in their behavior but which does not exist as a physical object. Humanity is in a global "accelerating culture change period", driven by the expansion of international commerce, the mass media, and above all, the human population explosion, among other factors. Cultures are internally affected by both forces encouraging change and forces resisting change. These forces are related to both social structures and natural events, and are involved in the perpetuation of cultural ideas and practices within current structures, which themselves are subject to change. (See structuration.) Social conflict and the development of technologies can produce changes within a society by altering social dynamics and promoting new cultural models, and spurring or enabling generative action. These social shifts may accompany ideological shifts and other types of cultural change. For example, the U. S. feminist movement involved new practices that produced a shift in gender relations, altering both gender and economic structures. Environmental conditions may also enter as factors. For example, after tropical forests returned at the end of the last ice age, plants suitable for domestication were available, leading to the invention of agriculture, which in turn brought about many cultural innovations and shifts in social dynamics. Cultures are externally affected via contact between societies, which may also produce—or inhibit—social shifts and changes in cultural practices. War or competition over resources may impact technological development or social dynamics. Additionally, cultural ideas may transfer from one society to another, through diffusion or acculturation.

In diffusion, the form of something (though not necessarily its meaning) moves from one culture to another. For example, hamburgers, mundane in the United States, seemed exotic when introduced into China. "Stimulus Diffusion" (the sharing of ideas) refers to an element of one culture leading to an invention or propagation in another. "Direct Borrowing" on the other hand tends to refer to technological or tangible diffusion from one culture to another. Diffusion of innovations theory presents a research-based model of why and when individuals and cultures adopt new ideas, practices, and products. Acculturation has different meanings, but in this context refers to replacement of the traits of one culture with those of another, such has happened to certain Native American tribes and to many indigenous peoples across the globe during the process of colonization. Related processes on an individual level include assimilation (adoption of a different culture by an individual) and transculturation.

Questions or Topics for Pondering and Further Discussion for Unit One-2:

1. Do you think culture is a very elusive term that is beyond accurate definition?
2. What is the core part of a culture broadly defined?
3. Do you believe there are such things as high-brow, middle-brow and low-brow cultures?
4. Do you think a world of cultural diversity is better than a world of cultural hegemony? Why or why not?
5. What are the major variables of cultural studies?
6. *Culture refers to a pan-human capacity and the totality of non-Genetic human phenomena.* Please make some further comment or explanation on it.
7. What role does a given language play in understanding a given culture?
8. Do you think there is a possibility of emergence of a global culture against the background of economic globalization in the future? Why and why not?

3. History, a Riddle for Humans

Those who cannot remember the past are condemned to repeat it.

—George Santayana

Editor's remarks: it is hotly disputed if there is a universally accepted view of history. Most likely there is no such view concerning history accepted by all. People of different social, political, economic, cultural and religious backgrounds definitely possess totally different views about history. It is in this regard that history is more subjective than objective even though some of the historic events existed objectively. In spite of this, history as one of the three foundation disciplines of social sciences is indispensable to human society and civilization studies. Theists hold that the whole universe is created by God. Thus, history is sometimes referred to as His Story, which means that He, almighty God, arranges everything according to His view and will and the whole world revolves around His Story. Marxist historians view common people as creator of history while some so-called bourgeois historians claim that it is heroes who create history. Whatever history may imply, it is of vital importance for people to know what has happened in the past and its implication to the present and future.

History is the discovery, collection, organization, and presentation of information about past events. History can also mean the period of time after writing was invented. Scholars who write about history are called historians. It is a field of research which uses a narrative to examine and analyze the sequence of events, and it sometimes attempts to investigate objectively the patterns of cause and effect that determine events. Historians debate the nature of history and its usefulness. This includes discussing the study of the discipline as an end in itself and as a way of providing "perspective" on the problems of the present. The stories common to a particular culture, but not supported by external sources (such as the legends surrounding King Arthur) are usually classified as cultural heritage rather than the "disinterested investigation" needed by the discipline of history. Events of the past prior to written record are considered prehistory. Among scholars, the 5th-century BC Greek historian Herodotus is considered to be the "father of history", and, along with his contemporary Thucydides, forms the foundations for the modern study of history. Their influence, along with other historical traditions in other parts of their world, have spawned many different interpretations of the nature of history which has evolved over the centuries and are continuing to change. The modern study of history has many different fields including those that focus on certain regions and those which focus on certain topical or thematical elements of historical investigation. Often history is taught as part of primary and secondary education, and the academic study of history is a major discipline in University studies. A derivation from *weid-* "know" or "see" is attested as "the reconstructed etymon *wid-tor* ['one who knows'] (compare to English *wit*) a suffixed zero-grade form of the PIE root *weid-*—'see' and so is related to Greek *eidénai*, to know "...

Ancient Greek στορία (*hístōr*) means "inquiry", "knowledge from inquiry", or "judge". It was in that sense that Aristotle used the word in his Περ Τ Ζα στορίαι (*Perì Tà Zôa Historíai* "Inquiries about Animals"). The ancestor word ἴστωρ is attested early on in Homeric Hymns, Heraclitus, the Athenian ephebes' oath, and in Boiotic inscriptions (in a legal sense, either "judge" or "witness", or similar). The word entered the English language in 1390 with the meaning of "relation of incidents, story". In Middle English, the meaning was "story" in general. The restriction to the meaning "record of past events" arises in the late 15th century. It was still in the Greek sense that Francis Bacon used the term in the late 16th century, when he wrote about "Natural History". For him, *historia* was "the knowledge of objects determined by space and time", that sort of knowledge provided by memory (while science was provided by reason, and poetry was provided by fantasy). In an expression of the linguistic synthetic vs. analytic/isolating dichotomy, English like Chinese now designates separate words for human history and storytelling in general. In modern German, French, and most Germanic and Romance languages, which are solidly synthetic and highly inflected, the same word is still used to mean both "history" and "story". The adjective *historical* is attested from 1661, and *historic* from 1669. *Historian* in the sense of a "researcher of history" is attested from 1531. In all European languages, the substantive "history" is still used to mean both "what happened with men", and "the scholarly study of the happened", the latter sense sometimes distinguished with a capital letter, "History", or the word *historiography*.

Description

Historians write in the context of their own time, and with due regard to the current dominant ideas of how to interpret the past, and sometimes write to provide lessons for their own society. In the words of Benedetto Croce, "All history is contemporary history". History is facilitated by the formation of a "true discourse of past" through the production of narrative and analysis of past events relating to the human race. The modern discipline of history is dedicated to the institutional production of this discourse. All events that are remembered and preserved in some authentic form constitute the historical record. The task of historical discourse is to identify the sources which can most usefully contribute to the production of accurate accounts of past. Therefore, the constitution of the historian's archive is a result of circumscribing a more general archive by invalidating the usage of certain texts and documents (by falsifying their claims to represent the "true past"). The study of history has sometimes been classified as part of the humanities and at other times as part of the social sciences. It can also be seen as a bridge between those two broad areas, incorporating methodologies from both. Some individual historians strongly support one or the other classification. In the 20th century, French historian Fernand Braudel revolutionized the study of history, by using such outside disciplines as economics, anthropology, and geography in the study of global history. Traditionally, historians have recorded events of the past, either in writing or by passing on an oral tradition, and have attempted to answer historical questions through the study of written documents and oral accounts. For the beginning, historians have also used such sources as monuments, inscriptions, and pictures. In general, the sources of historical knowledge can be separated into three categories: what is written, what is said, and what is physically preserved, and historians often consult all three. But writing is the marker that separates history from what comes before. Archaeology is a discipline that is especially helpful in dealing with buried sites and objects, which, once unearthed, contribute to the study of history. But archaeology rarely stands alone. It uses narrative sources to complement its discoveries. However, archaeology is constituted by a range of methodologies and approaches which are independent from history; that is to say, archaeology does not "fill the gaps" within textual sources. Indeed, Historical Archaeology is a specific branch of archaeology, often contrasting its conclusions against those of contemporary textual sources. For example, Mark Leone, the excavator and interpreter of historical Annapolis, Maryland, USA has sought to understand the contradiction between textual documents and the material record, demonstrating the possession of slaves and the inequalities of wealth apparent via the study of the total historical environment, despite the ideology of "liberty" inherent in written documents at this time.

There are varieties of ways in which history can be organized, including chronologically, culturally, territorially, and thematically. These divisions are not mutually exclusive, and significant overlaps are often present, as in "The International Women's Movement in an Age of Transition, 1830—1975". It is possible for historians to concern themselves with both the very specific and the very general, although the modern trend has been toward specialization. The area called Big History resists this specialization, and searches for universal patterns or trends. History has often been studied with some practical or theoretical aim, but also may be studied out of simple intellectual curiosity. The history of the world is the memory of the past experience of *Homo sapiens* around the world, as that experience has been preserved, largely in written records. By "prehistory", historians mean the recovery of knowledge of the past in an area where no written records exist, or where the writing of a culture is not understood. By studying painting, drawings, carvings, and other artifacts, some information can be recovered even in the absence of a written record. Since the 20th century, the study of prehistory is considered essential to avoid history's implicit exclusion of certain civilizations, such as those of Sub-Saharan Africa and pre-Columbian America. Historians in the West have been criticized for focusing disproportionately on the western world. In 1961, British historian E. H. Carr wrote:

> *The line of demarcation between prehistoric and historical times is crossed when people cease to live only in the present, and become consciously interested both in their past and in their future. History begins with the handing down of tradition; and tradition means the carrying of the habits and lessons of the past into the future. Records of the past begin to be kept for the benefit of future generations.*

This definition includes within the scope of history the strong interests of peoples, such as Australian Aboriginals and New Zealand Māori in the past, and the oral records maintained and transmitted to succeeding generations, even before their contact with European civilization.

Many of the advocates of history as a social science were or are noted for their multi-disciplinary approach. Braudel combined history with geography, Bracher history with political science, Fogel history with economics, Gay history with psychology, Trigger history with archaeology while Wehler, Bloch, Fischer, Stone, Febvre and Le Roy Ladurie have in varying and differing ways amalgamated history with sociology, geography, anthropology, and economics. More recently, the field of digital history has begun to address ways of using computer technology to pose new questions to historical data and generate digital scholarship. In opposition to the claims of history as a social science, historians such as Hugh Trevor-Roper, John Lukacs, Donald Creighton, Gertrude Himmelfarb and Gerhard Ritter argued that the key to the historians' work was the power of the imagination, and hence contended that history should be understood as an art. French historians associated with the Annales School introduced quantitative history, using raw data to track the lives of typical individuals, and were prominent in the establishment of cultural history (cf. *histoire des mentalités*). Intellectual historians such as Herbert Butterfield, Ernst Nolte and George Mosse have argued for the significance of ideas in history. American historians, motivated by the civil rights era, focused on formerly overlooked ethnic, racial, and socio-economic groups.

Another genre of social history to emerge in the post-WW II era was *Alltagsgeschichte* (History of Everyday Life). Scholars such as Martin Broszat, Ian Kershaw and Detlev Peukert sought to examine what everyday life was like for ordinary people in 20th-century Germany, especially in the Nazi period. Marxist historians such as Eric Hobsbawm, E. P. Thompson, Rodney Hilton, Georges Lefebvre, Eugene D. Genovese, Isaac Deutscher, C. L. R. James, Timothy Mason, Herbert Aptheker, Arno J. Mayer and Christopher Hill have sought to validate Karl Marx's theories by analyzing history from a Marxist perspective. In response to the Marxist interpretation of history, historians such as François Furet, Richard Pipes, J. C. D. Clark, Roland Mousnier, Henry Ashby Turner and Robert Conquest have offered anti-marxist interpretations of history. Feminist historians such as Joan Wallach Scott, Claudia Koonz, Natalie Zemon Davis, Sheila Rowbotham, Gisela Bock, Gerda Lerner, Elizabeth Fox-Genovese, and Lynn Hunt have argued for the importance of studying the experience of women in the past. In recent years, postmodernists have challenged the validity and need for the study of history on the basis that all history is based on the personal interpretation of sources. In his 1997 book *In Defense of History*, Richard J. Evans, a professor of modern history at Cambridge University, defended the worth of history. Another defense of history from post-modernist criticism was the Australian historian Keith Windschuttle's 1994 book, *The Killing of History*.

World General History

World history is the study of major civilizations over the last 3,000 years or so. It has led to highly controversial interpretations by Oswald Spengler and Arnold J. Toynbee, among others. World history is especially important as a teaching field. It has increasingly entered the university curriculum in the U.S., in many cases replacing courses in western Civilization, that had a focus on Europe and the U.S. World history adds extensive new material on Asia, Africa and Latin America.

Regions

- History of Africa begins with the first emergence of modern human beings on the continent, continuing into its modern present as a patchwork of diverse and politically developing nation states.
- History of the Americas is the collective history of North and South America, including Central America and the Caribbean.
  - History of North America is the study of the past passed down from generation to generation on the continent in the Earth's northern and western hemisphere.
  - History of Central America is the study of the past passed down from generation to generation on the continent in the Earth's western hemisphere.
  - History of the Caribbean is said to begin with the oldest evidence where 7,000-year-old

remains have been found.
- History of South America is the study of the past passed down from generation to generation on the continent in the Earth's southern and western hemisphere.
- History of Antarctica emerges from early western theories of a vast continent, known as Terra Australis, believed to exist in the far south of the globe.
- History of Australia starts with the documentation of the Makassar trading with Indigenous Australians on Australia's north coast.
- History of New Zealand dates back at least 700 years when it was discovered and settled by Polynesians, who developed a distinct Māori culture centered on kinship links and land.
- History of the Pacific Islands covers the history of the islands in the Pacific Ocean.
- History of Eurasia is the collective history of several distinct peripheral coastal regions: the Middle East, South Asia, East Asia, Southeast Asia, and Europe, linked by the interior mass of the Eurasian steppe of Central Asia and eastern Europe.
  - History of Europe describes the passage of time from humans inhabiting the European continent to the present day.
  - History of Asia can be seen as the collective history of several distinct peripheral coastal regions, East Asia, South Asia, and the Middle East linked by the interior mass of the Eurasian steppe.
  - History of East Asia refers to the study of the past passed down from generation to generation in East Asia.
  - History of the Middle East begins with the earliest civilizations in the region now known as the Middle East that were established around 3,000 BC, in Mesopotamia (Iraq).
  - History of South Asia is the study of the past passed down from generation to generation in the Sub-himalayan region.
  - History of Southeast Asia has been characterized as interaction between regional players and foreign powers.

Cultural History, an Interaction Between Culture and History

Cultural history replaced social history as the dominant form in the 1980s and 1990s. It typically combines the approaches of anthropology and history to look at language, popular cultural traditions and cultural interpretations of historical experience. It examines the records and narrative descriptions of past knowledge, customs, and arts of a group of people. How peoples constructed their memory of the past is a major topic.

Cultural History Further Studied

The term **cultural history** refers both to an academic discipline and to its subject matter. Cultural history, as a discipline, at least in its common definition since the 1970s, often combines the approaches of anthropology and history to look at popular cultural traditions and cultural interpretations of historical experience. It examines the records and narrative descriptions of past knowledge, customs, and arts of a group of people. Its subject matter encompasses the continuum of events occurring in succession leading from the past to the present and even into the future pertaining to a culture. Cultural history records and interprets past events involving human beings through the social, cultural, and political milieu of or relating to the arts and manners that a group favors. Jacob Burckhardt helped found cultural history as a discipline. Cultural history studies and interprets the record of human societies by denoting the various distinctive ways of living built up by a group of people under consideration. Cultural history involves the aggregate of past cultural activity, such as ceremony, class in practices, and the interaction with locales.

Description

Cultural history overlaps in its approaches with the French movements of *histoire des mentalités* (Philippe Poirrier, 2004) and the so-called new history, and in the U.S. it is closely associated with the field of American studies. As originally conceived and practiced by 19th century Swiss historian Jakob Burckhardt with regard to the Italian Renaissance, cultural history was oriented to the study of a particular historical period in its entirety, with regard not only for its painting, sculpture and architecture, but for the economic basis underpinning society, and the social institutions of its daily life as well. Most often the focus is on phenomena shared by non-elite groups in a society, such as: carnival, festival, and public rituals; performance traditions of tale, epic, and other verbal forms; cultural evolutions in human relations (ideas, sciences, arts, techniques); and cultural expressions of social movements such as nationalism. Also examines main historical concepts as power, ideology, class, culture, cultural identity, attitude, race, perception and new historical methods as narration of body. Many studies consider adaptations of traditional culture to mass media (television, radio, newspapers, magazines, posters, etc.), from print to film and, now, to the Internet (culture of capitalism). Its modern approaches come from art history, annales, Marxist school, microhistory and new cultural history. Common theoretical touchstones for recent cultural history have included: Jürgen Habermas's formulation of the public sphere in *The Structural Transformation of the Bourgeois Public Sphere*; Clifford Geertz's notion of "thick description" (expounded in, for example, *The Interpretation of Cultures*); and the idea of memory as a cultural-historical category, as discussed in Paul Connerton's *How Societies Remember*.

Questions or Topics for Pondering and Further Discussion for Unit One-3:

1. Do you believe the study of history can reflect a true picture of the past events?
2. Quotation: *People have learned from history that people have learned nothing from history*. Comment.
3. Some historians define history as an art that needs imagination for its research. Make further comment.
4. Some people say that human civilization began when people had a sense of history, which means that they started to pay attention to and learn from their past experience. Do you agree with this statement?
5. Why is history classified as a foundation discipline of social sciences?
6. History is further divided into many sub-branches such as diplomatic history or military history. Why is that?
7. Cultural history is a branch of cultural studies. Please point out its significance in cultural studies.
8. Francis Bacon once said, "history makes people wise." Please make some further comment on it.

Unit Two

1. West Is Not a Directional Concept Alone

Editor's remarks: *West as a terms means a lot as it carries implications much more than a geographical connotation. Geographically, economically, culturally, or even genetically, the world is divided into East and West, posing an eternal antithetical concept for human beings. It is in this sense that for easterners, learning something about the West is significant and rewarding.*

West is a noun, adjective, or adverb indicating direction or geography. West is one of the four cardinal directions or compass points. It is the opposite of East and is perpendicular to North and South. To go West using a compass for navigation, one needs to set a bearing or azimuth of 270°. West is the direction opposite that of the Earth's rotation on its axis, and is therefore the general direction towards which the Sun sets. During the Cold War "the West" was often used to refer to the NATO camp as opposed to the Warsaw Pact and non-aligned nations. The expression survives, with an increasingly ambiguous meaning. Moving continuously West is following a circle of latitude, which, except in the case of the equator, is not a great circle. The word *West* is derived from the name of one of the four dwarves in Norse mythology, Norðri, Suðri, Austri and Vestri, who each represented one of the directions of the world. cf Greek hesperus and Roman vesper.

Symbolic Meanings

In Chinese Buddhism, the West represents movement toward the Buddha or enlightenment (see *Journey to the West*). The ancient Aztecs believed that the West was the realm of the great goddess of water, mist, and maize. In ancient Egypt, the West was considered to be the portal to the netherworld, and is the cardinal direction regarded in connection with death, though not always with a negative connotation. Ancient Egyptians also believed that the Goddess Amunet was a personification of the West. The Celts believed that beyond the western sea off the edges of all maps lay the Otherworld, or Afterlife. In American literature (e. g. in *The Great Gatsby*) moving West has sometimes symbolized gaining freedom, perhaps as an association with the settling of the Old West (see also Manifest Destiny). The term **Occidentalism** is used to refer to images of "the West". in one of two main ways: a) stereotyped and sometimes dehumanizing views on the western world, including Europe and the English-speaking world; and b) ideologies or visions of the West developed in either the West or non-West. The former definition stresses negative constructions of the West and is often focused on the Islamic world. The latter approach has a broader range and includes both positive and negative representations. The term was used in the latter sense by James G. Carrier in his book *Occidentalism: Images of the West* (1995), and subsequently by Ian Buruma and Avishai Margalit in their book *Occidentalism: the West in the Eyes of its Enemies* (2004). The term is an inversion of Orientalism, Edward Said's label for stereotyped western views of the East. A number of earlier books had also used the term, sometimes with different meanings, such as Chen Xiaomei's *Occidentalism: A Theory of Counter-discourse in Post-Mao China* (New York: Oxford, 1995).

Picturing the West and Its Peculiar Image

In China "Traditions Regarding western Countries" became a regular part of dynastic histories from the fifth-century CE (Bonnett, 2004). With the spread of European trade and imperialism during the 18th and 19th centuries the modern concept of an East/West distinction came to be more clearly articulated. Stereotyped portrayals of westerners appear in many works of Indian, Chinese and Japanese artists during this period. At the same time western influence in politics, culture, economics and science came to be constructed through an imaginative geography of West and East. In the late 19th century many western cultural themes and images began appearing in Asian art and culture, especially in Japan. English words and phrases are prominent in Japanese advertising and popular culture, and many Japanese comics and cartoons are written around characters, settings, themes, and mythological figures derived from various western cultural traditions. Another way Occidentalism has been manifested is through the attempt to forge "non-western" identities and cultures. Notions of "spiritual Asia" are an example, since they depend upon constructions of the "materialist West". These images can be read as forms of resistance but they also demonstrate the power of western models.

Debates on Occidentalism

Buruma and Margalit argue that this nationalist and nativist resistance to the "West" actually replicates responses to forces of modernization that have their roots in western culture itself, among both Utopian radicals and nationalist conservatives who saw capitalism, liberalism and secularism as destructive forces. They argue that while early responses to the West represent a genuine encounter between alien cultures, many of the later manifestations of Occidentalism betray the influence on eastern intellectuals of western ideas, such as the supremacy of the Nation-state, the Romantic rejection of rationality and the alleged spiritual impoverishment of the citizens of liberal democracies. They trace this to German Romanticism and to the debates between the "westernisers" and "Slavophiles" in 19th century Russia, asserting that similar arguments appear under differing guises in Maoism, Islamism, wartime Japanese nationalism and other movements. However, Alastair Bonnett rejects this analysis as Eurocentric and makes a case for Occidentalism emerging from the interconnection of non-western and western intellectual traditions. In a departure from Buruma and Margalit's focus upon the non-western deployment of western ideas, Bonnett argues in *The Idea of the West* (2004) that both Occidentalism and the West can be understood as non-western inventions. Images of the West are employed and deployed, he says, sometimes with very positive connotations, to develop distinct, non-western, traditions of modernity. Bonnett's approach stresses the importance of visions of the occident in developing pan-national and ethnic identities around the world.

Questions or Topics for Pondering and Further Discussion for Unit Two-1:

1. How do you account for the rise of the West in modern time?
2. What are core elements of Westernization?
3. Is Westernization equal to modernization?
4. What is the essence of Occidentalism?
5. What is the etymological origin of West in the first place?
6. What is the symbolic meaning of the West?
7. Proverb: East and West, home is the best. Please make some comment on it.
8. Is Russia a western country? Why or why not?

2. Western Culture and Its Deep Implications

western culture, sometimes equated with **western civilization** or **European civilization**, is a term used very broadly to refer to a heritage of social norms, ethical values, traditional customs, religious beliefs, political systems, and specific artifacts and technologies. The term has come to apply to countries whose history is strongly marked by European immigration, such as the Americas, and Australasia, and is not restricted to western Eurasia (Europe). western culture stems from two sources: the Classical Period of the Graeco-Roman era and the influence of Christianity which have been an important part of the shaping of western civilization, at least since the 4th century. The artistic, philosophic, literary, and legal themes and traditions; the heritages of especially Latin, Celtic, Germanic, and Hellenic ethnic or linguistic groups; as well as a tradition of rationalism in various spheres of life, developed mainly by Hellenistic philosophy, Scholasticism, Humanism, the Scientific Revolution and Enlightenment; and including, in political thought, widespread rational arguments in favor of free thought, human rights, equality and democracy. Historical records of western culture in its European geographical range begin with Ancient Greece, and then Ancient Rome, Christianization during the European Middle Ages, and reform and modernization starting by Renaissance, and globalized by successive European empires that spread the European ways of life and education between the sixteenth and twentieth centuries. European Culture developed with a complex range of philosophy, medieval scholasticism and mysticism, Christian and secular humanism. Rational thinking developed through a long age of change and formation with the experiments of Enlightenment, Naturalism, Romanticism, Science, Democracy, and Socialism. With its global connection, European culture grew with an all-inclusive urge to adopt, adapt, and ultimately influence other trends of culture. Some tendencies that have come to define modern western societies are the existence of political pluralism, prominent subcultures or countercultures (such as New Age movements), and increasing cultural syncretism resulting from globalization and human migration. The Greeks contrasted themselves to their eastern neighbors, such as the Trojans in *Iliad*, setting an example for later contrasts between East and West. In the Middle Ages, Islam in the Near East provided a contrast to the West though it had been Hellenized since the time of Alexander the Great, and had been ruled by Rome and Constantinople and part of "Christendom". In the later 20th to early 21st century, with the advent of increasing globalism, it has become more difficult to determine which individuals fit into which category, and the East—West contrast is sometimes criticized as relativistic and arbitrary.

Globalism has, especially since the end of the Cold War, spread western ideas so widely that almost all modern countries or cultures are to some extent influenced by aspects of western culture which they have absorbed. Recent stereotyped western views of "the West" have been labeled *Occidentalism*, paralleling Orientalism, the term for the 19th century stereotyped views of "the East". Geographically, "the West" today would normally be said to include western Europe as well as certain territories belonging to the Anglosphere, the Hispanidad, the Lusofonia or the Francophonie. western culture is neither homogeneous nor unchanging. As with all other cultures it has evolved and gradually changed over time. All generalities about it have their exceptions at some time and place. The organization and tactics of the Greek Hoplites differed in many ways from the Roman legions. The *polis* of the Greeks is not the same as the American superpower of the 21st century. The gladiatorial games of the Roman Empire are not identical to present-day football. The art of Pompeii is not the art of Hollywood. Nevertheless, it is possible to follow the evolution and history of the West, and appreciate its similarities and differences, its borrowings from, and contributions to, other cultures of humanity. Concepts of what is the West arose out of legacies of the western Roman Empire and the eastern Roman Empire. Later, ideas of the West were formed by the concepts of Christendom and the Holy Roman Empire. What we think of as western thought today is generally defined as Greco-Roman and Judeo-Christian culture, and includes the ideals of the Renaissance and the Enlightenment.

The Classical West

In Homeric literature, and right up until the time of Alexander the Great, for example in the accounts of the Persian Wars of Greeks against Persians by Herodotus, we see the paradigm of a contrast between the West and East. Nevertheless the Greeks felt they were the most civilized and saw themselves (in the formulation of Aristotle) as something between the wild barbarians of most of Europe and the soft, slavish easterners. Ancient Greek science, philosophy, democracy, architecture, literature, and art provided a foundation embraced and built upon by the Roman Empire as it swept up Europe, including the Hellenic World in its conquests in the 1st century BC. In the meantime however, Greece, under Alexander, had become a capital of the East, and part of an empire. The idea that the later Orthodox or eastern Christian cultural descendants of the Greek-speaking eastern Roman Empire, are a happy mean between eastern slavishness and western barbarism is promoted to this day, for example in Russia, creating a zone which is highly context-depending. For about five hundred years, the Roman Empire maintained the Greek East and consolidated a Latin West, but an East-West division remained, reflected in many cultural norms of the two areas, including language. Although Rome, like Greece, was no longer democratic, the idea of democracy remained a part of the education of citizens, as if the emperors were a temporary emergency measure. Eventually the empire came to be increasingly officially split into a western and eastern part, reviving old ideas of a contrast between an advanced East, and a rugged West. In the Roman world one could speak of three main directions: North (Celtic tribes and Parthians), the East, and finally South which implied danger, historically via the Punic wars. The West was peaceful—it contained only the Mediterranean. With the rise of Christianity in the midst of the Roman world, much of Rome's tradition and culture were absorbed by the new religion, and transformed into something new, which would serve as the basis for the development of western civilization after the fall of Rome. Also, Roman culture mixed with the pre-existing Celtic, Germanic and Slavic cultures, which slowly became integrated into western culture starting, mainly, with their acceptance of Christianity.

The Medieval West

The Medieval West was at its broadest the same as Christendom, including both the "Latin" or "Frankish" West, and the Orthodox eastern part, where Greek remained the language of empire. After the crowning of Charlemagne, Charlemagne's part of Europe was referred to by its neighbors in Byzantium and the Muslim world as "Frankish". After the fall of Rome much of Greco-Roman art, literature, science and even technology were all but lost in the western part of the old empire, centered around Italy, and Gaul (France). However, this would become the center of a new West. Europe fell into political anarchy, with many warring kingdoms and principalities. Under the Frankish kings, it eventually reunified and evolved into feudalism. Charlemagne was crowned Emperor of the Romans by the Pope in 800. His reign is associated with the Carolingian Renaissance, a revival of art, religion, and culture through the medium of the Catholic Church. Through his foreign conquests and internal reforms, Charlemagne helped define both western Europe and the Middle Ages. He is numbered as Charles I in the regnal lists of France, Germany (where he is known as Karl der Große), and the Holy Roman Empire. The re-establishment of a western "Roman" imperium challenged the status of the eastern Roman Emperor in Constantinople and strained relations between them.

Much of the basis of the post-Roman cultural world had been set before the fall of the Empire, mainly through the integrating and reshaping of Roman ideas through Christian thought. The Greek and Roman paganism had been completely replaced by Christianity around the 4th and 5th centuries, since it became the official State religion following the baptism of emperor Constantine I. Roman Catholic Christianity and the Nicene Creed served as a unifying force in Christian parts of Europe, and in some respects replaced or competed with the secular authorities. Art and literature, law, education, and politics were preserved in the teachings of the Church, in an environment that, otherwise, would have probably seen their loss. The Church founded many cathedrals, universities, monasteries and seminaries, some of which continue to exist today. In the Medieval period, the route to power for many men was in the Church. In a broader sense, the Middle Ages, with its fertile encounter between Greek reasoning and Levantine monotheism was not confined to the West but also stretched into the old East, in what was to become the Islamic world. The philosophy and science of Classical Greece was largely forgotten in western and Northern Europe after the collapse of the western Roman Empire, other than in isolated monastic enclaves (notably in Ireland, which had become Christian but which was never conquered by Rome). Although the Byzantine Emperor Justinian (the last Emperor to speak Latin as a first tongue) closed the Academy in 529 AD (a date that is often cited as the end of Antiquity), the learning of Classical Antiquity was better preserved in the Byzantine eastern Roman Empire, whose capital at Constantinople stood for another millennium, before being captured by the Ottoman Turks. Justinian's Corpus Juris Civilis Roman civil law code was preserved in the East and Constantinople maintained trade and intermittent political control over outposts such as Venice in the West for centuries. Classical Greek learning was also subsumed, preserved and elaborated in the rising Islamic world, which gradually supplanted Roman-byzantine control over the Mediterranean, Middle East, North Africa, Iberia and even Greece itself—becoming a dominant cultural-political force in those regions. Thus, from the margins of the Roman world much of the learning of Classical Antiquity was slowly reintroduced to western Europe in the centuries following the collapse of the western Roman Empire. Irish missionaries such as St Columba propagated Christianity and Latin learning in western Europe during the Early Medieval Period and Byzantine Greeks and Islamic Arabs reintroduced texts from Antiquity to western Europe during the Late Middle Ages and Renaissance of the 12th century.

The Discovery of the New World by Columbus: the Beginning of the Rise of the West

The rediscovery of the Justinian Code in western Europe early in the 10th century rekindled a passion for the discipline of law, which crossed many of the re-forming boundaries between East and West. Eventually, it was only in the Catholic or Frankish West, that Roman law became the foundation on which all legal concepts and systems were based. Its influence can be traced to this day in all western legal systems (although in different manners and to different extents in the common [England] and the civil [continental European] legal traditions). The study of canon law, the legal system of the Catholic Church, fused with that of Roman law to form the basis of the refounding of western legal scholarship. The ideas of civil rights, equality before the law, equality of women, procedural justice, and democracy as the ideal form of society were principles which formed the basis of modern western culture. The West actively encouraged the spreading of Christianity, which was inexorably linked to the spread of western culture. Owing to the influence of Islamic culture and Islamic civilization—a culture that had preserved some of the knowledge of ancient Mesopotamia, Egypt, India, Persia, Greece, and Rome—in Islamic Spain and southern Italy, and in the Levant during the Crusades, Europeans translated many Arabic texts into Latin during the Middle Ages. Later, with the fall of Constantinople and the Ottoman conquest of the Byzantine Empire, followed by a massive exodus of Greek Christian priests and scholars to Italian towns like Venice, bringing with them as many scripts from the Byzantine archives as they could, scholars' interest in the Greek language and classic works, topics and lost files was revived. Both the Greek and Arabic influences eventually led to the beginnings of the Renaissance. From the late 15th century to the 17th century, western culture began to spread to other parts of the world by intrepid explorers and missionaries during the Age of Discovery, followed by imperialists from the 17th century to the early 20th century.

The Modern Era of the West: the Age of the West?

Coming into the modern era, the historical understanding of the East-West contrast—as the opposition of Christendom to its geographical neighbors—began to weaken. As religion became less important, and Europeans came into increasing contact with far away peoples, the old concept of western culture began a slow evolution towards what it is today. The Early Modern "Age of Discovery," first led by Portugal and Spain in the 15th and 16th centuries with France and England following in the 17th century, faded into the "Age of Enlightenment" of the 18th century, both characterized by the military advantages coming to Europeans from their development of firearms and other military technologies. The "Great Divergence" became more pronounced, making the West the bearer of science and the accompanying revolutions of technology and industrialisation. western political thinking also, eventually spread in many forms around the world.

With the early 19th century "Age of Revolution," the West entered a period of world empires, massive economic and technological advance, and bloody international conflicts continuing into the 20th century. As Europe discovered the wider world, old concepts adapted. The Islamic world which had formerly been considered "the Orient" ("the East") more specifically became the "Near East" as the interests of the European powers for the first time interfered with Qing China and Meiji Japan in the 19th century. Thus, the Sino-Japanese War in 1894—1895 occurred in the "Far East", while the troubles surrounding the decline of the Ottoman Empire simultaneously occurred in the "Near East". The "Middle East" in the mid-19th century included the territory East of the Ottoman empire but West of China, i. e. Greater Persia and Greater India, but is now used synonymously with "Near East" in most languages.

Ten Major Themes and Traditions of Western Culture

western culture has developed many themes and traditions, the most significant of which are listed as follows:

- Greco-Latin classic letters, arts, architecture, philosophical and cultural tradition, that include the influence of preeminent authors such as Plato, Aristotle, Homer, Herodotus, and Cicero, as well as a long mythologic tradition.
- A tradition of the importance of the rule of law which has its roots in Ancient Greece.
- The Catholic and Protestant Christian cultural tradition and ethic.
- Secular humanism, rationalism and Enlightenment thought, as opposed to traditionally

preeminent Catholicism and Protestant Christianity, religious and moral doctrines in lifestyle. This set the basis for a new critical attitude and open questioning of religion, favoring freethinking and questioning of the church as an authority, which resulted in open-minded and reformist ideals inside, such as liberation theology, which partly adopted these currents, and secular and political tendencies such as laicism, agnosticism, materialism and atheism.

- Widespread usage of terms and specific vocabulary borrowed, based or derived from Greek and Latin roots or etymologies for almost any field of arts, science and human knowledge, becoming easily understandable and common to almost any European language, and being a source for inventing internationalized neologisms for nearly any purpose. It is not rare for full loan Latin phrases or expressions, such as *in situ*, *habeas corpus* or *tempus fugit*, to be in usage, many of them giving name to artistic or literary concepts or currents. The usage of such roots and phrases is standardized in giving official scientific names for biological species (such as *Homo sapiens* or *Tyrannosaurus rex*). This shows a reverence for these languages, called classicism.
- Generalized usage of some form of the Latin or Greek alphabet. The latter includes the standard cases of Greece and other derived forms, such as Cyrillic, the case of those Balkan and eastern Slavic countries of Christian Orthodox tradition, historically under the Byzantine and later Russian czarist or Soviet area of influence. Other variants of it are encountered for Gothic and Coptic alphabets, that historically substituted older scripts, such as Runic, and Demotic or Hieroglyphic systems.
- Scholasticism and Renaissance arts and letters.
- Natural law, human rights, constitutionalism, parliamentarism (or presidentialism) and formal liberal democracy in recent times—prior to the 19th century, most western governments were still monarchies.
- A large influence, in modern times, of many of the ideals and values developed and inherited from Romanticism.
- Several subcultures (sometimes deriving into urban tribes) and countercultural movements, such as hippie lifestyle or New Age, that have left several influences on contemporary mainstream or subcultural tendencies (some of them, especially in the mainstream, can become merely aesthetic).

Widespread Influence of the Western Cultural Values

Elements of western culture have had a very influential effect on other cultures worldwide. People of many cultures, both western and non-western, equate *modernization* (adoption of technological progress) with *Westernization* (adoption of western culture). Some members of the non-western world, such as M. K. Gandhi, have suggested that the link between technological progress and certain harmful western values provides a reason why much of "modernity" should be rejected as being incompatible with their vision and the values of their societies. These types of argument referring to imperialism and stressing the importance of freedom from it and the relativist argument that different cultural norms should be treated equally, are also present in western philosophy.

Questions or Topics for Pondering and Further Discussion for Unit Two-2:

1. What are fundamental differences between western culture and eastern culture in general?
2. Do you think the rise of the West is the precondition of the dominance of western culture

or vice versa?
3. What are the core tenets of western culture as you see them?
4. Some people claim that American culture is the apex of western culture. Make some further comment, please.
5. Do you believe there is a such thing as cultural superiority or inferiority?
6. Does western culture stress more on material success? If so, why?
7. Can you point out some disadvantages of western culture in the view of cultural diversity?
8. Why did western culture become a more aggressive cultural form in the modern era?

Unit Three

1. Religion, a Human Spiritual Pillar and Faith

Editor's remarks: it is said that the core of a culture is its religion and the core of a religion is faith which serves as a spiritual and theological justification of one's life existence, physical and metaphysical. Religion is a spiritual and ritual phenomenon common in human society in all periods of human history. The western culture is in a sense a religious culture. More specifically, it is a Christian culture based upon Judeo-Christian tradition. Therefore, it is of vital importance to form some basic understanding of what religion implies and conveys to people in their daily life. Even for atheists, it is useful to know how theists think, act and live within the framework of a religious faith.

Religion is a collection of cultural systems, belief systems, and worldviews that relate humanity to spirituality and, sometimes, to moral values. Many religions have narratives, symbols, traditions and sacred histories that are intended to give meaning to life or to explain the origin of life or the universe. They tend to derive morality, ethics, religious laws or a preferred lifestyle from their ideas about the cosmos and human nature. The word *religion* is sometimes used interchangeably with *faith* or *belief system*, but religion differs from private belief in that it has a social aspect. Many religions have organized behaviors, clergy, a definition of what constitutes adherence or membership, congregations of laity, regular meetings or services for the purposes of veneration of a deity or for prayer, holy places (either natural or architectural), and/or scriptures. The practice of a religion may also include sermons, commemoration of the activities of a god or gods, sacrifices, festivals, feasts, trance, initiations, funerary services, matrimonial services, meditation, music, art, dance, public service, or other aspects of human culture. However, there are examples of religions for which some or many of these aspects of structure, belief, or practices are absent.

Etymology of Religion

Religion (from O. Fr. *religion* "religious community", from L. *religionem* [nom. *religio*] "respect for what is sacred, reverence for the gods", "obligation, the bond between man and the gods") is derived from the Latin *religiō*, the ultimate origins of which are obscure. One possibility is derivation from a reduplicated *le-ligare*, an interpretation traced to Cicero connecting *lego* "read", i. e. *re* (again) + *lego* in the sense of "choose", "go over again" or "consider carefully". Modern scholars such as Tom Harpur and Joseph Campbell favor the derivation from *ligare* "bind, connect", probably from a prefixed *re-ligare*, i. e. *re* (again) + *ligare* or "to reconnect", which was made prominent by St. Augustine, following the interpretation of Lactantius. The medieval usage alternates with *order* in designating bonded communities like those of monastic orders: "we hear of the 'religion' of the Golden Fleece, of a knight 'of the religion of Avys'." According to the philologist Max Müller, the root of the English word "religion", the Latin *religiō*, was originally used to mean only "reverence for God or the gods, careful pondering of divine things, piety" (which Cicero further derived to mean "diligence"). Max Müller characterized many other cultures around the world, including Egypt, Persia, and India, as having a similar power structure at this point in history. What is called ancient religion today, they would have only called "law". Many languages have words that can be translated as "religion", but they may use them in a very different way, and some have no word for religion at all.

Definitions of Religion

There are numerous definitions of religion and only a few are stated here. The typical dictionary definition of religion refers to a "belief in, or the worship of, a god or gods" or the "service and worship of God or the supernatural". However, many writers and scholars have noted that this basic "belief in god" definition fails to capture the diversity of religious thought and experience. Tylor defined religion as simply "the belief in spiritual beings". He argued, back in 1871, that narrowing the definition to mean the belief in a supreme deity or judgment after death or idolatry and so on, would exclude many peoples from the category of religious, and thus "has the fault of identifying religion rather with particular developments than with the deeper motive which underlies them". He also argued that the belief in spiritual beings exists in all known societies. The anthropologist Clifford Geertz defined religion as a "system of symbols which acts to establish powerful, pervasive, and long-lasting moods and motivations in men by formulating conceptions of a general order of existence and clothing these conceptions with such an aura of factuality that the moods and motivations seem uniquely realistic. Alluding perhaps to Tylor's "deeper motive", Geertz remarked that "we have very little idea of how, in empirical terms, this particular miracle is accomplished. We just know that it is done, annually, weekly, daily, for some people almost hourly; and we have an enormous ethnographic literature to demonstrate it". The theologian Antoine Vergote also emphasized the "cultural reality" of religion, which he defined as "the entirety of the linguistic expressions, emotions and, actions and signs that refer to a supernatural being or supernatural beings"; he took the term "supernatural" simply to mean whatever transcends the powers of nature or human agency.

The sociologist Durkheim, in his seminal book *The Elementary Forms of the Religious Life*, defined religion as a "unified system of beliefs and practices relative to sacred things". By sacred things he meant things "set apart and forbidden—beliefs and practices which unite into one single moral community called a Church, all those who adhere to them". Sacred things are not, however, limited to gods or spirits. On the contrary, a sacred thing can be "a rock, a tree, a spring, a pebble, a piece of wood, a house, in a word, anything can be sacred". Religious beliefs, myths, dogmas and legends are the representations that express the nature of these sacred things, and the virtues and powers which are attributed to them. In his book *The Varieties of Religious Experience* the psychologist William James defined religion as "the feelings, acts, and experiences of individual men in their solitude, so far as they apprehend themselves to stand in relation to whatever they may consider the divine". By the term "divine" James meant "any object that is god *like*, whether it be a concrete deity or not" to which the individual feels impelled to respond with solemnity and gravity. Echoes of James' and Durkheim's definitions are to be found in the writings of, for example, Frederick Ferré who defined religion as "one's way of valuing most comprehensively and intensively". Similarly, for the theologian Paul Tillich, faith is "the state of being ultimately concerned", which "is itself religion. Religion is the substance, the ground, and the depth of man's spiritual life." When religion is seen in terms of "sacred", "divine", intensive "valuing", or "ultimate concern", then it is possible to understand why scientific findings and philosophical criticisms (e.g. Richard Dawkins) do not necessarily disturb its adherents.

Origins and Development of Religion

There are a number of theories regarding the origins of religion. According to anthropologists John

Monaghan and Peter Just, many of the great world religions appear to have begun as revitalization movements of some sort, as the vision of a charismatic prophet fires the imaginations of people seeking a more comprehensive answer to their problems than they feel is provided by everyday beliefs. Charismatic individuals have emerged at many times and places in the world. It seems that the key to long-term success—and many movements come and go with little long-term effect—has relatively little to do with the prophets, who appear with surprising regularity, but more to do with the development of a group of supporters who are able to institutionalize the movement. The development of religion has taken different forms in different cultures. Some religions place an emphasis on belief, while others emphasize practice. Some religions focus on the subjective experience of the religious individual, while others consider the activities of the religious community to be most important. Some religions claim to be universal, believing their laws and cosmology to be binding for everyone, while others are intended to be practiced only by a closely defined or localized group. In many places religion has been associated with public institutions such as education, hospitals, the family, government, and political hierarchies. Anthropologists John Monoghan and Peter Just state that, "it seems apparent that one thing religion or belief helps us do is deal with problems of human life that are significant, persistent, and intolerable. One important way in which religious beliefs accomplish this is by providing a set of ideas about how and why the world is put together that allows people to accommodate anxieties and deal with misfortune." One modern academic theory of religion, social constructionism, says that religion is a modern concept that suggests all spiritual practice and worship follows a model similar to the Abrahamic religions as an orientation system that helps to interpret reality and define human beings, and thus religion, as a concept, has been applied inappropriately to non-western cultures that are not based upon such systems, or in which these systems are a substantially simpler construct.

Types of Religion: Categories

Some scholars classify religions as either *universal religions* that seek worldwide acceptance and actively look for new converts, or *ethnic religions* that are identified with a particular ethnic group and do not seek converts. Others reject the distinction, pointing out that all religious practices, whatever their philosophical origin, are ethnic because they come from a particular culture. In the 19th and 20th centuries, the academic practice of comparative religion divided religious belief into philosophically defined categories called "world religions". However, some recent scholarship has argued that not all types of religion are necessarily separated by mutually exclusive philosophies, and furthermore that the utility of ascribing a practice to a certain philosophy, or even calling a given practice religious, rather than cultural, political, or social in nature, is limited. The current state of psychological study about the nature of religiousness suggests that it is better to refer to religion as a largely invariant phenomenon that should be distinguished from cultural norms (i.e. "religions").

Some academics studying the subject have divided religions into three broad categories:

- world religions, a term which refers to transcultural, international faiths;
- indigenous religions, which refers to smaller, culture-specific or nation-specific religious groups;
- new religious movements, which refers to recently developed faiths.

Interfaith Cooperation

Because religion continues to be recognized in western thought as a universal impulse, many religious practitioners have aimed to band together in interfaith dialogue, cooperation, and religious peacebuilding. The first major dialogue was the Parliament of the World's Religions at the 1893 Chicago World's Fair, which remains notable even today both in affirming "universal values" and recognition of the diversity of practices among different cultures. The 20th century has been especially fruitful in use of interfaith dialogue as a means of solving ethnic, political, or even religious conflict, with Christian-Jewish reconciliation representing a complete reverse in the attitudes of many Christian communities towards Jews. Recent interfaith initiatives include "A Common Word", launched in 2007 and focused on bringing Muslim and Christian leaders together, the "C1 World Dialogue", the "Common Ground" initiative between Islam and Buddhism, and a United Nations sponsored "World Interfaith Harmony Week".

Abrahamic Religions: Religion of All Major Religions in the Middle East

Abrahamic religions are monotheistic religions which believe they descend from Abraham.

- **Judaism** is the oldest Abrahamic religion, originating in the people of ancient Israel and Judea. Judaism is based primarily on the Torah, a text which some Jews believe was handed down to the people of Israel through the prophet Moses. This along with the rest of the Hebrew Bible and the Talmud are the central texts of Judaism. The Jewish people were scattered after the destruction of the Temple in Jerusalem in 70 CE. Today there are about 13 million Jews, about 40 percent living in Israel and 40 percent in the United States.
- **Christianity** is based on the life and teachings of Jesus of Nazareth (1st century) as presented in the New Testament. The Christian faith is essentially faith in Jesus as the Christ, the Son of God, and as Savior and Lord. Almost all Christians believe in the Trinity, which teaches the unity of Father, Son (Jesus Christ), and Holy Spirit as three persons in one Godhead. Most Christians can describe their faith with the Nicene Creed. As the religion of Byzantine Empire in the first millennium and of western Europe during the time of colonization, Christianity has been propagated throughout the world. The main divisions of Christianity are, according to the number of adherents:
  - **Catholic Church**, headed by the Pope in Rome, is a communion of the western church and 22 eastern Catholic churches.
  - **Protestantism**, separated from the Catholic Church in the 16th-century Reformation and split in many denominations.
  - **eastern Christianity** which include eastern Orthodoxy, Oriental Orthodoxy and the Church of the East.

  There are other smaller groups, such as Jehovah's Witnesses and the Latter Day Saint movement, whose inclusion in Christianity is sometimes disputed.
- **Islam** refers to the religion taught by the Islamic prophet Muhammad, a major political and religious figure of the 7th century CE. Islam is the dominant religion of northern Africa, the Middle East, and South Asia. As with Christianity, there is no single orthodoxy in Islam but a multitude of traditions which are generally categorized as Sunni and Shia, although there are other minor groups as well. Wahhabi is the dominant Muslim schools of thought in the Kingdom of Saudi Arabia. There are also several Islamic republics, including Iran, which is run by a Shia Supreme Leader.
- Smaller regional Abrahamic groups, including Samaritanism (primarily in Israel and the West Bank), the Rastafari movement (primarily in Jamaica), and Druze (primarily in Syria and Lebanon).

Questions or Topics for Pondering and Further Discussion for Unit Three-1:

1. The core element of a religion is faith. How do you define faith?
2. The core element of a culture is religion? How do you understand this statement?
3. Does a religion have any secular function in the modern era?
4. Why do people in the modern era become less and less religious?
5. What is the difference between a religion and superstition, and between a religion and a cult?
6. It seems that western religions and eastern religions share something in common. What is that?
7. Why are people as a whole divided into atheists and theists? What basically determines such division?
8. What is the relationship between religion and philosophy?

2. Judaism, a Mother Religion of Some Religions

Judaism is the religion, philosophy, and way of life of the Jewish people. A monotheistic religion originating in the Hebrew Bible (also known as the Tanakh) and explored in later texts such as the Talmud, Judaism is considered by religious Jews to be the expression of the covenantal relationship God developed with the Children of Israel. Rabbinic Judaism holds that God revealed his laws and commandments to Moses on Mount Sinai in the form of both the written and oral Torah. This assertion was historically challenged by the Karaites, a movement that flourished in the medieval period, which retains several thousand followers today and maintains that only the written Torah was revealed. In modern times, liberal movements such as Humanistic Judaism may be nontheistic. Judaism claims a historical continuity spanning more than 3,000 years. It is one of the oldest monotheistic religions, and the oldest to survive into the present day. The Hebrews / Israelites were already referred to as "Jews" in later books of the Tanakh such as the Book of Esther, with the term "Jews" replacing the title "Children of Israel". Judaism's texts, traditions and values strongly influenced later Abrahamic religions, including Christianity, Islam and the Baha'i Faith. Many aspects of Judaism have also directly or indirectly influenced secular western ethics and civil law. Jews are an ethnoreligious group and include those born Jewish and converts to Judaism. In 2010, the world Jewish population was estimated at 13.4 million, or roughly 0.2% of the total world population. About 42% of all Jews reside in Israel and about 42% reside in the United States and Canada, with most of the remainder living in Europe. The largest Jewish religious movements are Orthodox Judaism (Hareidi Judaism and Modern Orthodox Judaism), Conservative Judaism and Reform Judaism. A major source of difference between these groups is their approach to Jewish law. Orthodox Judaism maintains that the Torah and Jewish law are divine in origin, eternal and unalterable, and that they should be strictly followed. Conservative and Reform Judaism are more liberal, with Conservative Judaism generally promoting a more "traditional" interpretation of Judaism's requirements than Reform Judaism. A typical Reform position is that Jewish law should be viewed as a set of general guidelines rather than as a set of restrictions and obligations whose observance is required of all Jews. Historically, special courts enforced Jewish law; today, these courts still exist but the practice of Judaism is mostly voluntary. Authority on theological and legal matters is not vested in any one person or organization, but in the sacred texts and rabbis and scholars who interpret them.

Defining Character and Principles of Faith

Unlike other ancient Near eastern gods, the Hebrew God is portrayed as unitary and solitary; consequently, the Hebrew God's principal relationships are not with other gods, but with the world, and more specifically, with the people He created. Judaism thus begins with an ethical monotheism: the belief that God is one, and concerned with the actions of humankind. According to the Hebrew Bible, God promised Abraham to make of his offspring a great nation. Many generations later, he commanded the nation of Israel to love and worship only one God; that is, the Jewish nation is to reciprocate God's concern for the world. He also commanded the Jewish people to love one another; that is, Jews are to imitate God's love for people. These commandments are but two of a large corpus of commandments and laws that constitute this covenant, which is the substance of Judaism. Thus, although there is an esoteric tradition in Judaism (Kabbalah), rabbinic scholar Max Kadushin has characterized normative Judaism as "normal mysticism", because it involves everyday personal experiences of God through ways or modes that are common to all Jews. This is played out through the observance of the halakhot and given verbal expression in the Birkat Ha-Mizvot, the short blessings that are spoken every time a positive commandment is to be fulfilled.

The ordinary, familiar, everyday things and occurrences, we have constitute occasions for the experience of God. Such things as one's daily sustenance, the very day itself, are felt as manifestations of God's loving-kindness, calling for the Berakhot. Kedushah, holiness, which is nothing else than the imitation of God, is concerned with daily conduct, with being gracious and merciful, with keeping oneself from defilement by idolatry, adultery, and the shedding of blood. The Birkat Ha-Mitzwot evokes the consciousness of holiness at a rabbinic rite, but the objects employed in the majority of these rites are non-holy and of general character, while the several holy objects are non-theurgic. And not only do ordinary things and occurrences bring with them the experience of God, everything that happens to a man evokes that experience, evil as well as good, for a Berakah is said also at evil tidings. Hence, although the experience of God is like none other, the occasions for experiencing Him, for having a consciousness of Him, are manifold, even if we consider only those that call for Berakot.

Whereas Jewish philosophers often debate whether God is immanent or transcendent, and whether people have free will or their lives are determined, Halakha is a system through which any Jew acts to bring God into the world. Ethical monotheism is central in all sacred or normative texts of Judaism. However, monotheism has not always been followed in practice. The Jewish Bible (Tanakh) records and repeatedly condemns the widespread worship of other gods in ancient Israel. In the Greco-Roman era, many different interpretations of monotheism existed in Judaism, including the interpretations that gave rise to Christianity. Moreover, as a non-creedal religion, some have argued that Judaism does not require one to believe in God. For some, observance of Jewish law is more important than belief in God *per se*. In modern times, some liberal Jewish movements do not accept the existence of a personified deity active in history.

Core Tenets/13 Principles of Faith

- I believe with perfect faith that the Creator, Blessed be His Name, is the Creator and Guide of everything that has been created; He alone has made, does make, and will make all things.

- I believe with perfect faith that the Creator, Blessed be His Name, is One, and that there is no unity in any manner like His, and that He alone is our God, who was, and is, and will be.
- I believe with perfect faith that the Creator, Blessed be His Name, has no body, and that He is free from all the properties of matter, and that there can be no (physical) comparison to Him whatsoever.
- I believe with perfect faith that the Creator, Blessed be His Name, is the first and the last.
- I believe with perfect faith that to the Creator, Blessed be His Name, and to Him alone, it is right to pray, and that it is not right to pray to any being besides Him.
- I believe with perfect faith that all the words of the prophets are true.
- I believe with perfect faith that the prophecy of Moses our teacher, peace be upon him, was true, and that he was the chief of the prophets, both those who preceded him and those who followed him.
- I believe with perfect faith that the entire Torah that is now in our possession is the same that was given to Moses our teacher, peace be upon him.
- I believe with perfect faith that this Torah will not be exchanged, and that there will never be any other Torah from the Creator, Blessed be His Name.
- I believe with perfect faith that the Creator, Blessed be His Name, knows all the deeds of human beings and all their thoughts, as it is written, "Who fashioned the hearts of them all, Who comprehends all their actions" (Psalms 33:15).
- I believe with perfect faith that the Creator, Blessed be His Name, rewards those who keep His commandments and punishes those that transgress them.
- I believe with perfect faith in the coming of the Messiah; and even though he may tarry, nonetheless, I wait every day for his coming.
- I believe with perfect faith that there will be a revival of the dead at the time when it shall please the Creator, Blessed be His name, and His mention shall be exalted for ever and ever.

Jewish Legal Literature

The basis of Jewish law and tradition (halakha) is the Torah (also known as the Pentateuch or the Five Books of Moses). According to rabbinic tradition there are 613 commandments in the Torah. Some of these laws are directed only to men or to women, some only to the ancient priestly groups, the Kohanim and Leviyim (members of the tribe of Levi), some only to farmers within the Land of Israel. Many laws were only applicable when the Temple in Jerusalem existed, and fewer than 300 of these commandments are still applicable today. While there have been Jewish groups whose beliefs were claimed to be based on the written text of the Torah alone (e.g., the Sadducees, and the Karaites), most Jews believed in what they call the oral law. These oral traditions were transmitted by the Pharisee sect of ancient Judaism, and were later recorded in written form and expanded upon by the rabbis. Rabbinic Judaism (which derives from the Pharisees) has always held that the books of the Torah (called the written law) have always been transmitted in parallel with an oral tradition. To justify this viewpoint, Jews point to the text of the Torah, where many words are left undefined, and many procedures mentioned without explanation or instructions; this, they argue, means that the reader is assumed to be familiar with the details from other, i.e., oral, sources. This parallel set of material was originally transmitted orally, and came to be known as "the oral law". By the time of Rabbi

Judah haNasi (200 CE), after the destruction of Jerusalem, much of this material was edited together into the Mishnah. Over the next four centuries this law underwent discussion and debate in both of the world's major Jewish communities (in Israel and Babylonia), and the commentaries on the Mishnah from each of these communities eventually came to be edited together into compilations known as the two Talmuds. These have been expounded by commentaries of various Torah scholars during the ages. Halakha, the rabbinic Jewish way of life, then, is based on a combined reading of the Torah, and the oral tradition—the Mishnah, the halakhic Midrash, the Talmud and its commentaries. The Halakha has developed slowly, through a precedent-based system. The literature of questions to rabbis, and their considered answers, is referred to as responsa (in Hebrew, *Sheelot U-Teshuvot*.) Over time, as practices develop, codes of Jewish law are written that are based on the responsa; the most important code, the Shulchan Aruch, largely determines Orthodox religious practice today.

Jewish Philosophy

Jewish philosophy refers to the conjunction between serious study of philosophy and Jewish theology. Major Jewish philosophers include Solomon ibn Gabirol, Saadia Gaon, Judah Halevi, Maimonides, and Gersonides. Major changes occurred in response to the Enlightenment (late 18th to early 19th century) leading to the post-enlightenment Jewish philosophers. Modern Jewish philosophy consists of both Orthodox and non-Orthodox oriented philosophy. Notable among Orthodox Jewish philosophers are Eliyahu Eliezer Dessler, Joseph B. Soloveitchik, and Yitzchok Hutner. Well-known non-Orthodox Jewish philosophers include Martin Buber, Franz Rosenzweig, Mordecai Kaplan, Abraham Joshua Heschel, Will Herberg, and Emmanuel Lévinas.

Rabbinic Hermeneutics/13 Principles of Hermeneutics

- A law that operates under certain conditions will surely be operative in other situations where the same conditions are present in a more acute form.
- A law operating in one situation will also be operative in another situation, if the text characterizes both situations in identical terms.
- A law that clearly expresses the purpose it was meant to serve will also apply to other situations where the identical purpose may be served.
- When a general rule is followed by illustrative particulars, only those particulars are to be embraced by it.
- A law that begins with specifying particular cases, and then proceeds to an all-embracing generalization, is to be applied to particulars cases not specified but logically falling into the same generalization.
- A law that begins with a generalization as to its intended applications, then continues with the specification of particular cases, and then concludes with a restatement of the generalization, can be applied only to the particular cases specified.
- The rules about a generalization being followed or preceded by specifying particulars (rules 4 and 5) will not apply if it is apparent that the specification of the particular cases or the statement of the generalization is meant purely for achieving a greater clarity of language.
- A particular case already covered in a generalization that is nevertheless treated separately suggests that the same particularized treatment be applied to all other cases which are covered in that generalization.

- A penalty specified for a general category of wrong-doing is not to be automatically applied to a particular case that is withdrawn from the general rule to be specifically prohibited, but without any mention of the penalty.
- A general prohibition followed by a specified penalty may be followed by a particular case, normally included in the generalization, with a modification in penalty, either toward easing it or making it more severe.
- A case logically falling into a general law but treated separately remains outside the provisions of the general law except in those instances where it is specifically included in them.
- Obscurities in Biblical texts may be cleared up from the immediate context or from subsequently occurring passages.
- Contradictions in Biblical passages may be removed through the mediation of other passages.

Orthodox and many other Jews do not believe that the revealed Torah consists solely of its written contents, but of its interpretations as well. The study of Torah (in its widest sense, to include both poetry, narrative, and law, and both the Hebrew Bible and the Talmud) is in Judaism itself a sacred act of central importance. For the sages of the Mishnah and Talmud, and for their successors today, the study of Torah was therefore not merely a means to learn the contents of God's revelation, but an end in itself. According to the Talmud,

> *These are the things for which a person enjoys the dividends in this world while the principal remains for the person to enjoy in the world to come; they are: honoring parents, loving deeds of kindness, and making peace between one person and another. But the study of the Torah is equal to them all. (Talmud Shabbat 127a)*

In Judaism, "the study of Torah can be a means of experiencing God". Reflecting on the contribution of the Amoraim and Tanaim to contemporary Judaism, Professor Jacob Neusner observed:

> *The rabbi's logical and rational inquiry is not mere logic-chopping. It is a most serious and substantive effort to locate in trivialities the fundamental principles of the revealed will of God to guide and sanctify the most specific and concrete actions in the workaday world... Here is the mystery of Talmudic Judaism: the alien and remote conviction that the intellect is an instrument not of unbelief and desacralization but of sanctification.*

To study the written Torah and the oral Torah in light of each other is thus also to study how to study the word of God. In the study of Torah, the sages formulated and followed various logical and hermeneutical principles. According to David Stern, all rabbinic hermeneutics rest on two basic axioms:

> *First, the belief in the omnisignificance of Scripture, in the meaningfulness of its every word, letter, even (according to one famous report) scribal flourish; second, the claim of the essential unity of Scripture as the expression of the single divine will.*

These two principles make possible a great variety of interpretations. According to the Talmud,

> *A single verse has several meanings, but no two verses hold the same meaning. It was taught in the school of R. Ishmael: "Behold, My word is like fire—declares the Lord—and like a hammer that shatters rock" (Jer 23:29). Just as this hammer produces many*

sparks (when it strikes the rock), so a single verse has several meanings. (Talmud Sanhedrin 34a)

Observant Jews thus view the Torah as dynamic, because it contains within it a host of interpretations. According to rabbinic tradition, all valid interpretations of the written Torah were revealed to Moses at Sinai in oral form, and handed down from teacher to pupil (The oral revelation is in effect coextensive with the Talmud itself). When different rabbis forwarded conflicting interpretations, they sometimes appealed to hermeneutic principles to legitimize their arguments; some rabbis claim that these principles were themselves revealed by God to Moses at Sinai. Thus, Hillel called attention to seven commonly used in the interpretation of laws (baraita at the beginning of Sifra); R. Ishmael, thirteen (baraita at the beginning of Sifra; this collection is largely an amplification of that of Hillel). Eliezer b. Jose ha-gelili listed 32, largely used for the exegesis of narrative elements of Torah. All the hermeneutic rules scattered through the Talmudim and Midrashim have been collected by Malbim in *Ayyelet ha-shachar*, the introduction to his commentary on the Sifra. Nevertheless, R. Ishmael's 13 principles are perhaps the ones most widely known; they constitute an important, and one of Judaism's earliest, contributions to logic, hermeneutics, and jurisprudence. Judah Hadassi incorporated Ishmael's principles into Karaite Judaism in the 12th century. Today R. Ishmael's 13 principles are incorporated into the Jewish prayer book to be read by observant Jews on a daily basis.

Distinction Between Jews as a People and Judaism

According to Daniel Boyarin, the underlying distinction between religion and ethnicity is foreign to Judaism itself, and is one form of the dualism between spirit and flesh that has its origin in Platonic philosophy and that permeated Hellenistic Judaism. Consequently, in his view, Judaism does not fit easily into conventional western categories, such as religion, ethnicity, or culture. Boyarin suggests that this in part reflects the fact that much of Judaism's more than 3,000-year history predates the rise of western culture and occurred outside the West (that is, Europe, particularly medieval and modern Europe). During this time, Jews have experienced slavery, anarchic and theocratic self-government, conquest, occupation, and exile; in the Diasporas, they have been in contact with and have been influenced by ancient Egyptian, Babylonian, Persian, and Hellenic cultures, as well as modern movements such as the Enlightenment (see Haskalah) and the rise of nationalism, which would bear fruit in the form of a Jewish state in the Levant. They also saw an elite convert to Judaism (the Khazars), only to disappear as the centers of power in the lands once occupied by that elite fell to the people of Rus and then the Mongols. Thus, Boyarin has argued that "Jewishness disrupts the very categories of identity, because it is not national, not genealogical, not religious, but all of these, in dialectical tension." In contrast to this point of view, practices such as Humanistic Judaism reject the religious aspects of Judaism, while retaining certain cultural traditions.

Who Is a Jew?

According to traditional Jewish Law, a Jew is anyone born of a Jewish mother or converted to Judaism in accordance with Jewish Law. American Reform Judaism and British Liberal Judaism accept the child of one Jewish parent (father or mother) as Jewish if the parents raise the child with a Jewish identity. All mainstream forms of Judaism today are open to sincere converts, although conversion has traditionally been discouraged since the time of the Talmud. The conversion process is evaluated by an authority, and the convert is examined on his or her sincerity and knowledge. Converts are given the name "ben Abraham" or "bat Abraham", (son or daughter of Abraham). Traditional Judaism maintains that a Jew, whether by birth or conversion, is a Jew forever. Thus a Jew who claims to be an atheist or converts to another religion is still considered by traditional Judaism to be Jewish. According to some sources, the Reform movement has maintained that a Jew who has converted to another religion is no longer a Jew, and the Israeli Government has also taken that stance after Supreme Court cases and statutes. However, the Reform movement has indicated that this is not so cut and dry, and different situations call for consideration and differing actions. For example, Jews who have converted under duress may be permitted to return to Judaism "without any action on their part but their desire to rejoin the Jewish community" and "a proselyte who has become an apostate remains, nevertheless, a Jew". The question of what determines Jewish identity in the State of Israel was given new impetus when, in the 1950s, David Ben-Gurion requested opinions on *mihu Yehudi* ("who is a Jew") from Jewish religious authorities and intellectuals worldwide in order to settle citizenship questions. This is still not settled, and occasionally resurfaces in Israeli politics.

Jewish Religious Movements/Rabbinic Judaism

Rabbinic Judaism (or in some Christian traditions, Rabbinism) has been the mainstream form of Judaism since the 6th century CE, after the codification of the Talmud. It is characterized by the belief that the written Torah (Law) cannot be correctly interpreted without reference to the oral Torah and by the voluminous literature specifying what behavior is sanctioned by the law (called halakha, "the way"). The Jewish Enlightenment of the late 18th century resulted in the division of Ashkenazi (western) Jewry into religious movements or denominations, especially in North America and anglophone countries. The main denominations today outside Israel (where the situation is rather different) are Orthodox, Conservative, and Reform.

- Orthodox Judaism holds that both the written and oral Torah were divinely revealed to Moses, and that the laws within it are binding and unchanging. Orthodox Jews generally consider commentaries on the *Shulchan Aruch* (a condensed codification of halakha that largely favored Sephardic traditions) to be the definitive codification of Jewish law. Orthodoxy places a high importance on Maimonides' 13 principles as a definition of Jewish faith.
- Orthodoxy is often divided into Modern Orthodox Judaism and Haredi Judaism. Haredi Judaism is less accommodating to modernity and has less interest in non-Jewish disciplines, and it may be distinguished from Modern Orthodox Judaism in practice by its styles of dress and more stringent practices. Subsets of Haredi Judaism include: Hasidic Judaism, which is rooted in the Kabbalah and distinguished by reliance on a Rebbe or religious teacher; and Sephardic Haredi Judaism, which emerged among Sephardic (Asian and North African) Jews in Israel.
- Conservative Judaism, known as Masorti outside the United States and Canada, is characterized by a commitment to traditional Jewish laws and customs, including observance of Shabbat and kashrut, a deliberately non-Fundamentalist teaching of Jewish principles of faith, a positive attitude toward modern culture, and an acceptance of both traditional rabbinic and modern scholarship when considering Jewish religious texts. Conservative Judaism teaches that Jewish law is not static, but has always developed in response to changing conditions. It holds that the Torah is a divine document written by prophets inspired by God and reflecting his will, but rejects the Orthodox position that it was dictated by God to Moses. Conservative Judaism holds that the oral Law is divine and normative, but holds that both the written and oral Law may be interpreted by the rabbis

to reflect modern sensibilities and suit modern conditions.
- Reform Judaism, called Liberal or Progressive Judaism in many countries, defines Judaism as a religion rather than as a race or culture, rejects most of the ritual and ceremonial laws of the Torah while observing moral laws, and emphasizes the ethical call of the Prophets. Reform Judaism has developed an egalitarian prayer service in the vernacular (along with Hebrew in many cases) and emphasizes personal connection to Jewish tradition.
- Reconstructionist Judaism, like Reform Judaism, does not hold that Jewish law, as such, requires observance, but unlike Reform, reconstructionist thought emphasizes the role of the community in deciding what observances to follow.
- Jewish Renewal is a recent North American movement which focuses on spirituality and social justice, but does not address issues of Jewish law. Men and women participate equally in prayer.
- Humanistic Judaism is a small non-theistic movement centered in North America and Israel that emphasizes Jewish culture and history as the sources of Jewish identity.

Jewish Movements in Israel

Most Jewish Israelis classify themselves as "secular" (*hiloni*), "traditional" (*masorti*), "religious" (*dati*) or *Haredi*. The term "secular" is more popular as a self-description among Israeli families of western (European) origin, whose Jewish identity may be a very powerful force in their lives, but who see it as largely independent of traditional religious belief and practice. This portion of the population largely ignores organized religious life, be it of the official Israeli rabbinate (Orthodox) or of the liberal movements common to diaspora Judaism (Reform, Conservative). The term "traditional" (*masorti*) is most common as a self-description among Israeli families of "eastern" origin (i.e., the Middle East, Central Asia, and North Africa). This term, as commonly used, has nothing to do with the official Masorti (Conservative) movement. There is a great deal of ambiguity in the ways "secular" and "traditional" are used in Israel: they often overlap, and they cover an extremely wide range in terms of ideology and religious observance. The term "Orthodox" is not popular in Israeli discourse, although the percentage of Jews who come under that category is far greater than in the diaspora. What would be called "Orthodox" in the diaspora includes what is commonly called *dati* (religious) or *haredi* (ultra-Orthodox) in Israel. The former term includes what is called "Religious Zionism" or the "National Religious" community, as well as what has become known over the past decade or so as *haredi-leumi* (nationalist *haredi*), or "Hardal", which combines a largely *haredi* lifestyle with nationalist ideology. (Some people, in Yiddish, also refer to observant Orthodox Jews as *frum*, as opposed to *frei* [more liberal Jews]). *Haredi* applies to a populace that can be roughly divided into three separate groups along both ethnic and ideological lines: (1) Lithuanian (non-hasidic) *haredim* of Ashkenazic origin; (2) Hasidic *haredim* of Ashkenazic origin; and (3) Sephardic *haredim*.

Life-Cycle Events

Life-cycle events, or rites of passage, occur throughout a Jew's life that serve to strengthen Jewish identity and bind him/her to the entire community.
- Brit milah—Welcoming male babies into the covenant through the rite of circumcision on their eighth day of life. The baby boy is also given his Hebrew name in the ceremony. A naming ceremony intended as a parallel ritual for girls, named *zeved habat* or brit bat,

enjoys limited popularity.
- Bar mitzvah and Bat mitzvah—This passage from childhood to adulthood takes place when a female Jew is twelve and a male Jew is thirteen years old among Orthodox and some Conservative congregations. In the Reform movement, both girls and boys have their bat/bar mitzvah at age thirteen. This is often commemorated by having the new adults, male only in the Orthodox tradition, lead the congregation in prayer and publicly read a "portion" of the Torah.
- Marriage—Marriage is an extremely important lifecycle event. A wedding takes place under a *chupah*, or wedding canopy, which symbolizes a happy house. At the end of the ceremony, the groom breaks a glass with his foot, symbolizing the continuous mourning for the destruction of the Temple, and the scattering of the Jewish people.
- Death and Mourning—Jiudaism has a multi-staged mourning practice. The first stage is called the shiva (literally "seven", observed for one week) during which it is traditional to sit at home and be comforted by friends and family, the second is the *shloshim* (observed for one month) and for those who have lost one of their parents, there is a third stage, *avelut yud bet chodesh*, which is observed for eleven months.

Specialized Religious Roles

- *Dayan* (judge)—An ordained rabbi with special legal training who belongs to a *beth din* (rabbinical court). In Israel, religious courts handle marriage and divorce cases, conversion and financial disputes in the Jewish community.
- Mohel (circumciser)—An expert in the laws of circumcision who has received training from a previously qualified *mohel* and performs the *brit milah* (circumcision).
- Shochet (ritual slaughterer)—In order for meat to be kosher, it must be slaughtered by a *shochet* who is an expert in the laws of kashrut and has been trained by another *shochet*.
- Sofer (scribe)—Torah scrolls, *tefillin* (phylacteries), *mezuzot* (scrolls put on doorposts), and *gittin* (bills of divorce) must be written by a *sofer* who is an expert in Hebrew calligraphy and has undergone rigorous training in the laws of writing sacred texts.
- Rosh yeshiva—A Torah scholar who runs a yeshiva.
- Mashgiach of a yeshiva—Depending on which yeshiva, might either be the person responsible for ensuring attendance and proper conduct, or even supervise the emotional and spiritual welfare of the students and give lectures on mussar (Jewish ethics).
- Mashgiach—Supervises manufacturers of kosher food, importers, caterers and restaurants to ensure that the food is kosher. Must be an expert in the laws of kashrut and trained by a rabbi, if not a rabbi himself.

The Enlightenment and New Religious Movements

In the late 18th century CE, Europe was swept by a group of intellectual, social and political movements known as the Enlightenment. The Enlightenment led to reductions in the European laws that prohibited Jews to interact with the wider secular world, thus allowing Jews access to secular education and experience. A parallel Jewish movement, Haskalah or the "Jewish Enlightenment", began, especially in Central Europe and western Europe, in response to both the Enlightenment and these new freedoms. It placed an emphasis on integration with secular society and a pursuit of non-religious knowledge through reason. With the promise of political emancipation many Jews saw no reason to continue to observe Jewish law and increasing numbers of Jews assimilated into Christian Europe. Modern religious movements of Judaism all formed in reaction to this trend. In Central Europe, followed by Great Britain and the United States, Reform Judaism and Liberal Judaism developed, relaxing legal obligations (especially those that limited Jewish relations with non-Jews), emulating Protestant decorum in prayer, and emphasizing the ethical values of Judaism's Prophetic tradition. Modern Orthodox Judaism developed in reaction to Reform Judaism, by leaders who argued that Jews could participate in public life as citizens equal to Christians, while maintaining the observance of Jewish law. Meanwhile, in the United States, wealthy Reform Jews helped European scholars, who were Orthodox in practice but critical (and skeptical) in their study of the Bible and Talmud, to establish a seminary to train rabbis for immigrants from eastern Europe. These left-Wing Orthodox rabbis were joined by right-Wing Reform rabbis who felt that Jewish law should not be entirely abandoned, to form the Conservative movement. Orthodox Jews who opposed the Haskalah formed Haredi Orthodox Judaism. After massive movements of Jews following the Holocaust and the creation of the state of Israel, these movements have competed for followers from among traditional Jews in or from other countries.

Spectrum of Observance

Countries such as the United States, Israel, Canada, United Kingdom, Argentina and South Africa contain large Jewish populations. Jewish religious practice varies widely through all levels of observance. According to the 2001 edition of the National Jewish Population Survey, in the United States' Jewish community—the world's second largest—4.3 million Jews out of 5.1 million had some sort of connection to the religion. Of that population of connected Jews, 80% participated in some sort of Jewish religious observance, but only 48% belonged to a synagogue, and fewer than 16% attend regularly. Birth rates for American Jews have dropped from 2.0 to 1.7. (Replacement rate is 2.1.) Intermarriage rates range from 40%—50% in the US, and only about a third of children of intermarried couples are raised as Jews. Due to intermarriage and low birth rates, the Jewish population in the US shrank from 5.5 million in 1990 to 5.1 million in 2001. This is indicative of the general population trends among the Jewish community in the Diaspora, but a focus on total population obscures growth trends in some denominations and communities, such as Haredi Judaism. The Baal teshuva movement is a movement of Jews who have "returned" to religion or become more observant.

Christianity and Judaism:
They Have as Much in Common as in Difference

Historians and theologians regularly review the changing relationship between some Christian groups and the Jewish people.

Islam and Judaism: They Have a Common Ancestor

The relationship between Islam and Judaism is special and close. Both religions claim to arise from the patriarch Abraham, and are therefore considered Abrahamic religions. As fellow monotheists, Muslims view Jews as "people of the book", a term that Jews have subsequently adopted as a way of describing their own connection to the Torah and other holy texts. In turn, many Jews maintain that Muslims adhere to the Seven Laws of Noah. Thus, Judaism views Muslims as righteous people of God. Jews have interacted with Muslims since the 7th century, when Islam originated and spread in the Arabian peninsula, and many aspects of Islam's core values, structure, jurisprudence and practice are based on Judaism. Muslim culture and philosophy have heavily influenced practitioners of Judaism in the Islamic world. In premodern

Muslim countries, Jews rarely faced martyrdom, exile or forcible conversion, and were mostly free in their choice of residence and profession. Indeed, the years 712 to 1066 CE under the Ummayad and the Abbasid rulers have been called the Golden age of Jewish culture in Spain. Non-muslim monotheists living in these countries, including Jews, were known as dhimmis. Dhimmis were allowed to practice their religion and to administer their internal affairs, but they were subject to certain restrictions that were not imposed on Muslims. For example, they had to pay the jizya, a per capita tax imposed on free adult non-Muslim males, and they were also forbidden to bear arms or testify in court cases involving Muslims. Many of the laws regarding dhimmis were highly symbolic. For example, dhimmis in some countries were required to wear distinctive clothing, a practice not found in either the Qur'an or hadiths but invented in early medieval Baghdad and inconsistently enforced. Jews in Muslim countries were not entirely free from persecution—for example, many were killed, exiled or forcibly converted in the 12th century, in Persia and by the rulers of the Almohad dynasty in North Africa and Al-Andalus. At times, Jews were also restricted in their choice of residence—in Morocco, Jews were confined to walled quarters (mellahs) beginning in the 15th century and increasingly since the early 19th century. In the late 20th century, Jews were expelled from nearly all the Arab countries. Most have chosen to live in Israel. Today, antisemitic themes have become commonplace in the propaganda of Arab Islamic movements such as Hizbullah and Hamas, in the pronouncements of various agencies of the Islamic Republic of Iran, and even in the newspapers and other publications of Refah Partisi.

Questions or Topics for Pondering and Further Discussion for Unit Three-2:

1. The significance of Judaism in shaping the evolution of Christianity can never be over-stressed. Comment.
2. What are the major divergences between Judaism and Christianity?
3. What are basic theological principles of Judaism?
4. What role does Judaism play in influencing Jewish people's way of thinking and living?
5. Why do Jewish people stand so firm on their spiritual belief?
6. Why was there a wide-spread anti-Jewish movement in Europe in history, culminated in the Holocaust?
7. Why do Jewish suffer so much? Do you think Jewish people themselves bear something to blame for?
8. What can you find out from Israeli-Palestine conflict when the fact is taken into consideration that they were originally brothers and sisters?

3. Christianity, a Spiritual Rock of the West

Christianity is a monotheistic and Abrahamic religion based on the life and teachings of Jesus as presented in canonical gospels and other New Testament writings. It also considers the Hebrew Bible, which is known as the Old Testament, to be canonical. Adherents of the Christian faith are known as Christians. The mainstream Christian belief is that Jesus is the Son of God, fully divine and fully human and the saviour of humanity. Because of this, Christians commonly refer to Jesus as Christ or Messiah. Jesus' ministry, sacrificial death, and subsequent resurrection, are often referred to as the Gospel message ("good news"). In short, the Gospel is news of God the Father's eternal victory over evil, and the promise of salvation and eternal life for all people, through divine grace. Jesus stated that love is the greatest commandment: "Thou shalt love the Lord thy God with all thy heart, and with all thy soul, and with all thy mind [and] thou shalt love thy neighbour as thyself."

Worldwide the three largest groups of Christianity are the Roman Catholic Church, the eastern Orthodox churches, and the various denominations of Protestantism. The Roman Catholic and eastern Orthodox patriarchates split from one another in the East-West Schism of 1054 AD, and Protestantism came into existence during the Protestant Reformation of the 16th century, splitting from the Roman Catholic Church. Christianity began as a Jewish sect in the mid-1st century. Originating in the Levant region of the Middle East (modern Israel and Palestine), it quickly spread to Syria, Mesopotamia, Asia Minor and Egypt. It grew in size and influence over a few decades, and by the 4th century replaced paganism as the dominant religion within the Roman Empire. During the Middle Ages, most of the remainder of Europe was Christianized, with Christians also being a sometimes large religious minority in the Middle East, North Africa, Ethiopia and parts of India. Following the Age of Discovery, through missionary work and colonization, Christianity spread to the Americas, Australasia, sub-Saharan Africa, and the rest of the world.

Christians believe that Jesus is the Messiah prophesied in the Hebrew Bible, referred to as the "Old Testament" in Christianity. The foundation of Christian theology is expressed in the early Christian ecumenical creeds which contain claims predominantly accepted by followers of the Christian faith. These professions state that Jesus suffered, died, was buried, and was resurrected from the dead in order to grant eternal life to those who believe in him and trust him for the remission of their sins (salvation). They further maintain that Jesus bodily ascended into heaven where he rules and reigns with God the Father. Most denominations teach that Jesus will return to judge all humans, living and dead, and grant eternal life to his followers. He is considered the model of a virtuous life, and both the revealer and physical incarnation of God. Christians call the message of Jesus Christ the Gospel ("good news") and generally adhere to the Ten Commandments. As of the early 21st century, Christianity has approximately 2.2 billion adherents. Christianity represents about a third of the world's population and is the world's largest religion. Christianity is the state religion of several countries. Among all Christians, 37.5% live in the Americas, 25.7% live in Europe, 22.5% live in Africa, 13.1% live in Asia, 1.2% live in Oceania and 0.9% live in the Middle East. Christianity has played a role in shaping of western civilization. Though there are many important differences of interpretation and opinion of the Bible on which Christianity is based, Christians share a set of beliefs that they hold as essential to their faith.

Creeds

Creeds (from Latin *"credo"*, meaning "I believe") are concise doctrinal statements or confessions, usually of religious beliefs. They began as baptismal formulae and were later expanded during the Christological controversies of the 4th and 5th centuries to become statements of faith. Many evangelical Protestants reject creeds as definitive statements of faith, even while agreeing with some or all of the substance of the creeds. The Baptists have been non-creedal "in that they have not sought to establish binding authoritative confessions of faith on one another". Also rejecting creeds are groups with roots in the Restoration Movement, such as the Christian Church (Disciples of Christ), the Evangelical Christian Church in Canada and the Churches of Christ. The Apostles' Creed remains the most popular statement of the articles of Christian faith that are generally acceptable to most Christian denominations that are creedal. It is widely used by a number of Christian denominations for both liturgical and catechetical purposes, most visibly by liturgical Churches of western Christian tradition, including the Latin Rite of the Catholic Church, Lutheranism, Anglicanism, and western Orthodoxy. It is also used by Presbyterians, Methodists, and Congregationalists. This particular creed was developed between the 2nd and 9th centuries. Its central doctrines are those of the Trinity and God the Creator. Each of the doctrines found in this creed can be traced to statements current in the apostolic period. The creed was apparently used as a summary of Christian doctrine for baptismal candidates in the churches of Rome.

Its Main Points of Faith:

- *belief in God the Father, Jesus Christ as the Son of God and the Holy Spirit*
- *the death, descent into hell, resurrection, and ascension of Christ*
- *the holiness of the Church and the communion of saints*
- *Christ's second coming, the Day of Judgement and salvation of the faithful*

The Nicene Creed, largely a response to Arianism, was formulated at the Councils of Nicaea and Constantinople in 325 and 381 respectively and ratified as the universal creed of Christendom by the First Council of Ephesus in 431. The Chalcedonian Creed, developed at the Council of Chalcedon in 451, though rejected by the Oriental Orthodox Churches, taught Christ "to be acknowledged in two natures, unconfusedly, unchangeably, indivisibly, inseparably": one divine and one human, and that both natures are perfect but are nevertheless perfectly united into one person. The Athanasian Creed, received in the western Church as having the same status as the Nicene and Chalcedonian, says, "We worship one God in Trinity, and Trinity in Unity; neither confounding the Persons nor dividing the Substance." Most Christians (Roman Catholics, eastern Orthodox, eastern Rite and Protestants alike) accept the use of creeds, and subscribe to at least one of the creeds mentioned above.

Trinity: the Core Idea of Christianity

Trinity refers to the teaching that the one God comprises three distinct, eternally co-existing persons; the *Father*, the *Son* (incarnate in Jesus Christ), and the *Holy Spirit*. Together, these three persons are sometimes called the Godhead, although there is no single term in use in Scripture to denote the unified Godhead. In the words of the Athanasian Creed, an early statement of Christian belief, "the Father is God, the Son is God, and the Holy Spirit is God, and yet there are not three Gods but one God". They are distinct from another: the Father has no source, the Son is begotten of the Father, and the Spirit proceeds from the Father. Though distinct, the three persons cannot be divided from one another in being or in operation. The Trinity is an essential doctrine of mainstream Christianity. "Father, Son and Holy Spirit" represents both the immanence and transcendence of God. God is believed to be infinite and God's presence may be perceived through the actions of Jesus Christ and the Holy Spirit. According to this doctrine, God is not divided in the sense that each person has a third of the whole; rather, each person is considered to be fully God (see Perichoresis). The distinction lies in their relations, the Father being unbegotten; the Son being begotten of the Father; and the Holy Spirit proceeding from the Father and (in western Christian theology) from the Son. Regardless of this apparent difference, the three "persons" are each eternal and omnipotent. The word *trias*, from which *trinity* is derived, is first seen in the works of Theophilus of Antioch. He wrote of "the Trinity of God (the Father), His Word (the Son) and His Wisdom (Holy Spirit)". The term may have been in use before this time. Afterwards it appears in Tertullian. In the following century the word was in general use. It is found in many passages of Origen.

Scriptures

Christianity, like other religions, has adherents whose beliefs and biblical interpretations vary. Christianity regards the Biblical canon, the Old Testament and New Testament, as the inspired word of God. The traditional view of inspiration is that God worked through human authors so that, what they produced was what God wished to communicate. The Greek word used to describe inspiration in 2 Timothy 3:16 is *Theopneustos*, which literally means "God-breathed". Some believe that divine inspiration makes our present Bibles "inerrant". Others claim inerrancy for the Bible in its original manuscripts, though none of those are extant. Still others maintain that only a particular translation is inerrant, such as the King James Version. Another view closely related is Biblical infallibility or Limited inerrancy, which affirms that the Bible is free of error as a guide to salvation, but may include errors on matters such as history, geography, or science. The Books of the Bible, considered to be inspired, among Judaism, and the Catholic, Orthodox and Protestant churches vary, thus each define the canon differently, although there is substantial overlap.

These variations are a reflection of the range of traditions and councils that have convened on the subject. Every version of the Bible always includes books of the Tanakh, the canon of the Hebrew Bible. This makes up what Christians regard as the Old Testament. The Catholic and Orthodox canons, in addition to the Tanakh, also include the Deuterocanonical Books, as part of the Old Testament. These Books appear in the Septuagint, but are regarded by Protestants to be apocryphal. However, they are considered to be important historical documents which help to inform the understanding of words, grammar and syntax used in the historical period of their conception. Some versions of the Bible include a separate Apocrypha section between the Old Testament and the New Testament. The New Testament, originally written in Koine Greek, contains 27 books which are agreed upon by all churches.

Catholic and Orthodox Interpretations

In antiquity, two schools of exegesis developed in Alexandria and Antioch. Alexandrine interpretation, exemplified by Origen, tended to read Scripture allegorically, while Antiochene interpretation adhered to the literal sense, holding that other meanings (called *theoria*) could only be accepted if based on the literal meaning. Catholic theology distinguishes two senses of scripture: the literal and the spiritual. The *literal* sense of understanding scripture is the meaning conveyed by the words of Scripture. The *spiritual* sense is further subdivided into:

- the *allegorical* sense, which includes typology. An example would be the parting of the Red Sea being understood as a "type" (sign) of baptism.
- the *moral* sense, which understands the scripture to contain some ethical teaching.
- the *anagogical* sense, which applies to eschatology, eternity and the consummation of the world.

Regarding exegesis, following the rules of sound interpretation, Catholic theology holds:

- the injunction that all other senses of sacred scripture are based on the *literal*
- that the historicity of the Gospels must be absolutely and constantly held
- that scripture must be read within the "living Tradition of the whole Church"
- that "the task of interpretation has been entrusted to the bishops in communion with the successor of Peter, the Bishop of Rome"

Protestant Interpretation: Clarity of Scripture

Protestant Christians believe that the Bible is a self-sufficient revelation, the final authority on all Christian doctrine, and revealed all truth necessary for salvation. This concept is known as *sola scriptura*. Protestants characteristically believe that ordinary believers may reach an adequate understanding of Scripture because Scripture itself is clear (or "perspicuous"), because of the help of the Holy Spirit, or both. Martin Luther believed that without God's help Scripture would be "enveloped in darkness". He advocated "one definite and simple understanding of Scripture". John Calvin wrote, "all who... follow the Holy Spirit as their guide, find in the Scripture a clear light." The Second Helvetic Confession, composed by the pastor of the Reformed church in Zurich (successor to Protestant reformer Zwingli) was adopted as a declaration of doctrine by most European Reformed churches.

Original Intended Meaning of Scripture

Protestants strongly stress the meaning conveyed by the words of Scripture, the historical grammatical method. The historical-grammatical method or grammatico-historical method is an effort in Biblical hermeneutics to find the intended original meaning in the text. This original intended meaning of the text is drawn out through examination of the passage in light of the grammatical and syntactical aspects, the historical background, the literary genre as well as theological (canonical) considerations. The historical-grammatical method distinguishes between the one original meaning and the significance of the text. The significance of the text includes the ensuing use of the text or application. The original passage is seen as having only a single meaning or sense. As Milton S. Terry said, "A fundamental principle in grammatico-historical exposition is that the words and sentences can have but one significance in one and the same connection. The moment we neglect this principle we drift out upon a sea of uncertainty and conjecture." Technically speaking, the grammatical-historical method of interpretation is distinct from the determination of the passage's significance in light of that interpretation. Taken together, both define the term (Biblical) hermeneutics. Some Protestant interpreters make use of typology.

Eschaton

The end of things, whether the end of an individual life, the end of the age, or the end of the world, broadly speaking is Christian eschatology; the study of the destiny of humans as it is revealed in the Bible. The major issues in Christian eschatology are the Tribulation, death and the afterlife, the Rapture, the Second Coming of Jesus, Resurrection of the Dead, Heaven and Hell, Millennialism, the Last Judgment, the end of the world, and the New Heavens and New Earth. Christians believe that the second coming of Christ will occur at the end of time after a period of severe persecution (the Great Tribulation). All who have died will be resurrected bodily from the dead for the Last Judgment. Jesus will fully establish the Kingdom of God in fulfillment of scriptural prophecies.

Death and Afterlife

Most Christians believe that human beings experience divine judgment and are rewarded either with eternal life or eternal damnation. This includes the general judgement at the Resurrection of the dead as well as the belief (held by Roman Catholics, Orthodox and most

Protestants) in a judgment particular to the individual soul upon physical death. In Roman Catholicism, those who die in a state of grace, i. e., without any mortal sin separating them from God, but are still imperfectly purified from the effects of sin, undergo purification through the intermediate state of purgatory to achieve the holiness necessary for entrance into God's presence. Those who have attained this goal are called *saints* (Latin *sanctus*, "holy"). Some Christian groups, including Anglicans, Lutherans and Seventh-day Adventists hold to mortalism, the belief that the human soul is not naturally immortal, and is unconscious during the intermediate state between bodily death and resurrection. These Christians also hold to Annihilationism, the belief that subsequent to the final judgment, the wicked will cease to exist rather than suffer everlasting torment. Jehovah's Witnesses hold to a similar view.

Worship

Justin Martyr described 2nd century Christian liturgy in his *First Apology* (c. 150) to Emperor Antoninus Pius, and his description remains relevant to the basic structure of Christian liturgical worship:

> *And on the day called Sunday, all who live in cities or in the country gather together to one place, and the memoirs of the apostles or the writings of the prophets are read, as long as time permits; then, when the reader has ceased, the president verbally instructs, and exhorts to the imitation of these good things. Then we all rise together and pray, and, as we before said, when our prayer is ended, bread and wine and water are brought, and the president in like manner offers prayers and thanksgivings, according to his ability, and the people assent, saying Amen; and there is a distribution to each, and a participation of that over which thanks have been given, and to those who are absent a portion is sent by the deacons. And they who are well to do, and willing, give what each thinks fit; and what is collected is deposited with the president, who succors the orphans and widows and those who, through sickness or any other cause, are in want, and those who are in bonds and the strangers sojourning among us, and in a word takes care of all who are in need.*

Sacraments: Mystic and Mysterious Rite

In Christian belief and practice, a **sacrament** is a rite, instituted by Christ, that mediates grace, constituting a sacred mystery. The term is derived from the Latin word *sacramentum*, which was used to translate the Greek word for *mystery*. Views concerning both what rites are sacramental, and what it means for an act to be a sacrament vary among Christian denominations and traditions. The most conventional functional definition of a sacrament is that it is an outward sign, instituted by Christ, that conveys an inward, spiritual grace through Christ. The two most widely accepted sacraments are Baptism and the Eucharist, however, the majority of Christians recognize seven Sacraments or Divine Mysteries: Baptism, Confirmation (Chrismation in the Orthodox tradition), and the Eucharist, Holy Orders, Reconciliation of a Penitent (confession), Anointing of the Sick, and Matrimony. Taken together, these are the Seven Sacraments as recognised by churches in the High church tradition—notably Roman Catholic, eastern Orthodox, Oriental Orthodox, Independent Catholic, Old Catholic, most Anglicans, and some Lutherans. Most other denominations and traditions typically affirm only Baptism and Eucharist as sacraments, while some Protestant groups, such as the Quakers, reject sacramental theology. Most Protestant Christian denominations who believe these rites do not communicate grace prefer to call them *ordinances*.

Liturgical Calendar and Symbols

Roman Catholics, Anglicans, eastern Christians, and traditional Protestant communities frame worship around a liturgical calendar. This includes holy days, such as solemnities which commemorate an event in the life of Jesus or the saints, periods of fasting such as Lent, and other pious events such as memoria or lesser festivals commemorating saints. Christian groups that do not follow a liturgical tradition often retain certain celebrations, such as Christmas, Easter and Pentecost. A few churches make no use of a liturgical calendar. The cross, which is today one of the most widely recognised symbols in the world, was used as a Christian symbol from the earliest times. Tertullian, in his book *De Corona*, tells how it was already a tradition for Christians to trace repeatedly on their foreheads the sign of the cross. Although the cross was known to the early Christians, the crucifix did not appear in use until the 5th century. Among the symbols employed by the primitive Christians, that of the fish seems to have ranked first in importance. From monumental sources such as tombs it is known that the symbolic fish was familiar to Christians from the earliest times. The fish was depicted as a Christian symbol in the first decades of the 2nd century. Its popularity among Christians was due principally, it would seem, to the famous acrostic consisting of the initial letters of five Greek words forming the word for fish (Ichthys), which words briefly but clearly described the character of Christ and the claim to worship of believers: *Iesous Christos Theou Yios Soter*, meaning, *Jesus Christ, Son of God, Savior*. Christians from the very beginning adorned their tombs with paintings of Christ, of the saints, of scenes from the Bible and allegorical groups. The catacombs are the cradle of all Christian art. The first Christians had no prejudice against images, pictures, or statues. The idea that they must have feared the danger of idolatry among their new converts is disproved in the simplest way by the pictures, even statues, that remain from the 1st centuries. Other major Christian symbols include the chi-rho monogram, the dove (symbolic of the Holy Spirit), the sacrificial lamb (symbolic of Christ's sacrifice), the vine (symbolizing the necessary connectedness of the Christian with Christ) and many others. These all derive from writings found in the New Testament.

Baptism: an Important Ritual Act for Believers

Baptism is the ritual act, with the use of water, by which a person is admitted to membership of the Church. Beliefs on baptism vary among denominations. Differences occur firstly, on whether the act has any spiritual significance, some churches hold to the doctrine of Baptismal Regeneration, which affirms that baptism creates or strengthens a person's faith, and is intimately linked to salvation, this view is held by Catholic and eastern Orthodox churches as well as Lutherans and Anglicans, while others simply acknowledge it as a purely symbolic act, an external public declaration of the inward change which has taken place in the person. Secondly, there are differences of opinion on the methodology of the act. These methods being: Baptism by Immersion; if immersion is total, Baptism by Submersion; and Baptism by Affusion (pouring) and Baptism by Aspersion (sprinkling). Those who hold the first view may also adhere to the tradition of Infant Baptism.

History of Christianity

Christianity began as a Jewish sect in the Levant of the middle East in the mid-1st century. Its earliest development took place under the leadership of the Twelve Apostles, particularly Saint Peter and Paul the Apostle, followed by the early bishops, whom Christians consider the successors of the Apostles. According to the scriptures, Christians were from the beginning subject to persecution by some Jewish religious authorities, who disagreed with the apostles' teachings (See Split of early Christianity and Judaism). This involved punishments, including death, for Christians such as Stephen and James, son of Zebedee. Larger-scale persecutions followed at the hands of the authorities of the Roman Empire, first in the year 64, when Emperor Nero blamed them for the Great Fire of Rome. According to Church tradition, it was under Nero's persecution that early Church leaders Peter and Paul of Tarsus were each martyred in Rome. Further widespread persecutions of the Church occurred under nine subsequent Roman emperors, most intensely under Decius and Diocletian. From the year 150, Christian teachers began to produce theological and apologetic works aimed at defending the faith. These authors are known as the Church Fathers, and study of them is called Patristics. Notable early Fathers include Ignatius of Antioch, Polycarp, Justin Martyr, Irenaeus, Tertullian, Clement of Alexandria, and Origen. However, Armenia is considered the first nation to accept Christianity in 301 AD. State persecution ceased in the 4th century, when Constantine I issued an edict of toleration in 313. On 27 February 380, Emperor Theodosius I enacted a law establishing Christianity as the official religion of the Roman Empire. From at least the 4th century, Christianity has played a prominent role in the shaping of western civilization. Constantine was also instrumental in the convocation of the First Council of Nicaea in 325, which sought to address the Arian heresy and formulated the Nicene Creed, which is still used by the Roman Catholic Church, eastern Orthodoxy, Anglican Communion, and many Protestant churches. Nicaea was the first of a series of Ecumenical (worldwide) Councils which formally defined critical elements of the theology of the Church, notably concerning Christology. The Assyrian Church of the East did not accept the third and following Ecumenical Councils, and are still separate today.

In 395, the most Christianized regions of the world were Crete, Cyprus, Anatolia, Armenia, the Nile delta, and Numidia (present-day Tunisia and Algeria). The presence of Christianity in Africa began in the middle of the 1st century in Egypt, and by the end of the 2nd century in the region around Carthage. Important Africans who influenced the early development of Christianity includes Tertullian, Clement of Alexandria, Origen of Alexandria, Cyprian, Athanasius and Augustine of Hippo. The later rise of Islam in North Africa reduced the size and numbers of Christian congregations, leaving only the Coptic Church in Egypt and the Ethiopian Orthodox Tewahedo Church in the Horn of Africa. The History of Christianity in Africa began in the 1st century when Mark the Evangelist started the Orthodox Church of Alexandria in about 43 AD.

Early Middle Ages

With the decline and fall of the Roman Empire in the West, the papacy became a political player, first visible in Pope Leo's diplomatic dealings with Huns and Vandals. The church also entered into a long period of missionary activity and expansion among the various tribes. Whilst arianists instituted the death penalty for practicing pagans (see Massacre of Verden as example), Catholicism also spread among the Germanic peoples, the Celtic and Slavic peoples, the Hungarians, and the Baltic peoples. Christianity has been an important part of the shaping of western civilization, at least since the 4th century. Around 500, St. Benedict set out his Monastic Rule, establishing a system of regulations for the foundation and running of monasteries. Monasticism became a powerful force throughout Europe, and gave rise to many early centers of learning, most famously in Ireland, Scotland and Gaul, contributing to the Carolingian Renaissance of the 9th century. In the 7th century Muslims conquered Syria (including Jerusalem), North Africa and Spain. Part of the Muslims' success was due to the exhaustion of the Byzantine empire in its decades long conflict with Persia. Beginning in the 8th century, with the rise of Carolingian leaders, the papacy began to find greater political support in the Frankish Kingdom. The Middle Ages brought about major changes within the church. Pope Gregory the Great dramatically reformed ecclesiastical structure and administration. In the early 8th century, iconoclasm became a divisive issue, when it was sponsored by the Byzantine emperors. The Second Ecumenical Council of Nicaea (787) finally pronounced in favor of icons. In the early 10th century, western Christian monasticism was further rejuvenated through the leadership of the great Benedictine monastery of Cluny. Hebraism, like Hellenism, has been an all-important factor in the development of western Civilization; Judaism, as the precursor of Christianity, has indirectly had had much to do with shaping the ideals and morality of western nations since the christian era.

High and Late Middle Ages

In the West, from the 11th century onward, older cathedral schools developed into universities (see University of Oxford, University of Paris, and University of Bologna). The traditional medieval universities—evolved from Catholic and Protestant church schools—then established specialized academic structures for properly educating greater numbers of students as professionals. Prof. Walter Rüegg, editor of *A History of the University in Europe*, reports that universities then only trained students to become clerics, lawyers, civil servants, and physicians. Originally teaching only theology, these steadily added subjects including medicine, philosophy and law, became the direct ancestors of modern institutions of learning. Accompanying the rise of the "new towns" throughout Europe, mendicant orders were founded, bringing the consecrated religious life out of the monastery and into the new urban setting. The two principal mendicant movements were the Franciscans and the Dominicans founded by St. Francis and St. Dominic respectively. Both orders made significant contributions to the development of the great universities of Europe. Another new order were the Cistercians, whose large isolated monasteries spearheaded the settlement of former wilderness areas. In this period church building and ecclesiastical architecture reached new heights, culminating in the orders of Romanesque and Gothic architecture and the building of the great European cathedrals. From 1095 under the pontificate of Urban II, the Crusades were launched. These were a series of military campaigns in the Holy Land and elsewhere, initiated in response to pleas from the Byzantine Emperor Alexios I for aid against Turkish expansion.

The Crusades ultimately failed to stifle Islamic aggression and even contributed to Christian enmity with the sacking of Constantinople during the Fourth Crusade. Over a period stretching from the 7th to the 13th century, the Christian Church underwent gradual alienation, resulting in a schism dividing it into a so-called Latin or western Christian branch, the Roman Catholic Church, and an eastern, largely Greek, branch, the Orthodox Church. These two churches disagree on a number of administrative, liturgical, and doctrinal issues, most notably papal primacy of jurisdiction. The Second Council of Lyon (1274) and the Council of Florence (1439) attempted to reunite the churches, but in both cases the eastern Orthodox refused to implement the decisions and the two principal churches remain in schism to the present day. However, the Roman Catholic Church has achieved union with various smaller eastern churches. Beginning around 1184, following the crusade against the Cathar heresy, various institutions, broadly referred to as the Inquisition, were established with the aim of suppressing heresy and securing religious and doctrinal unity within Christianity through conversion and prosecution.

Post-Enlightenment Period

In the era known as the Great Divergence, when in the West the Age of Enlightenment and the Scientific revolution brought about great societal changes, Christianity was confronted with various forms of skepticism and with certain modern political ideologies such as versions of socialism and liberalism. Events ranged from mere anti-clericalism to violent outbursts against Christianity such as the Dechristianisation during the French Revolution, the Spanish Civil War, and general hostility of Marxist movements, especially the Russian Revolution. Especially pressing in Europe was the formation of nation states after the Napoleonic era. In all European countries, different Christian denominations found themselves in competition, to greater or lesser extents, with each other and with the state. Variables are the relative sizes of the denominations and the religious, political, and ideological orientation of the state. Urs Altermatt of the University of Fribourg, looking specifically at Catholicisms in Europe, identifies four models for the European nations. In traditionally Catholic countries such as Belgium, Spain, and to some extent Austria, religious and national communities are more or less identical. Cultural symbiosis and separation are found in Poland, Ireland, and Switzerland, all countries with competing denominations. Competition is found in Germany, the Netherlands, and again Switzerland, all countries with minority Catholic populations who to a greater or lesser extent did identify with the nation.

Finally, separation between religion (again, specifically Catholicism) and the state is found to a great degree in France and Italy, countries where the state actively opposed itself to the authority of the Catholic Church. The combined factors of the formation of nation states and ultramontanism, especially in Germany and the Netherlands but also in England (to a much lesser extent), often forced Catholic churches, organizations, and believers to choose between the national demands of the state and the authority of the Church, specifically the papacy. This conflict came to a head in the First Vatican Council, and in Germany would lead directly to the Kulturkampf, where liberals and Protestants under the leadership of Bismarck managed to severely restrict Catholic expression and organization. Christian commitment in Europe dropped as modernity and secularism came into their own in Europe, particularly in the Czech Republic and Estonia, while religious commitments in America have been generally high in comparison to Europe. The late 20th century has shown the shift of Christian adherence to the Third World and southern hemisphere in general, with the western civilization no longer the chief standard bearer of Christianity. Some Europeans (including diaspora), indigenous peoples of the Americas, and natives of other continents have revived their respective peoples' historical folk religions. Approximately 7.1 to 10% of Arabs are Christians most prevalent in Egypt, Syria and Lebanon.

Demographics

With around 2.23 billion adherents, split into 3 main branches of Catholic, Protestant and Orthodox, Christianity is the world's largest religion. The Christian share of the world's population has stood at around 33% for the last hundred years, which says that one in three persons on earth are Christians. This masks a major shift in the demographics of Christianity; large increases in the developing world (around 23,000 per day) have been accompanied by substantial declines in the developed world, mainly in Europe and North America (around 7,600 per day). It is still the predominant religion in Europe, the Americas and Southern Africa. In Asia, it is the dominant religion in Georgia, Armenia, East Timor and the Philippines. However, it is declining in many areas including the Northern and western United States, Oceania

(Australia and New Zealand), northern Europe (including Great Britain, Scandinavia and other places), France, Germany, the Canadian provinces of Ontario, British Columbia, and Quebec, and parts of Asia (especially the Middle East, South Korea, Taiwan, The Philippines and Macau). The Christian population is not decreasing in Brazil, the Southern United States and the province of Alberta, Canada, but the percentage is decreasing. In countries such as Australia and New Zealand, the Christian population are declining in both numbers and percentage. Despite the declining numbers, Christianity remains the dominant religion in the western World, where 70% are Christians, in Europe 76.2% of the population considering themselves Christians, and 86.0% of the Americas and 73.36% in Oceania still practice Christianity. However, there are many charismatic movements that have become well established over large parts of the world, especially Africa, Latin America and Asia. A leading Saudi Arabian Muslim leader Sheikh Ahmad al Qatanni reported on Aljazeera that every day 16,000 African Muslims convert to Christianity. He claimed that Islam was losing 6 million African Muslims a year to becoming Christians, including Muslims in Algeria, France, Iran, India, Morocco, Russia, Turkey, and Central Asia. It is also reported that Christianity is popular in Malaysia, Mongolia, Nigeria, Vietnam, Singapore, Indonesia, China, Japan, and South Korea. In most countries in the developed world, church attendance among people who continue to identify themselves as Christians has been falling over the last few decades. Some sources view this simply as part of a drift away from traditional membership institutions, while others link it to signs of a decline in belief in the importance of religion in general. Christianity, in one form or another, is the sole state religion of the following nations: Costa Rica (Roman Catholic), Denmark (Evangelical Lutheran), El Salvador (Roman Catholic), England (Anglican), Finland (Evangelical Lutheran & Orthodox), Georgia (Georgian Orthodox), Greece (Greek Orthodox), Iceland (Evangelical Lutheran), Liechtenstein (Roman Catholic), Malta (Roman Catholic), Monaco (Roman Catholic), and Vatican City (Roman Catholic). There are numerous other countries, such as Cyprus, which although do not have an established church, still give official recognition to a specific Christian denomination.

Major Groupings within Christianity

The three primary divisions of Christianity are Catholicism, eastern Orthodoxy, and Protestantism. There are other Christian groups that do not fit neatly into one of these primary categories. The Nicene Creed is "accepted as authoritative by the Roman Catholic, eastern Orthodox, Anglican, and major Protestant churches." There is a diversity of doctrines and practices among groups calling themselves Christian. These groups are sometimes classified under denominations, though for theological reasons many groups reject this classification system. Another distinction that is sometimes drawn is between eastern Christianity and western Christianity. However, one should note that Christianity was never a unified movement. There were many diverse Christian communities with wildly different Christologies, eschatologies, soteriologies, and cosmologies that existed alongside the "Early Church" which is itself a projected concept to indicate which communities were "proto-orthodox", in that their views would become dominate. In many ways, the first three centuries of Christianity was significantly more diverse than modern Christianity.

Catholic Church

The Catholic Church comprises those particular churches, headed by bishops, in communion with the Pope, the Bishop of Rome, as its highest authority in matters of faith, morality and

Church governance. Like the eastern Orthodox, the Roman Catholic Church through Apostolic succession traces its origins to the Christian community founded by Jesus Christ. Catholics maintain that the "one, holy, catholic and apostolic church" founded by Jesus subsists fully in the Roman Catholic Church, but also acknowledges other Christian churches and communities and works towards reconciliation among all Christians. The Catholic faith is detailed in the *Catechism of the Catholic Church*. The 2,834 sees are grouped into 23 particular rites, the largest being the Latin Rite, each with distinct traditions regarding the liturgy and the administering the sacraments. With more than 1.1 billion baptized members, the Catholic Church is the largest church representing over half of all Christians and one sixth of the world's population. Various smaller communities, such as the Old Catholic and Independent Catholic Churches, include the word *Catholic* in their title, and share much in common with Roman Catholicism but are no longer in communion with the See of Rome. The Old Catholic Church is in communion with the Anglican Communion.

Orthodox Church

eastern Orthodoxy comprises those churches in communion with the Patriarchal Sees of the East, such as the Ecumenical Patriarch of Constantinople. Like the Roman Catholic Church, the eastern Orthodox Church also traces its heritage to the foundation of Christianity through Apostolic succession and has an episcopal structure, though the autonomy of the individual, mostly national churches is emphasized. A number of conflicts with western Christianity over questions of doctrine and authority culminated in the Great Schism. eastern Orthodoxy is the second largest single denomination in Christianity, with over 200 million adherents. The Oriental Orthodox Churches (also called *Old Oriental Churches*) are those eastern churches that recognize the first three ecumenical councils—Nicaea, Constantinople and Ephesus—but reject the dogmatic definitions of the Council of Chalcedon and instead espouse a Miaphysite christology. The Oriental Orthodox communion comprises six groups: Syriac Orthodox, Coptic Orthodox, Ethiopian Orthodox, Eritrean Orthodox, Malankara Orthodox Syrian Church (India) and Armenian Apostolic churches. These six churches, while being in communion with each other are completely independent hierarchically. These churches are generally not in communion with eastern Orthodox Churches with whom they are in dialogue for erecting a communion.

Protestant/Reformed Christianity

In the 16th century, Martin Luther, Huldrych Zwingli, and John Calvin inaugurated what has come to be called Protestantism. Luther's primary theological heirs are known as Lutherans. Zwingli and Calvin's heirs are far broader denominationally, and are broadly referred to as the Reformed Tradition. Most Protestant traditions branch out from the Reformed tradition in some way. In addition to the Lutheran and Reformed branches of the Reformation, there is Anglicanism after the English Reformation. The Anabaptist tradition was largely ostracized by the other Protestant parties at the time, but has achieved a measure of affirmation in more recent history. Some but not most Baptists prefer not to be called Protestants, claiming a direct ancestral line going back to the apostles in the 1st century. The oldest Protestant groups separated from the Catholic Church in the 16th century Protestant Reformation, followed in many cases by further divisions. For example, the Methodist Church grew out of Anglican minister John Wesley's evangelical and revival movement in the Anglican Church. Several Pentecostal and non-denominational Churches, which emphasize the cleansing power of the Holy Spirit, in turn grew out of the Methodist Church. Because Methodists, Pentecostals, and other evangelicals stress "accepting Jesus as your personal Lord and Savior", which comes from John Wesley's emphasis of the New Birth, they often refer to themselves as being born-again. Estimates of the total number of Protestants are very uncertain, partly because of the difficulty in determining which denominations should be placed in these categories, but it seems clear that Protestantism is the second largest major group of Christians after Catholicism in number of followers (although the Orthodox Church is larger than any single Protestant denomination). A special grouping are the Anglican churches descended from the Church of England and organized in the Anglican Communion. Some Anglican churches consider themselves both Protestant and Catholic. Some Anglicans consider their church a branch of the "One Holy Catholic Church" alongside of the Roman Catholic and eastern Orthodox Churches, a concept rejected by the Roman Catholic Church and some eastern Orthodox. Some groups of individuals who hold basic Protestant tenets identify themselves simply as "Christians" or "born-again Christians". They typically distance themselves from the confessionalism and/or creedalism of other Christian communities by calling themselves "non-denominational". Often founded by individual pastors, they have little affiliation with historic denominations.

Cultural Christian

Cultural Christian is a broad term used to describe people with either ethnic or religious Christian heritage who may not believe in the religious claims of Christianity, but who retain an affinity for the culture, art, music, and so on related to it. Many of the population of the western hemisphere could broadly be described as cultural Christians, due to the predominance of the Christian faith in western culture, as well as widely celebrated religious holidays such as Easter and Christmas. Another frequent application of the term is to distinguish political groups in areas of mixed religious backgrounds.

Role in Western Culture: Dominant and Persistent, but Declining

western culture, throughout most of its history, has been nearly equivalent to Christian culture. Though western culture contained several polytheistic religions during its early years under the Greek and Roman empires, as the centralized Roman power waned, the dominance of the Catholic Church was the only consistent force in Europe. Therefore, until the Age of Enlightenment, Christian culture took over as the predominant force in western civilization guiding the course of philosophy, art, and science.

Criticism of Christianity

Criticism of Christianity and Christians goes back to the Apostolic age, with the New Testament recording friction between the followers of Jesus and the Pharisees and scribes (e. g. Mark 7:1—23 and Matthew 15:1—20). In the second century Christianity was criticized by the Jews on a various grounds, e. g. that the prophecies of the Hebrew Bible could not have been fulfilled by Jesus, given that he did not have a successful life. By the third century criticism of Christianity had mounted, partly as a defense against it, and the 15 volume *Adversus Christianos* by Porphyry was written as a comprehensive attack on Christianity, in part building on the pre-Christian concepts of Plotinus. By the 12th century, the Mishneh Torah (i. e., Rabbi Moses Maimonides) was criticizing Christianity on the grounds of idol worship, in that Christians attributed divinity to Jesus who had a physical body. In the 19th century, Nietzsche began to write a series of attacks on the "unnatural" teachings of Christianity (e. g. avoidance of temptations), and continued anti-christian attacks to the end of his life. In the 20th century, the philosopher Bertrand Russell expressed his criticism of Christianity in *Why I Am Not a Christian*, formulating his rejection of Christianity in the setting of logical arguments. Karl Marx was also highly critical of Christianity and argued that it is detrimental to progress because it "protects the weak", while society needs strong people to flourish. Criticism of Christianity continues to date, e.g. Jewish and Muslim theologians criticize the doctrine of the Trinity held by most Christians, stating that this doctrine in effect assumes that there are three Gods, running against the basic tenet of monotheism.

Questions or Topics for Pondering and Further Discussion for Unit Three-3:

1. The core concept of Christianity is Trinity? Please elaborate on it.
2. How do you account for the reason behind "the Great Schism"?
3. Why are there so many denominations or sects within one religion as the case in Christianity?
4. Can you briefly tell the historical process of the evolution of Christianity?
5. Please name one important event that greatly facilitated the flourishing of Christianity?
6. Karl Marx was highly critical of Christianity. What was his main argument for his criticism?
7. Some people say that western culture is mainly Christian culture. Please make some further comment.
8. Do you believe miraculous story of Jesus Christ as described in the Bible? Why and why not?

4. Religious Reformation, a Milestone Event that Paved the Way for the Rise of Western Capitalism and Power

Editor's remarks: *it is little disputed that two major abstract pillars support the western civilization. One is its religion, Christianity and the other is secular ideological institution, Capitalism. Connecting these two pillars is a famous movement called Reformation. The significance of this movement links these seemingly two conflicting ideas together and bridges the gap between the two. Max Weber in his Magus Opus entitled "The Protestant Ethic and Spirit of Capitalism" presents an in-depth analysis of the inherent and interdependent connections between a religious ethic that glorifies such virtues as thrift, diligence and self-denial of material comfort and capitalism that worships the accumulation of wealth and making profits. Thus, Reformation is what must be studied in the exploration of the western civilization.*

The Protestant Reformation was the 16th-century schism within western Christianity initiated by Martin Luther, John Calvin and other early Protestants. It was sparked by the 1517 posting of Luther's *Ninety-Five Theses*. The efforts of the self-described "reformers", who objected to ("protested") the doctrines, rituals, and ecclesiastical structure of the Roman Catholic Church, led to the creation of new national Protestant churches. The Reformation was precipitated by earlier events within Europe, such as the Black Death and the western Schism—in which, over the course of almost a century, there were at times three men claiming to be Pope simultaneously—which eroded people's faith in the Catholic Church and the Papacy which governed it. This, as well as many other factors, such as the mid 15th-century invention of the printing press, the fall of the eastern Roman Empire, the end of the Middle Ages, and the beginning of the modern era, contributed to the creation of Protestantism. The Roman Catholic Church responded with a Counter-Reformation put in to motion by the Council of Trent—the most important ecumenical council since Nicaea II 800 years earlier (at the time, there had not been an ecumenical council since Lateran IV over 300 years prior, a length only to be matched by the interval between Trent and Vatican I)—and spearheaded by the Society of Jesus. In general, northern Europe, with the exception of Ireland and pockets of Britain, turned Protestant. Southern Europe remained Roman Catholic, while fierce battles which turned into warfare took place in central Europe. The largest of the new churches were the Lutherans (mostly in Germany and Scandinavia) and the Reformed churches (mostly in Germany, Switzerland, the Netherlands and Scotland). There were many smaller bodies as well. The most common dating of the Protestant Reformation begins in 1517, when Luther published *The Ninety-Five Theses*, and concludes in 1648 with the Treaty of Westphalia that ended years of European religious wars.

Religious Situation in Europe

The Reformation began as an attempt to reform the Roman Catholic Church, by priests who opposed what they perceived as false doctrines and ecclesiastic malpractice—especially the teaching and the sale of indulgences or the abuses thereof, and simony, the selling and buying of clerical offices—that the reformers saw as evidence of the systemic corruption of the Church's Roman hierarchy, which included the Pope. In Germany, reformation ideals developed in 1520 when Martin Luther expressed doubts over the legitimacy of indulgences and the *plenitudo potestatis* of the pope. Martin Luther's excommunication on January 3, 1521, from the Catholic Church, was a main cause for the Protestant Reformation. Martin Luther's spiritual predecessors included John Wycliffe and Jan Hus, who likewise had attempted to reform the Roman Catholic Church. The Protestant Reformation began on 31 October 1517, in Wittenberg, Saxony, where Martin Luther nailed his *Ninety-Five Theses on the Power and Efficacy of Indulgences* to the door of the Castle Church, in Wittenberg. The theses debated and criticized the Church and the Pope, but concentrated upon the selling of indulgences and doctrinal policies about purgatory, particular judgment, Catholic devotion to Mary, "The Mother of God", the intercession of and devotion to the saints, most of the sacraments, the mandatory clerical celibacy, including monasticism, and the authority of the Pope. In the event, other religious reformers, such as Ulrich Zwingli, soon followed Martin Luther's example. The reformers soon disagreed among themselves and divided their movement according to doctrinal differences—first between Luther and Zwingli, later between Luther and John Calvin—consequently resulting in the establishment of different and rival Protestant Churches (denominations), such as the Lutheran, the Reformed, the Puritans, and the Presbyterian. Elsewhere, the religious reformation causes, processes, and effects were different; Anglicanism arose in England with the English Reformation, and most Protestant denominations derived from the Germanic denominations. The reformers also accelerated the development of the Counter-Reformation by the Catholic Church.

History and Origins

All mainstream Protestants generally date their doctrinal separation from the Roman Catholic Church to the 16th century, occasionally called the "Magisterial Reformation" because the ruling magistrates supported them; unlike the "Radical Reformation", which the State did not support. Older Protestant churches, such as the Unitas Fratrum (Unity of the Brethren), Moravian Brethren (Bohemian Brethren) date their origins to Jan Hus in the early 15th century. As it was led by a Bohemian noble majority, and recognized, for a time, by the Basel Compacts, the Hussite Reformation was Europe's first Magisterial Reformation. One hundred years later, in Germany the protests erupted simultaneously, whilst under threat of Islamic Ottoman invasion, which especially distracted the German princes responsible for military defense.

Corruption

Unrest due to the Great Schism of western Christianity (1378—1416) excited wars between princes, uprisings among the peasants, and widespread concern over corruption in the church. The first of a series of disruptive and new perspectives came from John Wycliffe at Oxford University, then from Jan Hus at the University of Prague. The Roman Catholic Church officially concluded this debate at the Council of Constance (1414—1417). The conclave condemned Jan Hus, who was executed by burning in spite of a promise of safe-conduct. Wycliffe was posthumously burned as a heretic. The Council of Constance confirmed and strengthened the traditional medieval conception of church and empire. It did not address the national tensions, or the theological tensions stirred up during the previous century. The council could not prevent schism and the Hussite Wars in Bohemia. Sixtus Ⅳ (1471—1484) established the practice of selling indulgences to be applied to the dead, thereby establishing a new stream of revenue with agents across Europe. Pope Alexander Ⅵ (1492—1503) was one of the most controversial of the Renaissance Popes. He fathered seven children, including Lucrezia and Cesare Borgia, by at least two mistresses. Fourteen years after his death, the corruption of the papacy that Pope Alexander Ⅵ exemplified—particularly the sale of indulgences—prompted Luther to write the *The Ninety-Five Theses*, which he nailed to the door of a church at Wittenberg in Saxony.

Sixteenth Century

The protests against the corruption emanating from Rome began in earnest when Martin Luther, an Augustinian monk at the university of Wittenberg, called in 1517 for a reopening of the debate on the sale of indulgences and the authority to absolve sin and remit one from purgatory. Luther's dissent marked a sudden outbreak of a new and irresistible force of discontent. The Reformers made heavy use of inexpensive pamphlets (using the relatively new printing press invented by Johannes Gutenberg) so there was swift movement of both ideas and documents, including *The Ninety-Five Theses*. Parallel to events in Germany, a movement began in Switzerland under the leadership of Ulrich Zwingli. These two movements quickly agreed on most issues, but some unresolved differences kept them separate. Some followers of Zwingli believed that the Reformation was too conservative, and moved independently toward more radical positions, some of which survive among modern day Anabaptists. Other Protestant movements grew up along lines of mysticism or humanism, sometimes breaking from Rome or from the Protestants, or forming outside of the churches. After this first stage of the Reformation, following the excommunication of Luther and condemnation of the Reformation by the Pope, the work and writings of John Calvin were influential in establishing a loose consensus among various groups in Switzerland, Scotland, Hungary, Germany and elsewhere. The Reformation foundations engaged with Augustinianism. Both Luther and Calvin thought along lines linked with the theological teachings of Augustine of Hippo. The Augustinianism of the Reformers struggled against Pelagianism, a heresy that they perceived in the Roman Catholic Church of their day. In the course of this religious upheaval, the German Peasants' War of

1524—1525 swept through the Bavarian, Thuringian and Swabian principalities, including the Black Company of Florian Geier, a knight from Giebelstadt who joined the peasants in the general outrage against the Roman Catholic hierarchy. Martin Luther, however, condemned the revolt, thus contributing to its eventual defeat. Some 100,000 peasants were killed. Even though Luther and Calvin had very similar theological teachings, the relationship between their followers turned quickly to conflict. Frenchman Michel de Montaigne told a story of a Lutheran pastor who declared over dinner that he would rather hear a hundred masses than take part in one of Calvin's sacraments. The political separation of the Church of England from Rome under Henry VIII, beginning in 1529 and completed in 1536, brought England alongside this broad Reformed movement. However, religious changes in the English national church proceeded more conservatively than elsewhere in Europe. Reformers in the Church of England alternated, for centuries, between sympathies for Roman Catholic traditions and Protestantism, progressively forging a stable compromise between adherence to ancient tradition and Protestantism, which is now sometimes called the via media.

Magisterial Reformers

Martin Luther, John Calvin, and Huldrych Zwingli are considered Magisterial Reformers because their reform movements were supported by ruling authorities or "magistrates". Frederick the Wise did not support Luther, who was a professor at the university he founded, but he protected him by hiding Luther in Wartburg Castle in Eisenach. Frederick the Wise was a very devout Roman Catholic, but only protected Luther in hopes of obtaining greater political autonomy from the Church. Zwingli and Calvin were supported by the city councils in Zurich and Geneva. Since the term "magister" also means "teacher", the Magisterial Reformation is also characterized by an emphasis on the authority of a teacher. This is made evident in the prominence of Luther, Calvin, and Zwingli as leaders of the reform movements in their respective areas of ministry. Because of their authority, they were often criticized by Radical Reformers as being too much like the Roman Popes. For example, Radical Reformer Andreas Karlstadt referred to the Wittenberg theologians as the "new papists".

Literacy

The Reformation was a triumph of literacy and the new printing press. Luther's translation of the Bible into German was a decisive moment in the spread of literacy, and stimulated as well the printing and distribution of religious books and pamphlets. From 1517 onward religious pamphlets flooded Germany and much of Europe. By 1530 over 10,000 publications are known, with a total of ten million copies. The Reformation was thus a media revolution. Luther strengthened his attacks on Rome by depicting a "good" against "bad" church. From there, it became clear that print could be used for propaganda in the Reformation for particular agendas. Reform writers used pre-reformation styles, clichés, and stereotypes and changed items as needed for their own purposes. Especially effective were writings in German, including Luther's translation of the Bible, his *Small Catechism* for parents teaching their children, and his *Larger Catechism* for pastors. Using the German vernacular they expressed the Apostles' Creed in simpler, more personal, Trinitarian language. Illustrations in the German Bible and in many tracts popularized Luther's ideas. Lucas Cranach the Elder (1472—1553), the great painter patronized by the electors of Wittenberg, was a close friend of Luther, and illustrated Luther's theology for a popular audience. He dramatized Luther's views on the relationship between the Old and New Testaments, while remaining mindful of Luther's careful distinctions about proper and improper uses of visual imagery.

From Humanism to Protestantism: a Revolutionary Shift in Religion

The frustrated reformism of the humanists, ushered in by the Renaissance, contributed to a growing impatience among reformers. Erasmus and later figures like Martin Luther and Zwingli would emerge from this debate and eventually contribute to another major schism of Christendom. The crisis of theology beginning with William of Ockham in the 14th century was occurring in conjunction with the new burgher discontent. Since the breakdown of the philosophical foundations of scholasticism, the new nominalism did not bode well for an institutional church legitimized as an intermediary between man and God. New thinking favored the notion that no religious doctrine can be supported by philosophical arguments, eroding the old alliance between reason and faith of the medieval period laid out by Thomas Aquinas. The major individualistic reform movements that revolted against medieval scholasticism and the institutions that underpinned it were humanism, devotionalism, (see for example, the Brothers of the Common Life and Jan Standonck) and the observantine tradition. In Germany, "the modern way" or devotionalism caught on in the universities, requiring a redefinition of God, who was no longer a rational governing principle but an arbitrary, unknowable will that cannot be limited. God was now a ruler, and religion would be more fervent and emotional. Thus, the ensuing revival of Augustinian theology, stating that man cannot be saved by his own efforts but only by the grace of God would erode the legitimacy of the rigid institutions of the church meant to provide a channel for man to do good works and get into heaven. Humanism, however, was more of an educational reform movement with origins in the Renaissance's revival of classical learning and thought. A revolt against Aristotelian logic, it placed great emphasis on reforming individuals through eloquence as opposed to reason. The European Renaissance laid the foundation for the Northern humanists in its reinforcement of the traditional use of Latin as the great unifying language of European culture.

The polarization of the scholarly community in Germany over the Reuchlin (1455—1522) affair, attacked by the elite clergy for his study of Hebrew and Jewish texts, brought Luther fully in line with the humanist educational reforms who favored academic freedom. At the same time, the impact of the Renaissance would soon backfire against traditional Roman Catholicism, ushering in an age of reform and a repudiation of much of medieval Latin tradition. Led by Erasmus, the humanists condemned various forms of corruption within the church, forms of corruption that might not have been any more prevalent than during the medieval zenith of the church. Erasmus held that true religion was a matter of inward devotion rather than outward symbols of ceremony and ritual. Going back to ancient texts, scriptures, from this viewpoint the greatest culmination of the ancient tradition, are the guides to life. Favoring moral reforms and de-emphasizing didactic ritual, Erasmus laid the groundwork for Luther. Humanism's intellectual anti-clericalism would profoundly influence Luther. The increasingly well-educated middle sectors of Northern Germany, namely the educated community and city dwellers would turn to Luther's rethinking of religion to conceptualize their discontent according to the cultural medium of the era. The great rise of the burghers, the desire to run their new businesses free of institutional barriers or outmoded cultural practices, contributed to the appeal of humanist individualism. To many, papal institutions were rigid, especially regarding their views on just price and usury. In the North, burghers and monarchs were united in their frustration for not paying any taxes to the nation, but collecting taxes from subjects and sending the revenues disproportionately to the Pope in Italy.

These trends heightened demands for significant reform and revitalization along with anticlericalism. New thinkers began noticing the divide between the priests and the flock. The clergy, for instance, were not always well-educated. Parish priests often did not know Latin and rural parishes often did not have great opportunities for theological education for many at the time. Due to its large landholdings and institutional rigidity, a rigidity the excessively large ranks of the clergy contributed to, many bishops studied law, not theology, being relegated to the role of property managers trained in administration. While priests emphasized works of religiosity, the respectability of the church began diminishing, especially among well educated urbanites, and especially considering the recent strings of political humiliation, such as the apprehension of Pope Boniface VIII by Philip IV of France, the "Babylonian Captivity", the Great Schism, and the failure of conciliar reformism. In a sense, the campaign by Pope Leo X to raise funds to rebuild St. Peter's Basilica was too much of an excess by the secular Renaissance church, prompting high-pressure indulgences that rendered the clergy establishments even more disliked in the cities. Luther borrowed from the humanists the sense of individualism, that each man can be his own priest (an attitude likely to find popular support considering the rapid rise of an educated urban middle class in the North), and that the only true authority is the Bible, echoing the reformist zeal of the conciliar movement and opening up the debate once again on limiting the authority of the Pope. While his ideas called for the sharp redefinition of the dividing lines between the laity and the clergy, his ideas were still, by this point, reformist in nature. Luther's contention that the human will was incapable of following good, however, resulted in his rift with Erasmus finally distinguishing Lutheran reformism from humanism.

John Calvin: a Reformist Figure for Christianity

Following the excommunication of Luther and condemnation of the Reformation by the Pope, the work and writings of John Calvin were influential in establishing a loose consensus among various groups in Switzerland, Scotland, Hungary, Germany and elsewhere. After the expulsion of its Bishop in 1526, and the unsuccessful attempts of the Berne reformer Guillaume (William) Farel, Calvin was asked to use the organizational skill he had gathered as a student of law to discipline the "fallen city" of Geneva. His "Ordinances" of 1541 involved a collaboration of Church affairs with the City council and consistory in order to bring morality to all areas of life. After the establishment of the Geneva academy in 1559, Geneva became the unofficial capital of the Protestant movement, providing refuge for Protestant exiles from all over Europe and educating them as Calvinist missionaries.

These missionaries dispersed Calvinism widely, and formed the French Huguenots in Calvin's own lifetime, as well as causing the conversion of Scotland under the leadership of the cantankerous John Knox in 1560. The faith continued to spread after Calvin's death in 1564 and reached as far as Constantinople by the start of the 17th century. The Reformation foundations engaged with Augustinianism. Both Luther and Calvin thought along lines linked with the theological teachings of Augustine of Hippo. The Augustinianism of the Reformers struggled against Pelagianism, a heresy that they perceived in the Roman Catholic Church of their day. Ironically, even though both Luther and Calvin had very similar theological teachings, the relationship between Lutherans and Calvinists evolved into one of conflict.

England/Church of England: a Front Beach for Protestantism

The separation of the Church of England (or Anglican Church) from Rome under Henry VIII, beginning in 1529 and completed in 1537, brought England alongside this broad Reformation movement; however, religious changes in the English national church proceeded more conservatively than elsewhere in Europe. Reformers in the Church of England alternated, for centuries, between sympathies for ancient Catholic tradition and more Reformed principles, gradually developing into a tradition considered a middle way (*via media*) between the Roman Catholic and Protestant traditions. The English Reformation followed a different course from the Reformation in continental Europe. There had long been a strong strain of anti-clericalism and England had already given rise to the Lollard movement of John Wycliffe, which played an important part in inspiring the Hussites in Bohemia. Lollardy was suppressed and became an underground movement so the extent of its influence in the 1520s is difficult to assess. The different character of the English Reformation came rather from the fact that it was driven initially by the political necessities of Henry VIII. Henry had once been a sincere Roman Catholic and had even authored a book strongly criticizing Luther, but he later found it expedient and profitable to break with the Papacy. His wife, Catherine of Aragon, bore him only a single child that survived infancy, Mary. As England had recently gone through a lengthy dynastic conflict (see Wars of the Roses), Henry feared that his lack of a male heir might jeopardize his descendants' claim to the throne. However, Pope Clement VII, concentrating more on Charles V's sack of Rome, denied his request for an annulment. Had Clement granted the annulment and therefore admitted that his predecessor, Julius II, had erred, Clement would have given support to the Lutheran assertion that Popes replaced their own judgment for the will of God. King Henry decided to remove the Church of England from the authority of Rome.

In 1534, the Act of Supremacy made Henry the Supreme Head of the Church of England. Between 1535 and 1540, under Thomas Cromwell, the policy known as the Dissolution of the Monasteries was put into effect. The veneration of some saints, certain pilgrimages and some pilgrim shrines were also attacked. Huge amounts of church land and property passed into the hands of the Crown and ultimately into those of the nobility and gentry. The vested interest thus created made for a powerful force in support of the dissolutions. There were some notable opponents to the Henrician Reformation, such as St. Thomas More and Bishop John Fisher, who were executed for their opposition. There was also a growing party of reformers who were imbued with the Zwinglian and Calvinistic doctrines now current on the Continent. When Henry died he was succeeded by his Protestant son Edward VI, who, through his empowered councilors (with the King being only nine years old at his succession and not yet sixteen at his death) the Duke of Somerset and the Duke of Northumberland, ordered the destruction of images in churches, and the closing of the chantries. Under Edward VI the reform of the Church of England was established unequivocally in doctrinal terms. Yet, at a popular level, religion in England was still in a state of flux. Following a brief Roman Catholic restoration during the reign of Mary 1553—1558, a loose consensus developed during the reign of Elizabeth I, though this point is one of considerable debate among historians. Yet it is this "Elizabethan Religious Settlement" which largely formed Anglicanism into a distinctive church tradition. The compromise was uneasy and was capable of veering between extreme Calvinism on the one hand and Roman Catholicism on the other, but compared to the bloody and chaotic state of affairs in France, it was relatively successful until the Puritan Revolution or English Civil War in the 17th century.

Puritan Movement: It Is Not a Religious Movement Alone

The success of the Counter-Reformation on the Continent and the growth of a Puritan party dedicated to further Protestant reform polarized the Elizabethan Age, although it was not until the 1640s that England underwent religious strife comparable to what its neighbors had suffered some generations before. The early *Puritan Movement* (late 16th—17th centuries) was Reformed or Calvinist and was a movement for reform in the Church of England. Its origins lay in the discontent with the Elizabethan Religious Settlement. The desire was for the Church of England to resemble more closely the Protestant churches of Europe, especially Geneva. The Puritans objected to ornaments and ritual in the churches as idolatrous (vestments, surplices, organs, genuflection), which they castigated as "popish pomp and rags". (See Vestments controversy) They also objected to ecclesiastical courts. They refused to endorse completely all of the ritual directions and formulas of the *Book of Common Prayer*; the imposition of its liturgical order by legal force and inspection sharpened Puritanism into a definite opposition movement. The later Puritan movement were often referred to as dissenters and nonconformists and eventually led to the formation of various reformed denominations. The most famous and well-known emigration to America was the migration of the Puritan separatists from the Anglican Church of England, who fled first to Holland, and then later to America, to establish the English colony of Massachusetts in New England, which later became one of the original United States.

These Puritan separatists were also known as "the Pilgrims". After establishing a colony at Plymouth (which became part of the colony of Massachusetts) in 1620, the Puritan pilgrims received a charter from the King of England that legitimized their colony, allowing them to do trade and commerce with merchants in England, in accordance with the principles of mercantilism. This successful, though initially quite difficult, colony marked the beginning of the Protestant presence in America (the earlier French, Spanish and Portuguese settlements had been Roman Catholic), and became a kind of oasis of spiritual and economic freedom, to which persecuted Protestants and other minorities from the British Isles and Europe (and later, from all over the world) fled to for peace, freedom and opportunity. The Pilgrims of New England disapproved of Christmas and celebration was outlawed in Boston from 1659 to 1681. The ban was revoked in 1681 by Sir Edmund Andros, who also revoked a Puritan ban against festivities on Saturday night. However, it wasn't until the mid-19th century that celebrating Christmas became fashionable in the Boston region. The original intent of the colonists was to establish spiritual Puritanism, which had been denied to them in England and the rest of Europe, to engage in peaceful commerce with England and the native American Indians, and to Christianize the peoples of the Americas.

Conclusion and Legacy

The Reformation led to a series of religious wars that culminated in the Thirty Years' War (1618—1648), which devastated much of Germany, killing between 24.9 and 40% of its population. From 1618 to 1648 the Roman Catholic House of Habsburg and its allies fought against the Protestant princes of Germany, supported at various times by Denmark, Sweden and France. The Habsburgs, who ruled Spain, Austria, the Spanish Netherlands and much of Germany and Italy, were staunch defenders of the Roman Catholic Church. Some historians believe that the era of the Reformation came to a close when Roman Catholic France allied itself, first in secret and later on the battlefields, with Protestant states against the Habsburg dynasty. For the first time since the days of Luther, political and national convictions again outweighed religious convictions in Europe.

The main tenets of the Peace of Westphalia, which ended the Thirty Years' War, were listed as follows:

- All parties would now recognize the Peace of Augsburg of 1555, by which each prince

would have the right to determine the religion of his own state, the options being Roman Catholicism, Lutheranism, and now Calvinism. (the principle of *cuius regio, eius religio*)
- Christians living in principalities where their denomination was *not* the established church were guaranteed the right to practice their faith in public during allotted hours and in private at their will.

The treaty also effectively ended the Pope's pan-european political power. Fully aware of the loss, Pope Innocent X declared the treaty "null, void, invalid, iniquitous, unjust, damnable, reprobate, inane, empty of meaning and effect for all times". European sovereigns, Roman Catholic and Protestant alike, ignored his verdict. In *The Protestant Ethic and the Spirit of Capitalism*, Max Weber first suggested that cultural values could affect economic success, arguing that the Protestant Reformation led to values that drove people toward worldly achievements, a hard work ethic, and saving to accumulate wealth for investment. The new religions (in particular, Calvinism and other more austere Protestant groups) effectively forbade wastefully using hard earned money and identified the purchase of luxuries a sin.

Questions or Topics for Pondering and Further Discussion for Unit Three-4:

1. What is the true nature of the Reformation?
2. What prompted the Reformation?
3. Is the Reformation a religious movement or political movement in the name of religion?
4. What are the chief purposes of the Reformation?
5. What are the basic demands of those who imitated the Reformation?
6. Why did some countries in Europe become protestant countries after the Reformation while some others remained Catholic ones?
7. What is the relationship between Protestant ethic and spirit of capitalism as expounded by Max Weber?
8. What is the relationship between Puritanism and Protestantism?

Unit Four

1. Roman Empire, the First Western Power

The **Roman Empire** (Latin: *IMPERIVM ROMANVM*) was an ancient empire centered around the Mediterranean Sea, commonly dated from the accession of the Emperor Augustus in 27 BC through the abdication of the last emperor in 476 AD. It was the successor state to the Roman Republic, and constituted the final period of classical antiquity. The 500-year-old Roman Republic, which preceded it, had been weakened through several civil wars. Several events are commonly proposed to mark the transition from Republic to Empire, including Julius Caesar's appointment as perpetual dictator (44 BC), and the Battle of Actium (2 September 31 BC), though the Roman Senate's granting to Octavian the honorific *Augustus* is most common (16 January 27 BC). The first two centuries of the empire were characterized by the Pax Romana, which was a period of unprecedented peace and prosperity. Though Roman expansion was mostly accomplished under the republic, it continued under the emperors. Notably, parts of northern Europe were conquered in the 1st century AD, while Roman dominion in Europe, Africa and especially Asia was strengthened during this time. Numerous uprisings were successfully put down, notably those in Britain and Judea, though the latter uprising triggered the suicide of the unpopular Emperor Nero and a brief civil war. The empire would reach its greatest territorial extent under the emperor Trajan in 117 AD, though most of his gains were given up under his successor. In the view of Dio Cassius, a contemporary observer, the accession of the emperor Commodus in 180 AD marked the descent "from a kingdom of gold to one of rust and iron" a famous comment which has led some historians, notably Edward Gibbon, to take Commodus' reign as the beginning of the decline of the Roman Empire. Following the collapse of the troubled Severan dynasty, the Roman Empire was engulfed by period of civil wars and social unrest termed the Crisis of the Third Century. In the late third-century, the emperor Diocletian stabilized the empire and established the practice of dividing authority between four co-emperors (known as the tetrarchy). Disorder began again soon after his reign, but order was resorted by Constantine, who was the first emperor to convert to Christianity and who established the new capital of the eastern empire, Constantinople. During the following decades the empire was often divided along an East/West (Constantinople/Rome) axis. Theodosius I was the last emperor to rule over East and West, and died in 395 AD after making Christianity the official religion of the empire. Beginning in the late 4th century, the empire began to disintegrate as barbarians from the north overwhelmed Roman control. The crumbling western Roman Empire ended in 476 when Romulus Augustus was forced to abdicate to the Germanic warlord Odoacer. The empire in the East (known today as the Byzantine Empire but referred to in its own day as simply the "Roman Empire") continued in various forms until 1453 with the death of Constantine XI and the capture of Constantinople by Mehmed II, leader of the Ottoman Turks. Because of the Empire's vast extent and long endurance, the institutions and culture of Rome had a profound and lasting influence on the development of language, religion, architecture, philosophy, law, and forms of government in the territory it governed, particularly Europe, and by means of European expansionism throughout the modern world.

Government/Emperor

The powers of an emperor (his *imperium*) existed, in theory at least, by virtue of his "tribunician powers" (*potestas tribunicia*) and his "proconsular powers" (*imperium proconsulare*). In theory, the tribunician powers (which were similar to those of the Plebeian Tribunes under the old republic) made the Emperor's person and office sacrosanct, and gave the Emperor authority over Rome's civil government, including the power to preside over and to control the Senate. The proconsular powers (similar to those of military governors, or Proconsuls, under the old Republic) gave him authority over the Roman army. He was also given powers that, under the Republic, had been reserved for the Senate and the assemblies, including the right to declare war, to ratify treaties, and to negotiate with foreign leaders. The emperor also had the authority to carry out a range of duties that had been performed by the censors, including the power to control Senate membership. In addition, the emperor controlled the religious institutions, since, as emperor, he was always *Pontifex Maximus* and a member of each of the four major priesthoods. While these distinctions were clearly defined during the early Empire, eventually they were lost, and the emperor's powers became less constitutional and more monarchical. Realistically, the main support of an emperor's power and authority was the military. Being paid by the imperial treasury, the legionaries also swore an annual military oath of loyalty towards him, called the Sacramentum. The death of an emperor led to a crucial period of uncertainty and crisis. In theory the Senate was entitled to choose the new emperor, but most emperors chose their own successors, usually a close family member. The new emperor had to seek a swift acknowledgement of his new status and authority in order to stabilize the political landscape. No emperor could hope to survive, much less to reign, without the allegiance and loyalty of the Praetorian Guard and of the legions. To secure their loyalty, several emperors paid the *donativum*, a monetary reward.

Senate: a Governing Body for All?

While the Roman assemblies continued to meet after the founding of the Empire, their powers were all transferred to the Roman Senate, and so senatorial decrees (*senatus consulta*) acquired the full force of law. In theory, the Emperor and the Senate were two equal branches of government, but the actual authority of the Senate was negligible and it was largely a vehicle through which the Emperor disguised his autocratic powers under a cloak of republicanism. Although the Senate still commanded much prestige and respect, it was largely a glorified rubber stamp institution. Stripped of most of its powers, the Senate was largely at the Emperor's mercy. Many emperors showed a certain degree of respect towards this ancient institution, while others were notorious for ridiculing it. During Senate meetings, the Emperor sat between the two consuls, and usually acted as the presiding officer. Higher ranking senators spoke before lower ranking senators, although the Emperor could speak at any time. By the 3rd century, the Senate had been reduced to a glorified municipal body.

Senators and Equestrians

No emperor could rule the Empire without the Senatorial order and the Equestrian order. Most of the more important posts and offices of the government were reserved for the members of these two aristocratic orders. It was from among their ranks that the provincial governors, legion commanders, and similar officials were chosen. These two classes were hereditary and mostly closed to outsiders. Very successful and favored individuals could enter, but this was a rare occurrence. The career of a young aristocrat was influenced by his family connections and the favor of patrons. As important as ability, knowledge, skill, or competence, patronage was considered vital for a successful career and the highest posts and offices required the Emperor's favor and trust.

Military/Legions

During and after the civil war, Octavian reduced the huge number of the legions (over 60) to a much more manageable and affordable size (28). Several legions, particularly those with doubtful loyalties, were simply disbanded. Other legions were amalgamated, a fact suggested by the title *Gemina* (Twin). In 9 AD, Germanic tribes wiped out three full legions in the Battle of the Teutoburg Forest. This disastrous event reduced the number of the legions to 25. The total of the legions would later be increased again and for the next 300 years always be a little above or below 30. Augustus also created the Praetorian Guard: nine cohorts ostensibly to maintain the public peace which were garrisoned in Italy. Better paid than the legionaries, the Praetorians also served less time; instead of serving the standard 25 years of the legionaries, they retired after 16 years of service.

Navy

The Roman navy (Latin: *Classis*, lit. "fleet") not only aided in the supply and transport of the legions, but also helped in the protection of the frontiers in the rivers Rhine and Danube. Another of its duties was the protection of the very important maritime trade routes against the threat of pirates. Therefore it patrolled the whole of the Mediterranean, parts of the North Atlantic (coasts of Hispania, Gaul, and Britannia), and also had a presence in the Black Sea. Nevertheless the army was considered the senior and more prestigious branch.

Provinces

Until the Tetrarchy (296 AD) Roman provinces (lat. *provincae*) were administrative and territorial units of the Roman Empire outside of Italy. In the old days of the Republic the governorships of the provinces were traditionally awarded to members of the Senatorial Order. Augustus' reforms changed this policy.

Imperial Provinces

Augustus created the Imperial provinces. Most, but not all, of the Imperial provinces were relatively recent conquests and located at the borders. Thereby the overwhelming majority of legions, which were stationed at the frontiers, were under direct Imperial control. Very important was the Imperial province of Egypt, the major breadbasket of the Empire, whose grain supply was vital to feed the masses in Rome. It was considered the personal fiefdom of the Emperor, and Senators were forbidden to even visit this province. The governor of Egypt and the commanders of any legion stationed there were not from the Senatorial Order, but were chosen by the Emperor from among the members of the lower Equestrian Order.

Senatorial Provinces

The old traditional policy continued largely unchanged in the Senatorial provinces. Due to their location, away from the borders, and to the fact that they were under longer Roman sovereignty and control, these provinces were largely peaceful and stable. Only a single legion was based in a Senatorial province: Legio III Augusta, stationed in the Senatorial province of Africa (modern northern Algeria). The status of a province was subject to change; it could change from Senatorial to Imperial, or vice-versa. This happened several times during Augustus' reign. Another trend was to create new provinces, mostly by dividing older ones, or by expanding the Empire.

Religion

As the Empire expanded, and came to include people from a variety of cultures, the worship of an ever increasing number of deities was tolerated and accepted. The Imperial government, and the Romans in general, tended to be very tolerant towards most religions and cults, so long as they did not cause trouble. This could easily be accepted by other faiths as Roman liturgy and ceremonies were frequently tailored to fit local culture and identity. Since the Romans practiced polytheism they were also able to easily assimilate the gods of the peoples the Empire conquered. An individual could attend to both the Roman gods representing his Roman identity and his own personal religion, which was considered part of his personal identity. There were periodic persecutions of various religions at various points in time, most notably that of Christians.

Imperial Cult

In an effort to enhance loyalty, the inhabitants of the Empire were called to participate in the Imperial cult to revere (usually deceased) emperors as demigods. Few emperors claimed to be Gods while living, the exceptions being emperors who were widely regarded at the time to be insane (such as Caligula). Doing so in the early Empire would have risked revealing the shallowness of what the Emperor Augustus called the "restored Republic" and would have had a decidedly eastern quality to it. Since the tool was mostly one the Emperor used to control his subjects, its usefulness would have been greatest in the chaotic later Empire, when the emperors were often Christians and unwilling to participate in the practice. Usually, an emperor was deified after his death by his successor in an attempt by that successor to enhance his own prestige. This practice can be misunderstood, however, since "deification" was to the ancient world what canonization is to the Christian world. Likewise, the term "god" had a different context in the ancient world. This could be seen during the years of the Roman Republic with religio-political practices such as the disbanding of a Senate session if it was believed the gods disapproved of the session or wished a particular vote. Deification was one of the many honors a dead emperor was entitled to, as the Romans (more than modern societies) placed great prestige on honors and national recognitions. The importance of the Imperial cult slowly grew, reaching its peak during the Crisis of the Third Century. Especially in the eastern half of the Empire, imperial cults grew very popular. As such it was one of the major agents of romanization. The central elements of the cult complex were, apart from a temple; a theatre or amphitheatre for gladiator displays and other games and a public bath complex. Sometimes the imperial cult was added to the cults of an existing temple or celebrated in a special hall in the bath complex. The seriousness of this belief is unclear. Some Romans ridiculed the notion that a Roman emperor was to be considered a living god, or even made fun of the deification of an emperor after his death. Seneca the Younger parodied the notion of apotheosis in his only known satire *The Pumpkinification of Claudius*, in which the clumsy and ill-spoken Claudius is transformed not into a god, but a pumpkin or gourd. An element of mockery was present even at Claudius' funeral, and Vespasian's purported last words were *Vé, puto deus fio*, "Oh dear! I think I'm becoming a god!"

Absorption of Foreign Cults

Since Roman religion did not have a core belief that excluded other religions, several foreign gods and cults became popular. The worship of Cybele was the earliest, introduced from around 200 BC. Isis and Osiris were introduced from Egypt a century later. Bacchus and Sol Invictus were quite important and Mithras became very popular with the military. Several of these were Mystery cults. In the 1st century BC Julius Caesar granted Jews the freedom to worship in Rome as a reward for their help in Alexandria.

Languages

The language of Rome before its expansion was Latin, and this became the empire's official language. By the time of the imperial period Latin had developed two registers: the "high" written Classical Latin and the "low" spoken Vulgar Latin. While Classical Latin remained relatively stable, even through the Middle Ages, Vulgar Latin as with any spoken language was fluid and evolving. Vulgar Latin became the lingua franca in the western provinces, later evolving into the modern Romance languages: Italian, French, Portuguese, Spanish, Romanian, etc. Greek and Classical Latin were the languages of literature, scholarship, and education. Although Latin remained the most widely spoken language in the West, through to the fall of Rome and for some centuries afterwards, in the East the Greek language was the literary language and the lingua franca. The Romans generally did not attempt to supplant local languages. They generally left established customs in place and only gradually introduced typical Roman cultural elements including the Latin language. Along with Greek, many other languages of different tribes were used but almost without expression in writing. Greek was already widely spoken in many cities in the East, and as such, the Romans were quite content to retain it as an administrative language there rather than impede bureaucratic efficiency. Hence, two official secretaries served in the Roman Imperial court, one charged with correspondence in Latin and the other with correspondence in Greek for the East. Thus in the eastern Province, as with all provinces, original languages were retained.

Moreover, the process of hellenization widened its scope during the Roman period, for the Romans perpetuated "Hellenistic" culture, but with all the trappings of Roman improvements. This further spreading of "Hellenistic" culture (and therefore language) was largely due to the extensive infrastructure (in the form of entertainment, health, and education amenities, and extensive transportation networks, etc.) put in place by the Romans and their tolerance of, and inclusion of, other cultures, a characteristic which set them apart from the xenophobic nature of the Greeks preceding them. Since the Roman annexation of Greece in 146 BC, the Greek language gradually obtained a unique place in the Roman world, owing initially to the large number of Greek slaves in Roman households. In Rome itself Greek became the second language of the educated elite. It became the common language in the early Church (as its major centers in the early Christian period were in the East), and the language of scholarship and the arts. However, due to the presence of other widely spoken languages in the densely populated East, such as Coptic, Syriac, Armenian, Aramaic and Phoenician (which was also extensively spoken in North Africa), Greek never took as strong a hold beyond Asia Minor (some urban enclaves notwithstanding) as Latin eventually did in the West. This is partly evident in the extent to which the derivative languages are spoken today. Like Latin, the language gained a dual nature with the literary language, an Attic Greek variant, existing alongside spoken language, Koine Greek, which evolved into Medieval or Byzantine Greek (Romaic). By the 4th century AD, Greek no longer held such dominance over Latin in the arts and sciences as it had previously, resulting to a great extent from the growth of the western provinces. This was true also of Christian literature, reflected, for example, in the publication in the early 5th century AD of the

Vulgate Bible, the first officially accepted Latin Bible. As the western Empire declined, the number of people who spoke both Greek and Latin declined as well, contributing greatly to the future East—West/ Orthodox—Catholic cultural divide in Europe. Important as both languages were, today the descendants of Latin are widely spoken in many parts of the world, while the Greek dialects are limited mostly to Greece, Cyprus, and small enclaves in Turkey and Southern Italy (where the eastern Empire retained control for several more centuries). To some degree this can be attributed to the fact that the western provinces fell mainly to "Latinized" Christian tribes whereas the eastern provinces fell to Muslim Arabs and Turks for whom Greek held less cultural significance.

Culture of Rome

Life in the Roman Empire revolved around the city of Rome, and its famed seven hills. The city also had several theatres, gymnasia, and many taverns, baths and brothels. Throughout the territory under Rome's control, residential architecture ranged from very modest houses to country villas, and in the capital city of Rome, to the residences on the elegant Palatine Hill, from which the word *palace* is derived. The vast majority of the population lived in the City center, packed into apartment blocks. Most Roman towns and cities had a forum and temples, as did the city of Rome itself. Aqueducts were built to bring water to urban centres and served as an avenue to import wine and oil from abroad. Landlords generally resided in cities and their estates were left in the care of farm managers. To stimulate a higher labor productivity, many landlords freed a large numbers of slaves. By the time of Augustus, cultured Greek household slaves taught the Roman young (sometimes even the girls). Greek sculptures adorned Hellenistic landscape gardening on the Palatine or in the villas. Many aspects of Roman culture were taken from the Etruscans and the Greeks. In architecture and sculpture, the difference between Greek models and Roman paintings are apparent. The chief Roman contributions to architecture were the arch and the dome. The center of the early social structure was the family, which was not only marked by blood relations but also by the legally constructed relation of patria potestas. The Pater familias was the absolute head of the family; he was the master over his wife, his children, the wives of his sons, the nephews, the slaves and the freedmen, disposing of them and of their goods at will, even putting them to death. Originally, only patrician aristocracy enjoyed the privilege of forming familial clans, or *gens*, as legal entities; later, in the wake of political struggles and warfare, clients were also enlisted. Thus, such plebian *gentes* were the first formed, imitating their patrician counterparts. Slavery and slaves were part of the social order; there were slave markets where they could be bought and sold. Many slaves were freed by the masters for services rendered; some slaves could save money to buy their freedom. Generally mutilation and murder of slaves was prohibited by legislation. It is estimated that over 25% of the Roman population was enslaved. Professor Gerhard Rempel from the western New England College claims that in the city of Rome alone, during the Empire, there were about 400,000 slaves. The city of Rome had a place called the Campus Martius ("Field of Mars"), which was a sort of drill ground for Roman soldiers. Later, the Campus became Rome's track and field playground. In the Campus, the youth assembled to play and exercise, which included jumping, wrestling, boxing and racing. Riding, throwing, and swimming were also preferred physical activities. In the countryside, pastimes also included fishing and hunting. Board games played in Rome included Dice (Tesserae or Tali), Roman Chess (Latrunculi), Roman Checkers (Calculi), Tic-tac-toe (Terni Lapilli), and Ludus duodecim scriptorum and Tabula, predecessors of backgammon. There were several other activities to keep people engaged like chariot races, musical and theatrical performances,

Romans had simple food habits. Staple food was simple, generally consumed at around 11 o'clock, and consisted of bread, salad, cheese, fruits, nuts, and cold meat left over from the dinner the night before. The Roman poet, Horace mentions another Roman favourite, the olive, in reference to his own diet, which he describes as very simple: "As for me, olives, endives, and smooth mallows provide sustenance." The family ate together, sitting on stools around a table. Fingers were used to eat solid foods and spoons were used for soups. Wine was considered a staple drink, consumed at all meals and occasions by all classes and was quite cheap. Many types of drinks involving grapes and honey were consumed as well. Drinking on an empty stomach was regarded as boorish and a sure sign for alcoholism, whose debilitating physical and psychological effects were known to the Romans. An accurate accusation of being an alcoholic was an effective way to discredit political rivals. Roman literature was from its very inception influenced heavily by Greek authors. Some of the earliest works we possess are of historical epics telling the early military history of Rome. As the empire expanded, authors began to produce poetry, comedy, history, and tragedy. Virgil represents the pinnacle of Roman epic poetry. His *Aeneid* tells the story of flight of Aeneas from Troy and his settlement of the city that would become Rome. The genre of satire was common in Rome, and satires were written by, among others, Juvenaland Persius. Many Roman homes were decorated with landscapes by Greek artists. Portrait sculpture during the period utilized youthful and classical proportions, evolving later into a mixture of realism and idealism. Advancements were also made in relief sculptures, often depicting Roman victories. Music was a major part of everyday life. The word itself derives from Greek μουσική (*mousike*), "(art) of the Muses". Many private and public events were accompanied by music, ranging from nightly dining to military parades and maneuvers. In a discussion of any ancient music, however, non-specialists and even many musicians have to be reminded that much of what makes our modern music familiar to us is the result of developments only within the last 1,000 years; thus, our ideas of melody, scales, harmony, and even the instruments we use would not be familiar to Romans who made and listened to music many centuries earlier. Over time, Roman architecture was modified as their urban requirements changed, and the civil engineering and building construction technology became developed and refined. The Roman concrete has remained a riddle, and even after more than 2,000 years some Roman structures still stand magnificently. The architectural style of the capital city was emulated by other urban centers under Roman control and influence.

Education

Following various military conquests in the Greek East, Romans adapted a number of Greek educational precepts to their own system. Home was often the learning center, where children were taught Roman law, customs, and physical training to prepare the boys for eventual recruitment into the Roman army. Conforming to discipline was a point of great emphasis. Girls generally received instruction from their mothers in the art of spinning, weaving, and sewing. Education nominally began at the age of six. During the next six to seven years, both boys and girls were taught the basics of reading, writing and arithmetic. From the age of twelve, they would be learning Latin, Greek, grammar and literature, followed by training for public speaking. Oratory was an art to be practiced and learned, and good orators commanded respect. To become an effective orator was one of the objectives of education and learning. In some cases, services of gifted slaves were utilized for imparting education.

Economy and Industry

The invention and widespread application of hydraulic mining, namely hushing and ground-sluicing, aided by the ability of the Romans to plan and execute mining operations on a large scale, allowed various base and precious metals to be extracted on a proto-Industrial scale. The annual total iron output is estimated at 82,500 t, assuming a productive capacity of c. 1.5 kg per capita. Copper was produced at an annual rate of 15,000 t, and lead at 80,000 t, both production levels not to be paralleled until the Industrial Revolution; Spain alone had a 40% share in world lead production. The high lead output was a by-product of extensive silver mining which reached an amount of 200 t per annum. At its peak around the mid-2nd century AD, the Roman silver stock is estimated at 10,000 t, five to ten times larger than the combined silver mass of medieval Europe and the Caliphate around 800 AD. Any one of the *Imperium's* most important mining provinces produced as much silver as the contemporary Han empire as a whole, and more gold by an entire order of magnitude. The high amount of metal coinage in circulation meant that more coined money was available for trading or saving in the economy (monetization). The imperial government was, as all governments, interested in the issue and control of the currency in circulation. To mint coins was an important political act: the image of the ruling emperor appeared on most issues, and coins were a means of showing his image throughout the empire. Also featured were predecessors, empresses, other family members, and heirs apparent. By issuing coins with the image of an heir his legitimacy and future succession was proclaimed and reinforced. Political messages and imperial propaganda such as proclamations of victory and acknowledgments of loyalty also appeared in certain issues. Legally only the emperor and the Senate had the authority to mint coins inside the empire. However the authority of the Senate was mainly in name only. In general, the imperial government issued gold and silver coins while the Senate issued bronze coins marked by the legend "*SC*", short for *Senatus Consulto* "by decree of the Senate". However, bronze coinage could be struck without this legend. Some Greek cities were allowed to mint bronze and certain silver coins, which today are known as *Greek Imperials* (also *Roman Colonials* or *Roman Provincials*). The imperial mints were under the control of a chief financial minister, and the provincial mints were under the control of the imperial provincial procurators. The Senatorial mints were governed by officials of the Senatorial treasury.

Demography

In recent years, questions relating to ancient demographics have received increasingly more scholarly attention, with estimates of the population size of the Roman empire at its demographic peak now varying between 60 and 70 million ("low count") and over 100 million ("high count"). Adhering to the more traditional value of 55 million inhabitants, the Roman Empire constituted the most populous western political unity until the mid-19th century and remained unsurpassed on a global scale through the first millennium.

History: Augustus (27 BC—14 AD)

Octavian, the grandnephew and heir of Julius Caesar, had made himself a central military figure during the chaotic period following Caesar's assassination. In 43 BC at the age of twenty he held his first consulship and became one of the three members of the Second Triumvirate, a political alliance with Lepidus, and Mark Antony. In 36 BC, he was given the power of a Plebeian Tribune, which gave him veto power over the Senate and the ability to control the Plebeian Council, the principal legislative assembly. These powers made himself and his position sacrosanct. The triumvirate ended in 32 BC, torn apart by the competing ambitions of its members: Lepidus was forced into exile and Antony, who had allied himself with his lover Queen Cleopatra Ⅶ of Egypt, committed suicide in 30 BC following his defeat at the Battle of Actium (31 BC) by the fleet of Octavian commanded by his general Agrippa. Octavian subsequently annexed Egypt to the empire. Now sole ruler of Rome, Octavian began a full-scale reformation of military, fiscal and political matters. In 29 BC, he was given the authority of a Roman Censor and thus the power to appoint new senators. The senate also granted him a unique grade of proconsular *imperium*, giving him authority over all proconsuls, the military governors of the Empire. The powers had now secured for himself were in effect those that his predecessor Julius Caesar had secured for himself years earlier as Roman Dictator. The provinces at the frontiers where the vast majority of legions were stationed, newly classified as imperial provinces, were now under the control of Octavian. The peaceful provinces were given to the authority of the Senate and were classified as senatorial provinces. The legions, which had reached an unprecedented number of around fifty because of the civil wars, were concentrated and reduced to twenty-eight. Octavian also created nine special cohorts to maintain peace in Italy, keeping at least three stationed in Rome. The cohorts in the capital became known as the Praetorian Guard. In 27 BC, Octavian offered to transfer control of the state back to the Senate. The Senate refused the offer, which in effect was a ratification of his position within the state. Octavian was also granted the title of "Augustus" by the Senate, and took the title of *Princeps* or "first citizen". As the adopted heir of Julius Caesar, Octavian, now referred to as "Augustus", took "Caesar" as a component of his name. By the time of the reign of Vespasian, the term "Caesar" had evolved from a family name into a formal title. Augustus completed the conquest of Hispania, while subordinate generals expanded Roman possessions in Africa and Asia Minor. Augustus' final task was to ensure an orderly succession of his powers. His greatest general and stepson Tiberius had conquered Pannonia, Dalmatia, Raetia, and temporarily Germania for the Empire, and was thus a prime candidate. In 6 BC, Augustus granted tribunician powers to his stepson, and soon after he recognized Tiberius as his heir. In 13 AD, a law was passed which extended Augustus' powers over the provinces to Tiberius, so that Tiberius' legal powers were equivalent to, and independent from, those of Augustus. In 14 AD Augustus died at the age of seventy-five, having ruled the empire for forty years.

Tiberius to Alexander Severus (14—235)

Augustus was succeeded by his stepson Tiberius, the son of his wife Livia from her first marriage. Augustus was a scion of the *gens* Julia (the Julian family), one of the most ancient patrician clans of Rome, while Tiberius was a scion of the *gens* Claudia. Their three immediate successors were all descended from the *gens* Claudia, through Tiberius's brother Nero Claudius Drusus. They also descended from the *gens* Julia, emperors Caligula and Nero through Julia the Elder, Augustus's daughter from his first marriage, and emperor Claudius through Augustus's sister Octavia Minor. Historians refer to their dynasty as the "Julio-Claudian Dynasty". The early years of Tiberius's reign were relatively peaceful. However, his rule soon became characterized by paranoia. He began a series of treason trials and executions, which continued until his death in 37. The logical successor to the much hated Tiberius was his 24-year-old grandnephew Caligula. Caligula's reign began well, but after an illness he became tyrannical and insane. In 41 Caligula was assassinated, and for two days following his assassination, the senate debated the merits of restoring the Republic.

Due to the demands of the army, however, Claudius was ultimately declared emperor.

Claudius was neither paranoid like his uncle Tiberius, nor insane like his nephew Caligula, and was therefore able to administer the Empire with reasonable ability. In his own family life he was less successful, as he married his niece, who may very well have poisoned him in 54. Nero, who succeeded Claudius, focused much of his attention on diplomacy, trade, and increasing the cultural capital of the Empire. Nero, though, is remembered as a tyrant, and was forced to commit suicide in 68. Nero was followed by a brief period of civil war, known as the "Year of the Four Emperors". Augustus had established a standing army, where individual soldiers served under the same military governors over an extended period of time. The consequence was that the soldiers in the provinces developed a degree of loyalty to their commanders, which they did not have for the emperor. Thus the Empire was, in a sense, a union of inchoate principalities, which could have disintegrated at any time. Between June 68 and December 69, Rome witnessed the successive rise and fall of Galba, Otho and Vitellius until the final accession of Vespasian, first ruler of the Flavian dynasty. These events showed that any successful general could legitimately claim a right to the throne. Vespasian, though a successful emperor, continued the weakening of the Senate which had been going on since the reign of Tiberius. Through his sound fiscal policy, he was able to build up a surplus in the treasury, and began construction on the Colosseum. Titus, Vespasian's successor, quickly proved his merit, although his short reign was marked by disaster, including the eruption of Mount Vesuvius in Pompeii. He held the opening ceremonies in the still unfinished Colosseum, but died in 81. His brother Domitian succeeded him. Having exceedingly poor relations with the Senate, Domitian was murdered in September 96. The next century came to be known as the period of the "Five Good Emperors", in which the successions were peaceful and the Empire was prosperous. Each emperor of this period was adopted by his predecessor. The last two of the "Five Good Emperors" and Commodus are also called Antonines. After his accession, Nerva, who succeeded Domitian, set a new tone: he restored much confiscated property and involved the Senate in his rule.

Starting with 101Trajan undertook two military campaigns against the gold rich Dacia, which he finally conquered in 106 (see Trajan's Dacian Wars). In 112, Trajan marched on Armenia and annexed it to the Roman Empire. Then he turned south into Parthia, taking several cities before declaring Mesopotamia a new province of the Empire, and lamenting that he was too old to follow in the steps of Alexander the Great. During his rule, the Roman Empire expanded to its largest extent, and would never again advance so far to the East. Hadrian's reign was marked by a general lack of major military conflicts, but he had to defend the vast territories that Trajan had acquired. Antoninus Pius's reign was comparatively peaceful. During the reign of Marcus Aurelius, Germanic tribes launched many raids along the northern border. The period of the "Five Good Emperors" also commonly described as the Pax Romana, or "Roman Peace" was brought to an end by the reign of Commodus. Commodus was the son of Marcus Aurelius, breaking the scheme of adoptive successors that had turned out so well. Commodus became paranoid and slipped into insanity before being murdered in 192. Third-century Roman soldiers battling Gothic troops, as depicted on a contemporary Roman sarcophagus, c. 250 AD (National Museum of Rome, Rome). The Severan Dynasty, which lasted from 193 until 235, included several increasingly troubled reigns. A generally successful ruler, Septimius Severus, the first of the dynasty, cultivated the army's support and substituted equestrian officers for senators in key administrative positions. His son, Caracalla, extended full Roman citizenship to all free inhabitants of the Empire. Increasingly unstable and autocratic, Caracalla was assassinated by Macrinus, who succeeded him, before being killed and succeeded by Elagabalus. Alexander Severus, the last of the dynasty, was increasingly unable to control the army, and was assassinated in 235.

Crisis of the Third Century and the Later Emperors (235—395)

The Crisis of the Third Century is a commonly applied name for the near-collapse of the Roman Empire between 235 and 284. During this time, 25 emperors reigned, and the empire experienced extreme military, political, and economic crises. Additionally, in 251, the Plague of Cyprian broke out, causing large-scale mortality which may have seriously affected the ability of the Empire to defend itself. This period ended with the accession of Diocletian, who reigned from 284 until 305, and who solved many of the acute problems experienced during this crisis. However, the core problems would remain and cause the eventual destruction of the western empire. Diocletian saw the vast empire as ungovernable, and therefore split the Roman Empire in half and created two equal emperors to rule under the title of *Augustus*. In doing so, he effectively created what would become the western Roman Empire and the eastern Roman Empire. In 293 authority was further divided, as each *Augustus* took a junior Emperor called a *Caesar* to provide a line of succession. This constituted what is now known as the Tetrarchy ("rule of four"). The transitions of this period mark the beginnings of Late Antiquity. The Tetrarchy effectively collapsed with the death of Constantius Chlorus, the first of the Constantinian dynasty, in 306. Constantius's troops immediately proclaimed his son Constantine the Great as *Augustus*. A series of civil wars broke out, which ended with the entire empire being united under Constantine, who legalized Christianity definitively in 313 through the *Edict of Milan*. In 361, after further episodes of civil war, Julian became emperor. His edict of toleration in 362 ordered the reopening of pagan temples, and, more problematically for the Christian Church, the recalling of previously exiled Christian bishops. Julian eventually resumed the war against Shapur Ⅱ of Persia, although he received a mortal wound in battle and died in 363. His officers then elected Jovian as emperor. Jovian ceded territories won from the Persians as far back as Trajan's time, and restored the privileges of Christianity, before dying in 364.

Upon Jovian's death, Valentinian I, the first of the Valentinian dynasty, was elected Augustus, and chose his brother Valens to serve as his co-emperor. In 365, Procopius managed to bribe two legions, who then proclaimed him Augustus. War between the two rival eastern Roman Emperors continued until Procopius was defeated, although in 367, eight-year-old Gratian was proclaimed emperor by the other two. In 375 Valentinian I led his army in a campaign against a Germanic tribe, but died shortly thereafter. Succession did not go as planned. Gratian was then a 16-year-old and arguably ready to act as Emperor, but the troops proclaimed his infant half-brother emperor under the title Valentinian Ⅱ, and Gratian acquiesced. Meanwhile, the eastern Roman Empire faced its own problems with Germanic tribes. One tribe fled their former lands and sought refuge in the eastern Roman Empire. Valens let them settle on the southern bank of the Danube in 376, but they soon revolted against their Roman hosts. Valens personally led a campaign against them in 378. However this campaign proved disastrous for the Romans. The two armies approached each other near Adrianople, but Valens was apparently overconfident of the numerical superiority of his own forces over the enemy. Valens, eager to have all of the glory for himself, rushed into battle, and on 9 August 378, the Battle of Adrianople resulted in a crushing defeat for the Romans, and the death of Valens. Contemporary historian Ammianus Marcellinus estimated that two-thirds of the Roman soldiers on the field were lost in the battle. The battle had far-reaching consequences, as veteran soldiers and valuable administrators were among the heavy casualties, which left the Empire with the problem of finding suitable leadership. Gratian was now effectively responsible for the whole of the Empire. He sought however a replacement Augustus for the eastern Roman Empire, and in 379 chose Theodosius I.

Theodosius, the founder of the Theodosian dynasty, proclaimed his five-year-old son Arcadius an Augustus in 383 in an attempt to secure succession. Hispanic Celt general Magnus Maximus, stationed in Roman Britain, was proclaimed Augustus by his troops in 383 and rebelled against Gratian when he invaded Gaul. Gratian fled, but was assassinated. Following Gratian's death, Maximus had to deal with Valentinian II, at the time only twelve years old, as the senior Augustus. Maximus soon entered negotiations with Valentinian II and Theodosius, attempting and ultimately failing to gain their official recognition. Theodosius campaigned West in 388 and was victorious against Maximus, who was captured and executed. In 392 Valentinian II was murdered, and shortly thereafter Arbogast arranged for the appointment of Eugenius as emperor. The eastern emperor Theodosius I refused to recognise Eugenius as emperor and invaded the West again, defeating and killing Arbogast and Eugenius. He thus reunited the entire Roman Empire under his rule. Theodosius was the last Emperor who ruled over the whole Empire. As emperor, he made Christianity the official religion of the Roman Empire. After his death in 395, he gave the two halves of the Empire to his two sons Arcadius and Honorius. The Roman state would continue to have two different emperors with different seats of power throughout the 5th century, though the eastern Romans considered themselves Roman in full. The two halves were nominally, culturally and historically, if not politically, the same state.

Decline of the Western Roman Empire (395—476)

After 395, the emperors in the western Roman Empire were usually figureheads, while the actual rulers were military strongmen. In 475 Orestes had revolted against Emperor Julius Nepos, causing him to flee to Dalmatia. Orestes then proclaimed his own son Romulus Augustus to be emperor, but could not get sanction from the eastern Empire nor homage from scattered remnants of the western Empire outside Italy (which was under his immediate military control.) A few months later, in 476 Orestes refused to honor his promises to the Foederati, (Germanic mercenaries in the service of the empire) who had supported his revolt against Nepos, for lands in Italy. The dissatisfied mercenaries, led by Odoacer, revolted, killing Orestes and removing Romulus Augustus. Odoacer ruled Italy as a king and refused imperial titulature, so the year 476 is generally used to mark the end of the western Roman Empire. Odoacer quickly conquered the remaining provinces of Italy, and was greeted as a liberator by the Roman Senate. eastern Roman Emperor Zeno soon received two deputations. One was from the Senate returned the Imperial regalia and requested that the division of the empire be formally abolished and Zeno reign alone, and endorsing Odoacer's governance of Italy. The second deputation was from Nepos, asking for military support to regain control of the Italian Peninsula. Zeno declined to abolish the western Empire, but acceded to the requests to legitimize Odoacer's, naming him *patrician*. He urged the Odoacer and the Senate, however, to recognize Nepo's authority and invite him to return to Italy. Nepos was not invited back, but Odoacer was careful to observe the formalities of the exiled emperor's titular status, often invoking his name and even minting coins with his image. Upon Nepos' death in 480, Zeno claimed Dalmatia for the East, but Odoacer, claiming his duty as vassal to arrest and punish the killers of the western Emperor, invaded and took control of the country. He also did try and execute the assassins. When Odoacer supported the revolt of Illus and Leonitus (484—488), Zeno responded by declaring his own menacing ally Theodoric the Great, Ostrogoths, to be King of Italy. Theodoric invaded, crushed Odoacer, and took possession of Italy in 489. The Empire became gradually less Romanised and increasingly Germanic in nature: although the Empire buckled under Visigothic assault, the overthrow of the last Emperor Romulus Augustus was carried out by federated Germanic troops from within the

Roman army rather than by foreign troops. In this sense had Odoacer not renounced the title of Emperor and named himself "King of Italy" instead, the Empire might have continued in name. Its identity, however, was no longer Roman—it was increasingly populated and governed by Germanic peoples long before 476. The Roman people were by the 5th century "bereft of their military ethos" and the Roman army itself a mere supplement to federated troops of Goths, Huns, Franks and others fighting on their behalf. Many theories have been advanced in explanation of the decline of the Roman Empire, and many dates given for its fall, from the onset of its decline in the 3rd century to the fall of Constantinople in 1453. Militarily, however, the Empire finally fell after first being overrun by various non-Roman peoples and then having its heart in Italy seized by Germanic troops in a revolt. The historicity and exact dates are uncertain, and some historians do not consider that the Empire fell at this point. Disagreement persists since the decline of the Empire had been a long and gradual process rather than a single event. The Huns, a nomadic Mongoloid people from the steppes of central Eurasia, may have stimulated the barbarian invasions, a contributing factor in the collapse of the western Roman Empire.

Eastern Roman Empire/Byzantine Empire (476—1453)

As the western Roman Empire declined during the 5th century, the richer eastern Roman Empire would be relieved of much destruction, and in the mid 6th century the eastern Roman Empire (generally today called the Byzantine Empire) under the emperor Justinian I reconquered Italy and parts of Illyria from the Ostrogoths, North Africa from the Vandals, and southern Hispania from the Visigoths. The reconquest of southern Hispania was somewhat ephemeral, but North Africa served the Byzantines for another century, parts of Italy for another five centuries, and parts of Illyria even longer. Of the many accepted dates for the end of the classical Roman state, the latest is 610. This is when the Emperor Heraclius made sweeping reforms, forever changing the face of the empire. Greek was readopted as the language of government and Latin influence waned. By 610, the eastern Roman Empire had come under definite Greek influence, and could be considered to have become what many modern historians now call the Byzantine Empire. However, the Empire was never called thus by its inhabitants, who used terms such as "Romania", "Basileia Romaion" or "Pragmata Romaion", meaning "Land of the Romans" or "Kingdom of the Romans", and who still saw themselves as Romans, and their state as the rightful continuation of the ancient empire of Rome. During the Muslim conquests in the 7th century, the Empire lost its possessions in Africa and the Levant to the Arab-Islamic Caliphate, reducing Byzantine lands to Anatolia, the Balkans and southern Italy. The sack of Constantinople at the hands of the Fourth Crusade in 1204 is sometimes used to date the end of eastern Roman Empire: the destruction of Constantinople and most of its ancient treasures, total discontinuity of leadership, and the division of its lands into rival states with a Catholic-controlled "Emperor" in Constantinople itself was a blow from which the Empire never fully recovered. Nevertheless, the Byzantines recovered Constantinople itself and reestablished the Empire in 1261, and continued to call themselves Romans until their fall to the Ottoman Turks in 1453. That year the eastern part of the Roman Empire was ultimately ended by the Fall of Constantinople. Even though Mehmed II, the conqueror of Constantinople, declared himself the Emperor of the Roman Empire (*Caesar of Rome/Kayser-i Rum*), and even though this capture was in some ways far less catastrophic than the sack, Constantine XI is usually considered the last Roman Emperor. The Greek ethnic self-descriptive name "Rhomios" (*Roman*) survives to this day.

Collapse of the Western Empire (395—476)

After the death of Theodosius I in 395, the Visigoths renounced their treaty with the Empire and invaded northern Italy under their new king Alaric, but were repeatedly repulsed by the western commander-in-chief Stilicho. However, the limes on the Rhine had been depleted of Roman troops, and in early 407 Vandals, Alans, and Suevi invaded Gaul *en masse* and, meeting little resistance, proceeded to cross the Pyrenees, entering Spain in 409. Stilicho became a victim of court intrigues in Ravenna (where the imperial court resided since 402) and was executed for high treason in 408. After his death, the government became increasingly ineffective in dealing with the barbarians, and in 410 Rome was sacked by the Visigoths. Under Alaric's successors, the Goths then settled in Gaul (412—418) as *foederati* and for a while were successfully employed against the Vandals, Alans, and Suevi in Spain. Meanwhile, in the turmoil of the preceding years, Roman Britain had been abandoned. After Honorius' death in 423, the eastern empire installed the weak Valentinian III as western Emperor in Ravenna. After a violent struggle with several rivals, Aetius rose to the rank of *magister militum*. Aetius was able to stabilize the Empire's military situation somewhat, relying heavily on his Hunnic allies. With their help he defeated the Burgundians, who had occupied part of southern Gaul after 407, and settled them as Roman allies in the Savoy (433). Later that century, as Roman power faded away, the Burgundians extended their rule to the Rhone valley. Meanwhile, pressure from the Visigoths and a rebellion by the governor of Africa, Bonifacius, had induced the Vandals under their king Gaiseric to cross over from Spain in 429. After capturing Carthage, they established an independent state with a powerful navy (439), which was officially recognised by the Empire in 442. The Vandal fleet from then on formed a constant danger to Roman seafare and the coasts and islands of the western and Central Mediterranean. In 444, the Huns, who had been employed as Roman allies by Aetius, were united under their king Attila, who invaded Gaul and was only stopped with great effort by a combined Roman-Germanic force led by Aetius in the Battle of Châlons (451). The next year, Attila invaded Italy and proceeded to march upon Rome, but he halted his campaign and died a year later in 453. Aetius was murdered by Valentinian in 454, who was then himself murdered by the dead general's supporters a year later. With the end of the Theodosian dynasty, a new period of dynastic struggle ensued. The Vandals took advantage of the unrest, sailed up to Rome, and plundered the city in 455. As the barbarians settled in the former provinces, nominally as allies but *de facto* operating as independent polities, the territory of the western Empire was effectively reduced to Italy and parts of Gaul. From 455 onward, several emperors were installed in the West by the government of Constantinople, but their authority only reached as far as the barbarian commanders of the army and their troops (Ricimer [456—472], Gundobad [473—475]) allowed it to. In 475, Orestes, a former secretary of Attila, drove Emperor Julius Nepos out of Ravenna and proclaimed his own son Romulus Augustus as emperor. In 476, Orestes refused to grant Odoacer and the Heruli federated status, prompting the latter to kill him, depose his son and send the imperial insignia to Constantinople, installing himself as king over Italy. Although isolated pockets of Roman rule continued even after 476, the city of Rome itself was under the rule of the barbarians, and the control of Rome over the West had effectively ended. The eastern Roman or Byzantine Empire ended in 1453 with the capture of Constantinople by the Ottoman Turks led by Mehmed II.

Legacy of the Empire: Immense and Persistent

The American magazine *National Geographic* described the legacy of the Roman Empire in an article entitled "The World According to Rome":

> *The enduring Roman influence is reflected pervasively in contemporary language, literature, legal codes, government, architecture, engineering, medicine, sports, arts, etc. Much of it is so deeply embedded that we barely notice our debt to ancient Rome. Consider language, for example. Fewer and fewer people today claim to know Latin—and yet, go back to the first sentence in this paragraph. If we removed all the words drawn directly from Latin, that sentence would read: "The".*

Several states claimed to be the Roman Empire's successors after the fall of the western Roman Empire. The Holy Roman Empire, an attempt to resurrect the Empire in the West, was established in 800 when Pope Leo III crowned Frankish King Charlemagne as Roman Emperor on Christmas Day, though the empire and the imperial office did not become formalized for some decades. After the fall of Constantinople, the Russian Tsardom, as inheritor of the Byzantine Empire's Orthodox Christian tradition, counted itself the Third Rome (Constantinople having been the second). These concepts are known as *Translatio imperii*. When the Ottomans, who based their state on the Byzantine model, took Constantinople in 1453, Mehmed II established his capital there and claimed to sit on the throne of the Roman Empire. He even went so far as to launch an invasion of Italy with the purpose of "re-uniting the Empire", although Papal and Neapolitan armies stopped his march on Rome at Otranto in 1480. Constantinople was not officially renamed Istanbul until 28 March 1930. Excluding these states claiming its heritage, if the traditional date for the founding of Rome is accepted as fact, the Roman state can be said to have lasted in some form from 753 BC to the fall in 1461 of the Empire of Trebizond (a successor state and fragment of the Byzantine Empire which escaped conquest by the Ottomans in 1453), for a total of 2,214 years. The Roman impact on western and eastern civilianizations lives on. In time most of the Roman achievements were duplicated by later civilianizations. For example, the technology for cement was rediscovered 1755—1759 by John Smeaton. The Empire contributed many things to the world, such as a calendar with leap years, the institutions of Christianity and aspects of modern neo-classicistic and Byzantine architecture. The extensive system of roads that was constructed by the Roman Army lasts to this day. Because of this network of roads, the time necessary to travel between destinations in Europe did not decrease until the 19th century, when steam power was invented. Even modern astrology comes to us directly from the Romans. The Roman Empire also contributed its form of government, which influences various constitutions including those of most European countries and many former European colonies. In the United States, for example, the framers of the Constitution remarked, in creating the Presidency, that they wanted to inaugurate an "Augustan Age". The modern world also inherited legal thinking from Roman law, fully codified in Late Antiquity. Governing a vast territory, the Romans developed the science of public administration to an extent never before conceived or necessary, creating an extensive civil service and formalized methods of tax collection. While in the West the term "Roman" acquired a new meaning in connection with the church and the Pope of Rome the Greek form Romaioi remained attached to the Greek-speaking Christian population of the eastern Roman Empire and is still used by Greeks in addition to their common appellation. The Roman Empire's territorial legacy of controlling the Italian peninsula would serve as an influence to Italian nationalism and the unification (*Risorgimento*) of Italy in 1861.

Questions and Topics for Pondering for Unit Four-1:
1. What can you learn from the rise and fall of the Roman Empire?
2. Why was the first trans-continental empire born in Rome?

3. What are the characteristics of Roman political rule?
4. Rome was not build in a day. What is the implication of this proverb?
5. Every road leads to Rome. Please make some further comment on it.
6. What are the root cause for the fall of the Roman Empire?
7. What are the cultural implications of the Roman Empire within the framework of western culture?
8. What legacies did the Roman Empire leave to the world after its demise?

2. Hellenistic Civilization, a Beauty of the West

Hellenistic civilization (Greek civilization beyond classical Greece) represents the zenith of Greek influence in the ancient world from 323 BC to about 146 BC (or arguably as late as 30 BC). Hellenistic civilization was preceded by the Classical Hellenic period, and followed by Roman rule over the areas Greece had earlier dominated—even though much of Greek culture, religion, art and literature still permeated Rome's rule, whose elite spoke and read Greek as well as Latin. The spread of Hellenistic cultures was sparked by the conquests of Alexander the Great. After his ventures of the Persian Empire, Hellenistic kingdoms were established throughout south-West Asia (the "Near" and "Middle East") and north-East Africa (ancient Egypt and Cyrene in ancient Libya). This resulted in the export of Greek culture and language to these new realms, and moreover Greek colonists themselves. Equally, however, these new kingdoms were influenced by the indigenous cultures, adopting local practices where beneficial, necessary or convenient. Hellenistic civilization thus represents a fusion of the Ancient Greek world with that of the Near East, Middle East and Southwest Asia, and a departure from earlier Greek attitudes towards "barbarian" cultures. The extent to which genuinely hybrid Greco-asian cultures emerged is contentious; consensus tends to point towards pragmatic cultural adaptation by the elites of society, but for much of the populations, life would probably have continued much as it had before. The Hellenistic period was characterized by a new wave of Greek colonization (as distinguished from that occurring in the 8th-6th centuries BC) which established Greek cities and kingdoms in Asia and Africa. Those new cities were composed of Greek colonists who came from different parts of the Greek world, and not, as before, from a specific "mother city". The main cultural centers expanded from mainland Greece to Pergamon, Rhodes, and new Greek colonies such as Seleucia, Antioch and Alexandria. This mixture of Greek-speakers gave birth to a common Attic-based dialect, known as Hellenistic Greek, which became the *lingua franca* through the Hellenistic world. The term "Hellenistic" itself is derived from Ελλην (Héllēn), the Greeks' traditional name for themselves. It was coined by the historian Johann Gustav Droysen to refer to the spreading of Greek culture and colonization over the non-Greek lands that were conquered by Alexander the Great in the 4th century BC, compared to "Hellenic" which describes Greek culture in its native form. There has been much debate about the validity of Droysen's ideas, leading many to reject the label "Hellenistic" (at least in the specific meaning of Droysen). However, the term "Hellenistic" can still be usefully applied to this period in history, and, moreover, no better general term does so.

History

The nominal start of the Hellenistic period is usually taken as the 323 BC death of Alexander the Great in Babylon. During the previous decade of campaigning (from 334 BC), Alexander had conquered the whole Persian Empire, overthrowing the Persian King Darius Ⅲ. The conquered lands included Asia Minor, Assyria, the Levant, Egypt, Mesopotamia, Media, Persia, and parts of modern Afghanistan, Pakistan and the steppes of central Asia. Alexander had made no special preparations for his succession in his newly founded empire, dying as he did at a young age, and thus on his death-bed (apocryphally), he willed it to "the strongest". The result was a state of internecine warfare between his generals (the Diadochi, or "successors"), which lasted for forty years before a more-or-less stable arrangement was established, consisting of four major domains:

- The Antigonid dynasty in Macedon and central Greece;
- The Ptolemaic dynasty in Egypt based at Alexandria;
- The Seleucid dynasty in Syria and Mesopotamia based at Antioch;
- The Attalid dynasty in Anatolia based at Pergamum.

A further two kingdoms later emerged, the so-called Greco-Bactrian and Indo-Greek kingdom. Each of these kingdoms had, thereafter, a noticeably individual development and history. For the most part, the latter parts of those histories are of gradual decline, with most ending in absorption by the Republic of Rome. We find numerous cycles of alliances, marriages and wars between these states. However, it is clear that the rulers of these kingdoms still considered themselves Greek, and furthermore, recognized that the other Hellenistic realms were also Greek and not "robbing barbarians". The end of the Hellenistic period is often considered to be 146 BC, when the Roman Republic conquered most of mainland Greece, and absorbed all of ancient Macedon. By this time the rise of Rome to absolute political prominence in the Mediterranean was complete, and this might therefore mark the start of the "Roman period". An alternative date is 30 BC, when the final Hellenistic kingdom of Ptolemaic Egypt was conquered by Rome (the last remnants of the Seleucid empire having been taken over thirty years earlier). This more obviously represents the absolute end of the power of the Hellenistic civilizations.

The Hellenistic World

In addition to the four main successor kingdoms, there was a wider sphere of Greek influence during the period of Hellenistic rule. Much of mainland Greece and the Greek islands remained at least nominally independent, although often dominated by Macedon. The kingdom of Epirus, bordering Macedon, was also heavily influenced by the Greeks, and is often counted as a Hellenistic kingdom. Further West, the Greek cities of Sicily and southern Italy ("Magna Graecia") would remain independent for the early part of the period, until conquered by Rome; but they would in turn contribute to the growing Hellenization of the Roman Republic itself. In Asia Minor, the non-Greek kingdoms of Pontus and Cappadocia emerged, and though not directly hellenized, were heavily influenced by the Greeks. Carthage also was heavily hellenized by the 3rd century BCE. At the eastern extremes of the Hellenistic world, the Greco-Bactrian kingdom was established as a secession from the Seleucid empire. During the 2nd century BC, the Greco-Bactrians seem to have conquered north-West India, forming an Indo-Greek kingdom, and furthering the spread of Greek influence (into what would otherwise have been a neglected part of the Seleucid realm). Indeed, the Indo-Greek kingdom may technically have been the last Hellenistic state remaining (until c. 10 AD), although almost nothing is known of it, such was its profit from European affairs; thus, by the end it may not have been particularly "Hellenistic".

Arabian Peninsula

Bahrain was referred to by the Greeks as **Tylos**, the center of pearl trading, when Nearchus came to discover it serving under Alexander the Great. From the 6th to 3rd century BC Bahrain was included in Persian Empire by Achaemenians, an Iranian dynasty. The Greek admiral Nearchus is believed to have been the first of Alexander's commanders to visit this islands, and he found a verdant land that was part of a wide trading network; he recorded: "That in the island of Tylos, situated in the Persian Gulf, are large plantations of cotton tree, from which are manufactured clothes called *sindones*, a very different degrees of value, some being costly, others less expensive. The use of these is not confined to India, but extends to Arabia." The Greek historian, Theophrastus, states that much of the islands were covered in these cotton trees and that Tylos was famous for exporting walking canes engraved with emblems that were customarily carried in Babylon. It is not known whether Bahrain was part of the Seleucid Empire, although the archaeological site at Qalat Al Bahrain has been proposed as a Seleucid base in the Persian Gulf. Alexander had planned to settle the eastern shores of the Persian Gulf with Greek colonists, and although it is not clear that this happened on the scale he envisaged, Tylos was very much part of the Hellenised world: the language of the upper classes was Greek (although Aramaic was in everyday use), while Zeus was worshiped in the form of the Arabian sun-God Shams. Tylos even became the site of Greek athletic contests. The name Tylos is thought to be a Hellenization of the Semitic, Tilmun (from Dilmun). The term "Tylos" was commonly used for the islands until Ptolemy's *Geographia* when the inhabitants are referred to as "thilouanoi". Some place names in Bahrain go back to the Tylos era, for instance, the residential suburb of Arad in Muharraq, is believed to originate from "Arados", the ancient Greek name for Muharraq island. The ancient Greeks speculated as to whether the Phoenicians were originally from Tylos. According to the 19th century German classicist, Arnold Heeren: "In the Greek geographers, for instance, we read of two islands, named Tyrus or Tylos, and Aradus, which boasted that they were the mother country of the Phoenicians, and exhibited relics of Phoenician temples." The people of Tyre in particular have long maintained Persian Gulf origins, and the similarity in the words "Tylos" and "Tyre" has been commented upon.

With the waning of Seleucid Greek power, Tylos was incorporated into Characene or Mesenian, the state founded in what today is Kuwait by Hyspaosines in 127 BC. A building inscriptions found in Bahrain indicate that Hyspoasines occupied the islands, (and it also mention his wife, Thalassia). From the third century BC to arrival of Islam in the seventh AD, Bahrain was controlled by two other Iranian dynasties of Parthians and Sassanids. By about 250 BC, Seleucids lost their tritories to Parthians, an Iranian tribe from Central Asia. Parthian dynasty brought the Persian Gulf under their control and extended their influence as far as Oman. Because they needed to control the Persian Gulf trade route, the Parthians established garrisons in the southern coast of Persian Gulf. In the third century AD, the Sasanids succeeded the Parthians and held area until the rise of Islam four centuries later. Ardashir, the first ruler of Iranian Sassanians dynasty marched forward Oman and Bahrain and defeat Sanatruq (or Satiran), probably the Parthian governor of Bahrain. He appointed his son Shapur I as governor of Bahrain. Shapur constructed a new city there and named it Batan Ardashir after his father. At this time, Bahrain incorporated in the southern Sassanid province covering over the Persian Gulfs southern shore plus the archipelago of Bahrain. The southern province of Sasanids was subdivided into three districts of Haggar (Now al-hafuf province, Saudi Arabia), Batan Ardashir(Now al-Qatif province, Saudi Arabia), and Mishmahig (Now Bahrain Island) (In Middle-persian it means "ewe-fish"), included the Bahrain archipelago which earlier called Awal, but later, in the Islamic era, became known as Bahrain. The name "ewe-fish" would appear to suggest that the name /Tulos/ is related to Hebrew /tāleh/ "lamb" (Strong's 2924). By the fifth century Bahrain was a center for Nestorian Christianity, with Samahij the seat of bishops. In 410, according to the Oriental Syriac Church synodal records, a bishop named Batai was excommunicated from the church in Bahrain. It was also the site Bahrain of worship of a shark deity called Awal. Worshippers reputedly built a large statue to Awal in Muharraq, although it has now been lost, and for many centuries after Tylos, the islands of Bahrain were known as "Awal".

Hellenization

The concept of Hellenization, meaning the spread of Greek culture, has long been controversial. Undoubtedly Greek influence did spread through the Hellenistic realms, but to what extent, and whether this was a deliberate policy or mere cultural diffusion, have been hotly debated.

Alexander the Great

It seems likely that Alexander himself pursued deliberate "Hellenization" policies, but the exact motives behind those policies are unclear. Whilst it may have been a deliberate attempt to spread Greek culture, it is more likely that it was a series of pragmatic measures designed to aid in the rule of his enormous empire. These policies can also be interpreted as the result of Alexander's probable megalomania during his later years. The first tenet of Alexander's policies was the founding (or re-founding) of cities across the empire. This has, in the past, been interpreted as part of Alexander's desire to spread Greek culture throughout the empire. These cities were presumably intended to be administrative headquarters in the regions, and to have been settled by Greeks; many were settled by veterans of Alexander's campaigns. Undoubtedly, this would have resulted in the spread of Greek influence across the empire; however, the primary purpose could have been to control his new subjects, rather than specifically to spread Greek culture. Arrian explicitly says that a city founded in Bactria was "meant to civilize the natives"; however, this comment could be interpreted in either way (with civilize as a euphemism for "control"). Certainly, the cities would have been garrison points, and thus allowed control of the surrounding areas. Secondly, Alexander attempted to create a unified ruling class of Persians and Greeks, bound by marriage ties. He used both Greeks and Persians in positions of power, although he depended more on Greeks in unstable positions, and also replaced many Persian satraps in a purge after his return from India. He also tried to mix the two cultures, adopting elements of the Persian court (such as a version of the royal robes and some of the court ceremony and attendants) and also attempting to insist on the practice of proskynesis for his Greek subjects. This is probably an attempt to equalize the two races in their behavior towards Alexander as "Great King", but it was bitterly resented by the Macedonians, as the Greek custom was reserved solely for the gods. This policy can be interpreted as an attempt to spread Greek culture, or to create a hybrid culture. However, again, it is probably better seen as an attempt to help control the unwieldy empire; Alexander needed loyalty from Persian nobles as much as from his Macedonian officers. A hybrid court culture may have been created so as not to exclude the Persians. Furthermore, Alexander's marriage to, and child with the Bactrian princess Roxana can be interpreted as an attempt to create a royal dynasty which would be acceptable to both Asians and Greeks. Alexander also unified the army, placing Persian soldiers (some trained in the Macedonian way of fighting and some in their original styles) in the

Macedonian ranks. However, again, this can simply be seen as a pragmatic solution to chronic manpower problems. Alexander's increasing megalomania can be seen in his plan to completely homogenize the populations of Europe and Asia by mass re-settlement. Whilst this thoroughly impractical plan could be interpreted as an attempt to create a new hybrid culture, the sheer ambitiousness of the plan suggests some other process at work. In short, Alexander's policies did undoubtedly result in the spread of Greek culture, but whether this was their primary aim must remain doubtful. They probably represent, instead, pragmatic attempts by Alexander to control his extensive new territories, in part by presenting himself as the heir to both Greek and Asian legacies, rather than an outsider.

Hellenization under the Successors

After Alexander's death in 323 BC, the Empire was split into satrapies under his generals. Most of Alexander's cultural changes were rejected by the Diadochi, including the cross-cultural marriages they entered into. However, the influx of Greek colonists into the new realms continued to spread Greek culture into Asia. The founding of new cities continued to be a major part of the Successors' struggle for control of any particular region, and these continued to be centers of cultural diffusion. The spread of Greek culture under the Successors seems mostly to have occurred with the spreading of Greeks themselves, rather than as an active policy. Despite their initial reluctance, the Successors seem to have later deliberately naturalized themselves to their different regions, presumably in order to help maintain control of the population. Thus, for instance, we find the Ptolemies, as early as Ptolemy I Soter, the first Hellenistic king of Egypt, portrayed as pharaohs. Similarly, in the Indo-Greek kingdom, we find kings who were converts to Buddhism (e.g. Menander). The Greeks in the regions therefore gradually become "localized", adopting local customs as appropriate. In this way, hybrid "Hellenistic" cultures naturally emerged, at least among the upper echelons of society. In summary, Alexander's conquests and the Successor kingdoms allowed widespread Greek colonization and cultural diffusion, but it is unlikely this was ever a deliberate policy. Furthermore, such Hellenization was accompanied by the opposite spread of Asian culture to Europe. Nevertheless, the upheavals which occurred during this period do seem to have resulted in the development of hybrid "Hellenistic" cultures. As a final point, it should be noted that the degree of influence that Greek culture had throughout the Hellenistic regions is often exaggerated because of the great influence on later generations of a small number of extensively Hellenized cities, particularly Alexandria.

Hellenistic Culture: Genetic Root of the Western Culture

Many 19th century scholars contended that the Hellenistic period represented a cultural decline from the brilliance of classical Greece. Though this comparison is now seen as unfair and meaningless, it has been noted that even commentators of the time saw the end of a cultural era which could not be matched again. This may be inextricably linked with the nature of government. It has been noted that after the establishment of the Athenian democracy:

> ...the Athenians found themselves suddenly a great power. Not just in one field, but in everything they set their minds to... As subjects of a tyrant, what had they accomplished?... Held down like slaves they had shirked and slacked; once they had won their freedom, not a citizen but he could feel like he was laboring for himself.

Thus, with the decline of the Greek polis, and the establishment of monarchical states, the environment and social freedom in which to excel may have been reduced. A parallel can be drawn with the productivity of the city states of Italy during the Renaissance, and their subsequent decline under autocratic rulers. However, in some fields Hellenistic culture thrived, particularly in its preservation of the past. As has been noted, the states of the Hellenistic period were deeply fixated with the past and its seemingly lost glories. Athens retained its position as the most prestigious seat of higher education, especially in the domains of philosophy and rhetoric, with considerable libraries. Alexandria was arguably the second most important center of Greek learning. The Library of Alexandria had 700,000 volumes. The city of Pergamon became a major center of book production, possessing a library of some 200,000 volumes, second only to Alexandria's. The island of Rhodes boasted a famous finishing school for politics and diplomacy. Cicero was educated in Athens and Mark Antony in Rhodes. Antioch was founded as a metropolis and center of Greek learning which retained its status into the era of Christianity. Seleucia replaced Babylon as the metropolis of the lower Tigris. The spread of Greek culture throughout the Near East and Asia owed much to the development of cities. Settlements such as Ai-Khanoum, situated on trade routes, allowed cultures to mix and spread. The identification of local gods with similar Greek deities facilitated the building of Greek-style temples, and the Greek culture in the cities also meant that buildings such as gymnasia became common. Many cities maintained their autonomy while under the nominal rule of the local king or satrap, and often had Greek-style institutions. Greek dedications, statues, architecture and inscriptions have all been found. However, local cultures were not replaced, and often mixed to create a new culture. Greek language and literature spread throughout the former Persian Empire. The development of the Alexander Romance (mainly in Egypt) owes much to Greek theater as well as other styles of story. The Library at Alexandria, set up by Ptolemy I Soter, became a center for learning and was copied by various other monarchs. An example that shows the spread of Greek theater is Plutarch's story of the death of Crassus, in which his head was taken to the Parthian court and used as a prop in a performance of The Bacchae. Theaters have also been found: for example, in Ai-Khanoum on the edge of Bactria, the theater has 35 rows—larger than the theater in Babylon. The spread of Greek influence and language is also shown through Ancient Greek coinage. Portraits became more realistic, and the obverse of the coin was often used to display a propaganda image, commemorating an event or displaying the image of a favored god. The use of Greek-style portraits and Greek language continued into the Parthian period, even as the use of Greek was in decline.

Indian Reference

Several references in Indian literature praise the knowledge of the Yavanas or the Greeks. The Mahabharata compliments them as "the all-knowing Yavanas" i.e. "The Yavanas, O king, are all-knowing; the Suras are particularly so. The mlecchas are wedded to the creations of their own fancy." and the creators of flying machines that are generally called vimanas. The "Brihat-Samhita" of the mathematician Varahamihira says: "The Greeks, though impure, must be honored since they were trained in sciences and therein, excelled others...". Yet another Indian text (Gargi-samhita), also similarly compliments the Yavanas saying: "The Yavanas are barbarians yet the science of astronomy originated with them and for this they must be revered like gods".

The Post-Hellenistic Period

In the 2nd to 1st centuries BC, Rome conquered Greece piece by piece until, with the conquest of Egypt in 30 BC, the Roman Empire controlled the Mediterranean. However, as

Horace gently put it: " *Graecia capta ferum victorim cepit et artis intulit agresti Latio* " ("Conquered Greece has conquered the brute victor and brought her arts into rustic Latium"). Roman art and literature were calqued upon Hellenistic models. Koine Greek remained the dominant language in the eastern part of the Roman Empire. In the city of Rome, Koine Greek was in widespread use among ordinary people, and the elite spoke and wrote Greek as fluently as Latin.

Questions and Topics for Pondering and Further Discussion for Unit Four-2:

1. What is the essence of Hellenistic civilization or spirit?
2. In western tradition, there is Double H (Hellenistic and Hebraic Culture) assumption? Please elaborate on it.
3. What role did Alexander the Great play in the spread of Hellenistic culture?
4. What legacy did Hellenistic culture leave to its successor, the Roman Empire?
5. Some people disagree with the statement that Hellenistic represents the zenith of the influence of ancient Greek civilization. Can you make some comment on it?
6. Some scholars claim that the Hellenistic period signified the decline of ancient Greek culture. Do you agree with it or disagree with it? Why?
7. Why is Greek culture regarded as a beauty of the West?
8. In the West, there is a saying that Greece must be mentioned in talking about western civilization. Why is that?

3. Greek Mythology, a Treasure of the West

Greek mythology is the body of myths and legends belonging to the ancient Greeks, concerning their gods and heroes, the nature of the world, and the origins and significance of their own cult and ritual practices. They were a part of religion in ancient Greece and are part of religion in modern Greece and around the world as Hellenismos. Modern scholars refer to, and study, the myths in an attempt to throw light on the religious and political institutions of Ancient Greece, its civilization, and to gain understanding of the nature of myth-making itself. Greek mythology is embodied, explicitly, in a large collection of narratives, and implicitly in Greek representational arts, such as vase-paintings and votive gifts. Greek myth attempts to explain the origins of the world, and details the lives and adventures of a wide variety of gods, goddesses, heroes, heroines, and mythological creatures. These accounts initially were disseminated in an oral-poetic tradition; today the Greek myths are known primarily from Greek literature. The oldest known Greek literary sources, Homer's epic poems *Iliad* and *Odyssey*, focus on events surrounding the Trojan War. Two poems by Homer's near contemporary Hesiod, the *Theogony* and the *Works and Days*, contain accounts of the genesis of the world, the succession of divine rulers, the succession of human ages, the origin of human woes, and the origin of sacrificial practices. Myths also are preserved in the Homeric Hymns, in fragments of epic poems of the Epic Cycle, in lyric poems, in the works of the tragedians of the fifth century BC, in writings of scholars and poets of the Hellenistic Age and in texts from the time of the Roman Empire by writers such as Plutarch and Pausanias. Archaeological findings provide a principal source of detail about Greek mythology, with gods and heroes featured prominently in the decoration of many artifacts. Geometric designs on pottery of the eighth century BC depict scenes from the Trojan cycle as well as the adventures of Heracles. In the succeeding Archaic, Classical, and

Hellenistic periods, Homeric and various other mythological scenes appear, supplementing the existing literary evidence. Greek mythology has exerted an extensive influence on the culture, the arts, and the literature of western civilization and remains part of western heritage and language. Poets and artists from ancient times to the present have derived inspiration from Greek mythology and have discovered contemporary significance and relevance in these mythological themes.

Literary Sources

Mythical narration plays an important role in nearly every genre of Greek literature. Nevertheless, the only general mythographical handbook to survive from Greek antiquity was the *Library* of Pseudo-apollodorus. This work attempts to reconcile the contradictory tales of the poets and provides a grand summary of traditional Greek mythology and heroic legends. Apollodorus of Athens lived from c. 180—120 BC and wrote on many of these topics. His writings may have formed the basis for the collection; however the "Library" discusses events that occurred long after his death, hence the name Pseudo-apollodorus. Among the Earliest literary sources are Homer's two epic poems, the *Iliad* and the *Odyssey*. Other poets completed the "epic cycle", but these later and lesser poems now are lost almost entirely. Despite their traditional name, the "Homeric Hymns" have no direct connection with Homer. They are choral hymns from the earlier part of the so-called Lyric age. Hesiod, a possible contemporary with Homer, offers in his *Theogony (Origin of the Gods)* the fullest account of the earliest Greek myths, dealing with the creation of the world; the origin of the gods, Titans, and Giants; as well as elaborate genealogies, folktales, and etiological myths. Hesiod's *Works and Days*, a didactic poem about farming life, also includes the myths of Prometheus, Pandora, and the Four Ages. The poet gives advice on the best way to succeed in a dangerous world, rendered yet more dangerous by its gods. Lyrical poets often took their subjects from myth, but their treatment became gradually less narrative and more allusive. Greek lyric poets including Pindar, Bacchylides, Simonides and bucolic poets such as Theocritus and Bion, relate individual mythological incidents. Additionally, myth was central to classical Athenian drama. The tragic playwrights Aeschylus, Sophocles, and Euripides took most of their plots from myths of the age of heroes and the Trojan War. Many of the great tragic stories (e. g. Agamemnon and his children, Oedipus, Jason, Medea, etc.) took on their classic form in these tragedies. The comic playwright Aristophanes also used myths, in *The Birds* and *The Frogs*. Historians Herodotus and Diodorus Siculus, and geographers Pausanias and Strabo, who traveled throughout the Greek world and noted the stories they heard, supplied numerous local myths and legends, often giving little-known alternative versions. Herodotus in particular, searched the various traditions presented him and found the historical or mythological roots in the confrontation between Greece and the East. Herodotus attempted to reconcile origins and the blending of differing cultural concepts.

The poetry of the Hellenistic and Roman ages was primarily composed as a literary rather than cultic exercise. Nevertheless, it contains many important details that would otherwise be lost. This category includes the works of:

- The Roman poets Ovid, Statius, Valerius Flaccus, Seneca, and Virgil with Servius's commentary.
- The Greek poets of the Late Antique period: Nonnus, Antoninus Liberalis, and Quintus Smyrnaeus.
- The Greek poets of the Hellenistic period: Apollonius of Rhodes, Callimachus, Pseudo-eratosthenes, and Parthenius.

- The ancient novels of Greeks and Romans such as Apuleius, Petronius, Lollianus, and Heliodorus.

The *Fabulae* and *Astronomica* of the Roman writer styled as Pseudo-hyginus are two important, non-poetical compendiums of myth. The *Imagines* of Philostratus the Elder and Philostratus the Younger and the *Descriptions* of Callistratus, are two other useful sources that were drawn upon for themes. Finally, Arnobius and a number of Byzantine Greek writers provide important details of myth, much derived from earlier now lost Greek works. These preservers of myth include a lexicon of Hesychius, the *Suda*, and the treatises of John Tzetzes and Eustathius. The Christian moralizing view of Greek myth is encapsulated in the saying, *en panti muthōi kai to Daidalou musos* ("In every myth there is also the defilement of Daidalos"). In this fashion, the encyclopedic Sudas reported the role of Daedalus in satisfying the "unnatural lust" of Pasiphaë for the bull of Poseidon: "Since the origin and blame for these evils were attributed to Daidalos and he was loathed for them, he became the subject of the proverb."

Archaeological Sources

The Roman poet Virgil, here depicted in the fifth-century manuscript, the *Vergilius Romanus*, preserved details of Greek mythology in many of his writings. The discovery of the Mycenaean civilization by the German amateur archaeologist, Heinrich Schliemann, in the nineteenth century, and the discovery of the Minoan civilization in Crete by British archaeologist, Sir Arthur Evans, in the twentieth century, helped to explain many existing questions about Homer's epics and provided archaeological evidence for many of the mythological details about gods and heroes. Unfortunately, the evidence about myth and ritual at Mycenaean and Minoan sites is entirely monumental, as the Linear B script (an ancient form of Greek found in both Crete and Greece) was used mainly to record inventories, although the names of gods and heroes doubtfully have been revealed. Geometric designs on pottery of the eighth century BC depict scenes from the Trojan cycle, as well as the adventures of Heracles. These visual representations of myths are important for two reasons. For one, many Greek myths are attested on vases earlier than in literary sources: of the twelve labors of Heracles, for example, only the Cerberus adventure occurs in a contemporary literary text. In addition, visual sources sometimes represent myths or mythical scenes that are not attested in any extant literary source. In some cases, the first known representation of a myth in geometric art predates its first known representation in late archaic poetry, by several centuries. In the Archaic (c. 750—c. 500 BC), Classical (c. 480—323 BC), and Hellenistic (323—146 BC) periods, Homeric and various other mythological scenes appear, supplementing the existing literary evidence.

Survey of Mythic History

Greek mythology has changed over time to accommodate the evolution of their culture, of which mythology, both overtly and in its unspoken assumptions, is an index of the changes. In Greek mythology's surviving literary forms, as found mostly at the end of the progressive changes, is inherently political, as Gilbert Cuthbertson has urged. The earlier inhabitants of the Balkan Peninsula were an agricultural people who, using Animism, assigned a spirit to every aspect of nature. Eventually, these vague spirits assumed human forms and entered the local mythology as gods. When tribes from the north of the Balkan Peninsula invaded, they brought with them a new pantheon of gods, based on conquest, force, prowess in battle, and violent heroism. Other older gods of the agricultural world fused with those of the more powerful invaders or else faded into insignificance. After the middle of the Archaic period, myths about relationships between male gods and male heroes became more and more frequent, indicating the parallel development of pedagogic pederasty (*eros paidikos*, παιδικξ ρωζ), thought to have been introduced around 630 BC. By the end of the fifth century BC, poets had assigned at least one eromenos, an adolescent boy who was their sexual companion, to every important god except Ares and to many legendary figures. Previously existing myths, such as those of Achilles and Patroclus, also then were cast in a pederastic light. Alexandrian poets at first, then more generally literary mythographers in the early Roman Empire, often readapted stories of Greek mythological characters in this fashion. The achievement of epic poetry was to create story-cycles and, as a result, to develop a new sense of mythological chronology. Thus Greek mythology unfolds as a phase in the development of the world and of humans. While self-contradictions in these stories make an absolute timeline impossible, an approximate chronology may be discerned. The resulting mythological "history of the world" may be divided into three or four broader periods:

1. The myths of originor age of gods (Theogonies, "births of gods"): myths about the origins of the world, the gods, and the human race.
2. The age when gods and mortals mingled freely: stories of the early interactions between gods, demigods, and mortals.
3. The age of heroes (heroic age), where divine activity was more limited. The last and greatest of the heroic legends is the story of the Trojan War and after (which is regarded by some researchers as a separate fourth period).

While the age of gods often has been of more interest to contemporary students of myth, the Greek authors of the archaic and classical eras had a clear preference for the age of heroes, establishing a chronology and record of human accomplishments after the questions of how the world came into being were explained. For example, the heroic *Iliad* and *Odyssey* dwarfed the divine-focused *Theogony* and Homeric Hymns in both size and popularity. Under the influence of Homer the "hero cult" leads to a restructuring in spiritual life, expressed in the separation of the realm of the gods from the realm of the dead (heroes), of the Chthonic from the Olympian. In the *Works and Days*, Hesiod makes use of a scheme of Four Ages of Man (or Races): Golden, Silver, Bronze, and Iron. These races or ages are separate creations of the gods, the Golden Age belonging to the reign of Cronos, the subsequent races the creation of Zeus. The poet regards it as the worst; the presence of evil was explained by the myth of Pandora, when all of the best of human capabilities, save hope, had been spilled out of her overturned jar. In *Metamorphoses*, Ovid follows Hesiod's concept of the four ages.

Era of Gods: Cosmogony and Cosmology

"Myths of origin" or "creation myths" represent an attempt to render the universe comprehensible in human terms and explain the origin of the world. The most widely accepted version at the time, although a philosophical account of the beginning of things, is reported by Hesiod, in his *Theogony*. He begins with Chaos, a yawning nothingness. Out of the void emerged Gaia (the Earth) and some other primary divine beings: Eros (Love), the Abyss (the Tartarus), and the Erebus. Without male assistance, Gaia gave birth to Uranus (the Sky) who then fertilized her. From that union were born first the Titans—six males: Coeus, Crius, Cronus, Hyperion, Iapetus, and Oceanus; and six females: Mnemosyne, Phoebe, Rhea, Theia, Themis, and Tethys. After Cronus was born, Gaia and Uranus decreed no more Titans were to be born. They were followed by the one-eyed Cyclopes and the Hecatonchires or Hundred-handed Ones, who were both thrown into Tartarus by Uranus. This made Gaia furious. Cronus (the wily, youngest and most terrible of Gaia's children), was convinced by Gaia to castrate his father. He did this, and became the ruler of the Titans with his sister-wife Rhea as his consort, and the other Titans became his court. A motif of father-against-son conflict was repeated when Cronus was confronted by his son, Zeus. Because Cronus had betrayed his father, he feared that his offspring would do the same, and so each time Rhea gave birth, he snatched up the child and ate it. Rhea hated this and tricked him by hiding Zeus and wrapping a stone in a baby's blanket, which Cronus ate. When Zeus was full grown, he fed Cronus a drugged drink which caused him to vomit, throwing up Rhea's other children and the stone, which had been sitting in Cronus's stomach all along. Zeus then challenged Cronus to war for the kingship of the gods. At last, with the help of the Cyclopes (whom Zeus freed from Tartarus), Zeus and his siblings were victorious, while Cronus and the Titans were hurled down to imprisonment in Tartarus. Attic black-figured amphora depicting Athena being "reborn" from the head of Zeus, who had swallowed her mother, Metis, the goddess of childbirth. Eileithyia, on the right assists, circa 550—525 BC. Zeus was plagued by the same concern and, after a prophecy that the offspring of his first wife, Metis, would give birth to a god "greater than he"—Zeus swallowed her. She was already pregnant with Athena, however, and she burst forth from his head—fully-grown and dressed for war.

The earliest Greek thought about poetry considered the theogonies to be the prototypical poetic genre—the prototypical *mythos*—and imputed almost magical powers to it. Orpheus, the archetypal poet, also was the archetypal singer of theogonies, which he uses to calm seas and storms in Apollonius' *Argonautica*, and to move the stony hearts of the underworld gods in his descent to Hades. When Hermes invents the lyre in the *Homeric Hymn to Hermes*, the first thing he does is sing about the birth of the gods. Hesiod's *Theogony* is not only the fullest surviving account of the gods, but also the fullest surviving account of the archaic poet's function, with its long preliminary invocation to the Muses.

Theogony also was the subject of many lost poems, including those attributed to Orpheus, Musaeus, Epimenides, Abaris, and other legendary seers, which were used in private ritual purifications and mystery-rites. There are indications that Plato was familiar with some version of the Orphic theogony. A silence would have been expected about religious rites and beliefs, however, and that nature of the culture would not have been reported by members of the society while the beliefs were held. After they ceased to become religious beliefs, few would have known the rites and rituals. Allusions often existed, however, to aspects that were quite public. Images existed on pottery and religious artwork that were interpreted and more likely, misinterpreted in many diverse myths and tales. A few fragments of these works survive in quotations by Neoplatonist philosophers and recently unearthed papyrus scraps. One of these scraps, the Derveni Papyrus now proves that at least in the fifth century BC a theogonic-cosmogonic poem of Orpheus was in existence. The first philosophical cosmologists reacted against, or sometimes built upon, popular mythical conceptions that had existed in the Greek world for some time. Some of these popular conceptions can be gleaned from the poetry of Homer and Hesiod. In Homer, the Earth was viewed as a flat disk afloat on the river of Oceanus and overlooked by a hemispherical sky with sun, moon, and stars. The Sun (Helios) traversed the heavens as a charioteer and sailed around the Earth in a golden bowl at night. Sun, earth, heaven, rivers, and winds could be addressed in prayers and called to witness oaths. Natural fissures were popularly regarded as entrances to the subterranean house of Hades and his predecessors, home of the dead. Influences from other cultures always afforded new themes.

Greek Pantheon

According to Classical-era mythology, after the overthrow of the Titans, the new pantheon of gods and goddesses was confirmed. Among the principal Greek gods were the Olympians, residing atop Mount Olympus under the eye of Zeus. (The limitation of their number to twelve seems to have been a comparatively modern idea.) Besides the Olympians, the Greeks worshiped various gods of the countryside, the satyr-god Pan, Nymphs (spirits of rivers), Naiads (who dwelled in springs), Dryads (who were spirits of the trees), Nereids (who inhabited the sea), river gods, Satyrs, and others. In addition, there were the dark powers of the underworld, such as the Erinyes (or Furies), said to pursue those guilty of crimes against blood-relatives. In order to honor the Ancient Greek pantheon, poets composed the Homeric Hymns (a group of thirty-three songs). Gregory Nagy regards "the larger Homeric Hymns as simple preludes (compared with *Theogony*), each of which invokes one god".

In the wide variety of myths and legends that Greek mythology consists of, the gods that were native to the Greek peoples are described as having essentially corporeal but ideal bodies. According to Walter Burkert, the defining characteristic of Greek anthropomorphism is that "the Greek gods are persons, not abstractions, ideas or concepts". Regardless of their underlying forms, the Ancient Greek gods have many fantastic abilities; most significantly, the gods are not affected by disease, and can be wounded only under highly unusual circumstances. The Greeks considered immortality as the distinctive characteristic of their gods; this immortality, as well as unfading youth, was insured by the constant use of nectar and ambrosia, by which the divine blood was renewed in their veins. Each god descends from his or her own genealogy, pursues differing interests, has a certain area of expertise, and is governed by a unique personality; however, these descriptions arise from a multiplicity of archaic local variants, which do not always agree with one another. When these gods are called upon in poetry, prayer or cult, they are referred to by a combination of their name and epithets, that identify them by these distinctions from other manifestations of themselves (e.g. *Apollo Musagetes* is "Apollo, [as] leader of the Muses").

Alternatively the epithet may identify a particular and localized aspect of the god, sometimes thought to be already ancient during the classical epoch of Greece. Most gods were associated with specific aspects of life. For example, Aphrodite was the goddess of love and beauty, Ares was the god of war, Hades the god of the dead, and Athena the goddess of wisdom and courage. Some gods, such as Apollo and Dionysus, revealed complex personalities and mixtures of functions, while others, such as Hestia (literally "hearth") and Helios (literally "sun"), were little more than personifications. The most impressive temples tended to be dedicated to a limited number of gods, who were the focus of large pan-hellenic cults. It was, however, common for individual regions and villages to devote their own cults to minor gods. Many cities also honored the more well-known gods with unusual local rites and associated strange myths with them that were unknown elsewhere. During the heroic age, the cult of heroes supplemented that of the gods.

Age of Gods and Mortals

Bridging the age when gods lived alone and the age when divine interference in human affairs was limited was a transitional age in which gods and mortals moved together. These were the early days of the world when the groups mingled more freely than they did later. Most of these tales were later told by Ovid's *Metamorphoses* and they are often divided into two thematic groups: tales of love, and tales of punishment. Tales of love often involve incest, or the seduction or rape of a mortal woman by a male god, resulting in heroic offspring. The stories generally suggest that relationships between gods and mortals are something to avoid; even consenting relationships rarely have happy endings. In a few cases, a female divinity mates with a mortal man, as in the *Homeric Hymn to Aphrodite*, where the goddess lies with Anchises to produce Aeneas. The second type (tales of punishment) involves the appropriation or invention of some important cultural artifact, as when Prometheus steals fire from the gods, when Tantalus steals nectar and ambrosia from Zeus' table and gives it to his own subjects—revealing to them the secrets of the gods, when Prometheus or Lycaon invents sacrifice, when Demeter teaches agriculture and the Mysteries to Triptolemus, or when Marsyas invents the aulos and enters into a musical contest with Apollo. Ian Morris considers Prometheus' adventures as "a place between the history of the gods and that of man".

An anonymous papyrus fragment, dated to the third century, vividly portrays Dionysus' punishment of the king of Thrace, Lycurgus, whose recognition of the new god came too late, resulting in horrific penalties that extended into the afterlife. The story of the arrival of Dionysus to establish his cult in Thrace was also the subject of an Aeschylean trilogy. In another tragedy, Euripides' *The Bacchae*, the king of Thebes, Pentheus, is punished by Dionysus, because he disrespected the god and spied on his Maenads, the female worshippers of the god. In another story, based on an old folktale-motif, and echoing a similar theme, Demeter was searching for her daughter, Persephone, having taken the form of an old woman called Doso, and received a hospitable welcome from Celeus, the King of Eleusis in Attica. As a gift to Celeus, because of his hospitality, Demeter planned to make his son Demophon a god, but she was unable to complete the ritual because his mother Metanira walked in and saw her son in the fire and screamed in fright, which angered Demeter, who lamented that foolish mortals do not understand the concept and ritual.

Heroic Age

The age in which the heroes lived is known as the heroic age. The epic and genealogical poetry created cycles of stories clustered around particular heroes or events and established the family relationships between the heroes of different stories; they thus arranged the stories in sequence. According to Ken Dowden, "there is even a saga effect: we can follow the fates of some families in successive generations". After the rise of the hero cult, gods and heroes constitute the sacral sphere and are invoked together in oaths and prayers which are addressed to them. In contrast to the age of gods, during the heroic age the roster of heroes is never given fixed and final form; great gods are no longer born, but new heroes can always be raised up from the army of the dead. Another important difference between the hero cult and the cult of gods is that the hero becomes the center of local group identity. The monumental events of Heracles are regarded as the dawn of the age of heroes. To the Heroic Age are also ascribed three great events: the Argonautic expedition, the Theban Cycle and the Trojan War. Some scholars believe that behind Heracles' complicated mythology there was probably a real man, perhaps a chieftain-vassal of the kingdom of Argos. Some scholars suggest the story of Heracles is an allegory for the sun's yearly passage through the twelve constellations of the zodiac. Others point to earlier myths from other cultures, showing the story of Heracles as a local adaptation of hero myths already well established. Traditionally, Heracles was the son of Zeus and Alcmene, granddaughter of Perseus. His fantastic solitary exploits, with their many folk-tale themes, provided much material for popular legend. He is portrayed as a sacrificier, mentioned as a founder of altars, and imagined as a voracious eater himself; it is in this role that he appears in comedy, while his tragic end provided much material for tragedy—Heracles is regarded by Thalia Papadopoulou as "a play of great significance in examination of other Euripidean dramas". In art and literature Heracles was represented as an enormously strong man of moderate height; his characteristic weapon was the bow but frequently also the club. Vase paintings demonstrate the unparalleled popularity of Heracles, his fight with the lion being depicted many hundreds of times.

Heracles also entered Etruscan and Roman mythology and cult, and the exclamation "mehercule" became as familiar to the Romans as "Herakleis" was to the Greeks. In Italy he was worshiped as a god of merchants and traders, although others also prayed to him for his characteristic gifts of good luck or rescue from danger. Heracles attained the highest social prestige through his appointment as official ancestor of the Dorian kings. This probably served as a legitimation for the Dorian migrations into the Peloponnese. Hyllus, the eponymous hero of one Dorian phyle, became the son of Heracles and one of the Heracleidae or Heraclids (the numerous descendants of Heracles, especially the descendants of Hyllus—other Heracleidae included Macaria, Lamos, Manto, Bianor, Tlepolemus, and Telephus). These Heraclids conquered the Peloponnesian kingdoms of Mycenae, Sparta and Argos, claiming, according to legend, a right to rule them through their ancestor. Their rise to dominance is frequently called the "Dorian invasion". The Lydian and later the Macedonian kings, as rulers of the same rank, also became Heracleidae. Other members of this earliest generation of heroes, such as Perseus, Deucalion, Theseus and Bellerophon, have many traits in common with Heracles. Like him, their exploits are solitary, fantastic and border on fairy tale, as they slay monsters such as the Chimera and Medusa. Bellerophon's adventures are commonplace types, similar to the adventures of Heracles and Theseus. Sending a hero to his presumed death is also a recurrent theme of this early heroic tradition, used in the cases of Perseus and Bellerophon.

Argonauts

The only surviving Hellenistic epic, the *Argonautica* of Apollonius of Rhodes (epic poet, scholar, and director of the Library of Alexandria) tells the myth of the voyage of Jason and the Argonauts to retrieve the Golden Fleece from the mythical land of Colchis. In the *Argonautica*, Jason is impelled on his quest by king Pelias, who receives a prophecy that a man with one sandal would be his nemesis. Jason loses a sandal in a river, arrives at the court of Pelias, and the epic is set in motion. Nearly every member of the next generation of heroes, as well as Heracles, went with Jason in the ship *Argo* to fetch the Golden Fleece. This generation also included Theseus, who went to Crete to slay the Minotaur; Atalanta, the female heroine; and Meleager, who once had an epic cycle of his own to rival the *Iliad* and *Odyssey*. Pindar, Apollonius and the *Bibliotheca* endeavor to give full lists of the Argonauts. Although Apollonius wrote his poem in the 3rd century BC, the composition of the story of the Argonauts is earlier than *Odyssey*, which shows familiarity with the exploits of Jason (the wandering of Odysseus may have been partly founded on it). In ancient times the expedition was regarded as a historical fact, an incident in the opening up of the Black Sea to Greek commerce and colonization. It was also extremely popular, forming a cycle to which a number of local legends became attached. The story of Medea, in particular, caught the imagination of the tragic poets.

Trojan War and Aftermath

In *The Rage of Achilles* by Giovanni Battista Tiepolo (1757, Fresco, 300cm x 300cm, Villa Valmarana, Vicenza) Achilles is outraged that Agamemnon would threaten to seize his war prize,

Briseis, and he draws his sword to kill Agamemnon. The sudden appearance of the goddess Athena, who, in this fresco, has grabbed Achilles by the hair, prevents the act of violence. Greek mythology culminates in the Trojan War, fought between the Greeks and Troy, and its aftermath. In Homer's works, such as the *Iliad*, the chief stories have already taken shape and substance, and individual themes were elaborated later, especially in Greek drama. The Trojan War also elicited great interest in the Roman culture because of the story of Aeneas, a Trojan hero whose journey from Troy led to the founding of the city that would one day become Rome, as recounted in Virgil's *Aeneid* (Book Ⅱ of Virgil's *Aeneid* contains the best-known account of the sack of Troy). Finally there are two pseudo-Chronicles written in Latin that passed under the names of Dictys Cretensis and Dares Phrygius. The Trojan War cycle, a collection of epic poems, starts with the events leading up to the war: Eris and the golden apple of Kallisti, the Judgement of Paris, the abduction of Helen, the sacrifice of Iphigenia at Aulis.

To recover Helen, the Greeks launched a great expedition under the overall command of Menelaus' brother, Agamemnon, king of Argos or Mycenae, but the Trojans refused to return Helen. The *Iliad*, which is set in the tenth year of the war, tells of the quarrel between Agamemnon and Achilles, who was the finest Greek warrior, and the consequent deaths in battle of Achilles' beloved comrade Patroclus and Priam's eldest son, Hector. After Hector's death the Trojans were joined by two exotic allies, Penthesilea, queen of the Amazons, and Memnon, king of the Ethiopians and son of the dawn-Goddess Eos. Achilles killed both of these, but Paris then managed to kill Achilles with an arrow in the heel. Achilles' heel was the only part of his body which was not invulnerable to damage by human weaponry. Before they could take Troy, the Greeks had to steal from the citadel the wooden image of Pallas Athena (the Palladium). Finally, with Athena's help, they built the Trojan Horse. Despite the warnings of Priam's daughter Cassandra, the Trojans were persuaded by Sinon, a Greek who feigned desertion, to take the horse inside the walls of Troy as an offering to Athena; the priest Laocoon, who tried to have the horse destroyed, was killed by sea-serpents. At night the Greek fleet returned, and the Greeks from the horse opened the gates of Troy. In the total sack that followed, Priam and his remaining sons were slaughtered; the Trojan women passed into slavery in various cities of Greece. The adventurous homeward voyages of the Greek leaders (including the wanderings of Odysseus and Aeneas [the *Aeneid*], and the murder of Agamemnon) were told in two epics, the Returns (the lost *Nostoi*) and Homer's *Odyssey*.

The Trojan Cycle also includes the adventures of the children of the Trojan generation (e.g. Orestes and Telemachus). The Trojan War provided a variety of themes and became a main source of inspiration for Ancient Greek artists (e.g. metopes on the Parthenon depicting the sack of Troy); this artistic preference for themes deriving from the Trojan Cycle indicates its importance to the Ancient Greek civilization. The same mythological cycle also inspired a series of posterior European literary writings. For instance, Trojan Medieval European writers, unacquainted with Homer at first hand, found in the Troy legend a rich source of heroic and romantic storytelling and a convenient framework into which to fit their own courtly and chivalric ideals. The 12th century authors, such as Benoît de Sainte-maure (*Roman de Troie* [*Romance of Troy*, 1154—60]) and Joseph of Exeter (*De Bello Troiano* [*On the Trojan War*, 1183]) describe the war while rewriting the standard version they found in *Dictys* and *Dares*. They thus follow Horace's advice and Virgil's example: they rewrite a poem of Troy instead of telling something completely new.

Greek and Roman Conceptions of Myth

Mythology was at the heart of everyday life in Ancient Greece. Greeks regarded mythology as a part of their history. They used myth to explain natural phenomena, cultural variations, traditional enmities and friendships. It was a source of pride to be able to trace one's leaders' descent from a mythological hero or a god. Few ever doubted that there was truth behind the account of the Trojan War in the *Iliad* and *Odyssey*. According to Victor Davis Hanson, a military historian, columnist, political essayist and former Classics professor, and John Heath, associate professor of Classics at Santa Clara University, the profound knowledge of the Homeric epos was deemed by the Greeks the basis of their acculturation. Homer was the "education of Greece" (λλάδοζ παίδευσιζ), and his poetry "the Book".

Philosophy and Myth

Raphael's Plato in *The School of Athens* fresco (probably in the likeness of Leonardo da Vinci). The philosopher expelled the study of Homer, of the tragedies and of the related mythological traditions from his utopian *Republic*. After the rise of philosophy, history, prose and rationalism in the late 5th century BC, the fate of myth became uncertain, and mythological genealogies gave place to a conception of history which tried to exclude the supernatural (such as the Thucydidean history). While poets and dramatists were reworking the myths, Greek historians and philosophers were beginning to criticize them. A few radical philosophers like Xenophanes of Colophon were already beginning to label the poets' tales as blasphemous lies in the 6th century BC; Xenophanes had complained that Homer and Hesiod attributed to the gods "all that is shameful and disgraceful among men; they steal, commit adultery, and deceive one another". This line of thought found its most sweeping expression in Plato's *Republic* and *Laws*. Plato created his own allegorical myths (such as the vision of Er in the *Republic*), attacked the traditional tales of the gods' tricks, thefts and adulteries as immoral, and objected to their central role in literature. Plato's criticism was the first serious challenge to the Homeric mythological tradition, referring to the myths as "old wives' chatter". For his part Aristotle criticized the pre-socratic quasi-mythical philosophical approach and underscored that "Hesiod and the theological writers were concerned only with what seemed plausible to themselves, and had no respect for us ... But it is not worth taking seriously writers who show off in the mythical style; as for those who do proceed by proving their assertions, we must cross-examine them".

Nevertheless, even Plato did not manage to wean himself and his society from the influence of myth; his own characterization for Socrates is based on the traditional Homeric and tragic patterns, used by the philosopher to praise the righteous life of his teacher. But perhaps someone might say: "Are you then not ashamed, Socrates, of having followed such a pursuit, that you are now in danger of being put to death as a result?" But I should make to him a just reply: "You do not speak well, Sir, if you think a man in whom there is even a little merit ought to consider danger of life or death, and not rather regard this only, when he does things, whether the things he does are right or wrong and the acts of a good or a bad man. For according to your argument all the demigods would be bad who died at Troy, including the son of Thetis, who so despised danger, in comparison with enduring any disgrace, that when his mother (and she was a goddess) said to him, as he was eager to slay Hector, something like this, I believe,

> My son, if you avenge the death of your friend Patroclus and kill Hector, you yourself shall die; for straightway, after Hector, is death appointed unto you. (Hom. Il. 18.96)

He, when he heard this, made light of death and danger, and feared much more to live as a coward and not to avenge his friends, and said,

> *Straightway may I die, after doing vengeance upon the wrongdoer, that I may not stay here, jeered at beside the curved ships, a burden of the earth.*

Hanson and Heath estimate that Plato's rejection of the Homeric tradition was not favorably received by the grassroots Greek civilization. The old myths were kept alive in local cults; they continued to influence poetry and to form the main subject of painting and sculpture. More sportingly, the 5th century BC tragedian Euripides often played with the old traditions, mocking them, and through the voice of his characters injecting notes of doubt. Yet the subjects of his plays were taken, without exception, from myth. Many of these plays were written in answer to a predecessor's version of the same or similar myth. Euripides mainly impugns the myths about the gods and begins his critique with an objection similar to the one previously expressed by Xenocrates: the gods, as traditionally represented, are far too crassly anthropomorphic. Cicero saw himself as the defender of the established order, despite his personal skepticism with regard to myth and his inclination towards more philosophical conceptions of divinity. In Roman religion the worship of the Greek god Apollo (early Imperial Roman copy of a fourth century Greek original, Louvre Museum) was combined with the cult of Sol Invictus. The worship of Sol as special protector of the emperors and of the empire remained the chief imperial religion until it was replaced by Christianity.

Hellenistic and Roman Rationalism

During the Hellenistic period, mythology took on the prestige of elite knowledge that marks its possessors as belonging to a certain class. At the same time, the skeptical turn of the Classical age became even more pronounced. Greek mythographer Euhemerus established the tradition of seeking an actual historical basis for mythical beings and events. Although his original work (*Sacred Scriptures*) is lost, much is known about it from what is recorded by Diodorus and Lactantius. Rationalizing hermeneutics of myth became even more popular under the Roman Empire, thanks to the physicalist theories of Stoic and Epicurean philosophy. Stoics presented explanations of the gods and heroes as physical phenomena, while the Euhemerists rationalized them as historical figures. At the same time, the Stoics and the Neoplatonists promoted the moral significations of the mythological tradition, often based on Greek etymologies. Through his Epicurean message, Lucretius had sought to expel superstitious fears from the minds of his fellow-citizens. Livy, too, is skeptical about the mythological tradition and claims that he does not intend to pass judgment on such legends (fabulae). The challenge for Romans with a strong and apologetic sense of religious tradition was to defend that tradition while conceding that it was often a breeding-ground for superstition. The antiquarian Varro, who regarded religion as a human institution with great importance for the preservation of good in society, devoted rigorous study to the origins of religious cults. In his *Antiquitates Rerum Divinarum* (which has not survived, but Augustine's *City of God* indicates its general approach) Varro argues that whereas the superstitious man fears the gods, the truly religious person venerates them as parents. In his work he distinguished three kinds of gods:

1. The gods of nature: personifications of phenomena like rain and fire.
2. The gods of the poets: invented by unscrupulous bards to stir the passions.
3. The gods of the city: invented by wise legislators to soothe and enlighten the populace.

Roman Academic Cotta ridicules both literal and allegorical acceptance of myth, declaring roundly that myths have no place in philosophy. Cicero is also generally disdainful of myth, but, like Varro, he is emphatic in his support for the state religion and its institutions. It is difficult to know how far down the social scale this rationalism extended. Cicero asserts that no one (not even old women and boys) is so foolish as to believe in the terrors of Hades or the existence of Scyllas, centaurs or other composite creatures, but, on the other hand, the orator elsewhere complains of the superstitious and credulous character of the people. *De Natura Deorum* is the most comprehensive summary of Cicero's line of thought.

Modern Interpretations

The genesis of modern understanding of Greek mythology is regarded by some scholars as a double reaction at the end of the eighteenth century against "the traditional attitude of Christian animosity", in which the Christian reinterpretation of myth as a "lie" or fable had been retained. In Germany, by about 1795, there was a growing interest in Homer and Greek mythology. In Göttingen, Johann Matthias Gesner began to revive Greek studies, while his successor, Christian Gottlob Heyne, worked with Johann Joachim Winckelmann, and laid the foundations for mythological research both in Germany and elsewhere.

Comparative and Psychoanalytic Approaches

Max Müller is regarded as one of the founders of comparative mythology. In his *Comparative Mythology* (1867) Müller analyzed the "disturbing" similarity between the mythologies of "savage races" with those of the early Europeans. The development of comparative philology in the 19th century, together with ethnological discoveries in the 20th century, established the science of myth. Since the Romantics, all study of myth has been comparative. Wilhelm Mannhardt, Sir James Frazer, and Stith Thompson employed the comparative approach to collect and classify the themes of folklore and mythology. In 1871 Edward Burnett Tylor published his *Primitive Culture*, in which he applied the comparative method and tried to explain the origin and evolution of religion. Tylor's procedure of drawing together material culture, ritual and myth of widely separated cultures influenced both Carl Jung and Joseph Campbell. Max Müller applied the new science of comparative mythology to the study of myth, in which he detected the distorted remains of Aryan nature worship. Bronisław Malinowski emphasized the ways myth fulfills common social functions. Claude Lévi-strauss and other structuralists have compared the formal relations and patterns in myths throughout the world.

Sigmund Freud introduced a transhistorical and biological conception of man and a view of myth as an expression of repressed ideas. Dream interpretation is the basis of Freudian myth interpretation and Freud's concept of dream work recognizes the importance of contextual relationships for the interpretation of any individual element in a dream. This suggestion would find an important point of rapprochement between the structuralist and psychoanalytic approaches to myth in Freud's thought. Carl Jung extended the transhistorical, psychological approach with his theory of the "collective unconscious" and the archetypes (inherited "archaic" patterns), often encoded in myth, that arise out of it. According to Jung, "myth-forming structural elements must be present in the unconscious psyche". Comparing Jung's methodology with Joseph Campbell's theory, Robert A. Segal concludes that "to interpret a myth Campbell simply identifies the archetypes in it. An interpretation of the *Odyssey*, for example, would show how Odysseus's life conforms to a heroic pattern. Jung, by contrast, considers the identification of archetypes merely the first step in the interpretation of a myth". Karl Kerényi, one of the founders of modern studies in Greek mythology, gave up his early views of myth, in order to apply Jung's theories of archetypes to Greek myth.

Origin Theories

For Karl Kerényi mythology is "a body of material contained in tales about gods and god-like beings, heroic battles and journeys to the Underworld—*mythologem* is the best Greek word for them—tales already well-known but not amenable to further re-shaping". There are various modern theories about the origins of Greek mythology. According to the Scriptural Theory, all mythological legends are derived from the narratives of the Scriptures, although the real facts have been disguised and altered. According to the Historical Theory all the persons mentioned in mythology were once real human beings, and the legends relating to them are merely the additions of later times. Thus the story of Aeolus is supposed to have arisen from the fact that Aeolus was the ruler of some islands in the Tyrrhenian Sea. The Allegorical Theory supposes that all the ancient myths were allegorical and symbolical; while the Physical Theory subscribed to the idea that the elements of air, fire, and water were originally the objects of religious adoration, thus the principal gods were personifications of these powers of nature.

Max Müller attempted to understand an Indo-European religious form by tracing it back to its Aryan, "original" manifestation. In 1891, he claimed that "the most important discovery which has been made during the nineteenth century with respect to the ancient history of mankind was this sample equation: Sanskrit Dyaus-pitar = Greek Zeus = Latin Jupiter = Old Norse Tyr". In other cases, close parallels in character and function suggest a common heritage, yet lack of linguistic evidence makes it difficult to prove, as in the comparison between Uranus and the Sanskrit Varuna or the Moirai and the Norns. Archaeology and mythography, on the other hand, have revealed that the Greeks were inspired by some of the civilizations of Asia Minor and the Near East. Adonis seems to be the Greek counterpart—more clearly in cult than in myth—of a Near eastern "dying god". Cybele is rooted in Anatolian culture while much of Aphrodite's iconography springs from Semitic goddesses. There are also possible parallels between the earliest divine generations (Chaos and its children) and Tiamat in the *Enuma Elish*. According to Meyer Reinhold, "Near eastern theogonic concepts, involving divine succession through violence and generational conflicts for power, found their way ... into Greek mythology". In addition to Indo-European and Near eastern origins, some scholars have speculated on the debts of Greek mythology to the pre-Hellenic societies: Crete, Mycenae, Pylos, Thebes and Orchomenus. Historians of religion were fascinated by a number of apparently ancient configurations of myth connected with Crete (the god as bull, Zeus and Europa, Pasiphaë who yields to the bull and gives birth to the Minotaur, etc.) Professor Martin P. Nilsson concluded that all great classical Greek myths were tied to Mycenaen centers and were anchored in prehistoric times. Nevertheless, according to Burkert, the iconography of the Cretan Palace Period has provided almost no confirmation for these theories.

Motifs in Western Art and Literature

Botticelli's *The Birth of Venus* (c. 1485—1486, oil on canvas, Uffizi, Florence)—a revived Venus Pudica for a new view of pagan Antiquity—is often said to epitomize for modern viewers the spirit of the Renaissance. The widespread adoption of Christianity did not curb the popularity of the myths. With the rediscovery of classical antiquity in the Renaissance, the poetry of Ovid became a major influence on the imagination of poets, dramatists, musicians and artists. From the early years of Renaissance, artists such as Leonardo da Vinci, Michelangelo, and Raphael, portrayed the Pagan subjects of Greek mythology alongside more conventional Christian themes. Through the medium of Latin and the works of Ovid, Greek myth influenced Medieval and

Renaissance poets such as Petrarch, Boccaccio and Dante in Italy. In Northern Europe, Greek mythology never took the same hold of the visual arts, but its effect was very obvious on literature. The English imagination was fired by Greek mythology starting with Chaucer and John Milton and continuing through Shakespeare to Robert Bridges in the 20th century. Racine in France and Goethe in Germany revived Greek drama, reworking the ancient myths. Although during the Enlightenment of the 18th century reaction against Greek myth spread throughout Europe, the myths continued to provide an important source of raw material for dramatists, including those who wrote the libretti for many of Handel's and Mozart's operas. By the end of the 18th century, Romanticism initiated a surge of enthusiasm for all things Greek, including Greek mythology. In Britain, new translations of Greek tragedies and Homer inspired contemporary poets (such as Alfred Lord Tennyson, Keats, Byron and Shelley) and painters (such as Lord Leighton and Lawrence Alma-Tadema). Christoph Gluck, Richard Strauss, Jacques Offenbach and many others set Greek mythological themes to music. American authors of the 19th century, such as Thomas Bulfinch and Nathaniel Hawthorne, held that the study of the classical myths was essential to the understanding of English and American literature. In more recent times, classical themes have been reinterpreted by dramatists Jean Anouilh, Jean Cocteau, and Jean Giraudoux in France, Eugene O'Neill in America, and T. S. Eliot in Britain and by novelists such as James Joyce and André Gide.

Questions and Topics for Pondering and Further Discussion for Unit Four-3:

1. What is the relationship between Greek mythology and Roman mythology?
2. What human mentality does mythology reflect?
3. What is the relationship between philosophy and mythology?
4. Some people say that mythology represents human imagination about and aspiration for something that is beyond understanding or reach. Please make some further comment on this statement.
5. What are the motifs in western art and literature as reflected in Greek mythology?
6. Can you briefly illustrate origin of theories about Greek mythology?
7. What is Freud's idea about mythology at large?
8. Can you name some of the literary giants of the West, especially of Britain who are influenced by Greek mythology in their literary production and creation?

Unit Five

1. Colonialism, a Global Expansion Idea

Colonialism is the establishment, maintenance, acquisition and expansion of colonies in one territory by people from another territory. It is a process whereby the metropole claims sovereignty over the colony, and the social structure, government, and economics of the colony are changed by colonizers from the metropole. Colonialism is a set of unequal relationships between the metropole and the colony and between the colonists and the indigenous population. The European colonial period was the era from the 1500s to, arguably, the 1990s when several European powers (particularly [but not exclusively] Spain, Portugal, Britain, the Netherlands and France) established colonies in Asia, Africa, and the Americas. At first the countries followed mercantilist policies designed to strengthen the home economy at the expense of rivals, so the colonies were usually allowed to trade only with the mother country.

By the mid-19th century, however, the powerful British Empire gave up mercantilism and trade restrictions and introduced the principle of free trade, with few restrictions or tariffs. *Collins English Dictionary* defines colonialism as "the policy and practice of a power in extending control over weaker peoples or areas." The *Merriam-webster Dictionary* offers four definitions, including "something characteristic of a colony" and "control by one power over a dependent area or people".

The 2006 *Stanford Encyclopedia of Philosophy* uses the term "colonialism" to describe the process of European settlement and political control over the rest of the world, including Americas, Australia, and parts of Africa and Asia. It discusses the distinction between colonialism and imperialism and states that "given the difficulty of consistently distinguishing between the two terms, this entry will use colonialism as a broad concept that refers to the project of European political domination from the sixteenth to the twentieth centuries that ended with the national liberation movements of the 1960s." In his preface to Jürgen Osterhammel's *Colonialism: A Theoretical Overview*, Roger Tignor says, "For Osterhammel, the essence of colonialism is the existence of colonies, which are by definition governed differently from other territories such as protectorates or informal spheres of influence." In the book, Osterhammel asks, "How can 'colonialism' be defined independently from 'colony?'" He settles on a three-sentence definition:

> *Colonialism is a relationship between an indigenous (or forcibly imported) majority and a minority of foreign invaders. The fundamental decisions affecting the lives of the colonized people are made and implemented by the colonial rulers in pursuit of interests that are often defined in a distant metropolis. Rejecting cultural compromises with the colonized population, the colonizers are convinced of their own superiority and their ordained mandate to rule.*

Types of Colonialism

Historians often distinguish between two overlapping forms of colonialism:

1. Settler colonialism involves large-scale immigration, often motivated by religious, political, or economic reasons.
2. Exploitation colonialism involves fewer colonists and focuses on access to resources for

export, typically to the metropole. This category includes trading posts as well as larger colonies where colonists would constitute much of the political and economic administration, but would rely on indigenous resources for labour and material. Prior to the end of the slave trade and widespread abolition, when indigenous labor was unavailable, slaves were often imported to the Americas, first by the Spanish Empire, and later by the Dutch, French and British. Plantation colonies would be considered exploitation colonialism; but colonizing powers would utilize either type for different territories depending on various social and economic factors as well as climate and geographic conditions. Surrogate colonialism involves a settlement project supported by colonial power, in which most of the settlers do not come from the mainstream of the ruling power. Internal colonialism is a notion of uneven structural power between areas of a nation state. The source of exploitation comes from within the state.

Sociocultural Evolution

As colonialism often played out in pre-populated areas sociocultural evolution included the creation of various ethnically hybrid populations. Colonialism gave rise to culturally and ethnically mixed populations such as the mestizos of the Americas, as well as racially divided populations as found in French Algeria or Southern Rhodesia. In fact everywhere where colonial powers established a consistent and continued presence hybrid communities existed. Notable examples in Asia include the Anglo-Burmese people, Anglo-Indian, Burgher people, Eurasian Singaporean, Filipino mestizo, Kristang people and Macanese people. In the Dutch East Indies (now Indonesia) the vast majority of Dutch settlers were in fact Eurasians known as Indo-europeans, formally belonging to the European legal class in the colony.

History

Activity that could be called colonialism has a long history. The Egyptians, Phoenicians, Greeks and Romans all built colonies in antiquity. The word "metropole" comes from the Greek *metropolis* or "mother city". The word "colony" comes from the Latin *colonia* —"a place for agriculture". Between the 11th and 18th centuries, the Vietnamese established military colonies south of their original territory and absorbed the territory, in a process known as *nam tiên*. Modern colonialism started with the Age of Discovery. Portugal and Spain discovered new lands across the oceans and built trading posts or conquered large extensions of land. For some people, it is this building of colonies across oceans that differentiates colonialism from other types of expansionism. These new lands were divided between the Portuguese Empire and Spanish Empire, first by the papal bull Inter caetera and then by the Treaty of Tordesillas and the Treaty of Zaragoza (1529). This period is also associated with the Commercial Revolution. The late Middle Ages saw reforms in accountancy and banking in Italy and the eastern Mediterranean. These ideas were adopted and adapted in western Europe to the high risks and rewards associated with colonial ventures. The 17th century saw the creation of the French colonial empire and the Dutch Empire, as well as the English colonial empire, which later became the British Empire. It also saw the establishment of a Danish colonial empire and some Swedish overseas colonies.

The spread of colonial empires was reduced in the late 18th and early 19th centuries by the American Revolutionary War and the Latin American wars of independence. However, many new colonies were established after this time, including the German colonial empire and Belgian colonial empire. In the late 19th century, many European powers were involved in the scramble for Africa. The Russian Empire, Ottoman Empire and Austrian Empire existed at the same time as the above empires, but did not expand over oceans. Rather, these empires expanded through the more traditional route of conquest of neighboring territories. There was, though, some Russian colonization of the Americas across the Bering Strait. The Empire of Japan modeled itself on European colonial empires. The United States of America gained overseas territories after the Spanish-American War for which the term "American Empire" was coined. After the First World War, the victorious allies divided up the German colonial empire and much of the Ottoman Empire between themselves as League of Nations mandates. These territories were divided into three classes according to how quickly it was deemed that they would be ready for independence. However, decolonisation outside the Americas lagged until after the Second World War. In 1962 the United Nations set up a Special Committee on Decolonization, often called the Committee of 24, to encourage this process. Further, dozens of independence movements and global political solidarity projects such as the Non-aligned Movement were instrumental in the decolonization efforts of former colonies.

Neocolonialism

The term "neocolonialism" has been used to refer to a variety of contexts since decolonization that took place after World War II. Generally it does not refer to a type of direct colonization, rather, colonialism by other means. Specifically, neocolonialism refers to the theory that former or existing economic relationships, such as the General Agreement on Tariffs and Trade and the Central American Free Trade Agreement, created by former colonial powers were or are used to maintain control of their former colonies and dependencies after the colonial independence movements of the post-World War II period.

Colonialism and the History of Thought: Universalism

The conquest of vast territories brings multitudes of diverse cultures under the central control of the imperial authorities. From the time of Ancient Greece and Ancient Rome, this fact has been addressed by empires adopting the concept of universalism, and applying it to their imperial policies towards their subjects far from the imperial capitol. The capitol, the metropole, was the source of ostensibly enlightened policies imposed throughout the distant colonies. The empire that grew from Athenian conquest spurred the spread of Greek language, religion, science and philosophy throughout the colonies. The Athenians considered their own culture superior to all others. They referred to people speaking foreign languages as barbarians, dismissing foreign languages as inferior mutterings that sounded to Greek ears like "bar-bar". Romans found efficiency in imposing a universalist policy towards their colonies in many matters. Roman law was imposed on Roman citizens, as well as colonial subjects, throughout the empire. Latin spread as the common language of government and trade, the lingua franca, throughout the Empire. Romans also imposed peace between their diverse foreign subjects, which they described in beneficial terms as the Pax Romana. The use of universal regulation by the Romans marks the emergence of a European concept of universalism and internationalism. Tolerance of other cultures and beliefs has always been secondary to the aims of empires, however. The Roman Empire was tolerant of diverse cultures and religious practices, so long as these did not threaten Roman authority. Napoleon's foreign minister, Charles Maurice de Talleyrand, once remarked: "Empire is the art of putting men in their place".

Colonialism and Geography

Settlers acted as the link between the natives and the imperial hegemony, bridging the geographical, ideological and commercial gap between the colonizers and colonized. Advanced technology made possible the expansion of European states. With tools such as cartography, shipbuilding, navigation, mining and agricultural productivity colonizers had an upper hand. Their awareness of the Earth's surface and abundance of practical skills provided colonizers with a knowledge that, in turn, created power. Painter and Jeffrey argue that geography as a discipline was not and is not an objective science, rather it is based on assumptions about the physical world. Whereas it may have given "The West" an advantage when it came to exploration, it also created zones of racial inferiority. Geographical beliefs such as environmental determinism, the view that some parts of the world are underdeveloped, legitimized colonialism and created notions of skewed evolution. These are now seen as elementary concepts. Political geographers maintain that colonial behavior was reinforced by the physical mapping of the world, visually separating "them" and "us". Geographers are primarily focused on the spaces of colonialism and imperialism, more specifically, the material and symbolic appropriation of space enabling colonialism.

Colonialism and Imperialism

A colony is part of an empire and so colonialism is closely related to imperialism. Assumptions are that colonialism and imperialism are interchangeable, however Robert Young suggests that imperialism is the concept while colonialism is the practice. Colonialism is based on an imperial outlook, thereby creating a consequential relationship. Through an empire, colonialism is established and capitalism is expanded, on the other hand a capitalist economy naturally enforces an empire. In the next section Marxists make a case for this mutually reinforcing relationship.

Marxist View of Colonialism

Marxism views colonialism as a form of capitalism, enforcing exploitation and social change. Marx thought that working within the global capitalist system, colonialism is closely associated with uneven development. It is an "instrument of wholesale destruction, dependency and systematic exploitation producing distorted economies, socio-psychological disorientation, massive poverty and neocolonial dependency". According to some Marxist historians, in all of the colonial countries ruled by western European countries "the natives were robbed of more than half their natural span of life by undernourishment". Colonies are constructed into modes of production. The search for raw materials and the current search for new investment opportunities is a result of inter-capitalist rivalry for capital accumulation. Lenin regarded colonialism as the root cause of imperialism, as imperialism was distinguished by monopoly capitalism via colonialism and as Lyal S. Sunga explains: "Vladimir Lenin advocated forcefully the principle of self-determination of peoples in his 'Theses on the Socialist Revolution and the Right of Nations to Self-determination' as an integral plank in the programme of socialist internationalism" and he quotes Lenin who contended that "The right of nations to self-determination implies exclusively the right to independence in the political sense, the right to free political separation from the oppressor nation. Specifically, this demand for political democracy implies complete freedom to agitate for secession and for a referendum on secession by the seceding nation."

Liberalism, Capitalism and Colonialism

Classical liberals generally opposed colonialism (as opposed to colonization) and imperialism, including Adam Smith, Frédéric Bastiat, Richard Cobden, John Bright, Henry Richard, Herbert

Spencer, H. R. Fox Bourne, Edward Morel, Josephine Butler, W. J. Fox and William Ewart Gladstone. Moreover, American Revolution was the first anti-colonial rebellion, inspiring others. Adam Smith wrote in *Wealth of Nations* that Britain should liberate all of its colonies and also noted that it would be economically beneficial for British people in the average, although the merchants having mercantilist privileges would lose out.

Post-Colonialism

Post-colonialism (or post-colonial theory) can refer to a set of theories in philosophy and literature that grapple with the legacy of colonial rule. In this sense, post-colonial literature may be considered a branch of post-modern literature concerned with the political and cultural independence of peoples formerly subjugated in colonial empires. Many practitioners take Edward Saïd's book *Orientalism* (1978) as the theory's founding work (although French theorists such as Aimé Césaire and Frantz Fanon made similar claims decades before Saïd). Saïd analyzed the works of Balzac, Baudelaire and Lautréamont, exploring how they both absorbed and helped to shape a societal fantasy of European racial superiority. Writers of post-colonial fiction interact with the traditional colonial discourse, but modify or subvert it; for instance by retelling a familiar story from the perspective of an oppressed minor character in the story. Gayatri Chakravorty Spivak's *Can the Subaltern Speak?* (1998) gave its name to Subaltern Studies. In *A Critique of Postcolonial Reason* (1999), Spivak explored how major works of European metaphysics (such as those of Kant and Hegel) not only tend to exclude the subaltern from their discussions, but actively prevent non-Europeans from occupying positions as fully human subjects. Hegel's *Phenomenology of Spirit* (1807), famous for its explicit ethnocentrism, considers western civilization as the most accomplished of all, while Kant also allowed some traces of racialism to enter his work.

Impact of Colonialism and Colonization

The impacts of colonization are immense and pervasive. Various effects, both immediate and protracted, include the spread of virulent diseases, the establishment of unequal social relations, exploitation, enslavement, medical advances, the creation of new institutions, and technological progress. Colonial practices also spur the spread of languages, literature and cultural institutions. The native cultures of the colonized peoples can also have a powerful influence on the imperial country.

Expansion of Trade

Imperial expansion has been accompanied by economic expansion since ancient times. Greek trade networks spread throughout the Mediterranean region, while Roman trade expanded with the main goal of directing tribute from the colonized areas towards the Roman metropole. With the development of trade routes under the Ottoman Empire, Gujari Hindus, Syrian Muslims, Jews, Armenians, Christians from south and central Europe operated trading routes that supplied Persian and Arab horses to the armies of all three empires, Mocha coffee to Delhi and Belgrade, Persian silk to India and Istanbul. Aztec civilization developed into a large empire that, much like the Roman Empire, had the goal of exacting tribute from the conquered colonial areas. For the Aztecs, the most important tribute was the acquisition of sacrificial victims for their religious rituals.

Military Innovation

Imperial expansion follows military conquest in most instances. Imperial armies therefore have a long history of military innovation in order to gain an advantage over the armies of the people they aim to conquer. Greeks developed the phalanx system, which enabled their military units to present themselves to their enemies as a wall, with foot soldiers using shields to cover one another during their advance on the battlefield. Under Philip II of Macedon, they were able to organize thousands of soldiers into a formidable battle force, bringing together carefully trained infantry and cavalry regiments. Alexander the Great exploited this military foundation further during his conquests. The Spanish Empire held a major advantage over Mesoamerican warriors through the use of weapons made of stronger metal, predominantly iron, which was able to shatter the blades of axes used by the Aztec civilization and others. The European development of firearms using gunpowder cemented their military advantage over the peoples they sought to subjugate in the Americas and elsewhere.

The End of Empire

The populations of some colonial territories, such as Canada, enjoyed relative peace and prosperity as part of a European power, at least among the majority; however, minority populations such as First Nations peoples and French-Canadians experienced marginalization and resented colonial practices. Francophone residents of Quebec, for example, were vocal in opposing conscription into the armed services to fight on behalf of Britain during World War I, resulting in the Conscription crisis of 1917. Other European colonies had much more pronounced conflict between European settlers and the local population. Rebellions broke out in the later decades of the imperial era, such as India's Sepoy Rebellion. The territorial boundaries imposed by European colonizers, notably in central Africa and south Asia, defied the existing boundaries of native populations that had previously interacted little with one another. European colonizers disregarded native political and cultural animosities, imposing peace upon people under their military control. Native populations were relocated at the will of the colonial administrators. Once independence from European control was achieved, civil war erupted in some former colonies, as native populations fought to capture territory for their own ethnic, cultural or political group. The Partition of India, a 1947 civil war that came in the aftermath of India's independence from Britain, became a conflict with 500,000 killed. Fighting erupted between Hindu, Sikh and Muslim communities as they fought for territorial dominance. Muslims fought for an independent country to be partitioned where they would not be a religious minority, resulting in the creation of Pakistan.

Post-Independence Population Movement

In a reversal of the migration patterns experienced during the modern colonial era, post-independence era migration followed a route back towards the imperial country. In some cases, this was a movement of settlers of European origin returning to the land of their birth, or to an ancestral birthplace. 900,000 French colonists (known as the *Pied-Noirs*) resettled in France following Algeria's independence in 1962. A significant number of these migrants were also of Algerian descent. 800,000 people of Portuguese origin migrated to Portugal after the independence of former colonies in Africa between 1974 and 1979; 300,000 settlers of Dutch origin migrated to the Netherlands from the Dutch West Indies after Dutch military control of the colony ended. After WW II 300,000 Dutchmen from the Dutch East Indies, of which the majority were people of Eurasian descent called Indo-Europeans, repatriated to the Netherlands. A significant number later migrated to the US, Canada, Australia and New Zealand. Global travel and migration in general developed at an increasingly brisk pace throughout the era of European colonial expansion. Citizens of the former colonies of European countries may have a privileged status in some respects with regard to immigration rights when settling in the former European imperial nation. For example, rights to dual citizenship may be generous, or larger immigrant quotas may be extended to former colonies. In some cases, the former European imperial nations continue to foster close political and economic ties with former colonies. The Commonwealth of Nations is an organization that promotes cooperation between and among Britain and its former colonies, the Commonwealth members. A similar organization exists for former colonies of France, the Francophonie; the Community of Portuguese Language Countries plays a similar role for former Portuguese colonies, and the Dutch Language Union is the equivalent for former colonies of the Netherlands. Migration from former colonies has proven to be problematic for European countries, where the majority population may express hostility to ethnic minorities who have immigrated from former colonies. Cultural and religious conflict have often erupted in France in recent decades, between immigrants from the Maghreb countries of north Africa and the majority population of France. Nonetheless, immigration has changed the ethnic composition of France; by the 1980s, 25% of the total population of "inner Paris" and 14% of the metropolitan region were of foreign origin, mainly Algerian.

Questions and Topics for Pondering and Further Discussion for Unit Five-1:

1. Is colonialism an idea of human design or a true reflection of human nature?
2. Some people say that colonialism is the first human attempt for globalization. Please make some comment.
3. What are the real motivations behind the rise of colonialism?
4. Is colonialism an evil for human beings?
5. Is colonialism predecessor for free trade or trade liberalization?
6. Sea power plays an important role in pushing the spread or expansion of colonies. Tell your opinions about it.
7. What is the relationship between colonization and population?
8. Some historians list colonialism as one of the five great ideas that changed the world along with industrialism, communism, nationalism and globalism. Please make some further comments on it.

2. Capitalism, a Crazy Devil for Angels

Editor's remarks: *capitalism is not something that is only about capital as its term implies on surface. It is a comprehensive and inclusive concept upon which the West has been established. As an ideological concept, capitalism in a sense represents the West and its past, present and future. It is safe to say that capitalism has existed for its own logic and rationale or it would have otherwise disappeared. As a dominant social, political and economic system, a careful study of capitalism is necessary and useful if the whole human beings still keep striving for a better future. Since its birth, capitalism itself has undergone some sort of transformation in which some of its defects have been eliminated and it has adopted positive elements from other ideological systems, such as socialism. The worst form of capitalism is crony or nepotistic capitalism which denotes an alliance between political power and business interest that aims at material gains at the cost of public interest. If capitalism shall be abolished, it is crony capitalism that should be on the top of the list for abolition.*

Capitalism is an economic system that is based on private ownership of the means of production and the creation of goods or services for profit. Competitive markets, wage labor, capital accumulation, voluntary exchange, and personal finance are also considered capitalistic. There are multiple variants of capitalism, including laissez-faire, mixed economies, and state capitalism. Capitalism is considered to have applied in a variety of historical cases, varying in time, geography, politics, and culture. There is general agreement that capitalism became dominant in the western world following the demise of feudalism. Economists, political economists and historians have taken different perspectives on the analysis of capitalism. Economists usually emphasize the degree to which government does not have control over markets (laissez faire), as well as the importance of property rights. Most political economists emphasize private property as well, in addition to power relations, wage labor, class, and the uniqueness of capitalism as a historical formation. The extent to which different markets are free, as well as the rules defining private property, is a matter of politics and policy. Many states have what are termed mixed economies, referring to the varying degree of planned and market-driven elements in a state's economic system. A number of political ideologies have emerged in support of various types of capitalism, the most prominent being economic liberalism. Capitalism gradually spread throughout the western world in the 19th and 20th centuries.

Economic Elements

Capitalist economics developed out of the interactions of the following elements. A product is any good produced for exchange on a market. "Commodities" refers to standard products, especially raw materials such as grains and metals that are not associated with particular producers or brands and trade on organized exchanges.

There are two types of products:

- capital goods
- consumer goods

Capital goods (i.e. raw materials, tools, industrial machines, vehicles and factories) are used to produce consumer goods (e.g. televisions, cars, computers, houses) to be sold to others.

The three inputs required for production are:

- labor
- land (i.e. natural resources, which exist prior to human beings)
- capital goods
- entrepreneurship or management skills

Capitalism entails the private ownership of the latter two—natural resources and capital goods—by a class of owners called capitalists, either individually, collectively or through a state apparatus that operates for a profit or serves the interests of capital owners. Money was primarily a standardized medium of exchange, and final means of payment, that serves to measure the value of all goods and commodities in a standard of value. It eliminates the cumbersome system of barter by separating the transactions involved in the exchange of products, thus greatly facilitating specialization and trade through encouraging the exchange of commodities. Capitalism involves the further abstraction of money into other exchangeable assets and the accumulation of money through ownership, exchange, interest and various other financial instruments. Labor includes all physical and mental human resources, including entrepreneurial capacity and management skills, which are needed to produce products and services. Production is the act of making products or services by applying labor power to the means of production. Capitalism is the system of raising, conserving and spending a set monetary value in a specified market.

There are three main markets in a basic capitalistic economy: labor, goods and services, and financial. Labor markets (people) make products and get paid for work by the goods and services market (companies, firms, or corporations, etc.) which then sells the products back to the laborers. However, both of the first two markets pay into and receive benefits from the financial market, which handles and regulates the actual money in the economic system. This includes banks, credit-unions, stock exchanges, etc. From a monetary standpoint, governments control just how much money is in circulation worldwide, which plays an immense role on how money is spent in one's own country. Most of these institutes focus on a form of economics called macroeconomics which keeps its eyes on things such as inflation: the rate at which money loses its value over time; growth: how much money a government has and how quickly it accrues money; unemployment, and rates of trade between other countries. Whereas microeconomics deals with individual firms, people, and other institutions that work within a set framework of rules to balance prices and the workings of a singular government. Both micro-and macroeconomics work together to form a single set of evolving rules and regulations. Governments (the macroeconomic side) set both national and international regulations that keep track of prices and corporations' (microeconomics) growth rates, set prices, and trade, while the corporations influence what federal laws are set.

Types of Capitalism

There are many variants of capitalism in existence. All these forms of capitalism are based on production for profit, at least a moderate degree of market allocation, and capital accumulation. The dominant forms of capitalism are listed here.

Mercantilism

A nationalist form of early capitalism where national business interests are tied to state interests, and consequently, the state apparatus is utilized to advance national business interests abroad. An example of this is colonists living in America who were only allowed to trade with and purchase goods from their respective mother countries (Britain, France, etc.). Mercantilism holds that the wealth of a nation is increased through a positive balance of trade with other nations.

Free-market Capitalism

Free market capitalism consists of a free-price system where supply and demand are allowed to reach their point of equilibrium without intervention by the government. Productive enterprises are privately owned, and the role of the state is limited to protecting the rights to life, liberty, and property.

Social Market Economy

A social market economy is a nominally free-market system where government intervention in price formation is kept to a minimum but the state provides significant social security, unemployment benefits and recognition of labor rights through national collective bargaining laws. The social market is based on private ownership of businesses.

State Capitalism

State capitalism consists of state ownership of the means of production within a state. The debate between proponents of private versus state capitalism is centered around questions of managerial efficacy, productive efficiency, and fair distribution of wealth. According to Aldo Musacchio, a professor at Harvard Business School, it is a system in which governments, whether democratic or autocratic, exercise a widespread influence on the economy, through either direct ownership or various subsidies. Musacchio also emphasizes the difference between today's state capitalism and its predecessors. Gone are the days when governments appointed bureaucrats to run companies. The world's largest state-owned enterprises are traded on the public markets and kept in good health by large institutional investors.

Corporate Capitalism

Corporate capitalism is a free or mixed market characterized by the dominance of hierarchical, bureaucratic corporations, which are legally required to pursue profit. State monopoly capitalism was originally a Marxist concept referring to a form of corporate capitalism where the state is used to benefit, protect from competition and promote the interests of dominant or established corporations.

Mixed Economy

A largely market-based economy consisting of both public ownership and private ownership of the means of production. Most capitalist economies are defined as "mixed economies" to some degree although the balance between the public and private sectors may vary.

Etymology and Early Usage

The term "capitalist" as referring to an owner of capital (rather than its meaning of someone adherent to the economic system) shows earlier recorded use than the term "capitalism", dating back to the mid-seventeenth century. *Capitalist* is derived from *capital*, which evolved from *capitale*, a late Latin word based on proto-Indo-european *caput*, meaning "head"—also the origin of *chattel* and *cattle* in the sense of movable property (much later to refer only to livestock). Capitale emerged in the 12th to 13th centuries in the sense of referring to funds, stock of merchandise, sum of money, or money carrying interest. By 1283 it was used in the sense of the capital assets of a trading firm. It was frequently interchanged with a number of other words—wealth, money, funds, goods, assets, property and so on. The *Hollandische Mercurius* uses *capitalists* in 1633 and 1654 to refer to owners of capital.

In French, Étienne Clavier referred to *capitalistes* in 1788, six years before its first recorded English usage by Arthur Young in his work *Travels in France* (1792). David Ricardo, in his *Principles of Political Economy and Taxation* (1817), referred to "the capitalist" many times. Samuel Taylor Coleridge, an English poet, used *capitalist* in his work *Table Talk* (1823). Pierre-Joseph Proudhon used the term *capitalist* in his first work, *What is Property?* (1840) to refer to the owners of capital. Benjamin Disraeli used the term "capitalist" in his 1845 work *Sybil*. Karl Marx and Friedrich Engels used the term "capitalist" (*Kapitalist*) in *The Communist Manifesto* (1848) to refer to a private owner of capital. According to the *Oxford English*

Dictionary (OED), the term "capitalism" was first used by novelist William Makepeace Thackeray in 1854 in *The Newcomes*, where he meant "having ownership of capital". Also according to the OED, Carl Adolph Douai, a German-American socialist and abolitionist, used the term "private capitalism" in 1863. The initial usage of the term "capitalism" in its modern sense has been attributed to Louis Blanc in 1850 and Pierre-Joseph Proudhon in 1861. Marx and Engels referred to the *capitalistic system* (*kapitalistisches System*) and to the capitalist mode of production (*kapitalistische Produktionsform*) in *Das Kapital* (1867).

The use of the word "capitalism" in reference to an economic system appears twice in Volume I of *Das Kapital* (German edition, p. 124), and in *Theories of Surplus Value*, tome II (German edition, p. 493). Marx did not extensively use the form *capitalism*, but instead those of *capitalist* and *capitalist mode of production*, which appear more than 2,600 times in the trilogy *Das Kapital*. Marx's notion of the capitalist mode of production is characterized as a system of primarily private ownership of the means of production in a mainly market economy, with a legal framework on commerce and a physical infrastructure provided by the state. No legal framework was available to protect the laborers, so exploitation by the companies was rife. Engels made more frequent use of the term "capitalism"; volumes II and III of *Das Kapital*, both edited by Engels after Marx's death, contain the word "capitalism" four and three times, respectively. The three combined volumes of *Das Kapital* (1867, 1885, 1894) contain the word *capitalist* more than 2,600 times. An 1877 work entitled *Better Times* by Hugh Gabutt and an 1884 article in the *Pall Mall Gazette* also used the term "capitalism". A later use of the term "capitalism" to describe the production system was by the German economist Werner Sombart, in his 1902 book *The Jews and Modern Capitalism* (*Die Juden und das Wirtschaftsleben*). Sombart's close friend and colleague, Max Weber, also used *capitalism* in his 1904 book *The Protestant Ethic and the Spirit of Capitalism* (*Die protestantische Ethik und der Geist des Kapitalismus*).

History

Economic trade for profit has existed since the second millennium BC. However, capitalism in its modern form is usually traced to the Mercantilism of the 16th—18th Centuries.

Mercantilism

The period between the sixteenth and eighteenth centuries is commonly described as mercantilism. This period, the Age of Discovery, was associated with geographic exploration being exploited by merchant overseas traders, especially from England and the Low Countries; the European colonization of the Americas; and the rapid growth in overseas trade. Mercantilism was a system of trade for profit, although commodities were still largely produced by non-capitalist production methods. While some scholars see mercantilism as the earliest stage of capitalism, others argue that capitalism did not emerge until later. For example, Karl Polanyi, noted that "mercantilism, with all its tendency toward commercialization, never attacked the safeguards which protected [the] two basic elements of production—labor and land—from becoming the elements of commerce"; thus mercantilist attitudes towards economic regulation were closer to feudalist attitudes, "they disagreed only on the methods of regulation."

Moreover Polanyi argued that the hallmark of capitalism is the establishment of generalized markets for what he referred to as the "fictitious commodities": land, labor, and money. Accordingly, "not until 1834 was a competitive labor market established in England, hence industrial capitalism as a social system cannot be said to have existed before that date." Evidence of long-distance merchant-driven trade motivated by profit has been found as early as the second millennium BC, with the Old Assyrian merchants. The earliest forms of mercantilism date back to the Roman Empire. When the Roman Empire expanded, the mercantilist economy expanded throughout Europe. After the collapse of the Roman Empire, most of the European economy became controlled by local feudal powers, and mercantilism collapsed there. However, mercantilism persisted in Arabia. Due to its proximity to neighboring countries, the Arabs established trade routes to Egypt, Persia, and Byzantium. As Islam spread in the seventh century, mercantilism spread rapidly to Spain, Portugal, Northern Africa, and Asia. Mercantilism finally revived in Europe in the fourteenth century, as mercantilism spread from Spain and Portugal.

Among the major tenets of mercantilist theory was bullionism, a doctrine stressing the importance of accumulating precious metals. Mercantilists argued that a state should export more goods than it imported so that foreigners would have to pay the difference in precious metals. Mercantilists argued that only raw materials that could not be extracted at home should be imported; and promoted government subsidies, such as the granting of monopolies and protective tariffs, which mercantilists thought were necessary to encourage home production of manufactured goods. European merchants, backed by state controls, subsidies, and monopolies, made most of their profits from the buying and selling of goods. In the words of Francis Bacon, the purpose of mercantilism was "the opening and well-balancing of trade; the cherishing of manufacturers; the banishing of idleness; the repressing of waste and excess by sumptuary laws; the improvement and husbanding of the soil; the regulation of prices..." Similar practices of economic regimentation had begun earlier in the medieval towns. However, under mercantilism, given the contemporaneous rise of absolutism, the state superseded the local guilds as the regulator of the economy.

During that time the guilds essentially functioned like cartels that monopolized the quantity of craftsmen to earn above-market wages. At the period from the eighteenth century, the commercial stage of capitalism originated from the start of the British East India Company and the Dutch East India Company. These companies were characterized by their colonial and expansionary powers given to them by nation-states. During this era, merchants, who had traded under the previous stage of mercantilism, invested capital in the East India Companies and other colonies, seeking a return on investment. In his "History of Economic Analysis", Joseph Schumpeter reduced mercantilist propositions to three main concerns: exchange controls, export monopolism and balance of trade.

Industrialism

A new group of economic theorists, led by David Hume and Adam Smith, in the mid-18th century, challenged fundamental mercantilist doctrines as the belief that the amount of the world's wealth remained constant and that a state could only increase its wealth at the expense of another state. During the Industrial Revolution, the industrialist replaced the merchant as a dominant actor in the capitalist system and affected the decline of the traditional handicraft skills of artisans, guilds, and journeymen. Also during this period, the surplus generated by the rise of commercial agriculture encouraged increased mechanization of agriculture. Industrial capitalism marked the development of the factory system of manufacturing, characterized by a complex division of labor between and within work process and the routine of work tasks; and finally established the global domination of the capitalist mode of production. Britain also abandoned its protectionist policy, as embraced by mercantilism. In the 19th century, Richard Cobden and John Bright, who based their beliefs on the Manchester School, initiated a movement to lower tariffs.

In the 1840s, Britain adopted a less protectionist policy, with the repeal of the Corn Laws and the Navigation Acts. Britain reduced tariffs and quotas, in line with Smith and Ricardo's advocacy for free trade. Karl Polanyi argued that capitalism did not emerge until the progressive commodification of land, money, and labor culminating in the establishment of a generalized labor market in Britain in the 1830s. For Polanyi, "the extension of the market to the elements of industry—land, labor and money—was the inevitable consequence of the introduction of the factory system in a commercial society." Other sources argued that mercantilism fell after the repeal of the Navigation Acts in 1849.

Keynesianism and Neoliberalism

In the period following the global depression of the 1930s, the state played an increasingly prominent role in the capitalistic system throughout much of the world. After World War II, a broad array of new analytical tools in the social sciences were developed to explain the social and economic trends of the period, including the concepts of post-industrial society and the welfare state. This era was greatly influenced by Keynesian economic stabilization policies. The postwar boom ended in the late 1960s and early 1970s, and the situation was worsened by the rise of stagflation. Exceptionally high inflation combined with slow output growth, rising unemployment, and eventually recession to cause a loss of credibility in the Keynesian welfare-statist mode of regulation. Under the influence of Friedrich Hayek and Milton Friedman, western states embraced policy prescriptions inspired by laissez-faire capitalism and classical liberalism. In particular, monetarism, a theoretical alternative to Keynesianism that is more compatible with laissez-faire, gained increasing prominence in the capitalist world, especially under the leadership of Ronald Reagan in the US and Margaret Thatcher in the UK in the 1980s. Public and political interest began shifting away from the so-called collectivist concerns of Keynes's managed capitalism to a focus on individual choice, called "remarketised capitalism". In the eyes of many economic and political commentators, the collapse of the Soviet Union brought further evidence of the superiority of market capitalism over planned economy.

Globalization

Although international trade has been associated with the development of capitalism for over five hundred years, some thinkers argue that a number of trends associated with globalization have acted to increase the mobility of people and capital since the last quarter of the 20th century, combining to circumscribe the room to maneuver of states in choosing non-capitalist models of development. Today, these trends have bolstered the argument that capitalism should now be viewed as a truly world system. However, other thinkers argue that globalization, even in its quantitative degree, is no greater now than during earlier periods of capitalist trade.

Perspectives/Classical Political Economy

The classical school of economic thought emerged in Britain in the late 18th century. The classical political economists Adam Smith, David Ricardo, Jean-baptiste Say, and John Stuart Mill published analyses of the production, distribution and exchange of goods in a market that have since formed the basis of study for most contemporary economists. In France, "physiocrats" like François Quesnay promoted free trade based on a conception that wealth originated from land. Quesnay's **Tableau Économique**, described the economy analytically and laid the foundation of the Physiocrats' economic theory, followed by Anne Robert Jacques Turgot who opposed tariffs and customs duties and advocated free trade. Richard Cantillon defined long-run equilibrium as the balance of flows of income, and argued that the supply and demand mechanism around land influenced short-term prices. Smith's attack on mercantilism and his reasoning for "the system of natural liberty" in *The Wealth of Nations* (1776) are usually taken as the beginning of classical political economy. Smith devised a set of concepts that remain strongly associated with capitalism today. His theories regarding the "invisible hand" are commonly misinterpreted to mean individual pursuit of self-interest unintentionally producing collective good for society. It was necessary for Smith to be so forceful in his argument in favor of free markets because he had to overcome the popular mercantilist sentiment of the time period. He criticized monopolies, tariffs, duties, and other state enforced restrictions of his time and believed that the market is the most fair and efficient arbitrator of resources. This view was shared by David Ricardo, second most important of the classical political economists and one of the most influential economists of modern times. In *The Principles of Political Economy and Taxation* (1817), he developed the law of comparative advantage, which explains why it is profitable for two parties to trade, even if one of the trading partners is more efficient in every type of economic production.

This principle supports the economic case for free trade. Ricardo was a supporter of Say's Law and held the view that full employment is the normal equilibrium for a competitive economy. He also argued that inflation is closely related to changes in quantity of money and credit and was a proponent of the law of diminishing returns, which states that each additional unit of input yields less and less additional output. The values of classical political economy are strongly associated with the classical liberal doctrine of minimal government intervention in the economy, though it does not necessarily oppose the state's provision of a few basic public goods. Classical liberal thought has generally assumed a clear division between the economy and other realms of social activity, such as the state. While economic liberalism favors markets unfettered by the government, it maintains that the state has a legitimate role in providing public goods. For instance, Adam Smith argued that the state has a role in providing roads, canals, schools and bridges that cannot be efficiently implemented by private entities. However, he preferred that these goods should be paid proportionally to their consumption (e. g. putting a toll). In addition, he advocated retaliatory tariffs to bring about free trade, and copyrights and patents to encourage innovation.

Marxist Political Economy

Karl Marx considered capitalism to be a historically specific mode of production (the way in which the productive property is owned and controlled, combined with the corresponding social relations between individuals based on their connection with the process of production) in which capitalism has become the dominant mode of production. The capitalist stage of development or "bourgeois society", for Marx, represented the most advanced form of social organization to date, but he also thought that the working classes would come to power in a worldwide socialist or communist transformation of human society as the end of the series of first aristocratic, then capitalist, and finally working class rule was reached. Following Adam Smith, Marx distinguished the use value of commodities from their exchange value in the market. Capital, according to Marx, is created with the purchase of commodities for the purpose of creating new commodities with an exchange value higher than the sum of the original purchases. For Marx, the use of labor power had itself become a commodity under capitalism; the exchange value of labor power, as reflected in the wage, is less than the value it produces for the capitalist. This difference in values, he argues, constitutes surplus value, which the capitalists extract and accumulate. In his book *Capital*, Marx argues that the capitalist mode of production is distinguished by how the owners of capital extract this surplus from workers—all prior class societies had extracted surplus labor, but capitalism was new in doing so via the sale-value of produced commodities. He argues that a core requirement of a capitalist society is that a large portion of the population must not possess sources of self-sustenance that would allow them to be independent, and must instead be compelled, to survive, to sell their labor for a living wage.

In conjunction with his criticism of capitalism was Marx's belief that exploited labor would be the driving force behind a revolution to a socialist-style economy. For Marx, this cycle of the extraction of the surplus value by the owners of capital or the bourgeoisie becomes the basis of class struggle. This argument is intertwined with Marx's version of the labor theory of value arguing that labor is the source of all value, and thus of profit. Vladimir Lenin, in ***Imperialism, the Highest Stage of Capitalism***, modified classic Marxist theory and argued that capitalism necessarily induced monopoly capitalism—which he also called "imperialism"—to find new markets and resources, representing the last and highest stage of capitalism. Some 20th-century Marxian economists consider capitalism to be a social formation where capitalist class processes dominate, but are not exclusive. Capitalist class processes, to these thinkers, are simply those in which surplus labor takes the form of surplus value, usable as capital; other tendencies for utilization of labor nonetheless exist simultaneously in existing societies where capitalist processes are predominant.

However, other late Marxian thinkers argue that a social formation as a whole may be classed as capitalist if capitalism is the mode by which a surplus is extracted, even if this surplus is not produced by capitalist activity, as when an absolute majority of the population is engaged in non-capitalist economic activity. In *Limits to Capital* (1982), David Harvey outlines an overdetermined, "spatially restless" capitalism coupled with the spatiality of crisis formation and resolution. Harvey used Marx's theory of crisis to aid his argument that capitalism must have its "fixes" but that we cannot predetermine what fixes will be implemented, nor in what form they will be. His work on contractions of capital accumulation and international movements of capitalist modes of production and money flows has been influential. According to Harvey, capitalism creates the conditions for volatile and geographically uneven development.

Weberian Political Sociology

In social science, the understanding of the defining characteristics of capitalism has been strongly influenced by German sociologist Max Weber. Weber considered market exchange, a voluntary supply of labor and a planned division of labor within the enterprises as defining features of capitalism. Capitalist enterprises, in contrast to their counterparts in prior modes of economic activity, were directed toward the rationalization of production, maximizing efficiency and productivity—a tendency embedded in a sociological process of enveloping rationalization that formed modern legal bureaucracies in both public and private spheres. According to Weber, workers in pre-capitalist economies understood work in terms of a personal relationship between master and journeyman in a guild, or between lord and peasant in a manor. For these developments of capitalism to emerge, Weber argued, it was necessary the development of a "capitalist spirit"; that is, ideas and habits that favor a rational pursuit of economic gain. These ideas, in order to propagate a certain manner of life and come to dominate others, "had to originate somewhere... as a way of life common to whole groups of men".

In his book *The Protestant Ethic and the Spirit of Capitalism* (1904—1905), Weber sought to trace how a particular form of religious spirit, infused into traditional modes of economic activity, was a condition of possibility of modern western capitalism. For Weber, the "spirit of capitalism" was, in general, that of ascetic protestantism; this ideology was able to motivate extreme rationalization of daily life, a propensity to accumulate capital by a religious ethic to advance economically through hard and diligent work, and thus also the propensity to reinvest capital. This was sufficient, then, to create "self-mediating capital" as conceived by Marx. This is pictured in the Protestant understanding of *beruf* —whose meaning encompasses at the same time profession, vocation and calling—as exemplified in Proverbs 22:29, "Seest thou a man diligent in his calling? He shall stand before kings". In the *Protestant Ethic*, Weber describes the developments of this idea of calling from its religious roots, through the understanding of someone's economic success as a sign of his salvation, until the conception that moneymaking is, within the modern economic order, the result and the expression of diligence in one's calling. Finally, as the social mores critical for its development became no longer necessary for its maintenance, modern western capitalism came to represent the order "now bound to the technical and economic conditions of machine production which today determine the lives of all the individuals who are born into this mechanism, not only those directly concerned with economic acquisition, with irresistible force. Perhaps it will so determine them until the last ton of fossilized coal is burnt". This is further seen in his criticism of "specialists without spirit, hedonists without a heart" that were developing, in his opinion, with the fading of the original Puritan "spirit" associated with capitalism.

Institutional Economics

Institutional economics, once the main school of economic thought in the United States, holds that capitalism cannot be separated from the political and social system within which it is embedded. It emphasizes the legal foundations of capitalism (seeJohn R. Commons) and the evolutionary, habituated, and volitional processes by which institutions are erected and then changed (see John Dewey, Thorstein Veblen, and Daniel Bromley.) One key figure in institutional economics was Thorstein Veblen who in his book **The Theory of the Leisure Class** (1899) analyzed the motivations of wealthy people in capitalism who conspicuously consumed their riches as a way of demonstrating success. The concept of conspicuous consumption was in direct contradiction to the neoclassical view that capitalism was efficient. In *The Theory of Business Enterprise* (1904) Veblen distinguished the motivations of industrial production for people to use things from business motivations that used, or misused, industrial infrastructure for profit, arguing that the former is often hindered because businesses pursue the latter. Output and technological advance are restricted by business practices and the creation of monopolies. Businesses protect their existing capital investments and employ excessive credit, leading to depressions and increasing military expenditure and war through business control of political power.

German Historical School and Austrian School

From the perspective of the German Historical School, capitalism is primarily identified in terms of the organization of production for markets. Although this perspective shares similar theoretical roots with that of Weber, its emphasis on markets and money lends it different focus. For followers of the German Historical School, the key shift from traditional modes of economic activity to capitalism involved the shift from medieval restrictions on credit and money to the modern monetary economy combined with an emphasis on the profit motive. In the late 19th century, the German Historical School of economics diverged, with the emerging Austrian School of economics, led at the time by Carl Menger.

Later generations of followers of the Austrian School continued to be influential in western economic thought in the early part of the 20th century. Austrian-born economist Joseph Schumpeter, sometimes associated with the School, emphasized the "creative destruction" of capitalism—the fact that market economies undergo constant change. Schumpeter argued that at any moment in time there are rising industries and declining industries. Schumpeter, and many contemporary economists influenced by his work, argues that resources should flow from the declining to the expanding industries for an economy to grow, but they recognized that sometimes resources are slow to withdraw from the declining industries because of various forms of institutional resistance to change. The Austrian economists Ludwig von Mises and Friedrich Hayek were among the leading defenders of market economy against 20th century proponents of socialist planned economies. Mises and Hayek argued that only market capitalism could manage a complex, modern economy. Since a modern economy produces such a large array of distinct goods and services, and consists of such a large array of consumers and enterprises, argued Mises and Hayek, the information problems facing any other form of economic organization other than market capitalism would exceed its capacity to handle information. Thinkers within Supply-side economics built on the work of the Austrian School, and particularly emphasize Say's Law: "Supply creates its own demand." Capitalism, to this school, is defined by lack of state restraint on the decisions of producers. Austrian economists such as Murray Rothbard argued that Marx failed to make the distinction between *capitalism* and *mercantilism*. They argue that Marx conflated the imperialistic, colonialistic, protectionist and interventionist doctrines of mercantilism with capitalism. Austrian economics has been a major influence on some forms of libertarianism, in which laissez-faire capitalism is considered to be the ideal economic system.

Keynesian Economics (Keynesian Revolution in Economics)

In his *The General Theory of Employment, Interest, and Money* (1937), the British economist John Maynard Keynes argued that capitalism suffered a basic problem in its ability to recover from periods of slowdowns in investment. Keynes argued that a capitalist economy could remain in an indefinite equilibrium despite high unemployment. Essentially rejecting Say's law, he argued that some people may have a liquidity preference that would see them rather hold money than buy new goods or services, which therefore raised the prospect that the Great Depression would not end without what he termed in the *General Theory* "a somewhat comprehensive socialization of investment". Keynesian economics challenged the notion that laissez-faire capitalist economics could operate well on their own, without state intervention used to promote aggregate demand, fighting high unemployment and deflation of the sort seen during the 1930s. He and his followers recommended "pump-priming" the economy to avoid recession: cutting taxes, increasing government borrowing, and spending during an economic down-turn.

This was to be accompanied by trying to control wages nationally partly through the use of inflation to cut real wages and to deter people from holding money. John Maynard Keynes tried to provide solutions to many of Marx's problems without completely abandoning the classical understanding of capitalism. His work attempted to show that regulation can be effective, and that economic stabilizers can rein in the aggressive expansions and recessions that Marx disliked. These changes sought to create more stability in the business cycle, and reduce the abuses of laborers. Keynesian economists argue that Keynesian policies were one of the primary reasons capitalism was able to recover following the Great Depression. The premises of Keynes's work have, however, since been challenged by neoclassical and supply-side economics and the Austrian

School. Another challenge to Keynesian thinking came from his colleague Piero Sraffa, and subsequently from the Neo-Ricardian school that followed Sraffa. In Sraffa's highly technical analysis, capitalism is defined by an entire system of social relations among both producers and consumers, but with a primary emphasis on the demands of production. According to Sraffa, the tendency of capital to seek its highest rate of profit causes a dynamic instability in social and economic relations.

Neoclassical Economics and the Chicago School

Today, the majority of academic research on capitalism in the English-speaking world draws on neoclassical economic thought. It favors extensive market coordination and relatively neutral patterns of governmental market regulation aimed at maintaining property rights; deregulated labor markets; corporate governance dominated by financial owners of firms; and financial systems depending chiefly on capital market-based financing rather than state financing. Milton Friedman took many of the basic principles set forth by Adam Smith and the classical economists and gave them a new twist. One example of this is his article in the September 1970 issue of *The New York Times* Magazine, where he argues that the social responsibility of business is "to use its resources and engage in activities designed to increase its profits... (through) open and free competition without deception or fraud." This is similar to Smith's argument that self-interest in turn benefits the whole of society. Work like this helped lay the foundations for the coming marketization (or privatization) of state enterprises and the supply-side economics of Ronald Reagan and Margaret Thatcher. The Chicago School of economics is best known for its free market advocacy and monetarist ideas. According to Friedman and other monetarists, market economies are inherently stable if left to themselves and depressions result only from government intervention. Friedman, for example, argued that the Great Depression was result of a contraction of the money supply, controlled by the Federal Reserve, and not by the lack of investment as Keynes had argued. Bernanke, current Chairman of the Fed, is among the economists today generally accepting Friedman's analysis of the causes of the Great Depression. Neoclassical economists, today the majority of economists, consider value to be subjective, varying from person to person and for the same person at different times, and thus reject the labor theory of value. Marginalism is the theory that economic value results from marginal utility and marginal cost (the marginal concepts). These economists see capitalists as earning profits by forgoing current consumption, by taking risks, and by organizing production.

Neoclassical Economic Theory

Neoclassical economics explain capitalism as made up of individuals, enterprises, markets and government. According to their theories, individuals engage in a capitalist economy as consumers, laborers, and investors. As laborers, individuals may decide which jobs to prepare for, and in which markets to look for work. As investors they decide how much of their income to save and how to invest their savings. These savings, which become investments, provide much of the money that businesses need to grow. Business firms decide what to produce and where this production should occur. They also purchase inputs (materials, labor, and capital). Businesses try to influence consumer purchase decisions through marketing and advertisement, as well as the creation of new and improved products. Driving the capitalist economy is the search for profits (revenues minus expenses). This is known as the profit motive, and it helps ensure that companies produce the goods and services that consumers desire and are able to buy. To be profitable, firms must sell a quantity of their product at a certain price to yield a profit. A business may lose money if sales fall too low or if its costs become too high. The profit motive encourages firms to operate more efficiently. By using less materials, labor or capital, a firm can cut its production costs, which can lead to increased profits. An economy grows when the total value of goods and services produced rises. This growth requires investment in infrastructure, capital and other resources necessary in production. In a capitalist system, businesses decide when and how much they want to invest. Income in a capitalist economy depends primarily on what skills are in demand and what skills are being supplied. Skills that are in scarce supply are worth more in the market and can attract higher incomes. Competition among workers for jobs—and among employers for skilled workers—help determine wage rates. Firms need to pay high enough wages to attract the appropriate workers; when jobs are scarce, workers may accept lower wages than they would when jobs are plentiful. Trade union and governments influence wages in capitalist systems. Unions act to represent their members in negotiations with employers over such things as wage rates and acceptable working conditions.

The Market

The price (P) of a product is determined by a balance between production at each price (supply, S) and the desires of those with purchasing power at each price (demand, D). This results in a market equilibrium, with a given quantity (Q) sold of the product. A rise in demand would result in an increase in price and an increase in output. Supply is the amount of a good or service produced by a firm and which is available for sale. Demand is the amount that people are willing to buy at a specific price. Prices tend to rise when demand exceeds supply, and fall when supply exceeds demand. In theory, the market is able to coordinate itself when a new equilibrium price and quantity is reached. Competition arises when more than one producer is trying to sell the same or similar products to the same buyers. In capitalist theory, competition leads to innovation and more affordable prices. Without competition, a monopoly or cartel may develop. A monopoly occurs when a firm supplies the total output in the market; the firm can therefore limit output and raise prices because it has no fear of competition. A cartel is a group of firms that act together in a monopolistic manner to control output and raise prices.

Role of Government

In a capitalist system, the government does not prohibit private property or prevent individuals from working where they please. The government does not prevent firms from determining what wages they will pay and what prices they will charge for their products. Many countries, however, have minimum wage laws and minimum safety standards. Under some versions of capitalism, the government carries out a number of economic functions, such as issuing money, supervising public utilities and enforcing private contracts. Many countries have competition laws that prohibit monopolies and cartels from forming. Despite anti-trust laws, large corporations can form near-monopolies in some industries. Such firms can temporarily drop prices and accept losses to prevent competition from entering the market, and then raise them again once the threat of entry is reduced. In many countries, public utilities (e.g. electricity, heating fuel, communications) are able to operate as a monopoly under government regulation, due to high economies of scale. Government agencies regulate the standards of service in many industries, such as airlines and broadcasting, as well as financing a wide range of programs. In addition, the government regulates the flow of capital and uses financial tools such as the interest rate to control factors such as inflation and unemployment.

Democracy, the State, and Legal Frameworks: Private Property

The relationship between the state, its formal mechanisms, and capitalist societies has been debated in many fields of social and political theory, with active discussion since the 19th century. Hernando de Soto is a contemporary economist who has argued that an important characteristic of capitalism is the functioning state protection of property rights in a formal property system where ownership and transactions are clearly recorded. According to de Soto, this is the process by which physical assets are transformed into capital, which in turn may be used in many more ways and much more efficiently in the market economy. A number of Marxian economists have argued that the Enclosure Acts in England, and similar legislation elsewhere, were an integral part of capitalist primitive accumulation and that specific legal frameworks of private land ownership have been integral to the development of capitalism.

Institutions

New institutional economics, a field pioneered by Douglass North, stresses the need of a legal framework in order for capitalism to function optimally, and focuses on the relationship between the historical development of capitalism and the creation and maintenance of political and economic institutions. In new institutional economics and other fields focusing on public policy, economists seek to judge when and whether governmental intervention (such as taxes, welfare, and government regulation) can result in potential gains in efficiency. According to Gregory Mankiw, a New Keynesian economist, governmental intervention can improve on market outcomes under conditions of "market failure", or situations in which the market on its own does not allocate resources efficiently. Market failure occurs when an externality is present and a market will either under-produce a product with a positive externalization or overproduce a product that generates a negative externalization. Air pollution, for instance, is a negative externalization that cannot be incorporated into markets as the world's air is not owned and then sold for use to polluters. So, too much pollution could be emitted and people not involved in the production pay the cost of the pollution instead of the firm that initially emitted the air pollution. Critics of market failure theory, like Ronald Coase, Harold Demsetz, and James M. Buchanan argue that government programs and policies also fall short of absolute perfection. Market failures are often small, and government failures are sometimes large. It is therefore the case that imperfect markets are often better than imperfect governmental alternatives. While all nations currently have some kind of market regulations, the desirable degree of regulation is disputed.

Democracy

The relationship between democracy and capitalism is a contentious area in theory and popular political movements. The extension of universal adult male suffrage in 19th century Britain occurred along with the development of industrial capitalism, and democracy became widespread at the same time as capitalism, leading many theorists to posit a causal relationship between them, or that each affects the other. However, in the 20th century, according to some authors, capitalism also accompanied a variety of political formations quite distinct from liberal democracies, including fascist regimes, absolute monarchies, and single-party states. While some thinkers argue that capitalist development more-or-less inevitably eventually leads to the emergence of democracy, others dispute this claim. Research on the democratic peace theory indicates that capitalist democracies rarely make war with one another and have little internal violence. However, critics of the democratic peace theory note that democratic capitalist states may fight infrequently and or never with other democratic capitalist states because of political similarity or stability rather than because they are democratic or capitalist.

Some commentators argue that though economic growth under capitalism has led to democratization in the past, it may not do so in the future, as authoritarian regimes have been able to manage economic growth without making concessions to greater political freedom. States that have highly capitalistic economic systems have thrived under authoritarian or oppressive political systems. Singapore, which maintains a highly open market economy and attracts lots of foreign investment, does not protect civil liberties such as freedom of speech and expression. The private (capitalist) sector in the People's Republic of China has grown exponentially and thrived since its inception, despite having an authoritarian government. Augusto Pinochet's rule in Chile led to economic growth by using authoritarian means to create a safe environment for investment and capitalism. In response to criticism of the system, some proponents of capitalism have argued that its advantages are supported by empirical research. Indices of Economic Freedom show a correlation between nations with more economic freedom (as defined by the indices) and higher scores on variables such as income and life expectancy, including the poor, in these nations.

Advocacy for Capitalism/Economic Growth

World's GDP per capita shows exponential growth since the beginning of the Industrial Revolution. Many theorists and policymakers in predominantly capitalist nations have emphasized capitalism's ability to promote economic growth, as measured by Gross Domestic Product (GDP), capacity utilization or standard of living. This argument was central, for example, to Adam Smith's advocacy of letting a free market control production and price, and allocate resources. Many theorists have noted that this increase in global GDP over time coincides with the emergence of the modern world capitalist system. In years 1000—1820 world economy grew six-fold, 50% per person. After capitalism had started to spread more widely, in years 1820—1998 world economy grew 50-fold, i.e. 9-fold per person. In most capitalist economic regions such as Europe, the United States, Canada, Australia and New Zealand, the economy grew 19-fold per person even though these countries already had a higher starting level, and in Japan, which was poor in 1820, to 31-fold, whereas in the rest of the world the growth was only 5-fold per person. Proponents argue that increasing GDP (per capita) is empirically shown to bring about improved standards of living, such as better availability of food, housing, clothing, and health care. The decrease in the number of hours worked per week and the decreased participation of children and the elderly in the workforce have been attributed to capitalism. Proponents also believe that a capitalist economy offers far more opportunities for individuals to raise their income through new professions or business ventures than do other economic forms. To their thinking, this potential is much greater than in either traditional feudal or tribal societies or in socialist societies.

Political Freedom: Precondition of Economic Freedom

Milton Friedman stated that the economic freedom of capitalism is a requisite of political freedom which has been continuously echoed by others such as Andrew Brennan and Ronald Reagan. Friedman stated that centralized operations of economic activity is always accompanied by political repression. In his view, transactions in a market economy are voluntary, and the wide diversity that voluntary activity permits is a fundamental threat to repressive political leaders and greatly diminish power to coerce. Friedman's view was also shared by Friedrich Hayek and John Maynard Keynes, both of whom believed that capitalism is vital for freedom to survive and thrive.

Self-Organization

Austrian School economists have argued that capitalism can organize itself into a complex system without an external guidance or central planning mechanism. Friedrich Hayek considered the phenomenon of self-organization as underpinning capitalism. Prices serve as a signal as to the urgent and unfilled wants of people, and the promise of profits gives entrepreneurs incentive to use their knowledge and resources to satisfy those wants. Thus the activities of millions of people, each seeking his own interest, are coordinated. Critics of capitalism associate it with: social inequality and unfair distribution of wealth and power; a tendency toward market monopoly or oligopoly (and government by oligarchy); imperialism, counter-revolutionary wars and various forms of economic and cultural exploitation; repression of workers and trade unionists; social alienation; economic inequality; unemployment; and economic instability. Individual property rights have also been associated with the tragedy of the anticommons.

Criticisms

The following illustration shows the social structure of capitalist economic system. It is like a pyramid, on top of which is capitalists and at the bottom of which lies working class. In the middle are a few social classes including armed forces and government bureaucratic officials who help to manage the whole system. Notable critics of capitalism have included: socialists, anarchists, communists, national socialists, social democrats, technocrats, some types of conservatives, Luddites, Narodniks, Shakers and some types of nationalists. Marxists have advocated a revolutionary overthrow of capitalism that would lead to socialism, before eventually transforming into communism. Many socialists consider capitalism to be irrational, in that production and the direction of the economy are unplanned, creating many inconsistencies and internal contradictions. Labor historians and scholars such as Immanuel Wallerstein have argued that unfree labor—by slaves, indentured servants, prisoners, and other coerced persons—is compatible with capitalist relations. Many aspects of capitalism have come under attack from the anti-globalization movement, which is primarily opposed to corporate capitalism. Environmentalists have argued that capitalism requires continual economic growth, and that it will inevitably deplete the finite natural resources of the Earth. Many religions have criticized or opposed specific elements of capitalism. Traditional Judaism, Christianity, and Islam forbid lending money at interest, although alternative methods of banking have been developed. Some Christians have criticized capitalism for its materialist aspects and its inability to account for the wellbeing of all people. Many of Jesus's parables deal with clearly economic concerns: farming, shepherding, being in debt, doing hard labor, being excluded from banquets and the houses of the rich, and have implications for wealth and power distribution.

Unpredictability of Market, Human Behavior and Psychology

Economists such as John Stuart Mill point out that the behavior of men and women in the marketplace is not "calculable". Stores go out of business for varied, often-overlapping reasons, which include: inadequate parking, shifting demand, excessive overhead, marketing problems, and competition. In addition, political and social elements affect economic result a lot, so much so that an economic issue is never a pure economic issue in reality.

Questions and Topics for Pondering and Further Discussion for Unit Five-2:

1. What is the basic logic behind capitalism?
2. What are the chief tenets of capitalism?
3. Why is the fact that capitalism rose and flourished in the West first?
4. Is capitalism simply an economic institution? Why or why not?
5. Is capitalism an end of ideology?
6. How many forms are there in capitalism? What are their respective features?
7. Why is capitalism more efficient than other economic system?
8. What secrets of capitalism did Karl Marx discover?

Unit Six

1. Renaissance: a Turning Point for the West

The Renaissance (French: *Renaissance*; Original Italian: *Rinascimento*, from *rinascere* "to be reborn") was a cultural movement that spanned the period roughly from the 14th to the 17th century, beginning in Italy in the Late Middle Ages and later spreading to the rest of Europe. Though the invention of printing sped the dissemination of ideas from the later 15th century, the changes of the Renaissance were not uniformly experienced across Europe. As a cultural movement, it encompassed innovative flowering of Latin and vernacular literatures, beginning with the 14th-century resurgence of learning based on classical sources, which contemporaries credited to Petrarch, the development of linear perspective and other techniques of rendering a more natural reality in painting, and gradual but widespread educational reform. In politics the Renaissance contributed the development of the conventions of diplomacy, and in science an increased reliance on observation. Historians often argue this intellectual transformation was a bridge between the Middle Ages and the Modern era. Although the Renaissance saw revolutions in many intellectual pursuits, as well as social and political upheaval, it is perhaps best known for its artistic developments and the contributions of such polymaths as Leonardo da Vinci and Michelangelo, who inspired the term "Renaissance man". There is a consensus that the Renaissance began in Florence, Italy, in the 14th century. Various theories have been proposed to account for its origins and characteristics, focusing on a variety of factors including the social and civic peculiarities of Florence at the time; its political structure; the patronage of its dominant family, the Medici; and the migration of Greek scholars and texts to Italy following the Fall of Constantinople at the hands of the Ottoman Turks. The Renaissance has a long and complex historiography, and in line with general skepticism of discrete periodizations, there has been much debate among historians reacting to the 19th-century glorification of the "Renaissance" and individual culture heroes as "Renaissance men", questioning the usefulness of Renaissance as a term and as a historical delineation. The art historian Erwin Panofsky observed of this resistance to the concept of Renaissance. It is perhaps no accident that the factuality of the Italian Renaissance has been most vigorously questioned by those who are not obliged to take a professional interest in the aesthetic aspects of civilization—historians of economic and social developments, political and religious situations, and, most particularly, natural science—but only exceptionally by students of literature and hardly ever by historians of Art. Some have called into question whether the Renaissance was a cultural "advance" from the Middle Ages, instead seeing it as a period of pessimism and nostalgia for the classical age, while social and economic historians of the *longue durée* especially have instead focused on the continuity between the two eras, linked, as Panofsky himself observed, "by a thousand ties". The word Renaissance has also been extended to other historical and cultural movements, such as the Carolingian Renaissance and the Renaissance of the 12th century.

Overview of Renaissance: Its Spirit and Logo

The Renaissance was a cultural movement that profoundly affected European intellectual life in the early modern period. Beginning in Italy, and spreading to the rest of Europe by the 16th century, its influence was felt in literature, philosophy, art, music, politics, science, religion, and other aspects of intellectual inquiry. Renaissance scholars employed the humanist method in study, and searched for realism and human emotion in art. Renaissance humanists such as Poggio Bracciolini sought out in Europe's monastic libraries the Latin literary, historical, and oratorical texts of Antiquity, while the Fall of Constantinople (1453) generated a wave of *émigré* Greek scholars bringing precious manuscripts in ancient Greek, many of which had fallen into obscurity in the West. It is in their new focus on literary and historical texts that Renaissance scholars differed so markedly from the medieval scholars of the Renaissance of the 12th century, who had focused on studying Greek and Arabic works of natural sciences, philosophy and mathematics, rather than on such cultural texts. In the revival of neo-platonism Renaissance humanists did not reject Christianity; quite the contrary, many of the Renaissance's greatest works were devoted to it, and the Church patronized many works of Renaissance art. However, a subtle shift took place in the way that intellectuals approached religion that was reflected in many other areas of cultural life. In addition, many Greek Christian works, including the Greek New Testament, were brought back from Byzantium to western Europe and engaged western scholars for the first time since Late Antiquity. This new engagement with Greek Christian works, and particularly the return to the original Greek of the New Testament promoted by humanists Lorenzo Valla and Erasmus, would help pave the way for the Protestant Reformation.

Well after the first artistic return to classicism had been exemplified in the sculpture of Nicola Pisano, Florentine painters led by Masaccio strove to portray the human form realistically, developing techniques to render perspective and light more naturally. Political philosophers, most famously Niccolò Machiavelli, sought to describe political life as it really was, that is to understand it rationally. A critical contribution to Italian Renaissance humanism Pico della Mirandola wrote the famous text *De hominis dignitate* (*Oration on the Dignity of Man*, 1486), which consists of a series of theses on philosophy, natural thought, faith and magic defended against any opponent on the grounds of reason. In addition to studying classical Latin and Greek, Renaissance authors also began increasingly to use vernacular languages; combined with the introduction of printing, this would allow many more people access to books, especially the Bible. In all, the Renaissance could be viewed as an attempt by intellectuals to study and improve the secular and worldly, both through the revival of ideas from antiquity, and through novel approaches to thought. Some scholars, such as Rodney Stark, play down the Renaissance in favor of the earlier innovations of the Italian city states in the High Middle Ages, which married responsive government, Christianity and the birth of capitalism. This analysis argues that, whereas the great European states (France and Spain) were absolutist monarchies, and others were under direct Church control, the independent city republics of Italy took over the principles of capitalism invented on monastic estates and set off a vast unprecedented commercial revolution which preceded and financed the Renaissance.

Origins of the Movement

Many argue that the ideas that characterized the Renaissance had their origin in late 13th century Florence, in particular with the writings of Dante Alighieri (1265—1321) and Francesco Petrarca (1304—1374), as well as the painting of Giotto di Bondone (1267—1337). Some writers date the Renaissance quite precisely; one proposed starting point is 1401, when the rival geniuses Lorenzo Ghiberti and Filippo Brunelleschi competed for the contract to build the bronze doors for the Baptistery of the Florence Cathedral (Ghiberti won). Others see more general competition between artists and polymaths such as Brunelleschi, Ghiberti, Donatello, and Masaccio for artistic commissions as sparking the creativity of the Renaissance. Yet it remains much debated why the Renaissance began in Italy, and why it began when it did. Accordingly, several theories have been put forward to explain its origins. During the Renaissance, money and art went hand in hand. Artists depended totally on patrons while the patrons needed money to sustain geniuses. Wealth was brought to Italy in the 14th, 15th, and 16th centuries by expanding trade into Asia and Europe. Silver mining in Tyrol increased the flow of money. Luxuries from the eastern world, brought home during the Crusades, increased the prosperity of Genoa and Venice. Michelet defined the 16th-century Renaissance in France as a period in Europe's cultural history that represented a break from the Middle Ages, creating a modern understanding of humanity and its place in the world.

Social and Political Structures in Italy

The unique political structures of late Middle Ages Italy have led some to theorize that its unusual social climate allowed the emergence of a rare cultural efflorescence. Italy did not exist as a political entity in the early modern period. Instead, it was divided into smaller city states and territories: the Kingdom of Naples controlled the south, the Republic of Florence and the Papal States at the center, the Milanese and the Genoese to the north and West respectively, and the Venetians to the East. Fifteenth-century Italy was one of the most urbanised areas in Europe. Many of its cities stood among the ruins of ancient Roman buildings; it seems likely that the classical nature of the Renaissance was linked to its origin in the Roman Empire's heartland. Historian and political philosopher Quentin Skinner points out that Otto of Freising (c. 1114—1158), a German bishop visiting north Italy during the 12th century, noticed a widespread new form of political and social organization, observing that Italy appeared to have exited from feudalism so that its society was based on merchants and commerce. Linked to this was anti-monarchical thinking, represented in the famous early Renaissance fresco cycle Allegory of Good and Bad Government in Siena by Ambrogio Lorenzetti (painted 1338—1340) whose strong message is about the virtues of fairness, justice, republicanism and good administration. Holding both Church and Empire at bay, these city republics were devoted to notions of liberty. Skinner reports that there were many defenses of liberty such as Matteo Palmieri's (1406—1475) celebration of Florentine genius not only in art, sculpture and architecture, but "the remarkable efflorescence of moral, social and political philosophy that occurred in Florence at the same time". Even cities and states beyond central Italy, such as the Republic of Florence at this time, were also notable for their merchant Republics, especially the Republic of Venice. Although in practice these were oligarchical, and bore little resemblance to a modern democracy, they did have democratic features and were responsive states, with forms of participation in governance and belief in liberty. The relative political freedom they afforded was conducive to academic and artistic advancement. Likewise, the position of Italian cities such as Venice as great trading centers made them intellectual crossroads. Merchants brought with them ideas from far corners of the globe, particularly the Levant. Venice was Europe's gateway to trade with the East, and a producer of fine glass, while Florence was a capital of textiles. The wealth such business brought to Italy meant large public and private artistic projects could be commissioned and individuals had more leisure time for study.

Black Death/Plague

One theory that has been advanced is that the devastation caused by the Black Death in Florence, which hit Europe between 1348 and 1350, resulted in a shift in the world view of people in 14th-century Italy. Italy was particularly badly hit by the plague, and it has been speculated that the resulting familiarity with death caused thinkers to dwell more on their lives on

Earth, rather than on spirituality and the afterlife. It has also been argued that the Black Death prompted a new wave of piety, manifested in the sponsorship of religious works of art. However, this does not fully explain why the Renaissance occurred specifically in Italy in the 14th century. The Black Death was a pandemic that affected all of Europe in the ways described, not only Italy. The Renaissance's emergence in Italy was most likely the result of the complex interaction of the above factors. The plague was carried by fleas on sailing vessels returning from the ports of Asia, spreading quickly due to lack of proper sanitation: the population of England, then about 4.2 million, lost 1.4 million people to the bubonic plague. Florence's population was nearly halved in the year 1347. As a result of the decimation in the populace the value of the working class increased, and commoners came to enjoy more freedom. To answer the increased need for labor, workers traveled in search of the most favorable position economically. The demographic decline due to the plague had some economic consequences: the prices of food dropped and land values declined by 30 to 40% in most parts of Europe between 1350 and 1400. Landholders faced a great loss but for ordinary men and women, it was a windfall. The survivors of the plague found not only that the prices of food were cheaper but also found that lands were more abundant, and that most of them inherited property from their dead relatives. The spread of disease was significantly more rampant in areas of poverty. Epidemics ravaged cities, particularly children. Plagues were easily spread by lice, unsanitary drinking water, armies, or by poor sanitation. Children were hit the hardest because many diseases such as typhus and syphilis target the immune system and left young children without a fighting chance. Children in city dwellings were more affected by the spread of disease than the children of the wealthy. The Black Death caused greater upheaval to Florence's social and political structure than later epidemics. Despite a significant number of deaths among members of the ruling classes, the government of Florence continued to function during this period. Formal meetings of elected representatives were suspended during the height of the epidemic due to the chaotic conditions in the city, but a small group of officials was appointed to conduct the affairs of the city, which ensured continuity of government.

Characteristics/Humanism

In some ways **Humanism** was not a philosophy per se, but rather a method of learning. In contrast to the medieval scholastic mode, which focused on resolving contradictions between authors, humanists would study ancient texts in the original, and appraise them through a combination of reasoning and empirical evidence. Humanist education was based on the programme of "studia Humanitatis", that being the study of five humanities: poetry, grammar, history, moral philosophy and rhetoric. Although historians have sometimes struggled to define humanism precisely, most have settled on "a middle of the road definition... the movement to recover, interpret, and assimilate the language, literature, learning and values of ancient Greece and Rome". Above all, humanists asserted "the genius of man... the unique and extraordinary ability of the human mind." Humanist scholars shaped the intellectual landscape throughout the early modern period. Political philosophers such as Niccolò Machiavelli and Thomas More revived the ideas of Greek and Roman thinkers, and applied them in critiques of contemporary government. Pico della Mirandola wrote what is often considered the *manifesto* of the Renaissance, a vibrant defence of thinking, the Oration on the Dignity of Man. Matteo Palmieri (1406—1475), another humanist, is most known for his work *Della vita civile* (*On Civic Life*; printed 1528) which advocated civic humanism, and his influence in refining the Tuscan vernacular to the same level as Latin. Palmieri's written works drawn on Roman philosophers and theorists, especially Cicero, who, like Palmieri, lived an active public life as a citizen and official, as well as a theorist and philosopher and also Quintilian. Perhaps the most succinct expression of his perspective on humanism is in a 1465 poetic work *La città di vita*, but an earlier work *Della vita civile* (*On Civic Life*) is more wide-ranging. Composed as a series of dialogues set in a country house in the Mugello countryside outside Florence during the plague of 1430, Palmieri expounds on the qualities of the ideal citizen. The dialogues include ideas about how children develop mentally and physically, how citizens can conduct themselves morally, how citizens and states can ensure probity in public life, and an important debate on the difference between that which is pragmatically useful and that which is honest. The humanists believed that it is important to transcend to the afterlife with a perfect mind and body. This transcending belief can be done with education. The purpose of humanism was to create a universal man whose person combined intellectual and physical excellence and who was capable of functioning honorably in virtually any situation. This ideology was referred to as il uomo universal, an ancient Greco-Roman ideal. The education during Renaissance was mainly composed of ancient literature and history. It was thought that the classics provided moral instruction and an intensive understanding of human behavior.

Art

The Renaissance marks the period of European history at the close of the Middle Ages and the rise of the Modern world. It represents a cultural rebirth from the 14th through the middle of the 17th centuries. Early Renaissance, mostly in Italy, bridges the art period during the fifteenth century, between the Middle Ages and the High Renaissance in Italy. It is generally known that Renaissance matured in Northern Europe later, in 16th century. One of the distinguishing features of Renaissance art was its development of highly realistic linear perspective. Giotto di Bondone (1267—1337) is credited with first treating a painting as a window into space, but it was not until the demonstrations of architect Filippo Brunelleschi (1377—1446) and the subsequent writings of Leon Battista Alberti (1404—1472) that perspective was formalized as an artistic technique. The development of perspective was part of a wider trend towards realism in the arts. To that end, painters also developed other techniques, studying light, shadow, and, famously in the case of Leonardo da Vinci, human anatomy. Underlying these changes in artistic method, was a renewed desire to depict the beauty of nature, and to unravel the axioms of aesthetics, with the works of Leonardo, Michelangelo and Raphael representing artistic pinnacles that were to be much imitated by other artists. Other notable artists include Sandro Botticelli, working for the Medici in Florence, Donatello another Florentine and Titian in Venice, among others. Concurrently, in the Netherlands, a particularly vibrant artistic culture developed, the work of Hugo van der Goes and Jan van Eyck having particular influence on the development of painting in Italy, both technically with the introduction of oil paint and canvas, and stylistically in terms of naturalism in representation. (see *Renaissance in the Netherlands*). Later, the work of Pieter Brueghel the Elder would inspire artists to depict themes of everyday life. In architecture, Filippo Brunelleschi was foremost in studying the remains of ancient classical buildings, and with rediscovered knowledge from the 1st-century writer Vitruvius and the flourishing discipline of mathematics, formulated the Renaissance style which emulated and improved on classical forms. Brunelleschi's major feat of engineering was the building of the dome of Florence Cathedral. The first building to demonstrate this is claimed to be the church of St. Andrew built by Alberti in Mantua. The outstanding architectural work of the High Renaissance was the rebuilding of St. Peter's Basilica, combining the skills of Bramante,

Michelangelo, Raphael, Sangallo and Maderno. The Roman orders types of columns are used: Tuscan, Doric, Ionic, Corinthian and Composite. These can either be structural, supporting an arcade or architrave, or purely decorative, set against a wall in the form of pilasters. During the Renaissance, architects aimed to use columns, pilasters, and entablatures as an integrated system. One of the first buildings to use pilasters as an integrated system was in the Old Sacristy (1421—1440) by Filippo Brunelleschi. Arches, semi-circular or (in the Mannerist style) segmental, are often used in arcades, supported on piers or columns with capitals. There may be a section of entablature between the capital and the springing of the arch. Alberti was one of the first to use the arch on a monumental. Renaissance vaults do not have ribs. They are semi-circular or segmental and on a square plan, unlike the Gothic vault which is frequently rectangular. The Renaissance artists were not pagans although they admired antiquity and they also kept some ideas and symbols of the medieval past. Nicola Pisano (c. 1220—c. 1278) imitated classical forms by portraying scenes from the Bible. The Annunciation by Nicola Pisano, from the Baptistry at Pisa, demonstrates that classical models influenced Italian art before the Renaissance took root as a literary movement.

Science and Scientific Spirit

The rediscovery of ancient texts and the invention of printing democratized learning and allowed a faster propagation of ideas. In the first period of Italian Renaissance, humanists favoured the study of humanities over natural philosophy or applied mathematics. And their reverence for classical sources further enshrined the Aristotelian and Ptolemaic views of the universe. Even though, around 1450, the writings of Nicholas Cusanus were anticipating Copernicus' heliocentric world-view, it was made in a philosophical fashion. Science and art were very much intermingled in the early Renaissance, with polymath artists such as Leonardo da Vinci making observational drawings of anatomy and nature. He set up controlled experiments in water flow, medical dissection, and systematic study of movement and aerodynamics; he devised principles of research method that led to Fritjof Capra classifying him as "father of modern science". In 1492 the "discovery" of the "New World" by Christopher Columbus challenged the classical world-view, as the works of Ptolemy (geography) and Galen (medicine) were found not always to match everyday observations: a suitable environment was created to question scientific doctrine. As the Protestant Reformation and Counter-Reformation clashed, the Northern Renaissance showed a decisive shift in focus from Aristotelean natural philosophy to chemistry and the biological sciences (botany, anatomy, and medicine). The willingness to question previously held truths and search for new answers resulted in a period of major scientific advancements. Some have seen this as a "scientific revolution", heralding the beginning of the modern age. Others as an acceleration of a continuous process stretching from the ancient world to the present day. Regardless, there is general agreement that the Renaissance saw significant changes in the way the universe was viewed and the methods sought to explain natural phenomena. Traditionally held to have begun in 1543, when were first printed the books *De humani corporis fabrica* (*On the Workings of the Human Body*) by Andreas Vesalius, which gave a new confidence to the role of dissection, observation, and mechanistic view of anatomy, and also *De Revolutionibus*, by the Nicolaus Copernicus. The famous thesis of Copernicus' book was that the Earth moved around the Sun. Significant scientific advances were made during this time by Galileo Galilei, Tycho Brahe and Johannes Kepler. One important development was not any specific discovery, but rather the further development of the *process* for discovery, the scientific method. It focused on empirical evidence, the importance of mathematics, and discarded

Aristotelian science. Early and influential proponents of these ideas included Copernicus and Galileo and Francis Bacon. The new scientific method led to great contributions in the fields of astronomy, physics, biology, and anatomy.

Religion

The new ideals of humanism, although more secular in some aspects, developed against a Christian backdrop, especially in the Northern Renaissance. Much, if not most, of the new art was commissioned by or in dedication to the Church. However, the Renaissance had a profound effect on contemporary theology, particularly in the way people perceived the relationship between man and God. Many of the period's foremost theologians were followers of the humanist method, including Erasmus, Zwingli, Thomas More, Martin Luther, and John Calvin. The Renaissance began in times of religious turmoil. The late Middle Ages saw a period of political intrigue surrounding the papacy, culminating in the western schism, in which three men simultaneously claimed to be true Bishop of Rome. While the schism was resolved by the Council of Constance (1414), the 15th century saw a resulting reform movement known as Conciliarism, which sought to limit the pope's power. Although the papacy eventually emerged supreme in ecclesiastical matters by the Fifth Council of the Lateran (1511), it was dogged by continued accusations of corruption, most famously in the person of Pope Alexander Ⅵ, who was accused variously of simony, nepotism and fathering four illegitimate children whilst Pope, whom he married off to gain more power. Churchmen such as Erasmus and Luther proposed reform to the Church, often based on humanist textual criticism of the New Testament. It was Luther who in October 1517 published the 95 Theses, challenging papal authority and criticizing its perceived corruption, particularly with regard to its sale of indulgences. The 95 Theses led to the Reformation, a break with the Roman Catholic Church that previously claimed hegemony in western Europe. Humanism and the Renaissance therefore played a direct role in sparking the Reformation, as well as in many other contemporaneous religious debates and conflicts. In an era following the sack of Rome in 1527 and prevalent with uncertainties in the Catholic Church following the Protestant Reformation, Pope Paul Ⅲ came to the papal throne (1534—1549), to whom Nicolaus Copernicus dedicated *De revolutionibus orbium coelestium* (*On the Revolutions of the Celestial Spheres*) and who became the grandfather of Alessandro Farnese (cardinal), who had paintings by Titian, Michelangelo, and Raphael, and an important collection of drawings and who commissioned the masterpiece of Giulio Clovio, arguably the last major illuminated manuscript, the *Farnese Hours*.

Self-Awareness

By the 15th century, writers, artists, and architects in Italy were well aware of the transformations that were taking place and were using phrases such as, *modi antichi* (in the antique manner) or *alle romana et alla antica* (in the manner of the Romans and the ancients) to describe their work. In the 1330s Petrarch referred to pre-Christian times as *antiqua* (ancient) and to the Christian period as *nova* (new). From Petrarch's Italian perspective, this new period (which included his own time) was an age of national eclipse. Leonardo Bruni was the first to use tripartite periodization in his *History of the Florentine People* (1442). Bruni's first two periods were based on those of Petrarch, but he added a third period because he believed that Italy was no longer in a state of decline. Flavio Biondo used a similar framework in *Decades of History from the Deterioration of the Roman Empire* (1439—1453). Humanist historians argued that contemporary scholarship restored direct links to the classical period, thus bypassing the

Medieval period, which they then named for the first time the "Middle Ages". The term first appears in Latin in 1469 as *media tempestas* (middle times). The term *la rinascita* (rebirth) first appeared, however, in its broad sense in Giorgio Vasari's *Vite de più eccellenti architetti, pittori, et scultori Italiani* (*The Lives of the Artists*, 1550, revised 1568). Vasari divides the age into three phases: the first phase contains Cimabue, Giotto, and Arnolfo di Cambio; the second phase contains Masaccio, Brunelleschi, and Donatello; the third centers on Leonardo da Vinci and culminates with Michelangelo. It was not just the growing awareness of classical antiquity that drove this development, according to Vasari, but also the growing desire to study and imitate nature.

Spread

In the 15th century, the Renaissance spread with great speed from its birthplace in Florence, first to the rest of Italy, and soon to the rest of Europe. The invention of the printing press allowed the rapid transmission of these new ideas. As it spread, its ideas diversified and changed, being adapted to local culture. In the 20th century, scholars began to break the Renaissance into regional and national movements.

England

What a piece of work is a man, how noble in reason, how infinite in faculties, in form and moving how express and admirable, in action how like an angel, in apprehension how like a god!

—from William Shakespeare's *Hamlet*

In England, the Elizabethan era marked the beginning of the English Renaissance with the work of writers William Shakespeare, Christopher Marlowe, Edmund Spenser, Sir Thomas More, Francis Bacon, Sir Philip Sidney, John Milton, as well as great artists, architects (such as Inigo Jones who introduced Italianate architecture to England), and composers such as Thomas Tallis, John Taverner, and William Byrd.

France

In 1495 the Italian Renaissance arrived in France, imported by King Charles Ⅷ after his invasion of Italy. A factor that promoted the spread of secularism was the Church's inability to offer assistance against the Black Death. Francis I imported Italian art and artists, including Leonardo da Vinci, and built ornate palaces at great expense. Writers such as François Rabelais, Pierre de Ronsard, Joachim du Bellay and Michel de Montaigne, painters such as Jean Clouet and musicians such as Jean Mouton also borrowed from the spirit of the Italian Renaissance. In 1533, a fourteen-year-old Caterina de' Medici (1519—1589), born in Florence to Lorenzo Ⅱ de' Medici and Madeleine de la Tour d'Auvergne, married Henry, second son of King Francis I and Queen Claude. Though she became famous and infamous for her role in France's religious wars, she made a direct contribution in bringing arts, sciences and music (including the origins of ballet) to the French court from her native Florence.

Germany

In the second half of the 15th century, the spirit of the age spread to Germany and the Low Countries, where the development of the printing press (c. 1450) and early Renaissance artists such as the painters Jan van Eyck (1395—1441) and Hieronymus Bosch (1450—1516) and the composers Johannes Ockeghem (1410—1497), Jacob Obrecht (1457—1505) and Josquin des Prez (1455—1521), predated the influence from Italy. In the early Protestant areas of the country humanism became closely linked to the turmoil of the Protestant Reformation, and the art and writing of the German Renaissance frequently reflected this dispute. However, the gothic style and medieval scholastic philosophy remained exclusively until the turn of the 16th century. Emperor Maximilian I of Habsburg (Ruling 1493—1519) was the first truly Renaissance monarch of the Holy Roman Empire, later known as "Holy Roman Empire of the German Nation" (Diet of Cologne 1512).

Historiography/Conception

The term was first used retrospectively by the Italian artist and critic Giorgio Vasari (1511—1574) in his book *The Lives of the Artists* (published 1550). In the book Vasari was attempting to define what he described as a break with the barbarities of gothic art: the arts had fallen into decay with the collapse of the Roman Empire and only the Tuscan artists, beginning with Cimabue (1240—1301) and Giotto (1267—1337) began to reverse this decline in the arts. According to Vasari, antique art was central to the rebirth of Italian art. However, it was not until the 19th century that the French word *Renaissance* achieved popularity in describing the self-conscious cultural movement based on revival of Roman models that began in the late-13th century. The Renaissance was first defined by French historian Jules Michelet (1798—1874), in his 1855 work, *Histoire de France*. For Michelet, the Renaissance was more a development in science than in art and culture. He asserted that it spanned the period from Columbus to Copernicus to Galileo; that is, from the end of the 15th century to the middle of the 17th century. Moreover, Michelet distinguished between what he called "the bizarre and monstrous" quality of the Middle Ages and the democratic values that he, as a vocal Republican, chose to see in its character. As a French nationalist, Michelet also sought to claim the Renaissance as a French movement. The Swiss historian Jacob Burckhardt (1818—1897) in his *Die Cultur der Renaissance in Italien* (1860), by contrast, defined the Renaissance as the period between Giotto and Michelangelo in Italy, that is, the 14th to mid-16th centuries. He saw in the Renaissance the emergence of the modern spirit of individuality, which had been stifled in the Middle Ages. His book was widely read and was influential in the development of the modern interpretation of the Italian Renaissance. However, Buckhardt has been accused of setting forth a linear Whiggish view of history in seeing the Renaissance as the origin of the modern world. More recently, historians have been much less keen to define the Renaissance as a historical age, or even a coherent cultural movement. Randolph Starn, historian at the University of California Berkeley, stated:

> *Rather than a period with definitive beginnings and endings and consistent content in between, the Renaissance can be (and occasionally has been) seen as a movement of practices and ideas to which specific groups and identifiable persons variously responded in different times and places. It would be in this sense a network of diverse, sometimes converging, sometimes conflicting cultures, not a single, time-bound culture.*

Debates about Progress

There is debate about the extent to which the Renaissance improved on the culture of the Middle Ages. Both Michelet and Burckhardt were keen to describe the progress made in the Renaissance towards the modern age. Burckhardt likened the change to a veil being removed from man's eyes, allowing him to see clearly. In the Middle Ages both sides of human consciousness—that which was turned within as that which was turned without—lay dreaming or half awake beneath a common veil. The veil was woven of faith, illusion, and childish prepossession, through which the world and history were seen clad in strange hues.

—Jacob Burckhardt, *The Civilization of the Renaissance in Italy*

On the other hand, many historians now point out that most of the negative social factors popularly associated with the medieval period—poverty, warfare, religious and political persecution, for example—seem to have worsened in this era which saw the rise of Machiavellian politics, the Wars of Religion, the corrupt Borgia Popes, and the intensified witch-hunts of the 16th century. Many people who lived during the Renaissance did not view it as the "golden age" imagined by certain 19th-century authors, but were concerned by these social maladies. Significantly, though, the artists, writers, and patrons involved in the cultural movements in question believed they were living in a new era that was a clean break from the Middle Ages. Some Marxist historians prefer to describe the Renaissance in material terms, holding the view that the changes in art, literature, and philosophy were part of a general economic trend from feudalism towards capitalism, resulting in a bourgeois class with leisure time to devote to the arts. Johan Huizinga (1872—1945) acknowledged the existence of the Renaissance but questioned whether it was a positive change. In his book *The Waning of the Middle Ages*, he argued that the Renaissance was a period of decline from the High Middle Ages, destroying much that was important. The Latin language, for instance, had evolved greatly from the classical period and was still a living language used in the church and elsewhere. The Renaissance obsession with classical purity halted its further evolution and saw Latin revert to its classical form. Robert S. Lopez has contended that it was a period of deep economic recession. Meanwhile George Sarton and Lynn Thorndike have both argued that scientific progress was perhaps less original than has traditionally been supposed. Finally, Joan Kelly argued that the Renaissance led to greater gender dichotomy, lessening the agency women had had during the Middle Ages. Some historians have begun to consider the word *Renaissance* to be unnecessarily loaded, implying an unambiguously positive rebirth from the supposedly more primitive "Dark Ages" (Middle Ages). Many historians now prefer to use the term "Early Modern" for this period, a more neutral designation that highlights the period as a transitional one between the Middle Ages and the modern era. Others such as Roger Osborne have come to consider the Italian Renaissance as a repository of the myths and ideals of western history in general, and instead of rebirth of ancient ideas as a period of great innovation.

Questions and Topics for Pondering and Further Discussion for Unit Six-1:
1. What is the fundamental significance of Renaissance?
2. What is the paramount spirit of Renaissance?
3. What does Renaissance try to revive?
4. Why did Renaissance first occur in Italy?
5. What was the social climate before the occurrence of Renaissance?
6. What is meant by humanism promoted during the Renaissance era?
7. Is Renaissance simply a cultural movement or what?
8. A famous person once said that Renaissance is a period in which giants are needed and giants can be produced. Please make some comment on it.

2. The Enlightenment, an Age of Soul Liberation

Editor's remarks: *as one of the three movements that have propelled social progress of the West, the Enlightenment Movement has played a crucial role in freeing people from unscientific way of thinking, greatly facilitating the following industrial revolution that once and for all fundamentally changed the way people worked, produced and lived. The Enlightenment Movement is like a torch in darkness, illuminating people's mind and broadening their horizon. People's mentality in the West changed once and for all through this intellectual movement that greatly helped the West control the commanding heights of thinking and thought in the modern era. Many ideas and concepts promoted during the Enlightenment Movement era have ever since then become universal values of human beings, encouraging people to aspire for their own freedom and personal happiness.*

The Age of Enlightenment (or simply the **Enlightenment** or **Age of Reason**) was a cultural movement of intellectuals in 18th century Europe and the United States, whose purpose was to reform society and advance knowledge. It promoted science and intellectual interchange and opposed superstition, intolerance and abuses by church and state. Originating about 1650 to 1700, it was sparked by philosophers Baruch Spinoza (1632—1677), John Locke (1632—1704), Pierre Bayle (1647—1706), physicist Isaac Newton (1643—1727), and philosopher Voltaire (1694—1778). The wide distribution of the printing press, invented in Europe in 1450, made possible the rapid dispersion of knowledge and ideas which precipitated the Enlightenment. Ruling princes often endorsed and fostered figures and even attempted to apply their ideas of government in what was known as Enlightened Despotism. The Enlightenment flourished until about 1790—1800, after which the emphasis on reason gave way to Romanticism's emphasis on emotion and a Counter-enlightenment gained force. In France, Enlightenment was based in the salons and culminated in the great *Encyclopédie* (1751—72) edited by Denis Diderot (1713—1784) with contributions by hundreds of leading philosophers (intellectuals) such as Voltaire (1694—1778), Rousseau (1712—1778) and Montesquieu (1689—1755). Some 25,000 copies of the 35 volume set were sold, half of them outside France. The new intellectual forces spread to urban centers across Europe, notably England, Scotland, the German states, the Netherlands, Russia, Italy, Austria, and Spain, then jumped the Atlantic into the European colonies, where it influenced Benjamin Franklin and Thomas Jefferson, among many others, and played a major role in the American Revolution. The political ideals of the Enlightenment influenced the American Declaration of Independence, the United States Bill of Rights, the French Declaration of the Rights of Man and of the Citizen, and the Polish-Lithuanian Constitution of May 3, 1791.

Use of the Term

The term "Enlightenment" did not come into use in English until the mid-18th century, with particular reference to French philosophy, as the equivalent of the French term "Lumières" (used first by Dubos 1733 and already well established by 1751). From Immanuel Kant's 1784 essay "Beantwortung der Frage: Was ist Aufklärung?" ("Answering the Question: What Is Enlightenment?") the German term became "Aufklärung".

"For Kant, Enlightenment was mankind's final coming of age, the emancipation of the human consciousness from an immature state of ignorance and error." According to historian Roy Porter, the thesis of the liberation of the human mind from the dogmatic state of ignorance that he argues was prevalent at the time is the epitome of what the age of enlightenment was trying to capture. According to Bertrand Russell, however, the enlightenment was a phase in a progressive development, which began in antiquity, and that reason and challenges to the established order were constant ideals throughout that time. Russell argues that the enlightenment was ultimately born out of the Protestant reaction against the Catholic counter-Reformation, when the philosophical views of the past two centuries crystallized into a coherent world view. He argues that many of the philosophical views, such as affinity for democracy against monarchy, originated among Protestants in the early 16th century to justify their desire to break away from the pope and the Catholic Church. Though many of these philosophical ideals were picked up by Catholics, Russell argues, by the 18th century the Enlightenment was the principal manifestation of the schism that began with Martin Luther. Chartier (1991) argues that the Enlightenment was only invented after the fact for a political goal. He claims the leaders of the French Revolution created an Enlightenment canon of basic text, by selecting certain authors and identifying them with the Enlightenment in order to legitimize their republican political agenda.

Historian Jonathan Israel dismisses the post-modern interpretation of the Enlightenment and the attempts of modern historians to link social and economical reasons for the revolutionary aspect of the period. He instead focuses on the history of ideas in the period from 1650 to the end of the 18th century, and claims that it was the ideas themselves that caused the change that eventually led to the revolutions of the later half of the 18th century and the early 19th century. Israel argues that until the 1650s western civilization "was based on a largely shared core of faith, tradition and authority". Up until this date most intellectual debates revolved around "confessional"—that is Catholic, Lutheran, Reformed (Calvinist), or Anglican issues, and the main aim of these debates was to establish which bloc of faith ought to have the "monopoly of truth and a God-given title to authority". After this date everything thus previously rooted in tradition was questioned and often replaced by new concepts in the light of philosophical reason. After the second half of the 17th century and during the 18th century a "general process of rationalization and secularization set in which rapidly overthrew theology's age-old hegemony in the world of study", and thus confessional disputes were reduced to a secondary status in favor of the "escalating contest between faith and incredulity".

This period saw the shaping of two distinct lines of enlightenment thought: Firstly the radical enlightenment, largely inspired by the one-substance philosophy of Spinoza, which in its political form adhered to: "democracy; racial and sexual equality; individual liberty of lifestyle; full freedom of thought, expression, and the press; eradication of religious authority from the legislative process and education; and full separation of church and state". Secondly the moderate enlightenment, which in a number of different philosophical systems, like those in the writings of Descartes, John Locke, Isaac Newton or Christian Wolff, expressed some support for critical review and renewal of the old modes of thought, but in other parts sought reform and accommodation with the old systems of power and faith. These two lines of thought were again met by the conservative counter-enlightenment, encompassing those thinkers who held on to the traditional belief-based systems of thought.

Time Span

There is little consensus on the precise beginning of the age of Enlightenment; the beginning of the 18th century (1701) or the middle of the 17th century (1650) are often used as an approximate starting point. If taken back to the mid-17th century, the Enlightenment would trace its origins to Descartes' *Discourse on Method*, published in 1637. Others define the Enlightenment as beginning in Britain's Glorious Revolution of 1688 or with the publication of Isaac Newton's *Principia Mathematica* in 1687. Jonathan Israel argues, "after 1650, everything, no matter how fundamental or deeply rooted, was questioned in the light of philosophic reason". Israel makes the detailed case that, from 1650 to 1750, Spinoza was "the chief challenger of the fundamentals of revealed religion, received ideas, tradition, morality, and what was everywhere regarded, in absolutist and non-absolutist states alike, as divinely constituted political authority". As to its end, most scholars use the last years of the century—often choosing the French Revolution of 1789 or the beginning of the Napoleonic Wars (1804—1815) as a convenient point in time with which to date the end of the Enlightenment.

National Variations

The Enlightenment operated in most countries, but often with a specific local emphasis. For example in France it became associated with anti-government and anti-church radicalism, while in Germany it reached deep into the middle classes and expressed a spiritualistic and nationalistic tone without threatening governments or established churches. Government responses varied widely. In France the government was hostile, and the philosophers fought against its censorship. They were sometimes imprisoned or hounded into exile. The British government generally ignored the Enlightenment's leaders in England and Scotland, although it did give Newton a knighthood and a very lucrative government office in charge of the mint.

Enlightened Absolutism

In several nations, powerful rulers—called "enlightened despots" by historians—welcomed leaders of the Enlightenment at court and had them help design laws and programs to reform the system, typically to build stronger national states. The most prominent of those rulers were Frederick the Great of Prussia, Catherine the Great, Empress of Russia from 1762 to 1796, and Joseph II, Emperor of Austria 1780—1790. Joseph was over-enthusiastic, announcing so many reforms that had so little support, that revolts broke out and his regime became a comedy of errors and nearly all his programs were reversed. Senior ministers Pombal in Portugal and Struensee in Denmark governed according to Enlightenment ideals.

North America

The Americans closely followed English and Scottish political ideas, as well as some French thinkers such as Montesquieu. During the Enlightenment there as a great emphasis upon liberty, democracy, republicanism and religious tolerance—culminating in the drafting of the United States Declaration of Independence. Attempts to reconcile science and religion resulted in a widespread rejection of prophecy, miracle and revealed religion in preference for Deism—especially by Thomas Paine in "The Age of Reason" and by Thomas Jefferson in his short Jefferson Bible—from which all supernatural aspects were removed.

Prussia and the German States

By the mid-18th century the German Enlightenment in music, philosophy, science and literature emerged as an intellectual force. Frederick the Great (1712—1786), the king of Prussia (1740—1786), saw himself as a leader of the Enlightenment and patronized philosophers and scientists at his court in Berlin. He was an enthusiast for French ideas as he ridiculed German culture and was unaware of the remarkable advances it was undergoing. Voltaire, who had been imprisoned and maltreated by the French government, was eager to accept Frederick's invitation to live at his palace. Frederick explained, "My principal occupation is to combat ignorance and prejudice and to enlighten minds, cultivate morality, and to make people as happy as it suits human nature, and as the means at my disposal permit." Other rulers were supportive, such as Karl Friedrich, Grand Duke of Baden, who ruled Baden for 73 years (1738—1811). *Weimar's Courtyard of the Muses* demonstrates the importance of Weimar. Schiller is reading; on the far left (seated) Wieland and Herder, Goethe standing on the right in front of the pillar. 1860 painting by Theobald von Oer Christian Wolff (1679—1754) was the pioneer as a writer who expounded the Enlightenment to German readers; he legitimized German as a philosophic language.

Johann Gottfried von Herder (1744—1803) broke new ground in philosophy and poetry, specifically in the Sturm und Drang movement of proto-Romanticism. Weimar Classicism (Weimarer Klassik) was a cultural and literary movement based in Weimar that sought to establish a new humanism by synthesizing Romantic, Classical and Enlightenment ideas. The movement, from 1772 until 1805, involved Herder as well as polymath Johann Wolfgang von Goethe (1749—1832) and Friedrich Schiller (1759—1805), a poet and historian. Herder argued that every folk had its own particular identity, which was expressed in its language and culture. This legitimized the promotion of German language and culture and helped shape the development of German nationalism. Schiller's plays expressed the restless spirit of his generation, depicting the hero's struggle against social pressures and the force of destiny. German music, sponsored by the upper classes, came of age under composers Johann Sebastian Bach (1685—1750), Franz Joseph Haydn (1732—1809), and Wolfgang Amadeus Mozart (1756—1791). In remote Königsberg philosopher Immanuel Kant (1724—1804) tried to reconcile rationalism and religious belief, individual freedom and political authority. Kant's work contained basic tensions that would continue to shape German thought—and indeed all of European philosophy—well into the 20th century. The German Enlightenment won the support of princes, aristocrats and the middle classes and permanently reshaped the culture.

England

John Locke was one of the most influential Enlightenment thinkers. He influenced other thinkers such as Rousseau, Voltaire, among others. He is one of the dozen or so thinkers who are remembered for their influential contributions across a broad spectrum of philosophical subfields—in Locke's case, across epistemology, the philosophy of language, the philosophy of mind, metaphysics, rational theology, ethics, and political philosophy. Closely associated with the First Earl of Shaftesbury, who instigated the Glorious Revolution and led the parliamentary grouping that later became the Whig party, he is still known today for his liberalism in political theory. The main goal that most people remember about him is his famous words of "Life, Liberty and Property". With property he stated that it is a natural right derived from labor. He was more of a positive Enlightenment thinker and often disagreed with others that related to Thomas Hobbes.

Scotland

One leader of the Scottish Enlightenment was Adam Smith, the father of modern economic science. In the 18th-century, influential thinkers as Francis Hutcheson, Adam Smith and David Hume, paved the way for the modernization of Scotland and the entire Atlantic world.

Hutcheson, the father of the Scottish Enlightenment, championed political liberty and the right of popular rebellion against tyranny. Smith, in his monumental *Wealth of Nations* (1776), advocated liberty in the sphere of commerce and the global economy. Hume developed philosophical concepts that directly influenced James Madison and thus the U. S. Constitution. In 19th-century Britain, the Scottish Enlightenment, as popularized by Dugald Stewart, became the basis of classical liberalism. Scientific progress was led by James Hutton, William Thomson, 1st Baron Kelvin, and James Watt (instrument maker to the University of Glasgow), who perfected the crucial technology of the Industrial Revolution: the steam engine.

Russia: Meeting Point Between the West and East

In Russia Enlightenment of the mid-eighteenth century saw the government begin to actively encourage the proliferation of arts and sciences. This era produced the first Russian university, library, theatre, public museum, and independent press. Like other enlightened despots, Catherine the Great played a key role in fostering the arts, sciences, and education. She used her own interpretation of Enlightenment ideals, assisted by notable international experts such as Voltaire (by correspondence) and, in residence, world class scientists such as Leonhard Euler, Peter Simon Pallas, Fedor Ivanovich Iankovich de Mirievo (also spelled Teodor Jankovic-Mirijevski), and Anders Johan Lexell. The national Enlightenment differed from its western European counterpart in that it promoted further Modernization of all aspects of Russian life and was concerned with attacking the institution of serfdom in Russia. Historians argue that the Russian enlightenment centered on the individual instead of societal enlightenment and encouraged the living of an enlightened life.

Goals

No brief summary can do justice to the diversity of enlightened thought in 18th-century Europe. Because it was a value system rather than a set of shared beliefs, there are many contradictory trains to follow. As Outram notes, the Enlightenment comprised "many different paths, varying in time and geography, to the common goals of progress, of tolerance, and the removal of abuses in Church and state."In his famous essay "What is Enlightenment?" (1784), Immanuel Kant described it simply as freedom to use one's own intelligence. More broadly, the Enlightenment period is marked by increasing empiricism, scientific rigor, and reductionism, along with increasing questioning of religious orthodoxy. Historian Peter Gay asserts the Enlightenment broke through "the Sacred Circle", whose dogma had circumscribed thinking. The Sacred Circle is a term he uses to describe the interdependent relationship between the hereditary aristocracy, the leaders of the church and the text of the Bible. This interrelationship manifests itself as kings invoking the doctrine "Divine Right of Kings" to rule. Thus church sanctioned the rule of the king and the king defended the church in return. Zafirovski, argues that the Enlightenment is the source of critical ideas, such as the centrality of freedom, democracy, and reason as primary values of society—as opposed to the divine right of kings or traditions as the ruling authority. (2010) This view argues that the establishment of a contractual basis of rights would lead to the market mechanism and capitalism, the scientific method, religious tolerance, and the organization of states into self-governing republics through democratic means. In this view, the tendency of the philosophes in particular to apply rationality to every problem is considered the essential change. Later critics of the Enlightenment, such as the Romantics of the 19th century, contended that its goals for rationality in human affairs were too ambitious to ever be achieved. A variety of 19th-century movements, including liberalism and neo-Classicism, traced their intellectual heritage back to the Enlightenment.

Social and Cultural Interpretation of the Movement

In opposition to the intellectual historiographical approach of the Enlightenment, which examines the various currents, or discourses of intellectual thought within the European context during the 17th and 18th centuries, the cultural (or social) approach examines the changes that occurred in European society and culture. Under this approach, the Enlightenment is less a collection of thought than a process of changing sociabilities and cultural practices—both the "content" and the processes by which this content was spread are now important. Roger Chartier describes it as follows:

> *This movement [from the intellectual to the cultural/social] implies casting doubt on two ideas: first, that practices can be deduced from the discourses that authorize or justify them; second, that it is possible to translate into the terms of an explicit ideology the latent meaning of social mechanisms. One of the primary elements of the cultural interpretation of the Enlightenment is the rise of the public sphere in Europe. Jürgen Habermas has influenced thinking on the public sphere more than any other, though his model is increasingly called into question. The essential problem that Habermas attempted to answer concerned the conditions necessary for "rational, critical, and genuinely open discussion of public issues". Or, more simply, the social conditions required for Enlightenment ideas to be spread and discussed. His response was the formation in the late 17th century and 18th century of the "bourgeois public sphere", a "realm of communication marked by new arenas of debate, more open and accessible forms of urban public space and sociability, and an explosion of print culture". More specifically, Habermas highlights three essential elements of the public sphere:*
> - *it was egalitarian;*
> - *it discussed the domain of "common concern";*
> - *argument was founded on reason.*

German explorer Alexander von Humboldt showed his disgust for slavery and often criticized the colonial policies. He always acted out of a deeply humanistic conviction, borne by the ideas of the Enlightenment. James Van Horn Melton provides a good summary of the values of this bourgeois public sphere: its members held reason to be supreme; everything was open to criticism (the public sphere is critical); and its participants opposed secrecy of all sorts. This helps explain what Habermas meant by the domain of "common concern". Habermas uses the term to describe those areas of political/social knowledge and discussion that were previously the exclusive territory of the state and religious authorities, now open to critical examination by the public sphere. Habermas credits the creation of the bourgeois public sphere to two long-term historical trends: the rise of the modern nation state and the rise of capitalism. The modern nation state in its consolidation of public power created by counterpoint a private realm of society independent of the state—allowing for the public sphere. Capitalism likewise increased society's autonomy and self-awareness, along with creating an increasing need for the exchange of information. As the nascent public sphere expanded, it embraced a large variety of institutions; the most commonly cited being coffee houses and cafés, salons and the literary public sphere, figuratively localized in the Republic of Letters. Dorinda Outram provides further description of the rise of the public sphere. The context of the rise of the public sphere was the economic and social change commonly grouped under the effects of the Industrial Revolution: "economic expansion, increasing urbanization, rising population and improving communications in comparison to the stagnation of the previous century". Rising efficiency in production techniques and communication lowered the prices of consumer goods at the same time as it increased the amount and variety of goods available to consumers (including the literature essential to the public sphere).

Meanwhile, the colonial experience (most European states had colonial empires in the 18th century) began to expose European society to extremely heterogeneous cultures. Outram writes that the end result was the breaking down of "barriers between cultural systems, religious divides, gender differences and geographical areas". In short, the social context was set for the public sphere to come into existence. A reductionist view of the Habermasian model has been used as a springboard to showcase historical investigations into the development of the public sphere. There are many examples of noble and lower class participation in areas such as the coffeehouses and the freemasonic lodges, demonstrating that the bourgeois-era public sphere was enriched by cross-class influences. A rough depiction of the public sphere as independent and critical of the state is contradicted by the diverse cases of government-sponsored public institutions and government participation in debate, along with the cases of private individuals using public venues to promote the status quo.

Exclusivity of the Public Sphere

The word "public" implies the highest level of inclusivity—the public sphere by definition should be open to all. However, as the analysis of many "public" institutions of the Enlightenment will show, this sphere was only public to relative degrees. Indeed, as Roger Chartier emphasizes, Enlightenment thinkers frequently contrasted their conception of the "public" with that of the people: Chartier cites Condorcet, who contrasted "opinion" with populace; Marmontel with "the opinion of men of letters" versus "the opinion of the multitude"; and d'Alembert, who contrasted the "truly enlightened public" with "the blind and noisy multitude". As Mona Ozouf underlines, public opinion was defined in opposition to the opinion of the greater population. While the nature of public opinion during the Enlightenment is as difficult to define as it is today, it is nonetheless clear that the body that held it (i. e. the public sphere) was exclusive rather than inclusive. This observation will become more apparent during the descriptions of the institutions of the public sphere, most of which excluded both women and the lower classes from getting involved in public affairs.

Social and Cultural Implications in Music

Because of the focus on reason over superstition, the Enlightenment cultivated the arts. Emphasis on learning, art and music became more widespread, especially with the growing middle class. Areas of study such as literature, philosophy, science, and the fine arts increasingly explored subject matter that the general public in addition to the previously more segregated professionals and patrons could relate to. As musicians depended more and more on public support, public concerts became increasingly popular and helped supplement performers and composers incomes. The concerts also helped them to reach a wider audience. Handel, for example, epitomized this with his highly public musical activities in London. He gained considerable fame there with performances of his operas and oratorios. The music of Haydn and Mozart, with their Viennese Classical styles, are usually regarded as being the most in line with the Enlightenment ideals. Another important text that came about as a result of Enlightenment values was Charles Burney's *A General History of Music : From the Earliest Ages to the Present Period*, originally published in 1776. This text was a historical survey and an attempt to rationalize elements in music systematically over time. As the economy and the middle class expanded, there was an increasing number of amateur musicians. One manifestation of this involves women; this movement allowed women to become more involved with music on a social level. Though women were not yet in professional roles (except for singers), they contributed to the amateur performers scene, especially with keyboard music. The desire to explore, record and systematize knowledge had a meaningful impact on music publications. Jean-Jacques Rousseau's *Dictionnaire de musique* (published 1767 in Geneva and 1768 in Paris) was a leading text in the late 18th century. This widely-available dictionary gave short definitions of words like genius and taste, and was clearly influenced by the Enlightenment movement. Additionally, music publishers began to cater to amateur musicians, putting out music that they could understand and play. The majority of the works that were published were for keyboard, voice and keyboard, and chamber ensemble. After these initial genres were popularized, from the mid-century on, amateur groups sang choral music, which then became a new trend for publishers to capitalize on. The increasing study of the fine arts, as well as access to amateur-friendly published works, led to more people becoming interested in reading and discussing music. Music magazines, reviews, and critical works which suited amateurs as well as connoisseurs began to surface. Although the ideals of the Enlightenment were rejected in postmodernism, they held fast in modernism and have extended well beyond the 18th century even to the present. Recently, musicologists have shown renewed interest in the ideas and consequences of the Enlightenment. For example, Rose Rosengard Subotnik's *Deconstructive Variations* (subtitled *Music and Reason in western Society*) compares Mozart's *Die Zauberflöte* (1791) using the Enlightenment and Romantic perspectives, and concludes that the work is "an ideal musical representation of the Enlightenment".

Dissemination of Ideas

The philosophers spent a great deal of energy disseminating their ideas among educated men and women in cosmopolitan cities. They used many venues, some of them quite new.

Schools and Universities: Cradle of Knowledge and New Ideas

In Germany and Scotland, the Enlightenment leaders were based in universities. However, in general the universities and schools of France and most of Europe were bastions of traditionalism and were not hospitable to the Enlightenment. In France the major exception was the medical university at Montpellier.

It is widely accepted that "modern science" arose in the Europe of the 17th century, introducing a new understanding of the natural world.

—Peter Barrett

The history of Academies in France during the Enlightenment begins with the Academy of Science, founded in 1666 in Paris. It was closely tied to the French state, acting as an extension of a government seriously lacking in scientists. It helped promote and organize new disciplines, and it trained new scientists. It also contributed to the enhancement of scientists' social status, considered them to be the "most useful of all citizens". Academies demonstrate the rising interest in science along with its increasing secularization, as evidenced by the small number of clerics who were members (13 percent). The presence of the French academies in the public sphere cannot be attributed to their membership; although the majority of their members were bourgeois, the exclusive institution was only open to elite Parisian scholars. They did perceive themselves to be "interpreters of the sciences for the people". Indeed, it was with this in mind that academians took it upon themselves to disprove the popular pseudo-science of mesmerism.

However, the strongest case for the French Academies being part of the public sphere comes the concours académiques (roughly translated as academic contests) they sponsored throughout France. As Jeremy L. Caradonna argues in a recent article in the *Annales*, "Prendre part au siècle des Lumières: Le concours académique et la culture intellectuelle au XVIIIe siècle", these academic contests were perhaps the most public of any institution during the Enlightenment. *L'Académie française* revived a practice dating back to the Middle Ages when it revived public contests in the mid-17th century. The subject matter was generally religious and/or monarchical, and featured essays, poetry, and painting. By roughly 1725, however, this subject matter had radically expanded and diversified, including "royal propaganda, philosophical battles, and critical ruminations on the social and political institutions of the Old Regime". Controversial topics were not always avoided: Caradonna cites as examples the theories of Newton and Descartes, the slave trade, women's education, and justice in France. More importantly, the contests were open to all, and the enforced anonymity of each submission guaranteed that neither gender nor social rank would determine the judging. Indeed, although the "vast majority" of participants belonged to the wealthier strata of society ("the liberal arts, the clergy, the judiciary, and the medical profession"), there were some cases of the popular classes submitting essays, and even winning. Similarly, a significant number of women participated—and won—the competitions. Of a total of 2 300 prize competitions offered in France, women won 49—perhaps a small number by modern standards, but very significant in an age in which most women did not have any academic training. Indeed, the majority of the winning entries were for poetry competitions, a genre commonly stressed in women's education. In England, the Royal Society of London also played a significant role in the public sphere and the spread of Enlightenment ideas. In particular, it played a large role in spreading Robert Boyle's experimental philosophy around Europe, and acted as a clearinghouse for intellectual correspondence and exchange. As Steven Shapin and Simon Schaffer have argued, Robert Boyle was "a founder of the experimental world in which scientists now live and operate". Boyle's method based knowledge on experimentation, which had to be witnessed to provide proper empirical legitimacy. This is where the Royal Society came into play: witnessing had to be a "collective act", and the Royal Society's assembly rooms were ideal locations for relatively public demonstrations. However, not just any witness was considered to be credible; "Oxford professors were accounted more reliable witnesses than Oxfordshire peasants." Two factors were taken into account: a witness's knowledge in the area; and a witness's "moral constitution". In other words, only civil society were considered for Boyle's public.

The Book Industry: a New Instrument for Spreading Knowledge and Ideas

The increased consumption of reading materials of all sorts was one of the key features of the "social" Enlightenment. Developments in the Industrial Revolution allowed consumer goods to be produced in greater quantities at lower prices, encouraging the spread of books, pamphlets, newspapers and journals—"media of the transmission of ideas and attitudes". Commercial development likewise increased the demand for information, along with rising populations and increased urbanization. However, demand for reading material extended outside of the realm of the commercial, and outside the realm of the upper and middle classes, as evidenced by the Bibliothèque Bleue. Literacy rates are difficult to gauge, but Robert Darnton writes that, in

France at least, the rates doubled over the course of the 18th century. Reading underwent serious changes in the 18th century. In particular, Rolf Engelsing has argued for the existence of a "reading revolution". Until 1750, reading was done intensively: people tended to own a small number of books and read them repeatedly, often to small audience. After 1750, people began to read "extensively", finding as many books as they could, increasingly reading them alone. On the other hand, as Jonathan Israel writes, Gabriel Naudé was already campaigning for the "universal" library in the mid-17th century. And if this was an ideal only realistic for state institutions and the very wealthy (and indeed, an ideal that was seldom achieved), there are records for extremely large private and state-run libraries throughout Europe in the 17th and 18th-centuries. Of course, the vast majority of the reading public could not afford to own a private library. And while most of the state-run "universal libraries" set up in the 17th and 18th centuries were open to the public, they were not the only sources of reading material. On one end of the spectrum was the *Bibliothèque Bleue*, a collection of cheaply produced books published in Troyes, France. Intended for a largely rural and semi-literate audience these books included almanacs, retellings of medieval romances and condensed versions of popular novels, among other things. While historians, such as Roger Chartier and Robert Darnton, have argued against the Enlightenment's penetration into the lower classes, the *Bibliothèque Bleue*, at the very least, represents a desire to participate in Enlightenment sociability, and it does not matter too much whether or not this was actually achieved.

Moving up the classes, a variety of institutions offered readers access to material without needing to buy anything. Libraries that lent out their material for a small price started to appear, and occasionally bookstores would offer a small lending library to their patrons. Coffee houses commonly offered books, journals and sometimes even popular novels to their customers. *The Tatler* and *The Spectator*, two influential periodicals sold from 1709 to 1714, were closely associated with coffee house culture in London, being both read and produced in various establishments in the city. Indeed, this is an example of the triple or even quadruple function of the coffee house: reading material was often obtained, read, discussed and even produced on the premises. As Darnton describes in *The Literary Underground of the Old Regime*, it is extremely difficult to determine what people actually read during the Enlightenment. For example, examining the catalogs of private libraries not only gives an image skewed in favor of the classes wealthy enough to afford libraries, it also ignores censured works unlikely to be publicly acknowledged. For this reason, Darnton argues that a study of publishing would be much more fruitful for discerning reading habits. All across continental Europe, but in France especially, booksellers and publishers had to negotiate censorship laws of varying strictness. The *Encyclopédie*, for example, narrowly escaped seizure and had to be saved by Malesherbes, the man in charge of the French censure. Indeed, many publishing companies were conveniently located outside of France so as to avoid overzealous French censors. They would smuggle their merchandise—both pirated copies and censured works—across the border, where it would then be transported to clandestine booksellers or small-time peddlers. Darnton provides a detailed record of one clandestine bookseller's (one de Mauvelain) business in the town of Troyes. At the time, the town's population was 22,000. It had one masonic lodge and an "important" library, even though the literacy rate seems to have been less than 50 percent. Mauvelain's records give us a good representation of what literate Frenchmen might have truly read, since the clandestine nature of his business provided a less restrictive product choice. The most popular category of books was political (319 copies ordered). This included five copies of D'Holbach's *Système social*, but around 300 libels and pamphlets. Readers were far more interested in sensationalist stories about criminals and political corruption than they were in political theory itself. The second most popular category, "general works" (those books "that did not have a dominant motif and that contained something to offend almost everyone in authority") likewise betrayed the high demand for generally low-brow subversive literature. These works, however, like the vast majority of work produced by Darnton's "grub street hacks", never became part of literary canon, and are largely forgotten today as a result. Nevertheless, the Enlightenment was not the exclusive domain of illegal literature, as evidenced by the healthy, and mostly legal, publishing industry that existed throughout Europe. "Mostly legal" because even established publishers and book sellers occasionally ran afoul of the law. The *Encyclopédie*, for example, condemned not only by the King but also by Clement XIII, nevertheless found its way into print with the help of the aforementioned Malesherbes and creative use of French censorship law. But many works were sold without running into any legal trouble at all. Borrowing records from libraries in England, Germany and North America indicate that more than 70 percent of books borrowed were novels; that less than 1 percent of the books were of a religious nature supports a general trend of declining religiosity.

Natural History

A genre that greatly rose in importance was that of scientific literature. Natural history in particular became increasingly popular among the upper classes. Works of natural history include René-Antoine Ferchault de Réaumur's *Histoire naturelle des insectes* and Jacques Gautier d' Agoty's *La Myologie complète, ou description de tous les muscles du corps humain* (1746). However, as François-Alexandre Aubert de La Chesnaye des Bois's *Dictionaire de la Noblesse* (1770) indicates, natural history was very often a political affair. As E. C. Spary writes, the classifications used by naturalists "slipped between the natural world and the social... to establish not only the expertise of the naturalists over the natural, but also the dominance of the natural over the social". From this basis, naturalists could then develop their own social ideals based on their scientific works. The target audience of natural history was French polite society, evidenced more by the specific discourse of the genre than by the generally high prices of its works. Naturalists catered to polite society's desire for erudition—many texts had an explicit instructive purpose. But the idea of taste was the real social indicator: to truly be able to categorize nature, one had to have the proper taste, an ability of discretion shared by all members of polite society. In this way natural history spread many of the scientific development of the time, but also provided a new source of legitimacy for the dominant class.

Scientific and Literary Journals

The many scientific and literary journals (predominantly composed of book reviews) that were published during this time are also evidence of the intellectual side of the Enlightenment. In fact, Jonathan Israel argues that the learned journals, from the 1680s onwards, influenced European intellectual culture to a greater degree than any other "cultural innovation". The first journal appeared in 1665—the Parisian *Journal des Sçavans* —but it was not until 1682 that periodicals began to be more widely produced. French and Latin were the dominant languages of publication, but there was also a steady demand for material in German and Dutch. There was generally low demand for English publications on the Continent, which was echoed by England's similar lack of desire for French works. Languages commanding less of an international market—such as Danish, Spanish and Portuguese—found journal success more difficult, and more often than not, a more international language was used instead. Although German did have an international quality to it, it was French that slowly took over Latin's status as the *lingua franca* of learned circles. This in turn gave precedence to the publishing industry in Holland, where the vast majority of these French language periodicals were produced. Israel divides the journals' intellectual importance into four elements. First was their role in shifting the attention of the "cultivated public" away from "established authorities" to "what was new, innovative, or challenging." Secondly, they did much to promote the "'enlightened' ideals of toleration and intellectual objectivity." Thirdly, the journals were an implicit critique of existing notions of universal truth monopolized by monarchies, parliaments, and religious authorities. The journals suggested a new source of knowledge—through science and reason—that undermined these sources of authority. And finally, they advanced the "Christian Enlightenment", a notion of Enlightenment that, despite its advocacy for new knowledge sources, upheld "the legitimacy of God-ordained authority."

Debating Societies: Truths Achieved Through Arguments and Counter-Arguments

The Debating Societies that rapidly came into existence in 1780 London present an almost perfect example of the public sphere during the Enlightenment. Donna T Andrew provides four separate origins:

- Clubs of fifty or more men who, at the beginning of the 18th century, met in pubs to discuss religious issues and affairs of state.
- Mooting clubs, set up by law students to practice rhetoric.
- Spouting clubs, established to help actors train for theatrical roles.
- John Henley's Oratory, which mixed outrageous sermons with even more absurd questions, like "Whether Scotland be anywhere in the world?".

In any event, popular debating societies began, in the late 1770s, to move into more "genteel", or respectable rooms, a change which helped establish a new standard of sociability: "order, decency, and liberality", in the words of the Religious Society of Old Portugal Street. Respectability was also encouraged by the higher admissions prices (ranging from 6d. to 3s.), which also contributed to the upkeep of the newer establishments. The backdrop to these developments was what Andrew calls "an explosion of interest in the theory and practice of public elocution". The debating societies were commercial enterprises that responded to this demand, sometimes very successfully. Indeed, some societies welcomed from 800 to 1200 spectators a night. These societies discussed an extremely wide range of topics. One broad area was women: societies debated over "male and female qualities", courtship, marriage, and the role of women in the public sphere. Societies also discussed political issues, varying from recent events to "the nature and limits of political authority", and the nature of suffrage. Debates on religion rounded out the subject matter. It is important to note, however, that the critical subject matter of these debates did not necessarily translate into opposition to the government. In other words, the results of the debate quite frequently upheld the status quo. From a historical standpoint, one of the most important features of the debating society was their openness to the public; women attended and even participated in almost every debating society, which were likewise open to all classes providing they could pay the entrance fee. Once inside, spectators were able to participate in a largely egalitarian form of sociability that helped spread "Enlightening ideas".

Freemasonic Lodges

Historians have recently been debating the extent to which Freemasonry was part of, or even a main factor in the Enlightenment. On the one hand, historians agree that the famous leaders of the Enlightenment included Freemasons such as Montesquieu, Voltaire, Pope, Horace Walpole, Sir Robert Walpole, Mozart, Goethe, Frederick the Great, Benjamin Franklin, and George Washington. On the other side, historians such as Robert Roswell Palmer concluded that even in France, Masons were politically "innocuous if not ridiculous" and did not act as a group. American historians, while noting that Benjamin Franklin and George Washington were indeed active Masons, have downplayed the importance of Freemasonry in the era of the American Revolution because the movement was non-political and included both Patriots and their enemy, the Loyalists. Regarding the movement's influence on the European continent, German historian Reinhart Koselleck claimed that "On the Continent there were two social structures that left a decisive imprint on the Age of Enlightenment: the Republic of Letters and the Masonic lodges.", while professor at University of Glasgow Thomas Munck argues that "although the Masons did promote international and cross-social contacts which were essentially non-religious and broadly in agreement with enlightened values, they can hardly be described as a major radical or reformist network in their own right."

Freemasonic lodges originated from English and Scottish stonemasonic guilds in the 17th century. In the 18th century, they expanded into an extremely widespread collection of interconnected (to varying degrees) men's, and occasionally women's, associations which Margaret Jacob contends had their own mythologies and special codes of conduct—including a communal understanding of liberty and equality inherited from guild sociability—"liberty, fraternity, and equality". The remarkable similarity between these values, which were generally common in Britain as on the Continent, and the French Revolutionary slogan of "Liberté, égalité, fraternité" spawned many conspiracy theories. Notably, Abbé Barruel traced the origins of the Jacobins—and hence the Revolution—to the French freemasons. Freemasonry was officially established on the continent of Europe in 1734, when a lodge was set up in the Hague, although the first "fully formed lodge" appears to have met in 1721 in Rotterdam. Similarly, there are records of a Parisian lodge meeting in 1725 or 1726. As Daniel Roche writes, freemasonry was particularly prevalent in France—by 1789, there were perhaps as many as 100,000 French Masons, making Freemasonry the most popular of all Enlightenment associations. Freemasonry does not appear to have been confined to western Europe, however, as Margaret Jacob writes of lodges in Saxony in 1729 and in Russia in 1731. Conspiracy theories aside, it is likely that masonic lodges had an effect on society as a whole. Jacob argues that they "reconstituted the polity and established a constitutional form of self-government, complete with constitutions and laws, elections and representatives". In other words, the micro-society set up within the lodges constituted a normative model for society as a whole. This was especially true on the Continent: when the first lodges began to appear in the 1730s, their embodiment of British values was often seen as threatening by state authorities. For example, the Parisian lodge that met in the mid 1720s was composed of English Jacobite exiles. Furthermore, freemasons all across Europe made reference to the Enlightenment in general in the 18th century. In French lodges, for example, the line "As the means to be enlightened I search for the enlightened" was a part of their initiation rites. British lodges assigned themselves the duty to "initiate the unenlightened". This did not necessarily link lodges to the irreligious, but neither did this exclude them from the occasional heresy. In fact, many lodges praised the Grand Architect, the masonic terminology for the divine being who created a scientifically ordered universe. On the other hand, Daniel Roche contests freemasonry's claims for egalitarianism, writing that "the real equality of the lodges was elitist", only attracting men of similar social backgrounds. This lack of real equality was made explicit by the constitution of the Lausanne Switzerland lodge (1741):

> *The order of freemasons is a society of confraternity and equality, and to this end is represented under the emblem of a level ... a brother renders to another brother the honor and deference that is justly due him in proportion to his rank in the civil society.*

Elitism was beneficial for some members of society. The presence, for example, of noble women in the French "lodges of adoption" that formed in the 1780s was largely due to the close ties shared between these lodges and aristocratic society.

Salons: a Historiographical Overview

Enlightenment historiography began in the period itself, from what "Enlightenment figures" said about their work. A dominant element was the intellectual angle they took. D'Alembert's *Preliminary Discourse of l'Encyclopédie* provides a history of the Enlightenment which comprises a chronological list of developments in the realm of knowledge—of which the *Encyclopédie* forms the pinnacle. A more philosophical example of this was the 1783 essay contest (in itself an activity typical of the Enlightenment) announced by the Berlin newspaper *Berlinische Monatsschrift*, which asked that very question: "What is Enlightenment?" Jewish philosopher Moses Mendelssohn was among those who responded, referring to Enlightenment as a process by which man was educated in the use of reason (*Jerusalem*, 1783). Immanuel Kant also wrote a response, referring to Enlightenment as "man's release from his self-incurred tutelage", tutelage being "man's inability to make use of his understanding without direction from another". This intellectual model of interpretation has been adopted by many historians since the 18th century, and is perhaps the most commonly used interpretation today. Dorinda Outram provides a good example of a standard, intellectual definition of the Enlightenment:

> *Enlightenment was a desire for human affairs to be guided by rationality rather than by faith, superstition, or revelation; a belief in the power of human reason to change society and liberate the individual from the restraints of custom or arbitrary authority; all backed up by a world view increasingly validated by science rather than by religion or tradition.*

Like the French Revolution, the Enlightenment has long been hailed as the foundation of modern western political and intellectual culture. It has been frequently linked to the French Revolution of 1789. However, as Roger Chartier points out, it was perhaps the Revolution that "invented the Enlightenment by attempting to root its legitimacy in a corpus of texts and founding authors reconciled and united ... by their preparation of a rupture with the old world". In other words, the revolutionaries elevated to heroic status those philosophers, such as Voltaire and Rousseau, who could be used to justify their radical break with the Ancien Régime. In any case, two 19th-century historians of the Enlightenment, Hippolyte Taine and Alexis de Tocqueville, did much to solidify this link of Enlightenment causing revolution and the intellectual perception of the Enlightenment itself. In his *Le Régime* (1876), Hippolyte Taine traced the roots of the French Revolution back to French Classicism. However, this was not without the help of the scientific view of the world [of the Enlightenment], which wore down the "monarchical and religious dogma of the old regime". In other words then, Taine was only interested in the Enlightenment insofar as it advanced scientific discourse and transmitted what he perceived to be the intellectual legacy of French classicism. Alexis de Tocqueville painted a more elaborate picture of the Enlightenment in *L'Ancien Régime et la Révolution* (1850). For de Tocqueville, the Revolution was the inevitable result of the radical opposition created in the 18th century between the monarchy and the men of letters of the Enlightenment. These men of letters constituted a sort of "substitute aristocracy that was both all-powerful and without real power". This illusory power came from the rise of "public opinion", born when absolutist centralization removed the nobility and the bourgeosie from the political sphere. The "literary politics" that resulted promoted a discourse of equality and was hence in fundamental opposition to the monarchical regime. From a historiographical point of view, de Tocqueville presents an interesting case. He was primarily concerned with the workings of political power under the Ancien Régime and the philosophical principles of the men of letters. However, there is a distinctly social quality to his analysis. In the words of Chartier, de Tocqueville "clearly designates ... the cultural effects of transformation in the forms of the exercise of power". Nevertheless, for a serious cultural approach, one has to wait another century for the work of historians such as Robert Darnton, *The Business of Enlightenment: A Publishing History of the Encyclopédie*, 1775—1800 (1979). In the meantime, though, intellectual history remained the dominant historiographical trend. The German scholar Ernst Cassirer is typical, writing in his *The Philosophy of the Enlightenment* that the Enlightenment was " a part and a special phase of that whole intellectual development through which modern philosophic thought gained its characteristic self-confidence and self-consciousness". Borrowing from Kant, Cassirer states that Enlightenment is the process by which the spirit "achieves clarity and depth in its understanding of its own nature and destiny, and of its own fundamental character and mission". In short, the Enlightenment was a series of philosophical, scientific and otherwise intellectual developments that took place mostly in the 18th century—the birthplace of intellectual modernity.

Recent Work

Only in the 1970s did interpretation of the Enlightenment allow for a more heterogeneous and even extra-European vision. A. Owen Aldridge demonstrated how Enlightenment ideas spread to Spanish colonies and how they interacted with indigenous cultures, while Franco Venturi explored how the Enlightenment took place in normally unstudied areas—Italy, Greece, the Balkans, Poland, Hungary, and Russia. Robert Darnton's cultural approach launched a new dimension of studies. He said:

> *Perhaps the Enlightenment was a more down-to-earth affair than the rarefied climate of opinion described by textbook writers, and we should question the overly highbrow, overly metaphysical view of intellectual life in the eighteenth century.*

Darnton examines the underbelly of the French book industry in the 18th century, examining the world of book smuggling and the lives of those writers (the "Grub Street Hacks") who never met the success of their *philosophe* cousins. In short, rather than concerning himself with Enlightenment canon, Darnton studies "what Frenchmen wanted to read", and who wrote, published and distributed it. Similarly, in *The Business of Enlightenment: A Publishing History of the Encyclopédie 1775—1800*, Darnton states that there is no need to further study the encyclopédia itself, as "the book has been analyzed and anthologized dozen of times: to recapitulate all the studies of its intellectual content would be redundant". He instead, as the title of the book suggests, examines the social conditions that brought about the production of the *Encyclopédie*. This is representative of the social interpretation as a whole—an examination of the social conditions that brought about Enlightenment ideas rather than a study of the ideas themselves. Another very important reform of Joseph II was the abolition of serfdom. The work of German philosopher Jürgen Habermas was central to this emerging social interpretation; his seminal work *The Structural Transformation of the Public Sphere* (published under the title *Strukturwandel der Öfentlicheit* in 1962) was translated into English in 1989. The book outlines the creation of the "bourgeois public sphere" in 18th century Europe. Essentially, this public sphere describes the new venues and modes of communication allowing for rational exchange that appeared in the 18th century. Habermas argued that the public sphere was bourgeois, egalitarian, rational, and independent from the state, making it the ideal venue for intellectuals to critically examine contemporary politics and society, away from the interference of established authority. Habermas's work, though influential, has come under criticism on all fronts. While the public sphere is generally an integral component of social interpretations of the Enlightenment, numerous historians have brought into question whether the public sphere was bourgeois, oppositional to the state, independent from the state, or egalitarian. These historiographical developments have done much to open up the study of Enlightenment to a multiplicity of interpretations. In *A Social History of Truth* (1994), for example, Steven Shapin makes the largely sociological argument that, in 17th-century England, the mode of sociability known as civility became the primary discourse of truth; for a statement to have the potential to be considered true, it had to be expressed according to the rules of civil society. Feminist interpretations have also appeared, with Dena Goodman being one notable example. In *The Republic of Letters: A Cultural History of the French Enlightenment* (1994), Goodman argues that many women in fact played an essential part in the French Enlightenment, due to the role they played as *salonnières* in Parisians salons. These salons "became the civil working spaces of the project of Enlightenment" and women, as *salonnières*, were "the legitimate governors of [the] potentially unruly discourse" that took place within. On the other hand, Carla Hesse, in *The Other Enlightenment: How French Women Became Modern* (2001), argues that "female participation in the public cultural life of the Old Regime was ... relatively marginal". It was instead the French Revolution, by destroying the old cultural and economic restraints of patronage and corporatism (guilds), that opened French society to female participation, particularly in the literary sphere.

Questions and Topics for Pondering and Further Discussion for Unit Six-2:

1. What does Enlightenment Movement try to enlighten?
2. Some people say that Enlightenment Movement is a soul liberation movement. Please comment.
3. Enlightenment Movement is a movement of ideas explosion. What ideas did the Movement ignite?
4. Who are the chief representatives of Enlightenment Movement thinkers? What are their chief ideas?
5. Montesquieu is one of the giant figures during Enlightenment Movement. Please list his contributions.
6. What is the main idea of John Locke?
7. How much do you know about Newton?
8. Modern science rose in Europe in the 17th century, introducing a new understanding of the natural world. What does this new understanding of the natural world imply?

3. Post-Modernity (POMO), a Rebellious Movement[①]

Postmodernity (also spelled **post-modernity** or termed the **postmodern condition**) is generally used to describe the economic or cultural state or condition of society which is said to exist after modernity. Some schools of thought hold that modernity ended in the late 20th century, in the 1980s or early 1990s replaced by postmodernity, while others would extend modernity to cover the developments denoted by postmodernity, while some believe that modernity ended after World War Ⅱ. Postmodernity can mean a personal response to a postmodern society, the conditions in a society which make it postmodern or the state of being that is associated with a postmodern society. In most contexts it should be distinguished from postmodernism, the conscious, unconscious and/or subconscious adoption of postmodern philosophies or traits in art, literature, culture and society. Postmodernity is the state or condition of being postmodern— after or in reaction to that which is modern, as in postmodern art (see postmodernism). Modernity is defined as a period or condition loosely identified with the Progressive Era, the Industrial Revolution, or the Enlightenment. In philosophy and critical theory postmodernity refers to the state or condition of society which is said to exist after modernity, a historical condition that marks the reasons for the end of modernity. This usage is ascribed to the philosophers Jean-François Lyotard and Jean Baudrillard. One "project" of modernity is said by Habermas to have been the fostering of progress by incorporating principles of rationality and hierarchy into public and artistic life. (See also postindustrial, Information Age.) Lyotard understood modernity as a cultural condition characterized by constant change in the pursuit of progress. Postmodernity then represents the culmination of this process where constant change has become the *status quo* and the notion of progress obsolete. Following Ludwig Wittgenstein's critique of the possibility of absolute and total knowledge Lyotard further argued that the various metanarratives of progress such as positivist science, Marxism, and structuralism were defunct as methods of achieving progress. The literary critic Fredric Jameson and the geographer David Harvey have identified postmodernity with "late capitalism" or "flexible accumulation", a stage of capitalism following finance capitalism, characterized by highly mobile labor and capital and what Harvey called "time and space compression". They suggest that this coincides with the breakdown of the Bretton Woods system which, they believe, defined the economic order following the Second World War. (See also consumerism, critical theory.) Those who generally view modernity as obsolete or an outright failure, a flaw in humanity's evolution leading to disasters like Auschwitz and Hiroshima, see postmodernity as a positive development. Many philosophers, particularly those seeing themselves as within the modern project, use postmodernity to imply the presumed results of holding postmodernist ideas. Most prominently Jürgen Habermas and others contend that postmodernity represents a resurgence of long running counter-enlightenment ideas, that the modern project is not finished and that universality cannot be so lightly dispensed with. Postmodernity, the consequence of holding postmodern ideas, is generally a negative term in this context.

[①] This material is the result of mixed information taken from *Wikipedia* entry of POMO and some other dictionary definitions of modernity and post-modernity such as *Free Dictionary* by Farlex on-line. Please visit its website at www.thefreedictionary.com for more information in this regard.

Postmodernism (POMO Movement)

Postmodernity is a condition or a state of being associated with changes to institutions and conditions (Giddens, 1990) and with social and political results and innovations, globally but especially in the West since the 1950s, whereas postmodernism is an aesthetic, literary, political or social philosophy, the "cultural and intellectual phenomenon", especially since the 1920s' new movements in the arts. Both of these terms are used by philosophers, social scientists and social critics to refer to aspects of contemporary culture, economics and society that are the result of features of late 20th century and early 21st century life, including the fragmentation of authority and the commoditization of knowledge. The relationship between postmodernity and critical theory, sociology and philosophy is fiercely contested. The terms "postmodernity" and "postmodernism" are often hard to distinguish, the former being often the result of the latter. The period has had diverse political ramifications: its "anti-ideological ideas" appear to have been positively associated with the feminist movement, racial equality movements, gay rights movements, most forms of late 20th century anarchism and even the peace movement as well as various hybrids of these in the current anti-globalization movement. Though none of these institutions entirely embraces all aspects of the postmodern movement in its most concentrated definition they all reflect, or borrow from, some of its core ideas.

History of Such Intellectual Movement

Some authors, such as Lyotard and Baudrillard, believe that modernity ended in the late 20th century and thus have defined a period subsequent to modernity, namely postmodernity, while others, such as Bauman and Giddens, would extend modernity to cover the developments denoted by postmodernity. Others still contend that modernity ended with the Victorian Age in the 1900s. Postmodernity has been said to have gone through two relatively distinct phases, the first beginning in the late 1940s and 1950s and ending with the Cold War (when analog media with limited bandwidth encouraged a few, authoritative media channels) and the second beginning at the end of the Cold War (marked by the spread of cable television and "new media" based on digital means of information dissemination and broadcast). The first phase of postmodernity overlaps the end of modernity and is regarded by many as being part of the modern period (see lumpers/splitters, periodization). Television became the primary news source, manufacturing decreased in importance in the economies of western Europe and the United States but trade volumes increased within the developed core. In 1967—1969 a crucial cultural explosion took place within the developed world as the baby boom generation, which had grown up with postmodernity as their fundamental experience of society, demanded entrance into the political, cultural and educational power structure. A series of demonstrations and acts of rebellion—ranging from nonviolent and cultural, through violent acts of terrorism—represented the opposition of the young to the policies and perspectives of the previous age. Opposition to the Algerian War and the Vietnam War, to laws allowing or encouraging racial segregation and to laws which overtly discriminated against women and restricted access to divorce, increased use of marijuana and hallucinogens, the emergence of pop cultural styles of music and drama, including rock music and the ubiquity of stereo, television and radio helped make these changes visible in the broader cultural context. This period is associated with the work of Marshall McLuhan, a philosopher who focused on the results of living in a media culture and argued that participation in a mass media culture both overshadows actual content disseminated and is liberating because it loosens the authority of local social normative standards.

The second phase of postmodernity is defined by "digitality"—the increasing power of personal and digital means of communication including fax machines, modems, cable and high speed internet, which has altered the condition of postmodernity dramatically: digital production of information allows individuals to manipulate virtually every aspect of the media environment. This has brought producers into conflict with consumers over intellectual capital and intellectual property and led to the creation of a new economy whose supporters argue that the dramatic fall in information costs will alter society fundamentally. It began to be argued that digitality or what Esther Dyson referred to as "being digital" had emerged as a separate condition from postmodernity. Those holding this position argued that the ability to manipulate items of popular culture, the World Wide Web, the use of search engines to index knowledge, and telecommunications were producing a "convergence" which would be marked by the rise of "participatory culture" in the words of Henry Jenkins and the use of media appliances, such as Apple's iPod. The simplest, but not necessarily most correct demarcation point of this era is the collapse of the Soviet Union in 1991 and the liberalization of China in 1949. Francis Fukuyama wrote "The End of History" in 1989 in anticipation of the fall of the Berlin wall. He predicted that the question of political philosophy had been answered, that large scale wars over fundamental values would no longer arise since "all prior contradictions are resolved and all human needs satisfied." This is a kind of "endism" also taken up Arthur Danto who in 1984 acclaimed that Andy Warhol's Brillo boxes asked the right question of art and hence art had ended.

Descriptions/Distinctions in Philosophy and Critical Theory

The debate on postmodernity has two distinct elements that are often confused: (1) the nature of contemporary society and (2) the nature of the critique of contemporary society. The first of these elements is concerned with the nature of changes that took place during the late 20th century. There are three principal analyses. Theorists such as Callinicos (1991) and Calhoun (1995) offer a conservative position on the nature of contemporary society, downplaying the significance and extent of socio-economic changes and emphasizing a continuity with the past. Second a range of theorists have tried to analyze the present as a development of the "modern" project into a second, distinct phase that is nevertheless still "modernity": this has been termed the "second" or "risk" society by Ulrich Beck (1986), "late" or "high" modernity by Giddens (1990, 1991), "liquid" modernity by Zygmunt Bauman (2000), and the "network" society by Castells (1996, 1997). Third are those who argue that contemporary society has moved into a literally post-modern phase distinct from modernity. The most prominent proponents of this position are Lyotard and Baudrillard. Another set of issues concerns the nature of critique, often replaying debates over (what can be crudely termed) universalism and relativism, where modernism is seen to represent the former and postmodernity the latter. Seyla Benhabib (1995) and Judith Butler (1995) pursue this debate can be found in relation to feminist politics, Benhabib arguing that postmodern critique comprises three main elements; an anti-foundationalist concept of the subject and identity, the death of history and of notions of teleology and progress, and the death of metaphysics defined as the search for objective truth. Benhabib argues forcefully against these critical positions, holding that they undermine the bases upon which feminist politics can be founded, removing the possibility of agency, the sense of self-hood and the appropriation of women's history in the name of an emancipated future. The denial of normative ideals removes the possibility for utopia, central for ethical thinking and democratic action. Butler responds to Benhabib by arguing that her use of postmodernism is an expression of a wider paranoia over anti-foundationalist philosophy, in particular, poststructuralism.

A number of positions are ascribed to postmodernism—Discourse is all there is, as if discourse were some kind of monistic stuff out of which all things are composed; the subject is dead, I can never say "I" again; there is no reality, only representation. These characterizations are variously imputed to postmodernism or poststructuralism, which are conflated with each other and sometimes conflated with deconstruction, and understood as an indiscriminate assemblage of French feminism, deconstruction, Lacanian psychoanalysis, Foucauldian analysis, Rorty's conversationalism, and cultural studies. In reality, these movements are opposed: Lacanian psychoanalysis in France positions itself officially against poststructuralism, that Foucauldian rarely relate to Derridideans and Lyotard champions the term, but he cannot be made into the example of what all the rest of the purported postmodernists are doing. Lyotard's work is, for instance, seriously at odds with that of Derrida. Butler uses the debate over the nature of the post-modernist critique to demonstrate how philosophy is implicated in power relationships and defends post-structuralist critique by arguing that the critique of the subject itself is the beginning of analysis, not the end, because the first task of inquiry is the questioning of accepted "universal" and "objective" norms. The Benhabib-Butler debate demonstrates that there is no simple definition of a postmodern theorist as the very definition of postmodernity itself is contested. Michel Foucault rejected the label of postmodernism explicitly in interviews yet is seen by many, such as Benhabib, as advocating a form of critique that is "postmodern" in that it breaks with Utopian and transcendental "modern" critiques by calling universal norms of the Enlightenment into question. Giddens (1990) rejects this characterization of "modern critique", pointing out that a critique of Enlightenment universals was central to philosophers of the modern period, most notably Nietzsche.

Postmodern Society Outlined

Jameson views a number of phenomena as distinguishing postmodernity from modernity. First of all, he speaks of "a new kind of superficiality" or "depthlessness" in which models that once explained people and things in terms of an "inside" and an "outside" (such as hermeneutics, the dialectic, Freudian repression, the existentialist distinction between authenticity and inauthenticity and the semiotic distinction of signifier and signified) have been rejected. The second is a rejection of the modernist "Utopian gesture", evident in Van Gogh, of the transformation through art of misery into beauty whereas in the postmodernism movement the object world has undergone a "fundamental mutation" so that it has "now become a set of texts or simulacra". Whereas modernist art sought to redeem and sacralize the world, to give life to world (we might say, following Graff, to give the world back the enchantment that science and the decline of religion had taken away from it), postmodernist art bestows upon the world a "deathly quality... whose glacéd X-ray elegance mortifies the reified eye of the viewer in a way that would seem to have nothing to do with death or the death obsession or the death anxiety on the level of content". Graff sees the origins of this transformative mission of art in an attempted substitution of art for religion in giving meaning to the world that the rise of science and Enlightenment rationality had removed—but in the postmodern period this is seen as futile. The third feature of the postmodern age that Jameson identifies is the "waning of affect"—not that all emotion has disappeared from the postmodern age but that it lacks a particular kind of emotion such as that found in "Rimbaud's magical flowers 'that look back at you'". He notes that "pastiche eclipses parody" as "the increasing unavailability of the personal style" leads to pastiche becoming a universal practice. Jameson argues that distance "has been abolished" in postmodernity, that we "are submerged in its henceforth filled and suffused volumes to the point where our now postmodern bodies are bereft of spatial co-ordinates". This "new global space" constitutes postmodernity's "moment of truth". The various other features of the postmodern that he identifies "can all now be seen as themselves partial (yet constitutive) aspects of the same general spatial object". The postmodern era has seen a change in the social function of culture. He identifies culture in the modern age as having had a property of "semi-autonomy", with an "existence... above the practical world of the existent" but, in the postmodern age, culture has been deprived of this autonomy, the cultural has expanded to consume the entire social realm so that all becomes "cultural". "Critical distance", the assumption that culture can be positioned outside "the massive Being of capital" upon which left-Wing theories of cultural politics are dependent, has become outmoded. The "prodigious new expansion of multinational capital ends up penetrating and colonizing those very pre-capitalist enclaves (Nature and the Unconscious) which offered extraterritorial and Archimedean footholds for critical effectivity".

Social Sciences Definition of Post-Modernity

Postmodern sociology can be said to focus on conditions of life which became increasingly prevalent in the late 20th century in the most industrialized nations, including the ubiquity of mass media and mass production, the rise of a global economy and a shift from manufacturing to service economies. Jameson and Harvey described it as consumerism, where manufacturing, distribution and dissemination have become exceptionally inexpensive but social connectedness and community have become rarer. Other thinkers assert that postmodernity is the natural reaction to mass broadcasting in a society conditioned to mass production and mass politics. The work of Alasdair MacIntyre informs the versions of postmodernism elaborated by such authors as Murphy (2003) and Bielskis (2005), for whom MacIntyre's postmodern revision of Aristotelianism poses a challenge to the kind of consumerist ideology that now promotes capital accumulation. The sociological view of postmodernity ascribes it to more rapid transportation, wider communication and the ability to abandon standardization of mass production, leading to a system which values a wider range of capital than previously and allows value to be stored in a greater variety of forms. Harvey argues that postmodernity is an escape from "Fordism", a term coined by Antonio Gramsci to describe the mode of industrial regulation and accumulation which prevailed during the Keynesian era of economic policy in OECD countries from the early 1930s to the 1970s. Fordism for Harvey is associated with Keynesianism in that the first concerns methods of production and capital-labor relations while the latter concerns economic policy and regulation. Post-fordism is therefore one of the basic aspects of postmodernity from Harvey's point of view. Artifacts of postmodernity include the dominance of television and popular culture, the wide accessibility of information and mass telecommunications. Postmodernity also exhibits a greater resistance to making sacrifices in the name of progress discernible in environmentalism and the growing importance of the anti-war movement. Postmodernity in the industrialized core is marked by increasing focus on civil rights and equal opportunity as well as movements such as feminism and multiculturalism and the backlash against these movements. The postmodern political sphere is marked by multiple arenas and possibilities of citizenship and political action concerning various forms of struggle against oppression or alienation (in collectives defined by sex or ethnicity) while the modernist political arena remains restricted to class struggle. Theorists such as Michel Maffesoli believe that postmodernity is corroding the circumstances that provide for its subsistence and will eventually result in a decline of individualism and the birth of a new neo-Tribal era.

Economic and technological conditions of our age have given rise to a decentralized, media-dominated society in which ideas are only simulacra, inter-referential representations and copies of each other with no real, original, stable or objective source of communication and meaning. Globalization, brought on by innovations in communication, manufacturing and transportation, is often cited as one force which has driven the decentralized modern life, creating a culturally pluralistic and interconnected global society lacking any single dominant center of political power, communication or intellectual production. The postmodernist view is that inter-subjective, not objective, knowledge will be the dominant form of discourse under such conditions and that ubiquity of dissemination fundamentally alters the relationship between reader and that which is read, between observer and the observed, between those who consume and those who produce. In *Spaces of Hope* Harvey argues that postmodern political movements have been indirectly responsible for weakening class issues (in the Marxist sense) and the critical consciousness of this field of action which, in his opinion, is now more significant than during the Fordist period. For Harvey this class conflict is far from solved (something postmodern theorists ignore, according to his argument); globalization has made it more difficult for labor organizations to tackle underpaid work in poor conditions without labour rights and the amount of surplus value earned by corporations is far larger because of the differential between the high prices paid by western consumers and the low wages earned by south-East Asian laborers.

Criticisms

Criticisms of the postmodern condition can broadly be put into four categories: criticisms of postmodernity from the perspective of those who reject modernism and its offshoots, criticisms from supporters of modernism who believe that postmodernity lacks crucial characteristics of the modern project, critics from within postmodernity who seek reform or change based on their understanding of postmodernism, and those who believe that postmodernity is a passing, and not a growing, phase in social organization.

> *We could say that every age has its own postmodern, just as every age has its own form of mannerism (in fact, I wonder if postmodern is not simply the modern name for Manierismus). I believe that every age reaches moments of crisis like those described by Nietzsche in the second of the Untimely Considerations, on the harmfulness of the study of history (Historiography). The sense that the past is restricting, smothering, blackmailing us.*

—Umberto Eco, "A Correspondence on Postmodernism" with Stefano Rosso in Hoesterey.

Questions and Topics for Pondering and Further Discussion for Unit Six-3:

1. What is modernity?
2. What is post-modernity?
3. Is modernity a relative term or absolute one?
4. What is the relationship between time and modernity?
5. What is the major spiritual tenet of postmodernism?
6. Does tradition imply backwardness?
7. What is meant by progress?
8. What are the main features of postmodern sociology? Any differences between traditional sociology and postmodern one?

Unit Seven

1. Commercial Revolution, in Hot Pursuit of Wealth

Editor's remarks: *one of the ideas that influenced the western way of thinking is business ethic and commercial mentality through trade on voluntary basis or sometimes by force. Commercial value and idea are key to the rise of the West, bringing huge material benefits to the West. Great geographical discoveries gave rise to the spirit of adventures of westerners who began to explore the unknown parts of the world, starting an age of global commerce. It is against this macro social background that Commercial Revolution began, which marked the beginning of the age of western dominance over the world. Such concepts as market value, material success, money worship and personal welfare and happiness all originated from this revolution. Commercial Revolution also paved the way for the rise and expansion of colonialism and capitalism as well as for the coming of the Industrial Revolution.*

The Commercial Revolution was a period of European economic expansion, colonialism, and mercantilism which lasted from approximately the 16th century until the early 18th century. It was succeeded in the mid-18th century by the Industrial Revolution. Beginning with the Crusades, Europeans rediscovered spices, silks, and other commodities rare in Europe. This development created a new desire for trade, and trade expanded in the second half of the Middle Ages. European nations, through voyages of discovery, were looking for new trade routes in the 15th and 16th centuries, which allowed the European powers to build vast, new international trade networks. Nations also sought new sources of wealth. To deal with this new-found wealth, new economic theories and practices were created. Because of competing national interest, nations had the desire for increased world power through their colonial empires. The Commercial Revolution is marked by an increase in general commerce, and in the growth of financial services such as banking, insurance, and investing.

Origins of the Term and Time Frame

The term itself was coined in the middle of the 20th century, by economic historian Roberto Sabatino Lopez, to shift focus away from the English Industrial Revolution. In his best-known book, *The Commercial Revolution of the Middle Ages* (1971, with numerous reprints), Lopez argued that the key contribution of the medieval period to European history was the creation of a commercial economy, centered at first in the Italo-Byzantine eastern Mediterranean, but eventually extending to the Italian city-states and over the rest of Europe. The commercial revolution ran from approximately the late 14th century, through the 18th century, with Walt Whitman Rostow saying the beginning is "arbitrarily" 1488, the year the first European sailed around the Cape of Good Hope. Historian Peter Spufford indicates that there was a commercial revolution of the 13th century, or that it began at this point, rather than later.

Factors of Commercial Revolution

Portuguese discoveries and explorations from 1415 to 1543: first arrival places and dates; main Portuguese spice trade routes in the Indian Ocean; territories of the Portuguese Empire under the rule of King John Ⅲ (1521—1557). A combination of factors drove the Age of Discovery. Among these were geopolitical, monetary, and technological factors. The Europeans involved in the Age of Discovery were mainly from Britain, France, the Netherlands, Spain, and Portugal. During this period (1450—17th century), the European economic center shifted from the Islamic Mediterranean to western Europe (Portugal, Spain, France, the Netherlands, and to some extent England). This shift was caused by the successful circumnavigation of Africa opening up sea-trade with the East; after Portugal's Vasco da Gama rounded the Cape of Good Hope and landed in Calicut, India in May 1498, a new path of eastern trade was possible ending the monopoly of the Ottoman Turks and their European allies, the Italian city-states. The wealth of the Indies was now open for the Europeans to explore; the Portuguese Empire was one of the early European empires to grow from spice trade. Following this, Portugal became the controlling state for trade between East and West, followed later by the Dutch city of Antwerp. Direct maritime trade between Europe and China started in the 16th century, after the Portuguese established the settlement of Goa, India in December 1510, and thereafter that of Macau in southern China in 1557. Since the English came late to the transatlantic trade, their commercial revolution was later as well.

Geopolitical Factors

In 1453, the Ottoman Turks took over Constantinople, which cut off (or significantly increased the cost of) overland trade routes to the Far East, so alternate routes had to be found. English laws were changed to benefit the navy, but had commercial implications in terms of farming. These laws also contributed to the demise of the Hanseatic League, which traded in northern Europe. Because of the Reconquista, the Spanish had a warrior culture ready to conquer still more people and places, so Spain was perfectly positioned to develop their vast overseas empire. Rivalry between the European powers produced intense competition for the creation of colonial empires, and fueled the rush to sail out of Europe.

Monetary Factors

The need for silver coinage also had an impact on the desire for expanded exploration as silver and gold were spent for trade to the Middle and Far East. The Europeans had a constant deficit in that silver and gold coin only went one way: out of Europe, spent on the very type of trade that they were now cut off from by the Ottomans. Another issue was that European mines were exhausted of silver and gold ore. What ore remained was too deep to recover, as water would fill the mine, and technology was not sufficiently advanced enough to successfully remove the water to get to the ore.

Technological Factors

In 1570 (May 20) Gilles Coppens de Diest at Antwerp published 53 maps created by Abraham Ortelius under the title *Theatrum Orbis Terrarum*, considered the "first modern atlas". Latin editions, besides Dutch, French and German editions appeared before the end of 1572; the atlas continued to be in demand till about 1612. This is the world map from this atlas. From the 16th to 18th centuries, Europeans made remarkable maritime innovations. These innovations enabled them to expand overseas and set up colonies, most notably during the 16th and 17th centuries. They developed new sail arrangements for ships, skeleton-based shipbuilding, the western "galea" (at the end of the 11th century), sophisticated navigational instruments, and detailed charts and maps. After Isaac Newton published the *Principia*, navigation was transformed, because sailors could predict the motion of the moon and other celestial objects using Newton's theories of motion. Starting in 1670, the entire world was measured using essentially modern latitude instruments. In 1676, the British Parliament declared that navigation was the greatest scientific problem of the age and in 1714 offered a substantial financial prize for the solution to finding longitude. This spurred the development of the marine chronometer, the lunar distance method and the invention of the octant after 1730. By the late 18th century, navigators replaced their prior instruments with octants and sextants.

Important People

Significant contributors to European exploration include Prince Henry the Navigator of Portugal, who was the first of the Europeans to venture out into the Atlantic Ocean, in 1420. Others are Bartolomeu Dias, who first rounded the Cape of Good Hope; Vasco da Gama, who sailed directly to India from Portugal; Ferdinand Magellan, the first to circumnavigate the Earth; Christopher Columbus, who significantly encountered the Americas; Jacques Cartier, who sailed for France, looking for the Northwest Passage; and others.

Key Features

The economy of the Roman Empire had been based on money, but after the Empire's fall, money became scarce; power and wealth became strictly land based, and local fiefs were self-sufficient. Because trade was dangerous and expensive, there were not many traders, and not much trade. The scarcity of money did not help; however, the European economic system had begun to change in the 14th century, partially as a result of the Black Death, and the Crusades.

Banks, stock exchanges, and insurance became ways to manage the risk involved in the renewed trade. New laws came into being. Travel became safer as nations developed. Economic theories began to develop in light of all of the new trading activity. The increase in the availability of money led to the emergence of a new economic system, and new problems to go with it. The Commercial Revolution is also marked by the formalization of pre-existing, informal methods of dealing with trade and commerce.

Inflation

Spain legally amassed approximately 180 tons of gold and 8,200 tons of silver through its endeavors in the New World, and another unknown amount through smuggling, spending this money to finance wars and the arts. The spent silver, suddenly being spread throughout a previously cash starved Europe, caused widespread inflation. The inflation was worsened by a growing population but a static production level, low employee salaries and a rising cost of living. This problem, combined with underpopulation (caused by the Black Death), affected the system of agriculture. The landholding aristocracy suffered under the inflation, since they depended on paying small, fixed wages to peasant tenants that were becoming able to demand higher wages. The aristocracy made failed attempts to counteract this situation by creating short-term leases of their lands to allow periodic revaluation of rent. The manorial system (manor system of lord and peasant tenant) eventually vanished, and the landholding aristocrats were forced to sell pieces of their land in order to maintain their style of living. Such sales attracted the rich bourgeois (from the French word referring to this dominant class, emerging with commerce), who wanted to buy land and thereby increased their social status. Former "common lands" were fenced by the landed bourgeois, a process known as "enclosure" which increased the efficiency of raising livestock (mainly sheep's wool for the textile industry). This "enclosure" forced the peasants out of rural areas and into the cities, resulting in urbanization and eventually the industrial revolution. On the other hand, the increase in the availability of silver coin allowed for commerce to expand in numerous ways. Inflation was not all bad.

Banks and Banking Industry

Various legal and religious developments in the late Middle Ages allowed for development of the modern banking system at the beginning of the 16th century. Interest was allowed to be charged, and profits generated from holding other people's money. Banks in the Italian Peninsula had great difficulty operating at the end of the 14th century, for lack of silver and gold coin. Nevertheless, by the later 16th century, enough bullion was available that many more people could keep a small amount hoarded and used as capital. In response to this extra available money, northern European banking interests came along; among them was the Fugger family. The Fuggers were originally mine owners, but soon became involved in banking, charging interest, and other financial activities. They dealt with everyone, from small time individuals, to the highest nobility. Their banks even loaned to the emperors and kings, eventually going bankrupt when their clients defaulted. This family, and other individuals, used Italian methods which outpaced the Hanseatic League's ability to keep up with the changes occurring in northern Europe. Antwerp had one of the first money exchanges in Europe, a Bourse, where people could change currency. After the Siege of Antwerp (1584—1585), the majority of business transactions were moved to Amsterdam. The Bank of Amsterdam, following the example of a private Stockholm corporation, began issuing paper money to lessen the difficulty of trade, replacing metal (coin and bullion) in exchanges. In 1609 the *Amsterdamsche Wisselbank* (Amsterdam Exchange Bank) was founded which made Amsterdam the financial center of the world until the Industrial Revolution. In a notable example of crossover between stock companies and banks, the Bank of England, which opened in 1694, was a joint-stock company. Banking offices were usually located near centers of trade, and in the late 17th century, the largest centers for commerce were the ports of Amsterdam, London, and Hamburg. Individuals could participate in the lucrative East India trade by purchasing bills of credit from these banks, but the price they received for commodities was dependent on the ships returning (which often did not happen on time) and on the cargo they carried (which often was not according to plan). The commodities market was very volatile for this reason, and also because of the many wars that led to cargo seizures and loss of ships.

Managing Risk of Production of Wealth

Trade in this period was a risky business: war, weather, and other uncertainties often kept merchants from making a profit, and frequently an entire cargo would disappear all together. To mitigate this risk, the wealthy got together to share the risk through stock: people would own shares of a venture, so that if there was a loss, it would not be an all consuming loss costing the individual investor everything in one transaction. Other ways of dealing with the risk and expense associated with all of the new trade activity include insurance and joint stock companies which were created as formal institutions. People had been informally sharing risk for hundreds of years, but the formal ways they were now sharing risk was new. Even though the ruling classes would not often directly assist in trade endeavors, and individuals were unequal to the task, rulers such as Henry VIII of England established a permanent Royal Navy, with the intention of reducing piracy, and protecting English shipping.

Joint Stock Companies and Stock Exchanges

Stock exchanges were developed as the volume of stock transactions increased. The London

Royal Exchange established in 1565 first developed as a securities market, though by 1801 it had become a stock exchange. Historian Fernand Braudel suggests that in Cairo in the 11th century Muslim and Jewish merchants had already set up every form of trade association and had knowledge of every method of credit and payment, disproving the belief that these were invented later by Italians. In 12th century France the *courratiers de change* were concerned with managing and regulating the debts of agricultural communities on behalf of the banks. Because these men also traded with debts, they could be called the first brokers. In late 13th century Bruges commodity traders gathered inside the house of a man called *Van der Beurse*, and in 1309 they became the "Bruges Beurse", institutionalizing what had been, until then, an informal meeting. The idea quickly spread around Flanders and neighboring counties and "Beurzen" soon opened in Ghent and Amsterdam.

In the middle of the 13th century Venetian bankers began to trade in government securities. In 1351 the Venetian government outlawed spreading rumors intended to lower the price of government funds. Bankers in Pisa, Verona, Genoa and Florence also began trading in government securities during the 14th century. This practice was only possible, because these independent city states were not ruled by a duke but a council of influential citizens. The Dutch later started joint stock companies, which let shareholders invest in business ventures and get a share of their profits—or losses. In 1602, the Dutch East India Company issued the first shares on the Amsterdam Stock Exchange. It was the first company to issue stocks and bonds. The Amsterdam Stock Exchange (or Amsterdam Beurs) is also said to have been the first stock exchange to introduce continuous trade in the early 17th century. The Dutch pioneered short selling, option trading, debt-equity swaps, merchant banking, unit trusts and other speculative instruments, much as we know them.

Insurance Companies: an Institution to Guard Against Risks and Potential Dangers

Insurance companies were another way to mitigate risk. Insurance in one form or another has been around as far back as there are records. What differed about insurance going into the 16th and 17th centuries was that these informal mechanisms became formalized. Lloyd's of London came into being in 1688 in English coffee shops that catered to sailors, traders, and others involved in trade. Interestingly, Lloyd's coffeehouse published a newspaper, which gave news from various parts of the world, and helped the underwriters of the insurance at the coffeehouse to determine the risk. This innovation was one of many that allowed for the categorization of risk. Another innovation was the use of ship catalogs and classifications. Other forms of insurance began to appear as well. After the Great Fire of London, Nicholas Barbon began to sell fire insurance in 1667. Laws were changed to deal with insurance issues, such as *l'Ordonnance de la Marine* (by Colbert in 1681).

Economic Theory

As the economy grew through the Commercial Revolution, so did attempts to understand and influence it. Economic theory as a separate subject of its own came into being as the stresses of the new global order brought about two opposing theories of how a nation accumulates wealth: mercantilistic and free-trade policies. Mercantilism inflamed the growing hostilities between the increasingly centralized European powers as the accumulation of precious metals by governments was seen as important to the prestige and power of a modern nation. This involvement in accumulating gold and silver (among other things) became important in the development of the nation-state. Governments' involvement in trade had an impact on the nobility of western European nations, because increased wealth by non-nobles threatened the nobility's place in society.

Mercantilism

Mercantilism is an economic policy that emphasizes the goal of each nation was to gain as much money as possible by whatever means. The belief was that the richer the nation the more powerful it was. The idea behind it was an outgrowth of the guild system, as guilds were monopolistic enterprises: they regulated trade within towns by controlling the creation of goods, regulated themselves through their system of apprenticeship, kept outside traders from selling goods in the town, and forced outsiders to pay tolls and other types of payments for the privilege of doing business in that town. Laws were passed to enforce this concept, such as the English Navigation Acts, and edicts issued by French Minister of Finance Jean-baptiste Colbert. Proponents of mercantilism included Thomas Mun, Philipp von Hörnigk, and others. An early critic of mercantilism was Nicholas Barbon.

Free Trade: Free Flow of Goods and Services and Removal of Trade Barriers

Capitalism as a theory developed toward the end of the Commercial Revolution, supplanting mercantilism as the prevailing economic theory. Briefly, capitalism can be described as the private ownership of the means of production and distribution. Capital is invested in order to produce more capital. The accumulation of capital in the hands of the entrepreneur made possible the purchase of raw material in greater bulk. The capitalist entrepreneur could now operate without the restrictions imposed by the urban guilds. This change became significant with the introduction of the Domestic System, which increased specialization of skills within a more efficient system of overall production, and allowed farm families to supplement their incomes. This system challenged the guild system directly, because these home based businesses were located on farms, away from urban centers.

Colonialism: First Attempt for Globalization

Mercantilism was a significant driver of Colonialism, as, according to the theory, the colony existed for the benefit of the mother country. This assumption meant that colonies were prohibited from engaging in their own independent commerce, and therefore competing with the mother country. Colonies were established to provide customers, raw materials, and investment opportunities. Other important goals of colonialism were European political considerations, and religious fervor. The administration of the colonies established by the Europeans mirrored in some part the mother country. Spain's encomienda system of forced labor in Latin America and the Philippines was an extension of the Spanish feudal system, with the granting of territory as part of a royal extension of power. After the Spanish acquisition of the Philippines, the pace of exchange between China and the West accelerated dramatically. Manila galleons brought in far more silver to China than the Silk Road. The Qing government attempted to limit contact with the outside world to a minimum. The Qing Dynasty only allowed trade through the port of Canton, what is now Guangzhou. Severe red-tape and licensed monopolies were set up to restrict the flow of trade, resulting in high retail prices for imported goods and limited demand. Spain began to sell opium, along with New World products such as tobacco and maize, to the Chinese in order to prevent a trade deficit. The English, for their part, used the British East India

Company as an agent of the crown, which was expected to govern and protect the people and commerce of the colony. The English also developed a commercial empire in North America, India, and Australia, creating colonies, with the intention of making a profit. As a result of high demand for tea, silk, and porcelain in Britain and the low demand for British commodities in China, Britain had a large trade deficit with China and had to pay for these goods with silver. Britain began illegally exporting opium to China from British India in the 18th century to counter its deficit. The opium trade took off rapidly, and the flow of silver began to reverse. The Yongzheng Emperor prohibited the sale and smoking of opium in 1729 because of the large number of addicts. The French followed the English to the New World, and settled Quebec in 1608. They did not populate North America as much as the English did, as they did not allow the Huguenots to travel to the New World. In addition, the heavy governmental regulations placed on trade in France discouraged settlement. The Portuguese Empire was created through commerce bases in South America, Africa, India, and across southeast Asia.

Trade Monopolies

Governments became involved in trade directly through the granting of royal trade monopolies. For example, Walter Raleigh had been granted a trade monopoly by Queen Elizabeth, for the export of broadcloth and wine. Ironically, competition between colonial powers led to their granting of trade monopolies to the East India Companies.

Triangular Trade: a Dark Page of the West

A triangular trade occurred in this period: between Africa, North America, and England; and it worked in the following way: Slaves came from Africa, and went to the Americas; raw materials came from the Americas and went to Europe; from there, finished goods came from Europe and were sold back to the Americas at a much higher price. Because of the massive die-off of the indigenous people, the Atlantic Slave Trade was established to import the labor required for the extraction of resources (such as gold and silver) and farming.

Law

Laws began to change to deal with commerce, both internationally, and locally within individual countries. In France, for example, the Ordinance of Marine of Louis XIV was published under the auspices of Colbert in 1691, and was the first complete code of maritime and commercial law; and "when we consider the originality and extent of the design and the ability with which it is executed, we shall not hesitate to admit that it deserves to be ranked among the noblest works that legislative genius and learning have ever accomplished." In England, the Navigation Acts were among the British effort to regulate trade.

Effects and Influences

The Commercial Revolution, coupled with other changes in the Early Modern Period, had dramatic effects on the globe. Christopher Columbus and the conquistadors, through their travels, were indirectly responsible for the massive depopulation of South America. They were directly responsible for destroying the civilizations of the Inca, Aztec, and Maya in their quest to build the Spanish Empire. Other Europeans similarly impacted the peoples of North America as well. An equally important consequence of the Commercial Revolution was the Columbian Exchange. Plants and animals moved throughout the world due to human movements. For example, Yellow Fever, previously unknown in North and South America, was imported through water that ships took on in Africa. Cocoa (chocolate), coffee, maize, cassava, and potatoes moved from one hemisphere to the other. For more than 2000 years, the Mediterranean Sea had been the focus of European trade with other parts of the world. After 1492, this focus shifted to the Atlantic Ocean by routes south around the Cape of Good Hope, and by trans-Atlantic trade. Another important change was the increase in population. Better food and more wealth allowed for larger families. The migration of peoples from Europe to the Americas allowed for European populations to increase as well. Population growth provided the expanding labor force needed for industrialization. Another important outcome of Europe's commercial revolution was a foundation of wealth needed for the industrial revolution. Economic prosperity financed new forms of cultural expression during this period.

Questions and Topics for Pondering and Further Discussion for Unit Seven-1:

1. What is the rationality behind commercial behavior?
2. What is the essence of commercialism?
3. Is gaining profit a human instinct or rational act?
4. What is the mechanism of commercial activity?
5. How is it that commercial act has got the significance of a revolution?
6. Is commercial revolution responsible for the demise of some of the brilliant civilizations in America?
7. Some historians find that Dutch people are especially good at commerce. Why is that?
8. Some people say that speculation is key to commercial success. Please make some comments on it.

2. Industrial Revolution, a Driving Force for Society

Editor's remarks: *in our modern age, few people can deny the significance of the Industrial Revolution that fundamentally changed the way of production and way of life for mass people. This process started around 200 years ago first in Europe and it is still going on in many parts of the world today. The Industrial Revolution has taken human beings into a new stage of social and economic development, greatly boosting human's ability to produce material wealth via the use of machinery and a new mode of production based upon factory system and advanced technology. Industrialization has freed people from their passive reliance upon the natural forces for survival and thriving in material well-being. Its effects can be felt in every field of human life.*

The Industrial Revolution was a period from 1750 to 1850 where changes in agriculture, manufacturing, mining, transportation, and technology had a profound effect on the social, economic and cultural conditions of the times. It began in the United Kingdom, then subsequently spread throughout western Europe, North America, Japan, and eventually the rest of the world. The Industrial Revolution marks a major turning point in history; almost every aspect of daily life was influenced in some way. Most notably, average income and population began to exhibit unprecedented sustained growth. In the two centuries following 1800, the world's average per capita income increased over tenfold, while the world's population increased over sixfold. In the words of Nobel Prize winner Robert E. Lucas, Jr., "For the first time in history, the living standards of the masses of ordinary people have begun to undergo sustained growth... Nothing remotely like this economic behavior has happened before". Great Britain provided the legal and cultural foundations that enabled entrepreneurs to pioneer the industrial revolution. Key factors fostering this environment were: (1) The period of peace and stability which followed the unification of England and Scotland, (2) no trade barriers between England and Scotland, (3) the rule of law (respecting the sanctity of contracts), (4) a straightforward legal system which allowed the formation of joint-stock companies (corporations), and (5) a free market (capitalism). Starting in the later part of the 18th century, there began a transition in parts of Great Britain's previously manual labor and draft-animal-based economy towards machine-based manufacturing. It started with the mechanization of the textile industries, the development of iron-making techniques and the increased use of refined coal. Trade expansion was enabled by the introduction of canals, improved roads and railways. With the transition away from an agricultural-based economy and towards machine-based manufacturing came a great influx of population from the countryside and into the towns and cities, which swelled in population.

The critical manufacturing change that marks the Industrial Revolution is the production of interchangeable parts. Lathes and other machine tools of the Industrial Revolution enabled (1) high precision, and (2) the mass reproduction of parts with that precision. Guns, for example, had previously been made one at a time, with the parts filed to mate together accurately on one gun, but they were not made to mate with any other gun. With the repeatable precision of the Industrial Revolution, interchangeable parts for guns or other products could be produced on a mass basis, which dramatically reduced the price of the product. The introduction of steam power fueled primarily by coal, wider utilization of water wheels and powered machinery (mainly in textile manufacturing) underpinned the dramatic increases in production capacity. The development of all-metal machine tools in the first two decades of the 19th century facilitated the manufacture of more production machines for manufacturing in other industries. The effects spread throughout western Europe and North America during the 19th century, eventually affecting most of the world, a process that continues as industrialisation. The impact of this change on society was enormous. The First Industrial Revolution, which began in the 18th century, merged into the Second Industrial Revolution around 1850, when technological and economic progress gained momentum with the development of steam-powered ships, railways, and later in the 19th century with the internal combustion engine and electrical power generation. The period of time covered by the Industrial Revolution varies with different historians. Eric Hobsbawm held that it "broke out" in Britain in the 1780s and was not fully felt until the 1830s or 1840s, while T. S. Ashton held that it occurred roughly between 1760 and 1830. Some 20th-century historians such as John Clapham and Nicholas Crafts have argued that the process of economic and social change took place gradually and the term "revolution" is a misnomer. This is still a subject of debate among historians. GDP per capita was broadly stable before the Industrial Revolution and the emergence of the modern capitalist economy. The Industrial Revolution began an era of per-capita economic growth in capitalist economies. Economic historians are in agreement that the onset of the Industrial Revolution is the most important event in the history of humanity since the domestication of animals and plants.

Etymology

The earliest use of the term "Industrial Revolution" seems to be a letter of 6 July 1799 by French envoy Louis-Guillaume Otto, announcing that France had entered the race to industrialize. In his *Keywords: A Vocabulary of Culture and Society* (1976), Raymond Williams states in the entry for "Industry": "The idea of a new social order based on major industrial change was clear in Southey and Owen, between 1811 and 1818, and was implicit as early as Blake in the early 1790s and Wordsworth at the turn of the century." The term "Industrial Revolution" applied to technological change was becoming more common by the late 1830s, as in Louis-Auguste Blanqui description in 1837 of *La révolution industrielle*. Friedrich Engels in *The Condition of the Working Class in England in* 1844 spoke of "an industrial revolution, a revolution which at the same time changed the whole of civil society". Credit for popularizing the term may be given to Arnold Toynbee, whose lectures given in 1881 gave a detailed account of it.

Innovations

The commencement of the Industrial Revolution is closely linked to a small number of innovations, made in the second half of the 18th century:

- **Textiles**—Cotton spinning using Richard Arkwright's water frame, James Hargreaves's Spinning Jenny, and Samuel Crompton's Spinning Mule (a combination of the Spinning Jenny and the Water Frame). This was patented in 1769 and so came out of patent in 1783. The end of the patent was rapidly followed by the erection of many cotton mills. Similar technology was subsequently applied to spinning worsted yarn for various textiles and flax for linen. The cotton revolution began in Derby, which has been known since this period as the "Powerhouse of the North".
- **Steam power**—The improved steam engine invented by James Watt and patented in 1775 was at first mainly used to power pumps for pumping water out of mines, but from the 1780s was applied to power other types of machines. This enabled rapid development of efficient semi-automated factories on a previously unimaginable scale in places where waterpower was not available. For the first time in history people did not have to rely on human or animal muscle, wind or water for power. The steam engine was used to pump water from coal mines; to lift trucks of coal to the surface; to blow air into the furnaces for the making of iron; to grind clay for pottery; and to power new factories of all kinds. For over a hundred years the steam engine was the king of the industries.
- **Iron making**—In the Iron industry, coke was finally applied to all stages of iron smelting, replacing charcoal. This had been achieved much earlier for lead and copper as well as for producing pig iron in a blast furnace, but the second stage in the production of bar iron depended on the use of potting and stamping (for which a patent expired in 1786) or puddling (patented by Henry Cort in 1784).

These represent three "leading sectors", in which there were key innovations, which allowed the economic take off by which the Industrial Revolution is usually defined. This is not to belittle many other inventions, particularly in the textile industry. Without some earlier ones, such as the Spinning Jenny and flying shuttle in the textile industry and the smelting of pig iron with coke, these achievements might have been impossible. Later inventions such as the power loom and Richard Trevithick's high pressure steam engine were also important in the growing industrialization of Britain. The application of steam engines to powering cotton mills and ironworks enabled these to be built in places that were most convenient because other resources were available, rather than where there was water to power a watermill. In the textile sector, such mills became the model for the organization of human labour in factories, epitomized by Cottonopolis, the name given to the vast collection of cotton mills, factories and administration offices based in Manchester. The assembly line system greatly improved efficiency, both in this and other industries. With a series of men trained to do a single task on a product, then having it moved along to the next worker, the number of finished goods also rose significantly. Also important was the 1756 rediscovery of concrete (based on hydraulic lime mortar) by the British engineer John Smeaton, which had been lost for 1300 years.

Transfer of Knowledge: a Power Behind the Revolution

Knowledge of innovation was spread by several means. Workers who were trained in the technique might move to another employer or might be poached. A common method was for someone to make a study tour, gathering information where he could. During the whole of the Industrial Revolution and for the century before, all European countries and America engaged in study-touring; some nations, like Sweden and France, even trained civil servants or technicians to undertake it as a matter of state policy. In other countries, notably Britain and America, this practice was carried out by individual manufacturers eager to improve their own methods. Study tours were common then, as now, as was the keeping of travel diaries. Records made by industrialists and technicians of the period are an incomparable source of information about their methods. Another means for the spread of innovation was by the network of informal philosophical societies, like the Lunar Society of Birmingham, in which members met to discuss "natural philosophy" (i. e. science) and often its application to manufacturing. The Lunar Society flourished from 1765 to 1809, and it has been said of them, "They were, if you like, the revolutionary committee of that most far reaching of all the eighteenth century revolutions, the Industrial Revolution". Other such societies published volumes of proceedings and transactions. For example, the London-based Royal Society of Arts published an illustrated volume of new inventions, as well as papers about them in its annual *Transactions*. There were publications describing technology. Encyclopaedias such as Harris's *Lexicon Technicum* (1704) and Abraham Rees's *Cyclopaedia* (1802—1819) contain much of value. *Cyclopaedia* contains an enormous amount of information about the science and technology of the first half of the Industrial Revolution, very well illustrated by fine engravings. Foreign printed sources such as the *Descriptions des Arts et Métiers* and Diderot's *Encyclopédie* explained foreign methods with fine engraved plates. Periodical publications about manufacturing and technology began to appear in the last decade of the 18th century, and many regularly included notice of the latest patents. Foreign periodicals, such as the *Annales des Mines*, published accounts of travels made by French engineers who observed British methods on study tours.

Technological Developments in Britain

In the early 18th century, British textile manufacture was based on wool which was processed by individual artisans, doing the spinning and weaving on their own premises. This system is called a cottage industry. Flax and cotton were also used for fine materials, but the processing was difficult because of the pre-processing needed, and thus goods in these materials made only a small proportion of the output. Use of the spinning wheel and hand loom restricted the production capacity of the industry, but incremental advances increased productivity to the extent that manufactured cotton goods became the dominant British export by the early decades of the 19th century. India was displaced as the premier supplier of cotton goods. Lewis Paul patented the Roller Spinning machine and the flyer-and-bobbin system for drawing wool to a more even thickness, developed with the help of John Wyatt in Birmingham. Paul and Wyatt opened a mill in Birmingham which used their new rolling machine powered by a donkey. In 1743, a factory was opened in Northampton with fifty spindles on each of five of Paul and Wyatt's machines. This operated until about 1764. A similar mill was built by Daniel Bourn in

Leominster, but this burnt down. Both Lewis Paul and Daniel Bourn patented carding machines in 1748. Using two sets of rollers that traveled at different speeds, it was later used in the first cotton spinning mill. Lewis's invention was later developed and improved by Richard Arkwright in his water frame and Samuel Crompton in his spinning mule. Other inventors increased the efficiency of the individual steps of spinning (carding, twisting and spinning, and rolling) so that the supply of yarn increased greatly, which fed a weaving industry that was advancing with improvements to shuttles and the loom or "frame". The output of an individual laborer increased dramatically, with the effect that the new machines were seen as a threat to employment, and early innovators were attacked and their inventions destroyed. To capitalize upon these advances, it took a class of entrepreneurs, of which the most famous is Richard Arkwright. He is credited with a list of inventions, but these were actually developed by people such as Thomas Highs and John Kay; Arkwright nurtured the inventors, patented the ideas, financed the initiatives, and protected the machines. He created the cotton mill which brought the production processes together in a factory, and he developed the use of power—first horse power and then water power—which made cotton manufacture a mechanized industry. Before long steam power was applied to drive textile machinery.

Metallurgy Techniques

The reverberatory furnace could produce wrought iron using mined coal. The burning coal remained separate from the iron ore and so did not contaminate the iron with impurities like sulphur. This opened the way to increased iron production. The major change in the metal industries during the era of the Industrial Revolution was the replacement of organic fuels based on wood with fossil fuel based on coal. Much of this happened somewhat before the Industrial Revolution, based on innovations by Sir Clement Clerke and others from 1678, using coal reverberatory furnaces known as cupolas. These were operated by the flames, which contained carbon monoxide, playing on the ore and reducing the oxide to metal. This has the advantage that impurities (such as sulphur) in the coal do not migrate into the metal. This technology was applied to lead from 1678 and to copper from 1687. It was also applied to iron foundry work in the 1690s, but in this case the reverberatory furnace was known as an air furnace. The foundry cupola is a different (and later) innovation. This was followed by Abraham Darby, who made great strides using coke to fuel his blast furnaces at Coalbrookdale in 1709. However, the coke pig iron he made was used mostly for the production of cast-iron goods such as pots and kettles. He had the advantage over his rivals in that his pots, cast by his patented process, were thinner and cheaper than theirs. Coke pig iron was hardly used to produce bar iron in forges until the mid-1750s, when his son Abraham Darby II built Horsehay and Ketley furnaces (not far from Coalbrookdale). By then, coke pig iron was cheaper than charcoal pig iron. Since cast iron was becoming cheaper and more plentiful, it also became a major structural material following the building of the innovative Iron Bridge in 1778 by Abraham Darby III. Matthew Boulton helped James Watt to get his business off the ground. he set up a massive factory called the Soho Factory, in the midlands. Bar iron for smiths to forge into consumer goods was still made in finery forges, as it long had been. However, new processes were adopted in the ensuing years. The first is referred to today as potting and stamping, but this was superseded by Henry Cort's puddling process. From 1785, perhaps because the improved version of potting and stamping was about to come out of patent, a great expansion in the output of the British iron industry began. The new processes did not depend on the use of charcoal at all and were therefore not limited by charcoal sources. Up to that time, British iron manufacturers had used considerable amounts of imported iron to supplement native supplies. This came principally from Sweden from the mid-17th century and later also from Russia from the end of the 1720s. However, from 1785, imports decreased because of the new iron making technology, and Britain became an exporter of bar iron as well as manufactured wrought iron consumer goods. An improvement was made in the production of steel, which was an expensive commodity and used only where iron would not do, such as for the cutting edge of tools and for springs. Benjamin Huntsman developed his crucible steel technique in the 1740s. The raw material for this was blister steel, made by the cementation process. The supply of cheaper iron and steel aided the development of boilers and steam engines, and eventually railways. Improvements in machine tools allowed better working of iron and steel and further boosted the industrial growth of Britain.

Mining: Tapping Natural Resources for More Wealth

Coal mining in Britain, particularly in South Wales started early. Before the steam engine, pits were often shallow bell pits following a seam of coal along the surface, which were abandoned as the coal was extracted. In other cases, if the geology was favorable, the coal was mined by means of an adit or drift mine driven into the side of a hill. Shaft mining was done in some areas, but the limiting factor was the problem of removing water. It could be done by hauling buckets of water up the shaft or to a sough (a tunnel driven into a hill to drain a mine). In either case, the water had to be discharged into a stream or ditch at a level where it could flow away by gravity. The introduction of the steam engine greatly facilitated the removal of water and enabled shafts to be made deeper, enabling more coal to be extracted. These were developments that had begun before the Industrial Revolution, but the adoption of James Watt's more efficient steam engine from the 1770s reduced the fuel costs of engines, making mines more profitable. Coal mining was very dangerous owing to the presence of firedamp in many coal seams. Some degree of safety was provided by the safety lamp which was invented in 1816 by Sir Humphry Davy and independently by George Stephenson. However, the lamps proved a false dawn because they became unsafe very quickly and provided a weak light. Firedamp explosions continued, often setting off coal dust explosions, so casualties grew during the entire 19th century. Conditions of work were very poor, with a high casualty rate from rock falls.

Steam Power: a Driving Power for the Revolution

The development of the stationary steam engine was an essential early element of the Industrial Revolution; however, for most of the period of the Industrial Revolution, the majority of industries still relied on wind and water power as well as horse-and man-power for driving small machines. The first real attempt at industrial use of steam power was due to Thomas Savery in 1698. He constructed and patented in London a low-lift combined vacuum and pressure water pump, that generated about one horsepower (hp) and was used in numerous water works and tried in a few mines (hence its "brand name", *The Miner's Friend*), but it was not a success since it was limited in pumping height and prone to boiler explosions. Newcomen's steam powered atmospheric engine was the first practical engine. Subsequent steam engines were to power the Industrial Revolution. The first safe and successful steam power plant was introduced by Thomas Newcomen before 1712. Newcomen apparently conceived the Newcomen steam engine quite independently of Savery, but as the latter had taken out a very wide-ranging patent, Newcomen and his associates were obliged to come to an arrangement with him, marketing the engine until 1733 under a joint patent. Newcomen's engine appears to have been based on Papin's experiments carried out 30 years earlier, and employed a piston and cylinder, one end of which was open to the atmosphere above the piston. Steam just above atmospheric pressure (all that the boiler could stand) was introduced into the lower half of the cylinder beneath the piston during the gravity-induced upstroke; the steam was then condensed by a jet of cold water injected into the steam space to produce a partial vacuum; the pressure differential between the atmosphere and the vacuum on either side of the piston displaced it downwards into the cylinder, raising the opposite end of a rocking beam to which was attached a gang of gravity-actuated reciprocating force pumps housed in the mineshaft. The engine's downward power stroke raised the pump, priming it and preparing the pumping stroke. At first the phases were controlled by hand, but within ten years an escapement mechanism had been devised worked by a vertical *plug tree* suspended from the rocking beam which rendered the engine self-acting. A number of Newcomen engines were successfully put to use in Britain for draining hitherto unworkable deep mines, with the engine on the surface; these were large machines, requiring a lot of capital to build, and produced about 5 hp (3.7 kW). They were extremely inefficient by modern standards, but when located where coal was cheap at pit heads, opened up a great expansion in coal mining by allowing mines to go deeper. Despite their disadvantages, Newcomen engines were reliable and easy to maintain and continued to be used in the coalfields until the early decades of the 19th century. By 1729, when Newcomen died, his engines had spread (first) to Hungary in 1722, Germany, Austria, and Sweden. A total of 110 are known to have been built by 1733 when the joint patent expired, of which 14 were abroad. In the 1770s, the engineer John Smeaton built some very large examples and introduced a number of improvements. A total of 1,454 engines had been built by 1800.

James Watt: the Man Who Set the Whole World in Motion

A fundamental change in working principles was brought about by James Watt. In close collaboration with Matthew Boulton, he had succeeded by 1778 in perfecting his steam engine, which incorporated a series of radical improvements, notably the closing off of the upper part of the cylinder thereby making the low pressure steam drive the top of the piston instead of the atmosphere, use of a steam jacket and the celebrated separate steam condenser chamber. All this meant that a more constant temperature could be maintained in the cylinder and that engine efficiency no longer varied according to atmospheric conditions. These improvements increased engine efficiency by a factor of about five, saving 75% on coal costs. Bolton and Watt opened the Soho Foundry, for the manufacture of such engines, in 1795. Nor could the atmospheric engine be easily adapted to drive a rotating wheel, although Wasborough and Pickard did succeed in doing so towards 1780. However by 1783 the more economical Watt steam engine had been fully developed into a double-acting rotative type, which meant that it could be used to directly drive the rotary machinery of a factory or mill. Both of Watt's basic engine types were commercially very successful, and by 1800, the firm Boulton & Watt had constructed 496 engines, with 164 driving reciprocating pumps, 24 serving blast furnaces, and 308 powering mill machinery; most of the engines generated from 5 to 10 hp (7.5 kW). The development of machine tools, such as the lathe, planing and shaping machines powered by these engines, enabled all the metal parts of the engines to be easily and accurately cut and in turn made it possible to build larger and more powerful engines. Until about 1800, the most common pattern of steam engine was the beam engine, built as an integral part of a stone or brick engine-house, but soon various patterns of self-contained portative engines (readily removable, but not on wheels) were developed, such as the table engine. Towards the turn of the 19th century, the Cornish engineer Richard Trevithick, and the American, Oliver Evans began to construct higher pressure non-condensing steam engines, exhausting against the atmosphere. This allowed an engine and boiler to be combined into a single unit compact enough to be used on mobile road and rail locomotives and steam boats. In the early 19th century after the expiration of Watt's patent, the steam engine underwent many improvements by a host of inventors and engineers.

Chemicals: a Magician of Wealth and of Change

The large scale production of chemicals was an important development during the Industrial Revolution. The first of these was the production of sulphuric acid by the lead chamber process invented by the Englishman John Roebuck (James Watt's first partner) in 1746. He was able to greatly increase the scale of the manufacture by replacing the relatively expensive glass vessels formerly used with larger, less expensive chambers made of riveted sheets of lead. Instead of making a small amount each time, he was able to make around 100 pounds (50 kg) in each of the chambers, at least a tenfold increase. The production of an alkali on a large scale became an important goal as well, and Nicolas Leblanc succeeded in 1791 in introducing a method for the production of sodium carbonate. The Leblanc process was a reaction of sulphuric acid with sodium chloride to give sodium sulphate and hydrochloric acid. The sodium sulphate was heated with limestone (calcium carbonate) and coal to give a mixture of sodium carbonate and calcium sulphide. Adding water separated the soluble sodium carbonate from the calcium sulphide. The process produced a large amount of pollution (the hydrochloric acid was initially vented to the air, and calcium sulphide was a useless waste product). Nonetheless, this synthetic soda ash proved economical compared to that from burning specific plants (barilla) or from kelp, which were the previously dominant sources of soda ash, and also to potash (potassium carbonate) derived from hardwood ashes. These two chemicals were very important because they enabled the introduction of a host of other inventions, replacing many small-scale operations with more cost-effective and controllable processes. Sodium carbonate had many uses in the glass, textile, soap, and paper industries. Early uses for sulphuric acid included pickling (removing rust) iron and steel, and for bleaching cloth. The development of bleaching powder (calcium hypochlorite) by Scottish chemist Charles Tennant in about 1800, based on the discoveries of French chemist Claude Louis Berthollet, revolutionized the bleaching processes in the textile industry by dramatically reducing the time required (from months to days) for the traditional process then in use, which required repeated exposure to the sun in bleach fields after soaking the textiles with alkali or sour milk. Tennant's factory at St Rollox, North Glasgow, became the largest chemical plant in the world. In 1824 Joseph Aspdin, a British bricklayer turned builder, patented a chemical process for making portland cement which was an important advance in the building trades. This process involves sintering a mixture of clay and limestone to about 1,400 °C (2,552 °F), then grinding it into a fine powder which is then mixed with water, sand and gravel to produce concrete. Portland cement was used by the famous English engineer Marc Isambard Brunel several years later when constructing the Thames Tunnel. Cement was used on a large scale in the construction of the London sewerage system a generation later. After 1860 the focus on chemical innovation was in dyestuffs, and Germany took world leadership, building a strong chemical industry. A large number of chemists flocked to German universities in the 1860—1914 era to learn the latest techniques. British scientists by contrast, lacked research universities and did not train advanced students; instead the practice was to hire German-trained chemists.

Machine Tools: Adding More Power to Humans

The Industrial Revolution could not have developed without machine tools, for they enabled manufacturing machines to be made. They have their origins in the tools developed in the 18th century by makers of clocks and watches and scientific instrument makers to enable them to batch-produce small mechanisms. The mechanical parts of early textile machines were sometimes called "clock work" because of the metal spindles and gears they incorporated. The manufacture of textile machines drew craftsmen from these trades and is the origin of the modern engineering industry. Machines were built by various craftsmen—carpenters made wooden framings, and smiths and turners made metal parts. A good example of how machine tools changed manufacturing took place in Birmingham, England, in 1830. The invention of a new machine by Joseph Gillott, William Mitchell and James Stephen Perry allowed mass manufacture of robust, cheap steel pen nibs; the process had been laborious and expensive. Because of the difficulty of manipulating metal and the lack of machine tools, the use of metal was kept to a minimum. Wood framing had the disadvantage of changing dimensions with temperature and humidity, and the various joints tended to rack (work loose) over time. As the Industrial Revolution progressed, machines with metal frames became more common, but they required machine tools to make them economically. Before the advent of machine tools, metal was worked manually using the basic hand tools of hammers, files, scrapers, saws and chisels. Small metal parts were readily made by this means, but for large machine parts, production was very laborious and costly. Apart from workshop lathes used by craftsmen, the first large machine tool was the cylinder boring machine used for boring the large-diameter cylinders on early steam engines. The planing machine, the slotting machine and the shaping machine were developed in the first decades of the 19th century. Although the milling machine was invented at this time, it was not developed as a serious workshop tool until somewhat later in the 19th century.

Military production, as well, had a hand in the development of machine tools. Henry Maudslay, who trained a school of machine tool makers early in the 19th century, was employed at the Royal Arsenal, Woolwich, as a young man where he would have seen the large horse-driven wooden machines for cannon boring made and worked by the Verbruggans. He later worked for Joseph Bramah on the production of metal locks, and soon after he began working on his own. He was engaged to build the machinery for making ships' pulley blocks for the Royal Navy in the Portsmouth Block Mills. These were all metal and were the first machines for mass production and making components with a degree of interchangeability. The lessons Maudslay learned about the need for stability and precision he adapted to the development of machine tools, and in his workshops he trained a generation of men to build on his work, such as Richard Roberts, Joseph Clement and Joseph Whitworth. James Fox of Derby had a healthy export trade in machine tools for the first third of the century, as did Matthew Murray of Leeds. Roberts was a maker of high-quality machine tools and a pioneer of the use of jigs and gauges for precision workshop measurement.

Gas Lighting: Illuminating the Mind of People and the World

Another major industry of the later Industrial Revolution was gas lighting. Though others made a similar innovation elsewhere, the large scale introduction of this was the work of William Murdoch, an employee of Boulton and Watt, the Birmingham steam engine pioneers. The process consisted of the large scale gasification of coal in furnaces, the purification of the gas (removal of sulphur, ammonia, and heavy hydrocarbons), and its storage and distribution. The first gas lighting utilities were established in London between 1812—1820. They soon became one of the major consumers of coal in the UK. Gas lighting had an impact on social and industrial organization because it allowed factories and stores to remain open longer than with tallow candles or oil. Its introduction allowed night life to flourish in cities and towns as interiors and streets could be lighted on a larger scale than before.

Glass Making: Creating a Window for People to Know More and See More

A new method of producing glass, known as the cylinder process, was developed in Europe during the early 19th century. In 1832, this process was used by the Chance Brothers to create sheet glass. They became the leading producers of window and plate glass. This advancement allowed for larger panes of glass to be created without interruption, thus freeing up the space planning in interiors as well as the fenestration of buildings. The Crystal Palace is the supreme example of the use of sheet glass in a new and innovative structure.

Paper Machine: Ink and Paper are More Powerful than Guns and Bullets

A machine for making a continuous sheet of paper on a loop of wire fabric was patented in 1798 by Nicholas Louis Robert who worked for Saint-Léger Didot family in France. The paper machine is known as a Fourdrinier after the financiers, brothers Sealy and Henry Fourdrinier, who were stationers in London. Although greatly improved and with many variations, the Fourdriner machine is the predominant means of paper production today.

Effects on Agriculture: an Initial Stage for Automated Agriculture and Mass Production of It

The invention of machinery played a big part in driving forward the British Agricultural Revolution. Agricultural improvement began in the centuries before the Industrial Revolution got going and it may have played a part in freeing up labor from the land to work in the new industrial mills of the 18th century. As the revolution in industry progressed a succession of machines became available which increased food production with ever fewer laborers. Jethro Tull's seed drill invented in 1701 was a mechanical seeder which distributed seeds efficiently across a plot of land. Joseph Foljambe's Rotherham plough of 1730, was the first commercially successful iron plough. Andrew Meikle's threshing machine of 1784 was the final straw for many farm laborers, and led to the 1830 agricultural rebellion of the Swing Riots.

Transport in Britain: Connecting the Whole Nation Within and to the Outside World

At the beginning of the Industrial Revolution, inland transport was by navigable rivers and roads, with coastal vessels employed to move heavy goods by sea. Railways or wagon ways were used for conveying coal to rivers for further shipment, but canals had not yet been constructed. Animals supplied all of the motive power on land, with sails providing the motive power on the sea. The Industrial Revolution improved Britain's transport infrastructure with a turnpike road network, a canal and waterway network, and a railway network. Raw materials and finished products could be moved more quickly and cheaply than before. Improved transportation also allowed new ideas to spread quickly.

Canals/Roads/Railways: Transportation Network Facilitating Economic Transactions

Canals began to be built in the late 18th century to link the major manufacturing centers in the Midlands and north with seaports and with London, at that time itself the largest manufacturing center in the country. Canals were the first technology to allow bulk materials to be easily transported across the country. A single canal horse could pull a load dozens of times larger than a cart at a faster pace. By the 1820s, a national network was in existence. Canal construction served as a model for the organization and methods later used to construct the railways. They were eventually largely superseded as profitable commercial enterprises by the spread of the railways from the 1840s on. Britain's canal network, together with its surviving mill buildings, is one of the most enduring features of the early Industrial Revolution to be seen in Britain. Much of the original British road system was poorly maintained by thousands of local parishes, but from the 1720s (and occasionally earlier) turnpike trusts were set up to charge tolls and maintain some roads. Increasing numbers of main roads were turnpiked from the 1750s to the extent that almost every main road in England and Wales was the responsibility of some turnpike trust. New engineered roads were built by John Metcalf, Thomas Telford and John Macadam. The major turnpikes radiated from London and were the means by which the Royal Mail was able to reach the rest of the country. Heavy goods transport on these roads was by means of slow, broad wheeled, carts hauled by teams of horses. Lighter goods were conveyed by smaller carts or by teams of pack horse. Stage coaches carried the rich, and the less wealthy could pay to ride on carriers carts.

Wagonways for moving coal in the mining areas had started in the 17th century and were often associated with canal or river systems for the further movement of coal. These were all horse drawn or relied on gravity, with a stationary steam engine to haul the wagons back to the top of the incline. The first applications of the steam locomotive were on wagon or plate ways (as they were then often called from the cast-iron plates used). Horse-drawn public railways did not begin until the early years of the 19th century. Steam-hauled public railways began with the Stockton and Darlington Railway in 1825 and the Liverpool and Manchester Railway in 1830. Construction of major railways connecting the larger cities and towns began in the 1830s but only gained momentum at the very end of the first Industrial Revolution. After many of the workers had completed the railways, they did not return to their rural lifestyles but instead remained in the cities, providing additional workers for the factories. Railways helped Britain's trade enormously, providing a quick and easy way of transport and an easy way to transport mail and news.

Social Effects of Industrial Revolution are Immense and Immeasurable

In terms of social structure, the Industrial Revolution witnessed the triumph of a middle class of industrialists and businessmen over a landed class of nobility and gentry. Ordinary working people found increased opportunities for employment in the new mills and factories, but these were often under strict working conditions with long hours of labour dominated by a pace set by machines. As late as the year 1900, most industrial workers in the United States still worked a 10-hour day (12 hours in the steel industry), yet earned from 20 to 40 percent less than the minimum deemed necessary for a decent life. However, harsh working conditions were prevalent long before the Industrial Revolution took place. Pre-industrial society was very static and often cruel—child labour, dirty living conditions, and long working hours were just as prevalent before the Industrial Revolution.

Factories and Urbanization: a New Life Style for Mass People

Industrialization led to the creation of the factory. Arguably the first was John Lombe's water-powered silk mill at Derby, operational by 1721. However, the rise of the factory came somewhat later when cotton spinning was mechanized. The factory system was largely responsible for the rise of the modern city, as large numbers of workers migrated into the cities in search of employment in the factories. Nowhere was this better illustrated than the mills and associated industries of Manchester, nicknamed "Cottonopolis", and arguably the world's first industrial city. For much of the 19th century, production was done in small mills, which were typically water-powered and built to serve local needs. Later each factory would have its own steam engine and a chimney to give an efficient draft through its boiler. The transition to industrialization was not without difficulty. For example, a group of English workers known as Luddites formed to protest against industrialization and sometimes sabotaged factories. In other industries the transition to factory production was not so divisive. Some industrialists themselves tried to improve factory and living conditions for their workers.

One of the earliest such reformers was Robert Owen, known for his pioneering efforts in improving conditions for workers at the New Lanark mills, and often regarded as one of the key thinkers of the early socialist movement. By 1746, an integrated brass mill was working at Warmley near Bristol. Raw material went in at one end, was smelted into brass and was turned into pans, pins, wire, and other goods. Housing was provided for workers on site. Josiah Wedgwood and Matthew Boulton (whose Soho Manufactory was completed in 1766) were other prominent early industrialists, who employed the factory system.

Child Labor: Evil of Early Capitalism of Primitive Wealth Accumulation

In Britain laws passed in 1842 and 1844 improved working conditions in mines. The Industrial Revolution led to a population increase, but the chances of surviving childhood did not improve throughout the Industrial Revolution (although *infant* mortality rates were reduced markedly). There was still limited opportunity for education, and children were expected to work. Employers could pay a child less than an adult even though their productivity was comparable; there was no need for strength to operate an industrial machine, and since the industrial system was completely new there were no experienced adult laborers.

This made child labor the labor of choice for manufacturing in the early phases of the Industrial Revolution between the 18th and 19th centuries. In England and Scotland in 1788, two-thirds of the workers in 143 water-powered cotton mills were described as children. Child labour had existed before the Industrial Revolution, but with the increase in population and education it became more visible. Many children were forced to work in relatively bad conditions for much lower pay than their elders, 10—20% of an adult male's wage. Children as young as four were employed. Beatings and long hours were common, with some child coal miners and hurriers working from 4 am until 5 pm. Conditions were dangerous, with some children killed when they dozed off and fell into the path of the carts, while others died from gas explosions. Many children developed lung cancer and other diseases and died before the age of 25. Workhouses would sell orphans and abandoned children as "pauper apprentices", working without wages for board and lodging. Those who ran away would be whipped and returned to their masters, with some masters shackling them to prevent escape. Children employed as mule scavenger by cotton mills would crawl under machinery to pick up cotton, working 14 hours a day, six days a week. Some lost hands or limbs, others were crushed under the machines, and some were decapitated. Young girls worked at match factories, where phosphorus fumes would cause many to develop phossy jaw. Children employed at glassworks were regularly burned and blinded, and those working at potteries were vulnerable to poisonous clay dust. Reports were written detailing some of the abuses, particularly in the coal mines and textile factories and these helped to popularize the children's plight. The public outcry, especially among the upper and middle classes, helped stir change in the young workers' welfare. Politicians and the government tried to limit child labor by law, but factory owners resisted; some felt that they were aiding the poor by giving their children money to buy food to avoid starvation, and others simply welcomed the cheap labor. In 1833 and 1844, the first general laws against child labor, the Factory Acts, were passed in England: Children younger than nine were not allowed to work, children were not permitted to work at night, and the work day of youth under the age of 18 was limited to twelve hours. Factory inspectors supervised the execution of the law, however, their scarcity made enforcement difficult. About ten years later, the employment of children and women in mining was forbidden. These laws decreased the number of child laborers; however, child labor remained in Europe and the United States up to the 20th century.

Housing: a Sign of Urbanization Movement

Living conditions during the Industrial Revolution varied from the splendor of the homes of the owners to the squalor of the lives of the workers. Poor people lived in very small houses in cramped streets. These homes would share toilet facilities, have open sewers and would be at risk of developing pathologies associated with persistent dampness. Disease was spread through a contaminated water supply. Conditions did improve during the 19th century as public health acts were introduced covering things such as sewage, hygiene and making some boundaries upon the construction of homes. Not everybody lived in homes like these. The Industrial Revolution created a larger middle class of professionals such as lawyers and doctors. Health conditions for improved over the course of the 19th century because of better sanitation; the famines that troubled rural areas did not happen in industrial areas. However, urban people—especially small children—died due to diseases spreading through the cramped living conditions. Tuberculosis (spread in congested dwellings), lung diseases from the mines, cholera from polluted water and typhoid were also common. A description of housing of the mill workers in England in 1844 was given by **Friedrich Engels**, a co-founder of Marxism. In the introduction of the 1892 edition of *Engels* (1844) he notes that most of the conditions he wrote about in 1844 had been greatly improved.

Luddites: a Working Class Rebellious Movement

The rapid industrialization of the English economy cost many craft workers their jobs. The movement started first with lace and hosiery workers near Nottingham and spread to other areas of the textile industry owing to early industrialization. Many weavers also found themselves suddenly unemployed since they could no longer compete with machines which only required relatively limited (and unskilled) labor to produce more cloth than a single weaver. Many such unemployed workers, weavers and others, turned their animosity towards the machines that had taken their jobs and began destroying factories and machinery. These attackers became known as Luddites, supposedly followers of Ned Ludd, a folklore figure. The first attacks of the Luddite movement began in 1811. The Luddites rapidly gained popularity, and the British government took drastic measures using the militia or army to protect industry. Those rioters who were caught were tried and hanged, or transported for life. Unrest continued in other sectors as they industrialize, such as agricultural laborers in the 1830s, when large parts of southern Britain were affected by the Captain Swing disturbances. Threshing machines were a particular target, and rick burning was a popular activity. However, the riots led to the first formation of trade unions, and further pressure for reform.

Organization of Labor: a Budding Form of Labor Union

The Industrial Revolution concentrated labor into mills, factories and mines, thus facilitating the organization of *combinations* or trade unions to help advance the interests of working people. The power of a union could demand better terms by withdrawing all labor and causing a consequent cessation of production. Employers had to decide between giving in to the union demands at a cost to themselves or suffering the cost of the lost production. Skilled workers were hard to replace, and these were the first groups to successfully advance their conditions through this kind of bargaining. The main method the unions used to effect change was strike action. Many strikes were painful events for both sides, the unions and the management. In England, the Combination Act forbade workers to form any kind of trade union from 1799 until its repeal in 1824. Even after this, unions were still severely restricted. In 1832, the year of the Reform Act which extended the vote in England but did not grant universal suffrage, six men from Tolpuddle in Dorset founded the Friendly Society of Agricultural Laborers to protest against the gradual lowering of wages in the 1830s. They refused to work for less than 10 shillings a week, although by this time wages had been reduced to seven shillings a week and were due to be further reduced to six shillings.

In 1834 James Frampton, a local landowner, wrote to the Prime Minister, Lord Melbourne, to complain about the union, invoking an obscure law from 1797 prohibiting people from swearing oaths to each other, which the members of the Friendly Society had done. James Brine, James Hammett, George Loveless, George's brother James Loveless, George's brother in-law Thomas Standfield, and Thomas's son John Standfield were arrested, found guilty, and transported to Australia. They became known as the Tolpuddle martyrs. In the 1830s and 1840s the Chartist Movement was the first large scale organized working class political movement which campaigned for political equality and social justice.

Its *Charter* of reforms received over three million signatures but was rejected by Parliament without consideration. Working people also formed friendly societies and co-operative societies as mutual support groups against times of economic hardship. Enlightened industrialists, such as Robert Owen also supported these organizations to improve the conditions of the working class. Unions slowly overcame the legal restrictions on the right to strike. In 1842, a General Strike involving cotton workers and colliers was organized through the Chartist Movement which stopped production across Great Britain. Eventually effective political galvanization for working people was achieved through the trades unions who, after the extensions of the franchise in 1867 and 1885, began to support socialist political parties that later merged to became the British Labour Party.

Standards of Living: Improvement for All or for Few?

The history of the change of living conditions during the industrial revolution has been very controversial, and was the topic that from the 1950s to the 1980s caused most heated debate among economic and social historians. A series of 1950s essays by Henry Phelps Brown and

Sheila V. Hopkins later set the academic consensus that the bulk of the population, that was at the bottom of the social ladder, suffered severe reductions in their living standards. Chronic hunger and malnutrition were the norm for the majority of the population of the world including England and France, until the latter part of the 19th century. Until about 1750, in large part due to malnutrition, life expectancy in France was about 35 years, and only slightly higher in England. The U. S. population of the time was adequately fed, were much taller and had life expectancies of 45—50 years. A vivid description of living standards of the mill workers in England in 1844 was given by Friedrich Engels. During the period 1813—1913, there was a significant increase in worker wages.

Population Increase: Boon or the Opposite?

According to Robert Hughes in *The Fatal Shore*, the population of England and Wales, which had remained steady at 6 million from 1700 to 1740, rose dramatically after 1740. The population of England had more than doubled from 8.3 million in 1801 to 16.8 million in 1850 and, by 1901, had nearly doubled again to 30.5 million. As living conditions and health care improved during the 19th century, Britain's population doubled every 50 years. Europe's population increased from about 100 million in 1700 to 400 million by 1900.

Other Effects: More Yet to Be Seen

The application of steam power to the industrial processes of printing supported a massive expansion of newspaper and popular book publishing, which reinforced rising literacy and demands for mass political participation. During the Industrial Revolution, the life expectancy of children increased dramatically. The percentage of the children born in London who died before the age of five decreased from 74.5% in 1730—1749 to 31.8% in 1810—1829. The growth of modern industry from the late 18th century onward led to massive urbanisation and the rise of new great cities, first in Europe and then in other regions, as new opportunities brought huge numbers of migrants from rural communities into urban areas. In 1800, only 3% of the world's population lived in cities, a figure that has risen to nearly 50% at the beginning of the 21st century. In 1717 Manchester was merely a market town of 10,000 people, but by 1911 it had a population of 2.3 million. The greatest killer in the cities was tuberculosis (TB). According to the *Harvard University Library*, "By the late 19th century, 70 to 90% of the urban populations of Europe and North America were infected with the TB bacillus, and about 80% of those individuals who developed active tuberculosis died of it. About 40% of working-class deaths in cities were from tuberculosis."

Continental Europe: Cradle of Western Power

The Industrial Revolution on Continental Europe came a little later than in Great Britain. In many industries, this involved the application of technology developed in Britain in new places. Often the technology was purchased from Britain or British engineers and entrepreneurs moved abroad in search of new opportunities. By 1809 part of the Ruhr Valley in Westphalia was called "Miniature England" because of its similarities to the industrial areas of England. The German, Russian and Belgian governments all provided state funding to the new industries. In some cases (such as iron), the different availability of resources locally meant that only some aspects of the British technology were adopted.

Demographic Effects

Wallonia was also the birthplace of a strong Socialist party and strong trade-unions in a particular sociological landscape. At the left, the *Sillon industriel*, which runs from Mons in the West, to Verviers in the East (except part of North Flanders, in another period of the industrial revolution, after 1920). Even if Belgium is the second industrial country after England, the effect of the industrial revolution there was very different. In "Breaking Stereotypes", Muriel Neven and Isabelle Devious say:

> *The industrial revolution changed a mainly rural society into an urban one, but with a strong contrast between northern and southern Belgium. During the Middle Ages and the Early Modern Period, Flanders was characterized by the presence of large urban centers (...) at the beginning of the nineteenth century this region (Flanders), with an urbanization degree of more than 30 per cent, remained one of the most urbanized in the world. By comparison, this proportion reached only 17 per cent in Wallonia, barely 10 percent in most West European countries, 16 per cent in France and 25 per cent in England. Nineteenth century industrialization did not affect the traditional urban infrastructure, except in Ghent. Also, in Wallonia the traditional urban network was largely unaffected by the industrialization process, even though the proportion of city-dwellers rose from 17 to 45 per cent between 1831 and 1910. Especially in the Haine, Sambre and Meuse valleys, between the Borinage and Liège, where there was a huge industrial development based on coal-mining and iron-making, urbanization was fast. During these eighty years the number of municipalities with more than 5,000 inhabitants increased from only 21 to more than one hundred, concentrating nearly half of the Walloon population in this region. Nevertheless, industrialization remained quite traditional in the sense that it did not lead to the growth of modern and large urban centers, but to a conurbation of industrial villages and towns developed around a coal-mine or a factory. Communication routes between these small centers only became populated later and created a much less dense urban morphology than, for instance, the area around Liège where the old town was there to direct migratory flows.*

France

The industrial revolution in France was a particular process for it did not correspond to the main model followed by other countries. Notably, most French historians argue that France did not go through a clear *take-off*. Instead, France's economic growth and industrialization process was slow and steady along the 18th and 19th centuries. However, some stages were identified by Maurice Lévy-leboyer:

1. French Revolution and Napoleonic wars (1789—1815),
2. Industrialization, along with Britain (1815—1860),
3. economic slowdown (1860—1905),
4. rnewal of the growth after 1905.

Germany and Sweden

Based on its leadership in chemical research in the universities and industrial laboratories, Germany became dominant in the world's chemical industry in the late 19th century. At first the production of dyes based on aniline was critical. Germany's political disunity—with three dozen states—and a pervasive conservatism made it difficult to build railways in the 1830s. However, by the 1840s, trunk lines linked the major cities; each German state was responsible for the lines within its own borders. Lacking a technological base at first, the Germans imported their engineering and hardware from Britain, but quickly learned the skills needed to operate and expand the railways. In many cities, the new railway shops were the centers of technological awareness and training, so that by 1850, Germany was self-sufficient in meeting the demands of railroad construction, and the railways were a major impetus for the growth of the new steel industry. Observers found that even as late as 1890, their engineering was inferior to Britain's. However, German unification in 1870 stimulated consolidation, nationalization into state-owned companies, and further rapid growth. Unlike the situation in France, the goal was support of industrialization, and so heavy lines crisscrossed the Ruhr and other industrial districts, and provided good connections to the major ports of Hamburg and Bremen. By 1880, Germany had 9,400 locomotives pulling 43,000 passengers and 30,000 tons of freight, and pulled ahead of France. During the period 1790—1815 Sweden experienced two parallel economic movements: an **agricultural revolution** with larger agricultural estates, new crops and farming tools and a commercialization of farming, and a **proto industrialization**, with small industries being established in the countryside and with workers switching between agricultural work in the summer season and industrial production in the winter season. This led to economic growth benefiting large sections of the population and leading up to a **consumption revolution** starting in the 1820s. In the period 1815—1850 the proto industries developed into more specialized and larger industries. This period witnessed increasing regional specialization with mining in Bergslagen, textile mills in Sjuhäradsbygden and forestry in Norrland. Several important institutional changes took place in this period, such as free and mandatory schooling introduced in 1842 (as first country in the world), the abolishment of a previous national monopoly on trade in handicrafts in 1846, and a stock company law in 1848. During the period 1850—1890 Sweden witnessed a veritable explosion in its export sector, with agricultural crops, wood and steel being the three dominating categories. Sweden abolished most tariffs and other barriers to free trade in the 1850s and joined the gold standard in 1873. During the period 1890—1930 the second industrial revolution took place in Sweden. During this period new industries developed with their focus on the domestic market: mechanical engineering, power utilities, papermaking and textile industries.

The United States: Emergence of a New Global Power

The United States originally used horse-powered machinery to power its earliest factories, but eventually switched to water power, with the consequence that industrialization was essentially limited to New England and the rest of the Northeastern United States, where fast-moving rivers were located. Horse-drawn production proved to be economically challenging and a more difficult alternative to the newer water-powered production lines. However, the raw materials (cotton) came from the Southern United States. It was not until after the Civil War in the 1860s that steam-powered manufacturing overtook water-powered manufacturing, allowing the industry to fully spread across the nation. Thomas Somers and the Cabot Brothers founded the Beverly Cotton Manufactory in 1787, the first cotton mill in America, the largest cotton mill of its era, and a significant milestone in the research and development of cotton mills in the future. This cotton mill was designed to utilize horse-powered production, however the operators quickly learned that the economic stability of their horse-drawn platform was unstable, and had fiscal issues for years after it was built. Despite the losses, the Manufactory served as a playground of innovation, both in turning a large amount of cotton, but also developing the water-powered milling structure used in Slater's Mill. Samuel Slater (1768—1835) is the founder of the Slater Mill. As a boy apprentice in Derbyshire, England, he learned of the new techniques in the textile industry and defied laws against the emigration of skilled workers by leaving for New York in 1789, hoping to make money with his knowledge. Slater founded Slater's Mill at Pawtucket, Rhode Island, in 1793. He went on to own thirteen textile mills. Daniel Day established a wool carding mill in the Blackstone Valley at Uxbridge, Massachusetts in 1809, the third woolen mill established in the U. S. (The first was in Hartford, Connecticut, and the second at Watertown, Massachusetts.)

The John H. Chafee Blackstone River Valley National Heritage Corridor retraces the history of "America's Hardest-Working River", the Blackstone. The Blackstone River and its tributaries, which cover more than 45 miles (72 km) from Worcester to Providence, was the birthplace of America's Industrial Revolution. At its peak over 1100 mills operated in this valley, including Slater's mill, and with it the earliest beginnings of America's Industrial and Technological Development. While on a trip to England in 1810, Newburyport merchant Francis Cabot Lowell was allowed to tour the British textile factories, but not take notes. Realizing the War of 1812 had ruined his import business but that a market for domestic finished cloth was emerging in America, he memorialized the design of textile machines, and on his return to the United States, he set up the Boston Manufacturing Company. Lowell and his partners built America's second cotton-to-cloth textile mill at Waltham, Massachusetts, second to the Beverly Cotton Manufactory After his death in 1817, his associates built America's first planned factory town, which they named after him. This enterprise was capitalized in a public stock offering, one of the first uses of it in the United States. Lowell, Massachusetts, utilizing 5.6 miles (9.0 km) of canals and ten thousand horsepower delivered by the Merrimack River, is considered by some to be a major contributor to the success of the American Industrial Revolution. The short-lived utopia-like Lowell System was formed, as a direct response to the poor working conditions in Britain.

However, by 1850, especially following the Irish Potato Famine, the system had been replaced by poor immigrant labor. The industrialization of the watch industry started in 1854 also in Waltham, Massachusetts, at the Waltham Watch Company, with the development of machine tools, tools, gauges and assembling methods adapted to the micro precision required for watches.

Japan: a Newcomer but a Giant Power

The Industrial Revolution began about 1870 as Meiji period leaders decided to catch up with the West. The government built railroads, improved roads, and inaugurated a land reform program to prepare the country for further development. It inaugurated a new western-based education system for all young people, sent thousands of students to the United States and Europe, and hired more than 3,000 westerners to teach modern science, mathematics, technology, and foreign languages in Japan (O-yatoi gaikokujin). In 1871 a group of Japanese politicians known as the Iwakura Mission toured Europe and the USA to learn western ways. The result was a deliberate state led industrialization policy to enable Japan to quickly catch up. The Bank of Japan, founded in 1877, used taxes to fund model steel and textile factories. Education was expanded and Japanese students were sent to study in the West. Modern industry first appeared in textiles, including cotton and especially silk, which was based in home workshops in rural areas.

Second Industrial Revolution: a Revolution after the Revolution

Steel is often cited as the first of several new areas for industrial mass-production, which are said to characterize a "Second Industrial Revolution", beginning around 1850, although a method for mass manufacture of steel was not invented until the 1860s, when Sir Henry Bessemer invented a new furnace which could convert wrought iron into steel in large quantities. However, it only became widely available in the 1870s after the process was modified to produce more uniform quality. This second Industrial Revolution gradually grew to include the chemical industries, petroleum refining and distribution, electrical industries, and, in the 20th century, the automotive industries, and was marked by a transition of technological leadership from Britain to the United States and Germany. The introduction of hydroelectric power generation in the Alps enabled the rapid industrialization of coal-deprived northern Italy, beginning in the 1890s. The increasing availability of economical petroleum products also reduced the importance of coal and further widened the potential for industrialization. By the 1890s, industrialization in these areas had created the first giant industrial corporations with burgeoning global interests, as companies like U. S. Steel, General Electric, Standard Oil and Bayer AG joined the railroad companies on the world's stock markets.

Intellectual Paradigms and Criticism/Capitalism: Antithetical Theme

The advent of the Age of Enlightenment provided an intellectual framework which welcomed the practical application of the growing body of scientific knowledge—a factor evidenced in the systematic development of the steam engine, guided by scientific analysis, and the development of the political and sociological analyses, culminating in Adam Smith's *The Wealth of Nations*. One of the main arguments for capitalism, presented for example in the book *The Improving State of the World*, is that industrialization increases wealth for all, as evidenced by raised life expectancy, reduced working hours, and no work for children and the elderly.

Socialism: Pushing Power of Social Progress

Socialism emerged as a critique of capitalism. Marxism began essentially as a reaction to the Industrial Revolution. According to Karl Marx, industrialization polarized society into the bourgeoisie (those who own the means of production, the factories and the land) and the much larger proletariat (the working class who actually perform the labour necessary to extract something valuable from the means of production). He saw the industrialization process as the logical dialectical progression of feudal economic modes, necessary for the full development of capitalism, which he saw as in itself a necessary precursor to the development of socialism and eventually communism.

Romanticism: Spirit Lingering On

During the Industrial Revolution an intellectual and artistic hostility towards the new industrialization developed. This was known as the Romantic movement. Its major exponents in English included the artist and poet William Blake and poets William Wordsworth, Samuel Taylor Coleridge, John Keats, Lord Byron and Percy Bysshe Shelley. The movement stressed the importance of "nature" in art and language, in contrast to "monstrous" machines and factories; the "Dark Satanic Mills" of Blake's poem "And Did Those Feet in Ancient Time". Mary Shelley's novel *Frankenstein* reflected concerns that scientific progress might be two-edged.

Causes: Too Many to Identify

The causes of the Industrial Revolution were complicated and remain a topic for debate, with some historians believing the Revolution was an outgrowth of social and institutional changes brought by the end of feudalism in Britain after the English Civil War in the 17th century. As national border controls became more effective, the spread of disease was lessened, thereby preventing the epidemics common in previous times. The percentage of children who lived past infancy rose significantly, leading to a larger workforce. The Enclosure Movement and the British Agricultural Revolution made food production more efficient and less labor-intensive, forcing the surplus population who could no longer find employment in agriculture into cottage industry, for example weaving, and in the longer term into the cities and the newly developed factories. The colonial expansion of the 17th century with the accompanying development of international trade, creation of financial markets and accumulation of capital are also cited as factors, as is the scientific revolution of the 17th century. Until the 1980s, it was universally believed by academic historians that technological innovation was the heart of the Industrial Revolution and the key enabling technology was the invention and improvement of the steam engine. However, recent research into the Marketing Era has challenged the traditional, supply-oriented interpretation of the Industrial Revolution. Lewis Mumford has proposed that the Industrial Revolution had its origins in the Early Middle Ages, much earlier than most estimates. He explains that the model for standardized mass production was the printing press and that "the archetypal model for the industrial era was the clock". He also cites the monastic emphasis on order and time-keeping, as well as the fact that medieval cities had at their center a church with bell ringing at regular intervals as being necessary precursors to a greater synchronization necessary for later, more physical, manifestations such as the steam engine. The presence of a large domestic market should also be considered an important driver of the Industrial Revolution, particularly explaining why it occurred in Britain. In other nations, such as France, markets were split up by local regions, which often imposed tolls and tariffs on goods traded among them. Internal tariffs were abolished by Henry Ⅷ of England, they survived in Russia till 1753, 1789 in France and 1839 in Spain.

Governments' grant of limited monopolies to inventors under a developing patent system (the Statute of Monopolies 1623) is considered an influential factor. The effects of patents, both good and ill, on the development of industrialization are clearly illustrated in the history of the steam engine, the key enabling technology. In return for publicly revealing the workings of an invention the patent system rewarded inventors such as James Watt by allowing them to monopolize the production of the first steam engines, thereby rewarding inventors and increasing the pace of technological development. However, monopolies bring with them their own inefficiencies which may counterbalance, or even overbalance, the beneficial effects of publicizing ingenuity and rewarding inventors. Watt's monopoly may have prevented other inventors, such as Richard Trevithick, William Murdoch or Jonathan Hornblower, from introducing improved steam engines, thereby retarding the Industrial Revolution by about 16 years.

Causes for Occurrence in Europe

European 17th century colonial expansion, international trade, and creation of financial markets produced a new legal and financial environment, one which supported and enabled 18th century industrial growth. One question of active interest to historians is why the industrial revolution occurred in Europe and not in other parts of the world in the 18th century, particularly China, India, and the Middle East, or at other times like in Classical Antiquity or the Middle Ages. Numerous factors have been suggested, including education, technological changes (see Scientific Revolution in Europe), "modern" government, "modern" work attitudes, ecology, and culture. The Age of Enlightenment not only meant a larger educated population but also more modern views on work. However, most historians contest the assertion that Europe and China were roughly equal because modern estimates of per capita income on western Europe in the late 18th century are of roughly 1,500 dollars in purchasing power parity (and Britain had a per capita income of nearly 2,000 dollars) whereas China, by comparison, had only 450 dollars. Some historians such as David Landes and Max Weber credit the different belief systems in China and Europe with dictating where the revolution occurred. The religion and beliefs of Europe were largely products of Judaeo-Christianity, and Greek thought. Conversely, Chinese society was founded on men like Confucius, Mencius, Han Feizi (Legalism), Lao Tzu (Taoism), and Buddha (Buddhism). Whereas the Europeans believed that the universe was governed by rational and eternal laws, the East believed that the universe was in constant flux and, for Buddhists and Taoists, not capable of being rationally understood. Other factors include the considerable distance of China's coal deposits, though large, from its cities as well as the then unnavigable Yellow River that connects these deposits to the sea. Regarding India, the Marxist historian Rajani Palme Dutt said: "The capital to finance the Industrial Revolution in India instead went into financing the Industrial Revolution in England." In contrast to China, India was split up into many competing kingdoms, with the three major ones being the Marathas, Sikhs and the Mughals. In addition, the economy was highly dependent on two sectors—agriculture of subsistence and cotton, and there appears to have been little technical innovation. It is believed that the vast amounts of wealth were largely stored away in palace treasuries by totalitarian monarchs prior to the British take over. Absolutist dynasties in China, India, and the Middle East failed to encourage manufacturing and exports, and expressed little interest in the well-being of their subjects.

Causes for Occurrence in Britain: Cradle of Industrial Revolution

As the Industrial Revolution developed British manufactured output surged ahead of other economies. After the Industrial Revolution, it was overtaken later by the United States. There were two main values that really drove the Industrial Revolution in Britain. These values were self interest and an entrepreneurial spirit. Because of these interests, many industrial advances were made that resulted in a huge increase in personal wealth. These advancements also greatly benefited the British society as a whole. Countries around the world started to recognize the changes and advancements in Britain and use them as an example to begin their own industrial revolutions. The debate about the start of the Industrial Revolution also concerns the massive lead that Great Britain had over other countries. Some have stressed the importance of natural or financial resources that Britain received from its many overseas colonies or that profits from the British slave trade between Africa and the Caribbean helped fuel industrial investment. However, it has been pointed out that slave trade and West Indian plantations provided only 5% of the British national income during the years of the Industrial Revolution. Even though slavery accounted for minimal economic profits in Britain during the Industrial Revolution, Caribbean-based demand accounted for 12% of England's industrial output. Instead, the greater liberalization of trade from a large merchant base may have allowed Britain to produce and use emerging scientific and technological developments more effectively than countries with stronger monarchies, particularly China and Russia. Britain emerged from the Napoleonic Wars as the only European nation not ravaged by financial plunder and economic collapse, and having the only merchant fleet of any useful size (European merchant fleets were destroyed during the war by the Royal Navy). Britain's extensive exporting cottage industries also ensured markets were already available for many early forms of manufactured goods. The conflict resulted in most British warfare being conducted overseas, reducing the devastating effects of territorial conquest that affected much of Europe. This was further aided by Britain's geographical position—an island separated from the rest of mainland Europe.

Another theory is that Britain was able to succeed in the Industrial Revolution due to the availability of key resources it possessed. It had a dense population for its small geographical size. Enclosure of common land and the related agricultural revolution made a supply of this labor readily available. There was also a local coincidence of natural resources in the North of England, the English Midlands, South Wales and the Scottish Lowlands. Local supplies of coal, iron, lead, copper, tin, limestone and water power, resulted in excellent conditions for the development and expansion of industry. Also, the damp, mild weather conditions of the North West of England provided ideal conditions for the spinning of cotton, providing a natural starting point for the birth of the textiles industry. The stable political situation in Britain from around 1688, and British society's greater receptiveness to change (compared with other European countries) can also be said to be factors favoring the Industrial Revolution. Peasant resistance to industrialization was largely eliminated by the Enclosure Movement, and the landed upper classes developed commercial interests that made them pioneers in removing obstacles to the growth of capitalism. (This point is also made in Hilaire Belloc's *The Servile State*.) Britain's population grew 280% 1550 — 1820, while the rest of western Europe grew 50 — 80%. 70% of European urbanization happened in Britain 1750—1800. By 1800, only the Netherlands was more urbanized than Britain. This was only possible because coal, coke, imported cotton, brick and slate had replaced wood, charcoal, flax, peat and thatch. The latter compete with land grown to feed people while mined materials do not. Yet more land would be freed when chemical fertilizers replaced manure and horse's work was mechanized. A workhorse needs 3 to 5 acres (1.21 to 2.02 ha) for fodder while even early steam engines produced 4 times more mechanical energy. In 1700, 5/6 of coal mined worldwide was in Britain, while the Netherlands had none; so despite having Europe's best transport, most urbanized, well paid, literate people and lowest taxes, it failed to industrialize. In the 18th century, it was the only European country whose cities and population shrank. Without coal, Britain would have run out of suitable river sites for mills by the 1830s.

Protestant Work Ethic: a Spiritual Power for Acquiring Wealth

Another theory is that the British advance was due to the presence of an entrepreneurial class which believed in progress, technology and hard work. The existence of this class is often linked to the Protestant work ethic (see Max Weber) and the particular status of the Baptists and the dissenting Protestant sects, such as the Quakers and Presbyterians that had flourished with the English Civil War. Reinforcement of confidence in the rule of law, which followed establishment of the prototype of constitutional monarchy in Britain in the Glorious Revolution of 1688, and the emergence of a stable financial market there based on the management of the national debt by the Bank of England, contributed to the capacity for, and interest in, private financial investment in industrial ventures. Dissenters found themselves barred or discouraged from almost all public offices, as well as education at England's only two universities at the time (although dissenters were still free to study at Scotland's four universities). When the restoration of the monarchy took place and membership in the official Anglican Church became mandatory due to the Test Act, they thereupon became active in banking, manufacturing and education. The Unitarians, in particular, were very involved in education, by running Dissenting Academies, where, in contrast to the universities of Oxford and Cambridge and schools such as Eton and Harrow, much attention was given to mathematics and the sciences—areas of scholarship vital to the development of manufacturing technologies. Historians sometimes consider this social factor to be extremely important, along with the nature of the national economies involved. While members of these sects were excluded from certain circles of the government, they were considered fellow Protestants, to a limited extent, by many in the middle class, such as traditional financiers or other businessmen. Given this relative tolerance and the supply of capital, the natural outlet for the more enterprising members of these sects would be to seek new opportunities in the technologies created in the wake of the scientific revolution of the 17th century.

Questions and Topics for Pondering and Further Discussion for Unit Seven-2:

1. Why is it that the Industrial Revolution occurred first in Britain?
2. What are the major features of the Industrial Revolution?
3. In what aspects do people call this Industrial Movement a revolution?
4. Some men of letters regard the Industrial Revolution as a disaster for human beings. What is your opinion?
5. What is the social significance of the Industrial Revolution?
6. Some people say that the Industrial Revolution ushered a new way of life. Can you elaborate on it?
7. What is the relationship between Industrialization and Urbanization?
8. Some people define the Industrial Revolution as being precondition for modernization. Make comment on it.

3. Scientific Revolution, a Miraculous Instrument for the Rise of the West and Its Leadership

The scientific revolution refers to the history of science in the early modern period, where development in physics, astronomy, biology, medicine and chemistry transformed views of society and nature. According to traditional accounts, the scientific revolution began in Europe towards the end of the Renaissance era and continued through the late 18th century, the later period known as The Enlightenment. While its dates are disputed, the publication in 1543 of Nicolaus Copernicus's *De revolutionibus orbium coelestium* (*On the Revolutions of the Heavenly Spheres*) and Andreas Vesalius's *De humani corporis fabrica* (*On the Fabric of the Human body*) are often cited as marking the beginning of the scientific revolution. By the end of the 18th century the scientific revolution gave way to the "Age of Reflection". Philosopher Alexandre Koyré coined the term "scientific revolution" in 1939 to describe this epoch.

Significance of the Revolution

The science of the middle ages was significant in establishing a base for modern science. The Marxist historian and scientist J. D. Bernal asserted that "the renaissance enabled a scientific revolution which let scholars look at the world in a different light. Religion, superstition, and fear were replaced by reason and knowledge". James Hannam says that, while most historians do think something revolutionary happened at this time, that "the term 'scientific revolution' is another one of those prejudicial historical labels that explain nothing. You could call any century from the twelfth to the twentieth a revolution in science" and that the concept "does nothing more than reinforce the error that before Copernicus nothing of any significance to science took place". Despite some challenges to religious views, however, many notable figures of the scientific revolution—including Nicolaus Copernicus, Tycho Brahe, Johannes Kepler, Galileo Galilei, Descartes, Isaac Newton and Gottfried Leibniz—remained devout in their faith. This period saw a fundamental transformation in scientific ideas across mathematics, physics, astronomy, and biology, in institutions supporting scientific investigation, and in the more widely held picture of the universe. The scientific revolution led to the establishment of several modern sciences. In 1984, Joseph Ben-david wrote:

> *Rapid accumulation of knowledge, which has characterized the development of science since the 17th century, had never occurred before that time. The new kind of scientific activity emerged only in a few countries of western Europe, and it was restricted to that small area for about two hundred years. (Since the 19th century, scientific knowledge has been assimilated by the rest of the world).*

Mid-20th century historian Herbert Butterfield was less disconcerted, but nevertheless saw the change as fundamental:

> *Since that revolution turned the authority in English not only of the Middle Ages but of the ancient world—since it started not only in the eclipse of scholastic philosophy but in the destruction of Aristotelian physics—it outshines everything since the rise of Christianity and reduces the Renaissance and Reformation to the rank of mere episodes, mere internal displacements within the system of medieval Christendom.... [It] looms so large as the real origin both of the modern world and of the modern mentality that our customary periodization of European history has become an anachronism and an encumbrance.*

More recently, sociologist and historian of science Steven Shapin opened his book, *The Scientific Revolution*, with the paradoxical statement: "There was no such thing as the Scientific Revolution, and this is a book about it." Although historians of science continue to debate the exact meaning of the term, and even its validity, the scientific revolution still remains a useful concept to interpret the many changes in science.

New Ideas Are Powerful and Everlasting

The scientific revolution was not marked by any single change. The following new ideas contributed to what is called the scientific revolution:

- The replacement of the Earth as center of the universe by Heliocentrism.
- Deprecation of the Aristotelian theory that matter was continuous and made up of the elements Earth, Water, Air, and Fire because its classic rival, Atomism, better lent itself to a "mechanical philosophy" of matter.

- The replacement of the Aristotelian idea that heavy bodies, by their nature, moved straight down toward their natural places; that light bodies, by their nature, moved straight up toward their natural place; and that ethereal bodies, by their nature, moved in unchanging circular motions with the idea that all bodies are heavy and move according to the same physical laws.
- Inertia replaced the medieval impetus theory, that unnatural motion ("forced" or "violent" rectilinear motion) is caused by continuous action of the original force imparted by a mover into that which is moved.
- The replacement of Galen's treatment of the venous and arterial systems as two separate systems with William Harvey's concept that blood circulated from the arteries to the veins "impelled in a circle, and is in a state of ceaseless motion".

However, according to Galileo, the core of what came to be known as the scientific method in modern physical sciences is stated in his book *Il Saggiatore* to be the concept of a systematic, mathematical interpretation of experiments and empirical facts:

Philosophy [i. e. physics] is written in this grand book—I mean the universe—which stands continually open to our gaze, but it cannot be understood unless one first learns to comprehend the language and interpret the characters in which it is written. It is written in the language of mathematics, and its characters are triangles, circles, and other geometrical figures, without which it is humanly impossible to understand a single word of it; without these, one is wandering around in a dark labyrinth.

Many of the important figures of the scientific revolution, however, shared in the Renaissance respect for ancient learning and cited ancient pedigrees for their innovations. Nicolaus Copernicus (1473—1543), Kepler (1571—1630), Newton (1642—1727) and Galileo Galilei (1564—1642) all traced different ancient and medieval ancestries for the heliocentric system. In the Axioms Scholium of his *Principia* Newton said its axiomatic three laws of motion were already accepted by mathematicians such as Huygens (1629—1695), Wallace, Wren and others, and also in memos in his draft preparations of the second edition of the *Principia* he attributed its first law of motion and its law of gravity to a range of historical figures. According to Newton himself and other historians of science, his *Principia*'s first law of motion was the same as Aristotle's counterfactual principle of interminable locomotion in a void stated in *Physics* and was also endorsed by ancient Greek atomists and others. As Newton expressed himself:

All those ancients knew the first law [of motion] who attributed to atoms in an infinite vacuum a motion which was rectilinear, extremely swift and perpetual because of the lack of resistance... Aristotle was of the same mind, since he expresses his opinion thus...[in Physics 4. 8. 215a19—22], speaking of motion in the void [in which bodies have no gravity and] where there is no impediment he writes: "Why a body once moved should come to rest anywhere no one can say. For why should it rest here rather than there? Hence either it will not be moved, or it must be moved indefinitely, unless something stronger impedes it."

As Newton attests, the *Principia*'s first law of motion was known in antiquity, even by Aristotle, although its significance, as such, went unappreciated. This refutes Kuhn's thesis of a scientific revolution in dynamics. The geocentric model was nearly universally accepted until 1543 when Nicolaus Copernicus published his book entitled *De revolutionibus orbium coelestium* and was widely accepted into the next century. At around the same time, the findings of Vesalius corrected the previous anatomical teachings of Galen, which were based upon the dissection of animals even though they were supposed to be a guide to the human body. Andreas Vesalius

(1514—1564) was an author of one of the most influential books on human anatomy, *De humani corporis fabrica*, also in 1543. French surgeon Ambroise Paré (c. 1510—1590) is considered as one of the fathers of surgery; he was leader in surgical techniques and battlefield medicine, especially the treatment of wounds. Partly based on the works by the Italian surgeon and anatomist Matteo Realdo Colombo (c. 1516—1559), the anatomist William Harvey (1578—1657) described the circulatory system. Herman Boerhaave (1668—1738) is sometimes referred to as a "father of physiology" due to his exemplary teaching in Leiden and textbook "Institutiones medicae" (1708). It was between 1650 and 1800 that the science of modern dentistry developed. It is said that the 17th century French physician Pierre Fauchard (1678—1761) started dentistry science as we know it today, and he has been named "the father of modern dentistry". Pierre Vernier (1580—1637) was inventor and eponym of the vernier scale used in measuring devices.

Evangelista Torricelli (1607—1647) was best known for his invention of the barometer. Although Franciscus Vieta (1540—1603) gave the first notation of modern algebra, John Napier (1550—1617) invented logarithms, and Edmund Gunter (1581—1626) created the logarithmic scales (lines, or rules) upon which slide rules are based. It was William Oughtred (1575—1660) who first used two such scales sliding by one another to perform direct multiplication and division; and thus is credited as the inventor of the slide rule in 1622. Blaise Pascal (1623—1662) invented the mechanical calculator in 1642. The introduction of his Pascaline in 1645 launched the development of mechanical calculators first in Europe and then all over the world. He also made important contributions to the study of fluid and clarified the concepts of pressure and vacuum by generalizing the work of Evangelista Torricelli. He wrote a significant treatise on the subject of projective geometry at the age of sixteen, and later corresponded with Pierre de Fermat (1601—1665) on probability theory, strongly influencing the development of modern economics and social science. Gottfried Leibniz (1646—1716), building on Pascal's work, became one of the most prolific inventors in the field of mechanical calculators; he was the first to describe a pinwheel calculator in 1685 and invented the Leibniz wheel, used in the arithmometer, the first mass-produced mechanical calculator. He also refined the binary number system, foundation of virtually all modern computer architectures. John Hadley (1682—1744) was mathematician inventor of the octant, the precursor to the sextant. Hadley also developed ways to make precision aspheric and parabolic objective mirrors for reflecting telescopes, building the first parabolic Newtonian telescope and a Gregorian telescope with accurately shaped mirrors. Denis Papin (1647—1712) was best known for his pioneering invention of the steam digester, the forerunner of the steam engine. Abraham Darby I (1678—1717) was the first, and most famous, of three generations with that name in an Abraham Darby family that played an important role in the Industrial Revolution. He developed a method of producing high-grade iron in a blast furnace fueled by coke rather than charcoal. This was a major step forward in the production of iron as a raw material for the Industrial Revolution. Thomas Newcomen (1664—1729) perfected a practical steam engine for pumping water, the Newcomen steam engine. Consequently, he can be regarded as a forefather of the Industrial Revolution. In 1672, Otto von Guericke (1602—1686), was the first human on record to knowingly generate electricity using a machine, and in 1729, Stephen Gray (1666—1736) demonstrated that electricity could be "transmitted" through metal filaments. The first electrical storage device was invented in 1745, the so-called "Leyden jar", and in 1749, Benjamin Franklin (1706—1790) demonstrated that lightning was electricity.

In 1698 Thomas Savery (c. 1650—1715) patented an early steam engine. German scientist Georg Agricola (1494—1555), known as "the father of mineralogy", published his great work *De re metallica*. Robert Boyle (1627—1691) was credited with the discovery of Boyle's Law. He is also credited for his landmark publication *The Sceptical Chymist*, where he attempts to develop an atomic theory of matter. The person celebrated as the "father of modern chemistry" is Antoine Lavoisier (1743—1794) who developed his law of Conservation of mass in 1789, also called *Lavoisier's Law*. Antoine Lavoisier proved that burning was caused by oxidation, that is, the mixing of a substance with oxygen. He also proved that diamonds were made of carbon and argued that all living processes were at their heart chemical reactions. In 1766, Henry Cavendish (1731—1810) discovered hydrogen. In 1774, Joseph Priestley (1733—1804) discovered oxygen. Gottfried Leibniz (1646—1716) refined the binary system, foundation of virtually all modern computer architectures. German physician Leonhart Fuchs (1501—1566) was one of the three founding fathers of botany, along with Otto Brunfels (1489—1534) and Hieronymus Bock (1498—1554) (also called Hieronymus Tragus). Valerius Cordus (1515—1554) authored one of the greatest pharmacopoeias and one of the most celebrated herbals in history, *Dispensatorium* (1546).

In his *Systema Naturae*, published in 1767, Carl von Linné (1707—1778) cataloged all the living creatures into a single system that defined their morphological relations to one another: the Linnean Classification System. He is often called the "father of taxonomy". Georges Buffon (1707—1788), was perhaps the most important of Charles Darwin's predecessors. From 1744 to 1788, he wrote his monumental *Histoire naturelle, générale et particulière*, which included everything known about the natural world up until that date. Along with the inventor and microscopist Robert Hooke (1635—1703), Sir Christopher Wren (1632—1723) and Sir Isaac Newton (1642—1727), English scientist and astronomer Edmond Halley (1656—1742) was trying to develop a mechanical explanation for planetary motion. Halley's star catalogue of 1678 was the first to contain telescopically determined locations of southern stars. Many historians of science have seen other ancient and medieval antecedents of these ideas. It is widely accepted that Copernicus's *De revolutionibus* followed the outline and method set by Ptolemy in his *Almagest* and employed geometrical constructions that had been developed previously by the Maragheh school in his heliocentric model, and that Galileo's mathematical treatment of acceleration and his concept of impetus rejected earlier medieval analyses of motion.

The standard theory of the history of the scientific revolution claims the 17th century was a period of revolutionary scientific changes. It is claimed that not only were there revolutionary theoretical and experimental developments, but that even more importantly, the way in which scientists worked was radically changed. An alternative anti-revolutionist view is that science as exemplified by Newton's *Principia* was anti-mechanist and highly Aristotelian, being specifically directed at the refutation of anti-aristotelian Cartesian mechanism, as evidenced in the *Principia* quotations below, and not more empirical than it already was at the beginning of the century or earlier in the works of scientists such as Benedetti, Galileo Galilei, or Johannes Kepler.

Ancient and Medieval Background

The scientific revolution was built upon the foundation of ancient Greek learning and science in the middle ages, as it had been elaborated and further developed by Roman/Byzantine science and medieval Islamic science. The "Aristotelian tradition" was still an important intellectual framework in the 17th century, although by that time natural philosophers had moved away from much of it. Key scientific ideas dating back to classical antiquity had changed drastically over the years, and in many cases been discredited. The ideas that remained, which would be transformed fundamentally during the scientific revolution, include:

Aristotle's cosmology which placed the Earth at the center of a spherical hierarchic cosmos. The terrestrial and celestial regions were made up of different elements which had different kinds of *natural movement*.

1. The terrestrial region, according to Aristotle, consisted of concentric spheres of the four elements—earth, water, air, and fire. All bodies naturally moved in straight lines until they reached the sphere appropriate to their elemental composition—their *natural place*. All other terrestrial motions were non-natural, or *violent*.
2. The celestial region was made up of the fifth element, Aether, which was unchanging and moved naturally with uniform circular motion. In the Aristotelian tradition, astronomical theories sought to explain the observed irregular motion of celestial objects through the combined effects of multiple uniform circular motions.

The Ptolemaic model of planetary motion: Based on the geometrical model of Eudoxus of Cnidus, Ptolemy's *Almagest*, demonstrated that calculations could compute the exact positions of the Sun, Moon, stars, and planets in the future and in the past, and showed how these computational models were derived from astronomical observations. As such they formed the model for later astronomical developments. The physical basis for Ptolemaic models invoked layers of spherical shells, though the most complex models were inconsistent with this physical explanation. It is important to note that ancient precedent existed for alternative theories and developments which prefigured later discoveries in the area of physics and mechanics; but in the absence of a strong empirical tradition, dominance of the Aristotelian school, and in light of the limited number of works to survive translation in an era when many books were lost to warfare, such developments remained obscure for centuries and are traditionally held to have had little effect on the re-discovery of such phenomena; whereas the invention of the printing press made the wide dissemination of such incremental advances of knowledge commonplace. Meanwhile, however, significant progress in geometry, mathematics, and astronomy was made in the medieval era, particularly in the Islamic world as well as Europe.

New Approaches to Nature

Historians of the scientific revolution traditionally maintain that its most important changes were in the way in which scientific investigation was conducted, as well as the philosophy underlying scientific developments. Among the main changes are the mechanical philosophy, the chemical philosophy, empiricism, and the increasing role of mathematics.

The Mechanical Philosophy

Aristotle recognized four kinds of causes, and where applicable, the most important of them is the "final cause". The final cause was the aim, goal, or purpose of some natural process or man-made thing. Until the scientific revolution, it was very natural to see such aims, such as a child's growth, for example, leading to a mature adult. Intelligence was assumed only in the purpose of man-made artifacts; it was not attributed to other animals or to nature. In "mechanical philosophy" no field or action at a distance is permitted, particles or corpuscles of matter are fundamentally inert. Motion is caused by direct physical collision. Where nature substances had previously been understood organically, the mechanical philosophers viewed them as machines. As a result, Newton's theory seemed like some kind of throwback to "spooky action at a distance". According to Thomas Kuhn, he and Descartes held the teleological principle that God conserved the amount of motion in the universe:

> *Gravity, interpreted as an innate attraction between every pair of particles of matter, was an occult quality in the same sense as the scholastics' "tendency to fall" had been....*

By the mid eighteenth century that interpretation had been almost universally accepted, and the result was a genuine reversion (which is not the same as a retrogression) to a scholastic standard. Innate attractions and repulsions joined size, shape, position and motion as physically irreducible primary properties of matter. Newton had also specifically attributed the inherent power of inertia to matter, against the mechanist thesis that matter has no inherent powers. But whereas Newton vehemently denied gravity was an inherent power of matter, his collaborator Roger Cotes made gravity also an inherent power of matter, as set out in his famous preface to the Principia's 1713 second edition which he edited, and contra Newton himself. And it was Cotes's interpretation of gravity rather than Newton's that came to be accepted.

The Chemical Philosophy

Chemistry, and its antecedent alchemy, became an increasingly important aspect of scientific thought in the course of the 16th and 17th centuries. The importance of chemistry is indicated by the range of important scholars who actively engaged in chemical research. Among them were the astronomer Tycho Brahe, the chemical physician Paracelsus, the Irish philosopher Robert Boyle, and the English philosophers T Browne and Newton. Unlike the mechanical philosophy, the chemical philosophy stressed the active powers of matter, which alchemists frequently expressed in terms of vital or active principles—of spirits operating in nature.

Empiricism

The Aristotelian scientific tradition's primary mode of interacting with the world was through observation and searching for "natural" circumstances through reasoning. Coupled with this approach was the belief that rare events which seemed to contradict theoretical models were aberrations, telling nothing about nature as it "naturally" was. During the scientific revolution, changing perceptions about the role of the scientist in respect to nature, the value of evidence, experimental or observed, led towards a scientific methodology in which empiricism played a large, but not absolute, role. By the start of the scientific revolution, empiricism had already become an important component of science and natural philosophy. Prior thinkers, particularly nominalist William of Ockham in the early 14th century, had begun the intellectual movement toward empiricism. Under the influence of scientists and philosophers like Francis Bacon, a sophisticated empirical tradition was developed by the 16th century. Belief of natural and artificial circumstances was abandoned, and a research tradition of systematic experimentation was slowly accepted throughout the scientific community. Bacon's philosophy of using an inductive approach to nature—to abandon assumption and to attempt to simply observe with an open mind—was in strict contrast with the earlier, Aristotelian approach of deduction, by which analysis of known facts produced further understanding. In practice, of course, many scientists (and philosophers) believed that a healthy mix of both was needed—the willingness to question assumptions, yet also to interpret observations assumed to have some degree of validity. At the end of the scientific revolution the organic, qualitative world of book-reading philosophers had been changed into a mechanical, mathematical world to be known through experimental research. Though it is certainly not true that Newtonian science was like modern science in all respects, it conceptually resembled ours in many ways. Many of the hallmarks of modern science, especially in respect to the institution and profession of science, would not become standard until the mid-19th century.

Mathematization: Measurement Yardstick for All Existences in the World

Scientific knowledge, according to the Aristotelians, was concerned with establishing true and necessary causes of things. To the extent that medieval natural philosophers used mathematical problems, they limited social studies to theoretical analyses of local speed and other aspects of life. The actual measurement of a physical quantity, and the comparison of that measurement to a value computed on the basis of theory, was largely limited to the mathematical disciplines of astronomy and optics in Europe. In the 16th and 17th centuries, European scientists began increasingly applying quantitative measurements to the measurement of physical phenomena on the Earth. Galileo maintained strongly that mathematics provided a kind of necessary certainty that could be compared to God's:

> *With regard to those few mathematical propositions which the human intellect does understand, I believe its knowledge equals the Divine in objective certainty.*

Scientific Developments Listed and Summarized for Great Ideas

Key ideas and people that emerged from the 16th and 17th centuries are listed as follows:

1. First printed edition of Euclid's *Elements* in 1482.
2. Nicolaus Copernicus (1473—1543) published *On the Revolutions of the Heavenly Spheres* in 1543, which advanced the heliocentric theory of cosmology.
3. Andreas Vesalius (1514—1564) published *De Humani Corporis Fabrica* (*On the Fabric of the Human Body*) (1543), which discredited Galen's views. He found that the circulation of blood resolved from pumping of the heart. He also assembled the first human skeleton from cutting open cadavers.
4. Franciscus Vieta (1540—1603) published *In Artem Analycitem Isagoge* (1591), which gave the first symbolic notation of parameters in literal algebra.
5. William Gilbert (1544—1603) published *On the Magnet and Magnetic Bodies, and on the Great Magnet the Earth* in 1600, which laid the foundations of a theory of magnetism and electricity.
6. Tycho Brahe (1546—1601) made extensive and more accurate naked eye observations of the planets in the late 16th century. These became the basic data for Kepler's studies.
7. Sir Francis Bacon (1561—1626) published *Novum Organum* in 1620, which outlined a new system of logic based on the process of reduction, which he offered as an improvement over Aristotle's philosophical process of syllogism. This contributed to the development of what became known as the scientific method.
8. Galileo Galilei (1564—1642) improved the telescope, with which he made several important astronomical discoveries, including the four largest moons of Jupiter, the phases of Venus, and the rings of Saturn, and made detailed observations of sunspots. He developed the laws for falling bodies based on pioneering quantitative experiments which he analyzed mathematically.
9. Johannes Kepler (1571—1630) published the first two of his three laws of planetary motion in 1609.
10. William Harvey (1578—1657) demonstrated that blood circulates, using dissections and other experimental techniques.
11. René Descartes (1596—1650) published his *Discourse on the Method* in 1637, which helped to establish the scientific method.

12. Antonie van Leeuwenhoek (1632—1723) constructed powerful single lens microscopes and made extensive observations that he published around 1660, opening up the micro-world of biology.
13. Isaac Newton (1643—1727) built upon the work of Kepler and Galileo. He showed that an inverse square law for gravity explained the elliptical orbits of the planets, and advanced the law of universal gravitation. His development of infinitesimal calculus opened up new applications of the methods of mathematics to science. Newton taught that scientific theory should be coupled with rigorous experimentation, which became the keystone of modern science.

Numerous other great minds were produced during this period of time albeit with less influence in scientific fields. For example, French Encyclopedic School that made great contributions to the spread of knowledge that deepened human understanding of nature.

Theoretical Developments

In 1543 Copernicus' work on the heliocentric model of the solar system was published, in which he tried to demonstrate that the sun was the center of the universe. Few were bothered by this suggestion, and the pope and several archbishops were interested enough by it to want more detail. His model was later used to create the calendar of Pope Gregory XIII. For almost two millennia, the geocentric model had been accepted by all but a few astronomers. The idea that the earth moved around the sun, as advocated by Copernicus, was to most of his contemporaries doubtful. It contradicted not only empirical observation, due to the absence of an observable stellar parallax, but also Aristotelian philosophy. The discoveries of Johannes Kepler and Galileo gave the theory credibility. Kepler was an astronomer who, using the accurate observations of Tycho Brahe, proposed that the planets move around the sun not in circular orbits, but in elliptical ones. Together with his other laws of planetary motion, this allowed him to create a model of the solar system that was an improvement over Copernicus' original system. Galileo's main contributions to the acceptance of the heliocentric system were his mechanics, the observations he made with his telescope, as well as his detailed presentation of the case for the system. Using an early theory of inertia, Galileo could explain why rocks dropped from a tower fall straight down even if the earth rotates. His observations of the moons of Jupiter, the phases of Venus, the spots on the sun, and mountains on the moon all helped to discredit the Aristotelian philosophy and the Ptolemaic theory of the solar system. Through their combined discoveries, the heliocentric system gained support, and at the end of the 17th century it was generally accepted by astronomers. Kepler's laws of planetary motion and Galileo's mechanics culminated in the work of Isaac Newton. His laws of motion were to be the solid foundation of mechanics; his law of universal gravitation combined terrestrial and celestial mechanics into one great system that seemed to be able to describe the whole world in mathematical formulae. Not only astronomy and mechanics were greatly changed. Optics, for instance, was revolutionized by people like Robert Hooke, Christiaan Huygens, René Descartes and, once again, Isaac Newton, who developed mathematical theories of light as either waves (Huygens) or particles (Newton). Similar developments could be seen in chemistry, biology and other sciences, although their full development into modern science was delayed for a century or more.

Contrary Views: a Revolution or Natural Evolution?

Not all historians of science are agreed that there was any revolution in the sixteenth or 17th century. The continuity thesis is the hypothesis that there was no radical discontinuity between the intellectual development of the Middle Ages and the developments in the Renaissance and early modern period. Thus the idea of an intellectual or scientific revolution following the Renaissance is—according to the continuity thesis—a myth. Some continuity theorists point to earlier intellectual revolutions occurring in the Middle Ages, usually referring to either a European "Renaissance of the 12th century" or a medieval "Muslim scientific revolution", as a sign of continuity. Another contrary view has been recently proposed by Arun Bala in his dialogical history of the birth of modern science. Bala argues that the changes involved in the Scientific Revolution—the mathematical realist turn, the mechanical philosophy, the atomism, the central role assigned to the Sun in Copernican heliocentrism—have to be seen as rooted in multicultural influences on Europe. Islamic science gave the first exemplar of a mathematical realist theory with Alhazen's *Book of Optics* in which physical light rays traveled along mathematical straight lines. The swift transfer of Chinese mechanical technologies in the medieval era shifted European sensibilities to perceive the world in the image of a machine. The Hindu-Arabic numeral system, which developed in close association with atomism in India, carried implicitly a new mode of mathematical atomic thinking. And the heliocentric theory, which assigned central status to the Sun, as well as Newton's concept of force acting at a distance, were rooted in ancient Egyptian religious ideas associated with Hermeticism. Bala argues that by ignoring such multicultural impacts we have been led to a Eurocentric conception of the scientific revolution. A third approach takes the term "renaissance" literally. A closer study of Greek philosophy and Greek mathematics demonstrates that nearly all of the so-called revolutionary results of the so-called scientific revolution were in actuality restatements of ideas that were in many cases older than those of Aristotle and in nearly all cases at least as old as Archimedes. Aristotle even explicitly argues against some of the ideas that were demonstrated during the scientific revolution, such as heliocentrism. The basic ideas of the scientific method were well known to Archimedes and his contemporaries, as demonstrated in the well known discovery of buoyancy. Atomism was first thought of by Leucippus and Democritus. This view of the scientific revolution reduces it to a period of relearning classical ideas that is very much an extension of the renaissance, specifically relearning ideas that originated with somebody other than Aristotle and particularly those rooted in the schools of Plato and Pythagoras. This view of the scientific revolution does not deny that a change occurred but argues that it was a reassertion of previous knowledge (a renaissance) and not the creation of new knowledge. It cites statements from Newton, Copernicus and others in favor of the Pythagorean worldview as evidence.

Questions and Topics for Pondering and Further Discussion for Unit Seven-3:

1. Why was there a scientific revolution?
2. What are the ideological forces behind the Scientific Revolution?
3. Can you name some of the scientific giants in history? And briefly tell their major contributions.
4. What is the significance of Copernicus' scientific contribution?
5. What is the significance of Galileo's discovery?
6. What are the relations between alchemy & chemistry? What are the relations between philosophy & science?
7. What are the major substantial achievements of the Scientific Revolution?
8. What is the Pythagorean world-view about?

4. Science and Scientific Spirit

Editor's remarks: it is said that the West began to rise because of its scientific spirit that has dominated the way westerners think. No matter what, science did play a very important role in helping the West to rise in the modern era. Facts abound that many western countries, headed by the USA are strong in their scientific research and discoveries that are applied to the mode of production which in turn has produced a lot of material wealth. The rise of the West should be chiefly attributed to its highly developed awareness of science since the end of the Middle Ages, among other things. It should be pointed out that science defined below mainly refers to natural science even though the scientific spirit applies to other categories of science (social science and human science disciplines).

Science is a systematic enterprise that builds and organizes knowledge in the form of testable explanations and predictions about the universe. In an older and closely related meaning (found, for example, in Aristotle), "science" refers to the body of reliable knowledge itself, of the type that can be logically and rationally explained (see *History and Philosophy* below). Since classical antiquity science as a type of knowledge was closely linked to philosophy. In the early modern era the words "science" and "philosophy" were sometimes used interchangeably in the English language. By the 17th century, natural philosophy (which is today called "natural science") was considered a separate branch of philosophy. However, "science" continued to be used in a broad sense denoting reliable knowledge about a topic, in the same way it is still used in modern terms such as library science or political science. In modern use, "science" more often refers to a way of pursuing knowledge, not only the knowledge itself. It is "often treated as synonymous with 'natural and physical science', and thus restricted to those branches of study that relate to the phenomena of the material universe and their laws, sometimes with implied exclusion of pure mathematics. This is now the dominant sense in ordinary use." This narrower sense of "science" developed as scientists such as Johannes Kepler, Galileo Galilei and Isaac Newton began formulating *laws of nature* such as Newton's laws of motion. In this period it became more common to refer to natural philosophy as "natural science". Over the course of the 19th century, the word "science" became increasingly associated with scientific method, a disciplined way to study the natural world, including physics, chemistry, geology and biology. It is in the 19th century also that the term "scientist" was created by the naturalist-theologian William Whewell to distinguish those who sought knowledge on nature from those who sought knowledge on other disciplines. The *Oxford English Dictionary* dates the origin of the word "scientist" to 1834. This sometimes left the study of human thought and society in a linguistic limbo, which was resolved by classifying these areas of academic study as social science. Similarly, several other major areas of disciplined study and knowledge exist today under the general rubric of "science", such as formal science and applied science.

History and Philosophy

Both Aristotle and Kuan Tzu (4th C. BCE), in an example of simultaneous scientific discovery, mentioned that some marine animals were subject to a lunar cycle, and increase and decrease in size with the waxing and waning of the moon. Aristotle was referring specifically to the sea urchin, Science in a broad sense existed before the modern era, and in many historical civilizations, but modern science is so distinct in its approach and successful in its results that it now defines what science is in the strictest sense of the term. Much earlier than the modern era, another important turning point was the development of the classical natural philosophy in the ancient Greek-speaking world.

Pre-Philosophical

Science in its original sense is a word for a type of knowledge (Latin *scientia*, Ancient Greek *epistemē*), rather than a specialized word for the pursuit of such knowledge. In particular it is one of the types of knowledge which people can communicate to each other and share. For example, knowledge about the working of natural things was gathered long before recorded history and led to the development of complex abstract thinking, as shown by the construction of complex calendars, techniques for making poisonous plants edible, and buildings such as the pyramids. However no consistent distinction was made between knowledge of such things which are true in every community, and other types of communal knowledge such as mythologies and legal systems.

Philosophical Study of Nature

Before the invention or discovery of the concept of "nature" (Ancient Greek *phusis*), by the pre-Socratic philosophers, the same words tend to be used to describe the natural "way" in which a plant grows, and the "way" in which, for example, one tribe worships a particular god. For this reason it is claimed these men were the first philosophers in the strict sense, and also the first people to clearly distinguish "nature" and "convention". Science was therefore distinguished as the knowledge of nature, and the things which are true for every community, and the name of the specialized pursuit of such knowledge was philosophy—the realm of the first philosopher-physicists. They were mainly speculators or theorists, particularly interested in astronomy. In contrast, trying to use knowledge of nature to imitate nature (artifice or technology, Greek *technē*) was seen by classical scientists as a more appropriate interest for lower class artisans.

Philosophical Turn to Human Things

A major turning point in the history of early philosophical science was the controversial but successful attempt by Socrates to apply philosophy to the study of human things, including human nature, the nature of political communities, and human knowledge itself. He criticized the older type of study of physics as too purely speculative, and lacking in self-criticism. He was particularly concerned that some of the early physicists treated nature as if it could be assumed that it had no intelligent order, explaining things merely in terms of motion and matter. The study of human things had been the realm of mythology and tradition, and Socrates was executed. Aristotle later created a less controversial systematic programme of Socratic philosophy, which was teleological, and human-centered. He rejected many of the conclusions of earlier scientists. For example in his physics the Sun goes around the Earth, and many things have it as part of their nature that they are for humans. Each thing has a formal cause and final cause and a role in the rational cosmic order. Motion and change is described as the actualization of potentials already in things, according to what types of things they are. While the Socratics insisted that philosophy should be used to consider the practical question of the best way to live for a human being, they did not argue for any other types of applied science. Aristotle maintained the sharp distinction between science and the practical knowledge of artisans, treating theoretical speculation as the highest type of human activity, practical thinking about good living as something less lofty, and the knowledge of artisans as something only suitable for the lower classes. In contrast to modern science, Aristotle's influential emphasis was upon the "theoretical" steps of deducing universal rules from raw data, and did not treat the gathering of experience and raw data as part of science itself.

Medieval Science

During late Antiquity and the early Middle Ages, the Aristotelian approach to inquiries on natural phenomenon was used. Some ancient knowledge was lost, or in some cases kept in obscurity, during the fall of the Roman Empire and periodic political struggles. However, the general fields of science, or Natural Philosophy as it was called, and much of the general knowledge from the ancient world remained preserved though the works of the early encyclopedists like Isidore of Seville. During the early medieval period, Syrian Christians from eastern Europe such as Nestorians and Monophysites were the ones that translated much of the important Greek science texts from Greek to Syriac and later on they translated many of the works into Arabic and other languages under Islamic rule. This was a major line of transmission for the development of Islamic science which provided much of the activity during the early medieval period. In the later medieval period, Europeans recovered some ancient knowledge by translations of texts and they built their work upon the knowledge of Aristotle, Ptolemy, Euclid, and others works. In Europe, men like Roger Bacon learned Arabic and Hebrew and argued for more experimental science. By the late Middle Ages, a synthesis of Catholicism and Aristotelianism known as Scholasticism was flourishing in western Europe, which had become a new geographic center of science.

Renaissance, and Early Modern Science

By the late Middle Ages, especially in Italy there was an influx of texts and scholars from the collapsing Byzantine empire. Copernicus formulated a heliocentric model of the solar system unlike the geocentric model of Ptolemy's Almagest. All aspects of scholasticism were criticized in the 15th and 16th centuries; one author who was notoriously persecuted was Galileo, who made innovative use of experiment and mathematics. However the persecution began after Pope Urban VIII blessed Galileo to write about the Copernican system. Galileo had used arguments from the Pope and put them in the voice of the simpleton in the work "Dialogue Concerning the Two Chief World Systems" which caused great offense to him. In Northern Europe, the new technology of the printing press was widely used to publish many arguments including some that disagreed with church dogma. René Descartes and Francis Bacon published philosophical arguments in favor of a new type of non-Aristotelian science. Descartes argued that mathematics could be used in order to study nature, as Galileo had done, and Bacon emphasized the importance of experiment over contemplation. Bacon also argued that science should aim for the first time at practical inventions for the improvement of all human life. Bacon questioned the Aristotelian concepts of formal cause and final cause, and promoted the idea that science should study the laws of "simple" natures, such as heat, rather than assuming that there is any specific nature, or "formal cause", of each complex type of thing. This new modern science began to see itself as describing "laws of nature". This updated approach to studies in nature was seen as mechanistic.

Age of Enlightenment, a Booming Period of Science

In the 17th and 18th centuries, the project of modernity, as had been promoted by Bacon and Descartes, led to rapid scientific advance and the successful development of a new type of natural science, mathematical, methodically experimental, and deliberately innovative. Newton and

Leibniz succeeded in developing a new physics, now referred to as Newtonian physics, which could be confirmed by experiment and explained in mathematics. Leibniz also incorporated terms from Aristotelian physics, but now being used in a new non-teleological way, for example "energy" and "potential". But in the style of Bacon, he assumed that different types of things all work according to the same general laws of nature, with no special formal or final causes for each type of thing. It is, during this period that the word science gradually became more commonly used to refer to the pursuit of a type of knowledge, and especially knowledge of nature—coming close in meaning to the old term "natural philosophy".

19th Century and 20th Century

Both John Herschel and William Whewell systematized methodology: the latter coined the term "scientist". When Charles Darwin published *On the Origin of Species* he established descent with modification as the prevailing evolutionary explanation of biological complexity. His theory of natural selection provided a natural explanation of how species originated, but this only gained wide acceptance a century later. John Dalton developed the idea of atoms. The laws of thermodynamics and the electromagnetic theory were also established in the 19th century, which raised new questions which could not easily be answered using Newton's framework. Einstein's Theory of Relativity and the development of quantum mechanics led to the replacement of Newtonian physics with a new physics which contains two parts, that describe different types of events in nature. The extensive use of scientific innovation during the wars of this century, led to the space race and widespread public appreciation of the importance of modern science.

Philosophy of Science

Working scientists usually take for granted a set of basic assumptions that are needed to justify a scientific method: (1) that there is an objective reality shared by all rational observers; (2) that this objective reality is governed by natural laws; (3) that these laws can be discovered by means of systematic observation and experimentation. Philosophy of science seeks a deep understanding of what these underlying assumptions mean and whether they are valid. Most contributions to the philosophy of science have come from philosophers, who frequently view the beliefs of most scientists as superficial or naive—thus there is often a degree of antagonism between working scientists and philosophers of science. The belief that all observers share a common reality is known as realism. It can be contrasted with anti-realism, the belief that there is no valid concept of absolute truth such that things that are true for one observer are true for all observers. The most commonly defended form of anti-realism is idealism, the belief that the mind or spirit is the most basic essence, and that each mind generates its own reality. In an idealistic world-view, what is true for one mind need not be true for other minds. There are different schools of thought in philosophy of science. The most popular position is empiricism, which claims that knowledge is created by a process involving observation and that scientific theories are the result of generalizations from such observations. Empiricism generally encompasses inductivism, a position that tries to explain the way general theories can be justified by the finite number of observations humans can make and the hence finite amount of empirical evidence available to confirm scientific theories. This is necessary because the number of predictions those theories make is infinite, which means that they cannot be known from the finite amount of evidence using deductive logic only. Many versions of empiricism exist, with the predominant ones being Bayesianism and the hypothetico-deductive method. Empiricism has stood in contrast to rationalism, the position originally associated with Descartes, which holds that knowledge is created by the human intellect, not by observation. A significant twentieth century version of rationalism is critical rationalism, first defined by Austrian-british philosopher Karl Popper. Popper rejected the way that empiricism describes the connection between theory and observation. He claimed that theories are not generated by observation, but that observation is made in the light of theories and that the only way a theory can be affected by observation is when it comes in conflict with it. Popper proposed falsifiability as the landmark of scientific theories, and falsification as the empirical method, to replace verifiability and induction by purely deductive notions. Popper further claimed that there is actually only one universal method, and that this method is not specific to science: The negative method of criticism, trial and error. It covers all products of the human mind, including science, mathematics, philosophy, and art.

Another approach, instrumentalism, colloquially termed "shut up and calculate", emphasizes the utility of theories as instruments for explaining and predicting phenomena. It claims that scientific theories are black boxes with only their input (initial conditions) and output (predictions) being relevant. Consequences, notions and logical structure of the theories are claimed to be something that should simply be ignored and that scientists shouldn't make a fuss about (see interpretations of quantum mechanics). Finally, another approach often cited in debates of scientific skepticism against controversial movements like "scientific creationism", is methodological naturalism. Its main point is that a difference between natural and supernatural explanations should be made, and that science should be restricted methodologically to natural explanations. That the restriction is merely methodological (rather than ontological) means that science should not consider supernatural explanations itself, but should not claim them to be wrong either. Instead, supernatural explanations should be left a matter of personal belief outside the scope of science. Methodological naturalism maintains that proper science requires strict adherence to empirical study and independent verification as a process for properly developing and evaluating explanations for observable phenomena. The absence of these standards, arguments from authority, biased observational studies and other common fallacies are frequently cited by supporters of methodological naturalism as criteria for the dubious claims they criticize not to be true science.

Basic and Applied Research

Although some scientific research is applied research into specific problems, a great deal of our understanding comes from the curiosity-driven undertaking of basic research. This leads to options for technological advance that were not planned or sometimes even imaginable. This point was made by Michael Faraday when, allegedly in response to the question "what is the *use* of basic research?" he responded "Sir, what is the use of a new-born child?". For example, research into the effects of red light on the human eye's rod cells did not seem to have any practical purpose; eventually, the discovery that our night vision is not troubled by red light would lead search and rescue teams (among others) to adopt red light in the cockpits of jets and helicopters. In a nutshell: Basic research is the search for knowledge. Applied research is the search for solutions to practical problems using this knowledge. Finally, even basic research can take unexpected turns, and there is some sense in which the scientific method is built to harness luck.

Experimentation and Hypothesizing

Based on observations of a phenomenon, scientists may generate a model. This is an attempt to describe or depict the phenomenon in terms of a logical, physical or mathematical representation. As empirical evidence is gathered, scientists can suggest a hypothesis to explain the phenomenon. Hypotheses may be formulated using principles such as parsimony (also known as "Occam's Razor") and are generally expected to seek consilience—fitting well with other accepted facts related to the phenomena. This new explanation is used to make falsifiable predictions that are testable by experiment or observation. When a hypothesis proves unsatisfactory, it is either modified or discarded. Experimentation is especially important in science to help establish causational relationships (to avoid the correlation fallacy). Operationalization also plays an important role in coordinating research in/across different fields. Once a hypothesis has survived testing, it may become adopted into the framework of a scientific theory. This is a logically reasoned, self-consistent model or framework for describing the behavior of certain natural phenomena. A theory typically describes the behavior of much broader sets of phenomena than a hypothesis; commonly, a large number of hypotheses can be logically bound together by a single theory. Thus a theory is a hypothesis explaining various other hypotheses. In that vein, theories are formulated according to most of the same scientific principles as hypotheses. While performing experiments, scientists may have a preference for one outcome over another, and so it is important to ensure that science as a whole can eliminate this bias. This can be achieved by careful experimental design, transparency, and a thorough peer review process of the experimental results as well as any conclusions. After the results of an experiment are announced or published, it is normal practice for independent researchers to double-check how the research was performed, and to follow up by performing similar experiments to determine how dependable the results might be.

Certainty and Science

A scientific theory is empirical, and is always open to falsification if new evidence is presented. That is, no theory is ever considered strictly certain as science accepts the concept of fallibilism. The philosopher of science Karl Popper sharply distinguishes truth from certainty. He writes that scientific knowledge "consists in the search for truth", but it "is not the search for certainty... All human knowledge is fallible and therefore uncertain."

Although science values legitimate doubt, The Flat Earth Society is still widely regarded as an example of taking skepticism too far. New scientific knowledge very rarely results in vast changes in our understanding. According to psychologist Keith Stanovich, it may be the media's overuse of words like "breakthrough" that leads the public to imagine that science is constantly proving everything it thought was true to be false. While there are such famous cases as the theory of relativity that required a complete reconceptualization, these are extreme exceptions. Knowledge in science is gained by a gradual synthesis of information from different experiments, by various researchers, across different domains of science; it is more like a climb than a leap. Theories vary in the extent to which they have been tested and verified, as well as their acceptance in the scientific community. For example, heliocentric theory, the theory of evolution, and germ theory still bear the name "theory" even though, in practice, they are considered factual. Philosopher Barry Stroud adds that, although the best definition for "knowledge" is contested, being skeptical and entertaining the *possibility* that one is incorrect is compatible with being correct. Ironically then, the scientist adhering to proper scientific method will doubt themselves even once they possess the truth. The fallibilist C. S. Peirce argued that inquiry is the struggle to resolve actual doubt and that merely quarrelsome, verbal, or hyperbolic doubt is fruitless—but also that the inquirer should try to attain genuine doubt rather than resting uncritically on common sense. He held that the successful sciences trust, not to any single chain of inference (no stronger than its weakest link), but to the cable of multiple and various arguments intimately connected. Stanovich also asserts that science avoids searching for a "magic bullet"; it avoids the single-cause fallacy. This means a scientist would not ask merely "What is *the* cause of...", but rather "What *are* the most significant *causes* of...". This is especially the case in the more macroscopic fields of science (e. g. psychology, cosmology). Of course, research often analyzes few factors at once, but these are always added to the long list of factors that are most important to consider. For example, knowing the details of only a person's genetics, or their history and upbringing, or the current situation may not explain a behaviour, but a deep understanding of all these variables combined can be very predictive.

Scientific Practice

Astronomy became much more accurate after Tycho Brahe devised his scientific instruments for measuring angles between two celestial bodies, before the invention of the telescope. Brahe's observations were the basis for Kepler's laws.

If a man will begin with certainties, he shall end in doubts; but if he will be content to begin with doubts, he shall end in certainties.
—Francis Bacon (1605) *The Advancement of Learning*, Book 1, v, 8

A skeptical point of view, demanding a method of proof, was the practical position taken as early as 1000 years ago, with Alhazen, *Doubts Concerning Ptolemy*, through Bacon (1605), and C. S. Peirce (1839—1914), who note that a community will then spring up to address these points of uncertainty. The methods of inquiry into a problem have been known for thousands of years, and extend beyond theory to practice. The use of measurements, for example, are a practical approach to settle disputes in the community. John Ziman points out that intersubjective pattern recognition is fundamental to the creation of all scientific knowledge. Ziman shows how scientists can identify patterns to each other across centuries: Needham shows how today's trained western botanist can identify *Artemisia alba* from images taken from a 16th c. Chinese pharmacopia, and Ziman refers to this ability as "perceptual consensibility". Ziman then makes consensibility, leading to consensus, the touchstone of reliable knowledge.

Measurement

Measurement is often used in science to make definitive comparisons and reduce confusion. Even in cases of clear qualitative difference, increased precision through measurement is often preferred in order to aid in replication. For example, different colors may be reported based on wavelengths of light, instead of vague (qualitative) terms such as "green" and "blue" which are often interpreted differently by different people. Measurements are most commonly made in the SI system, which contains seven fundamental units: kilogram, meter, candela, second, ampere, kelvin, and mole. Six of these units are artifact-free (defined without reference to a particular physical object which serves as a standard); the definition of one remaining unit, the kilogram is still embodied in an artifact which rests at the BIPM outside Paris. Eventually, it is hoped that new SI definitions will be uniformly artifact-free. Artifact-free definitions fix measurements at an exact value related to a physical constant or other invariable phenomenon in nature, in contrast to standard artifacts which can be damaged or otherwise change slowly over time. Instead, the measurement unit can only ever change through increased accuracy in determining the value of the constant it is tied to.

Mathematics and Formal Sciences

Mathematics is essential to the sciences. One important function of mathematics in science is the role it plays in the expression of scientific *models*. Observing and collecting measurements, as well as hypothesizing and predicting, often require extensive use of mathematics. Arithmetic, algebra, geometry, trigonometry and calculus, for example, are all essential to physics. Virtually every branch of mathematics has applications in science, including "pure" areas such as number theory and topology. Statistical methods, which are mathematical techniques for summarizing and analyzing data, allow scientists to assess the level of reliability and the range of variation in experimental results. Statistical analysis plays a fundamental role in many areas of both the natural sciences and social sciences. Computational science applies computing power to simulate real-world situations, enabling a better understanding of scientific problems than formal mathematics alone can achieve. According to the Society for Industrial and Applied Mathematics, computation is now as important as theory and experiment in advancing scientific knowledge. Whether mathematics itself is properly classified as science has been a matter of some debate. Some thinkers see mathematicians as scientists, regarding physical experiments as inessential or mathematical proofs as equivalent to experiments. Others do not see mathematics as a science, since it does not require an experimental test of its theories and hypotheses. Mathematical theorems and formulas are obtained by logical derivations which presume axiomatic systems, rather than the combination of empirical observation and logical reasoning that has come to be known as scientific method. In general, mathematics is classified as formal science, while natural and social sciences are classified as empirical sciences.

Scientific Method

A scientific method seeks to explain the events of nature in a reproducible way. An explanatory thought experiment or hypothesis is put forward, as explanation, from which stem predictions. The predictions are to be posted before a confirming experiment or observation is sought, as proof that no tampering has occurred. Disproof of a prediction is evidence of progress. This is done partly through observation of natural phenomena, but also through experimentation, that tries to simulate natural events under controlled conditions, as appropriate to the discipline (in the observational sciences, such as astronomy or geology, a predicted observation might take the place of a controlled experiment). Taken in its entirety, a scientific method allows for highly creative problem solving while minimizing any effects of subjective bias on the part of its users (namely the confirmation bias). In the nineteenth century, the measurement of Earth's gravity was primarily dependent on pendulums for gravimetric surveys. An improved pendulum, designed by Friedrich Bessel, was manufactured by Repsold and Sons, Hamburg, Germany. The American C. S. Peirce was tasked with gravimetric research by the U. S. Coast and Geodetic Survey. Peirce developed a theory of the systematic errors in the mount of the Repsold pendulum. He was asked to present his theory for improving pendulums to a Special Committee of the International Geodetic Association. While underway to a conference of the IGA in Europe, September 1877, Peirce wrote an essay in French on scientific method, "How to Make Our Ideas Clear" and translated "The Fixation of Belief" into French. In these essays, he notes that our beliefs clash with real life, causing what Peirce denotes as the "irritation of doubt", for which he then lists multiple methods of coping, among them, scientific method.

Model-making, the imaginative and logical steps which precede the experiment, may be judged the most important part of scientific method because skill and insight in these matters are rare. Without them we do not know what experiment to do. But it is the experiment which provides the raw material for scientific theory. Scientific theory cannot be built directly from the conclusions of conceptual models.

—Herbert George Andrewartha (1907—92), Australian zoologist and entomologist, *Introduction to the Study of Animal Population* 1961, 181.

Scientific Community

The scientific community is the group of all interacting scientists. It includes many "sub-communities" working on particular scientific fields, and within particular institutions; interdisciplinary and cross-institutional activities are also significant.

Branches and Fields

Scientific fields are commonly divided into two major groups: natural sciences, which study natural phenomena (including biological life), and social sciences, which study human behavior and societies. These groupings are empirical sciences, which means the knowledge must be based on observable phenomena and capable of being tested for its validity by other researchers working under the same conditions. There are also related disciplines that are grouped into interdisciplinary and applied sciences, such as engineering and medicine. Within these categories are specialized scientific fields that can include parts of other scientific disciplines but often possess their own terminology and expertise. Mathematics, which is classified as a formal science, has both similarities and differences with the empirical sciences (the natural and social sciences). It is similar to empirical sciences in that it involves an objective, careful and systematic study of an area of knowledge; it is different because of its method of verifying its knowledge, using *a priori* rather than empirical methods. The formal sciences, which also include statistics and logic, are vital to the empirical sciences. Major advances in formal science have often led to major advances in the empirical sciences. The formal sciences are essential in the formation of hypotheses, theories, and laws, both in discovering and describing how things work (natural sciences) and how people think and act (social sciences). The word *field* has a technical meaning in physics, as occupying space, which uses the word *spacetime*, rather than space); that is the reason that a branch of science is taken as the meaning of field. Science divides into categories of specialized expertise, each typically embodying their own terminology and nomenclature. Each field will commonly be represented by one or more scientific journals, where peer reviewed research will be published.

Institutions

Learned societies for the communication and promotion of scientific thought and experimentation have existed since the Renaissance period. The oldest surviving institution is the Italian *Accademia dei Lincei* which was established in 1603. The respective National Academies of Science are distinguished institutions that exist in a number of countries, beginning with the British Royal Society in 1660 and the French *Académie des Sciences* in 1666. International scientific organizations, such as the International Council for Science, have since been formed to promote cooperation between the scientific communities of different nations. More recently, influential government agencies have been created to support scientific research, including the National Science Foundation in the U.S. Other prominent organizations include the National Scientific and Technical Research Council in Argentina, the academies of science of many nations,

CSIRO in Australia, Centre national de la recherche scientifique in France, Max Planck Society and Deutsche Forschungsgemeinschaft in Germany, and in Spain, CSIC.

Literature

An enormous range of scientific literature is published. Scientific journals communicate and document the results of research carried out in universities and various other research institutions, serving as an archival record of science. The first scientific journals, *Journal des Sçavans* followed by the *Philosophical Transactions*, began publication in 1665. Since that time the total number of active periodicals has steadily increased. As of 1981, one estimate for the number of scientific and technical journals in publication was 11,500. The United States National Library of Medicine currently indexes 5,516 journals that contain articles on topics related to the life sciences. Although the journals are in 39 languages, 91 percent of the indexed articles are published in English. Most scientific journals cover a single scientific field and publish the research within that field; the research is normally expressed in the form of a scientific paper. Science has become so pervasive in modern societies that it is generally considered necessary to communicate the achievements, news, and ambitions of scientists to a wider populace. Science magazines such as *New Scientist*, *Science & Vie* and *Scientific American* cater to the needs of a much wider readership and provide a non-technical summary of popular areas of research, including notable discoveries and advances in certain fields of research. Science books engage the interest of many more people. Tangentially, the science fiction genre, primarily fantastic in nature, engages the public imagination and transmits the ideas, if not the methods, of science. Recent efforts to intensify or develop links between science and non-scientific disciplines such as Literature or, more specifically, Poetry, include the *Creative Writing Science* resource developed through the Royal Literary Fund.

Science and Society/Women in Science

Science is largely a male-dominated field, with notable exceptions. Evidence suggests that this is due to stereotypes (e. g. science as "manly") as well as self-fulfilling prophecies. Experiments have shown that parents challenge and explain more to boys than girls, asking them to reflect more deeply and logically. Physicist Evelyn Fox Keller argues that science may suffer for its manly stereotypes when ego and competitiveness obstruct progress, since these tendencies prevent collaboration and sharing of information.

Calls for Certainty in Politics

As described in Certainty and Science above: "no theory is ever considered strictly certain as science accepts the concept of fallibilism." Researchers from the United States and Canada write about a rhetorical technique focussed on shifting the burden of proof in an argument: the rhetoric involves a very public call for absolute certainty from *one side* of the debate. For instance, laws that would control cigarette smoking were combated by lobby groups emphasizing that the evidence connecting smoking to cancer was not certain. The evidence that did exist was thus trivialized. The researchers call this a SCAM (Scientific Certainty Argumentation Method), and maintain that what is really needed is a balanced approach to science; an approach that admits scientific conclusions are always tentative. This means carefully considering the risks of both Type 1 and Type 2 errors in a situation (e. g. all the risks of over-reaction, but also the risks of under-reaction). Certainty, it should be clear, will not exist on either side of the debate. The authors conclude that politicians and lobby groups are too often able to make "successful efforts to argue for full 'scientific certainty' before a regulation can be said to be 'justified'—and that, in short, is a SCAM."

Science Policy

Science policy is an area of public policy concerned with the policies that affect the conduct of the science and research enterprise, including research funding, often in pursuance of other national policy goals such as technological innovation to promote commercial product development, weapons development, health care and environmental monitoring. Science policy also refers to the act of applying scientific knowledge and consensus to the development of public policies. Science policy thus deals with the entire domain of issues that involve the natural sciences. In accordance with public policy being concerned about the well-being of its citizens, science policy's goal is to consider how science and technology can best serve the public. State policy has influenced the funding of public works and science for thousands of years, dating at least from the time of the Mohists, who inspired the study of logic during the period of the Hundred Schools of Thought, and the study of defensive fortifications during the Warring States Period in China. In Great Britain, governmental approval of the Royal Society in the seventeenth century recognized a scientific community which exists to this day. The professionalization of science, begun in the nineteenth century, was partly enabled by the creation of scientific organizations such as the National Academy of Sciences, the Kaiser Wilhelm Institute, and State funding of universities of their respective nations. Public policy can directly affect the funding of capital equipment, intellectual infrastructure for industrial research, by providing tax incentives to those organizations that fund research. Vannevar Bush, director of the office of scientific research and development for the United States government, the forerunner of the National Science Foundation, wrote in July 1945 that "Science is a proper concern of government". Science and technology research is often funded through a competitive process, in which potential research projects are evaluated and only the most promising receive funding. Such processes, which are run by government, corporations or foundations, allocate scarce funds. Total research funding in most developed countries is between 1.5% and 3% of GDP. In the OECD, around two-thirds of research and development in scientific and technical fields is carried out by industry, and 20% and 10% respectively by universities and government. The government funding proportion in certain industries is higher, and it dominates research in social science and humanities. Similarly, with some exceptions (e.g. biotechnology) government provides the bulk of the funds for basic scientific research. In commercial research and development, all but the most research-oriented corporations focus more heavily on near-term commercialization possibilities rather than "blue-sky" ideas or technologies (such as nuclear fusion).

Pseudoscience, Fringe Science and Junk Science

An area of study or speculation that masquerades as science in an attempt to claim a legitimacy that it would not otherwise be able to achieve is sometimes referred to as pseudoscience, fringe science, or "alternative science". Another term, "junk science", is often used to describe scientific hypotheses or conclusions which, while perhaps legitimate in themselves, are believed to be used to support a position that is seen as not legitimately justified by the totality of evidence. Physicist Richard Feynman coined the term "cargo cult science" in reference to pursuits that have the formal trappings of science but lack "a principle of scientific thought that corresponds to a kind of utter honesty" that allows their results to be rigorously evaluated. Various types of commercial advertising, ranging from hype to fraud, may fall into these categories. There also can be an element of political or ideological bias on all sides of such debates. Sometimes, research may be characterized as "bad science", research that is well-intentioned but is seen as incorrect, obsolete, incomplete, or over-simplified expositions of scientific ideas. The term "scientific misconduct" refers to situations such as where researchers have intentionally misrepresented their published data or have purposely given credit for a discovery to the wrong person.

Criticism/Philosophical Criticisms

Historian Jacques Barzun termed science "a faith as fanatical as any in history" and warned against the use of scientific thought to suppress considerations of meaning as integral to human existence. Many recent thinkers, such as Carolyn Merchant, Theodor Adorno and E. F. Schumacher considered that the 17th century scientific revolution shifted science from a focus on understanding nature, or wisdom, to a focus on manipulating nature, i. e. power, and that science's emphasis on manipulating nature leads it inevitably to manipulate people, as well. Science's focus on quantitative measures has led to critiques that it is unable to recognize important qualitative aspects of the world. Philosopher of science Paul K Feyerabend advanced the idea of epistemological anarchism, which holds that there are no useful and exception-free methodological rules governing the progress of science or the growth of knowledge, and that the idea that science can or should operate according to universal and fixed rules is unrealistic, pernicious and detrimental to science itself. Feyerabend advocates treating science as an ideology alongside others such as religion, magic and mythology, and considers the dominance of science in society authoritarian and unjustified. He also contended (along with Imre Lakatos) that the demarcation problem of distinguishing science from pseudoscience on objective grounds is not possible and thus fatal to the notion of science running according to fixed, universal rules. Feyerabend also criticized science for not having evidence for its own philosophical precepts. Particularly the notion of Uniformity of Law and the Uniformity of Process across time and space. "We have to realize that a unified theory of the physical world simply does not exist" says Feyerabend, "We have theories that work in restricted regions, we have purely formal attempts to condense them into a single formula, we have lots of unfounded claims (such as the claim that all of chemistry can be reduced to physics), phenomena that do not fit into the accepted framework are suppressed; in physics, which many scientists regard as the one really basic science, we have now at least three different points of view... without a promise of conceptual (and not only formal) unification." Sociologist Stanley Aronowitz scrutinizes science for operating with the presumption that the only acceptable criticisms of science are those conducted within the methodological framework that science has set up for itself. That science insists that only those who have been inducted into its community, through means of training and credentials, are qualified to make these criticisms. Aronowitz also alleges that while scientists consider it absurd that Fundamentalist Christianity uses biblical references to bolster their claim that the Bible is true, scientists pull the same tactic by using the tools of science to settle disputes concerning its own validity. Several academics have offered critiques concerning ethics in science. In *Science and Ethics*, for example, the philosopher Bernard Rollin examines the relevance of ethics to science, and argues in favor of making education in ethics part and parcel of scientific training.

Fragmented View of World

Psychologist Carl Jung believed that though science attempted to understand all of nature, the experimental method imposed artificial and conditional questions that evoke equally artificial answers. Jung encouraged, instead of these "artificial" methods, empirically testing the world in a holistic manner. David Parkin compared the epistemological stance of science to that of divination. He suggested that, to the degree that divination is an epistemologically specific means of gaining insight into a given question, science itself can be considered a form of divination that is framed from a western view of the nature (and thus possible applications) of knowledge. In a similar vein, Sixel saw the scientific viewpoint as limited in scope without being conscious of its own limitations, so that science could be correct (within its framework) and yet not true (because it failed to take into account larger contexts).

Media Perspectives

The mass media face a number of pressures that can prevent them from accurately depicting competing scientific claims in terms of their credibility within the scientific community as a whole. Determining how much weight to give different sides in a scientific debate may require considerable expertise regarding the matter. Few journalists have real scientific knowledge, and even beat reporters who know a great deal about certain scientific issues may be ignorant about other scientific issues that they are suddenly asked to cover.

Politics and Public Perception of Science

Many issues damage the relationship of science to the media and the use of science and scientific arguments by politicians. As a very broad generalization, many politicians seek certainties and facts whilst scientists typically offer probabilities and caveats. However, politicians' ability to be heard in the mass media frequently distorts the scientific understanding by the public. Examples in Britain include the controversy over the MMR inoculation, and the 1988 forced resignation of a Government Minister, Edwina Currie for revealing the high probability that battery farmed eggs were contaminated with Salmonella.

Questions and Topics for Pondering and Further Discussion for Unit Seven-4:

1. What is the essential spirit of science?
2. Some people say that science is the major force behind the rise of the West. Please make comment on it.
3. Karl Popper once said that the test of science is falsification. Do you agree with it?
4. What is called pseudoscience?
5. What is philosophy of science?
6. What are the components of social sciences? How about humanity sciences?
7. Please elaborate on natural sciences?
8. What is the typical example of interdisciplinary science?

5. Information Revolution or Explosion

The term **information revolution** (sometimes called also the "information revolution") describes current economic, social and technological trends beyond the Industrial Revolution and its widespread influence upon human social and economic life. Many competing terms have been proposed that focus on different aspects of this societal development. The British polymath crystallographer J. D. Bernal (1939) introduced the term "scientific and technical revolution" in his book *The Social Function of Science* in order to describe the new role that science and technology are coming to play within society. He asserted that science is becoming a "productive force", using the Marxist Theory of Productive Forces. After some controversy, the term was taken up by authors and institutions of the then-soviet Bloc. Their aim was to show that socialism was a safe home for the scientific and technical ("technological" for some authors) revolution, referred to by the acronym **STR**. The book *Civilization at the Crossroads*, edited by the Czech philosopher Radovan Richta (1969), became a standard reference for this topic. Daniel Bell (1980) challenged this theory and advocated **post-industrial society**, which would lead to a service economy rather than socialism. Many other authors presented their views, including Zbigniew Brzezinski (1976) with his "Technetronic Society".

Information in Social and Economic Activities

The main feature of the information revolution is the growing economic, social and technological role of information. Information-related activities did not come up with the Information Revolution. They existed, in one form or the other, in all human societies, and eventually developed into institutions, such as the Platonic Academy, Aristotle's Peripatetic school in the Lyceum, the Musaeum and the Library of Alexandria, or the schools of Babylonian astronomy. The Agricultural Revolution and the Industrial Revolution came up when new informational inputs were produced by individual innovators, or by scientific and technical institutions. During the Information Revolution all these activities are experiencing continuous growth, while other information-oriented activities are emerging. Information is the central theme of several new sciences, which emerged in the 1940s, including Shannon's *Information Theory* (1949) and Wiener's *Cybernetics* (1948). Wiener (1948, p. 155) stated also: "information is information not matter or energy".

This aphorism suggests that information should be considered along with matter and energy as the third constituent part of the Universe; information is carried by matter or by energy. We can outline a hierarchy to distinguish between data, information, knowledge, and wisdom. Data are sensations, facts, figures, etc., that are independent and atomic in nature. Information can be described alternately as organized data, the patterns that exist in data, or the underlying meaning of interrelated pieces of data. Knowledge is the ability to comprehend and use information. Wisdom is the ability to make the best use of knowledge. Data and information are easily transferable in the modern world, whether through oral, written or electronic methods. Knowledge, however, is built by one person and transferred (more slowly) through education and human interaction. Wisdom is the least transferrable by virtue of being built upon the other three with the addition of personal experience and reflection on one's experience. Information is then further considered as an economic activity, since firms and institutions are involved in its production, collection, exchange, distribution, circulation, processing, transmission, and control. Labor is also divided into physical labor (use of muscle power) and informational labor (use of intellectual power). A new economic sector is thereby identified, the Information Sector, which amalgamates information-related labor activities.

The Theory of Information Revolution

The term "Information Revolution" may relate to, or contrast with, such widely used terms as Industrial Revolution and Agricultural Revolution. Note, however, that you may prefer mentalist to materialist paradigm. The following fundamental aspects of the theory of information revolution can be given (Veneris 1984, 1990):

- The object of economic activities can be conceptualized according to the fundamental distinction between matter, energy, and information. These apply both to the object of

each economic activity, as well as within each economic activity or enterprise. For instance, an industry may process matter (e. g. iron) using energy and information (production and process technologies, management, etc.).
- Information is a factor of production (along with capital, labor, land [economics]), as well as a product sold in the market, that is, a commodity. As such, it acquires use value and exchange value, and therefore a price.
- All products have use value, exchange value, and informational value. The latter can be measured by the information content of the product, in terms of innovation, design, etc.
- Industries develop information-generating activities, the so-called Research and Development (R&D) functions.
- Enterprises, and society at large, develop the information control and processing functions, in the form of management structures; these are also called "white-collar workers", "bureaucracy", "managerial functions", etc.
- Labor can be classified according to the object of labor, into information labor and non-information labor.
- Information activities constitute a large, new economic sector, the information sector along with the traditional primary sector, secondary sector, and tertiary sector, according to the three-sector hypothesis. These should be restated because they are based on the ambiguous definitions made by Colin Clark (1940), who included in the tertiary sector all activities that have not been included in the primary (agriculture, forestry, etc.) and secondary (manufacturing) sectors. The quaternary sector and the quinary sector of the economy attempt to classify these new activities, but their definitions are not based on a clear conceptual scheme, although the latter is considered by some as equivalent with the information sector.
- From a strategic point of view, sectors can be defined as information sector, means of production, means of consumption, thus extending the classical Ricardo-Marx model of the Capitalist mode of production (see Influences on Karl Marx). Marx stressed in many occasions the role of the "intellectual element" in production, but failed to find a place for it into his model.
- Innovations are the result of the production of new information, as new products, new methods of production, patents, etc. Diffusion of innovations manifests saturation effects (related term: market saturation), following certain cyclical patterns and creating "economic waves", also referred to as "business cycles". There are various types of waves, such as Kondratiev wave (54 years), Kuznets swing (18 years), Juglar cycle (9 years) and Kitchin (about 4 years, see also Joseph Schumpeter) distinguished by their nature, duration, and, thus, economic impact.
- Diffusion of innovations causes structural-sectoral shifts in the economy, which can be smooth or can create crisis and renewal, a process which Joseph Schumpeter called vividly "creative destruction".

From a different perspective, Irving E. Fang identified six "Information Revolutions": writing, printing, mass media, entertainment, the "tool shed" (which we call "home" now), and the Information Highway. In this work the term "Information Revolution" is used in a narrow sense, to describe trends in communication media.

Measuring and Modeling the Information Revolution

Porat (1976) measured the Information Sector in the US using the input-output analysis; OECD has included statistics on the Information Sector in the economic reports of its member countries. Veneris (1984, 1990) explored the theoretical, economic and regional aspects of the Informational Revolution and developed a systems dynamics simulation computer model. These works can be seen as following the path originated with the work of Fritz Machlup who in his book *The Production and Distribution of Knowledge in the United States* (1962), claimed that the "knowledge industry represented 29% of the US gross national product", which he saw as evidence that the Information Age has begun. He defines knowledge as a commodity and attempts to measure the magnitude of the production and distribution of this commodity within a modern economy. Machlup divided information use into three classes: instrumental, intellectual, and pastime knowledge. He identified also five types of knowledge: practical knowledge; intellectual knowledge, that is, general culture and the satisfying of intellectual curiosity; pastime knowledge, that is, knowledge satisfying non-intellectual curiosity or the desire for light entertainment and emotional stimulation; spiritual or religious knowledge; unwanted knowledge, accidentally acquired and aimlessly retained.

More recent estimates have reached the following results:

1. The world's technological capacity to receive information through one-way broadcast networks grew at a sustained compound annual growth rate of 7% between 1986 and 2007;
2. The world's technological capacity to store information grew at a sustained compound annual growth rate of 25% between 1986 and 2007;
3. The world's effective capacity to exchange information through two-way telecommunication networks grew at a sustained compound annual growth rate of 30 % during the same two decades;
4. The world's technological capacity to compute information with the help of humanly guided general-purpose computers grew at a sustained compound annual growth rate of 61% during the same period.

Questions and Topics for Pondering and Further Discussion for Unit Seven-5:

1. In what way does Information Revolution differ from any previous revolutions, such as the Industrial Revolution or the Scientific Revolution?
2. Is Information Revolution the end of human progress in science and technology? Why or why not?
3. What is meant by digital divide?
4. What is the relationship between Information Revolution and Knowledge economy?
5. Is the world going into an age of information? What is the key sign of such age?
6. What is the implication of information explosion?
7. What is the relationship between information technology and virtual economy?
8. What effects does information make in changing people's life style?

Unit Eight

1. A History of Economic Ideas, a Key for Wealth[①]

Editor's remarks: *the rise of the West first of all started with its rise of economic power driven by a few revolutions such as Industrial Revolution and Commercial Revolution. Economic power serves as a solid basis for the expansion of influence of other powers, such as political and cultural powers. What is the secret for the rise of western economic power is heatedly debated. However, facts and figures speak louder than words. For whatever reasons, the rise of western economic power has provided a strong and convincing rationale for its effective and efficient economic system based upon market principles highlighting competition and rule of law. It is believed that some useful lessons can be drawn through a careful review of the history of economic thought in the West.*

The history of economic thought deals with different thinkers and theories in the subject that became political economy and economics from the ancient world to the present day. It encompasses many disparate schools of economic thought. Greek writers such as the philosopher Aristotle examined ideas about the art of wealth acquisition and questioned whether property is best left in private or public hands. In medieval times, scholars such as Thomas Aquinas argued that it was a moral obligation of businesses to sell goods at a just price. Scottish philosopher Adam Smith is often cited as the father of modern economics for his treatise *The Wealth of Nations* (1776). His ideas built upon a considerable body of work from predecessors in the eighteenth century particularly the Physiocrats. His book appeared on the eve of the Industrial Revolution with associated major changes in the economy. Smith's successors included such classical economists as the Rev. Thomas Malthus, Jean-baptiste Say, David Ricardo, and John Stuart Mill. They examined ways the landed, capitalist and laboring classes produced and distributed national output and modeled the effects of population and international trade. In London, Karl Marx castigated the capitalist system, which he described as exploitative and alienating. From about 1870, neoclassical economics attempted to erect a positive, mathematical and scientifically grounded field above normative politics. After the wars of the early twentieth century, John Maynard Keynes led a reaction against what has been described as governmental abstention from economic affairs, advocating interventionist fiscal policy to stimulate economic demand and growth. With a world divided between the capitalist first world, the communist second world, and the poor of the third world, the post-war consensus broke down. Others like Milton Friedman and Friedrich von Hayek warned of *The Road to Serfdom* and socialism, focusing their theories on what could be achieved through better monetary policy and deregulation. As Keynesian policies seemed to falter in the 1970s there emerged the so-called New Classical school, with prominent theorists such as Robert Lucas and Edward Prescott. Governmental economic policies from the 1980s were challenged, and development economists like Amartya Sen and information economists like Joseph Stiglitz introduced new ideas to economic thought in the twenty-first century.

[①] The main contents of this section are chiefly based upon the materials adapted from the book entitled *The Mystery of Wealth* by John Hutton and the book entitled *The Growth of Economic Thought* by Henry W Spiegel and published by Duke University Press as well as being further enriched by the information collected from *Wikipedia*. Acknowledgments are hereby expressed for their intellectual contributions.

Early Economic Thought

The earliest discussions of economics date back to ancient times (e. g. Chanakya's *Arthashastra* or Xenophon's *Oeconomicus*). Back then, and until the Industrial Revolution, economics was not a separate discipline but part of philosophy. Plato's book *The Republic* contained references to specialization of labour and production. But it was his pupil Aristotle that made some of the most familiar arguments, still in economic discourse today.

Aristotle

Aristotle's *Politics* (c. 350 BC) was mainly concerned to analyze different forms of a state (monarchy, aristocracy, constitutional government, tyranny, oligarchy, democracy) as a critique of Plato's advocacy of a ruling class of "philosopher-kings". In particular for economists, Plato had drawn a blueprint of society on the basis of common ownership of resources. Aristotle viewed this model as an oligarchical anathema. In *Politics*, Book II, Part V, he argued that,

> *Property should be in a certain sense common, but, as a general rule, private; for, when everyone has a distinct interest, men will not complain of one another, and they will make more progress, because every one will be attending to his own business... And further, there is the greatest pleasure in doing a kindness or service to friends or guests or companions, which can only be rendered when a man has private property. These advantages are lost by excessive unification of the state.*

Though Aristotle certainly advocated there be many things held in common, he argued that not everything could be, simply because of the "wickedness of human nature". "It is clearly better that property should be private", wrote Aristotle, "but the use of it common; and the special business of the legislator is to create in men this benevolent disposition." In *Politics* Book I, Aristotle discusses the general nature of households and market exchanges. For him there is a certain "art of acquisition" or "wealth-getting". Money itself has the sole purpose of being a medium of exchange, which means on its own "it is worthless... not useful as a means to any of the necessities of life". Nevertheless, points out Aristotle, because the "instrument" of money is the same many people are obsessed with the simple accumulation of money. "Wealth-getting" for one's household is "necessary and honorable", while exchange on the retail trade for simple accumulation is "justly censured, for it is dishonourable". Of the people he stated they as a whole thought acquisition of wealth (chrematistike) as being either the same as, or a principle of *oikonomia* (household management—*oikonomos*), with *oikos* as house and *nomos* in fact translated as custom or law. Aristotle himself was highly disapproving of usury and cast scorn on making money through means of a monopoly.

Middle Ages

Thomas Aquinas (1225—1274) was an Italian theologian and writer on economic issues. He taught in both Cologne and Paris, and was part of a group of Catholic scholars known as the Schoolmen, who moved their inquiries beyond theology to philosophical and scientific debates. In the treatise *Summa Theologica* Aquinas dealt with the concept of a just price, which he considered necessary for the reproduction of the social order. Bearing many similarities with the modern concept of long run equilibrium a just price was supposed to be one just sufficient to cover the costs of production, including the maintenance of a worker and his family. He argued it was immoral for sellers to raise their prices simply because buyers were in pressing need for a product. Aquinas discusses a number of topics in the format of questions and replies, substantial tracts dealing with Aristotle's theory. Aquinas argued against any form of cheating and recommended compensation always be paid in lieu of good service. Whilst human laws might not impose sanctions for unfair dealing, divine law did, in his opinion. One of Aquinas' main critics was Duns Scotus (1265—1308) in his work *Sententiae* (1295). Originally from Duns Scotland, he taught in Oxford, Cologne and Paris. Scotus thought it possible to be more precise than Aquinas in calculating a just price, emphasizing the costs of labor and expenses—though he recognised that the latter might be inflated by exaggeration, because buyer and seller usually have different ideas of what a just price comprises. If people did not benefit from a transaction, in Scotus' view, they would not trade. Scotus defended merchants as performing a necessary and useful social role, transporting goods and making them available to the public.

Mercantilists and Nationalism

From the localism of the Middle Ages, the waning feudal lords, new national economic frameworks began to be strengthened. From 1492 and explorations like Christopher Columbus' voyages, new opportunities for trade with the New World and Asia were opening. New powerful monarchies wanted a powerful state to boost their status. Mercantilism was a political movement and an economic theory that advocated the use of the state's military power to ensure local markets and supply sources were protected. Mercantile theorists thought international trade could not benefit all countries at the same time. Because money and gold were the only source of riches, there was a limited quantity of resources to be shared between countries. Therefore, tariffs could be used to encourage exports (meaning more money comes into the country) and discourage imports (sending wealth abroad). In other words a positive balance of trade ought to be maintained, with a surplus of exports. The term "mercantilism" was not in fact coined until the late 1763 by Victor de Riqueti, marquis de Mirabeau and popularized by Adam Smith, who vigorously opposed its ideas.

Thomas Mun

English businessman Thomas Mun (1571—1641) represents early mercantile policy in his book *England's Treasure by Foreign Trade*. Although it was not published until 1664 it was widely circulated as a manuscript before then. He was a member of the East India Company and also wrote about his experiences there in *A Discourse of Trade from England unto the East Indies* (1621). According to Mun, trade was the only way to increase England's treasure (i.e. national wealth) and in pursuit of this end he suggested several courses of action. Important were frugal consumption to increase the amount of goods available for export, increased utilization of land and other domestic natural resources to reduce import requirements, lowering of export duties on goods produced domestically from foreign materials, and the export of goods with inelastic demand because more money could be made from higher prices.

Philipp von Hörnigk

Philipp von Hörnigk (1640—1712, sometimes spelt *Hornick* or *Horneck*) was born in Frankfurt am Main and became an Austrian civil servant writing in a time when his country was constantly threatened by Ottoman invasion. In *Österreich Über Alles, Wann es Nur Will* (1684, *Austria Over All, If She Only Will*) he laid out one of the clearest statements of mercantile policy. He listed nine principal rules of national economy.

To inspect the country's soil with the greatest care, and not to leave the agricultural possibilities of a single corner or clod of earth unconsidered... All commodities found in a country, which cannot be used in their natural state, should be worked up within the country... Attention should be given to the population, that it may be as large as the country can support... gold and silver once in the country are under no circumstances to be taken out for any purpose... The inhabitants should make every effort to get along with their domestic products... [Foreign commodities] should be obtained not for gold or silver, but in exchange for other domestic wares... and should be imported in unfinished form, and worked up within the country... Opportunities should be sought night and day for selling the country's superfluous goods to these foreigners in manufactured form... No importation should be allowed under any circumstances of which there is a sufficient supply of suitable quality at home. Nationalism, self-sufficiency and national power were the basic policies proposed.

Jean-Baptiste Colbert

Jean-Baptiste Colbert (1619—1683) was Minister of Finance under King Louis Ⅳ of France. He set up national guilds to regulate major industries. Silk, linen, tapestry, furniture manufacture and wine were examples of the crafts in which France specialized, all of which came to require membership of a guild to operate in. These remained until the French Revolution. According to Colbert, "It is simply, and solely, the abundance of money within a state [which] makes the difference in its grandeur and power."

British Enlightenment

Britain had gone through some of its most troubling times through the 17th century, enduring not only political and religious division in the English Civil War, King Charles I's execution and the Cromwellian dictatorship, but also the plagues and fires. The monarchy was restored under Charles Ⅱ, who had catholic sympathies, but his successor King James Ⅱ was swiftly ousted. Invited in his place were Protestant William of Orange and Mary, who assented to the Bill of Rights 1689 ensuring that the Parliament was dominant in what became known as the Glorious Revolution. The upheaval had seen a number of huge scientific advances, including Robert Boyle's discovery of the gas pressure constant (1660) and Sir Isaac Newton's publication of *Philosophiae Naturalis Principia Mathematica* (1687), which described the three laws of motion and his law of universal gravitation. All these factors spurred the advancement of economic thought. For instance, Richard Cantillon (1680—1734) consciously imitated Newton's forces of inertia and gravity in the natural world with human reason and market competition in the economic world. In his *Essay on the Nature of Commerce in General*, he argued rational self interest in a system of freely adjusting markets would lead to order and mutually compatible prices. Unlike the mercantilist thinkers however, wealth was found not in trade but in human labour. The first person to tie these ideas into a political framework was John Locke.

John Locke

John Locke (1632—1704) was born near Bristol and educated in London and Oxford. He is considered one of the most significant philosophers of his era mainly for his critique of Thomas Hobbes' defense of absolutism in *Leviathan* (1651) and the development of social contract theory. Locke believed that people contracted into society which was bound to protect their rights of property. He defined property broadly to include people's lives and liberties, as well as their wealth. When people combined their labor with their surroundings, then that created property rights. In his words from his *Second Treatise on Civil Government* (1689),

> God hath given the world to men in common... Yet every man has a property in his own person. The labor of his body and the work of his hands we may say are properly his. Whatsoever, then, he removes out of the state that nature hath provided and left it in, he hath mixed his labor with, and joined to it something that is his own, and thereby makes it his property.

Locke was arguing that not only should the government cease interference with people's property (or their "lives, liberties and estates") but also that it should positively work to ensure their protection. His views on price and money were laid out in a letter to a Member of Parliament in 1691 entitled *Some Considerations on the Consequences of the Lowering of Interest and the Raising of the Value of Money* (1691). Here Locke argued that the "price of any commodity rises or falls, by the proportion of the number of buyers and sellers", a rule which "holds universally in all things that are to be bought and sold".

Dudley North

Dudley North (1641—1691) was a wealthy merchant and landowner. He worked as an official for the Treasury and was opposed to most mercantile policy. In his *Discourses upon Trade* (1691), which he published anonymously, he argued that the assumption of needing a favorable trade balance was wrong. Trade, he argued, benefits both sides, it promotes specialisation, the division of labour and produces an increase in wealth for everyone. Regulation of trade interfered with these benefits by reducing the flow of wealth.

David Hume

David Hume (1711—1776) agreed with North's philosophy and denounced mercantile assumptions. His contributions were set down in *Political Discourses* (1752), later consolidated in his *Essays, Moral, Political, Literary* (1777). Added to the fact that it was undesirable to strive for a favorable balance of trade it is, said Hume, in any case impossible. Hume held that any surplus of exports that might be achieved would be paid for by imports of gold and silver. This would increase the money supply, causing prices to rise. That in turn would cause a decline in exports until the balance with imports is restored.

Francis Hutcheson

Francis Hutcheson (1694—1746) was teacher to Adam Smith during 1737—1740, and is considered to be at the end of a long tradition of thought on economics as "household or family management", stemming from Xenophon's work *Oeconomicus*.

The Circular Flow

Similarly disenchanted with regulation on trademarks inspired by mercantilism, a Frenchman named Vincent de Gournay (1712—1759) is reputed to have asked why it was so hard to *laissez faire, laissez passer* (free enterprise, free trade). He was one of the early physiocrats, a word from Greek meaning "government of nature", who held that agriculture was the source of wealth. As historian David B. Danbom wrote, the physiocrats "damned cities for their artificiality and praised more natural styles of living. They celebrated farmers." Over the end of the seventeenth and beginning of the eighteenth century big advances in natural science and anatomy were being made, including the discovery of blood circulation through the human body. This concept was mirrored in the physiocrats' economic theory, with the notion of a circular flow of income throughout the economy.

François Quesnay (1694—1774) was the court physician to King Louis XV of France. He believed that trade and industry were not sources of wealth, and instead in his book, *Tableau économique* argued that agricultural surpluses, by flowing through the economy in the form of rent, wages and purchases were the real economic movers. Firstly, said Quesnay, regulation impedes the flow of income throughout all social classes and therefore economic development. Secondly, taxes on the productive classes, such as farmers, should be reduced in favor of rises for unproductive classes, such as landowners, since their luxurious way of life distorts the income flow.

Jacques Turgot (1727—1781) was born in Paris and from an old Norman family. His best known work, *Réflexions sur la formation et la distribution des richesses* (1766, *Reflections on the Formation and Distribution of Wealth*) developed Quesnay's theory that land is the only source of wealth. Turgot viewed society in terms of three classes: the productive agricultural class, the salaried artisan class (*classe stipendice*) and the landowning class (*classe disponible*). He argued that only the net product of land should be taxed and advocated the complete freedom of commerce and industry. In August 1774, Turgot was appointed to be Minister of Finance and in the space of two years introduced many anti-mercantile and anti-feudal measures supported by the King. A statement of his guiding principles, given to the King were "no bankruptcy, no tax increases, no borrowing". Turgot's ultimate wish was to have a single tax on land and abolish all other indirect taxes, but measures he introduced before that were met with overwhelming opposition from landed interests. Two edicts in particular, one suppressing corvées (charges from farmers to aristocrats) and another renouncing privileges given to guilds inflamed influential opinion. He was forced from office in 1776.

Adam Smith and *The Wealth of Nations*: an Economic Bible for the West

Adam Smith (1723—1790) is popularly seen as the father of modern political economy. His publication of the *An Inquiry Into the Nature and Causes of the Wealth of Nations* in 1776 happened to coincide not only with the American Revolution, shortly before the Europe wide upheavals of the French Revolution, but also the dawn of a new industrial revolution that allowed more wealth to be created on a larger scale than ever before. Smith was a Scottish moral philosopher, whose first book was *The Theory of Moral Sentiments* (1759). He argued in it that people's ethical systems develop through personal relations with other individuals, that right and wrong are sensed through others' reactions to one's behavior. This gained Smith more popularity than his next work, *The Wealth of Nations*, which the general public initially ignored. Yet Smith's political economic magnum opus was successful in circles that mattered.

Context

William Pitt, the Tory Prime Minister in the late 1780s based his tax proposals on Smith's ideas and advocated free trade as a devout disciple of *The Wealth of Nations*. Smith was appointed a commissioner of customs and within twenty years Smith had a following of new generation writers who were intent on building the science of political economy.

Edmund Burke

Smith expressed an affinity himself to the opinions of Edmund Burke, known widely as a political philosopher, a Member of Parliament.

Burke is the only man I ever knew who thinks on economic subjects exactly as I do without any previous communication having passed between us.

Burke was an established political economist himself, with his book *Thoughts and Details on Scarcity*. He was widely critical of liberal politics, and condemned the French Revolution which began in 1789. In *Reflections on the Revolution in France* (1790) he wrote that the "age of chivalry is dead, that of sophisters, economists and calculators has succeeded, and the glory of Europe is extinguished forever." Smith's contemporary influences included François Quesnay and Jacques Turgot whom he met on a stay in Paris, and David Hume, his Scottish compatriot. The times produced a common need among thinkers to explain social upheavals of the Industrial Revolution taking place, and in the seeming chaos without the feudal and monarchical structures of Europe, showed there was order still.

The Invisible Hand

It is not from the benevolence of the butcher, the brewer or the baker, that we expect our dinner, but from their regard to their own self interest. We address ourselves, not to their humanity but to their self-love, and never talk to them of our own necessities but of their advantages.

—Adam Smith's famous statement on self interest

Smith argued for a "system of natural liberty" where individual effort was the producer of social good. Smith believed even the selfish within society were kept under restraint and worked for the good of all when acting in a competitive market. Prices are often unrepresentative of the true value of goods and services. Following John Locke, Smith thought true value of things derived from the amount of labor invested in them. Every man is rich or poor according to the degree in which he can afford to enjoy the necessaries, conveniences, and amusements of human life. But after the division of labour has once thoroughly taken place, it is but a very small part of these with which a man's own labor can supply him. The far greater part of them he must derive from the labor of other people, and he must be rich or poor according to the quantity of that labor which he can command, or which he can afford to purchase. The value of any commodity, therefore, to the person who possesses it, and who means not to use or consume it himself, but to exchange it for other commodities, is equal to the quantity of labor which it enables him to purchase or command. Labor, therefore, is the real measure of the exchangeable value of all commodities. The real price of every thing, what every thing really costs to the man who wants to acquire it, is the toil and trouble of acquiring it. When the butchers, the brewers and the bakers acted under the restraint of an open market economy, their pursuit of self interest, thought Smith, paradoxically drives the process to correct real life prices to their just values. His classic statement on competition goes as follows:

When the quantity of any commodity which is brought to market falls short of the effectual demand, all those who are willing to pay... cannot be supplied with the quantity which they want... Some of them will be willing to give more. A competition will begin among them, and the market price will rise... When the quantity brought to market exceeds the effectual demand, it cannot be all sold to those who are willing to pay the whole value of the rent, wages and profit, which must be paid to bring it thither... The market price will sink.

Smith believed that a market produced what he dubbed the "progress of opulence". This involved a chain of concepts, that the division of labour is the driver of economic efficiency, yet it is limited to the widening process of markets. Both labor division and market widening require more intensive accumulation of capital by the entrepreneurs and leaders of business and industry. The whole system is underpinned by maintaining the security of property rights.

Limitations of Smith's Ideas

Smith's vision of a free market economy, based on secure property, capital accumulation, widening markets and a division of labor contrasted with the mercantilist tendency to attempt to "regulate all evil human actions". Smith believed there were precisely three legitimate functions of government. The third function was erecting and maintaining certain public works and certain public institutions, which it can never be for the interest of any individual or small number of individuals, to erect and maintain. Every system which endeavors to draw towards a particular species of industry a greater share of the capital of the society than what would naturally go to it retards, instead of accelerating, the progress of the society toward real wealth and greatness. In addition to the necessity of public leadership in certain sectors Smith argued, secondly, that cartels were undesirable because of their potential to limit production and quality of goods and services. Thirdly, Smith criticized government support of any kind of monopoly which always charges the highest price "which can be squeezed out of the buyers". The existence of monopoly and the potential for cartels, which would later form the core of competition law policy, could distort the benefits of free markets to the advantage of businesses at the expense of consumer sovereignty.

Classical Political Economy

The classical economists were referred to as a group for the first time by Karl Marx. One unifying part of their theories was the labour theory of value, contrasting to value deriving from a general equilibrium of supply and demand. These economists had seen the first economic and social transformation brought by the Industrial Revolution: rural depopulation, precariousness, poverty, apparition of a working class. They wondered about the population growth, because the demographic transition had begun in Great Britain at that time. They also asked many fundamental questions, about the source of value, the causes of economic growth and the role of money in the economy. They supported a free-market economy, arguing it was a natural system based upon freedom and property. However, these economists were divided and did not make up a unified current of thought. A notable current within classical economics was under consumption theory, as advanced by the Birmingham School and Malthus in the early 19th century. These argued for government action to mitigate unemployment and economic downturns, and was an intellectual predecessor of what later became Keynesian economics in the 1930s. Another notable school was Manchester capitalism, which advocated free trade, against the previous policy of mercantilism.

Jeremy Bentham, Founder of Utilitarianism

Jeremy Bentham (1748—1832) was perhaps the most radical thinker of his time, and developed the concept of utilitarianism. Bentham was an atheist, a prison reformer, animal rights activist, believer in universal suffrage, free speech, free trade and health insurance at a time when few dared to argue for any. He was schooled rigorously from an early age, finishing university and being called to the bar at 18. His first book, *A Fragment on Government* (1776) published anonymously, was a trenchant critique of William Blackstone's *Commentaries of the laws of England*. This gained wide success until it was found that the young Bentham, and not a revered Professor had penned it. In *The Principles of Morals and Legislation* (1791) Bentham set out his theory of utility. The aim of legal policy must be to decrease misery and suffering so far as possible while producing the greatest happiness for the greatest number. Bentham even designed a comprehensive methodology for the calculation of aggregate happiness in society that a particular law produced, a felicific calculus.

Society, argued Bentham, is nothing more than the total of individuals, so that if one aims to produce net social good then one need only to ensure that more pleasure is experienced across the board than pain, regardless of numbers. For example, a law is proposed to make every bus in the city wheel chair accessible, but slower moving as a result than its predecessors because of the new design. Millions of bus users will therefore experience a small amount of displeasure (or "pain") in increased traffic and journey times, but a minority of people using wheel chairs will experience a huge amount of pleasure at being able to catch public transport, which outweighs the aggregate displeasure of other users. Interpersonal comparisons of utility were allowed by Bentham, the idea that one person's vast pleasure can count more than many others' pain. Much criticism later showed how this could be twisted, for instance, would the felicific calculus allow a vastly happy dictator to outweigh the dredging misery of his exploited population. Despite Bentham's methodology there were severe obstacles in measuring people's happiness.

Jean-Baptiste Say: Supply-side Spokesman

Say's law, that supply always equals demand, was unchallenged until the 20th century. Jean-Baptiste Say (1767—1832) was a Frenchman, born in Lyon who helped to popularize Adam Smith's work in France. His book, *A Treatise on Political Economy* (1803) contained a brief passage, which later became orthodoxy in political economics until the Great Depression and known as Say's Law of Markets. Say argued that there could never be a general deficiency of demand or a general glut of commodities in the whole economy. People produce things, said Say, to fulfill their own wants, rather than those of others. Production is therefore not a question of supply, but an indication of producers demanding goods. Say agreed that a part of the income is saved by the households, but in the long term, savings are invested. Investment and consumption are the two elements of demand, so that production is demand, so it is impossible for production to outrun demand, or for there to be a "general glut" of supply. Say also argued that money was neutral, because its sole role is to facilitate exchanges: therefore, people demand money only to buy commodities. Say said that "money is a veil". To sum up these two ideas, Say said "products are exchanged for products". At most, there will be different economic sectors whose demands are not fulfilled. But over time supplies will shift, businesses will retool for different production and the market will correct itself. An example of a "general glut" could be unemployment, in other words, too great a supply of workers, and too few jobs. Say's Law advocates would suggest that this necessarily means there is an excess demand for other products that will correct itself. This remained a foundation of economic theory until the 1930s. Say's Law was first put forward by James Mill (1773—1836) in English, and was advocated by David Ricardo, Henry Thornton and John Stuart Mill. However two political economists, Thomas

Malthus and Sismondi, were unconvinced.

Thomas Malthus: Pioneer in Population Economics

Thomas Malthus (1766—1834) was a Tory minister in the United Kingdom Parliament who, contrasting to Bentham, believed in strict government abstention from social ills. Malthus devoted the last chapter of his book *Principles of Political Economy* (1820) to rebutting Say's Law, and argued that the economy could stagnate with a lack of "effectual demand". In other words, wages if less than the total costs of production cannot purchase the total output of industry and that this would cause prices to fall. Price falls decrease incentives to invest, and the spiral could continue indefinitely. Malthus is more notorious however for his earlier work, *An Essay on the Principle of Population*. This argued that intervention was impossible because of two factors. "Food is necessary to the existence of man", wrote Malthus. "The passion between the sexes is necessary and will remain nearly in its present state", he added, meaning that the "power of the population is infinitely greater than the power in the Earth to produce subsistence for man." Nevertheless growth in population is checked by "misery and vice". Any increase in wages for the masses would cause only a temporary growth in population, which given the constraints in the supply of the Earth's produce would lead to misery, vice and a corresponding readjustment to the original population. However more labor could mean more economic growth, either one of which was able to be produced by an accumulation of capital.

David Ricardo: Labor Value Theory

Ricardo is renowned for his law of comparative advantage and his position in economic history can be paralleled to that of Adam Smith and Karl Marx. David Ricardo (1772—1823) was born in London. By the age of 26, he had become a wealthy stock market trader and bought himself a constituency seat in Ireland to gain a platform in the British Parliament's House of Commons. Ricardo's best known work is his *Principles of Political Economy and Taxation*, which contains his critique of barriers to international trade and a description of the manner the income is distributed in the population. Ricardo made a distinction between the workers, who receive a wage fixed to a level at which they can survive, the landowners, who earn a rent, and capitalists, who own capital and receive a profit, a residual part of the income. If population grows, it becomes necessary to cultivate additional land, whose fertility is lower than that of already cultivated fields, because of the law of decreasing productivity. Therefore, the cost of the production of the wheat increases, as well as the price of the wheat: The rents increase also, the wages, indexed to inflation (because they must allow workers to survive) too. Profits decrease, until the capitalists can no longer invest. The economy, Ricardo concluded, is bound to tend towards a steady state. To postpone the steady state, Ricardo advocates to promote international trade to import wheat at a low price to fight landowners.

The Corn Laws of the UK had been passed in 1815, setting a fluctuating system of tariffs to stabilize the price of wheat in the domestic market. Ricardo argued that raising tariffs, despite being intended to benefit the incomes of farmers, would merely produce a rise in the prices of rents that went into the pockets of landowners. Furthermore, extra labour would be employed leading to an increase in the cost of wages across the board, and therefore reducing exports and profits coming from overseas business. Economics for Ricardo was all about the relationship between the three "factors of production": land, labour and capital. Ricardo demonstrated mathematically that the gains from trade could outweigh the perceived advantages of protectionist policy. The idea of comparative advantage suggests that even if one country is inferior at producing all of its goods than another, it may still benefit from opening its borders since the inflow of goods produced more cheaply than at home, produces a gain for domestic consumers. According then to Ricardo, this concept would lead to a shift in prices, so that eventually England would be producing goods in which its comparative advantages were the highest.

John Stuart Mill: a Prodigy Who Serves an Example for Learners

Mill, weaned on the philosophy of Jeremy Bentham, wrote the most authoritative economics text of his time. John Stuart Mill (1806—1873) was the dominant figure of political economic thought of his time, as well as being a Member of Parliament for the seat of Westminster, and a leading political philosopher. Mill was a child prodigy, reading Ancient Greek from the age of 3, and being vigorously schooled by his father James Mill. Jeremy Bentham was a close mentor and family friend, and Mill was heavily influenced by David Ricardo. Mill's textbook, first published in 1848 and titled *Principles of Political Economy* was essentially a summary of the economic wisdom of the mid nineteenth century. It was used as the standard texts by most universities well into the beginning of the twentieth century. On the question of economic growth Mill tried to find a middle ground between Adam Smith's view of ever expanding opportunities for trade and technological innovation and Thomas Malthus' view of the inherent limits of population. In his fourth book Mill set out a number of possible future outcomes, rather than predicting one in particular. The first followed the Malthusian line that population grew quicker than supplies, leading to falling wages and rising profits. The second, per Smith, said if capital accumulated faster than population grew then real wages would rise. Third, echoing David Ricardo, should capital accumulate and population increase at the same rate, yet technology stay stable, there would be no change in real wages because supply and demand for labour would be the same. However growing populations would require more land use, increasing food production costs and therefore decreasing profits. The fourth alternative was that technology advanced faster than population and capital stock increased. The result would be a prospering economy. Mill felt the third scenario most likely, and he assumed technology advanced would have to end at some point. But on the prospect of continuing economic growth, Mill was more ambivalent. "I confess I am not charmed with the ideal of life held out by those who think that the normal state of human beings is that of struggling to get on; that the trampling, crushing, elbowing, and treading on each other's heels, which form the existing type of social life, are the most desirable lot of human kind, or anything but the disagreeable symptoms of one of the phases of industrial progress." Mill is also credited with being the first person to speak of supply and demand as a relationship rather than mere quantities of goods on markets, the concept of opportunity cost and the rejection of the wage fund doctrine.

Capitalism and Marx: from Utopian Socialism to Scientific Socialism

Karl Marx provided a fundamental critique of classical economics, based on the labour theory of value. Just as the term "mercantilism" had been coined and popularized by its critics, like Adam Smith, so was the term "capitalism" or *Kapitalismus* used by its dissidents, primarily Karl Marx. Karl Marx (1818—1883) was, and in many ways still remains the pre-eminent socialist economist. His combination of political theory represented in the *Communist Manifesto* and the dialectic theory of history inspired by Friedrich Hegel provided a revolutionary critique of capitalism as he saw it in the nineteenth century. The socialist movement that he joined had emerged in response to the conditions of people in the new industrial era and the classical economics which accompanied it. He wrote his magnum opus *Das Kapital* at the British

Museum's library. With Marx, Friedrich Engels co-authored the *Communist Manifesto*, and the second volume of *Das Kapital*.

Das Kapital

Karl Marx begins *Das Kapital* with the concept of commodities. Before capitalist societies, says Marx, the mode of production was based on slavery (e. g. in ancient Rome) before moving to feudal serfdom (e. g. in mediaeval Europe). As society has advanced, economic bondage has become looser, but the current nexus of labour exchange has produced an equally erratic and unstable situation allowing the conditions for revolution. People buy and sell their labor in the same way as people buy and sell goods and services. People themselves are disposable commodities. As he wrote in the *Communist Manifesto*,

> *The history of all hitherto existing society is the history of class struggles. Freeman and slave, patrician and plebeian, lord and serf, guild master and journeyman, in a word, oppressor and oppressed, stood in constant opposition to one another. The modern bourgeois society that has sprouted from the ruins of feudal society has not done away with class antagonisms. It has but established new classes, new conditions of oppression, new forms of struggle in place of the old ones.*

And furthermore from the first page of *Das Kapital*,

> *The wealth of those societies in which the capitalist mode of production prevails, presents itself as an immense accumulation of commodities, its unit being a single commodity. Our investigation must therefore begin with the analysis of a commodity.*

Marx's use of the word "commodity" is tied into an extensive metaphysical discussion of the nature of material wealth, how the objects of wealth are perceived and how they can be used. The concept of a commodity contrasts to objects of the natural world. When people mix their labor with an object it becomes a "commodity". In the natural world there are trees, diamonds, iron ore and people. In the economic world they become chairs, rings, factories and workers. However, says Marx, commodities have a dual nature, a dual value. He distinguishes the use value of a thing from its exchange value, which can be entirely different. The use value of a thing derives from the amount of labor used to produce it, says Marx, following the classical economists in the labour theory of value. However, Marx did not believe labor only was the source of use value in things. He believed value can derive too from natural goods and refined his definition of use value to "socially necessary labour time" (the time people need to produce things when they are not lazy or inefficient). Furthermore, people subjectively inflate the value of things, for instance because there's a commodity fetish for glimmering diamonds, and oppressive power relations involved in commodity production. These two factors mean exchange values differ greatly. An oppressive power relation, says Marx applying the use/exchange distinction to labor itself, in work-wage bargains derives from the fact that employers pay their workers less in "exchange value" than the workers produce in "use value". The difference makes up the capitalist's profit, or in Marx's terminology, "surplus value". Therefore, says Marx, capitalism is a system of exploitation. Marx explained the booms and busts, like the Panic of 1873, as part of an inherent instability in capitalist economies. Marx's work turned the labour theory of value, as the classicists used it, on its head. His dark irony goes deeper by asking what is the socially necessary labor time for the production of labor (i. e. working people) itself. Marx answers that this is the bare minimum for people to subsist and to reproduce with skills necessary in the economy. People are therefore alienated from both the fruits of production and the means to realize their potential, psychologically, by their oppressed position in the labor market. But the tale told alongside exploitation and alienation is one of capital accumulation and economic growth.

Employers are constantly under pressure from market competition to drive their workers harder, and at the limits invest in labor displacing technology (e. g. an assembly line packer for a robot). This raises profits and expands growth, but for the sole benefit of those who have private property in these means of production. The working classes meanwhile face progressive immiseration, having had the product of their labor exploited from them, having been alienated from the tools of production. And having been fired from their jobs for machines, they end unemployed. Marx believed that a reserve army of the unemployed would grow and grow, fueling a downward pressure on wages as desperate people accept work for less. But this would produce a deficit of demand as the people's power to purchase products lagged. There would be a glut in unsold products, production would be cut back, profits decline until capital accumulation halts in an economic depression. When the glut clears, the economy again starts to boom before the next cyclical bust begins. With every boom and bust, with every capitalist crisis, thought Marx, tension and conflict between the increasingly polarized classes of capitalists and workers heightens. Moreover smaller firms are being gobbled by larger ones in every business cycle, as power is concentrated in the hands of the few and away from the many. Ultimately, led by the Communist party, Marx envisaged a revolution and the creation of a classless society. How this may work, Marx never suggested. His primary contribution was not in a blue print for how society would be, but a criticism of what he saw it was.

After Marx: So Much Has Happened, Yet Basic Law Is Still There and Valid

The first volume of *Das Kapital* was the only one Marx alone published. The second and third volumes were done with the help of Friedrich Engels, and Karl Kautsky, who had become a friend of Engels, saw through the publication of volume four. Marx had begun a tradition of economists who concentrated equally on political affairs. Also in Germany, Rosa Luxemburg was a member of the SPD, who later turned towards the Communist Party because of their stance against the First World War. Beatrice Webb in England was a socialist, who helped found both the London School of Economics (LSE) and the Fabian Society.

Neoclassical Thought: Reformist or Otherwise?

In the 1860s, a revolution took place in economics. The new ideas were that of the Marginalist school. Writing simultaneously and independently, a Frenchman (Léon Walras), an Austrian (Carl Menger) and an Englishman (Stanley Jevons) were developing the theory, which had some antecedents. Instead of the price of a good or service reflecting the labor that has produced it, it reflects the marginal usefulness (utility) of the last purchase. This meant that in equilibrium, people's preferences determined prices, including, indirectly the price of labor. This current of thought was not united, and there were three main schools working independently. The Lausanne school, whose two main representatives were Walras and Vilfredo Pareto, developed the theories of general equilibrium and optimality. The main written work of this school was Walras' *Elements of Pure Economics*. The Cambridge school appeared with Jevons' *Theory of Political Economy* in 1871. This English school has developed the theories of the partial equilibrium and has insisted on markets' failures. The main representatives were Alfred Marshall, Stanley Jevons and Arthur Pigou. The Vienna school was made up of Austrian economists Menger, Eugen von Böhm-Bawerk and Friedrich von Wieser. They developed the theory of capital and has tried to explain the presence of economic crises. It appeared in 1871 with

Menger's *Principles of Economics*.

Marginal Utility: a Revolution in Economic Way of Thinking

William Stanley Jevons helped popularize marginal utility theory. Carl Menger (1840—1921), an Austrian economist stated the basic principle of marginal utility in *Grundsätze der Volkswirtschaftslehre* (1871, *Principles of Economics*). Consumers act rationally by seeking to maximize satisfaction of all their preferences. People allocate their spending so that the last unit of a commodity bought creates no more than a last unit bought of something else. Stanley Jevons (1835—1882) was his English counterpart, and worked as tutor and later professor at Owens College, Manchester and University College, London. He emphasized in the *Theory of Political Economy* (1871) that at the margin, the satisfaction of goods and services decreases. An example of the theory of diminishing returns is that for every orange one eats, the less pleasure one gets from the last orange (until one stops eating). Then Léon Walras (1834—1910), again working independently, generalized marginal theory across the economy in *Elements of Pure Economics* (1874). Small changes in people's preferences, for instance shifting from beef to mushrooms, would lead to a mushroom price rise, and beef price fall. This stimulates producers to shift production, increasing mushrooming investment, which would increase market supply and a new price equilibrium between the products—e.g. lowering the price of mushrooms to a level between the two first levels. For many products across the economy the same would go, if one assumes markets are competitive, people choose on self interest and no cost in shifting production. Early attempts to explain away the periodical crises of which Marx had spoken were not initially as successful. After finding a statistical correlation of sunspots and business fluctuations and following the common belief at the time that sunspots had a direct effect on weather and hence agricultural output, Stanley Jevons wrote,

> *When we know that there is a cause, the variation of the solar activity, which is just of the nature to affect the produce of agriculture, and which does vary in the same period, it becomes almost certain that the two series of phenomena—credit cycles and solar variations—are connected as effect and cause.*

Mathematical Analysis

- Alfred Marshall wrote the main alternative textbook to John Stuart Mill of the day, *Principles of Economics* (1882).
- Vilfredo Pareto (1848—1923) was an Italian economist, best known for developing the concept of an economy that would permit maximizing the utility level of each individual, given the feasible utility level of others from production and exchange. Such a result came to be called "Pareto efficient". Pareto devised mathematical representations for such a resource allocation, notable in abstracting from institutional arrangements and monetary measures of wealth or income distribution.
- Alfred Marshall is also credited with an attempt to put economics on a more mathematical footing. He was the first Professor of Economics at the University of Cambridge and his work, *Principles of Economics* coincided with the transition of the subject from "political economy" to his favored term, "economics". He viewed maths as a way to simplify economic reasoning, though had reservations, revealed in a letter to his student Arthur Cecil Pigou.
- (1) Use mathematics as shorthand language, rather than as an engine of inquiry. (2) Keep to them till you have done. (3) Translate into English. (4) Then illustrate by

examples that are important in real life. (5) Burn the mathematics. (6) If you can't succeed in 4, burn 3. This I do often.

- Coming after the marginal revolution, Marshall concentrated on reconciling the classical labor theory of value, which had concentrated on the supply side of the market, with the new marginalist theory that concentrated on the consumer demand side. Marshall's graphical representation is the famous supply and demand graph, the "Marshallian cross". He insisted it is the intersection of both supply and demand that produce an equilibrium of price in a competitive market. Over the long run, argued Marshall, the costs of production and the price of goods and services tend towards the lowest point consistent with continued production. Arthur Cecil Pigou in *Wealth and Welfare* (1920), insisted on the existence of market failures. Markets are inefficient in case of economic externalities, and the state must interfere. However, Pigou retained free-market beliefs, and in 1933, in the face of the economic crisis, he explained in *The Theory of Unemployment* that the excessive intervention of the state in the labor market was the real cause of massive unemployment, because the governments had established a minimal wage, which prevented the wages from adjusting automatically. This was to be the focus of attack from Keynes.

Austrian School: a Strong and Firm Defender for Market Economy

While the end of the nineteenth century and the beginning of the twentieth were dominated increasingly by mathematical analysis, the followers of Carl Menger, in the tradition of Eugen von Böhm-Bawerk, followed a different route, advocating the use of deductive logic instead. This group became known as the Austrian School, reflecting the Austrian origin of many of the early adherents. Thorstein Veblen in 1900, in his *Preconceptions of Economic Science*, contrasted neoclassical marginalists in the tradition of Alfred Marshall from the philosophies of the Austrian School. Joseph Alois Schumpeter (1883—1950) was an Austrian economist and political scientist most known for his works on business cycles and innovation. He insisted on the role of the entrepreneurs in an economy. In *Business Cycles: A theoretical, historical and statistical analysis of the Capitalist process* (1939), Schumpeter made a synthesis of the theories about business cycles. He suggested that those cycles could explain the economic situations. According to Schumpeter, capitalism necessarily goes through long-term cycles, because it is entirely based upon scientific inventions and innovations. A phase of expansion is made possible by innovations, because they bring productivity gains and encourage entrepreneurs to invest. However, when investors have no more opportunities to invest, the economy goes into recession, several firms collapse, closures and bankruptcy occur. This phase lasts until new innovations bring a creative destruction process, i.e. they destroy old products, reduce the employment, but they allow the economy to start a new phase of growth, based upon new products and new factors of production. Ludwig von Mises (1881—1973) was an Austrian economist who contributed the idea of praxeology, "the science of human action". Praxeology views economics as a series of voluntary trades that increase the satisfaction of the involved parties. Mises also argued that socialism suffers from an unsolvable economic calculation problem, which according to him, could only be solved through free market price mechanisms. Mises' outspoken criticisms of socialism had a large influence on the economic thinking of Friedrich von Hayek (1899—1992), who, while initially sympathetic to socialism, became one of the leading academic critics of collectivism in the 20th century. In echoes of Smith's "system of natural liberty", Hayek argued that the market is a "spontaneous order" and actively disparaged the concept of "social justice".

Hayek believed that all forms of collectivism (even those theoretically based on voluntary cooperation) could only be maintained by a central authority. In his book, *The Road to Serfdom* (1944) and in subsequent works, Hayek claimed that socialism required central economic planning and that such planning in turn would lead towards totalitarianism. Hayek attributed the birth of civilization to private property in his book *The Fatal Conceit* (1988). According to him, price signals are the only means of enabling each economic decision maker to communicate tacit knowledge or dispersed knowledge to each other, to solve the economic calculation problem. Along with his contemporary Gunnar Myrdal, Hayek was awarded the Nobel Prize in 1974.

Depression and Reconstruction

Alfred Marshall was still working on his last revisions of his *Principles of Economics* at the outbreak of the First World War (1914—1918). The new twentieth century's climate of optimism was soon violently dismembered in the trenches of the western front, as the civilized world tore itself apart. For four years the production of Britain, Germany and France was geared entirely towards the war economy's industry of death. In 1917 Russia crumbled into revolution led by Vladimir Lenin's Bolshevik Party. They carried Marxist theory as their savior, and promised a broken country "peace, bread and land" by collectivizing the means of production. Also in 1917, the United States of America entered the war on the side of France and Britain, President Woodrow Wilson carrying the slogan of "making the world safe for democracy". He devised a peace plan of Fourteen Points. In 1918 Germany launched a spring offensive which failed, and as the allies counter-attacked and more millions were slaughtered, Germany slid into revolution, its interim government suing for peace on the basis of Wilson's Fourteen Points. Europe lay in ruins, financially, physically, psychologically, and its future with the arrangements of the Versailles conference in 1919. John Maynard Keynes was the representative of Her Majesty's Treasury at the conference and the most vocal critic of its outcome.

John Maynard Keynes: Advocate of State Intervention

John Maynard Keynes (1883—1946) was born in Cambridge, educated at Eton and supervised by both A. C. Pigou and Alfred Marshall at Cambridge University. He began his career as a lecturer, before working in the British government during the Great War, and rose to be the British government's financial representative at the Versailles conference. His observations were laid out in his book *The Economic Consequences of the Peace* (1919) where he documented his outrage at the collapse of the Americans' adherence to the Fourteen Points and the mood of vindictiveness that prevailed towards Germany. Keynes quit from the conference and using extensive economic data provided by the conference records, Keynes argued that if the victors forced war reparations to be paid by the defeated Axis, then a world financial crisis would ensue, leading to a second world war. Keynes finished his treatise by advocating, first, a reduction in reparation payments by Germany to a realistically manageable level, increased intra-governmental management of continental coal production and a free trade union through the League of Nations; second, an arrangement to set off debt repayments between the Allied countries; third, complete reform of international currency exchange and an international loan fund; and fourth, a reconciliation of trade relations with Russia and eastern Europe. The book was an enormous success, and though it was criticized for false predictions by a number of people, without the changes he advocated, Keynes' dark forecasts matched the world's experience through the Great Depression which ensued in 1929, and the descent into a new outbreak of war in 1939. World War I had been the "war to end all wars", and the absolute failure of the peace settlement generated an even greater determination to not repeat the same mistakes. With the defeat of fascism, the Bretton Woods conference was held to establish a new economic order. Keynes was again to play a leading role.

The General Theory

During the Great Depression, Keynes had published his most important work, *The General Theory of Employment, Interest, and Money* (1936). The depression had been sparked by the Wall Street Crash of 1929, leading to massive rises in unemployment in the United States, leading to debts being recalled from European borrowers, and an economic domino effect across the world. Orthodox economics called for a tightening of spending, until business confidence and profit levels could be restored. Keynes by contrast, had argued in *A Tract on Monetary Reform* (1923) that a variety of factors determined economic activity, and that it was not enough to wait for the long run market equilibrium to restore itself. As Keynes famously remarked,

> ...this long run is a misleading guide to current affairs. In the long run we are all dead. Economists set themselves too easy, too useless a task if in tempestuous seasons they can only tell us that when the storm is long past the ocean is flat again.

On top of the supply of money, Keynes identified the propensity to consume, inducement to invest, the marginal efficiency of capital, liquidity preference and the multiplier effect as variables which determine the level of the economy's output, employment and level of prices. Much of this esoteric terminology was invented by Keynes especially for his *General Theory*, though some simple ideas lay behind. Keynes argued that if savings were being kept away from investment through financial markets, total spending falls. Falling spending leads to reduced incomes and unemployment, which reduces savings again. This continues until the desire to save becomes equal to the desire to invest, which means a new "equilibrium" is reached and the spending decline halts. This new "equilibrium" is a depression, where people are investing less, have less to save and less to spend. Keynes argued that employment depends on total spending, which is composed of consumer spending and business investment in the private sector. Consumers only spend "passively", or according to their income fluctuations. Businesses, on the other hand, are induced to invest by the expected rate of return on new investments (the benefit) and the rate of interest paid (the cost). So, said Keynes, if business expectations remained the same, and government reduces interest rates (the costs of borrowing), investment would increase, and would have a multiplied effect on total spending. Interest rates, in turn, depend on the quantity of money and the desire to hold money in bank accounts (as opposed to investing). If not enough money is available to match how much people want to hold, interest rates rise until enough people are put off. So if the quantity of money were increased, while the desire to hold money remained stable, interest rates would fall, leading to increased investment, output and employment. For both these reasons, Keynes therefore advocated low interest rates and easy credit, to combat unemployment. But Keynes believed in the 1930s, conditions necessitated public sector action. Deficit spending, said Keynes, would kick-start economic activity. This he had advocated in an open letter to U.S. President Franklin D. Roosevelt in the *New York Times* (1933). The New Deal programme in the U.S. had been well underway by the publication of the *General Theory*. It provided conceptual reinforcement for policies already pursued. Keynes also believed in a more egalitarian distribution of income, and taxation on unearned income arguing that high rates of savings (to which richer folk are prone) are not desirable in a developed economy. Keynes therefore advocated both monetary management and an active fiscal policy.

Keynesian Economics: a Complex System of Thoughts

During the Second World War, Keynes acted as adviser to HM Treasury again, negotiating major loans from the US. He helped formulate the plans for the International Monetary Fund, the World Bank and an International Trade Organisation at the Bretton Woods conference, a package designed to stabilize world economy fluctuations that had occurred in the 1920s and create a level trading field across the globe. Keynes passed away little more than a year later, but his ideas had already shaped a new global economic order, and all western governments followed the Keynesian prescription of deficit spending to avert crises and maintain full employment. One of Keynes' pupils at Cambridge was Joan Robinson, who contributed to the notion that competition is seldom perfect in a market, an indictment of the theory of markets setting prices. In *The Production Function and the Theory of Capital* (1953) Robinson tackled what she saw to be some of the circularity in orthodox economics. Neoclassicists assert that a competitive market forces producers to minimize the costs of production. Robinson said that costs of production are merely the prices of inputs, like capital. Capital goods get their value from the final products. And if the price of the final products determines the price of capital, then it is, argued Robinson, utterly circular to say that the price of capital determines the price of the final products. Goods cannot be priced until the costs of inputs are determined. This would not matter if everything in the economy happened instantaneously, but in the real world, price setting takes time—goods are priced before they are sold. Since capital cannot be adequately valued in independently measurable units, how can one show that capital earns a return equal to the contribution to production? Piero Sraffa came to England from fascist Italy in the 1920s, and worked with Keynes in Cambridge. In 1960 he published a small book called *Production of Commodities by Means of Commodities*, which explained how technological relationships are the basis for production of goods and services. Prices result from wage-profit trade-offs, collective bargaining, labor and management conflict and the intervention of government planning. Like Robinson, Sraffa was showing how the major force for price setting in the economy was not necessarily market adjustments.

The "American Way": Is It the Best Way for All?

After World War II, the United States had become the pre-eminent global economic power. Europe and the Soviet Union lay in ruins and the British Empire was at its end. Until then, American economists had played a minor role. The institutional economists had been largely critical of the "American Way" of life, especially regarding conspicuous consumption of the Roaring Twenties before the Wall Street Crash of 1929. After the war, however, a more orthodox body of thought took root, reacting against the lucid debating style of Keynes, and re-mathematizing the profession. The orthodox center was also challenged by a more radical group of scholars based at the University of Chicago. They advocated "liberty" and "freedom", looking back to 19th century-style non-Interventionist governments.

Institutionalism: Institution Is More Important than Resources

Thorsten Veblen (1857—1929), who came from rural mid-western America and worked at the University of Chicago, is one of the best known early critics of the "American Way". In *The Theory of the Leisure Class* (1899) he scorned materialistic culture and wealthy people who conspicuously consumed their riches as a way of demonstrating success and in *The Theory of Business Enterprise* (1904) Veblen distinguished production for people to use things and production for pure profit, arguing that the former is often hindered because businesses pursue the latter. Output and technological advance are restricted by business practices and the creation of monopolies. Businesses protect their existing capital investments and employ excessive credit, leading to depressions and increasing military expenditure and war through business control of political power. These two books, focusing on criticism first of consumerism, and second of profiteering, did not advocate change. However, in 1911, Veblen joined the faculty of the University of Missouri, where he had support from Herbert Davenport, the head of the economics department. Veblen remained at Columbia, Missouri through 1918. In that year, he moved to New York to begin work as an editor of a magazine called *The Dial*, and then in 1919, along with Charles A. Beard, James Harvey Robinson and John Dewey, helped found the New School for Social Research (known today as The New School). He was also part of the Technical Alliance, created in 1919 by Howard Scott. From 1919 through 1926 Veblen continued to write and to be involved in various activities at The New School. During this period he wrote *The Engineers and the Price System* (1921).

John Kenneth Galbraith: an Economist with a Goodwill and Sympathy for Common People

John K. Galbraith began his career as a high flying "new dealer", in the administration of Franklin Delano Roosevelt during the Great Depression. An interview from the early 1990s is here. After the war, John Kenneth Galbraith (1908—2006) became one of the standard bearers for pro-active government and liberal-democrat politics. In *The Affluent Society* (1958), Galbraith argued voters reaching a certain material wealth begin to vote against the common good. He argued that the "conventional wisdom" of the conservative consensus was not enough to solve the problems of social inequality. In an age of big business, he argued, it is unrealistic to think of markets of the classical kind. They set prices and use advertising to create artificial demand for their own products, distorting people's real preferences. Consumer preferences actually come to reflect those of corporations—a "dependence effect"—and the economy as a whole is geared to irrational goals. In *The New Industrial State* Galbraith argued that economic decisions are planned by a private-bureaucracy, a technostructure of experts who manipulate marketing and public relations channels. This hierarchy is self serving, profits are no longer the prime motivator, and even managers are not in control. Because they are the new planners, corporations detest risk, require steady economic and stable markets. They recruit governments to serve their interests with fiscal and monetary policy, for instance adhering to monetarist policies which enrich money-lenders in the city through increases in interest rates. While the goals of an affluent society and complicit government serve the irrational technostructure, public space is simultaneously impoverished. Galbraith paints the picture of stepping from penthouse villas onto unpaved streets, from landscaped gardens to unkempt public parks. In *Economics and the Public Purpose* (1973) Galbraith advocates a "new socialism" as the solution, nationalising military production and public services such as health care, introducing disciplined salary and price controls to reduce inequality.

Paul Samuelson: the First Comprehensive Economist

Paul Samuelson wrote the best selling economics texts and many of his textbooks are still in wide use in many economics schools. In contrast to Galbraith's linguistic style, the post-War economics profession began to synthesize much of Keynes' work with mathematical representations. Introductory university economics courses began to present economic theory as a unified whole in what is referred to as the neoclassical synthesis. "Positive economics" became the term created to describe certain trends and "laws" of economics that could be objectively observed and described in a value free way, separate from "normative economic" evaluations and judgments. The best selling textbook writer of this generation was Paul Samuelson (1915—2009). His Ph. D. was an attempt to show that mathematical methods could represent a core of testable economic theory. It was published as *Foundations of Economic Analysis* in 1947. Samuelson started with two assumptions. First, people and firms will act to maximise their self interested goals. Second, markets tend towards an equilibrium of prices, where demand matches supply. He extended the mathematics to describe equilibrating behavior of economic systems, including that of the then new macroeconomic theory of John Maynard Keynes. Whilst Richard Cantillon had imitated Isaac Newton's mechanical physics of inertia and gravity in competition and the market, the physiocrats had copied the body's blood system into circular flow of income models, William Jevons had found growth cycles to match the periodicity of sunspots, Samuelson adapted thermodynamics formulae to economic theory. Reasserting economics as a hard science was being done in the United Kingdom also, and one celebrated "discovery", of A. W. Phillips, was of a correlative relationship between inflation and unemployment. The workable policy conclusion was that securing full employment could be traded-off against higher inflation. Samuelson incorporated the idea of the Phillips curve into his work. His introductory textbook *Economics* was influential and widely adopted. It became the most successful economics text ever. Paul Samuelson was awarded the new Nobel Prize in Economics in 1970 for his merging of mathematics and political economy.

Kenneth Arrow: What Is Impossible?

Kenneth Arrow (born 1921) is Paul Samuelson's brother-in-law. His first major work, forming his doctoral dissertation at Columbia University was *Social Choice and Individual Values* (1951), which brought economics into contact with political theory. This gave rise to social choice theory with the introduction of his "Possibility Theorem". In his words,

> *if we exclude the possibility of interpersonal comparisons of utility, then the only methods of passing from individual tastes to social preferences which will be satisfactory and which will be defined for a wide range of sets of individual orderings are either imposed or dictatorial.*

This sparked widespread discussion over how to interpret the different conditions of the theorem and what implications it had for democracy and voting. Most controversial of his four (1963) or five (1950/1951) conditions is the independence of irrelevant alternatives. In the 1950s, Arrow and Gérard Debreu developed the Arrow—Debreu model of general equilibria. In 1971 Arrow with Frank Hahn co-authored *General Competitive Analysis* (1971), which reasserted a theory of general equilibrium of prices through the economy. In 1969 the Swedish Central Bank began awarding a prize in economics, as an analogy to the Nobel prizes awarded in Chemistry, Physics, Medicine as well as Literature and Peace (though Alfred Nobel never endorsed this in his will). With John Hicks, Arrow won the Bank of Sweden prize in 1972, the youngest recipient ever. The year before, US President Richard Nixon's had declared that "We are all Keynesians now". The irony was that this was the beginning of a new revolution in economic thought.

Monetarism and the Chicago School: Currency Is All

The interventionist monetary and fiscal policies that the orthodox post-War economics recommended came under attack in particular by a group of theorists working at the University of Chicago, which came to be known as the Chicago School. This more conservative strand of thought reasserted a "libertarian" view of market activity, that people are best left to themselves, free to choose how to conduct their own affairs.

Ronald Coase: Founder of Institutional School of Economics

Ronald Coase (born 1910) is the most prominent economic analyst of law and the 1991 Nobel Prize winner. His first major article, *The Nature of the Firm* (1937), argued that the reason for the existence of firms (companies, partnerships, etc.) is the existence of transaction costs. Rational individuals trade through bilateral contracts on open markets until the costs of transactions mean that using corporations to produce things is more cost-effective. His second major article, *The Problem of Social Cost* (1960), argued that if we lived in a world without transaction costs, people would bargain with one another to create the same allocation of resources, regardless of the way a court might rule in property disputes. Coase used the example of an old legal case about nuisance named *Sturges v Bridgman*, where a noisy sweet maker and a quiet doctor were neighbors and went to court to see who should have to move. Coase said that regardless of whether the judge ruled that the sweet maker had to stop using his machinery, or that the doctor had to put up with it, they could strike a mutually beneficial bargain about who moves house that reaches the same outcome of resource distribution. Only the existence of transaction costs may prevent this. So the law ought to preempt what would happen, and be guided by the most efficient solution. The idea is that law and regulation are not as important or effective at helping people as lawyers and government planners believe. Coase and others like him wanted a change of approach, to put the burden of proof for positive effects on a government that was intervening in the market, by analyzing the costs of action.

Milton Friedman: Strong Support of Free Market Economy

Milton Friedman (1912—2006) stands as one of the most influential economists of the late twentieth century. He won the Nobel Prize in Economics in 1976, among other things, for *A Monetary History of the United States* (1963). Friedman argued that the Great Depression had been caused by the Federal Reserve's policies through the 1920s, and worsened in the 1930s. Friedman argues that laissez-faire government policy is more desirable than government intervention in the economy. Governments should aim for a neutral monetary policy oriented toward long-run economic growth, by gradual expansion of the money supply. He advocates the quantity theory of money, that general prices are determined by money. Therefore active monetary (e.g. easy credit) or fiscal (e.g. tax and spend) policy can have unintended negative effects. In *Capitalism and Freedom* (1967) Friedman wrote:

> *There is likely to be a lag between the need for action and government recognition of the need; a further lag between recognition of the need for action and the taking of action; and a still further lag between the action and its effects.*

Friedman was also known for his work on the consumption function, the permanent income hypothesis (1957), which Friedman himself referred to as his best scientific work. This work contended that rational consumers would spend a proportional amount of what they perceived to be their permanent income. Windfall gains would mostly be saved. Tax reductions likewise, as rational consumers would predict that taxes would have to rise later to balance public finances. Other important contributions include his critique of the Phillips curve and the concept of the natural rate of unemployment (1968). This critique associated his name with the insight that a government that brings about higher inflation cannot permanently reduce unemployment by doing so. Unemployment may be temporarily lower, if the inflation is a surprise, but in the long run unemployment will be determined by the frictions and imperfections in the labor market.

Amartya Sen and Joseph E. Stiglitz: Call for More Justice in Economics

Amartya Sen (born 1933) is a leading development and welfare economist and has expressed considerable skepticism on the validity of neo-Classical assumptions. He was highly critical of rational expectations theory, and devoted his work to development and human rights. He won the Nobel Prize in Economics in 1998. Joseph Stiglitz (born 1943) received the Nobel Prize in 2001 for his work in information economics. He has served as chairman of President Clinton's Council of Economic Advisers and as chief economist for the World Bank. Stiglitz has taught at many universities, including Columbia, Stanford, Oxford, Manchester, Yale, and MIT. In recent years he has become an outspoken critic of global economic institutions. He is a popular and academic author. In *Making Globalization Work* (2007), he offers an account of his perspectives on issues of international economics. The fundamental problem with the neoclassical model and the corresponding model under market socialism is that they fail to take into account a variety of problems that arise from the absence of perfect information and the costs of acquiring information, as well as the absence or imperfections in certain key risk and capital markets. The absence or imperfection can, in turn, to a large extent be explained by problems of information.

Paul Krugman, an Economist with a Good Conscience

Paul Krugman (born 1953) is a contemporary economist. His textbook *International Economics* (2007) appears on many undergraduate reading lists. Well known as a representative of progressivism, he writes a weekly column on economics, American economic policy, and American politics more generally in the *New York Times*. He was awarded the Nobel Prize in Economics in 2008 for his work on New Trade Theory and economic geography.

Contemporary Economic Thought/Macroeconomics since the Bretton Woods Era

From the 1970s onwards Friedman's monetarist critique of Keynesian macroeconomics formed the starting point for a number of trends in macroeconomic theory opposed to the idea that government intervention can or should stabilize the economy. Robert Lucas criticized Keynesian thought for its inconsistency with microeconomic theory. Lucas's critique set the stage for a neoclassical school of macroeconomics, New Classical economics based on the foundation of classical economics. Lucas also popularized the idea of rational expectations, which was used as the basis for several new classical theories including the Policy Ineffectiveness Proposition. The standard model for new classical economics is the real business cycle theory, which sought to explain observed fluctuations in output and employment in terms of real variables such as changes in technology and tastes. Assuming competitive markets, real business cycle theory implied that cyclical fluctuations are optimal responses to variability in technology and tastes, and that macroeconomic stabilization policies must reduce welfare. Keynesian economics made a comeback among mainstream economists with the advent of New Keynesian macroeconomics. The central theme of new Keynesianism was the provision of a microeconomic foundation for Keynesian macroeconomics, obtained by identifying minimal deviations from the standard microeconomic assumptions which yield Keynesian macroeconomic conclusions, such as the possibility of significant welfare benefits from macroeconomic stabilization. Akerlof's "menu costs" arguments, showing that, under imperfect competition, small deviations from rationality generate significant (in welfare terms) price stickiness, are good example of this kind of work. Economists have combined the methodology of real business cycle theory with theoretical elements, like sticky prices, from new Keynesian theory to produce the new neoclassical synthesis. Dynamic stochastic general equilibrium (DSGE) models, large systems of microeconomic equations combined into models of the general economy, are central to this new synthesis. The synthesis dominates present day economics.

Questions and Topics for Pondering and Further Discussion for Unit Eight-1:
1. What is meant by the economic way of thinking?
2. Why do some people say that economics is not only a science, but also an art.
3. Why are such giant economists or thinkers as Smith, Ricardo, Marx, Keynes widely viewed as milestone figures in economic thoughts? Can you briefly illustrate their ideas respectively?
4. How much do you know about so-called "utility revolution"?
5. What is the fundamental issue of economics?
6. What are the standards to judge whether or not economists make progress?
7. In economics, there is an eternal dilemma between efficiency and fairness. Please make further comments.
8. A famous person once complained that economics is a science of dismal. What do you think of this statement?

2. A History of Political Philosophy of the West

Editor's remarks: *the article below is a brief account of political philosophy, which is not limited to western heritage in this aspect. However, after the Medieval Age, the West began to dominate the evolution of political philosophy which led to the modern political institution and system that are still influential globally. Some of the ideas expressed in its political philosophy have become universal values of whole human beings such as justice, equality, rule of law and individual freedom within the framework of legality. Political philosophy is an important and integral part of western culture and it has become its own embodied ideological system called political culture as a whole.*

Political philosophy is the study of such topics as politics, liberty, justice, property, rights, law, and the enforcement of a legal code by authority: what they are, why (or even if) they are needed, what, if anything, makes a government legitimate, what rights and freedoms it should protect and why, what form it should take and why, what the law is, and what duties citizens owe to a legitimate government, if any, and when it may be legitimately overthrown, if ever. In a vernacular sense, the term "political philosophy" often refers to a general view, or specific ethic, political belief or attitude, about politics that does not necessarily belong to the technical discipline of philosophy. Political philosophy can also be understood by analyzing it through the perspectives of metaphysics, epistemology and axiology. It provides insight into, among other things, the various aspects of the origin of the state, its institutions and laws...

Ancient Greece

western political philosophy originates in the philosophy of ancient Greece, where political philosophy begins with Plato's *Republic* in the 4th century BC. Ancient Greece was dominated by city-states, which experimented with various forms of political organization, grouped by Plato into four categories: timocracy, tyranny, democracy and oligarchy. One of the first, extremely important classical works of political philosophy is Plato's *Republic*, which was followed by Aristotle's *Nichomachean Ethics and Politics*. Roman political philosophy was influenced by the Stoics, including the Roman statesman Cicero.

Medieval Christianity/Saint Augustine

The early Christian philosophy of Augustine of Hippo was heavily influenced by Plato. The main change that Christian thought brought was to moderate the Stoicism and theory of justice of the Roman world, and emphasize the role of the state in applying mercy as a moral example. Augustine also preached that one was not a member of his or her city, but was either a citizen of the City of God (Civitas Dei) or the City of Man (Civitas Terrena). Augustine's *City of God* is an influential work of this period that refuted the thesis, after the First Sack of Rome, that the Christian view could be realized on Earth at all—a view many Christian Romans held.

Saint Thomas Aquinas

In political philosophy, Aquinas is most meticulous when dealing with varieties of law. According to Aquinas, there are four different kinds of laws:
1. God's cosmic law.
2. God's scriptural law.
3. Natural law or rules of conduct universally applicable within reason.
4. Human law or specific rules applicable to specific circumstances.

Medieval Europe

Medieval political philosophy in Europe was heavily influenced by Christian thinking. It had much in common with the Mutazalite Islamic thinking in that the Roman Catholics though subordinating philosophy to theology did not subject reason to revelation but in the case of contradictions, subordinated reason to faith as the Asharite of Islam. The Scholastics by combining the philosophy of Aristotle with the Christianity of St. Augustine emphasized the potential harmony inherent in reason and revelation. Perhaps the most influential political philosopher of medieval Europe was St. Thomas Aquinas who helped reintroduce Aristotle's works, which had only been preserved by the Muslims, along with the commentaries of Averroes. Aquinas's use of them set the agenda, for scholastic political philosophy dominated European thought for centuries even unto the Renaissance. Medieval political philosophers, such as Aquinas in *Summa Theologica*, developed the idea that a king who is a tyrant is no king at all and could be overthrown. Magna Carta, viewed by many as a cornerstone of Anglo-American political liberty, explicitly proposes the right to revolt against the ruler for justice sake. Other documents similar to Magna Carta are found in other European countries such as Spain and Hungary.

Niccolò Machiavelli: a Leading Figure for Political Realist and Pragmatist

One of the most influential works during this burgeoning period was Niccolò Machiavelli's *The Prince*, written between 1511—1512 and published in 1532, after Machiavelli's death. That work, as well as *The Discourses*, a rigorous analysis of the classical period, did much to influence modern political thought in the West. A minority (including Jean-Jacques Rousseau) could interpret *The Prince* as a satire meant to be given to the Medici after their recapture of Florence and their subsequent expulsion of Machiavelli from Florence. Though the work was written for the di Medici family in order to perhaps influence them to free him from exile, Machiavelli supported the Republic of Florence rather than the oligarchy of the di Medici family. At any rate, Machiavelli presents a pragmatic and somewhat consequentialist view of politics, whereby good and evil are mere means used to bring about an end, i. e. the secure and powerful state. Thomas Hobbes, well known for his theory of the social contract, goes on to expand this view at the start of the 17th century during the English Renaissance. Although neither Machiavelli nor Hobbes believed in the divine right of kings, they both believed in the inherent selfishness of the individual. It was necessarily this belief that led them to adopt a strong central power as the only means of preventing the disintegration of the social order.

John Locke: Founding Father of Modern Political Science

John Locke in particular exemplified this new age of political theory with his work *Two Treatises of Government*. In it Locke proposes a state of nature theory that directly complements his conception of how political development occurs and how it can be founded through contractual obligation. Locke stood to refute Sir Robert Filmer's paternally founded political theory in favor of a natural system based on nature in a particular given system. The theory of the divine right of kings became a passing fancy, exposed to the type of ridicule with which John Locke treated it. Unlike Machiavelli and Hobbes but like Aquinas, Locke would accept Aristotle's dictum that man seeks to be happy in a state of social harmony as a social animal. Unlike Aquinas's preponderant view on the salvation of the soul from original sin, Locke believes man's mind comes into this world as tabula rasa. For Locke, knowledge is neither innate, revealed nor based on authority but subject to uncertainty tempered by reason, tolerance and moderation. According to Locke, an absolute ruler as proposed by Hobbes is unnecessary, for natural law is based on reason and seeking peace and survival for man.

European Age of Enlightenment

Eugène Delacroix's *Liberty Leading the People* (1830, Louvre), a painting created at a time where old and modern political philosophies came into violent conflict. During the Enlightenment period, new theories about what the human was and is and about the definition of reality and the way it was perceived, along with the discovery of other societies in the Americas, and the changing needs of political societies (especially in the wake of the English Civil War, the American Revolution and the French Revolution) led to new questions and insights by such thinkers as Jean-Jacques Rousseau, Montesquieu and John Locke. These theorists were driven by two basic questions: one, by what right or need do people form states; and two, what the best form for a state could be. These fundamental questions involved a conceptual distinction between the concepts of "state" and "government". It was decided that "state" would refer to a set of enduring institutions through which power would be distributed and its use justified.

The term "government" would refer to a specific group of people who occupied the institutions of the state, and create the laws and ordinances by which the people, themselves included, would be bound. This conceptual distinction continues to operate in political science, although some political scientists, philosophers, historians and cultural anthropologists have argued that most political action in any given society occurs outside of its state, and that there are societies that are not organized into states which nevertheless must be considered in political terms. As long as the concept of natural order was not introduced, the social sciences could not evolve independently of theistic thinking. Since the cultural revolution of the 17th century in England, which spread to France and the rest of Europe, society has been considered subject to natural laws akin to the physical world. Political and economic relations were drastically influenced by these theories as the concept of the guild was subordinated to the theory of free trade, and Roman Catholic dominance of theology was increasingly challenged by Protestant churches subordinate to each nation-state, which also (in a fashion the Roman Catholic Church often decried angrily) preached in the vulgar or native language of each region. However, the Enlightenment was an outright attack on religion, particularly Christianity. The publication of Denis Diderot's and Jean d'Alembert's *Encyclopédie ou Dictionnaire raisonné des sciences, des arts et des métiers* marked the crowning intellectual achievement of the epoch. The most outspoken critic of the church in France was François Marie Arouet de Voltaire, a representative figure of the enlightenment. After Voltaire, religion would never be the same again in France.

In the Ottoman Empire, these ideological reforms did not take place and these views did not integrate into common thought until much later. As well, there was no spread of this doctrine within the New World and the advanced civilizations of the Aztec, Maya, Inca, Mohican, Delaware, Huron and especially the Iroquois. The Iroquois philosophy in particular gave much to Christian thought of the time and in many cases actually inspired some of the institutions adopted in the United States: for example, Benjamin Franklin was a great admirer of some of the methods of the Iroquois Confederacy, and much of early American literature emphasized the political philosophy of the natives.

Contemporary Political Philosophy

From the end of World War II until 1971, when John Rawls published *A Theory of Justice*, political philosophy declined in the Anglo-American academic world, as analytic philosophers expressed skepticism about the possibility that normative judgments had cognitive content, and political science turned toward statistical methods and behavioralism. In continental Europe, on the other hand, the postwar decades saw a huge blossoming of political philosophy, with Marxism dominating the field. This was the time of Jean-Paul Sartre and Louis Althusser, and the victories of Mao Zedong in China and Fidel Castro in Cuba, as well as the events of May 1968 led to increased interest in revolutionary ideology, especially by the New Left. A number of continental European émigrés to Britain and the United States—including Hannah Arendt, Karl Popper, Friedrich Hayek, Leo Strauss, Isaiah Berlin, Eric Voegelin and Judith Shklar— encouraged continued study in political philosophy in the Anglo-American world, but in the 1950s and 1960s they and their students remained at odds with the analytic establishment. Communism remained an important focus especially during the 1950s and 1960s. Colonialism and racism were important issues that arose.

In general, there was a marked trend towards a pragmatic approach to political issues, rather than a philosophical one. Much academic debate regarded one or both of two pragmatic topics: how (or whether) to apply utilitarianism to problems of political policy, or how (or whether) to apply economic models (such as rational choice theory) to political issues. The rise of feminism, LGBT social movements and the end of colonial rule and of the political exclusion of such minorities as African Americans and sexual minorities in the developed world has led to feminist, postcolonial, and multicultural thought becoming significant. This led to a challenge to the social contract by philosophers Charles W. Mills in his book *The Racial Contract* and Carole Patemen in her book *The Sexual Contract* that the social contract excluded persons of color and women respectively. In Anglo-American academic political philosophy, the publication of John Rawls's *A Theory of Justice* in 1971 is considered a milestone. Rawls used a thought experiment, the original position, in which representative parties choose principles of justice for the basic structure of society from behind a veil of ignorance. Rawls also offered a criticism of utilitarian approaches to questions of political justice. Robert Nozick's book *Anarchy, State, and Utopia*, which won a National Book Award, responded to Rawls from a libertarian perspective and gained academic respectability for libertarian viewpoints.

Contemporaneously with the rise of analytic ethics in Anglo-American thought, in Europe several new lines of philosophy directed at critique of existing societies arose between the 1950s and 1980s. Most of these took elements of Marxist economic analysis, but combined them with a more cultural or ideological emphasis. Out of the Frankfurt School, thinkers like Herbert Marcuse, Theodor W. Adorno, Max Horkheimer, and Jürgen Habermas combined Marxian and Freudian perspectives. Along somewhat different lines, a number of other continental thinkers—still largely influenced by Marxism—put new emphases on structuralism and on a "return to Hegel". Within the (post-) structuralist line (though mostly not taking that label) are thinkers such as Gilles Deleuze, Michel Foucault, Claude Lefort, and Jean Baudrillard. The Situationists were more influenced by Hegel; Guy Debord, in particular, moved a Marxist analysis of commodity fetishism to the realm of consumption, and looked at the relation between consumerism and dominant ideology formation. Another debate developed around the (distinct) criticisms of liberal political theory made by Michael Sandel and Charles Taylor. The liberal—communitarian debate is often considered valuable for generating a new set of philosophical problems, rather than a profound and illuminating clash of perspectives. Charles Blattberg has offered an account which distinguishes between four different contemporary political philosophies: neutralism, postmodernism, pluralism, and patriotism. There is fruitful interaction between political philosophers and international relations theorists. The rise of globalization has created the need for an international normative framework, and political theory has moved to fill the gap.

Questions and Topics for Pondering and Further Discussion for Unit Eight-2:

1. What are the prominent features of western philosophy?
2. What are the components of traditional western philosophy?
3. What is the definition of law according to Thomas Aquinas?
4. What are the major conflicts between the old and modern philosophy in Europe?
5. What are the major sources of Marxian philosophy?
6. How much do you know about ancient Greek philosophy?
7. What is political philosophy about?
8. Why did socialism and communism become an influential social trend in the late 19th century?

Unit Nine

1. The Culture of the United States[①]

   Editor's remarks: *the American culture is the apex of western culture, symbolizing its highest stage in the developmental process so far. The dominance of western culture nowadays in the world is best represented by American global cultural influence based on its core values evolved mainly from western cultural system. From Jerusalem via Rome and London to Washington/New York western culture has undergone a path of rapid and brutal expansion, growth and eventually dominance. Therefore, a basic understanding of western culture must be established on the full appreciation of American culture as its sign and symbol. In a sense, American culture is an equation to western culture at large.*

   The Culture of the United States is an offshoot and a symbolic flagship of western culture originally influenced by Native American cultures. American culture started its formation over 10,000 years ago with the migration of Paleo-Indians from Asia into the region that is today the continental United States. It has its own unique social and cultural characteristics such as dialect, music, arts, social habits, cuisine, and folklore. Today, the United States of America is an ethnically and racially diverse country as a result of large-scale immigration from many different countries throughout its history. Its chief early European influences came from English, Scottish, Welsh and Irish settlers of colonial America during British rule. British culture, due to colonial ties with Britain that spread the English language, legal system and other cultural inheritances, had a formative influence. Other important influences came from other parts of western Europe, especially Germany, France, and Italy. Original elements also play a strong role, such as the invention of Jeffersonian Democracy. Thomas Jefferson's *Notes on the State of Virginia* was perhaps the first influential domestic cultural critique by an American and a reactionary piece to the prevailing European consensus that America's domestic originality was degenerate. Prevalent ideas and ideals that evolved domestically, such as national holidays, uniquely American sports, military tradition, and innovations in the arts and entertainment give a strong sense of national pride among the population as a whole. American culture includes both conservative and liberal elements, scientific and religious competitiveness, political structures, risk taking and free expression, materialist and moral elements.

   Despite some certain consistent ideological principles (e. g. individualism, egalitarianism, and faith in freedom and democracy), American culture has a variety of expressions due to its geographical scale and demographic diversity. The flexibility of U. S. culture and its highly symbolic nature lead some researchers to categorize American culture as a *mythic* identity; others see it as American exceptionalism. It also includes elements that evolved from indigenous Americans, and other ethnic cultures—most prominently the culture of African Americans and different cultures from Latin America. Many American cultural elements, especially from popular culture, have spread across the globe through modern mass media. The United States has often been thought of as a melting pot, but recent developments trend towards cultural diversity, pluralism and the image of a salad bowl rather than a melting pot. Due to the extent of

---

   ① The information contained in this introductory article about American culture is the edited and revised intellectual result of many sources and materials including *Wikipedia* and *Columbia Encyclopedia* as well as some other books about American culture. For more detailed information, one can visit the website of US government for cultural part at www.usa.gov.

American culture there are many integrated but unique social subcultures within the United States. The cultural affiliations an individual in the United States may have commonly depend on social class, political orientation and a multitude of demographic characteristics such as religious background, occupation and ethnic group membership.

Languages: English Has Become an International Language for the USA

Although the United States has no official language at the federal level, 30 states have passed legislation making English the official language and it is and 3 considered to be the *de facto* national language. According to the 2000 U.S. Census, more than 97% of Americans can speak English well, and for 81% it is the only language spoken at home. More than 300 languages besides English have native speakers in the United States—some of which are spoken by the indigenous peoples (about 150 living languages) and others imported by immigrants. Spanish has official status in the commonwealth of Puerto Rico and the state of New Mexico; Spanish is the primary spoken language in Puerto Rico and various smaller linguistic enclaves. According to the 2000 census, there are nearly 30 million native speakers of Spanish in the United States. Bilingual speakers may use both English and Spanish reasonably well but code-switch according to their dialogue partner or context. Some refer to this phenomenon as Spanglish. Indigenous languages of the United States include the Native American languages, which are spoken on the country's numerous Indian reservations and Native American cultural events such as pow wows; Hawaiian, which has official status in the state of Hawaii; Chamorro, which has official status in the commonwealths of Guam and the Northern Mariana Islands; Carolinian, which has official status in the commonwealth of the Northern Mariana Islands; and Samoan, which has official status in the commonwealth of American Samoa. American Sign Language, used mainly by the deaf, is also native to the country. The national dialect is known as American English. There are four major regional dialects in the United States: northeastern, south, inland north, and midwestern. The midwestern accent (considered the "standard accent" in the United States, and analogous in some respects to the received pronunciation elsewhere in the English-speaking world) extends from what were once the "Middle Colonies" across the Midwest to the Pacific states. There is also a growing consensus that there is an accent/dialect native to the Pacific Northwest that is unique to that area.

Religion: America Is Very Religious, in Name or in Reality Alike

Completed in 1716, San Antonio Missions National Historical Park is one of numerous surviving colonial Spanish missions in the United States. These were primarily used to convert the Native Americans to Roman Catholicism. Among developed countries, the U.S. is one of the most religious in terms of its demographics. According to a 2002 study by the Pew Global Attitudes Project, the U.S. was the only developed nation in the survey where a majority of citizens reported that religion played a "very important" role in their lives, an opinion similar to that found in Latin America. Today, governments at the national, state, and local levels are a secular institution, with what is often called the "separation of church and state". But like federal politics, the topic of religion in the United States can cause an emotionally heated debate over moral, ethical and legal issues affecting Americans of all faiths in everyday life, such as polarizing issues of abortion, gay marriage and obscenity. Several of the original Thirteen Colonies were established by English and Irish settlers who wished to practice their own religion without discrimination or persecution: Pennsylvania was established by Quakers, Maryland by Roman

Catholics and the Massachusetts Bay Colony by Puritans. The first Bible printed in a European language in the Colonies was by German immigrant Christopher Sauer. Nine of the thirteen colonies had official public religions. By the time of the Philadelphia Convention of 1787, the United States became one of the first countries in the world to codify freedom of religion into law, although this originally applied only to the federal government, and not to state governments or their political subdivisions.

Modeling the provisions concerning religion within the Virginia Statute for Religious Freedom, the framers of the United States Constitution rejected any religious test for office, and the First Amendment specifically denied the central government any power to enact any law respecting either an establishment of religion, or prohibiting its free exercise. In following decades, the animating spirit behind the constitution's Establishment Clause led to the disestablishment of the official religions within the member states. The framers were mainly influenced by secular, Enlightenment ideals, but they also considered the pragmatic concerns of minority religious groups who did not want to be under the power or influence of a state religion that did not represent them. Thomas Jefferson, author of the Declaration of Independence said "The priest has been hostile to liberty. He is always in alliance with the despot."

Questions and Topics for Pondering and Further Discussion for Unit Nine-1:

1. It is widely viewed in the West as well as in many parts of the world that the culture of the USA is a flagship of the western culture. Do you agree with this statement? Why or why not?
2. Why does American culture spread so aggressively around the world?
3. Is American culture equal to culture of consumption or culture of enjoyment?
4. What are the unique features of American culture?
5. Compared with European culture, American culture seems to be more influential. Why is that?
6. What is the essence of American culture?
7. Are Americans still very religious?
8. What is the relationship between American culture and US hard power?

2. A Book Excerpt Illustrating Cultural Contradictions of Modern Capitalism[①]

Editor's remarks: *the following selected article is a famous book excerpt. More specifically, it is taken from the Introduction part of the book entitled <u>The Cultural Contradictions of Capitalism</u> written by Daniel Bell, a famous American sociologist and scholar for cultural and humanistic studies. Daniel Bell is known for his famous trilogy book series respectively entitled <u>The End of Ideology</u> published in 1960, <u>The Coming of the Post-industrial Society</u> published in 1973 and <u>The Cultural Contradictions of Capitalism</u> (first edition in*

---

① This book excerpt is adopted and adapted from the Introduction to a book entitled *The Cultural Contradictions of Capitalism* written by Daniel Bell for a small part of its introduction section. The current version is based upon the 20th anniversary edition of the book with the same title. It is selected here in order to provide a unique angle of analysis of major contradictions of capitalism from the eye of a liberal-conservative scholar who seems to know better the nature of capitalism, especially American capitalism.

1976), which he believed to be his last *Magnum Opus*. Daniel Bell has established his academic reputation with the publication of these three books in addition to many other books and articles and essays, expressing his unique views on many of the hot issues and topics concerning modern social development in terms of cultural and economic perspectives. He is a Professor Emeritus at Harvard University and he has claimed himself to be a liberalist in politics, socialist in economics and conservatist in culture, a famous trinity capacity for his intellectual stance. With his famous axial conflict assumption, Daniel Bell dissects the fundamental contradictions of capitalism, especially American capitalism. In <u>The Cultural Contradictions of Capitalism</u>, Bell contends that the culture created by modern capitalism generates a strong need for personal gratification through material consumption among the successful and prestigious, and that this will harm and eventually destroy the work ethic that has caused that initial success of capitalism in the first place. This book has been selected by New York Times Book Review Column as one of the ONE hundred most influential and intellectually profound books published in the 20th century. To read this book carefully and critically is to get some basic understanding of the deeply hidden contradictions of capitalism as represented by American capitalism and its capitalistic cultural logic.

Introduction/The Disjunctions of Realms[①]

A Statement of Themes

IN THE SPRING of 1888, Friedrich Nietzsche sketched the Preface of his last book, **The Will to Power**, which he planned to be his magnum opus, as follows:

> What I relate is the history of the next two centuries. I describe what is coming, what can no longer come differently: the advent of nihilism. This history can be related even now; for necessity itself is at work here. This future speaks even now in a hundred signs.... For some time now our whole European culture has been moving as toward a catastrophe, with a tortured tension that is growing from decade to decade: restlessly, violently, headlong, like a river that wants to reach the end, that no longer reflects, that is afraid to reflect.

The source of this nihilism for Nietzsche was rationalism and calculation, a temper of life whose intention was to destroy "unreflective spontaneity". If there was a single symbol for him which summed up the force of nihilism, it was modern science. For Nietzsche, what had happened was that tradition, the unwitting, unquestioning "means for obtaining homogeneous, enduring characters for long generations", had been destroyed. Instead, "we have [now] reached the opposite point; indeed, we wanted to reach it: the most extreme consciousness, man's ability to see through himself and history." The organic ties to the soil, "the inalienability of property", had been ruptured, and in their place had come a commercial civilization. Nietzsche speaks of the disorganizing principles of the time: "newspapers (in place of daily prayers), the railway, the telegraph, the centralization of a tremendous number of different interests in a single soul, which for that reason must be very strong and protean." This theme is foreshadowed in Nietzsche's first book, *The Birth of Tragedy*, written in 1870—1871, when he was 26 years old. His great demon, that monster of consciousness, is Socrates, the "despotic logician", whose "great

---

① For the sake of protection of copyrights, the author of this textbook can only quote the first paragraph of the book as the sample reading material. For the original contents of the book, the reader can read the book itself for detail. The book is entitled *The Cultural Contradictions of Capitalism* written by Daniel Bell, published by Basic Books in 1996. For more information about the contents of the book, the reader should read the original book.

Cyclops eye" never "glowed with the artist's divine frenzy", whose "voice always spoke to *dissuade* ". Socrates begins the devitalization of culture by introducing distance and questioning, the skepticism of knowledge that is gained by intoxication and dream. Socrates is "the great exemplar of ... *theoretical man* ", who has "the insatiable zest for knowledge" and who "finds his highest satisfaction in the unveiling process itself, which proves to him his own power".

Questions and Topics for Pondering and Further Discussion for Unit Nine-2:

1. In what way are cultural contradictions as discussed in the article different from other contradictions of capitalism? For example, economic or political contradictions of capitalism?
2. Nietzsche predicted that something would be bound to happen in the next 125 years in 1888. What is that?
3. Daniel Bell claims himself to be in trinity in his ideological approach. Please elaborate more specifically on this point. What are you in terms of ideology?
4. What calamity, according to Bell, is capitalism going to encounter sooner or later?
5. What is the Bell's definition of culture?
6. Do you agree with his axial analysis of capitalism as a whole with American capitalistic society as an example?
7. What is the assumption of the philosophers of the Enlightenment about the world?
8. What are the major academic contributions made by Daniel Bell?

3. Introduction to and Postscript of a Book Entitled *American Culture since WW II* by Paul Levine

Editor's remarks: America by the end of 19th or the beginning of 20th century had overtaken Great Britain to be the top one industrial nation on earth with its comprehensive state power ranked number 1 in the world, which, in the words of Henry Luce, heralded a century widely acclaimed as "the America Century". Shortly before WWI, America already enjoyed a status of power that was in parallel with the then declining British Empire. The Empire where the sun never sets was a sun-setting power while the United States of America loomed large as a sun-rising giant. However, America suffered a heavy setback in late 1920's when the worst economic depression, historically known as "the Great Depression" inflicted a sudden and fatal blow to capitalist economy at large, and to American economy in particular. The total GDP of the US dropped to the level well before WWI and the so-called "the Gilded Age" became an age of national disaster and popular depression. However, as FDR stated with a firm belief to the effect in his first Inauguration Address that this nation has endured so many hardships and would come out stronger. With his New Deal, FDR not only saved capitalist economic system, but also led America out of trouble and then continued its journey toward a much stronger nation through the trials and tribulations of WW II. When WW II ended with America as one of the triumphant powers, America stood firmly and proudly as the flagship of capitalist countries and erected as a arch-representative of western civilization. The process of "American Century", interrupted and shadowed briefly by the worst economic crisis ever experienced so far in the West, seemed to have been developing in full swing. The book <u>The American Culture</u>

Since WW Ⅱ provides a vivid and expressive account of American culture in a new era when the West, led by the United Stated, started to compete, ideologically and economically, with the eastern Bloc headed by the then Soviet Union, dawning a period of time in human history known to all as "the Cold War Period", which came to a dramatic stop when the Soviet Union all of sudden disintegrated. With the disintegration of the USSR, the United States has remained the sole super-power, greatly enhancing the westerners' confidence about the superiority of their social and political system. American-Japanese scholar Francis Fukuyama hailed the end of the Cold War as the end of history. However, as time goes by, a more true picture about the current world status has appeared and people have started to reflect the heritage of the Cold War. Now, it can be safely concluded that the disintegration of the USSR should be viewed more of the failure of a unreasonable and unjustifiable social structure than a manifest victory of capitalistic system as a whole. History is not always progressively, but developing in a spiral way full of turns and twists. But one thing is indisputable, which is that American capitalism has not disappeared as predicted by some Utopian left-Wing revolutionary idealists. Rather, it has undergone some form of radical or even fundamental transformation. To know something about American culture is not to emulate it blindly or adore it humbly. As an objective existence, the influence of American culture is global and such influence seems to be on ascendance, at least for some time to come. Therefore, it is beneficial to follow its path and to predict its future orientation. After all, this world still cannot by and large escape the influence of American culture as represented not only by its fancy commodities, but also by its soft power, ranging from its higher education, its entertainment apparatus to its omnipresent cultural images of Mickey Mouse, Lady Gaga, Ipads and NBA.

In February 1941, Henry Luce, the publisher of *Life* Magazine, wrote an editorial with the prophetic title "The American Century". Luce was one of those innovative entrepreneurs who shaped American life in the twentieth century. Like John D. Rockefeller, he combined the Protestant ethic and the spirit of Capitalism in his business magazine *Fortune*. Like William Randolph Hearst, he shaped modern journalism by inventing the weekly news magazine *Time*. And like Walt Disney he altered the way we see the world with *Life*, the famous magazine of photojournalism. Today, 40 years after Luce's death, his magazine empire is a global "infotainment" colossus that includes *Time* magazine, Warner Brothers movies, and CNN television.

Like his legendary contemporaries, Henry Luce was an American patriot. But he was more of an internationalist than they were. Born in 1898 in China, Luce grew up with a strong sense of America's global mission. His parents were Protestant missionaries and he became the journalistic apostle of the American century. "To him America was not just a country, it was an idea and an ideal," wrote David Halberstam in *The Powers That Be* (1979). "His magazines would celebrate this." Beginning in the 1920s, Luce sought to promote American values in his increasingly influential magazines. By mid-century, he had become the major media spokesman for the American dream. "He sought to make America what it should be and thus, of course, in the pages of *Time*, America *became* what it should be. The dream realized."

In his 1941 editorial, "The American Century", Luce urged his fellow countrymen to break with their traditional isolationism and lead the global fight against fascism. In World War I, the United States became a reluctant combatant after German submarines sank three American vessels. In 1919 a triumphant President Woodrow Wilson attended the Versailles Peace Conference with a sweeping plan to create a new world order; but he was thwarted by his French and British allies. After Wilson's failure, the US Congress rejected the peace treaty and refused to join the newly formed League of Nations that Wilson had proposed. After the outbreak of

World War Ⅱ in 1939, skeptical Americans were once again asked to come to the aid of their European allies. With France defeated and Britain beleaguered, the United States had become the last bulwark of western democracy against Nazi Germany. Now, as citizens of the world's most powerful nation, Luce argued, Americans had an obligation to promote democratic principles throughout the world. Nine months later, the Japanese attacked Pearl Harbor and the United States embarked on a course of action that ultimately transformed modern times into what he called "the American century".

Luce's editorial proved to be prophetic; but with some important reservations, as we shall see. Though the United States entered the conflict reluctantly only after the Japanese attack, Americans pursued the war enthusiastically. "World War Ⅱ was the most popular in American history," notes the historian John Patrick Diggins in *The Proud Decade* (1988). "It was truly a people's war." While Europe exhausted itself in a brutal conflict, the United States set out to create the most awesomely productive economic and military machine the world had ever seen. Moreover, American losses, though considerable, were slight in comparison to the devastation in Europe and Asia. The Americans suffered 400,000 deaths in battle whereas 35,000,000 Europeans—soldiers and civilians alike—died in just five years. "In the years since Pearl Harbor the United States had overcome the greatest crisis facing the country since the Civil War," says Diggins. "A war that most Americans originally did not want to fight turned into one of the proudest triumphs in the history of the Republic."

Thus at the end of World War Ⅱ, the United States emerged as an economic, political and military superpower, a position it has held for more than half a century. As we entered a new millennium, Luce's idea of "the American Century" took on a new currency. With the collapse of the Soviet Union, economic turmoil in Asia and political disunity in Europe, the United States remained by default the only global superpower. In the realm of culture, too, we have all experienced the long arm of American hyperpower. The world sees American films, hears American music, reads American books, copies American television programs and grumbles about the dangers of American cultural hegemony. The cultivation of efficient techniques of global distribution has created mass culture and spread American values all over the world. Today critics speak anxiously of Globalization and Americanization as if they were the same thing.

We all recognize forms of "American cultural imperialism", but what is American culture? For many skeptics, it is only McDonald's, Levi's and Hollywood. But a culture is more than a hamburger. When the Nobel Prize-winning novelist Saul Bellow was growing up in Chicago in the 1920s, the city was famous for its stockyards, steel mills, railroads and gangsters. "What Chicago gave to the world was goods—a standard of living sufficient for millions. Bread, bacon, overalls, gas ranges, radio sets, telephone directories, false teeth, light bulbs, tractors, steel rails, gasoline," Bellow wrote, "If you looked here for the sort of natural beauty described by Shakespeare, Milton, Wordsworth, Yeats, you would never find it."

Yet, as the son of Russian Jewish immigrants, Bellow found something else in Chicago. As he recalled 60 years later in *It All Adds Up* (1994):

> *The children of Chicago bakers, tailors, peddlers, insurance agents, pressers, cutters, grocers, the sons of families on relief, were reading buckram-bound books from the public library and were in a state of enthusiasm, having found themselves on the shore of a novelistic land to which they really belonged, discovering their birthright, hearing incredible news from the great world of culture, talking to one another about the mind, society, art, religion, epistemology, and doing this in Chicago, of all places.*

But critics of American material culture are partly right.

In *Land of Desire* (1993) William Leach describes how Americans created the modern world by combining corporate capitalism and consumer culture. "In the decades following the Civil War, American capitalism began to produce a distinct culture, unconnected to traditional family or community values, to religion in any conventional sense, or to political democracy," he says. "The cardinal features of this culture were acquisition and consumption as a means of achieving happiness; the cult of the new; the democratization of desire; and money value as the predominant measure of all value in society."

Leach traces the evolution of the consumer society from its humble beginnings in retailing through its institutionalization in the consumer and service sectors, to its total acceptance as the American Way of Life. The flamboyant entrepreneurs of the late nineteenth century were transformed into anonymous corporations in the early twentieth century, comprising a network of department stores, investment bankers, advertising agencies, hotels, restaurants, movie theaters, model agencies, fashion groups and public relations firms. In creating a new culture of consumption, the modern captains of industry found unlikely partners in new institutions of higher learning like the Harvard Business School (founded in 1908) and high culture like the Metropolitan Museum of Art (its division of industrial design began in 1914). "A new society has come to life in America," noted a French observer in 1928. "From a *moral point of view*, it is obvious that Americans have come to consider their standard of living as a somewhat sacred acquisition, which they will defend at any price."

In redefining modern democracy as a mass consumer society, Americans followed a different path from the Europeans. In *Why the American Century?* (1993) Olivier Zunz writes, "As its size increased and its standard of living improved, the middle class became the hallmark of the 'American century'. In the 'America-as-model' paradigm, the middle class, not the working class, is the revolutionary ideal. Promoting its values became the American alternative to Marxism." Instead of the Marxist ideology of class conflict, Americans pointed to an expanding middle-class society as the material expression of "the American dream". In the postwar years, this celebration of affluence became the hallmark of "the American Way of Life" and the cornerstone of the ideology of "the American Century". Zunz concludes, "In contrast to the situation in Europe, consumption, not welfare, was the American means of social cohesion."

Of course, these achievements have had their costs, especially among those groups who were excluded from the American mainstream. But, despite its failures, the United States continues to pursue the prophesy of Henry Luce's "American Century". We know how American ideas about the organization of knowledge, the consumer society and multiculturalism have become part of the global cultural landscape as well. After the collapse of the Soviet empire in 1989, the French historian Francois Furet argued that while the Soviet Union had been a superpower, it had never been a civilization. The proof was that it could vanish without leaving any substantial legacy behind. But the opposite is true of the United States. The idea of "the American Century" became the basis for the establishment of the "Pax Americana". Unlike the Soviet Union, says Zunz, "The United States became a superpower precisely because of its civilization."

This book is an exploration of American civilization in the period between World War II and the present. If this does not constitute an American Century, it can be seen as the American Moment: the time when, for good or ill, the United States became the predominant political, military, economic and cultural power in the world. In this book, we wish to examine the American Moment in a global context. Our approach is both interdisciplinary and dialogic. By using elements of political science and international relations, media and cultural studies, and social, intellectual and literary history, we try to present a multidimensional picture of the United States in its relation to the larger world. The odd-numbered chapters are written by a political scientist, Harry Papasotiriou; they move chronologically through major events in international relations and American domestic politics. The even-numbered chapters are written by a literary historian, Paul Levine; they explore thematically the central developments in American culture and society. By structuring our book in alternating chapters emphasizing political and cultural developments respectively, we hope to establish a dialogue between the authors and with the reader.

Meanwhile a generation of cultural icons have died: civil rights activist Rosa Parks, conservative movement godfather William Buckley, diplomat George F. Kennan, economist John Kenneth Galbraith, feminist Betty Friedan, journalist David Halberstam, political scientist Samuel P. Huntington, President Gerald R. Ford, pop idol Michael Jackson, urban critic Jane Jacobs, and three veterans of the Vietnam conflict: General William Westmoreland; antiwar, candidate Senator Eugene McCarthy and former Secretary of Defense Robert McNamara. The world of letters lost dramatists Arthur Miller and August Wilson, and novelists Saul Bellow, Norman Mailer, J. D. Salinger, John Updike and Kurt Vonnegut, Jr. Finally, in 2009 a modern political dynasty ended with the deaths of President John Kennedy's sister, Eunice Shriver, and his youngest brother, Senator Edward Kennedy.

As we enter the second decade of the twenty-first century the world looks different. With the economic rise of Brazil, Russia, India and China, some analysts predict the decline of the United States in the next decades. "Look around," says Fareed Zakaria. "The tallest building in the world is in Taipei, and it will soon be overtaken by one being built in Dubai. The world's richest man is Mexican, and its largest publicly traded corporation is Chinese." Even traditional American icons have been supplanted: the largest Ferris Wheel is in Singapore, the largest gambling casino is in Macao, the largest shopping center is in Beijing. Globalization has transformed the postmodern world in surprising ways. These are some of the issues we try to address in this new edition.

Postscript

And what of Henry Luce's prophesy of "the American Century"? During the 70 years since his famous *Life* Magazine editorial, the United States rose to dominate global politics, economics and culture. But in the new millennium its sustaining power has been challenged. The neoconservative strategists surrounding President George W. Bush had hoped to extend the American Century into the distant future; but their disastrous policies undermined the American economy at home and subverted American prestige abroad. Even a sympathetic critic, Francis Fukuyama, acknowledged its failures in *America at the Crossroads* (2007): "One of the striking things about the performance of the Bush administration is how poorly it has followed through in accomplishing the ambitious objectives it has set for itself." Perhaps the most revealing epitaph of the Bush years came inadvertently from the grammatically challenged president himself, when he said, "Our enemies are innovative and resourceful, and so are we. They never stop thinking about new ways to harm our country and our people, and neither do we."

The breathtaking election of Barack Obama and his message of hope created a new wave of optimism in America. His dazzling rise to the American presidency reached its apogee in the premature awarding of the Nobel Peace Prize in 2009, only months after he had assumed office and weeks after he had made the controversial decision to increase American troop levels in Afghanistan. Now Obama must deliver more than soaring rhetoric if he is to achieve the

Herculean tasks of resuscitating the economy, regulating Wall Street, reforming the health care system, rescuing the environment and raising America's standing in the world.

Though many analysts pronounce this mission impossible and predict the decline of the United States in the twenty-first century, perhaps Fareed Zakaria provides the shrewdest assessment of the future in *The Post-American World* (2008). He predicts not the fall of the United States but "the rise of the rest", especially emerging Asian powers like China and India. Meanwhile the American public grapples with global problems of social, economic and technological change. "The irony is that the rise of the rest is a consequence of American ideas and actions," says Zakaria. "Generations from now, when historians write about these times, they might note that, in the early decades of the twenty-first century, the United States succeeded in its great and historic mission—it globalized the world. But along the way, they might write, it forgot to globalize itself." It may be that the dream of the American Century is coming to a close. But we still live in the American Moment.

Unit Ten

An Understanding of Western Culture[①]

Introduction: Theme Stated

The concept of a "clash of civilizations" was first drafted in 1990 by Bernard Lewis, a committed Zionist, to describe the conflict between political Islam and the West. A few years later, in 1993, Samuel Huntington, elevated the thesis of a clash of civilizations into a universal historical principle. Lewis, Huntington, and many other thinkers who have discussed the theory, have seen the western civilization as a monolith with no internal fault lines or contradictions. It is common for many western thinkers to treat western civilization as the ultimate development of human species and treat every other culture as a lower level of civilization and culture. Before any discussion on clash of civilizations, it is important to understand the essential features of western civilization. Many American and European universities have (at least they used to have till a few years ago) courses on western civilization. Most of these courses state that western civilization has been formed from three distinct traditions that are listed as follows:

1. The classical culture of Greece and Rome;
2. The Christian religion;
3. The Enlightenment of the modern era.

Many have seen western civilization as a synthesis of all three traditions; others have emphasized the conflicts among them, the struggle between the Christian religion and the Enlightenment being especially consequential. These views of western civilization do not reflect an external observer's objective view. It is the perspective of western thinkers biased by their ideas of how they would like themselves to be seen.

Romans and Tribes

Western thinkers, in their analysis of western civilization, make a jump from Greek and Roman civilization straight to modern renaissance. The fact that Roman Empire did not cover most of present-day western Europe is glossed over. Influence of tribes like Vikings, Normans, Goths, Franks, Saxons, Thuringians, Alamanni, Macromanni, Teutons, Norse, Celts, Cherusci, etc. is also ignored when discussing the mindset of present western civilization. Most of these tribes were described as "barbarians" by Greek and Roman historians. Needless to say, that this description arose from a deep-seated bias against the tribes, and not from any in-depth understanding of these tribes. Yet, it can well be concluded that these tribes were fierce, warlike and had strong family links. They were, generally speaking, loyal to their mates for life. They were not known for leading a life of luxury. In fact they led a hard life and were content to live and let live. It was the Roman insatiable desire for luxury and riches that brought the Roman Empire in conflict with the tribes. Though the western thinkers like to recall the philosophy and

---

[①] The original article of more or less the same title concerning one's understanding was written and was published on the Internet by Anil Chawla, an American Studies scholar of Indian origins. This article has been revised, simplified and edited by the editor with some of the new ideas added while keep the basic ideas in the original article. Acknowledgments are hereby demonstrated with gratitude.

theology of Rome and Greece, the fact is that philosophy and theology were not central to the life of Greece and Rome. Gluttonous banquets and orgies thrown by Grecian and Roman elite (not to mention the depths of depravity and sexual license incurred among such festivities) dominated the Greek and Roman mind. Greek and Roman philosophers were just a shade better than gladiators and court jesters—dazzling everyone with their brilliant wit and arguments, without in any way disturbing the applecart of unbridled luxury.

Roman luxury needed direct and indirect slaves. Direct slaves were the ones who toiled in the Roman towns doing all menial jobs while their masters enjoyed the pleasures of food and flesh. But more important than these urban slaves were the indirect ones who worked in the vast country-land that fed the Roman cities. Much before the words colonialism and imperialism were even coined, the city republics of Greek and Rome had converted the villages around the cities into colonies from where there was an incessant transfer of resources that helped the city folks lead a life of luxury, even while the countrymen just about managed to eke out a living. As the demand for luxuries grew in the cities, the kings were forced to expand the catchment area from where resources flowed into the cities. This expansion brought the Romans in conflict with the "barbaric" tribes. Initially, the tribes were content with just resisting the Roman onslaught, but soon they realized that people used to a life of luxury could not be good warriors. Romans had become too soft to fight. Tribes exploited this. To fight the tribes, the Romans started employing "barbarians" as soldiers in their army. In due course, all positions of power in the Roman Government were in the hands of the so-called barbarians. This led to the end of the Roman civilization, but only an apparent end. The economic model of Greek and Roman civilization was adopted by the "barbarian" tribes who were no longer content to just live and let live. Now they had the benefit of Roman "education", which told them that the only aim of life worth pursuing is to strive for continuous increase of wealth and luxury by all means, fair or foul. Contentment is a dirty word in western civilization. In recent times, a liberal thinker (John Stuart Mill) said, "I would rather be a pig than be a contented man". From the Romans to the tribesmen to the modern day, the first commandment of western civilization has been an unrestrained pursuit of wealth and luxury. Each individual doggedly pursues pleasures and luxuries stepping on toes and necks, if necessary, of everyone else. This reflects in the collective psyche of the societies. Imperialism, slave trade and even the western world's espousal of the drug trade in China and other places, as long as it suited them, were expressions of this collective psyche. The mindset that looks at every other human being as either an obstacle or a stepping-stone in one's mad pursuit for wealth, luxury and pleasures is not confined to matters of collective psyche only. As a fundamental building block of psychology, it affects every aspect of a person's behavior, including mundane day-to-day matters. The following two examples may help to clarify the point:

Traveling in a long-distance train in India or China, one notices that it is customary for passengers to offer food to co-passengers, even though they may be perfect strangers. This is unimaginable in Europe and America. In USA, it is said, "there is nothing like a free lunch". Quite in contrast, free lunch (called 'langar') is an essential feature of all Sikh places of worship. When Swami Prabhupad (founder of International Society for Krishna Consciousness) reached USA, he had hardly any money. Yet, Swami Prabhupad would offer to share his limited meals with anyone who happened to come along. ISKCON temples across the world continue this tradition till today. A culture built on snatching the other man's bread cannot understand this sharing of one's food. Free food being served at a Sikh Gurudwara.

Sharing of food is central to the Oriental psyche. In a restaurant in India, if four persons are eating together, they will share every dish that is brought to the table. Quite often a guest will just tell the host to order whatever pleases the host. It will be considered extremely discourteous for four people eating together on a table to order four entirely different dishes and then each one eats his own. But this is exactly what happens in Europe and America. Sharing of food, or for that matter anything else, is not a virtue that western civilization practices. One does not know whether the so-called barbarian tribes used to share food. But we do know that the tribes did not have sexual orgies of the type Rome was famous for. We also know that Roman orgies had bestiality, child molestation, sado-masochism and many such acts, which were unheard of in the barbarian cultures that valued family life. Europe today, probably, has more family life than Rome had in its most glorious days. One cannot say the same with confidence about United States of America. Though, of course, family life remains alive in both Europe and USA. On the other hand, when one looks at the fact that the USA and parts of Europe have almost five times more incidents of rape and sexual crimes per hundred thousand of population than India, one is forced to seek the underlying psychological factors. The explanation, which comes to one's mind, is that a culture that seeks maximization of wealth, luxury and pleasures at all costs tends to look at women and even children as objects to be used for one's pleasure. If collectively speaking one does not bother about killing thousands in Iraq or Vietnam or Bengal to further one's self-interests, it stands to logic that, in an individual's mind, one does not respect the modesty of a woman or care for a child.

Surely, most people in Europe and America take good care of their children—it is a human instinct. western civilization cannot undo the natural programming of caring for children built into human instinct. Yet, the western civilization's influence runs counter to the natural instinct of caring. Put differently, the western culture teaches one to emphasize the instinct of maximization of pleasures, while de-emphasizing the instinct of care. With the instinct of pleasure-seeking getting upper hand over the instinct of caring, a western man grudgingly takes care of his children (till they reach adulthood) but ignores all other relationships. A couple of years ago (2003), about 15000 people died in Paris when summer temperatures rose too high. Most of Paris was on vacation and there were not sufficient persons to take care of the elderly, sick and weak. When some young people on vacation were informed that their father/mother/grandparent had died, they refused to cancel their vacation. President of France issued an appeal to the people to take care of their elders but refused to cancel his vacation. Obviously, in the western world, care for one's parents or grand parents cannot take precedence over one's immediate pleasures. Indian businessmen routinely extend hearty hospitality and courtesies to their business associates from Europe and America on visit to India even if there is no likelihood of any business being transacted in immediate future. With experience, Indian business class is now learning that the European or American, who enjoyed their hospitality for days or even weeks, may even refuse a ten-minute appointment at his / her office if there is no possibility of transacting business immediately. European/American attitude is—why waste time. Indian attitude is—we can be friends, even though we may not do any business. It takes an Indian some time to realize the western man's sharp focus on self-interests.

Christianity

The irony is that a civilization that emphasizes pleasures and self-interest to such a high degree professes Christianity—a religion founded on pain and suffering of Jesus Christ. A possible explanation for this irony is that Christianity, as it has evolved, has more to do with

Church and less to do with Jesus. To understand the role of Christianity in western mind, let us look at the evolution of Christianity as an organized religion. Christianity originated in Jerusalem, which is located in present-day Israel. So in a way, Christianity is an Asian religion and came to Europe almost two centuries after its birth. Jesus was a Jew who revolted against the ruling elite of his day and preached a system of religious practices that offended the people in power. He was crucified by the ruling elite but he did not retaliate or even ask his followers to rise up in arms. If he had compromised with his tormentors, he could have lived a life of luxury ever after. Story of Jesus Christ was not written down for a long time after his going to heaven, since his followers believed that he would come back. It was only about a century later that New Testament was written. For the first two or three centuries, followers of Jesus Christ used to meet and sing hymns; the Church was in its nascent form and had no powers.

Emperor Constantine's conversion to Christianity in 312 AD was the turning point in the history of Church. Before spread of Christianity, each country of Europe had its own religious traditions. Roman Empire was pagan (Mithraism) though there were a few Jews and Christians living in Rome. Emperor Constantine's conversion came at a point when Roman civilization was on the decline. The period after decline of Roman civilization saw the emergence of various tribes as the new invaders. They had tasted their first blood on the peripheries of Roman Empire. They had also seen what a life of luxury could be. Now, they wanted the same luxuries that the Roman elite had enjoyed. This pursuit of riches by various tribes took the form of bloody wars in Europe that lasted for more than a thousand years (some would say that World War II was the last of such wars). The victorious Kings used to encounter resistance from indigenous religions. It was at this point that Christianity came in handy. Church was too willing to provide the spiritual backup, needed by a victorious king, in return for money, land and new followers. The king benefited because the demolition of indigenous religions ensured that he could rule in peace without a fear of local revolt. Indigenous religions brought with them power structures deeply rooted in the psyche of the people. Destroying these structures was essential for ruling a country.

It may be mentioned that peaceful conversions to Christianity were rare. Saxons were converted at sword point in 804 AD. Danish and Norwegian Vikings were not Christianized till 11th century. Scandinavia and Balkans were the last to fall to Christianity—Poland in 966, Hungary in 1001, and Lithuania in 1387. From 312 to around fourteenth century, we see in Europe a period when each group of ruling elites wanted to capture as much power and wealth as possible by use of sword or by cunningness. Kings and royals had no concern for their own people. The indigenous unorganized pagan religions, which were close to the people's day-to-day lives, were systematically destroyed to ensure that people had no recourse to an alternative belief system, which could possibly threaten the excesses of the ruling elite. The Church emerged as the perfect handmaid for European despotic kings during this period. Church was providing, what Karl Marx later called as "opium for the masses". Church conducted charity programs, ran schools and hospitals, and in general provided the healing touch to populations brutalized by the oppressive monarchs. In the process, the Church controlled the minds of the people making them weak and pliant, making sure that they had no will to rise up in revolt against oppression and exploitation—just right for being ruled by despots.

The evolution of Church into a supporting institution for Kings is interesting. An Evangelical Christian friend recently wrote that Christianity is more than what is written in Bible. How true! Jesus did not write any portion of the Bible. In fact, Jesus never accepted the Old Testament in entirety as Church did a few centuries later. This was probably done as part of a compromise with some rulers and to acquire a higher level of acceptability among the educated classes that had a large number of Jews. Jesus had said, Love Thy Neighbor. He never said—

Love thy neighbor, if he is Christian and kill him if he is pagan. Jesus was a prophet of universal love, peace and kindness. Church does not (even today) believe in any love or kindness for pagans. A few months ago, Catholic Church issued an apology to Jews and women—not to pagans. From fourth century to fifteenth century or so, on one hand the Church helped soften up the Christian masses to be ruled by despotic Kings and on the other hand, the Church provided a moral basis for the most cruel and barbaric tormenting and killing of millions of people. The cruelty of the Church was extended to not just the pagans but also its own people. Recently there has been some interest in the killing of Knights Templar, who were soldier monks devoted to the Christian cause. From 1307 to 1314 all the Templars were arrested, brutally tortured and killed under an arrangement between the Kings and the Pope. Almost all historians accept that the charges against the Templars were baseless and ridiculous. It appears that the Templars had just become inconvenient for the Kings as well as the Pope. Hence, the wrath of God fell on these soldier monks of Christianity. Templars were probably a small group compared to the large number of so-called witches executed during 1400—1800.

The execution of about half a million witches in Europe in the period of 1400—1792, the majority of whom were female, some male or even children, and the majority of whom were burned at the stake or hanged after being extensively tortured, an event unparalleled in human history. Most of these victims probably would have viewed themselves as good Christians, and were not member of any secret cult; most of the confessions about secret meetings or convents can be shown to be the result of the torture on one hand, and the superstitions of the inquisitors on the other. The Burning Times was one of the foulest periods in the history of western Civilization, a time when reason and compassion gave way to prejudice and frenzy, when mere accusation or simply being "different" could result in the most sadistic and brutal tortures and eventually death.

The idea of burning witches, one of the cruelest forms of execution, is said to have originated with Saint Augustine (354—430), who said "that pagans, Jews, and heretics would burn forever in eternal fire with the Devil unless saved by the Catholic Church." Witches, also were classed as heretics, during the time of the Inquisition. Heretics were not only disbelieves of the church doctrine, but, many also were accused of beings servants of the Devil by forming compacts with him to get his help. The accused were sentenced to execution by burning when found guilty of heresy, and few escaped this conviction of the church, which practically controlled every aspect of human life, because "Fire itself is the element of purification, and nothing less than fire could negate the evil that was said to be witches." The 16th century demonologist, Jean Bodin, stated in "De la Demonomanie des Sorciers": Even if the witch has never killed or done evil to man, beast, or fruits, and even if he has always cured bewitched people, or driven away tempests, it is that he has renounced God and treated with Satan that he deserves to be burned alive... Even if there is no more than the obligation to the Devil, having denied God, this deserves the most cruel death that can be imagined. The idea of burning could also come from the "wicker man" of the pagan Celts. As reported in accounts by Julius Caesar and other Romans, the Celts would build a huge, cage-like structure in the shape of a large man made from wood or wicker. Inside it were stuffed living human beings. In bonfire-like fashion the "wicker man" was set ablaze, sacrificing the people inside. Jesus lived a simple and ascetic life. He never acquired any riches or property. Church preached the virtues of poverty to the gullible masses, even as it kept increasing its lands, wealth and riches. By the end of first millennium, Pope and Cardinals were living in palaces that might have put even some Kings to shame. This was the point when the cozy relationship between Church and Kings spoilt. The Church was no longer content to just play a second fiddle. It wanted more of the power. This led to a long drawn power struggle, about which much has been written.

When Europeans started moving out of Europe in search of colonies, it was in a sense repetition of history. Instead of Romans attacking "barbarian" tribes across Europe, it was Europeans (which mostly included tribesmen duly cultured in the ways of Rome) attacking the tribes across the world. The two key differences, between Roman times to the onset of colonialism, were technology and the Church. It is said that when Europeans landed in Africa, in one hand they had a gun and in the other hand was a Bible. In Africa and Asia, Church helped the colonialists in the same way that it had helped medieval European kings. The colonialists, in association with the Church, destroyed indigenous pagan religions and made local people weak and pliant. Wherever indigenous religions were too firmly established, the colonialists found life difficult. It is not a coincidence that independence movement in such countries had strong pagan religious overtones. For example, in India, leaders like Swami Vivekanand, Swami Dayanand, Bal Gangadhar Tilak and Mahatma Gandhi used Hindu religious symbols and practices to mobilize people against British colonialism. Church helped colonialists exploit Asia and Africa just as they had helped despotic kings to oppress and exploit the people of Europe. Christianity in association with the rulers destroyed indigenous religions of Europe—a job that is still unfinished in Asia and Africa, according to Church sources. Unfortunately for the Church, even in Europe the pagan religions are still alive and the process of Christianization is far from complete. In fact, paganism has been rising from its ashes across almost every part of Europe.

For centuries, Church had been in the forefront of campaign for most cruel torture and killing of traditional pagan healers like druids and witches across Europe. Druids and witches had been painted in the darkest colors by the propaganda machinery of Church. It is nothing short of miracle that now there is a growing understanding and respect for the useful role played by these traditional medical practitioners for centuries. Societies and associations of neo-converts to the faith of druids and witches are coming up across Europe and America. In the past five decades, power of Church has reduced considerably in every country of western Europe. Population surveys in every country reveal that the local population (excluding immigrants) has a significant percentage of Christians, non-Christians (including agnostics) as well as of pagans. Even among so-called Christians, a large percentage is of Church-less Christians—people who believe in Jesus Christ and go to church on special occasions but are not willing to let their life be controlled by the Church. Five hundred years ago it would have been unimaginable and would have surely invited death by burning on stakes, but today pagan festivals are celebrated openly at various places across Europe (and America). In addition to festivals that are declared to be pagan, there are number of festivals that are not Christian and are celebrated across the western world—Valentine Day, Mother's Day, Father's Day, Thanksgiving, and every local festival including national days of various countries. Church has never liked such non-Christian festivities by believers. It is only a sign of the times that the Church is unable to do anything about sheep going out of the control of the shepherd so blatantly.

The more worrying part for the clergy is the growing pagan influence that one sees in Christian festivals. Surprisingly, even celebration of Christmas is not free of pagan influence. It might surprise some to know that the most visible symbols of Christmas—Santa Claus and Christmas Tree—both are of pagan origin and have no connection whatsoever with Christianity or Church or Bible. Santa Claus, also known as Father Christmas, is typically like a pagan or Hindu god. One can see this when one looks at Santa riding on a reindeer driven-chariot. The association of every divine personality with some animal species is Hindu or pagan and no Christian saint rides an animal driven chariot. Surely, there have been muted protests by

Churches about the rising importance of Santa in Christmas celebrations across Europe and America. Catholic Church (as well as all other Churches) has also been warning its believers about adopting "non-Christian forms of meditation" (read Yoga) without much success.

There is a growing concern in Church circles about the modern western approach to religion, best described by the term "cafeteria attitude". Modern western mind looks at religion (often more than one religion) and picks what it likes and leaves what it does not like. A man might get baptized but still go to a Muslim friend's house on Eid; seek peace, solace and good health in Hindu Yoga classes; attend lectures on Buddhism by followers of Dalai Lama; take his girl friend for abortion; break bread with witches in a rock festival; and later come to the Church to get his marriage solemnized. This sort of behavior does not bother an Oriental mind. For example, in Japan marriages are held the Shinto way while rituals of death are generally Buddhist. It is rumored that Jesus had traveled to India and the Orient. But one sees none of the Oriental liberalism in the religion that his so-called followers have built. Christianity, as it has evolved, is a religion of power, of controlling minds and lives. Power of clergy is derived from the fact that they convert millions into sheep ready for sale to abattoirs under the promise of leading to heaven. As human beings learn to be human beings, the refuse to be sheep—that is the greatest challenge before Christianity and various Churches. In fact this is a clash that has been going on for past three centuries or so. Voltaire, Nietzsche, Marx and many other western thinkers led a frontal attack against religion, but they were attacking only the institutionalized form of Christian religion represented by the Church. Present civilization of Europe and USA includes a mix of various currents. On one hand, Christianity is still alive and orthodox elements have been trying to reclaim their lost glory. Loud anti-abortion voices in USA are evidence that Christian Churches are still a force to reckon with. On the other hand, there is a growing interest in pagan practices and festivals. It is impossible to look into the future and predict whether paganism will dominate or one of the Churches will rule again. Instead of trying to predict and forecast, let us try to understand paganism.

Paganism

Traditionally, "pagan" was a derogatory term used to describe anyone who was not a Jew or Muslim or Christian. In a way, it is the Christian equivalent of "kafir" (used by Muslims to describe non-believers). Muslims do not use the term "kafir" for Christians and Jews (who are called Ehle-Kitaab, followers of a book, in contrast with those who do not follow any one book). Similarly, the Christians abstain from calling Jews or Muslims as pagans. However, all other religions are called pagans. Contemporary paganism is the restoration of indigenous religion(s), especially those of ancient Europe. Paganism has grown in popularity greatly during the last hundred years. The growth coincides with a decline of Christianity in Europe, and the increase in knowledge of past and distant cultures. In modern world, the term "Contemporary Paganism" is used to describe a group of contemporary religions based on a reverence for nature. It encompasses a diverse community with some groups concentrating on specific traditions, practices or elements such as ecology, witchcraft, Celtic traditions or certain gods. Wiccans, Druids, Shamans, Sacred Ecologists, Odinists and Heathens all make up parts of the pagan community.

Whilst there are significant differences between these strands of contemporary paganism, most pagans share an ecological vision and involvement that comes from the pagan belief in the organic vitality and spirituality of the natural world. Moving beyond contemporary paganism and looking at pagan religions as a broad category, as against book-based religions like Judaism, Christianity and Islam, we see a vast array of pagan religions—Hinduism, Buddhism,

Confucianism, Taoism, Contemporary Paganism and many indigenous religions of various countries. In all pagan religions, whether modern or contemporary or ancient, the relationship of the individual with the cosmos or nature, which is considered divine, is direct and without any intermediary. In all one-book-based religions, human beings are prevented or even prohibited from being in direct communication with the divine; all communication between the divine and the layperson is through an established hierarchy. For example, in Christianity, God revealed himself through his son and the message was passed on by the apostles in the form of Gospels, which are handed down through the elaborate system of Church. All truth in Judaism, Christianity or Islam is revealed by the Almighty to a select person (prophet) who conveys it through a proper channel to all those who are not so privileged. It is blasphemy for anyone to attempt to bypass the "proper channel" and see or experience or talk to the divine Almighty. In contrast, paganism, in every part of the world, encourages a person to reach out to the cosmic whole or reality or Almighty. The role of the priest or guru is that of a guide. The priest or guru, claims no exclusive license or authority on behalf of the cosmic divinity. A pagan priest is supposed to hold the hand of a truth seeker, while he or she walks through the path. At some point in the journey of truth, the seeker is encouraged to let go of the hand and walk all alone and experience for himself or herself.

It is important to say—himself or herself—because in all pagan religions (exceptions aside), women and men do not have different standing in the eyes of the cosmic divinity. A woman can experience the ultimate truth as much as a man can. In one-book-based religions, this is not the case. The "proper channel" from cosmic divinity to layperson consists of a predominantly male institutionalized hierarchy (from the prophet downwards). This male-hierarchy pushes women to a lower status. No doubt, in pagan religions, there have been instances of atrocities on women, but these are isolated distortions without any underlying basis in the fundamental philosophy of any pagan religion. Second important differentiation between pagan and non-pagan religions is the concept of God or Ultimate Divine Being. For all prophet-based religions, God is an entity separate from the world; God is the creator while the world is created. The duality of the creator and creation is an essential feature of Judaism, Islam and Christianity. In paganism, the creator and the creation are one; the cosmos as a whole is the Ultimate Divine Being. Paganism denies the existence of a creator being separate from the cosmos. In a way, under the pagan view every human being is a part of the Ultimate Divine Being and may even be called as Son (or daughter) of God. For a Christian or Muslim, claiming to be Son of God will be considered to be the ultimate blasphemy.

Ultimate Divine Being is physical as well as spiritual. Pagan religions may differ in their approach or method of relating to the Ultimate Divine Being. Different pagan religions may worship vastly different multitude of spirits and entities, but underlying these diversities is a deep philosophy (which is rarely articulated) of reverence for nature. The philosophy emphasizes the divinity of nature as a cosmic whole of which human beings are a part. Pagan worship, rituals, festivals and customs are attempts to develop spiritual, emotional and physical bonding with nature. A pagan aims to observe, understand, experience, feel and internalize each element of nature in every possible way. Again, this is in total contrast with Christianity and Islam. An invading Muslim King is supposed to have ordered the burning of a massive ancient library in Egypt, since all that is worth knowing is contained in the Holy Book. In a similar vein, Christians destroyed centuries of traditional knowledge in the name of witch hunting.

It is obvious that an approach based on one-book has to necessarily lead to a closed mind—faith being the mechanism used for sealing the windows and doors of mind. One has to have faith in the book and not reason against it. And just in case faith starts losing to reason, there is the fear of death to reinforce faith. All one-book-based religions have at some time or the other enforced strict laws against blasphemy and heretics (providing capital punishment), while there are no accounts of such laws being passed in pagan regimes. The nature of paganism, where each person has a one-to-one communication with the cosmic Being, permits diversity, debate and disagreement. Christianity, Islam and Judaism—each one claims to have the objective truth, while denying the version of truth espoused by the other. Paganism is more subjective—no one is supposed to claim to have the total and ultimate truth. In fact, under paganism truth is a journey, rather than a destination. In this respect, paganism is like science. Not many in the western world will see paganism as science and Christianity (or Islam) as anti-science. Scientists do not generally accept the existence of spirits and the concept of cosmic divinity—two prominent features of pagan religions. After all one cannot provide any concrete evidence for the existence of spirits or cosmic divinity and common understanding is that science accepts only those facts as true for which there is undisputed evidence. Let us come back to what is science and what is not science a bit later. Spirits and cosmic divinity are prominent features of paganism, but the more important feature of paganism is its emphasis on observation, experience, and knowledge. Without the shackles imposed by what is written in the Holy Book, the mind is free to roam and explore. western world prospered after the Renaissance since it broke out of the medieval mindset imposed by the Church.

Spiritual or cosmic view aspects of paganism may or may not be explicitly accepted in the western world today, but at a practical level the reigning philosophy of western world is pagan and not Christian or Muslim or Jew. Faith, as opposed to reason, is no longer sufficiently strong in the western mind for it to blindly accept all that is contained in the Holy Book. Scientists, who deny the creation of universe by God in six days at some time around 3000 BC (or 4000 or 5000 BC), are neither burnt at the stakes nor ridiculed. Theories of evolution of species, though rejected by Church, are taught in all schools of Europe and America. Sociologists, psychologists, jurists and all other professionals do not look at the Bible to get the answers to their questions. In the western world today, the paradox is that even those who get their marriages solemnized by a Christian priest and get their children baptized believe in evolution and reject the worldview of the Church. It appears that the old split-up of life between the King and Church has taken on a different form in the western world. In the western mind, now, life is divided in two parts—secular and religious. No Church accepts the division. Yet, for a western person, there are subjects and issues for which one looks for answers towards the Church and for the rest one goes somewhere else. The dividing line is not sharp and each person defines the line as per one's own sense of conviction. But there is no denying that the line exists in the mind of every western person. Christianity, Islam and Judaism lay claim on the whole mind of each of their believers. The fact is that in modern western world, much of a person's mind and life is outside the control of Church (Islam and Judaism are small minorities, and here we are talking of mainstream). So even though a person may be known by a Christian name, he / she is Christian to a small degree only. If we look at the dictionary definition of "heretic" and if we consider the way Church has traditionally defined a "heretic", the modern western mind is more heretic than Christian. In other words, western world is more pagan than Christian.

Science & Scientific Temperament

Science evolved in Europe and America during the past few centuries as the iron hold of Church loosened. Initial developers of science had to encounter proactive opposition of the Church. There are innumerable instances of persecution and even execution of scientists, just because they held views that were considered heretic by the Church. Science grew, in spite of all opposition, because it could deliver results in terms of prosperity to the society. Massive transfer of resources from colonies aided the march of science and technology. Even though scientific discoveries and technological innovations were changing the face of the world, science avoided taking a holistic view of the world or of society. Scientists had (and generally speaking still have) a fragmented view. A scientist focuses on one problem, draws its boundaries and closes his eyes to all that is outside the boundary lines drawn by him. Epistemology of science is based on Law of Positive Truth—which states that every positive truth needs to be supported by evidence. The corollary of this is interpreted to mean that negative truth needs no evidence. If I have to prove that there is a mango tree in the ground opposite my house, I need to show either the tree or a photograph of the tree or have some people testify that they have seen the truth. On the other hand, if I say that there is no mango tree in the park opposite my house, I do not need to provide any evidence. Taken in a different context, Law of Positive Truth can be used to deny the existence of God. There is neither any evidence to prove that God exists, nor any evidence to show that God does not exist; so a scientist is supposed to follow Law of Positive Truth and deny the existence of God. However, in practical terms, a scientist just evades the question of existence of God, which is easy because it falls outside the boundary conditions set by each scientist.

The fragmented view focused within convenient boundaries helped science resist the onslaught of Church in initial years. But over time, scientists are discovering that they cannot push inconvenient questions under the carpet. Can a scientist who contributed to the making of the nuclear bombs, which destroyed Hiroshima and Nagasaki, escape from the moral responsibility for the same? What is moral responsibility in scientific terms? Is it possible to answer such questions without taking a holistic view? Can one take a holistic view, which is non-religious? These questions have been bothering scientists in the past century. They have been unable to come up with any consensus answer. It appears that scientific methodology has encountered its waterloo when it comes to answering some of the fundamental questions concerning mankind. The failure of science, which is the ruling ideology of modern western world, to provide a schema for human existence and behavior has led to a peculiar situation. There is a vacuum as western mind sheds away Church-ordained beliefs and does not find all the answers from science. At this point, Law of Positive Truth gives way to Law of Convenient Truth, which states—"In the absence of sufficient evidence for either affirming or denying a statement, accept what is more convenient". This principle of convenience is used by the western mind, bereft of any moral or religious shackles, to unabashedly pursue self-interest individually and collectively. The only shackles that the western mind seems to accept are those imposed by power equations. Having cast away the moral values that Church used to preach (and still preaches), there are no internal pressures within a western man's mind forcing him to abstain from acts that may be immoral or even criminal. With this mentality, one does not commit a crime only because there are the police and judiciary. If one is reasonably sure of police inaction, one has no hesitation in pilfering or looting or raping or even murdering. It is not surprising that western world has much higher crime rate than developing countries of Asia, even though the police-population ratio is much higher in Europe and America than in Asia. As and when there are situations when police cannot be effective, violence in western world jumps up still higher and becomes explosive. One is reminded of the July 1977 blackout of New York when 25 hours of power breakdown provided an opportunity for mass arson, looting and other crimes. There have been blackouts in New York after 1977 (last major one was on 15 August 2003) and now the police are better equipped to handle blackouts, so there is no collapse of law and order in a blackout. But in other situations, where police cannot intervene effectively, lawlessness continues to rage—domestic violence is a typical example.

In Section B (Romans and Tribes), we saw that Roman and Greek civilizations were based on selfish pursuit of luxury at the cost of poor slaves and country folks. This tradition inherited from the Romans and Greek was moderated to a small degree by Christian values of love and brotherhood (preached assiduously to masses for centuries). Church and Christianity have been considerably weakened in the western world, while the new religions of rationality and science have gained enormous strength. But the new religions prescribe no morality and do not talk of achieving any purpose in life beyond the mundane. Humanities and social sciences like psychology and sociology also follow the fragmented approach of physical sciences. While these new sciences devote considerable attention to "what is", they have no prescription for "what ought to be" on the most fundamental issues and even if they have any such prescriptions, more often than not such prescriptions are rooted in the cultural biases of western world and not based on any rational systematic approach. I remember attending a course on abnormal psychology many years ago when I was a teenager. Sophisticated data collection and statistical analysis techniques have been used to map what majority of men and women do in various situations.

This majority behavior is labeled as "normal"; everything else is "abnormal". At this point the learned psychologists make an intellectual jump—normal is considered as desirable and abnormal is classified as a diseased person requiring medical attention. Even as a teenager, I found this obsession with being a part of statistical majority as ridiculous, if not stupid. I tried to tell this to my learned teacher, who had just returned from USA. She brushed me aside. Morality and value systems based on psychology, sociology or economics are full of many ridiculous assumptions that are rarely stated explicitly. More often than not one encounters such contradictory suggestions and advice that one is forced to throw up one's hands in exasperation. No society can live without morality and value systems. In the western world, in the absence of any morality based on a holistic view of society and life, basic animal instincts of selfishness has taken over. Of course, the tradition from Greek and Roman civilizations to the brutal pursuit of power by Church has contributed to this move towards a society where everyone exerts to maximize one's own pleasures.

This process has been further strengthened by authors like Ayn Rand, who unabashedly argue for selfishness. Probably at no point in human history, there has been a civilization as devoted to selfishness as today's western civilization is. At an individual level, each person pursues his/her own selfish goals without any consideration for others. At the collective level, the country or state does the same. If you have read Ayn Rand, you will believe that this is most rational and scientific. Science and scientific temperament in western world has led on one hand to embracing of selfishness. On the other hand, the exasperation with collapse of social structures and family values has led to a journey back to religion, spirituality and Christianity. Orthodox religious groups have a higher presence, today, in USA than compared to ten years ago. In a way the western world has gone the full circle and is in a stage, which can be called the anti-thesis of renaissance. Science and technology are still viewed as the providers of new gadgets, instruments and gizmos. But no one believes that science and scientific temperament can provide a new morality or can help provide purpose to the life of a generation, which faces existentialist dilemmas, more than the previous ones. Around half a century ago, Bertrand Russell and others were proudly announcing philosophies based on scientific method and style. Around the same time, existentialist philosophers and authors were writing melancholic books about alienation and meaninglessness. Existentialist authors have fallen out of favor since their brilliant elucidation of the problem, though interesting and gripping, failed to offer any solutions. Similarly, Russell and all those swearing by science, dazzled everyone with their intellectual prowess, but failed to provide any solutions.

Summing Up: a Theme of Change as Eternity

Towards the end of nineteenth century, Nietzsche said, "God is dead". Less than a century later, another philosopher said, "God is dead, Marx is dead and I don't feel so good myself". But in the world of ideas, nothing ever dies. Christian Churches and Kings killed millions of pagans through centuries, but they could not kill paganism. Communists tried to kill Christianity in Russia, but they too failed. In any society, there always is a diversity of cross currents and under currents. No society or civilization is ever monolithic. In the western world, God—as defined by various Churches—lives on, just as Marx and communism continue to breathe in the hearts of millions of Russians in spite of the fall of the USSR. Along with God is the institution of Church—surely, reduced to a shadow of its grand (and scary) past, but still with the same genetic structure as it had a few centuries ago. In some countries, at a political level, Christianity and Church are getting back to center stage. George W Bush prays more often and more publicly than any US President in the middle of last century did.

On the other hand, there are more Church-less Christians, atheists and pagans in USA and Europe than ever before. Paganism is alive and kicking all over Europe and America, even among the Church-going Christians. Not many Church-going Christians are comfortable with the rising influence of orthodox Christian groups in political decision-making. Many of them would like to have a sharper division of secular and spiritual functions—keeping the Church restricted to spiritual arena. Christianity, paganism and scientific temperament—all three are influenced in Europe and America by the most important value of Greek and Roman city-states—unbridled pursuit of wealth, pleasures and luxuries. Some people call it consumerism. Ayn Rand calls it selfishness and declares it to be a virtue. Whether you see it as a virtue or vice depends on your perspective and value system. But, it surely is the most fundamental characteristic of western civilization. Another key characteristic of western civilization is violence. An American friend once told me that it is interesting to see Indians fight on the streets—there is so much sound and fury but hardly any blood. In contrast, when Americans fight, the only sound that is heard is of gunshots and blood flows more easily than Heinz ketchup does in nearby restaurants.

Greek/Roman city-states, Christianity and science—all of them have a history of perpetrating violence. Pagans were at the receiving end of violence through the past two thousand years of development of western civilization. Whether as receivers or as perpetrators, every stream of western civilization has been exposed to so much violence that most oriental thinkers cannot even imagine. Another feature of western mind that oriental thinkers find very disconcerting is arrogance. Hinduism, Buddhism and almost all pagan religions teach a person to be humble; one is taught to believe that learning is a never-ending process and in this journey as the circle of one's knowledge expands one comes into contact with more of one's ignorance. This is diametrically opposite of what every one-book-based religion teaches—one needs to just learn The Holy Book and one has all knowledge and there is no ignorance whatsoever. Anyone who believes that he / she has complete knowledge is bound to be free of all doubts and, as a result, becomes extremely arrogant. Arrogance, selfishness and wealth amassed from centuries of colonialism make a deadly combination in anyone's head and western mind is no exception. Let me at this point, before I close for the day, quote from Samuel P. Huntington: Civilization identity will be increasingly important in the future, and the world will be shaped in large measure by the interactions among seven or eight major civilizations. These include western,

Confucian, Japanese, Islamic, Hindu, Slavic-Orthodox, Latin American and possibly African civilization. The most important conflicts of the future will occur along the cultural fault lines separating these civilizations from one another.

The central axis of world politics in the future is likely to be, in Kishore Mahbubani's phrase, the conflict between "the West and the Rest" and the responses of non-western civilizations to western power and values. The fault lines that Samuel P Huntington talks about are not unreal. But, let us not forget that the western civilization has its own internal fault lines. If one looks at the history of the past one thousand years, more blood has been shed on the lands (and by the people of these lands) that are supposed to be presently under the influence of western civilization, than on lands under any other civilization. This bloodshed was on one hand due to clash of currents in the western world (Christianity, Paganism and Science) and on the other hand was due to Greek city-state mentality characterized by selfishness, greed, arrogance and a mindset of violence. In the past thousand years, inter-civilization conflict was more often not a result of Greek city-state mentality of the West or of West Asia. In a significant number of cases the conflicts were due to attempts by ruling elites of various one-book-based religions to carve out more territory and followers by violence. There are hardly any instances of pagan religions invading and initiating bloodshed. Europe and America are much richer now than they ever were. Rich people always look more beautiful, more intelligent, more sensible, more polished, more sophisticated than they actually are. Inherent in it is the danger that the West faces today. They believe that they are no longer what they were a hundred years ago—then they were not so rich and now they are, but that's not how they look at themselves. They genuinely believe that they have changed their cultural genetic structure in the past hundred years and have grown intellectually to become more responsible and less war-prone. But have they?

Postscript

Does the sun go round the earth or is it the other way round? This question was asked to three persons. The first one was sitting on the sun—he replied that earth goes round the sun. The second person was sitting on earth—in his view sun goes round the earth. The third person sitting on a distant star observed that earth goes round the sun. All three persons were speaking the truth. The man who said that the sun goes round the earth is neither wrong nor unscientific. The most important lesson, which I learned in my first course in Physics as a student at IIT, is that there can be no observation without an observer and there is no such thing as an objective truth, independent of observer. My understanding of western civilization is based on my cultural, religious and historical vantage point. Of course, it is also affected by the limitations of my small knowledge base and intellectual capabilities. I make no claims of offering any objective indisputable truths. I have only presented most humbly my view, which may well be wrong at various points. I was attracted to the idea of writing this after my recent visit to Switzerland. My trip was fully sponsored by a Swiss business family who wanted to collaborate for a business venture in India. Things went smooth in the first three days. We were able to agree on all key points.

A Draft of proposed Memorandum of Understanding providing for a partnership was prepared. On the morning when we were supposed to sign the MOU, the Swiss family backed out citing 2 Cor. 6V14 of Bible (apparently, it states that a Christian and non-Christian should not be partners). I was astounded. I had always thought that Christians had moved out of the dark medieval mindset into renaissance's sunrise. I was wrong. In this case the Swiss family was willing to forego three years of work and thousands of dollars of investment just because of a verse in Bible. In the mini-book on western civilization, which is in your hands I have attempted to be dispassionate but that is not always possible. I make no apologies for my views or passions. I only wish to clarify that I have no intentions of causing any hurt or insult or injury. And if I have caused so, I regret and apologize.

Questions and Topics for Pondering and Further Discussion for Unit Ten:

1. What is your understanding of the western culture?
2. Is the western culture an open and tolerant one? Why and why not?
3. What are the three pillars of the western culture or civilization?
4. The rise of the West is demonstrated by its economic success and cultural dominance in the modern era. Please make some further comments on it.
5. Is the western culture itself a homogeneous one or heterogeneous one?
6. The author of this article presents a view that there is no such thing as objective truth independent of observer. How do you understanding this view? Please state your idea about it.
7. "In the world of ideas, nothing ever dies." Please make some further comment on it.
8. In the western culture, there is a strong scientific temperament. Why is that?

Unit Eleven

The Millennium of the West, a Golden Age?[1]

THIS has been the millennium of the West: first Europe, later its offshoots too, above all the giant one in North America. It has exported worldwide its soldiers, missionaries and empire-builders, its religion and its ideas, its arts and its sciences, its goods and its technology, its political and business systems, even its principal currency. Like it or not (and much of the world often has not), for the moment the West has triumphed. Nothing proves the triumph will endure. Already one quite small Asian nation, Japan, has made a huge mark on the world economy. Who knows what will happen when China and (surely, one day) India really get moving? Already Christianity, the faith once almost synonymous with Europe, is decaying in its homelands—as its rival, Islam, is not. Electoral democracy, the rule of law, the tolerance of dissent, the belief in individual rights: all of these, which now seem characteristic of the West, are quite recent inventions, repeatedly trampled down in the region that proclaims them; and there is no guarantee (though fair reason to expect) that they will last, there or elsewhere. Still, for now, the world is one largely shaped by the West.

It is in this perspective that *The Economist* —part of that West, sharing its hopes, its beliefs and its prejudices—reports the millennium that has brought this world about. History is written by the victors, and those of 2500 or 3000 may have a very different view of what mattered in our past 1,000 years, let alone theirs. But here we are, now. The following pages report what seem, from that standpoint, the greatest changes of our millennium: such things as the astonishing multiplication of human wealth, of the human race, and of the knowledge, skills and communication that have enabled both to happen. We report too the events—not all great ones in themselves—that typify these: anything from the first crusade through the birth of banking to the Dutch purchase of Manhattan island, Japan's *zaibatsu*, the world wars and the contraceptive pill. The main trends get sizable articles of their own; that apart, the structure of this issue is much what readers are accustomed to—even to two pages of statistics, heroic ones some of them—seeking to do for a millennium what we usually do for a week. With one exception, our viewpoint too is the usual one: we write from the present day, with the happy benefit of some years, or centuries, of hindsight. The exception is our columnists. We have given them leave to step back in time. The results include an *Economics Focus* review of a new work on wealth by a Scottish economist called Adam Smith; and Lexington imagining the outlook for an ex-United States, after a post-War talk in the confederate capital with a happy President Jefferson Davis.

Questions and Topics for Pondering and Further Discussion for Unit Eleven:

1. The past one millennium witnessed the rise of the West and the decline of the East. Why is that?
2. It is said that history is written by the victors. Please make some comments on it.
3. In the past 1000 years, the West has exported to the world many things, tangible or

---

[1] This is the excerpt of an article entitled *The Millennium of the West* published for the millennium issue of *The Economist*, a renowned British magazine of intellectual and academic quality. Please go and visit its official website at www.economist.com for more detailed and comprehensive information or the full text. For the sake of protection of copyrights, only the first two paragraphs of the article are adopted here for reader's reference.

intangible. What is the most significant thing the West has exported to the world according to your opinion? Why?
4. Geographically the world is divided into the East and West. Do you think the world should be divided into the East and West? Why is that if the world has been divided into the East and West?
5. Is this West gold age going to continue for another five hundred years?
6. Can America continue to enjoy another "American century"?
7. What is the root cause of the Cold War? Is it a fact that the eastern block was defeated in the Cold War?
8. What do you think of the future of the world? Are you an optimist or pessimist?

Unit Twelve

An Introduction to the Clash of Civilizations

Editor's remarks: *as known to all intellectuals of cultural studies and scholars of international issues, the Clash of Civilizations is a theory, proposed by political scientist Samuel P. Huntington[①], that people's cultural and religious identities will be the primary source of conflict in the post-Cold War world. This theory was originally formulated in a 1992 lecture at the American Enterprise Institute, which was then developed in a 1993 Foreign Affairs article titled "The Clash of Civilizations?", in response to Francis Fukuyama's 1992 book, The End of History and the Last Man. Huntington later expanded his thesis in a 1996 book The Clash of Civilizations and the Remaking of World Order. The phrase itself was earlier used by Bernard Lewis in an article in the September 1990 issue of The Atlantic Monthly titled "The Roots of Muslim Rage". Even earlier, the phrase appears in a 1926 book regarding the Middle East by Basil Mathews: Young Islam on Trek: A Study in the Clash of Civilizations (p. 196). This expression derives from clash of cultures, already used during the colonial period and the Belle Époque.*

Overview of the Clash Theory

Huntington began his thinking by surveying the diverse theories about the nature of global politics in the post-Cold War period. Some theorists and writers argued that human rights, liberal democracy and capitalist free market economy had become the only remaining ideological alternative for nations in the post-Cold War world. Specifically, Francis Fukuyama argued that the world had reached the "end of history" in a Hegelian sense. Huntington believed that while the age of ideology had ended, the world had only reverted to a normal state of affairs characterized by cultural conflict. In his thesis, he argued that the primary axis of conflict in the future will be along cultural and religious lines. As an extension, he posits that the concept of different civilizations, as the highest rank of cultural identity, will become increasingly useful in analyzing the potential for conflict.

In the 1993 *Foreign Affairs* article, Huntington writes:

> It is my hypothesis that the fundamental source of conflict in this new world will not be primarily ideological or primarily economic. The great divisions among humankind and the dominating source of conflict will be cultural. Nation states will remain the most powerful actors in world affairs, but the principal conflicts of global politics will occur between nations and groups of different civilizations. The clash of civilizations will dominate global politics. The fault lines between civilizations will be the battle lines of the

---

① Samuel Phillips Huntington (1927—2008) was a political scientist known for his analysis of the relationship between the military and the civil government, his investigation of *coup d'états*, and his thesis that the central political actors of the 21st century will be civilizations rather than nation-states. Huntington stated his theory as follows: it is my hypothesis that the fundamental source of conflict in this new world will not be primarily ideological or primarily economic. The great divisions among humankind and the dominating source of conflict will be cultural. Nation-states will remain the most powerful actors in world affairs, but the principal conflicts of global politics will occur between nations and groups of different civilizations. The clash of civilizations will dominate global politics. The fault lines between civilizations will be the battle lines of the future. From "The Clash of Civilizations?", in *Foreign Affairs* (1993).

future.

In the end of the article, he writes:

This is not to advocate the desirability of conflicts between civilizations. It is to set forth descriptive hypothesis as to what the future may be like.

Major Civilizations According to Huntington

Huntington divided the world into the "major civilizations" in his thesis as such:
- western civilization, comprising North America, western and Central Europe, Australia and Oceania. Whether Latin America and the former member states of the Soviet Union are included, or are instead their own separate civilizations, will be an important future consideration for those regions, according to Huntington.
- Latin America, includes Central America, South America (excluding the Guianas), Cuba, the Dominican Republic, and Mexico. May be considered a part of western civilization, though it has slightly distinct social and political structures from Europe and Northern America. Many people of the Southern Cone, however, regard themselves as full members of the western civilization.
- The Orthodox world of the former Soviet Union (excluding the Baltic states and most of Central Asia), Armenia, Georgia, the former Yugoslavia (excluding Slovenia and Croatia), Bulgaria, Cyprus, Greece, Ukraine and Romania.
- The eastern world is the mix of the Buddhist, Chinese, Hindu, and Japonic civilizations.
  - The Buddhist areas of Bhutan, Cambodia, Laos, Mongolia, Myanmar, Sri Lanka, and Thailand are identified as separate from other civilizations, but Huntington believes that they do not constitute a major civilization in the sense of international affairs.
  - The Sinic civilization of China, the Koreas, Singapore, and Vietnam. This group also includes the Chinese diaspora, especially in relation to Southeast Asia.
  - Hindu civilization, located chiefly in India, Bhutan and Nepal, and culturally adhered to by the global Indian diaspora.
  - Japan, considered a hybrid of Chinese civilization and older Altaic patterns.
- The Muslim world of the Greater Middle East (excluding Armenia, Cyprus, Ethiopia, Georgia, Israel, Malta and South Sudan), northern West Africa, Albania, Bangladesh, Brunei, Comoros, Indonesia, Malaysia, Pakistan, and Maldives.
- The civilization of Sub-Saharan Africa located in Southern Africa, Middle Africa (excluding Chad), East Africa (excluding Ethiopia, Comoros, Kenya, Mauritius, and Tanzania), Cape Verde, Côte d'Ivoire, Ghana, Liberia, and Sierra Leone. Considered as a possible 8th civilization by Huntington.
- Instead of belonging to one of the "major" civilizations, Ethiopia and Haiti are labeled as "Lone" countries. Israel could be considered a unique state with its own civilization, Huntington writes, but one which is extremely similar to the West. Huntington also believes that the Anglophone Caribbean, former British colonies in the Caribbean, constitutes a distinct entity.
- There are also others which are considered "cleft countries" because they contain large groups of people identifying with separate civilizations. Examples include India (cleft between its Hindu majority and large Muslim minority), Ukraine (cleft between its eastern Rite Catholic-dominated western section and its Orthodox-dominated East), France (cleft between Sub-Saharan African, in the case of French Guiana; and the West), Benin, Chad, Kenya, Nigeria, Tanzania, and Togo (all cleft between Islam and

sub-Saharan Africa), Guyana and Suriname (cleft between Hindu and Sub-Saharan African), China (cleft between Sinic, Buddhist, in the case of Tibet; and the West, in the case of Hong Kong and Macau), and the Philippines (cleft between Islam, in the case of Mindanao; Sinic, and the West). Sudan was also included as "cleft" between Islam and sub-Saharan Africa; this division became a formal split in July 2011 following an overwhelming vote for independence by South Sudan in a January 2011 referendum.

Huntington's Thesis of Civilizational Clash

Russia, Japan, and India are what Huntington terms "swing civilizations" and may favor either side. Russia, for example, clashes with the many Muslim ethnic groups on its southern border (such as Chechnya) but—according to Huntington—cooperates with Iran to avoid further Muslim-Orthodox violence in Southern Russia, and to help continue the flow of oil. Huntington argues that a "Sino-Islamic connection" is emerging in which China will cooperate more closely with Iran, Pakistan, and other states to augment its international position. Huntington also argues that civilizational conflicts are "particularly prevalent between Muslims and non-Muslims", identifying the "bloody borders" between Islamic and non-Islamic civilizations. This conflict dates back as far as the initial thrust of Islam into Europe, its eventual expulsion in the Iberian reconquest, the attacks of the Ottoman Turks on eastern Europe and Vienna, and the European imperial division of the Islamic nations in the 1800s and 1900s.

Huntington also believes that some of the factors contributing to this conflict are that both Christianity (which has influenced western civilization) and Islam are:

- Missionary religions, seeking conversion of others.
- Universal, "all-or-nothing" religions, in the sense that it is believed by both sides that only their faith is the correct one.
- Teleological religions, that is, that their values and beliefs represent the goals of existence and purpose in human existence.
- Irreligious people who violate the base principles of those religions are perceived to be furthering their own pointless aims, which leads to violent interactions.

More recent factors contributing to a western-Islamic clash, Huntington wrote, are the Islamic Resurgence and demographic explosion in Islam, coupled with the values of western universalism—that is, the view that all civilizations should adopt western values—that infuriate Islamic fundamentalists. All these historical and modern factors combined, Huntington wrote briefly in his "Foreign Affairs" article and in much more detail in his 1996 book, would lead to a bloody clash between the Islamic and western civilizations. The political party Hizb ut-Tahrir also reiterate Huntington's views in their published book, *The Inevitability of Clash of Civilization*.

Why Civilizations Will Clash

Huntington offers six main explanations for why civilizations will clash:

1. Differences among civilizations are too basic in that civilizations are differentiated from each other by history, language, culture, tradition, and most important, religion. These fundamental differences are the product of centuries, so they will not soon disappear.
2. The world is becoming a smaller place. As a result, the interactions across the world are increasing, and they intend to intensify civilization consciousness and awareness of differences between civilizations and commonalities within civilizations.

3. Due to the economic modernization and social change, people are separated from longstanding local identities. Instead, religion has replaced this gap, which provides a basis for identity and commitment that transcends national boundaries and unites civilizations.
4. The growth of civilization-consciousness is enhanced by the dual role of the West. On the one hand, the West is at a peak of power. At the same time, a return to the roots phenomenon is occurring among non-western civilizations. A West at the peak of its power confronts non-western countries that increasingly have the desire, the will and the resources to shape the world in non-western ways.
5. Cultural characteristics and differences are less mutable and hence less easily compromised and resolved than political and economic ones.
6. Economic regionalism is increasing. Successful economic regionalism will reinforce to a large extent the civilization consciousness.

Modernization, Westernization, and "Torn Countries"

Critics of Huntington's ideas often extend their criticisms to traditional cultures and internal reformers who wish to modernize without adopting the values and attitudes of western culture. These critics sometimes claim that to modernize is necessarily to become Westernized to a very large extent. In reply, those who consider the *Clash of Civilizations* thesis accurate often point to the example of Japan, claiming that it is not a western state at its core. They argue that it adopted much western technology (also inventing technology of its own in recent times), parliamentary democracy, and free enterprise, but has remained culturally very distinct from the West, particularly in its conceptions of society as strictly hierarchical. Contradictory evidence on a more granular scale in turn comes from empirical evidence that greater exposure to factories, schools and urban living is associated with more "modern" attitudes to rationality, individual choice and responsibility. China is also cited by some as a rising non-western economy. Many also point out the East Asian Tigers or neighboring states as having adapted western economics, while maintaining traditional or authoritarian social government. Perhaps the ultimate example of non-western modernization is Russia, the core state of the Orthodox civilization. The variant of this argument that uses Russia as an example relies on the acceptance of a unique non-western civilization headed by an Orthodox state such as Russia or perhaps an eastern European country. Huntington argues that Russia is primarily a non-western state although he seems to agree that it shares a considerable amount of cultural ancestry with the modern West. Russia was one of the great powers during World War I. It also happened to be a non-western power. According to Huntington, the West is distinguished from Orthodox Christian countries by the experience of the Renaissance, Reformation, the Enlightenment, overseas colonialism rather than contiguous expansion and colonialism, and a recent re-infusion of classical culture through Rome rather than through the continuous trajectory of the Byzantine Empire. The differences among the modern Slavic states can still be seen today. This issue is also linked to the "universalizing factor" exhibited in some civilizations. Huntington refers to countries that are seeking to affiliate with another civilization as "torn countries." Turkey, whose political leadership has systematically tried to westernize the country since the 1920s, is his chief example. Turkey's history, culture, and traditions are derived from Islamic civilization, but Turkey's elite, beginning with Mustafa Kemal Atatürk, who took power as first President of the Republic of Turkey in 1923, imposed western institutions and dress, embraced the Latin alphabet, joined NATO, and is seeking to join the European Union. Mexico and Russia are also considered to be torn by Huntington. He also gives the example of Australia as a country torn between its western civilizational heritage and its growing economic engagement with Asia. According to Huntington, a torn country must meet three requirements to redefine its civilizational identity. Its political and economic elite must support the move. Second, the public must be willing to accept the redefinition. Third, the elites of the civilization that the torn country is trying to join must accept the country. The book claims that to date no torn country has successfully redefined its civilizational identity, this mostly due to the elites of the "host" civilization refusing to accept the torn country, though if Turkey gained membership of the European Union it has been noted that many of its people would support Westernization. If this were to happen it would be the first to redefine its civilizational identity.

Questions and Topics for Pondering and Further Discussion for Unit Twelve:

1. Do you think this theory of civilization clashes is a fact or fallacy?
2. What are the main arguments for Huntington in elaborating this theory?
3. Do you think civilization clashes mean religious confrontations between the East and West?
4. Why does Chomsky disagree with Huntington?
5. What are the main explanations offered by Huntington for his theory?
6. What is meant by modernization? Is modernization equal to westernization?
7. Do you think religious diversity will eventually lead to cultural conflicts? Why if so?
8. Based upon what does Huntington divide civilizations into different types?

Postscript

Western Culture: a Beast and a Beauty?

The topic of western Cultural Studies is at once an interesting and challenging one. It is also a rewarding one as well. The necessity of exploring this topic does not need any further explanation and the benefit of learning something about the western culture goes beyond the practical level. Not only is it part of human civilization, but also a vivid expressive record of human creativity and transcendental spirit of reason. It is true that, on the one hand, the western culture worships power, material success and conquest by force, which demonstrates its dialectical, paradoxical or maybe even negative and disastrous effect on human evolution and social development in the form of wars that claimed so many innocent lives, brutal conquests that extinguished some of the excellent civilizations and exploitation of nature and of man by man that destroyed so many natural wonders and created bloody and wicked inequality among human beings. However, on the other it is also a fact pure and simple that in the process of western civilization such positive values and ideals as scientific spirit, democratic tradition, rational way of thinking, humanistic approach have been promoted, glorified and maintained, which find their ultimate expression in the motto of French Revolution and pursuits as clearly expressed and firmly advocated in the Declaration of American Independence.

Liberty, Equality and Fraternity, these three capitalized words have become the flagship motto of an idealistic society for whole human beings and they have now become inalienable rights of entire human race regardless of their religious beliefs, political creeds, ethnic backgrounds and cultural traditions. Liberty, Equality, Fraternity, along with Justice, Progress and Social Harmony have become universal values of human society, the final goals human beings are struggling for. The history of the West, like that of whole human race, is one of replacements and social progress toward an idealistic society. Karl Marx, one of the greatest thinkers in the West, once said that socialists would like to see such a society eventually established with a lofty ideal prevalent and dominant that individual freedom is a precondition for the freedom of all people living in it.

Apples are delicious fruit and they are common fruits as well. In western traditions, apples carry some symbolic means. Some historians claim that the whole history of western civilization can be summed up with three and half apples. The first apple is the one grown on the tree of knowledge in the Garden of Eden, symbolizing the religious origin of western Culture. The second apple, the fallen apple, so to speak, is the one that has something to do with Sir Isaac Newton who through the fall of this apple down to ground discovered law of gravity, representing scientific spirit of western Culture, which has created western dominance in the modern world. That half apple refers to the golden apple of discord in Greek mythology, exhibiting western tradition found in Greek mythological heritage. The third apple is a new one, which means a whole series of electronic products under the name of Apple Company and ideas behind these Apple series products. This latest apple again has strongly demonstrated a clear and solid western tradition in science and technology. The whole world is now entering an information age of knowledge economy against the mega trend of economic globalization characterized by modern technology of communication and information transmission, which has assured the superior position of the West in modern era.

Science is like a modern religion and its pervasive power has influenced the way people live and work. It is easy to imagine that our life today would have been totally different from what we see it now or would have remained more or less the same as the one experienced by our ancestors living 3000 years ago without so many scientific inventions and technological innovations that on the one hand, have deepened our understanding of the natural world around us, and on the other hand have changed our life style. Sir Isaac Newton, one of the greatest scientific giants, has contributed so much to this world with his discoveries in science and he has beyond any doubt represented wisdom of not only the West, but also the whole world in terms of human minds and creativity. English poet Alexander Pope was moved by Newton's accomplishments to write the famous epitaph:

Nature and nature's laws lay hid in night;
God said "Let Newton be" and all was light.

The present day western dominance over world political and economic affairs is established on its great and glorious tradition of scientific discoveries and technological exploration as well as on its progressive ideas and ideals of democracy and social justice firmly backed up by the least harmful economic mechanism—market economy. For the past over 500 years beginning in 1492, the West has risen to the central position of the globe and has ever since then dominated the whole world with its economic, military, scientific or even cultural power and this pattern is more like to continue than otherwise. Given this hard fact, it is useful and beneficial to for an easterner know something about the West and its cultural history. This is the sole purpose for the editor to compile this short, yet concise anthology of the history of western Culture as a textbook for those interested in the West.

Some people claim that western culture presents a picture of paradox or of dialectical features vividly reflected by the image of a beast and a beauty. On the one hand, it demonstrates its beastly part of aggressiveness and brutality through the jungle law and nature of aggression, but on the other, the western cultural tradition also displays through its mythological and humanistic heritages a beautiful, rational and tender side of it, especially via many fables and fairy tales. As Abraham Lincoln once stated to the effect that throughout human history, there has always been a demarcation line clearly drawn between what is good and bad, between what is right and wrong and between what is virtuous and evil. According to Lincoln, it is wrong for some people to exploit others and it is wrong for some people to take bread out of others by force and it is wrong to be masters who view others as slaves. Lincoln is a great and milestone figure representing and symbolizing the ideals of democracy and equality. It might be the case that without Lincoln and his far-sightedness and resolution to save the Union of America and emancipate slaves, there would have been no present America. Were it the case, the whole human modern history would be definitely re-written or take on a totally different scenario. In a sense, the West should take pride in having such great figures as Plato, Aristotle, Socrates, Da Vince, Copernicus, Newton, Adam Smith, Shakespeare, Abraham Lincoln, Karl Marx, Beethoven, Einstein, Martin Luther King, etc. There should be a long list of them.

But everything has two sides and there are always two sides of the same coin. Truly and sadly, the history of the West is not all free from such bad, wrong and evil aspects. Just as the West has done a lot of good things and right things to contribute positively to human civilization. The West has also done a lot of bad and wrong things either for ignorance or prejudice, or for bigotry or for commercial benefits or for whatever reasons. Human civilized history and what has been confirmed as good and progressive ideas have clearly proved that, morally, ideologically and in reality, it is wrong for the West to burn Bruno for his defense of newly discovered scientific truths, it is wrong for the West to sentence Socrates to death for his advocacy and promotion of truths, it is wrong for the West to try Galileo for his spreading of, and insistence on truths, it is wrong for the West to engage in slave trade for commercial profits, it is wrong for the West to stage genocide to wipe out Indians and their civilization, it is wrong for the West to allow religious wars between Christians and so-called their heretics and among different Christian denominations under the name of God, it is wrong for the West to force children into employment and exploitation for the sake of primitive capital accumulation, it is wrong for the West to launch opium wars against an eastern state of ancient civilization even though that civilization was full of dirty spots itself, it is wrong for the West to try to extinguish Jewish population via brutal Holocaust, it is wrong for the West to stage persecution of so-called "Red Scare", it is wrong for the West to rob so many cultural treasures and relics of ancient civilizations from what they call "primitive regions" or "backward countries", it is wrong for the West to neglect extreme poverty of the LDCs while selfishly defending their own economic interest, it is wrong for the West to refuse to shoulder more responsibility for the costs of climate change, it is wrong for the West to protect the human rights of their own people at the costs of other people and it is wrong for the West to claim that their culture is superior to cultures of other regions. There are evidences enough in this aspect for the West to reflect, repent and review their own past evils so that they can contribute more of something positive to the whole world civilization system to bring a better tomorrow for whole human beings.

Admittedly, good and evil always coexist in one thing and it depends upon how people view it just as the statement in this regard expresses that what is good and bad stands interchangeable to each other in circumstances or against different contexts. That may be the true nature of some objective existences, social or natural, including human existence. It is said that two archetypes of hero summarize the human spirit of the West: one refers to Apollo's spirit and the other is called Dionysus's attitude, each representing different ethos of people and together encompassing the mentalities of all human beings. The world is complex and there is no easy and ready answer or solution to even one single difficult question or tough problem. However, the remedy or the way out lies in the promotion of mutual understanding among different cultures or civilizations, which is of vital importance for human beings as a whole. For non-westerners, it is of great benefit to know something about the West and its culture. Coincidentally, the late historian Spengler also pointed out two types of historical view of the West concerning human future destiny, each of which is represented by two famous mythological and theatrical names Apollo and Faust respectively. These two types of hero, if well studied, can best serve as torch guidance for western cultural studies. The history of western Culture is the one in which release and restraint of human desires alternately appear, vanish and replacement of each other co-exist in the long process of human civilization. It is like a river full of twists and turns, running to the sea where the earliest form of life is said to be born.

PART TWO

Special Case Study

Judaism and the Jews[①]

Editor's remarks: *reasons abound to choose Judaism and Jews as the topic for a special case study for western Cultural History Course. First of all, Judeo-Christian tradition or heritage is the fundamental pillar and logical starting point of western Culture. It is well acknowledged that Judaism serves as a foundation religion for Christianity which since its birth has exerted tremendous influence upon western cultural evolution. Religious faith has been an important and integral part of western culture. Secondly, given the influence of Judaism upon Christianity, it is an inseparable part to study Judaism in the course of western cultural history. Thirdly, Jewish people with their rich and eventful history and their ancestral place of residence have combined and connected the cultural traditions between the East and West. Jerusalem has been the convergent point for western and eastern cultures. Jewish people, geographically and ethnically speaking, are easterners. However, Jewish people, along with their traditional cultural heritages, have strong impact upon the evolution of the West. Finally, Jewish people are clever people and their contributions to the world civilization (not limited to western civilization) have been unique and unparallel in human history among diverse races. "Jews have made contributions in a broad range of human endeavors, including the sciences, arts, politics, and business. Although Jews comprise only 0.2% of the world's population, over 20% of Nobel Prize laureates have been Jewish, with multiple winners in each field." Jews are a famously accomplished group. They make up 0.2% of the world population, but 54% of the world chess champions, 27% of the Nobel physics laureates and 31% of the medicine laureates. Jews make up 2% of the U.S. population, but 21% of the Ivy League student bodies, 26% of the Kennedy Center honorees, 37% of the Academy Award-winning directors, 38% of those on a recent Business Week list of leading philanthropists, 51% of the Pulitzer Prize winners for nonfiction.*

In modern time, Jewish influence upon America is manifest and strong, which presents a strong argument for a careful study of Judaism and Jews. Judaism, through its effect on Christianity, is very worth studying. It should be noted that SIX distinguished Jews have been singled out as outstanding and representative figures with whose idea the nature of the whole world can be summed up with only a single word. Abraham, a Jewish religious leader, describes this world with one single word: covenant; Moses, a Jewish prophet, describes this world as governed by legal codes (Law); Jesus Christ devoted his life to this world full of sins with a good example of firm conviction in God (Faith); Karl Marx dissected this world with his comprehensive analysis of the nature of money or economic relations among people within a society (Capital); Sigmund Freud defined this world with interdependent relationship between a man and woman (Sex drive or Libido) and tried to see this world through his reflections on one phenomenon of human beings (Dream); Albert Einstein contributed to this world with his theory of relativity by claiming that everything in this world is relative, which means that nothing is absolute. The uniqueness and greatness of Jewish people are represented by six Jews

---

[①] In 2012, the famous British magazine *The Economist* published a feature column article series under the name of Special Report each year for some dozen issues. In 2012, the Magazine published a special topic "Judaism and Jews", outlining the history and current situation of Jewish people. Following the same title, this case study of Jewish people is dedicated to the excellent contributions Jewish people have made to world civilization. For reading the original articles or more detailed information, please visit its official website at www.economist.com.

whose simple profiles are listed below for further study of this group of people along with a summary of cultural implication for each one of these six Jews.

Abraham: Father and Founder of Abrahamic Religions

Abraham is one of the biblical patriarchs and a major character in the epic of the Israelites. His story is told in chapters 11—25 of the Book of Genesis, and he plays a prominent role in Judaism, Christianity and Islam. According to the account in Genesis, at the age of 75, Abram, obeying God's command, took his wife Sarai, and his household and traveled from Haran to Shechem in Canaan. Abram enters into a covenant with God, signified by the rite of circumcision. Abram is now known as Abraham ("father of many nations"), and Sarai becomes Sarah. As Abraham and Sarah are childless, Sarah suggests Abraham have a child by her handmaid, Hagar. Hagar bears Abraham his firstborn, Ishmael. Abraham and Sarah later become the parents of Isaac. In Jewish and Christian tradition, Abraham is the father of the Israelites through his son Isaac. In Islamic tradition, Abraham is considered a prophet of Islam, an ancestor of Muhammad, through Ishmael. Muslims regard him as an example of the perfect Muslim, and the revered reformer of the Kaaba in Mecca. Bahá'u'lláh, the prophet of the Baha'i Faith, affirms the highest religious station for Abraham. In the New Testament Abraham is described as a man of faith. He is regarded as the patron saint of those in the hospitality industry.

Abram's Origins and Calling

Terah, the tenth in descent from Noah, fathered Abram, Nahor and Haran, and Haran fathered Lot. Haran died in his native Ur of the Chaldees, and Abram married Sarai, who was barren. Terah, with Abram, Sarai and Lot, then departed for Canaan, but settled in a place named Haran, where Terah died at the age of 205. (Genesis 11:27—11:32) God appeared to Abram and told him to depart. After settling in Haran, where his father Terah died, God then told Abram to leave his country and his father's house for a land that He would show him, promising to make of him a great nation, bless him, make his name great, bless those who blessed him, and curse those who cursed him. (Genesis 12:1—3) Following God's command, at age 75, Abram took his wife Sarai, his nephew Lot, and the wealth and persons that they had acquired, and traveled to Shechem in Canaan.

Abrahamic Covenant with God

The word of God came to Abram in a vision and repeated the promise of the land and descendants as numerous as the stars. Abram and God made a covenant ceremony, and God told of the future bondage of Israel in Egypt. God described to Abram the land that his offspring would claim: "the land of the Kenites, Kenizzites, Kadmonites, Hittites, Perizzites, Rephaites, Amorites, Canaanites, Girgashites and Jebusites." (Genesis 15)

Abraham's Three Visitors

Not long afterward, during the heat of the day, Abraham had been sitting at the entrance of his tent by the terebinths of Mamre. He looked up and saw three men in the presence of God. Then he ran and bowed to the ground to welcome them. Abraham then offered to wash their feet and fetch them a morsel of bread of which they assented. Abraham rushed to Sarah's tent to order cakes made from choice flour, then he ordered a servant-boy to prepare a choice calf. When all was prepared, he set curds, milk and the calf before them waiting on them, under a tree, as they ate. (Genesis 18:1—8)

One of the visitors told Abraham that upon his return next year, Sarah would have a son. While at the tent entrance, Sarah overheard what was said and she laughed to herself about the prospect of having a child at their ages. The visitor inquired to Abraham why Sarah laughed at bearing a child for her age as nothing is too hard for God. Frightened, Sarah denied laughing.

Abraham's Plea

After eating, Abraham and the three visitors got up. They walked over to the peak that overlooked the *Cities of the Plain* to discuss the fate of Sodom and Gomorrah for their detestable sins that were so great, it moved God to action. Because Abraham's nephew was living in Sodom, God revealed plans to confirm and judge these cities. At this point, the two other visitors leave for Sodom. Then Abraham turned to the Lord and pleaded incrementally with Him (from fifty persons to less) that "if there were at least ten righteous men found in the city, would not God spare the city?" For the sake of ten righteous people, God declared that he would not destroy the city. (Genesis 18:17—33)

When the two visitors got to Sodom to conduct their report, they planned on staying in the city square. However, Abraham's nephew, Lot, met with them and strongly insisted that these two "men" stay at his house for the night. A rally of men stood outside of Lot's home and demanded that they bring out his guests so that they may "know" them. However, Lot objected and offered his virgin daughters to the rally of men instead. They rejected that notion and sought to break Lot's doors down to get to his male guests, thus confirming the "outcry against Sodom and Gomorrah" and sealing their doom. (Genesis 19:12—13) Early the next morning, Abraham awoke and went to the elevation that looked over the River Jordan plain, at the very spot where he stood before God, the day prior. From his vantage point, he saw what became of the cities of the plain as "dense smoke rising from the land, like smoke from a furnace." (Genesis 19:27—29) This meant that there was not even ten righteous people in any of those cities. (Genesis 18:32)

Abraham in Religious Traditions

In Islamic and Jewish traditions, Abraham is referred to as "our Father". In Jewish and Christian tradition, Abraham is the father of the Israelites through his son Isaac, whose mother was Sarah. His oldest son is Ishmael, whose mother is Hagar, Sarah's Egyptian handmaiden. In Islamic tradition, Abraham is considered a prophet of Islam, the ancestor of Muhammad, through his son Ishmael, whose mother is Hagar.

Summary of Cultural Implication of Abraham

It is said that the core or essential part of a way of life for a group of people is demonstrated through its culture defined in the broadest sense. The core of a culture is expressed by its religion. The statement thus given, the position of Abraham as a legendary figure in cultural history of human beings stands out so prominently not only because he has been worshiped by Jewish people, Christian believers and Islamic adherents, but also because his life experience has exerted everlasting influence upon world major religions through a system of religions by his name: Abrahamic Religions with the Abrahamic God as their central idea. The Abrahamic God in this sense is the conception of God that remains a common attribute of all three traditions. In all of Judaism, Christianity, Islam and Baha'i Faith God is conceived of as eternal, omnipotent, omniscient and as the creator of the universe. God by this definition is then further held to have the properties of holiness, justice, omni-benevolence and omnipresence. It is recorded and revealed in many religious documents that Abraham established a covenantal relationship with God who through Abraham extended its oracles of grace and redemption to his believers. Abraham with his life practice displayed a miraculous power based upon a very important concept: **Covenant**. Therefore, the cultural implication of Abraham revolves around this central idea of covenant, or in modern term, contract which is the core idea of capitalism that includes social contract, business contract, political contract or even personal contract. It goes without saying that the modern world would not go smoothly without the idea of contract to govern it.

Moses: a Figure That Has Left Strong Mark in Western Civilization with His Ten Commandments

The existence of Moses as well as the veracity of the Exodus story is disputed among archaeologists and Egyptologists, with experts in the field of biblical criticism citing logical inconsistencies, new archaeological evidence, historical evidence, and related origin myths in Canaanite culture. Other historians maintain that the biographical details, and Egyptian background, attributed to Moses imply the existence of a historical political and religious leader who was involved in the consolidation of the Hebrew tribes in Canaan towards the end of the Bronze Age. According to the Book of Exodus, Moses was born in a time when his people, the Children of Israel, were increasing in number and the Egyptian Pharaoh was worried that they might help Egypt's enemies. Moses' Hebrew mother, Jochebed, hid him when the Pharaoh ordered all newborn Hebrew boys to be killed, and the child was adopted as a foundling by the Egyptian royal family. After killing an Egyptian slave-master, Moses fled across the Red Sea to Midian where he encountered the God of Israel in the form of a "burning bush". God sent Moses to request the release of the Israelites. After the Ten Plagues, Moses led the Exodus of the Israelites out of Egypt and across the Red Sea, after which they based themselves at Mount Sinai, where Moses received the Ten Commandments. After 40 years of wandering in the desert, Moses died within sight of the Promised Land. Rabbinical Judaism calculated a lifespan of Moses corresponding to 1391—1271 BCE; Christian tradition has tended to assume an earlier date.

God commanded Moses to go to Egypt and deliver his fellow Hebrews from bondage. On the way Moses was nearly killed by God because his son was not circumcised. He was met on the way by his elder brother, Aaron, and gained a hearing with his oppressed kindred after they returned to Egypt, who believed Moses and Aaron after they saw the signs that were performed in the midst of the Israelite assembly. Moses and Aaron went to Pharaoh and told him that the Lord God of Israel wanted Pharaoh to permit the Israelites to celebrate a feast in the wilderness. Pharaoh replied that he did not know their God and would not permit them to go. They gained a second hearing with Pharaoh and changed Moses' rod into a serpent, but Pharaoh's magicians did the same with their rods. Moses and Aaron met Pharaoh at the Nile riverbank, and Moses had Aaron turn the river to blood, but Pharaoh's magicians could do the same. Moses obtained a fourth meeting, and had Aaron bring frogs from the Nile to overrun Egypt, but Pharaoh's magicians were able to do the same thing. Pharaoh asked Moses to remove the frogs and promised to let the Israelites go observe their feast in the wilderness in return. Pharaoh decided against letting the Israelites leave to observe the feast. Eventually Pharaoh let the Hebrews depart after Moses' God sent ten plagues upon the Egyptians. The third and fourth were the plague of gnats and flies. The fifth was diseases on the Egyptians' cattle, oxen, goats, sheep, camels, and horses. The sixth was boils on the skins of Egyptians. Seventh, fiery hail and thunder. The eighth plague was locusts. The ninth plague was total darkness. The tenth plague was the slaying of the Egyptian male first-born children, whereupon such terror seized the Egyptians that they ordered the Hebrews to leave. The events are commemorated as Passover, referring to how the plague "passed over" the houses of the Israelites while smiting the Egyptians.

The Crossing of the Red Sea

Moses then led his people eastward, beginning the long journey to Canaan. The procession moved slowly, and found it necessary to encamp three times before passing the Egyptian frontier—some believe at the Great Bitter Lake, while others propose sites as far south as the northern tip of the Red Sea. Meanwhile, Pharaoh had a change of heart, and was in pursuit of them with a large army. Shut in between this army and the sea, the Israelites despaired, but Exodus records that God divided the waters so that they passed safely across on dry ground. There is some contention about this passage, since an earlier incorrect translation of *Yam Suph* to Red Sea was later found to have meant Reed Sea. When the Egyptian army attempted to follow, God permitted the waters to return upon them and drown them. The people then continued to Marsa marching for three days along the wilderness of the Shur without finding water. Then they came to Elim where twelve water springs and 70 palm trees greeted them. From Elim they set out again and after 45 days they reached the wilderness of Sin between Elim and Sinai. From there they reached the plain of Rephidim, completing the crossing of the Red Sea.

Mount Sinai and the Ten Commandments

According to the Bible, after crossing the Red Sea and leading the Israelites towards the desert, Moses was summoned by God to Mount Sinai, also referred to as Mount Horeb, the same place where Moses had first talked to the Burning Bush, tended the flocks of Jethro his father-in-law, and later produced water by striking the rock with his staff and directed the battle with the Amalekites. Moses stayed on the mountain for 40 days and nights, a period in which he received the Ten Commandments directly from God. Moses then descended from the mountain with intent to deliver the commandments to the people, but upon his arrival he saw that the people were involved in the sin of the Golden Calf. In terrible anger, Moses broke the commandment tablets and ordered his own tribe (the Levites) to go through the camp and kill everyone, including family and friends, upon which the Levites killed about 3,000 people, some of whom were children. God later commanded Moses to inscribe two other tablets, to replace the ones Moses smashed, so Moses went to the mountain again, for another period of 40 days and nights, and when he returned, the commandments were finally given. In Jewish tradition, Moses is referred to as "The Lawgiver" for this singular achievement of delivering the Ten Commandments.

Death

Moses was warned that he would not be permitted to lead the Israelites across the Jordan river, because of his trespass at the waters of Meribah (Deut. 32:51) but would die on its eastern shores (Num. 20:12). He therefore assembled the tribes, and delivered to them a parting address, which is taken to form the Book of Deuteronomy. When Moses finished, he sang a song and pronounced a blessing on the people. He then went up Mount Nebo to the top of Pisgah, looked over the promised land of Israel spread out before him, and died, at the age of one hundred and twenty, according to Talmudic legend on 7 Adar, his 120th birthday exactly. God Himself buried him in an unknown grave in a valley in the land of Moab, over against Bethpeor (Deut. 34:6). Moses was thus the human instrument in the creation of the nation of Israel by communicating to it the Torah. More humble than any other man (Num. 12:3), he enjoyed unique privileges, for "there hath not arisen a prophet since in Israel like unto Moses, whom YHWH knew face to face" (Deut. 34:10). (See also Jude 1:9 and Zechariah 3.)

Mosaic Law

The Book of Kings relates how a "law of Moses" was discovered in the Temple during the reign of King Josiah (641 BC—609 BC). This book is mostly identified as an early version of the Book of Deuteronomy, perhaps chapters 5—26 and chapter 28 of the extant text. This text contains a number of laws, dated to the 8th century BC kingdom of Judah, a time when a minority Yahwist faction was actively attacking mainstream polytheism, succeeding in establishing official monolatry of the God of Israel under Josiah by the late 7th century BC. The law attributed to Moses, specifically the laws set out in Deuteronomy, as a consequence came to be considered supreme over all other sources of authority (the king and his officials), and the

Levite priests were the guardians and interpreters of the law.

Moses in Religious Traditions

Judaism

There is a wealth of stories and additional information about Moses in the Jewish apocrypha and in the genre of rabbinical exegesis known as Midrash, as well as in the primary works of the Jewish oral law, the Mishnah and the Talmud. Moses is also given a number of bynames in Jewish tradition. The Midrash identifies Moses as one of seven biblical personalities who were called by various names. Moses' other names were: Jekuthiel (by his mother), Heber (by his father), Jered (by Miriam), Avi Zanoah (by Aaron), Avi Gedor (by Kohath), Avi Soco (by his wet-nurse), Shemaiah ben Nethanel (by people of Israel). Moses is also attributed the names Toviah (as a first name), and Levi (as a family name) (Vayikra Rabbah 1:3), Heman, Mechoqeiq (lawgiver) and Ehl Gav Ish. (Numbers 12:3) Jewish historians who lived at Alexandria, such as Eupolemus, attributed to Moses the feat of having taught the Phoenicians their alphabet, similar to legends of Thoth. Artapanus of Alexandria explicitly identified Moses not only with Thoth / Hermes, but also with the Greek figure Musaeus (whom he calls "the teacher of Orpheus"), and ascribed to him the division of Egypt into 36 districts, each with its own liturgy. He names the princess who adopted Moses as Merris, wife of Pharaoh Chenephres. Ancient sources mention an Assumption of Moses and a Testimony of Moses. A Latin text was found in Milan in the 19th century by Antonio Ceriani who called it the Assumption of Moses, even though it does not refer to an assumption of Moses or contain portions of the Assumption which are cited by ancient authors, and it is apparently actually the Testimony. The incident which the ancient authors cite is also mentioned in the Epistle of Jude. To Orthodox Jews, Moses is called *Moshe Rabbenu*, *'Eved HaShem*, *Avi haNeviim zya "a*. He is defined "Our Leader Moshe", "Servant of God", and "Father of all the Prophets". In their view, Moses not only received the Torah, but also the revealed (written and oral) and the hidden (the *hokhmat nistar* teachings, which gave Judaism the Zohar of the Rashbi, the Torah of the Ari haQadosh and all that is discussed in the Heavenly Yeshiva between the Ramhal and his masters). He is also considered the greatest prophet. Arising in part from his age, but also because 120 is elsewhere stated as the maximum age for Noah's descendants (one interpretation of Genesis 6:3), "may you live to 120" has become a common blessing among Jews.

Christianity

For Christians, Moses—mentioned more often in the New Testament than any other Old Testament figure—is often a symbol of God's law, as reinforced and expounded on in the teachings of Jesus. New Testament writers often compared Jesus' words and deeds with Moses' to explain Jesus' mission. In Acts 7:39—43, 51—53, for example, the rejection of Moses by the Jews who worshiped the golden calf is likened to the rejection of Jesus by the Jews that continued in traditional Judaism. Moses also figures in several of Jesus' messages. When he met the Pharisees Nicodemus at night in the third chapter of the Gospel of John, he compared Moses' lifting up of the bronze serpent in the wilderness, which any Israelite could look at and be healed, to his own lifting up (by his death and resurrection) for the people to look at and be healed. In the sixth chapter, Jesus responded to the people's claim that Moses provided them *manna* in the wilderness by saying that it was not Moses, but God, who provided. Calling himself the "bread of life", Jesus stated that He was provided to feed God's people. Moses, along with Elijah, is presented as meeting with Jesus in all three Gospel accounts of the Transfiguration of Jesus in Matthew 17, Mark 9, and Luke 9, respectively. Later Christians found numerous other parallels between the life of Moses and Jesus to the extent that Jesus was likened to a "second Moses".

For instance, Jesus' escape from the slaughter by Herod in Bethlehem is compared to Moses' escape from Pharaoh's designs to kill Hebrew infants. Such parallels, unlike those mentioned above, are not pointed out in Scripture. His relevance to modern Christianity has not diminished. Moses is considered to be a saint by several churches; and is commemorated as a prophet in the respective Calendars of Saints of the eastern Orthodox Church, Roman Catholic Church, and Lutheran churches on September 4. He is commemorated as one of the Holy Forefathers in the Calendar of Saints of the Armenian Apostolic Church on July 30. Members of The Church of Jesus Christ of Latter-day Saints (colloquially called Mormons) generally view Moses in the same way that other Christians do. However, in addition to accepting the Biblical account of Moses, Mormons include Selections from the Book of Moses as part of their scriptural canon. This book is believed to be the translated writings of Moses, and is included in the Pearl of Great Price. Latter-day Saints are also unique in believing that Moses was taken to heaven without having tasted death (translated). In addition, Joseph Smith, Jr. and Oliver Cowdery stated that on April 3, 1836, Moses appeared to them in the Kirtland Temple in a glorified, immortal, physical form and bestowed upon them the "keys of the gathering of Israel from the four parts of the earth, and the leading of the ten tribes from the land of the north."

Islam

Moses is mentioned more in the Qur'an than any other individual and his life is narrated and recounted more than that of any other prophet. In general, Moses is described in ways which parallel the prophet Muhammad, and "his character exhibits some of the main themes of Islamic theology," including the "moral injunction that we are to submit ourselves to God." Moses is defined in the Qur'an as both prophet (*nabi*) and messenger (*rasul*), the latter term indicating that he was one of those prophets who brought a scripture and law to his people. Huston Smith (1991) describes an account in the Qur'an of meetings in heaven between Moses and Muhammad, which Huston states were "one of the crucial events in Muhammad's life", and resulted in Muslims observing 5 daily prayers. Moses is mentioned 502 times in the Qur'an; passages mentioning Moses include 2.49−61, 7.103−160, 10.75−93, 17.101−104, 20.9−97, 26.10−66, 27.7−14, 28.3−46, 40.23−30, 43.46−55, 44.17−31, and 79.15−25. and many others. Most of the key events in Moses' life which are narrated in the Bible are to be found dispersed through the different Surahs of Qur'an, with a story about meeting Khidr which is not found in the Bible. In the Moses story related by the Qur'an, Jochebed is commanded by God to place Moses in an ark and cast him on the waters of the Nile, thus abandoning him completely to God's protection. Pharaoh's wife Asiya, not his daughter, found Moses floating in the waters of the Nile. She convinced Pharaoh to keep him as their son because they were not blessed with any children. The Qur'an's account has emphasized Moses' mission to invite the Pharaoh to accept God's divine message as well as give salvation to the Israelites. According to the Qur'an, Moses encourages the Israelites to enter Canaan, but they are unwilling to fight the Canaanites, fearing certain defeat. Moses responds by pleading to Allah that he and his brother Aaron be separated from the rebellious Israelites.

Ten Commandments

The Ten Commandments, also known as the **Decalogue**, are a set of biblical laws relating to ethics and worship, which play a fundamental role in Judaism and Christianity. They include instructions to worship only God and to keep the sabbath, and prohibitions against idolatry, blasphemy, murder, theft, and adultery. Different groups follow slightly different traditions for interpreting and numbering them.

The Ten Commandments appear twice in the Hebrew Bible, in the books of Exodus and

Deuteronomy. According to the story in Exodus, God inscribed them on two stone tablets, which he gave to Moses on Mount Sinai. Modern scholarship has found likely influences in Hittite and Mesopotamian laws and treaties, but is divided over exactly when the Ten Commandments were written and who wrote them.

Importance Within Judaism and Christianity

The Ten Commandments concern only matters of fundamental importance: the greatest obligation (to worship only God), the greatest injury to a person (murder), the greatest injury to family bonds (adultery), the greatest injury to commerce and law (bearing false witness), the greatest intergenerational obligation (honor to parents), the greatest obligation to community (truthfulness), the greatest injury to moveable property (theft). Because they are fundamental, the Ten Commandments are written with room for varying interpretation. They are not as explicit or detailed as rules and regulations or many other biblical laws and commandments, because they provide guiding principles that apply universally, across changing circumstances. They do not specify punishments for their violation. Their precise import must be worked out in each separate situation. The Bible indicates the special status of the Ten Commandments among all other Old Testament laws in several ways. They have a uniquely terse style. Of all the biblical laws and commandments, the Ten Commandments alone were "written with the finger of God" (Exodus 31:18). And lastly, the stone tablets were placed in the Ark of the Covenant (Exodus 25:21). In Judaism, the Ten Commandments provide God's universal and timeless standard of right and wrong, unlike the other 603 commandments in the Torah, which describe various duties and ceremonies such as the kashrut dietary laws and now unobservable rituals to be performed by priests in the Holy Temple. They form the basis of Jewish law. During the period of the Second Temple, the Ten Commandments were recited daily. They were removed from daily liturgy to dispute a claim by early Christians that only the Ten Commandments were handed down at Mount Sinai rather than the whole Torah. In later centuries, rabbis continued to omit the Ten Commandments from daily liturgy in order to prevent a confusion among Jews that they are only bound by the Ten Commandments, and not also by many other biblical and talmudic laws, such as the requirement to observe holy days other than the sabbath. Today, the Ten Commandments are heard in the synagogue three times a year: as they come up during the readings of Exodus and Deuteronomy, and during the festival of Shavuot. In some traditions the worshipers rise for their reading to highlight their special significance.

The eastern Orthodox Church holds its moral truths to be chiefly contained in the Ten Commandments. A confession begins with the confessor reciting the Ten Commandments and asking the penitent which of them he has broken. In Roman Catholicism, Jesus freed Christians from the Jewish obligation to keep the 613 mitzvot, but not from their obligation to keep the Ten Commandments. They are to the moral order what the creation story is to the natural order. Even after rejecting the Roman Catholic moral theology, giving less importance to biblical law in order to better hear and be moved by the gospel, early Protestant theologians still took the Ten Commandments to be the starting point of Christian moral life. Different versions of Christianity have varied in how they have translated the bare principles into the specifics that make up a full Christian ethic. Where Catholicism emphasizes taking action to fulfill the Ten Commandments, Protestantism uses the Ten Commandments for two purposes: to outline the Christian life to each person, and to make each person realize, through their failure to live that life, that they lack the ability to do it on their own. Thus for Protestant Christianity, the Ten Commandments primarily serve to lead each Christian to the grace of God.

Attachment: The Ten Commandments—God's Revelation in the Old Testament

The Ten Commandments are found in the Bible's Old Testament at Exodus, Chapter 20.

They were given directly by God to the people of Israel at Mount Sinai after He had delivered them from slavery in Egypt:

And God spoke all these words, saying: "I am the LORD your God"
ONE: *"You shall have no other gods before Me."*
TWO: *"You shall not make for yourself a carved image—any likeness of anything that is in heaven above, or that is in the earth beneath, or that is in the water under the earth."*
THREE: *"You shall not take the name of the LORD your God in vain."*
FOUR: *"Remember the Sabbath day, to keep it holy."*
FIVE: *"Honor your father and your mother."*
SIX: *"You shall not murder."*
SEVEN: *"You shall not commit adultery."*
EIGHT: *"You shall not steal."*
NINE: *"You shall not bear false witness against your neighbor."*
TEN: *"You shall not covet your neighbor's house; you shall not covet your neighbor's wife, nor his male servant, nor his female servant, nor his ox, nor his donkey, nor anything that is your neighbor's."*

The Ten Commandments—Christ's Summation in the New Testament about 1,400 years later, the Ten Commandments were summed up in the New Testament at Matthew 22, when Jesus was confronted by the religious "experts" of the day:

" Teacher, which is the greatest commandment in the Law?" Jesus replied: "'Love the Lord your God with all your heart and with all your soul and with all your mind.' This is the first and greatest commandment. And the second is like it: 'Love your neighbor as yourself.' All the Law and the Prophets hang on these two commandments" (Matthew 22: 36—40).

A reflective reading of Christ's teaching reveals that the first four commandments given to the children of Israel are contained in the statement: " *Love the Lord your God with all your heart and with all your soul and with all your mind.* " It continues that the last six commandments are enclosed in the statement: " *Love your neighbor as yourself.* "

Summary of Cultural Implications of Moses

Moses was, according to the Hebrew Bible and the Qur'an, a religious leader, lawgiver and prophet, to whom the authorship of the Torah is traditionally attributed. Also called *Moshe Rabbenu* in Hebrew, he is the most important prophet in Judaism, and is also considered an important prophet in Christianity and Islam, as well as a number of other faiths. In this sense, Moses occupied a unique position in the western cultural realm, especially through his influence on Christianity. In addition to being widely claimed as a religious leader and prophet, Moses is most remembered as a lawgiver simply because of a whole series of legal codes known as Ten Commandments, which have laid an original and solid foundation for the spirit of law in the West. Among others, rule of law is one of a few pillars ideas in the West, which implies that the West has carried a strong tradition of legal spirit and such idea, although vividly expressed in Moses legal codes, has been amplified through the Enlightenment Movement. It is in this area that Moses has been esteemed not only by Jewish people, but also respected by Christians at large. In Moses' eyes through his lawful code, the whole world should be operated and governed strictly by law. Thus law is the central concept that can account for the nature of the world. And from this idea, legal spirit as a cultural symbol has become so unique in the West. It is not coincident that one of the three pillars of American political culture is found in the spirit and practice of rule of law, the other two being Constitutionalism and Federalism.

Jesus Christ: Savior and Spiritual Father of the West

Christian views of Jesus are based on the teachings and beliefs outlined in the Canonical gospels, New Testament letters, and the Christian creeds. These outline the key beliefs held by Christians about Jesus, including his divinity, humanity, and earthly life. The second sentence in the ICET version of the Nicene Creed states: "We believe in one Lord, Jesus Christ, the only Son of God...". In the New Testament Jesus indicates that he is the Son of God by calling God his father. Christians consider Jesus the Christ and believe that through his death and resurrection, humans can be reconciled to God and thereby are offered salvation and the promise of eternal life. These teachings emphasize that as the willing Lamb of God, Jesus chose to suffer in Calvary as a sign of his full obedience to the will of the Eternal Father, as an "agent and servant of God". The choice Jesus made thus counter-positions him as a new man of morality and obedience, in contrast to Adam's disobedience. Most Christians believe that Jesus was both human and the Son of God. While there have been theological debate over the nature of Jesus, Trinitarian Christians generally believe that Jesus is the Logos, God incarnate, God the Son, and "true God and true man" (or both fully divine and fully human). Jesus, having become fully human in all respects, suffered the pains and temptations of a mortal man, yet he did not sin. As fully God, he defeated death and rose to life again. According to the Bible, God raised him from the dead. He ascended to heaven, to sit at the "Right Hand of God", and he will return to earth again for the Last Judgment and the establishment of the Kingdom of God in the World to Come.

Overview

Although Christian views of Jesus vary, it is possible to summarize key elements of the shared beliefs among major denominations based on their catechetical or confessional texts. Christian views of Jesus are derived from various sources, but especially from the canonical Gospels, and New Testament letters, such as the Pauline Epistles. Christians predominantly hold that these works are historically true. The five major milestones in the gospel narrative of the life of Jesus are his Baptism, Transfiguration, Crucifixion, Resurrection and Ascension. These are usually bracketed by two other episodes: his Nativity at the beginning and the sending of the Paraclete at the end. The gospel accounts of the teachings of Jesus are often presented in terms of specific categories involving his "works and words", e. g. his ministry, parables and miracles. Christians not only attach theological significance to the works of Jesus, but also to his name. Devotions to the Holy Name of Jesus go back to the earliest days of Christianity. These devotions and feasts exist both in eastern and western Christianity. Christians predominantly profess that through his life, death, and resurrection, Jesus restored man's communion with God in the blood of the New Covenant. His death on a cross is understood as a redemptive sacrifice: the source of humanity's salvation and the atonement for sin, which had entered human history through the sin of Adam. However, not all Christian denominations agree on all doctrines, and both major and minor differences on teachings and beliefs persist throughout Christianity.

Christ, Logos and Son of God

Christians generally consider Jesus to be the Christ, the long awaited Messiah, as well as the one and only Son of God. The opening words in the Gospel of Mark (1:1), "The beginning of the gospel of Jesus Christ, the Son of God" provide Jesus with the two distinct attributions of Christ and the Son of God. The divinity being again re-affirmed in Mark 1:11. Matthew 1:1 also starts by calling Jesus Christ and Matthew 1:16 explains it again with: "Jesus, who is called

Christ". In the Letters of Saint Paul, the word "Christ" is so closely associated with Jesus that apparently for the early Christians there was no need to claim that Jesus was Christ, for that was considered widely accepted among them. Hence Paul could use the term *Christos* with no confusion about who it referred to, and as in 1 Corinthians 4:15 and Romans 12:5 he could use expressions such as "in Christ" to refer to the followers of Jesus.

In the New Testament, the title "Son of God" is applied to Jesus on many occasions. It is often used to refer to his divinity, from the beginning in the Annunciation up to the Crucifixion. The declaration that Jesus is the Son of God is made by many individuals in the New Testament, and on two separate occasions by God the Father as a voice from Heaven, and is asserted by Jesus himself. In Christology, the conception that *the Christ* is the *Logos* (i.e. The Word) has been important in establishing the doctrine of the divinity of Christ and his position as God the Son in the Trinity as set forth in the Chalcedonian Creed. The conception derives from the opening of the Gospel of John, commonly translated into English as: "In the beginning was the Word, and the Word was with God, and the Word was God." In the original Greek, *Logos* (λόγος) is used for "Word", and in theological discourse, this is often left untranslated. The *pre-existence of Christ* refers to the doctrine of the personal existence of Christ before his conception. One of the relevant Bible passages is John 1:1—18 where, in the Trinitarian view, Christ is identified with a pre-existent divine hypostasis called the Logos or Word. However, other non-trinitarian views question the aspect of personal pre-existence or question the aspect of divinity, or both. This doctrine is reiterated in John 17:5 when Jesus refers to the glory which he had with the Father "before the world was" during the Farewell discourse. John 17:24 also refers to the Father loving Jesus "before the foundation of the world". Following the Apostolic Age, from the 2nd century onwards, several controversies developed about how the human and divine are related within the person of Jesus. Eventually in 451 the *Hypostatic union* was decreed, namely that Jesus is both fully divine and fully human. However, differences among Christian denominations continued thereafter.

Incarnation, Nativity and Second Adam

Apostle Paul viewed the birth of Jesus as an event of cosmic significance which brought forth a "new man" who undid the damage caused by the fall of the first man, Adam. Just as the Johannine view of Jesus as the incarnate Logos proclaims the universal relevance of his birth, the Pauline perspective emphasizes the birth of a new man and a new world in the birth of Jesus. Paul's eschatological view of Jesus counter-positions him as a new man of morality and obedience, in contrast to Adam. Unlike Adam, the new man born in Jesus obeys God and ushers in a world of morality and salvation. In the Pauline view, Adam is positioned as the first man and Jesus as the second: Adam, having corrupted himself by his disobedience, also infected humanity and left it with a curse as inheritance. The birth of Jesus, on the other hand, counterbalanced the fall of Adam, bringing forth redemption and repairing the damage done by Adam. In the 2nd century Church Father Irenaeus writes:

> *When He became incarnate and was made man, He commenced afresh the long line of human beings, and furnished us, in a brief, comprehensive manner, with salvation; so that what we had lost in Adam—namely to be according to the image and likeness of God—that we might recover in Christ Jesus.*

In patristic theology, Paul's contrasting of Jesus as the new man versus Adam provided a framework for discussing the uniqueness of the birth of Jesus and the ensuing events of his life. The Nativity of Jesus thus began to serve as the starting point for "cosmic Christology" in which the birth, life and Resurrection of Jesus have universal implications. The concept of Jesus as the "new man" repeats in the cycle of birth and rebirth of Jesus from his Nativity to his Resurrection: following his birth, through his morality and obedience to the Father, Jesus began a new harmony in the relationship between God the Father and man. The Nativity and Resurrection of Jesus thus created the author and exemplar of a new humanity. In this view, the birth, death and Resurrection of Jesus brought about salvation, undoing the damage of Adam.

Teachings, Parables and Miracles

In the New Testament the teachings of Jesus are presented in terms of his "words and works". The words of Jesus include several sermons, as well as parables that appear throughout the narrative of the Synoptic Gospels (the gospel of John includes no parables). The works include the miracles and other acts performed during his ministry. Although the Canonical Gospels are the major source of the teachings of Jesus, the Pauline Epistles, which were likely written decades before the gospels, provide some of the earliest written accounts of the teachings of Jesus. The New Testament does not present the teachings of Jesus as merely his own teachings, but equates the words of Jesus with divine revelation, with John the Baptist stating in John 3:34: "he whom God hath sent speaketh the words of God" and Jesus stating in John 7:16: "My teaching is not mine, but his that sent me". In Matthew 11:27 Jesus claims divine knowledge, stating: "No one knows the Son except the Father and no one knows the Father except the Son", asserting the mutual knowledge he has with the Father.

Parables

The parables of Jesus represent a major component of his teachings in the gospels, the approximately thirty parables forming about one third of his recorded teachings. The parables may appear within longer sermons, as well as other places within the narrative. Jesus' parables are seemingly simple and memorable stories, often with imagery, and each conveys a teaching which usually relates the physical world to the spiritual world. In the 19th century, Lisco and Fairbairn stated that in the parables of Jesus, "the image borrowed from the visible world is accompanied by a truth from the invisible (spiritual) world" and that the parables of Jesus are not "mere similitudes which serve the purpose of illustration, but are internal analogies where nature becomes a witness for the spiritual world". Similarly, in the 20th century, calling a parable "an earthly story with a heavenly meaning", William Barclay states that the parables of Jesus use familiar examples to lead men's minds towards heavenly concepts. He suggests that Jesus did not form his parables merely as analogies but based on an "inward affinity between the natural and the spiritual order."

Miracles

In Christian teachings, the miracles of Jesus were as much a vehicle for his message as were his words. Many of the miracles emphasize the importance of faith, for instance in Cleansing Ten Lepers, Jesus did not say: "My power has saved you," but says, "Rise and go; your faith has saved you." Similarly, in the Walking on Water Miracle, Apostle Peter learns an important lesson about faith in that as his faith wavers, he begins to sink. One characteristic shared among all miracles of Jesus in the Gospel accounts is that he delivered benefits freely and never requested or accepted any form of payment for his healing miracles, unlike some high priests of his time who charged those who were healed. In Matthew 10:8 he advised his disciples to heal the sick without payment and stated: "Freely ye received, freely give." Christians in general believe that Jesus' miracles were actual historical events and that his miraculous works were an important part of his life, attesting to his divinity and the Hypostatic union, i.e. the dual natures of Jesus as God and Man. Christians believe that while Jesus' experiences of hunger, weariness, and death were evidences of his humanity, the miracles were evidences of his deity. Christian authors also view the miracles of Jesus not merely as acts of power and omnipotence, but as works of love and mercy; they were performed not to awe men by the feeling of omnipotence, but to show compassion for sinful and suffering humanity. And each miracle involves specific teachings. Since according to the Gospel of John it was impossible to narrate all the miracles performed by Jesus, the Catholic Encyclopedia states that the miracles presented in the Gospels were selected for a twofold reason: first for the manifestation of God's glory, and then for their evidential value. Jesus referred to his "works" as evidences of his mission and his divinity, and in John 5:36 he declared that his miracles have greater evidential value than the testimony of John the Baptist.

Crucifixion and Atonement

The accounts of the crucifixion and subsequent resurrection of Jesus provide a rich background for Christological analysis, from the Canonical Gospels to the Pauline Epistles. In Johannine "agent Christology" the submission of Jesus to crucifixion is a sacrifice made as an agent of God or servant of God, for the sake of eventual victory. This builds on the salvific theme of the Gospel of John which begins in John 1:36 with John the Baptist's proclamation: "The Lamb of God who takes away the sins of the world". Further reinforcement of the concept is provided in Revelation 21:14 where the "lamb slain but standing" is the only one worthy of handling the scroll (i. e. the book) containing the names of those who are to be saved. A central element in the Christology presented in the Acts of the Apostles is the affirmation of the belief that the death of Jesus by crucifixion happened "with the foreknowledge of God, according to a definite plan". In this view, as in Acts 2:23, the cross is not viewed as a scandal, for the crucifixion of Jesus "at the hands of the lawless" is viewed as the fulfillment of the plan of God. Paul's Christology has a specific focus on the death and resurrection of Jesus. For Paul, the crucifixion of Jesus is directly related to his resurrection and the term "the cross of Christ" used in Galatians 6:12 may be viewed as his abbreviation of the message of the gospels. For Paul, the crucifixion of Jesus was not an isolated event in history, but a cosmic event with significant eschatological consequences, as in 1 Corinthians 2:8. In the Pauline view, Jesus, obedient to the point of death (Philippians 2:8) died "at the right time" (Romans 4:25) based on the plan of God. For Paul the "power of the cross" is not separable from the Resurrection of Jesus. John Calvin supported the "agent of God" Christology and argued that in his trial in Pilate's Court Jesus could have successfully argued for his innocence, but instead submitted to crucifixion in obedience to the Father. This Christological theme continued into the 20th century, both in the eastern and western Churches. In the eastern Church Sergei Bulgakov argued that the crucifixion of Jesus was "pre-eternally" determined by the Father before the creation of the world, to redeem humanity from the disgrace caused by the fall of Adam. In the western Church, Karl Rahner elaborated on the analogy that the blood of the Lamb of God (and the water from the side of Jesus) shed at the crucifixion had a cleansing nature, similar to baptismal water.

Resurrection, Ascension and Second Coming

The New Testament teaches that the resurrection of Jesus is a foundation of the Christian faith. Christians, through faith in the working of God are spiritually resurrected with Jesus, and are redeemed so that they may walk in a new way of life. In the teachings of the apostolic Church, the resurrection was seen as heralding a new era. Forming a theology of the resurrection fell to Apostle Paul. It was not enough for Paul to simply repeat elementary teachings, but as Hebrews 6:1 states, "go beyond the initial teachings about Christ and advance to maturity". Fundamental to Pauline theology is the connection between Christ's resurrection and redemption. Paul explained the importance of the resurrection of Jesus as the cause and basis of the hope of Christians to share a similar experience in 1 Corinthians 15:20—22:

But Christ really has been raised from the dead. He is the first of all those who will rise. Death came because of what a man did. Rising from the dead also comes because of what a man did. Because of Adam, all people die. So because of Christ, all will be made alive.

If the cross stands at the center of Paul's theology, so does the Resurrection: unless the one died the death of *all*, the *all* would have little to celebrate in the resurrection of the one. Paul taught that, just as Christians share in Jesus' death in baptism, so they will share in his resurrection for Jesus was designated the Son of God by his resurrection. Paul's views went against the thoughts of the Greek philosophers to whom a bodily resurrection meant a new imprisonment in a corporeal body, which was what they wanted to avoid; given that for them the corporeal and the material fettered the spirit. At the same time, Paul believed that the newly resurrected body would be a heavenly body; immortal, glorified, powerful and pneumatic in contrast to an earthly body, which is mortal, dishonored, weak and psychic. According to theologian Peter Carnley, the Resurrection of Jesus was different from the Resurrection of Lazarus as: "In the case of Lazarus, the stone was rolled away so that he could walk out.... the raised Christ didn't have to have the stone rolled away, because he is transformed and can appear anywhere, at any time."

Summary of Cultural Implication of Jesus Christ

If one word must be chosen to describe the nature of western civilization, Christianity should top all the other words to be listed as the number one, which alone speaks volumes for the irreplaceable and unavoidable importance of Jesus Christ, the founder of this most important religion in the West. Cultural implication of Jesus Christ is so profound and rich that no other single person, or event or phenomenon in the West can replace this miraculous existence. Although Jesus Christ was born Jewish, he has been recognized in the West as a towering figure representing the eternal love and almighty power of God. With Christianity as its dominant religion, the western culture has found its spiritual and mental buttress forever. For more than 2000 years since the birth of Jesus Christ, the West has constantly traced its spiritual justification and mental power through this legendary figure who is said to redeem the sin of human beings through the sacrifice of his own life for the redemption of whole human beings. If religion is the core of a culture, this religious leader and son of God, by the Trinity, has glorified the whole bunch of the western culture with the most important and holy idea called faith. By this overwhelming idea of faith alone, the West has occupied a stronghold and commanding heights of human spiritual world and this influence has been ever felt even till today.

Karl Marx: the Top Thinker of the Millennium[①]

Marx's theories about society, economics and politics—collectively known as Marxism—hold that all societies progress through the dialectic of class struggle: a conflict between an ownership class which controls production and a lower class which produces the labor for goods. Heavily critical of the current socio-economic form of society, capitalism, he called it the "dictatorship of the bourgeoisie", believing it to be run by the wealthy classes purely for their own benefit; and he predicted that, like previous socioeconomic systems, capitalism would inevitably produce internal tensions which would lead to its self-destruction and replacement by a new system: socialism. He argued that under socialism society would be governed by the working class in what he called the "dictatorship of the proletariat", the "workers' state" or

---

① This title derives from a poll conducted by BBC. For the past 50 years, according to the poll result, Karl Marx has been singled out as the top thinker of the millennium. Please go to www.bbc.gov for more detailed information.

"workers' democracy". He believed that socialism would, in its turn, eventually be replaced by a stateless, classless society called pure communism. Along with believing in the inevitability of socialism and communism, Marx actively fought for the former's implementation, arguing that social theorists and underprivileged people alike should carry out organized revolutionary action to topple capitalism and bring about socio-economic change. Revolutionary socialist governments espousing Marxist concepts took power in a variety of countries in the 20th century, leading to the formation of such socialist states as the Soviet Union in 1922 and the People's Republic of China in 1949. Many labor unions and workers' parties worldwide were also influenced by Marxist ideas, while various theoretical variants, such as Leninism, Stalinism, Trotskyism, and Maoism, were developed from them. Marx is typically cited, with Émile Durkheim and Max Weber, as one of the three principal architects of modern social science. Marx has been described as one of the most influential figures in human history.

Thought

Marx's thought demonstrates influences from many thinkers, including but not limited to:

- Georg Wilhelm Friedrich Hegel's philosophy;
- the classical political economy (economics) of Adam Smith and David Ricardo;
- French socialist thought, in particular the thought of Jean-Jacques Rousseau, Henri de Saint-Simon, Pierre-Joseph Proudhon, and Charles Fourier;
- earlier German philosophical materialism, particularly that of Ludwig Feuerbach;
- the working class analysis by Friedrich Engels.

Marx's view of history, which came to be called historical materialism (controversially adapted as the philosophy of dialectical materialism by Engels and Lenin) certainly shows the influence of Hegel's claim that one should view reality (and history) dialectically. However, Hegel had thought in idealist terms, putting ideas in the forefront, whereas Marx sought to rewrite dialectics in materialist terms, arguing for the primacy of matter over idea. Where Hegel saw the "spirit" as driving history, Marx saw this as an unnecessary mystification, obscuring the reality of humanity and its physical actions shaping the world. He wrote that Hegelianism stood the movement of reality on its head, and that one needed to set it upon its feet. Though inspired by French socialist and sociological thought, Marx criticised utopian socialists, arguing that their favored small-scale socialistic communities would be bound to marginalization and poverty, and that only a large-scale change in the economic system can bring about real change. The other important contribution to Marx's revision of Hegelianism came from Engels's book, *The Condition of the Working Class in England* in 1844, which led Marx to conceive of the historical dialectic in terms of class conflict and to see the modern working class as the most progressive force for revolution. Marx believed that he could study history and society scientifically and discern tendencies of history and the resulting outcome of social conflicts. Some followers of Marx concluded, therefore, that a communist revolution would inevitably occur. However, Marx famously asserted in the eleventh of his *Theses on Feuerbach* that "philosophers have only interpreted the world, in various ways; the point however is to change it", and he clearly dedicated himself to trying to alter the world.

Philosophy and Social Thought

Marx polemic with other thinkers often occurred through critique, and thus he has been called "the first great user of critical method in social sciences". He criticized speculative philosophy, equating metaphysics with ideology. By adopting this approach, Marx attempted to separate key findings from ideological biases. This set him apart from many contemporary philosophers.

Human Nature

Fundamentally, Marx assumed that human history involves transforming human nature, which encompasses both human beings and material objects. Humans recognize that they possess both actual and potential selves. For both Marx and Hegel, self-development begins with an experience of internal alienation stemming from this recognition, followed by a realization that the actual self, as a subjective agent, renders its potential counterpart an object to be apprehended. Marx further argues that, by molding nature in desired ways, the subject takes the object as its own, and thus permits the individual to be actualized as fully human. For Marx, then, human nature—*Gattungswesen*, or species-being—exists as a function of human labor. Fundamental to Marx's idea of meaningful labor is the proposition that, in order for a subject to come to terms with its alienated object, it must first exert influence upon literal, material objects in the subject's world. Marx acknowledges that Hegel "grasps the nature of *work* and comprehends objective man, authentic because actual, as the result of his *own work*", but characterizes Hegelian self-development as unduly "spiritual" and abstract. Marx thus departs from Hegel by insisting that "the fact that man is a *corporeal*, actual, sentient, objective being with natural capacities means that he has *actual, sensuous objects* for his nature as objects of his life-expression, or that he can only *express* his life in actual sensuous objects." Consequently, Marx revises Hegelian "work" into material "labor", and in the context of human capacity to transform nature the term "labor power".

Labor, Class Struggle, and False Consciousness

The history of all hitherto existing society is the history of class struggles.

—Karl Marx, *The Communist Manifesto*

Marx had a special concern with how people relate to that most fundamental resource of all, their own labor power. He wrote extensively about this in terms of the problem of alienation. As with the dialectic, Marx began with a Hegelian notion of alienation but developed a more materialist conception. Capitalism mediates social relationships of production (such as among workers or between workers and capitalists) through commodities, including labor, that are bought and sold on the market. For Marx, the possibility that one may give up ownership of one's own labor—one's capacity to transform the world—is tantamount to being alienated from one's own nature; it is a spiritual loss. Marx described this loss as commodity fetishism, in which the things that people produce, commodities, appear to have a life and movement of their own to which humans and their behavior merely adapt. Commodity fetishism provides an example of what Engels called "false consciousness", which relates closely to the understanding of ideology. By "ideology", Marx and Engels meant ideas that reflect the interests of a particular class at a particular time in history, but which contemporaries see as universal and eternal. Marx and Engels's point was not only that such beliefs are at best half-truths; they serve an important political function. Put another way, the control that one class exercises over the means of production includes not only the production of food or manufactured goods; it includes the production of ideas as well (this provides one possible explanation for why members of a subordinate class may hold ideas contrary to their own interests). An example of this sort of analysis is Marx's understanding of religion, summed up in a passage from the preface to his 1843 *Contribution to the Critique of Hegel's Philosophy of Right*:

> *Religious suffering is, at one and the same time, the expression of real suffering and a protest against real suffering. Religion is the sigh of the oppressed creature, the heart of a heartless world, and the soul of soulless conditions. It is the opium of the people. The abolition of religion as the illusory happiness of the people is the demand for their real*

happiness. To call on them to give up their illusions about their condition is to call on them to give up a condition that requires illusions. Whereas his Gymnasium senior thesis argued that religion had as its primary social aim the promotion of solidarity, here Marx sees the social function of religion in terms of highlighting/preserving political and economic status quo and inequality.

Economy, History and Society

Marx's thoughts on labor were related to the primacy he gave to the economic relation in determining the society's past, present and future (see also economic determinism). Accumulation of capital shapes the social system. Social change, for Marx, was about conflict between opposing interests, driven, in the background, by economic forces. This became the inspiration for the body of works known as the conflict theory. In his evolutionary model of history, he argued that human history began with free, productive and creative work that was over time coerced and dehumanized, a trend most apparent under capitalism. Marx noted that this was not an intentional process; rather, no individual or even state can go against the forces of economy. The organization of society depends on means of production. Literally those things, like land, natural resources, and technology, necessary for the production of material goods and the relations of production, in other words, the social relationships people enter into as they acquire and use the means of production. Together these compose the mode of production, and Marx distinguished historical eras in terms of distinct modes of production. Marx differentiated between base and superstructure, with the base (or substructure) referring to the economic system, and superstructure, to the cultural and political system. Marx regarded this mismatch between (economic) base and (social) superstructure as a major source of social disruption and conflict. Despite Marx's stress on critique of capitalism and discussion of the new communist society that should replace it, his explicit critique of capitalism is guarded, as he saw it as an improved society compared to the past ones (slavery and feudal). Marx also never clearly discusses issues of morality and justice, although scholars agree that his work contained implicit discussion of those concepts. Marx's view of capitalism was two-sided. On one hand, Marx, in the 19th century's deepest critique of the dehumanizing aspects of this system, noted that defining features of capitalism include alienation, exploitation, and recurring, cyclical depressions leading to mass unemployment; on the other hand capitalism is also characterized by "revolutionizing, industrializing and universalizing qualities of development, growth and progressivity" (by which Marx meant industrialisation, urbanization, technological progress, increased productivity and growth, rationality and scientific revolution), that are responsible for progress. Marx considered the capitalist class to be one of the most revolutionary in history, because it constantly improved the means of production, more so than any other class in history, and was responsible for the overthrow of feudalism and its transition to capitalism. Capitalism can stimulate considerable growth because the capitalist can, and has an incentive to, reinvest profits in new technologies and capital equipment.

According to Marx capitalists take advantage of the difference between the labor market and the market for whatever commodity the capitalist can produce. Marx observed that in practically every successful industry input unit-costs are lower than output unit-prices. Marx called the difference "surplus value" and argued that this surplus value had its source in surplus labour, the difference between what it costs to keep workers alive and what they can produce. Marx's dual view of capitalism can be seen in his description of the capitalists: he refers to them as to vampires sucking worker's blood, but at the same time, he notes that drawing profit is "by no means an injustice" and that capitalists simply cannot go against the system. The true problem lies with the "cancerous cell" of capital, understood not as property or equipment, but the relations between workers and owners—the economic system in general. At the same time, Marx stressed that capitalism was unstable, and prone to periodic crises. He suggested that over time, capitalists would invest more and more in new technologies, and less and less in labor. Since Marx believed that surplus value appropriated from labor is the source of profits, he concluded that the rate of profit would fall even as the economy grew. Marx believed that increasingly severe crises would punctuate this cycle of growth, collapse, and more growth. Moreover, he believed that in the long-term this process would necessarily enrich and empower the capitalist class and impoverish the proletariat. In section one of *The Communist Manifesto* Marx describes feudalism, capitalism, and the role internal social contradictions play in the historical process:

We see then: the means of production and of exchange, on whose foundation the bourgeoisie built itself up, were generated in feudal society. At a certain stage in the development of these means of production and of exchange, the conditions under which feudal society produced and exchanged ... the feudal relations of property became no longer compatible with the already developed productive forces; they became so many fetters. They had to be burst asunder; they were burst asunder. Into their place stepped free competition, accompanied by a social and political constitution adapted in it, and the economic and political sway of the bourgeois class. A similar movement is going on before our own eyes ... The productive forces at the disposal of society no longer tend to further the development of the conditions of bourgeois property; on the contrary, they have become too powerful for these conditions, by which they are fettered, and so soon as they overcome these fetters, they bring order into the whole of bourgeois society, endanger the existence of bourgeois property. Marx believed that those structural contradictions within capitalism necessitate its end, giving way to socialism, or a post-capitalistic, communist society.

The development of Modern Industry, therefore, cuts from under its feet the very foundation on which the bourgeoisie produces and appropriates products. What the bourgeoisie, therefore, produces, above all, are its own grave-diggers. Its fall and the victory of the proletariat are equally inevitable. Thanks to various processes overseen by capitalism, such as urbanization, the working class, the proletariat, should grow in numbers and develop class consciousness, in time realizing that they have to and can change the system. Marx believed that if the proletariat were to seize the means of production, they would encourage social relations that would benefit everyone equally, abolishing exploiting class, and introduce a system of production less vulnerable to cyclical crises. Marx argued in *The German Ideology* that capitalism will end through the organized actions of an international working class:

Communism is for us not a state of affairs which is to be established, an ideal to which reality will have to adjust itself. We call communism the real movement which abolishes the present state of things. The conditions of this movement result from the premises now in existence.

In this new society the self-alienation would end, and humans would be free to act without being bound by the labor market. It would be a democratic society, enfranchising the entire population. In such a utopian world there would also be little if any need for a state, which goal was to enforce the alienation. He theorized that between capitalism and the establishment of a socialist/communist system, a dictatorship of the proletariat—a period where the working class holds political power and forcibly socializes the means of production—would exist. As he wrote in his "Critique of the Gotha Program", "between capitalist and communist society there lies the period of the revolutionary transformation of the one into the other. Corresponding to this is also a political transition period in which the state can be nothing but the revolutionary dictatorship of the proletariat." While he allowed for the possibility of peaceful transition in some countries with strong democratic institutional structures (such as Britain, the US and the Netherlands), he suggested that in other countries with strong centralized state-oriented traditions, like France and Germany, the "lever of our revolution must be force."

Legacy of Marx

Marx is widely considered one of the most influential thinkers in history, who has had a significant influence on both world politics and intellectual thought. BBC polls have consistently found Marx considered as the top "thinker of the millennium". Robert C. Tucker credits Marx with profoundly affecting ideas about history, society, economics, culture, politics, and the nature of social inquiry. Marx's biographer Francis Wheen considers the "history of the twentieth century" to be "Marx's legacy", whilst philosopher Peter Singer believes that Marx's impact can be compared with that of Jesus Christ and Muhammad. Singer notes that "Marx's ideas brought about modern sociology, transformed the study of history, and profoundly affected philosophy, literature and the arts." Paul Ricœur calls Marx one of the masters of the "school of suspicion", alongside Friedrich Nietzsche and Sigmund Freud. Karl Löwith considered Marx and Søren Kierkegaard to be the two greatest Hegelian philosophical successors. Erich Fromm identifies Marx, together with Freud and Albert Einstein, as the "architects of the modern age", but rejects the idea that Marx and Freud were equally significant, emphasizing that he sees Marx as both far more historically important than Freud and a finer thinker. Philip Stokes says that Marx's ideas led to him becoming "the darling of both European and American intellectuals up until the 1960s". Marx has influenced disciplines such as archaeology, anthropology, media studies, political science, theater, history, sociological theory, cultural studies, education, economics, geography, literary criticism, aesthetics, critical psychology, and philosophy. Marx's widespread influence has been understood to be a result of his work's "morally empowering language of critique" against the dominant capitalist society. Later commentators agree that no other body of work was so relevant to modern times and simultaneously so outspoken about the need for change.

Marxism

Followers of Marx have drawn on his work to propose grand, cohesive theoretical outlooks dubbed "Marxism". This body of works has had significant influence on both politics and science. Nevertheless, Marxists have frequently debated among themselves over how to interpret Marx's writings and apply his concepts to the modern world. The legacy of Marx's thought has become contested between numerous tendencies, each of which sees itself as Marx's most accurate interpreter. These tendencies include Leninism, Stalinism, Trotskyism, Maoism, Luxemburgism, and libertarian Marxism. Various currents have also developed in academic Marxism, often under influence of other views, resulting in Structuralist Marxism, Historical Marxism, Phenomenological Marxism, Analytical Marxism and Hegelian Marxism. The Marxist revolutionary Che Guevara summed up his own appeal to Marxism by stating that Marx produced "a qualitative change in the history of social thought. He interprets history, understands its dynamic, predicts the future, but in addition to predicting it, he expresses a revolutionary concept: the world must not only be interpreted, it must be transformed." The German philosopher Ernst Bloch attempted to reveal what he considered the hidden metaphysical meaning of Marx's thought, which Leszek Kołakowski summarizes as, "a picture of the world tending towards a universal synthesis of all forces and factors, not only social phenomena but the cosmos as a whole." Kołakowski credits Bloch with helping to reveal the neo-platonic roots of Marxism.

There is a distinction between "Marxism" and "what Marx believed"; for example, shortly before he died in 1883, Marx wrote a letter to the French workers' leader Jules Guesde, and to his own son-in-law Paul Lafargue, accusing them of "revolutionary phrase-mongering" and of lack of faith in the working class. After the French party split into a reformist and revolutionary party, some accused Guesde (leader of the latter) of taking orders from Marx; Marx remarked to Lafargue, "What is certain to me is [that, if this is Marxism, then] I myself am not [a] Marxist." (In a letter to Engels, Marx later accused Guesde of being a "Bakuninist".)

Summary of Cultural Influence and Implication of Karl Marx

Karl Marx is no doubt the most influential thinker in the modern time. In a sense, Marx can be summed up as "political and spiritual Jesus Christ" for workers of all lands. No single thinker can be matched up to the position held by Karl Marx in that he with his theory has changed the fate of modern history. One semi-eastern country, Russia, which is the largest country in the world in terms of territory and one totally eastern country, China, which is the largest nation on earth in terms of population, staged two epoch-making revolutions respectively that changed the political and social systems of these two big countries, which in turn changed the political pattern of the whole world for the 20th century. With the disintegration of the former USSR, a pure of product of one of the major and pioneering offshoots of Marxism, Leninism, Marxism was abandoned as the state guiding principle while in China, clearly and expressively written on the Constitution of the country's ruling party, is Marxism as its top guiding ideology, among others. Given this hard fact, the influence of Karl Marx is by no means confined to cultural arena. In effect, Marx has always been regarded as the political thinker that mercilessly exposed the evils of capitalism with his sharp critical views. As such, among all the famous thinkers or theoreticians in modern time, Karl Marx probably has been the one who has been quoted, referred to most, loved and hated most, interpreted and misinterpreted most, least understood and most misunderstood and arguably most controversial, which alone is a prominent and complex cultural phenomenon beyond comprehension. It is hotly disputed as for what is the essence of Marxism and his historical position in human history. No matter how people regard him, Marx and his influence will definitely linger on as time goes by, which testifies the eternity nature of his doctrine. For good or bad, Marx has changed the minds of tens of millions. It can be predicted that debates, discussion, interpretation and study of this German Jewish thinker will not diminish, let alone, stop, at least for a foreseeable future.

Sigmund Freud: a Man Who Sees the World Through Dreams

Development of Psychoanalysis

On the basis of his early clinical work Freud postulated that unconscious memories of sexual molestation in early childhood were a necessary precondition for the psychoneuroses (hysteria and obsessional neurosis), a formulation now known as Freud's seduction theory. By 1897, however, Freud had abandoned this theory, now arguing that the repressed sexual thoughts and fantasies of early childhood were the key causative factors in neuroses, whether or not derived from real events in the child's history. This would lead to the emergence of Freud's new theory of infantile sexuality, and eventually to the Oedipus complex. Freud's development of these new theories took place during a period in which he experienced several medical problems, including depression and heart irregularities, which became particularly acute after the death of his father in 1896. Suspecting them to be psychosomatic in origin and disturbed by a superstitious belief that he would die at the age of 51, Freud began exploring his own dreams and childhood memories. During this self-analysis, he became aware of the hostility he felt towards his father and also became convinced that he had developed sexual feelings towards his mother in infancy ("between two and two and a half years"), citing a memory of seeing her naked on a train journey. Richard Webster argues that Freud's account of his self-analysis shows that he "had remembered only a long train journey, from whose duration he deduced that he might have seen his mother undressing", and that Freud's memory was an artificial reconstruction.

Escape from Nazism

In 1930, Freud was awarded the Goethe Prize in recognition of his contributions to psychology and to German literary culture. In January 1933, the Nazis took control of Germany, and Freud's books were prominent among those they burned and destroyed. Freud quipped: "What progress we are making. In the Middle Ages they would have burned me. Now, they are content with burning my books." Freud continued to maintain his optimistic underestimation of the growing Nazi threat and remained determined to stay in Vienna, even following the Anschluss of 13 March 1938 in which Nazi Germany annexed Austria, and the outbursts of violent anti-semitism that ensued. Many famous names were soon to call on Freud to pay their respects, notably Salvador Dalí, Stefan Zweig, Leonard and Virginia Woolf, and H. G. Wells. Representatives of the Royal Society called with the Society's Charter for Freud to sign himself into membership. Bonaparte arrived towards the end of June to discuss the fate of Freud's four elderly sisters left behind in Vienna. Her subsequent attempts to get them exit visas failed and they were all to die in Nazi concentration camps. In the Spring of 1939 Anton Sauerwald arrived to see Freud, ostensibly to discuss matters relating to the assets of the IPA. He was able to do Freud one last favor. He returned to Vienna to drive Freud's Viennese cancer specialist, Hans Pichler, to London to operate on the worsening condition of Freud's cancerous jaw. Sauerwald was tried and imprisoned in 1945 by an Austrian court for his activities as a Nazi Party official. Responding to a plea from his wife, Anna Freud wrote to confirm that Sauerwald "used his office as our appointed commissar in such a manner as to protect my father". Her intervention helped secure his release from jail in 1947. In the Freud's new home at 20 Maresfield Garden, Hampstead, North London, Freud's Vienna consulting room was recreated in faithful detail. He continued to see patients there until the terminal stages of his illness. He also worked on his last books, *Moses and Monotheism*, published in German and English in 1938, and the uncompleted *Outline of Psychoanalysis* which was published posthumously.

Ideas

Freud began his study of medicine at the University of Vienna in 1873. He took almost nine years to complete his studies, due to his interest in neurophysiological research, specifically investigation of the sexual anatomy of eels and the physiology of the fish nervous system. He entered private practice in neurology for financial reasons, receiving his M. D. degree in 1881 at the age of 25. He was also an early researcher in the field of cerebral palsy, which was then known as "cerebral paralysis". He published several medical papers on the topic, and showed that the disease existed long before other researchers of the period began to notice and study it. He also suggested that William Little, the man who first identified cerebral palsy, was wrong about lack of oxygen during birth being a cause. Instead, he suggested that complications in birth were only a symptom. Freud hoped that his research would provide a solid scientific basis for his therapeutic technique. The goal of Freudian therapy, or psychoanalysis, was to bring repressed thoughts and feelings into consciousness in order to free the patient from suffering repetitive distorted emotions.

Classically, the bringing of unconscious thoughts and feelings to consciousness is brought about by encouraging a patient to talk about dreams and engage in free association, in which patients report their thoughts without reservation and make no attempt to concentrate while doing so. Another important element of psychoanalysis is transference, the process by which patients displace on to their analysts feelings and ideas which derive from previous figures in their lives. Transference was first seen as a regrettable phenomenon that interfered with the recovery of repressed memories and disturbed patients' objectivity, but by 1912 Freud had come to see it as an essential part of the therapeutic process. The origin of Freud's early work with psychoanalysis can be linked to Josef Breuer. Freud credited Breuer with opening the way to the discovery of the psychoanalytical method by his treatment of the case of Anna O. In November 1880, Breuer was called in to treat a highly intelligent 21-year-old woman (Bertha Pappenheim) for a persistent cough that he diagnosed as hysterical. He found that while nursing her dying father, she had developed a number of transitory symptoms, including visual disorders and paralysis and contractures of limbs, which he also diagnosed as hysterical. Breuer began to see his patient almost every day as the symptoms increased and became more persistent, and observed that she entered states of *absence*. He found that when, with his encouragement, she told fantasy stories in her evening states of *absence* her condition improved, and most of her symptoms had disappeared by April 1881. However, following the death of her father in that month her condition deteriorated again. Breuer recorded that some of the symptoms eventually remitted spontaneously, and that full recovery was achieved by inducing her to recall events that had precipitated the occurrence of a specific symptom. In the years immediately following Breuer's treatment, Anna O. spent three short periods in sanatoria with the diagnosis "hysteria" with "somatic symptoms", and some authors have challenged Breuer's published account of a cure. Richard Skues rejects this interpretation, which he sees as stemming from both Freudian and anti-psychoanalytical revisionism, that regards both Breuer's narrative of the case as unreliable and his treatment of Anna O. as a failure.

In the early 1890s Freud used a form of treatment based on the one that Breuer had described to him, modified by what he called his "pressure technique" and his newly developed analytic technique of interpretation and reconstruction. According to Freud's later accounts of this period, as a result of his use of this procedure most of his patients in the mid-1890s reported early childhood sexual abuse. He believed these stories, but then came to believe that they were fantasies. He explained these at first as having the function of "fending off" memories of infantile masturbation, but in later years he wrote that they represented Oedipal fantasies. Another version of events focuses on Freud's proposing that unconscious memories of infantile sexual abuse were at the root of the psychoneuroses in letters to Fliess in October 1895, before he reported that he had actually discovered such abuse among his patients. In the first half of 1896 Freud published three papers stating that he had uncovered, in all of his current patients, deeply repressed memories of sexual abuse in early childhood. In these papers Freud recorded that his patients were not consciously aware of these memories, and must therefore be present as *unconscious memories* if they were to result in hysterical symptoms or obsessional neurosis. The patients were subjected to considerable pressure to "reproduce" infantile sexual abuse "scenes" that Freud was convinced had been repressed into the unconscious. Patients were generally unconvinced that their experiences of Freud's clinical procedure indicated actual sexual abuse. He reported that even after a supposed "reproduction" of sexual scenes the patients assured him emphatically of their disbelief. As well as his pressure technique, Freud's clinical procedures involved analytic inference and the symbolic interpretation of symptoms to trace back to memories of infantile sexual abuse. His claim of one hundred percent confirmation of his theory only served to reinforce previously expressed reservations from his colleagues about the validity of findings obtained through his suggestive techniques.

The Unconscious

The concept of the unconscious was central to Freud's account of the mind. Freud believed that while poets and thinkers had long known of the existence of the unconscious, he had ensured that it received scientific recognition in the field of psychology. However, the concept made an informal appearance in Freud's writings. It was first introduced in connection with the phenomenon of repression, to explain what happens to ideas that are repressed; Freud stated explicitly that the concept of the unconscious was based on the theory of repression. He postulated a cycle in which ideas are repressed, but remain in the mind, removed from consciousness yet operative, then reappear in consciousness under certain circumstances. The postulate was based upon the investigation of cases of traumatic hysteria, which revealed cases where the behavior of patients could not be explained without reference to ideas or thoughts of which they had no awareness. This fact, combined with the observation that such behavior could be artificially induced by hypnosis, in which ideas were inserted into people's minds, suggested that ideas were operative in the original cases, even though their subjects knew nothing of them. Freud, like Breuer, found the hypothesis that hysterical manifestations were generated by ideas to be not only warranted, but given in observation. Disagreement between them arose, however, when they attempted to give causal explanations of their data: Breuer favored a hypothesis of hypnoid states, while Freud postulated the mechanism of defense. Richard Wollheim comments that given the close correspondence between hysteria and the results of hypnosis, Breuer's hypothesis appears more plausible, and that it is only when repression is taken into account that Freud's hypothesis becomes preferable.

Psychosexual Development

Freud hoped to prove that his model was universally valid and thus turned to ancient mythology and contemporary ethnography for comparative material. Freud named his new theory the Oedipus Complex after the famous Greek tragedy *Oedipus Rex* by Sophocles. "I found in myself a constant love for my mother, and jealousy of my father. I now consider this to be a universal event in childhood," Freud said. Freud sought to anchor this pattern of development in the dynamics of the mind. Each stage is a progression into adult sexual maturity, characterized by a strong ego and the ability to delay gratification (cf. *Three Essays on the Theory of Sexuality*). He used the Oedipus Conflict to point out how much he believed that people desire incest and must repress that desire. The Oedipus Conflict was described as a state of psychosexual development and awareness. He also turned to anthropological studies of totemism and argued that totemism reflected a ritualized enactment of a tribal Oedipal Conflict. Freud also believed that the Oedipus Complex was bisexual, involving an attraction to both parents.

Freud also believed that the libido developed in individuals by changing its object, a process codified by the concept of sublimation. He argued that humans are born "polymorphously perverse", meaning that any number of objects could be a source of pleasure. He further argued that, as humans develop, they become fixated on different and specific objects through their stages of development—first in the oral stage (exemplified by an infant's pleasure in nursing), then in the anal stage (exemplified by a toddler's pleasure in evacuating his or her bowels), then in the phallic stage. In the latter stage, Freud contended, male infants become fixated on the mother as a sexual object (known as the Oedipus Complex), a phase brought to an end by threats of castration, resulting in the *castration complex*, the severest trauma in his young life. (In his later writings Freud postulated an equivalent Oedipus situation for infant girls, the sexual fixation being on the father. Though not advocated by Freud himself, the term "Electra complex" is sometimes used in this context.) The repressive or dormant latency stage of psychosexual development preceded the sexually mature genital stage of psychosexual development. The child needs to receive the proper amount of satisfaction at any given stage in order to move on easily to the next stage of development; under or over gratification can lead to a fixation at that stage, which could cause a regression back to that stage later in life.

Id, Ego and Super-ego

In his later work, Freud proposed that the human psyche could be divided into three parts: Id, ego and super-ego. Freud discussed this model in the 1920 essay *Beyond the Pleasure Principle*, and fully elaborated upon it in *The Ego and the Id* (1923), in which he developed it as an alternative to his previous topographic schema (i. e. conscious, unconscious and preconscious). The id is the completely unconscious, impulsive, childlike portion of the psyche that operates on the "pleasure principle" and is the source of basic impulses and drives; it seeks immediate pleasure and gratification. Freud acknowledged that his use of the term "Id" (*das Es*, "the It") derives from the writings of Georg Groddeck. The super-ego is the moral component of the psyche, which takes into account no special circumstances in which the morally right thing may not be right for a given situation. The rational ego attempts to exact a balance between the impractical hedonism of the id and the equally impractical moralism of the super-ego; it is the part of the psyche that is usually reflected most directly in a person's actions. When overburdened or threatened by its tasks, it may employ defense mechanisms including denial, repression, and displacement. This concept is usually represented by the "Iceberg Model". This model represents the roles the id, ego, and super ego play in relation to conscious and unconscious thought. Freud compared the relationship between the ego and the id to that between a charioteer and his horses: the horses provide the energy and drive, while the charioteer provides direction.

Life and Death Drives

Freud believed that people are driven by two conflicting central desires: the life drive (libido or Eros) (survival, propagation, hunger, thirst, and sex) and the death drive. The death drive was also termed "Thanatos", although Freud did not use that term; "Thanatos" was introduced in this context by Paul Federn. Freud hypothesized that libido is a form of mental energy with which processes, structures and object-representations are invested. In *Beyond the Pleasure Principle*, Freud inferred the existence of the death instinct. Its premise was a regulatory principle that has been described as "the principle of psychic inertia", "the Nirvana principle", and "the conservatism of instinct". Its background was Freud's earlier *Project for a Scientific Psychology*, where he had defined the principle governing the mental apparatus as its tendency to divest itself of quantity or to reduce tension to zero. Freud had been obliged to abandon that definition, since it proved adequate only to the most rudimentary kinds of mental functioning, and replaced the idea that the apparatus tends toward a level of zero tension with the idea that it tends toward a minimum level of tension.

Legacy: Psychotherapy

Though not the first methodology in the practice of individual verbal psychotherapy, Freud's psychoanalytic system came to dominate the field from early in the twentieth century, forming the basis for many later variants. While these systems have adopted different theories and techniques, all have followed Freud by attempting to effect behavioral change through having patients talk about their difficulties. Psychoanalysis itself has, according to psychoanalyst Joel Kovel, declined as a distinct therapeutic practice, despite its pervasive influence on psychotherapy. The neo-Freudians, a group understood by Kovel to include Adler, Rank, Horney, Harry Stack Sullivan and Erich Fromm, rejected Freud's theory of instinctual drive, emphasized interpersonal relations and self-assertiveness, and made modifications to therapeutic practice that reflected these theoretical shifts. Adler originated the approach, although his influence was indirect due to his inability to systematically formulate his ideas. In Kovel's view, neo-Freudian practice shares the same assumption as most current therapeutic approaches in the United States: "If what is wrong with people follows directly from bad experience, then therapy can be in its basics nothing but good experience as a corrective." Neo-Freudian analysis therefore places more emphasis on the patient's relationship with the analyst and less on exploration of the unconscious.

Jung believed that the collective unconscious, which reflects the cosmic order and the history of the human species, is the most important part of the mind. It contains archetypes, which are manifested in symbols that appear in dreams, disturbed states of mind, and various products of culture. Jungians are less interested in infantile development and psychological conflict between wishes and the forces that frustrate them than in integration between different parts of the person. The object of Jungian therapy was to mend such splits. Jung focused in particular on problems of middle and later life. His objective was to allow people to experience the split-off aspects of themselves, such as the anima (a man's suppressed female self), the animus (a woman's suppressed male self), or the shadow (an inferior self-image), and thereby attain wisdom. Lacan approached psychoanalysis through linguistics and literature. Lacan believed that Freud's essential work had been done prior to 1905, and concerned the interpretation of dreams, neurotic symptoms, and slips, which had been based on a revolutionary way of understanding language and its relation to experience and subjectivity. Lacan believed that ego psychology and object relations theory were based upon misreadings of Freud's work; for Lacan, the determinative dimension of human experience is neither the self (as in ego psychology) nor relations with others (as in object relations theory), but language. Lacan saw desire as more important than need, and considered it necessarily ungratifiable.

Science

Research projects designed to empirically test Freud's theories have led to a vast literature on the topic. Seymour Fisher and Roger P. Greenberg concluded in 1977, on the basis of their analysis of research literature, that Freud's concepts of oral and anal personality constellations, his account of the role of Oedipal factors in certain aspects of male personality functioning, his formulations about the relatively greater concern about loss of love in women's as compared to men's personality economy, and his views about the instigating effects of homosexual anxieties on the formation of paranoid delusions were supported by empirical evidence. They also found limited and equivocal support for Freud's theories about the development of homosexuality. However, they found that several of Freud's other theories, including his portrayal of dreams as primarily containers of secret, unconscious wishes, as well as some of his views about the psychodynamics of women, were either not supported or contradicted by research. Reviewing the issues again in 1996, they concluded that much experimental data relevant to Freud's work exists, and supports some of his major ideas and theories. Fisher and Greenberg's similar conclusions in their more extensive earlier volume on experimental studies have, however, been strongly criticized for alleged methodological deficiencies by Paul Kline, who writes that they "accept results at their face value with almost no consideration of methodological adequacy", and by Edward Erwin.

Philosophy

Psychoanalysis has been interpreted as both radical and conservative. By the 1940s, it had come to be seen as conservative by the European and American intellectual community. Critics outside the psychoanalytic movement, whether on the political left or right, saw Freud as a conservative. Fromm had argued that several aspects of psychoanalytic theory served the interests of political reaction in his *The Fear of Freedom* (1942), an assessment confirmed by sympathetic writers on the right. Philip Rieff's *Freud: The Mind of the Moralist* (1959) portrayed Freud as a man who urged men to make the best of an inevitably unhappy fate, and admirable for that reason. Three books published in the 1950s challenged the then prevailing interpretation of Freud as a conservative: Herbert Marcuse's *Eros and Civilization* (1955), Lionel Trilling's *Freud and the Crisis of Our Culture*, and Norman O. Brown's *Life Against Death* (1959). *Eros and Civilization* helped make the idea that Freud and Marx were addressing similar questions from different perspectives credible to the left. Marcuse criticized neo-Freudian revisionism for discarding seemingly pessimistic theories such as the death instinct, arguing that they could be turned in a Utopian direction. Freud's theories also influenced the Frankfurt school and critical theory as a whole.

Jean-Paul Sartre critiques Freud's theory of the unconscious in *Being and Nothingness*, claiming that consciousness is essentially self-conscious. Sartre also attempts to adapt some of Freud's ideas to his own account of human life, and thereby develop an "existential psychoanalysis" in which causal categories are replaced by teleological categories. Maurice Merleau-Ponty considers Freud to be one of the anticipators of phenomenology, while Theodor W. Adorno considers Edmund Husserl, the founder of phenomenology, to be Freud's philosophical opposite, writing that Husserl's polemic against psychologism could have been directed against psychoanalysis. Paul Ricœur sees Freud as a master of the "school of suspicion", alongside Marx and Nietzsche. Ricœur and Jürgen Habermas have helped create "a distinctly hermeneutic version of Freud", one which "claimed him as the most significant progenitor of the shift from an objectifying, empiricist understanding of the human realm to one stressing subjectivity and interpretation." Louis Althusser drew on Freud's concept of overdetermination for his reinterpretation of Marx's *Capital*. Jean-François Lyotard developed a theory of the unconscious that reverses Freud's account of the dream-work: for Lyotard, the unconscious is a force whose intensity is manifest via disfiguration rather than condensation. Jacques Derrida finds Freud to be both a late figure in the history of western metaphysics and, with Nietzsche and Heidegger, an important precursor of his own brand of radicalism.

Gellner sees Freud as parallel to Plato, writing that they hold nearly the same theory of dreams and have similar theories of the tripartite structure of the human soul or personality. Gellner concludes that Freud's theories are an inversion of Plato's. Whereas Plato saw a hierarchy inherent in the nature of reality, and relied upon it to validate norms, Freud was a naturalist who could not follow such an approach. Both men's theories drew a parallel between the structure of the human mind and that of society, but while Plato wanted to strengthen the super-ego, which corresponded to the aristocracy, Freud wanted to strengthen the ego, which corresponded to the middle class. Michel Foucault writes that Plato and Freud meant different things when they claimed that dreams fulfill desires, since the meaning of a statement depends on its relation to other propositions. Paul Vitz compares Freudian psychoanalysis to Thomism, noting St. Thomas's belief in the existence of an "unconscious consciousness" and his "frequent use of the word and concept 'libido'—sometimes in a more specific sense than Freud, but always in a manner in agreement with the Freudian use." Vitz suggests that Freud may have been unaware that his theory of the unconscious was reminiscent of Aquinas. Bernard Williams writes that there has been hope that some psychoanalytical theories may "support some ethical conception as a necessary part of human happiness", but that in some cases the theories appear to support such hopes because they themselves involve ethical thought. In his view, while such theories may be better as channels of individual help because of their ethical basis, it disqualifies them from providing a basis for ethics.

Summary of Cultural Implication of Sigmund Freud

It is said that Freud read Shakespeare all his life, inspired and enlightened by the British playwright. No wonder he devoted his life time to the study of human being at different levels. Freud, with his rich imagination and intellectual talents, has gone deeper into human soul. No matter how abstractly systematic his theory about human psychology, Freud has been regarded as the founding father of psychoanalysis. Freud sees the whole world and human behavior through the lens of dream, a phenomenon that tells the sub-conscious or even unconscious mentality of human beings, which according to scientists, can't quantified with accurate data or experiments. It is true that any subject or discipline that falls into the category of social sciences is subject to the critical view that whenever something called science is involved in human behavior, it can't be pure science as human behavior itself can't be quantified to reveal its true nature. Many of Freud's theories are purely assumptive and as such can't be verified or falsified, which has led to many criticism of his theory. In spite of this, Freud's position as an outstanding fancy thinker or theorist in modern world can't be totally eradicated. Freud's contributions to psychoanalysis, interpretation of dreams or even to the study of libido, etc, don't demonstrate themselves so much in his own academic achievements as in the form of arousing and inspiring the widespread interest of other scholars and academicians in the field he served as a pioneer. Probably, Freud himself is not so clear about what he has been doing in his work effort for the sake of being sub-conscious or unconscious about his own existence. Culturally speaking, when people have begun to turn their attention to their own mental status and inner needs, that is a cultural manifestation of human behavior. Just as one commentator says, "Freud has no rivals among his successors because they think he wrote science, when he in fact wrote art." This gap for cognition reveals so much, which only cultural interpretations can tell.

Albert Einstein: a Contemporary Newton

Albert Einstein was a German-born Jewish theoretical physicist who developed the general theory of relativity, effecting a revolution in physics. For this achievement, Einstein is often regarded as the father of modern physics and the most influential physicist of the 20th century. While best known for his mass—energy equivalence formula $E = mc^2$ (which has been dubbed "the world's most famous equation"), he received the 1921 Nobel Prize in Physics "for his services to theoretical physics, and especially for his discovery of the law of the photoelectric effect". The latter was pivotal in establishing quantum theory. Near the beginning of his career, Einstein thought that Newtonian mechanics was no longer enough to reconcile the laws of classical mechanics with the laws of the electromagnetic field. This led to the development of his special theory of relativity. He realized, however, that the principle of relativity could also be extended to gravitational fields, and with his subsequent theory of gravitation in 1916, he published a paper on the general theory of relativity. He continued to deal with problems of statistical mechanics and quantum theory, which led to his explanations of particle theory and the motion of molecules. He also investigated the thermal properties of light which laid the foundation of the photon theory of light. In 1917, Einstein applied the general theory of relativity to model the structure of the universe as a whole. He was visiting the United States when Adolf Hitler came to power in 1933, and did not go back to Germany, where he had been a professor at the Berlin Academy of Sciences. He settled in the U.S., becoming a citizen in 1940. On the eve of World War II, he helped alert President Franklin D. Roosevelt that Germany might be developing an atomic weapon, and recommended that the U.S. begin similar research; this eventually led to what would become the Manhattan Project. Einstein was in support of defending the Allied forces, but largely denounced using the new discovery of nuclear fission as a weapon. Later, with the British philosopher Bertrand Russell, Einstein signed the Russell—

Einstein Manifesto, which highlighted the danger of nuclear weapons. Einstein was affiliated with the Institute for Advanced Study in Princeton, New Jersey, until his death in 1955. Einstein published more than 300 scientific papers along with over 150 non-scientific works. His great intellectual achievements and originality have made the word "Einstein" synonymous with genius.

Academic Career

In 1901, his paper "Folgerungen aus den Kapillarität Erscheinungen" ("Conclusions from the Capillarity Phenomena") was published in the prestigious *Annalen der Physik*. On 30 April 1905, Einstein completed his thesis, with Alfred Kleiner, Professor of Experimental Physics, serving as *pro-Forma* adviser. Einstein was awarded a PhD by the University of Zurich. His dissertation was entitled "A New Determination of Molecular Dimensions". That same year, which has been called Einstein's *annus mirabilis* (miracle year), he published four groundbreaking papers, on the photoelectric effect, Brownian motion, special relativity, and the equivalence of mass and energy, which were to bring him to the notice of the academic world. By 1908, he was recognized as a leading scientist, and he was appointed lecturer at the University of Bern. The following year, he quit the patent office and the lectureship to take the position of physics docent at the University of Zurich. He became a full professor at Karl-ferdinand University in Prague in 1911. In 1914, he returned to Germany after being appointed director of the Kaiser Wilhelm Institute for Physics (1914—1932) and a professor at the Humboldt University of Berlin, with a special clause in his contract that freed him from most teaching obligations. He became a member of the Prussian Academy of Sciences. In 1916, Einstein was appointed president of the German Physical Society (1916—1918). During 1911, he had calculated that, based on his new theory of general relativity, light from another star would be bent by the Sun's gravity. That prediction was claimed confirmed by observations made by a British expedition led by Sir Arthur Eddington during the solar eclipse of 29 May 1919. International media reports of this made Einstein world famous. On 7 November 1919, the leading British newspaper *The Times* printed a banner headline that read: "Revolution in Science—New Theory of the Universe—Newtonian Ideas Overthrown". Much later, questions were raised whether the measurements had been accurate enough to support Einstein's theory. In 1980 historians John Earman and Clark Glymour published an analysis suggesting that Eddington had suppressed unfavorable results. The two reviewers found possible flaws in Eddington's selection of data, but their doubts, although widely quoted and, indeed, now with a "mythical" status almost equivalent to the status of the original observations, have not been confirmed. Eddington's selection from the data seems valid and his team indeed made astronomical measurements verifying the theory. In 1921, Einstein was awarded the Nobel Prize in Physics for his explanation of the photoelectric effect, as relativity was considered still somewhat controversial. He also received the Copley Medal from the Royal Society in 1925.

Emigration to U.S. in 1933

In February 1933 while on a visit to the United States, Einstein decided not to return to Germany due to the rise to power of the Nazis under Germany's new chancellor. He visited American universities in early 1933 where he undertook his third two-month visiting professorship at the California Institute of Technology in Pasadena. He and his wife Elsa returned by ship to Belgium at the end of March. During the voyage they were informed that their cottage was raided by the Nazis and his personal sailboat had been confiscated. Upon landing in Antwerp on 28 March, he immediately went to the German consulate where he turned in his passport and formally renounced his German citizenship. In early April, he learned that the new German government had passed laws barring Jews from holding any official positions, including teaching at universities. A month later, Einstein's works were among those targeted by Nazi book burnings, and Nazi propaganda minister Joseph Goebbels proclaimed, "Jewish intellectualism is dead." Einstein also learned that his name was on a list of assassination targets, with a "$5,000 bounty on his head". One German magazine included him in a list of enemies of the German regime with the phrase, "not yet hanged". He resided in Belgium for some months, before temporarily living in England. In a letter to his friend, physicist Max Born, who also emigrated from Germany and lived in England, Einstein wrote, "... I must confess that the degree of their brutality and cowardice came as something of a surprise." In October 1933 he returned to the U.S. and took up a position at the Institute for Advanced Study at Princeton, New Jersey, that required his presence for six months each year. He was still undecided on his future (he had offers from European universities, including Oxford), but in 1935 he arrived at the decision to remain permanently in the United States and apply for citizenship. His affiliation with the Institute for Advance Studies would last until his death in 1955. He was one of the four first selected (two of the others being John von Neumann and Kurt Gödel) at the new Institute, where he soon developed a close friendship with Gödel. The two would take long walks together discussing their work.

World War II and the Manhattan Project

In 1939, a group of Hungarian scientists that included emigre physicist Leó Szilárd attempted to alert Washington of ongoing Nazi atomic bomb research. The group's warnings were discounted. Einstein and Szilárd, along with other refugees such as Edward Teller and Eugene Wigner, "regarded it as their responsibility to alert Americans to the possibility that German scientists might win the race to build an atomic bomb, and to warn that Hitler would be more than willing to resort to such a weapon." In the summer of 1939, a few months before the beginning of World War II in Europe, Einstein was persuaded to lend his prestige by writing a letter with Szilárd to President Franklin D. Roosevelt to alert him of the possibility. The letter also recommended that the U.S. government pay attention to and become directly involved in uranium research and associated chain reaction research. The letter is believed to be "arguably the key stimulus for the U.S. adoption of serious investigations into nuclear weapons on the eve of the U.S. entry into World War II". President Roosevelt could not take the risk of allowing Hitler to possess atomic bombs first. As a result of Einstein's letter and his meetings with Roosevelt, the U.S. entered the "race" to develop the bomb, drawing on its "immense material, financial, and scientific resources" to initiate the Manhattan Project. It became the only country to successfully develop an atomic bomb during World War II. For Einstein, "war was a disease and he called for resistance to war." But in 1933, after Hitler assumed full power in Germany, "he renounced pacifism altogether. In fact, he urged the western powers to prepare themselves against another German onslaught." In 1954, a year before his death, Einstein said to his old friend, Linus Pauling, "I made one great mistake in my life—when I signed the letter to President Roosevelt recommending that atom bombs be made; but there was some justification—the danger that the Germans would make them." Einstein became an American citizen in 1940. Not long after settling into his career at Princeton, he expressed his appreciation of the "meritocracy" in American culture when compared to Europe. According to Isaacson, he recognized the "right of individuals to say and think what they pleased", without social barriers, and as result, the individual was "encouraged" to be more creative, a trait he valued from his own early education. Einstein writes:

> *What makes the new arrival devoted to this country is the democratic trait among the people. No one humbles himself before another person or class... American youth has the*

good fortune not to have its outlook troubled by outworn traditions.

As a member of the National Association for the Advancement of Colored People (NAACP) at Princeton who campaigned for the civil rights of African Americans, Einstein corresponded with civil rights activist W. E. B. Du Bois, and in 1946 Einstein called racism America's "worst disease". He later stated, "Race prejudice has unfortunately become an American tradition which is uncritically handed down from one generation to the next. The only remedies are enlightenment and education". During the final stage of his life, Einstein transitioned to a vegetarian lifestyle, arguing that "the vegetarian manner of living by its purely physical effect on the human temperament would most beneficially influence the lot of mankind". After the death of Israel's first president, Chaim Weizmann, in November 1952, Prime Minister David Ben-Gurion offered Einstein the position of President of Israel, a mostly ceremonial post. The offer was presented by Israel's ambassador in Washington, Abba Eban, who explained that the offer "embodies the deepest respect which the Jewish people can repose in any of its sons". However, Einstein declined, and wrote in his response that he was "deeply moved", and "at once saddened and ashamed" that he could not accept it:

All my life I have dealt with objective matters, hence I lack both the natural aptitude and the experience to deal properly with people and to exercise official function. I am the more distressed over these circumstances because my relationship with the Jewish people became my strongest human tie once I achieved complete clarity about our precarious position among the nations of the world.

Scientific Career

Throughout his life, Einstein published hundreds of books and articles. In addition to the work he did by himself he also collaborated with other scientists on additional projects including the Bose—Einstein statistics, the Einstein refrigerator and others.

General Principles

He articulated the principle of relativity. This was understood by Hermann Minkowski to be a generalization of rotational invariance from space to space-time. Other principles postulated by Einstein and later vindicated are the principle of equivalence and the principle of adiabatic invariance of the quantum number.

Theory of Relativity and $E = MC^2$

Einstein's "Zur Elektrodynamik bewegter Körper" ("On the Electrodynamics of Moving Bodies") was received on 30 June 1905 and published 26 September of that same year. It reconciles Maxwell's equations for electricity and magnetism with the laws of mechanics, by introducing major changes to mechanics close to the speed of light. This later became known as Einstein's special theory of relativity.

Consequences of this include the time-space frame of a moving body appearing to slow down and contract (in the direction of motion) when measured in the frame of the observer. This paper also argued that the idea of a luminiferous aether—one of the leading theoretical entities in physics at the time—was superfluous. In his paper on *mass-energy equivalence* Einstein produced $E = mc^2$ from his special relativity equations. Einstein's 1905 work on relativity remained controversial for many years, but was accepted by leading physicists, starting with Max Planck.

General Relativity and the Equivalence Principle

General relativity (GR) is a theory of gravitation that was developed by Albert Einstein between 1907 and 1915. According to general relativity, the observed gravitational attraction between masses results from the warping of space and time by those masses. General relativity has developed into an essential tool in modern astrophysics. It provides the foundation for the current understanding of black holes, regions of space where gravitational attraction is so strong that not even light can escape. As Albert Einstein later said, the reason for the development of general relativity was that the preference of inertial motions within special relativity was unsatisfactory, while a theory which from the outset prefers no state of motion (even accelerated ones) should appear more satisfactory. So in 1908 he published an article on acceleration under special relativity. In that article, he argued that free fall is really inertial motion, and that for a free falling observer the rules of special relativity must apply. This argument is called the Equivalence Principle. In the same article, Einstein also predicted the phenomenon of gravitational time dilation. In 1911, Einstein published another article expanding on the 1907 article, in which additional effects such as the deflection of light by massive bodies were predicted.

Political and Religious Views

Albert Einstein's political view was in favor of socialism; his political views emerged publicly in the middle of the 20th century due to his fame and reputation for genius. Einstein offered to and was called on to give judgments and opinions on matters often unrelated to theoretical physics or mathematics. Einstein's views about religious belief have been collected from interviews and original writings. These views covered Judaism, theological determinism, agnosticism, and humanism. He also wrote much about ethical culture, opting for Spinoza's god over belief in a personal god.

Summary of Cultural Implications of Albert Einstein

Two things stand out as fundamental and solid pillars of the western culture, which means that they have constituted the very roots and foundations of the western cultural evolution and development. One is religious faith as solely represented by Christianity and the other is science vivified by technological development and rationalism that have enhanced the global position of the West since 14th century and changed the way people live, work and play forever. If Jesus Christ, and probably such earlier legendary figures as Abraham and Moses, coincidentally, all of them being Jewish sagas, represent the pillar of religious faith, then the other pillar of science is symbolized by two most important scientists in the West, Sir Isaac Newton (although Newton is not a Jew, his given name is very Jewish) and Albert Einstein, who each has made unique contributions to the West in terms of scientific discoveries and theoretical innovations that have pushed the whole human society forward, thus changing human history once and for all. Einstein is above all an outstanding scientist and his contributions to human beings go far beyond scientific field. His theory of relativity is said to have been related with the invention of atomic bombs and other weapons of mass destruction (WMD), a fact that has defined future fate of human beings. Even since the existence of WMDs, which is like a Damocles' Sword, human beings have been living in a threat that may lead to the total destruction of not only whole human beings, but also of total earth. It is in this sense that modern science has presented a double-face image and modern Frankenstein. The scientific discovery and rational spirit, which have made possible the hegemonic position of the West in modern world, may by accident or by fate exterminate human civilization as a whole. From the theory of relativity by Einstein, one lesson can be drawn that all is relative and what is good or bad, boon or otherwise, all depends on specific occasions and circumstance. Nothing is absolute including death and tax. If nothing is impossible, human beings shall run into an eternal fear of future uncertainty. A remedy for such fear, according to some people, lies in the return to religious faith, forgotten and forsaken in modern time by people who seem to fear nothing including God. If this world is full of fearless people, it is not far from being destroyed, at least spiritually.

Questions or Topics for Pondering and Further Discussion for the PART TWO:

1. It is said that the history of Jewish people is a history of trials and tribulations. Please make comment on it.
2. Jewish people in history were viewed with disrespect in many literary works. Please give some examples and tell the reasons behind this fact.
3. Jewish people are famous for their talents in doing business. Why is that?
4. What is the Jewish business ethic? Making money or testifying their own ability or both?
5. What are the life principles of Jewish people?
6. Why could such evil anti-human crime as Holocaust happen in Europe in the modern era?
7. Is it morally right or legally justified to establish the State of Israel?
8. What is the core knot of the conflict between Israel and Palestine?
9. How do you account for business success of so many Jewish people?
10. Is it coincidental that so many Jews have made remarkable contributions in so many fields?
11. Some people compare Chinese to Jews, claiming Chinese are eastern Jews. Please make some comment.
12. In addition to these six excellent Jews listed in the Case Study, are there any other Jews you know who have made great contributions to the world?
13. Why does Shakespeare portray such a figure as "Shylock" in his play?
14. Do you believe some races are superior to others? Why or why not?
15. What is the Jewish image as a whole around the world?

PART THREE

Exercises for the Textbook

Fact-finding Quiz on Western Culture Course

Designer's remarks: *this quiz is not designed to test the students concerned in a surprised way. Rather, it is provided as such that the instructor can find out through students' answers some basic information regarding the scope of knowledge and writing proficiency of the students who take this course so that the instructor can act accordingly in his lectures. However, the students' performance shall be taken into account when the instructor eventually evaluates the overall academic standings of the students for the course concerned. Therefore, the students are expected to complete this quiz seriously and in a self-motivated way.*

Ⅰ. **Answer the following questions briefly:**
 1. Why is the number 13 viewed as being unlucky in the West?
 2. Why do westerners regard SEVEN as a lucky number?
 3. There is a saying that western culture can be summed up with "three apples"(two and half apples) and the most updated version of "four apples" (three and half apples). Why is that?
 4. What are the seven deadly sins and their cultural significance?
 5. What are the seven Christian virtues?
 6. What is meant by so-called "Miller's Test?"
 7. In American movie check classification system, what does "PG" stand for? What does the idea as expressed in "PG" imply sociologically and culturally?
 8. In China, we normally put our family name first followed by given name while in the West, they put given name first followed by family name or last name as it is called. Why is that?
 9. What is the psychological and rational basis for the mentality of sympathizing the weak and worshipping the strong in the West?
 10. What is human nature? Is human nature more animal-like or culture-supported/determined?
 11. What is the principle hidden in the "jungle law"?
 12. What is the mechanism and driving force for human evolution?
 13. What is the relationship between civilization and geography?
 14. What is the relationship between culture and basic instinct?
 15. Why do westerners worship "force" or "power"?
 16. How much do you know about Alexander the Great of Macedonia?
 17. Why are lions and eagles regarded as strong cultural symbols in western Civilization?
 18. What can you see from American National Flag?
 19. What is the theme logo of French Revolution?
 20. Do you know the school motto of Harvard University or that of Yale? And please make some comments if you know.
 21. What is the greatness of William Shakespeare in western literature tradition?
 22. What is basic idea of commercial spirit?
 23. What is the true nature of American culture?
 24. What is meant by Kant's pure reason?
 25. How much do you know about existentialism?

II. A short essay question for you to answer in about 150 words each:

Note: you may choose any TWO of the following topics to answer.

1. Look at the following incomplete statement and complete your answer according to your own understanding. You are free to think about the answer in whatever way you can imagine.
   America is good only if...!
2. What has made the fundamental difference between Oriental Culture and Occidental Culture?
3. What is meant by Westernization in China's modernization drive?
4. What is the implication of so-called "Monkey Trial" in America in the 1950's?
5. Do you think a sudden accident like the death of a famous person can change the course of history? Why and why not, please cite one example to illustrate your view.
6. What is the difference between philosophical materialism and cultural/sociological materialism?
7. What are the three origins and components of Marxism?
8. How much do you know about the essence of Protestant work ethic?
9. What is meant by the Calvinist doctrine called "Justification by Faith Alone"?
10. Why is Jerusalem so important to the believers of Christianity, Judaism and Islam?
11. To err is humane, to forgive, divine.
12. "For Want of a Nail" is a proverbial rhyme showing that small actions can result in large consequences.

For Want of a Nail
For want of a nail the shoe was lost.
For want of a shoe the horse was lost.
For want of a horse the rider was lost.
For want of a rider the battle was lost.
For want of a battle the kingdom was lost.
And all for the want of a horseshoe nail.

A Sample Test Paper

Group One: Judge if each of the following statements is true or false.

1. Anthropologists and archaeologists in theory as well as in practice divide human races into four major ones: Caucasian race, Mongolian race, Hispanic race and Negroid race and Indians come out of Caucasian race.
2. It is said all human beings originated from Africa and all human beings in modern world are descendants of the people starting from present day East-central Africa. But there are still a lot of disagreements with this statement.
3. In the twentieth century, "culture" emerged as a concept central to anthropology, encompassing all human phenomena that are not purely results of human genetics.
4. Man must create culture in order to adapt himself to new environments so that he can obtain a sense of belongings and social identity.
5. The narrowest definition of culture is that culture as a value and behavior pattern demonstrates a way of life for a group of people in a society.
6. Pythagoras, philosopher and mathematician of ancient Greece, held the idea that all things in the world were related with number and he thought Number Seven is a holy and mystic number.
7. Protestant ethic is not widely regarded as the core value of traditional American culture even though WASP as a social group maintained a dominant position in American society for a long time.
8. Constantine the Great was the founder of Byzantine Empire, who was also the first Roman Empire that was converted to Christianity, which greatly enhanced the influence of Christian power in the West.
9. In any religion, faith is a core idea and concept. Faith is being sure of what we hope for and being not certain of what we do not see. Faith has to be tested via evidence and empirical data.
10. The components of traditional western philosophy include Astrology, Metaphysics, Epistemology, Ethics, Aesthetics, Mythology and Logics, to name only few.
11. Marxism firmly and persistently holds social being determines social consciousness, which is known as dialectical and historical idealism.
12. The core and central idea of Evolutionism is natural selection and elimination of species over time and the survival of the fittest as expressed in jungle law.
13. Every language is a special way of looking at the world and interpreting one's social experience. A language is, in a sense, a philosophy.
14. In terms of linguistic origins, English is closer to French than to German that falls in the category of Roman family of language that is within Indo-european language system.
15. The rise of agriculture and domestication of animals for living purposes led to stable human settlements, which marked a new era of human civilization.
16. All societies, urban or rural, complex or simple, possesses culture. However, not every society can be called one with civilization or civilized society. Civilization is a high degree of culture.
17. western culture is said to be deeply rooted in three traditions respectively represented by Greek and Roman humanistic heritages, Judeo-Christian religious doctrine or faith and scientific/technological innovation/revolution.

18. There are three great movements highlighting western Civilization, namely Renaissance, Crusade and Great Geographic Discovery.
19. Political conservatism is not among the six pillars of western Civilization, nor is liberalism.
20. Separation of church and state is among the core values of modern western culture. Theocracy is not accepted in western political ideas.
21. Two beliefs distinguish Christianity from all other religions: (1) Jesus Christ is the son of God, and God sent him to earth to live as humans live, suffer as humans suffer, and die to redeem mankind and (2) God gave his only begotten son, so that whosoever believes in him should not perish, but have ever-lasting life.
22. Colonialism is widely viewed as one of the five ideas that changed the world in modern age along with nationalism, socialism, romanticism and globalism or internationalism.
23. Clearly found in western Culture is a strong tradition of the importance of the rule of law which has its roots in Ancient Greece and Rome.
24. Mesopotamian civilization evolved from the region in the Lower Reach of the Nile between 4000 and 1000 BC marked by flood control and irrigation.
25. Hammurabi's Code, known as the earliest written laws in human civilization, provides the very basis, among others, for international commercial law concerning contracts, interest and mortgages.
26. Ancient Egyptian religion holds a belief in an immortal soul and reward for those who lived a just and honest life when they were alive.
27. The Ten Commandments of Moses, a covenant between Palestinians and their God, exert great influence upon the moral and ethic formation of western cultural tradition.
28. The fear of Number 13 in the West can find some origins in the Biblical stories and tales.
29. Feudalism in Europe was mainly a system of land holding—a system of holding land in exchange for military service. The word—feudalism was derived from the Latin—feudum, a grant of land.
30. The Trinity is an essential doctrine of mainstream Christianity. "Father, Son and Holy Spirit" represents both the immanence and transcendence of God.
31. There is a heavy and hot debate in terms of nature versus nurture concerning human nature. The idea that man is born both sinful and virtuous is deeply rooted in the western cultural tradition. Christianity holds that man can ascend to Heaven by doing good things in this life.
32. Out of the Reformation came Protestantism, the fundamental principles of which are three key ideas: (1) Scripture alone as the sole authority; (2) Justification by faith alone; and (3) Universal priesthood of believers.
33. The most distinguished spirit of any science, among others, is to challenge and question the established and authoritative doctrines and prove their validity through experiments. Three foundation sciences, namely, natural science, social science and humanity science all have three foundation disciplines each. For example, politics, economics and sociology are regarded as three basic disciplines of social science.
34. Religious Reformation in Europe is a social and intellectual movement to revive what has been lost in so-called Dark Ages, which refers to artistic and intellectual achievements of ancient Greco-Roman civilization.
35. Although the Crusades did not achieve their goal to regain the Holy land, they had an important effect on the future of both the East and the West. They brought the East into closer contact with the West. And they greatly influenced the history of Europe.

Crusades in general or on the whole helped to break down feudalism, which, in turn led to the rise of the monarchies.

36. Adam Smith, who has strong claim to being both the Adam and the Smith of systematic economics, was a professor of moral philosophy and it was at that forge that economics was made.

37. The modern history of human beings would have been more or less the same without Karl Marx and his theory. His role as a great thinker has been very much exaggerated in human history.

38. Newton's Third Law of Motion states that every object persists in its state of rest or uniform motion in a straight line unless it is compelled to change that state by forces impressed on it.

39. In 1099 the first crusade captured Jerusalem from the Muslims; in 1187 Saladin took it back. In 1453 Turkish Muslims took Constantinople. In 1492 Christians took Granada, the last Muslim state in Spain, thus the beginning of European expansion and domination over the world.

40. The Black Death in 13th century killed millions in Asia and North Africa, and maybe two Europeans in three.

41. In 1876 Alexander Bell showed off telephone, in 1879 Thomas Edison his electric lightening; in 1903 Orville and Wilbur Wright took to the air; in 1908 Henry Ford launched his Model T car; 1946 brought the first general-purpose computer; 1947 the first transistor. All of these events happened either in America or in Europe, which established and consolidated West position in modern world.

42. Three modern frontier sciences are evolution of heavenly bodies, origins of life and species and structure of elementary particles.

43. Two major outstanding themes of modern western culture are embodied in the idea of aristocracy of ancient Greece and Roman Empire and science and technology innovation of western Europe.

44. At the heart of the Renaissance Philosophy was the assertion of the greatness of man. Related to this is the belief in the promotion of wealth, pleasure and a frank admiration for the beauty of human body. This ran exactly counter to the medieval ascetical ideal of poverty and stoicism, and shifted man's interest from Christianity to humanity, from religion to philosophy, from heaven to earth, from beauty of God, and the house of God to the beauty of the human body.

45. Widely adored as Father of History, Herodotus wrote about the wars between Greeks and Persians. His history, full of anecdotes and digressions and lively dialogue, is wonderfully readable. He kept alive many traditional stories, which were not always accurate. His object in writing was that the great and wonderful deeds done by Greeks and Persians should not lack renown.

46. One of the most remarkable Marxian statements about human history is that all human history hereto is history of class struggle, especially the one between propertied class and propertyless class.

47. A Greek philosopher and a follower of Socrates, Aristotle founded the Academy, where he taught and wrote for much of the rest of his life. He presented his ideas in the form of dramatic dialogues, as in *The Republic*.

48. The Stoics were opposed to the Epicureans. To them, the most important thing in life was not—pleasure, but—duty. This developed into the theory that one should endure hardship and misfortune with courage. The history of western culture is one in which

people try to make alternate choice between restraints and abandonment in their attitudes towards enjoyment of life. Stoicism represents the latter attitude.
49. The history of western civilization, glorious and splendid as it is on the whole, is not all free from any evil or immorality. It also been smirched by such ugly spots as slave trade, destruction of aboriginal culture of Indians, religious wars and slaughters of pagans, drug business, military expansion and conquest of the weak and poor nations, and ruthless colonization of African and American continents and parts of Asia.
50. The rise of American pop culture has continued to maintain the hegemonic influence of the West upon the rest of the world although in many parts of the world. American pop culture, attractive as it is, sparkles lots of national resentments when brought into direct confrontation with local cultures.

Group Two: Judge if each of the following statements is true or false.
1. Sociologists and anthropologists in general agree to divide human races into three major ones: Caucasian race, Mongolian race and Negroid race and Indians come out of Mongolian race.
2. Creationists and evolutionists sharply disagree on the origins of human beings with the former holding that God creates everything including man and the latter insisting that human beings are product of long time evolution of animal species such as apes or monkeys.
3. In the eighteenth century, "culture" as an independent terminology emerged as a new concept central to anthropology and sociologists, including all human phenomena that are purely and directly results of human genetics.
4. Man must create culture in order to adapt himself to new environments so that he can obtain a sense of belongings and social identity.
5. The narrowest definition of culture is that culture demonstrates a way of life for a group of people in a society. In a sense, culture dictates a way of life for people living in a community.
6. Puritanism, which sets great store by asceticism that advocates plain-living life style, is widely regarded as foundation of traditional American culture. WASP used to represent the mainstream social power of American society. However, things have changed a lot in modern America.
7. Justin I was eastern Roman (Byzantine) Emperor from 518 to 527. He rose through the ranks of the Byzantine army and ultimately became its emperor, in spite of the fact he was illiterate and almost 70 years old at the time of accession.
8. The core of a culture is value, the core of which is religion. Faith or religious belief is being not sure of what we hope for and being certain of what we can't see.
9. The components of modern western philosophy include many branches such as Astrology, Metaphysics, Epistemology, Ethics, Aesthetics, Mythology and Logics, to name only few.
10. Dialectical idealism as represented by Hegel holds that social existence determines social consciousness, which is known as dialectical and historical idealism.
11. The fundamental idea of social Darwinism is jungle law applied to human society and the survival of the fittest among competitors.
12. Every language is a special way of looking at the world and interpreting one's social experience. A language is, in a sense, a philosophy.
13. The number of English native speakers is larger than that of Chinese. It is spoken

almost all over the world as a para-international language.
14. The rise of agriculture and domestication of animals for living purposes led to stable human settlements, which marked a new era of human civilization.
15. All societies, urban or rural, complex or simple, possesses culture. However, not every society can be called one with civilization or civilized society. Civilization is a low degree of culture.
16. western culture is deeply rooted in three traditions respectively represented by Greek and Roman humanistic heritages, Judeo-Christian religious doctrine and scientific/technological innovation and revolution.
17. It is widely accepted that there are three great movements highlighting western civilization, namely Renaissance, Crusade and Great Geographic Discovery.
18. Political realism is not among the six pillars of western civilization, nor is liberalism.
19. Separation of church and state is among the core values of modern western culture. Theocracy is not accepted in western political ideas.
20. Colonialism is widely viewed as one of the five ideas that changed the world in modern age along with nationalism, socialism, romanticism and globalism or internationalism.
21. Found in western culture is a tradition of the importance of the rule of law which has its roots in Ancient Greece and Rome.
22. Mycenaean civilization evolved from the region in the Lower Reach of the Nile between 4000 and 1000 BC marked by flood control and irrigation.
23. Napoleonic Code, known as the earliest written laws in human civilization, provides the very basis, among others, for international commercial law concerning contracts, interest and mortgages.
24. Ancient Persian religion holds a belief in an immortal soul and reward for those who lived a just life during their mortal life.
25. The Ten Commandments of Moses, a holy covenant between Hebrews and their God, exert great influence upon the moral and ethic formation of western cultural tradition.
26. Westerners have a strong inclination for the number "NINE" for some religious reasons.
27. In composition, Bible is a collection of religious writings comprising two parts: the Old Testament which is about God and the laws of God (consists of 39 books), the New Testament that conveys the doctrine of Jesus Christ (consists of 27 books).
28. The Trinity is an essential doctrine of mainstream Christianity. "Father, Son and Holy Spirit" represents both the immanence and transcendence of God.
29. Christianity is of the view that human beings are born with seven deadly sins that include wrath, avarice, gluttony, jealousy, lust, arrogance and laziness. Orthodox Christians also believe that human beings can't get rid of these sins unless they seek redemption of God by believing in Jesus Christ.
30. Out of the Reformation came Protestantism, the fundamental principles of which are three key ideas: (1) Scripture alone as the sole authority; (2) Justification by faith alone; and (3) Universal priesthood of believers.
31. The most outstanding and prominent spirit of any science, among others, is to challenge and question the established and authoritative doctrines and prove their validity through experiments. Karl Popper also firmly insists that falsification is one of the key features of any science.
32. The Enlightenment Movement is said to be a mass social and intellectual movement to revive what has been lost in so-called the Dark Ages, which refers to artistic and intellectual achievements of ancient Greco-Roman civilization that represented one of the

splendid peaks of the West.
33. John Alfred Marshall, who has strong claim to being both the Adam and the Smith of systematic economics, was a professor of moral philosophy and he concludes that almost all economic recessions, depressions or crises result from under-consumption and over-production.
34. The modern history of human beings would have been very much different without Karl Marx and his theory. His role as a great thinker can never be over-exaggerated in human history.
35. Newton's Second Law of Motion states that every object persists in its state of rest or uniform motion in a straight line unless it is compelled to change that state by forces impressed on it.
36. In 1099 the first crusade captured Jerusalem from the Muslims; in 1187 Saladin took it back. In 1453 Turkish Muslims took Constantinople. In 1492 Christians took Granada, the last Muslim state in Spain, thus the beginning of European expansion and domination over the world.
37. The Black Death in 14th century killed millions in Asia and North Africa, and maybe two Europeans in three. It is said that Black Death was brought to Europe via Mongolian arms led by Chengjisihan, a great Mongolian Warrior and Ruler.
38. In human history evolution process, the 19th and 20th centuries witnessed an age of scientific invention and revolution that greatly changed the way of life for common people. In 1876 Alexander Bell showed off telephone, in 1879 Thomas Edison his electric lightening; in 1903 Orville and Wilbur Wright took to the air; in 1908 Henry Ford launched his Model T car; 1946 brought the first general-purpose computer; 1947 the first transistor. All of these events happened either in America or in Europe, which assured the West a dominant position in modern world.
39. Three modern frontier sciences are evolution of heavenly bodies, origins of life and species and structure of elementary particles. Space exploration, genetic engineering including cloning and research into micro-world around us are closely related with these three fields.
40. Although American Revolution hails Liberty and Equality as its logo motto, slavery is no doubt a dirty page in its history even though some historians call it "necessary evil or peculiar institution". America has paid a heavy moral price for slavery.
41. Eros Cupid, a Greek mythological figure, a god for love, is son of Apollo who became a model for heroes.
42. William Shakespeare, one of the most understanding and productive playwright, who represents the spirit of Renaissance humanism, has produced so many famous tragic plays, among which are Hamlet, King Lear, Othello, to name only a few. In addition, he also wrote many chronicle plays.
43. One of the most significant themes of Renaissance Movement is to restore the value of human beings by placing them back in the center of the world by challenging and weakening the ecclesial authority.
44. Vasco da Gama, under the auspice of Spanish Queen Isabella, conducted a series of voyage that led to the discovery of the Cape of Hope, creating a sea route from Europe to India.
45. The ancient Greeks were curious about many things, including what made the universe. They had the spirit of free inquiry and were quite ready to drop established ideas, to speculate, to use their imagination and to form their own conclusions. They were also

not afraid to speak their minds.

46. A famous Greek philosopher and pupil of Plato, the tutor of Alexander the Great, and the author of works on logic, metaphysics, ethics, natural sciences, politics, and poetics, he profoundly influenced western thought. In his philosophical system theory follows empirical observation and logic, based on the syllogism, is the essential method of rational inquiry. The above-mentioned person is student of a famous student of Socrates.

47. Martin Luther was the German leader of the Protestant Reformation. His doctrine marked the first break in the unity of the Catholic Church, which heralded the rise of Protestantism.

48. Sigmund Freud, an Austrian social scientist and psychiatrist, divided human personality into three functional parts—Id, Ego and Superego. He has been widely claimed as founding father of psychoanalysis.

49. The history of western civilization, glorious and splendid as it is on the whole, is not free from any evil or immorality. It has also been smirched by such ugly spots as slave trade, opium transaction, military conquest and expansion, destruction of aboriginal culture of Indians, opium wars, and ruthless colonization of African continent.

50. Against the background of the age of information and economic globalization, the emergence and popularity of American pop culture, especially among younger generations, has continued to maintain the hegemonic influence of the West upon the rest of the world although in many parts of the world American pop culture, attractive as it is, sparkles many national resentments when brought into direct confrontation with local cultures.

Group Three: Judge if each of the following statements is true or false.

1. Archaeologists, anthropologists, historians and sociologists generally agree with the divisions of human races into four major ones: Caucasian race, Mongolian race, Hispanic race and Negroid race and Indians come out of Caucasian race.

2. It is generally accepted by academic world that all human beings originated from Africa and all human beings in modern world are descendants of the people starting from present day East-central Africa. But there are still a lot of disagreements with this statement.

3. In the twentieth century academic environment, the idea as expressed in "culture" emerged as a concept central to anthropology and sociology, encompassing all human phenomena that are not purely results of human genetics.

4. Man must create culture in order to adapt himself to new environments so that he can obtain a sense of belongings and social identity amid a fierce competitive biological and social world.

5. Culture entails many definitions at different levels. The narrowest definition of culture is that culture demonstrates a way of life for a group of people in a society.

6. Pythagoras, philosopher and mathematician of ancient Greece, held the idea that all things in the world were related with number and he thought Number Seven is a holy and mystic number. He is mostly remembered as the founder of Pythagorean Theorem that has something to do with triangles.

7. Puritan way of life based upon Protestant ethics is not widely regarded as the core value of traditional American culture even though WASP as a social group maintained a dominant position in American society for a long time.

8. Constantine the Great was the founder of Byzantine Empire, who was also the first Roman Empire that was converted to Christianity, which greatly enhanced the influence of Christian power in the West.
9. In any religion, eastern or western, faith is a central core idea. Faith is being sure of what we hope for and being not certain of what we do see around us in a natural world.
10. The chief components of traditional western philosophy include Astrology, Metaphysics, Epistemology, Ethics, Aesthetics, Mythology and Logics, to name only few. Philosophy in the old Greek time was not so important in people's academic pursuit.
11. Marxism holds that social existence determines social consciousness, which is known as dialectical and historical idealism that runs counter to materialism.
12. The central key idea of Evolutionism is natural selection and elimination of species over time and the survival of the fittest. Evolutionism as promulgated by Charles Darwin negates the theory of Creationism totally.
13. Every language is a special way of looking at the world and interpreting one's social experience. A language is, in a sense, a philosophy. Command of a language is the first step to understand the culture thus expressed by it.
14. In terms of linguistic origins, English is much closer to French than to German that falls in the category of Roman family of language which is within Indo-european language system. English is said to boast the largest number of native speakers in the world.
15. The appearance and development of agriculture and domestication of animals or taming animals for living purposes led to stable human settlements, which marked a new era of human civilization.
16. All societies, urban or rural, complex or simple, possesses culture. However, not every society can be called one with civilization or civilized society. Civilization is a high degree of culture. Nothing superior or inferior can be related with culture while civilization may have different degrees of its own evolution and development.
17. What is now understood as western culture is deeply rooted in three traditions respectively represented by Greek and Roman humanistic heritages, Judeo-Christian religious traditions and scientific/technological innovation/revolution, each of which stands for different features of western culture that demonstrate themselves in people's behavior that is responsible for their choice of actions.
18. Three great intellectual, social or religious movements such as Renaissance, Crusade and Great Geographic Discovery have highlighted the developmental process of western civilization.
19. western political theories abound and political conservatism is not among the six pillars of western Civilization, nor is liberalism.
20. In terms of state governing theory, separation of church and state is among the core values of modern western political culture. Theocracy is not accepted in western political institutional arrangement, nor in its practical political structure of power.
21. It is summed up that two fundamental beliefs distinguish Christianity from all other religions: (1) Jesus Christ is the son of God, and God sent him to earth to live as humans live, suffer as humans suffer, and die to redeem mankind and (2) God gave his only begotten son, so that whosoever believes in him should not perish, but have everlasting life.
22. Colonialism is widely viewed as one of the five ideas that changed the world in modern age along with nationalism, socialism, romanticism and globalism or internationalism. Value of ideas play very minor and little role in pushing human civilization forward.

23. Clearly found and deeply-rooted in western culture is a tradition of the importance of the rule of law which has its roots in Ancient Greece and Rome.
24. Mesopotamian civilization evolved from the region in the Lower Reach of the Nile between 4000 and 1000 BC marked by flood control and irrigation.
25. Hammurabi's Code, known as the earliest written laws in human civilization, provides the very basis, among others, for international commercial law concerning contracts, interest and mortgages.
26. Ancient religions pay much attention to what became of people after their death. Ancient Egyptian religion holds a firm belief in an immortal soul and reward for those who lived a just life when they were alive.
27. The Ten Commandments of Moses, a covenant between Palestinians and their God, exert great influence upon the moral and ethic formation of western cultural tradition.
28. Triskaidekaphobia can find some ancient origins in the Biblical story. So is Paraskavedekatriaphobia.
29. As a social structural system, feudalism in Europe was mainly a system of land holding — a system of holding land in exchange for military service. The word — feudalism was derived from the Latin — feudum which means a grant of land by kings to his lords.
30. The Trinity is an essential doctrine of mainstream Christianity. "Father, Son and Holy Spirit" represents both the immanence and transcendence of omnipotent and omnipresent God.
31. There is a heavy and hot debate in terms of nature versus nurture concerning human nature. The idea that man is born both sinful and virtuous is deeply rooted in the western cultural tradition. Christianity holds that man can ascend to Heaven by doing good things in this life.
32. Out of the Reformation came Protestantism, the fundamental principles of which are three key ideas: (1) Scripture alone as the sole authority; (2) Justification by faith alone; and (3) Universal priesthood of believers.
33. The most distinguished spirit of any science, among others, is to challenge and question the established and authoritative doctrines and prove their validity through experiments. Three foundation sciences, namely, natural science, social science and humanity science all have three foundation disciplines each. For example, politics, economics and sociology are regarded as three basic disciplines of social science.
34. Religious Reformation in Europe is a social and intellectual movement to revive what has been lost in so-called Dark Ages, which refers to artistic and intellectual achievements of ancient Greco-Roman civilization. It paved the way for Romantic literature to flourish in Europe.
35. Although the Crusades did not achieve their goal to regain the Holy Land, they had an important effect on the future of both the East and the West. They brought the East into closer contact with the West. And they greatly influenced the history of Europe. Crusades helped to break down feudalism, which, in turn led to the rise of the monarchies. In this sense, its significance is not totally negative.
36. Adam Smith, who has strong claim to being both the Adam and the Smith of systematic economics, was a professor of moral philosophy and it was at that forge that economics was made. Smith was a strong opponent of mercantilism that was not in favor of free trade.
37. The modern history of human beings would have been more or less the same without Karl Marx and his theory. His role as a great thinker has been very much exaggerated in

human history.

38. Newton's contribution to human world was of immense importance to present day society. Newton's Third Law of Motion states that every object persists in its state of rest or uniform motion in a straight line unless it is compelled to change that state by forces impressed on it.
39. The West started to rise especially after 1000. In 1099 the first crusade captured Jerusalem from the Muslims; in 1187 Saladin took it back. In 1453 Turkish Muslims took Constantinople. In 1492 Christians took Granada, the last Muslim state in Spain, thus the beginning of European expansion and domination over the world.
40. The notorious Black Death that occurred in 13th century killed millions of people in Asia and North Africa, and maybe two Europeans in three. However, it also purified and elevated quality of people then and there.
41. The West made rapid progress in scientific and technological fields after 19th century. In 1876 Alexander Bell showed off telephone, in 1879 Thomas Edison offered his electric lightening; in 1903 Orville and Wilbur Wright took to the air; in 1908 Henry Ford launched his Model T car; 1946 brought the first general-purpose computer; 1947 the first transistor. All of these events happened either in North America or in Europe, which established and consolidated West position in modern world.
42. Three modern frontier sciences are evolution of heavenly bodies, origins of life and species and structure of elementary particles, which in turn lead to rapid development of scientific and technological development in such fields as space exploration, genetic engineering, and peaceful use of nuclear energy.
43. Two major outstanding themes of modern western culture are obviously embodied in the idea of aristocracy of ancient Greece and Roman Empire and science and technology innovation of western Europe. Theocracy has been carried on till today in the West.
44. At the heart of the Renaissance Philosophy was the assertion of the greatness of man. Related to this is the belief in the promotion of wealth, pleasure and a frank admiration for the beauty of human body. This ran exactly counter to the medieval ascetical ideal of poverty and stoicism, and shifted man's interest from Christianity to humanity, from religion to philosophy, from heaven to earth, from beauty of God, and the house of God to the beauty of the human body.
45. Widely adored as Father of History in the West, Herodotus wrote about the wars between Greeks and Persians. His history, full of anecdotes and digressions and lively dialogues, is wonderfully readable. He kept alive many traditional stories, which were not always accurate. His object in writing was that the great and wonderful deeds done by Greeks and Persians should not lack renown.
46. One of the most remarkable Marxian statements about human history is that all human history hereto is history of class struggle. The nature of human life is exploitation of people by people and the final objective of Marxian revolution is to destroy this exploitative social system.
47. A Greek philosopher and a follower of Socrates, Aristotle founded the Academy, where he taught and wrote for much of the rest of his life. He presented his ideas in the form of dramatic dialogues, as in *The Republic*.
48. The Stoics were opposed to the Epicureans. To them, the most important thing in life was not—pleasure, but—duty. This developed into the theory that one should endure hardship and misfortune with courage. The history of western culture is one in which people try to make alternate choice between restraints and abandonment in their

attitudes towards enjoyment of life. Stoicism represents the latter attitudes.
49. The history of western civilization, glorious and splendid as it is on the whole, is not all free from any evil or immorality. It also been smirched by such ugly spots as slave trade, destruction of aboriginal culture of Indians, religious wars and slaughters of pagans, drug business, military expansion and conquest of the weak and poor nations, and ruthless colonization of African and American continents and parts of Asia.
50. The rise of American pop culture has continued to maintain the hegemonic influence of the West upon the rest of the world although in many parts of the world, American pop culture, attractive as it is, sparkles lots of national resentments when brought into direct confrontation with local cultures.
51. Islam, Christianity and Judaism along with Hinduism, Shintoism as well as Buddhism plus Taoism as major religions in the world all find their origins in Abrahamic religion that originated from Abraham, a legendary figure in the mid-East in ancient time.
52. The triple colors of French national flag represent the political ideals of French people. The logo slogan of French Revolution is liberty, equality and fraternity.
53. Britain has occupied a very unique position in western civilization in that it was birthplace of a few important revolutions. Without Britain, the world today would have been quite different.
54. Britain not only contributes to the world with a lot of brilliant ideas, but also great minds like Sir Issac Newton, William Shakespeare and so on.
55. A famous bridge in Beijing where a famous incident happened is more familiar to the West in the name of Marco Polo Bridge.
56. Matteo Ricci made great contributions to the cultural exchange between China and the then West and he was buried in China after his death.
57. T. S. Eliot is widely acclaimed as one of the greatest modern poet who was awarded Nobel Prize for literature in 1922 for his mastery of poetic language to express human dilemma in the modern world.
58. Sir is a noble title in Britain that can be inherited from generation to generation and the same is true of some other noble titles such as Marquis or Viscount.
59. The current monarch of the UK, Queen Elizabeth II would not have been in her current royal status but for her uncle who abdicated his crown for love.
60. American pop culture, a partial negation of its traditional Puritan or Protestant culture, represents an apex of western civilization with its popular cultural products that are spread out in a commercial way to the rest of the world, consolidating the western cultural domination of the world today.

Group Four: Judge if each of the following statements is true or false.
1. Historians, sociologists, anthropologists and archaeologist hold a general consensus that human races are divided into three major categories: Caucasian, Mongolian and Negroid races and Indians are of Mongolian race.
2. Evolutionists and Creationists have sharp disagreement concerning the origins of human beings with the latter holding that God creates everything including man and the former strongly insisting that human beings are product of long time evolution of animal species such as apes or monkeys.
3. In the history of intellectual development, around the 18th century, "culture" emerged as a new concept central to anthropology, including all human phenomena that are purely and directly results of human genetics.

4. Man must create culture in order to adapt himself to new environments so that he can obtain a sense of belongings and social identity that are so important for his mental and physical survival and thriving.
5. Culture presents itself with a diverse scope of definitions, which exhibits its complex feature. The broadest definition of culture is that culture demonstrates a way of life for a group of people in a society. In a sense, culture dictates a way of life for people living in a community.
6. As a theoretical as well as theological result of European Religious Reformation, Puritanism, which sets great store by asceticism that advocates plain-living life style, is widely regarded as foundation of traditional American culture. WASP used to represent the mainstream social power of American society. However, things have changed a lot in modern American society.
7. History records that Justin I was eastern Roman (Byzantine) Emperor from 518 to 527. He rose through the ranks of the Byzantine army and ultimately became its emperor, in spite of the fact he was illiterate and almost 70 years old at the time of accession.
8. The very core concept of a culture is value, the core concept of which is religion. And the core part of a religion is faith. Faith or religious belief is being cock sure of what people strongly hope for and being firmly certain of what people can't see around us in the world.
9. The major components of modern western philosophy include Astrology, Phrenology, Metaphysics, Epistemology, Ethics, Aesthetics, Mythology and Logics, to name only few. They all have played an important part or role in our mental and spiritual life.
10. Dialectical idealism held by Hegel holds that social existence determines social consciousness, which is known as dialectical and historical idealism that is against materialistic views about the universe.
11. The fundamental idea of social Darwinism is jungle law and the survival of the fittest. Along with biological Darwinism, there is a social Darwinism that is aimed at explaining the cruel reality of human world.
12. Every language is a special way of observing and interpreting the world and elucidating one's social and mental experience. A language is, in a sense, a philosophical way of expressing one's basic and fundamental ideas about life, love and other major themes of human existence.
13. The number of English native speakers is larger than that of Chinese. It is spoken almost all over the world as a para-international language. Spanish speakers are even more than native Chinese speakers.
14. The rise of agriculture and domestication of animals for living purposes led to stable human settlements, which marked a new era of human civilization. Agricultural civilization replaced hunting civilization and was replaced by industrial civilization.
15. All societies, urban or rural, complex or simple, possesses culture. However, not every society can be called one with civilization or civilized society. Civilization is a lower middle degree of culture that can be further improved through human efforts.
16. western culture is deeply rooted in three traditions as represented by Greek and Roman humanistic heritages, Judeo-Christian religious doctrine and scientific/technological innovation and revolution.
17. It is widely accepted that there are three great movements highlighting western civilization, namely Renaissance, Crusade and Great Geographic Discovery.
18. western history has undergone different stages of ideological development and gradually

formed some pillar ideas. Political realism is not among the six pillars of western civilization, nor is liberalism.

19. Within the political structure of western state theory, religious power should stay away from state affairs. Separation of church and state is among the core values of modern western culture. Theocracy is not accepted in western political ideas.
20. Colonialism is widely viewed as one of the five ideas that changed the world in modern age along with nationalism, socialism, romanticism and globalism or internationalism.
21. Found in western culture is a tradition of the importance of the rule of man or autocracy which has its deep roots in Ancient Greece and Rome, especially in Roman Oligarchy.
22. Mycenaean civilization evolved from the region in the Lower Reach of the Nile between 4000 and 1000 BC marked by flood control and irrigation.
23. Napoleonic Code, known as the earliest written laws in human civilization, provides the very basis, among others, for international commercial law concerning contracts, interest and mortgages.
24. Ancient Persian religion holds a belief in an immortal soul and reward for those who lived a just life during their mortal life.
25. The Ten Commandments of Moses, a covenant between Hebrews and their God, exert great influence upon the moral and ethic formation of western cultural tradition.
26. westerners have a strong inclination for the number "NINE" for some religious reasons and they seem to dislike or even hate No. 13.
27. Bible is a collection of religious writings comprising two parts: the Old Testament which is about God and the laws of God and the New Testament that conveys the doctrine of Jesus Christ.
28. The Trinity idea is essential to mainstream Christianity. "Father, Son and Holy Spirit" represents both the immanence and transcendence of God. No other religions have such concept in their doctrines.
29. Christianity is of the view that human beings are born with seven deadly sins that include wrath, avarice, gluttony, jealousy, lust, arrogance and laziness. Orthodox Christians also believe that human beings can't get rid of these sins unless they seek redemption of God by believing in Jesus Christ.
30. Out of the Religious Reformation came Protestantism, the fundamental principles of which are three key ideas listed as follows: (1) Scripture alone as the sole authority; (2) Justification by faith alone; (3) Universal priesthood of believers. Protestantism is a sort of mixture of liberalism and individualism in the disguise of religion.
31. Science was a concept in old time finding its origin in ancient Greece. The most outstanding and prominent spirit of any science, among others, is to challenge and question the established and authoritative doctrines and prove their validity through experiments. Karl Popper also firmly insists that falsification is one of the key features of any science.
32. Enlightenment Movement is said to be a social and intellectual movement to revive what has been lost in so called the Dark Ages, which refers to artistic and intellectual achievements of ancient Greco-Roman civilization.
33. John M Keynes, the author of "the General Theory", who has strong claim to being both the Adam and the Smith of systematic economics, was a professor of moral philosophy and he concludes that almost all economic recessions, depressions or crises result from under-consumption and over-production in economic affairs.
34. Many people have played a part in pushing human world forward. The modern history of

human beings would have been very much different without Karl Marx and his theory. His role as a great thinker can never be over-exaggerated in human history.

35. Newton's Second Law of Motion states that every object persists in its state of rest or uniform motion in a straight line unless it is compelled to change that state by forces impressed on it. Without Newton, human exploration into natural world would have been much delayed for sure.

36. The West began to overtake the East around 1000 when a series of wars were fought between Islamic world and Christian world. In 1099 the first crusade captured Jerusalem from the Muslims; in 1187 Saladin took it back. In 1453 Turkish Muslims took Constantinople. In 1492 Christians took Granada, the last Muslim state in Spain, thus the beginning of European expansion around the world.

37. Human history has witnessed a lot of disasters, natural or human. The Black Death in 14th century killed millions in Asia and North Africa, and maybe two Europeans in three.

38. History is full of milestone events that heralded new ages. The 19th and 20th centuries witnessed an age of scientific invention and revolution that greatly changed the way of life for common people. In 1876 Alexander Bell showed off telephone, in 1879 Thomas Edison his electric lightening; in 1903 Orville and Wilbur Wright took to the air; in 1908 Henry Ford launched his Model T car; 1946 brought the first general-purpose computer; 1947 the first transistor. All of these events happened either in North America or in Europe, which assured the West a dominant position in modern world.

39. Three modern frontier sciences are evolution of heavenly bodies, origins of life and species and structure of elementary particles. Space exploration, genetic engineering including cloning and research into micro-world around us are closely related with these three fields.

40. Although American Revolution hails Liberty and Equality as its logo motto, slavery is no doubt a dirty page in its history even though some historians call it "necessary evil or peculiar institution". America has paid a heavy moral price for slavery.

41. Ancient Greek mythology is one of the rich sources of western civilization, Eros Cupid, a Greek mythological figure, a god for love, is son of Apollo.

42. William Shakespeare, widely regarded as one of the most understanding playwrights, who represents the spirit of Renaissance humanism, has produced so many famous tragic plays, among which are Hamlet, King Lear, Othello, to name only a few.

43. One of the most significant themes of Renaissance Movement is to restore the value of human beings by placing them back in the center of the world and by challenging and weakening the ecclesial authority that used to be all-powerful and all-authoritative.

44. Vasco da Gama, under the auspice of Spanish Queen Isabella, conducted a series of voyage that led to the discovery of the Cape of Hope, creating a sea route from Europe to India, greatly shortening the distance between Europe and Asia for commercial transactions and transportation.

45. The ancient Greeks were curious about many things, including what made the universe. They had the spirit of free enquiry and were quite ready to drop established ideas, to speculate, to use their imagination and to form their own conclusions. They were also not afraid to speak their minds.

46. A famous Greek philosopher and pupil of Plato, the tutor of Alexander the Great, and the author of works on logic, metaphysics, ethics, natural sciences, politics, and poetics, he profoundly influenced western thought. In his philosophical system theory

follows empirical observation and logic, based on the syllogism, is the essential method of rational inquiry. The above-mentioned person is student of a famous student of Socrates.
47. Martin Luther was the German leader of the Protestant Reformation. His doctrine marked the first break in the unity of the Catholic Church, which heralded the rise of Protestantism as an antithetical theology to traditional Roman Catholic Church in many aspects.
48. Sigmund Freud, an Austrian social scientist and psychiatrist, divided human personality into three functional parts—Id, Ego and Superego. He has been widely claimed as founding father of psychoanalysis. Jung inherited much of Freud's intellectual achievements and made some of his own unique contributions to the science of psychoanalysis and psychiatrism.
49. History is like a mirror reflecting the true nature of human beings. The history of western civilization, glorious as it nay be in a way, is not free from any evil or immorality. It has also been smirched by such ugly spots as slave trade, opium transaction, military conquest and expansion, destruction of aboriginal culture of Indians, opium wars, and ruthless colonization of African continent.
50. Against the background of the age of information and economic globalization, the emergence and popularity of American pop culture, especially among younger generations, has continued to maintain the hegemonic influence of the West upon the rest of the world although in many parts of the world American pop culture, attractive as it is, sparkles many national resentments when brought into direct confrontation with local cultures.
51. Henry VIII was a leading figure in British religious reformation movement and he not only divorced his wives, but also conducted a divorce between English Church and Roman Catholic Church, which heralded a new age of England in terms of religion.
52. The major themes of Hamlet, among others, are about human choice and their dilemma in the process of making choices in life, which reflects tragic touch of human life.
53. Queen Elizabeth I was a key figure in helping Britain rise to its global power statues and she was the longest Monarch in reign only next to Queen Victoria who was in the reign from 1847 to 1901 when the British Empire reached its ace period.
54. Commercial civilization is a new stage of western civilization in that it is based upon the calculation of input and output ratio for the maximum returns of investment at a minimum cost.
55. The Great Geographical Discovery coupled with Great Ocean Voyage in the 13th and 14th centuries constituted the first peak of what is called today the process of globalization.
56. Marco Polo, Giuseppe Castiglione and Matteo Ricci made immense and magnificent contributions to the promotion of mutual understanding between the West and East. They came to China to discover the wonders of the land and brought back to their countries the glory of China or recorded what they saw as splendid achievements of eastern civilization.
57. 1812 War in the United States of America was also referred to as "the Second Independent War", after which Britain fully recognized the political independence of America.
58. The history of western civilization is clearly marred by some of its dirty records as expressed in such historic events as slave trade, the Opium War, Holocaust of Jewish people during WW II or genocidal elimination of American Indians and their aboriginal

culture in early colonial periods.
59. In the 19th and early 20th centuries, some of the letters of men were strong against so-called Industrial and Urban Civilization. Among these critics were famous British novelists Thomas Hardy, Charles Dickens, and philosophers Friedrich Wilhelm Nietzsche and Heinrich Floris Schopenhauer as well as the poets T. S. Eliot and Tennyson, to name only a few.
60. Nicolas Copernicus, a famous Austrian astrologist, created Epicureanism that modified the ancient idea about the relative position between the Moon and Sun and the rest of planets. His contribution to western civilization can never be paralleled by any other people in the world.

Paraphrase the Following Sentences:
1. I think, therefore I am.
2. Know thyself!
3. Waste not, want not.
4. A house divided against itself can't stand for long.
5. An empty sack can never stand upright.
6. The Achilles' heel of John is his Hamlet character.
7. It is always right to err on the side of life.
8. April showers bring May flowers.
9. Homer sometimes nods.
10. To err is human; to forgive, divine.
11. Things without remedy should be without regard.
12. Man proposes, God disposes.
13. God help those who help themselves.
14. A flower does not make a spring.
15. Plato is dear to me, but dearer still is truth.
16. A gentle man is, rather than does.
17. Money is like much, not good unless spread out.
18. To be or not to be, that is the question.
19. Love knows no bounds.
20. Nothing succeeds like success.
21. Beauty buys no beef.
22. Life is like a Damocles' banquet. The sword is ever suspended.
23. Today a man, tomorrow a mouse.
24. Nothing is absolute but tax and death.
25. Knowing truths sets people free.
26. Great minds think alike.
27. Rome is not built in one day.
28. No pains, no gains.
29. Speak little, trust a few and harm none.
30. East and West, home is the best.

Write an essay on the following sentences in about 150 words each:
Topic Group 1:
1. Adversity leads to prosperity.
2. The shortest distance between two points is always under-construction.
3. Love all, trust a few and do wrong to none or harm none.

4. A hedge between keeps friendship green.
5. Is it better to be a Jack of all trades than a master of one or otherwise?
6. A little absence makes heart grow fonder.
7. It is a house of card to predict what will exactly occur tomorrow.
8. Face the music and you will face the honor.
9. The name of the game is the game of the name in commercials industry.
10. Barking dogs never bite.
11. For when wine is in, the wit is out.
12. Change a lane, change a life.

Topic Group 2:
1. All roads lead to Rome.
2. The fear of God is beginning of wisdom.
3. Is it right morally to rob Peter to pay Paul. Or economically?
4. Luck is the residue of all designs.
5. Well begun, half done.
6. Love of wealth is spring of all evil.
7. Grasp all, lose all.
8. East and West, home is the best.
9. It is wrong to put a cart before a horse.
10. Fortune favors fools.
11. A fall into a pit, a gain in your wit.
12. Where there is despair, there is hope.

Topic Group 3:
1. There is no use crying over the split milk.
2. Birds of a feather flock together.
3. Still waters run deep.
4. The on-looker sees most of the game.
5. Nothing will come out of nothing.
6. Death ends all debts.
7. It is a house of card to predict what will exactly occur tomorrow.
8. One man's meat is another man's poison.
9. The friend of my enemy is my enemy and the enemy of my enemy is my friend.
10. Never say never.
11. It is a profitable wisdom to know when we have done enough. Much time and pains are spared in not flattering ourselves against probabilities.
12. Power comes from gun powder.

Topic Group 4:
1. Everybody's business is nobody's business.
2. The best is the enemy of good.
3. Ends justify means.
4. Might is right.
5. All is well that ends well.
6. Good and bad things average out in life in the end.
7. Do unto others as you would they should do unto you.
8. England's difficulty is Ireland's opportunity.
9. Of the two evils choose the less.

10. Hope smiles on efforts.
11. The grass is always greener on the other side of a mountain.
12. Never give up while there is hope; but hope not beyond reason for that shows more desire than judgment.

Ending remarks for this part: *these few sets of exercise papers are designed and prepared as a retrospective tool for the course participants to review and reflect upon what has been taught and discussed during the course time. They are not meant to test the course participants for their command of the course contents alone. Rather, they are intended to facilitate and deepen their understanding of the course contents and it is hoped that the course participants may from time to time spend some time doing these exercises so that they can get more familiar with what they have learned in the course. It should also be noted here that there are no accurate and authoritative answers to the statements listed above. Some of the historical facts are still subject to debates. People need to keep exploring the truths as reflected in these facts. It is one of the purposes for this course to promote the spirit of science which is expressed in a common proverb prevalent in the West that facts speak louder than words. Knowing truths sets people free and we must seek truths from facts to guide our life so that we can become less silly if not wiser in understanding the natural law that governs this universe in which we live and experience. People grow mentally through learning and experiencing something new, which marks a journey from a kingdom of necessity to a kingdom of freedom. This journey is too long for one individual to be able to cover it all for life time. However, for whole human beings, to cover this journey is like a relay running match in which one generation should pave the way for the next. So long as we keep running and exploring along the way, there is always something of a new view for us to appreciate. It is from this perspective that immense pleasure can be found in learning and exploring the unknown.*

Appendix Ⅰ

The Western Cultural Tradition Course Outline and Descriptions

Editor's remarks: *The following course outline is adapted from the western Tradition preview book written by Eugen Weber, professor of western Civilization at UCLA, first published by Macmillan Publishing Company. The course outline mentioned above has been creatively edited and revised and substantially enriched by Zhang Xiaoli, a faculty member of China Foreign Affairs University, who conducts a selective course of western Cultural Studies for graduate and undergraduate students. This course outline is intended for the course participants or attendants to try to form a clear picture of what is mentioned as highlights in the course through the introduction of the major themes in western cultural studies. The contents hereby included are chiefly theme-based and roughly chronologically arranged. It is believed that through this course, interested learners in western cultural studies will have a more in-depth understanding of the topic under discussion and envisage a systematic guidance in their future pursuit of the subject at a higher level. Please note that the units marked with asterisk are the ones for detailed and underlined study and the rest of the units are for general reference.*

Opening Unit * : Culture as a Key Concept Defined

Any discussion of the western cultural tradition begins with a clear understanding of what is meant by "Culture" which is so inclusive and comprehensive a term that it defies a simple and singular definition. It is a cultural phenomenon to define culture itself. Once defined within a framework commonly accepted, culture looms large as a key concept for this course. Cultural study is a new subject that is more of an interdisciplinary subject than an independent one based upon such subjects as history, anthropology, sociology, archaeology, theology, linguistics, economics and politics. Culture as an academic term has not been in existence for a long time. It is a result of human awareness of their own dilemmas and destinies. To promote cultural understanding among different cultural groups is of vital importance to the maintenance of world peace and stability. Cultural diversity and tolerance should be viewed as a sign of a civilized society in which peoples of different religious beliefs and political creeds can co-exist in harmony. (Please refer to Unit One-1/2/3 and Unit Two-2 of A Concise Textbook of western Cultural Studies, hereafter called the Textbook for short)

Unit One *

Episode 1. The Dawn of History
Episode 2. The Ancient Egyptians

A vivid account of the evolution of the human race, the origins of agriculture, and a look at one of the earliest civilizations that gave rise to the emergence of western civilization. Any topic concerning any civilization should begin with a review of the definition of culture and its history. Civilization of Ancient Egypt is viewed as the earliest ancestor of western civilization for simply geographical reason. Egypt developed the earliest form of agriculture in Mediterranean Region upon which people lived in settlements, ending the nomadic civilization. (Please refer to Unit One-2 of the Textbook)

Through or after this Unit, with the help of the class conductor and by reading relevant materials and viewing related video materials, it is expected that

Students should understand the following issues:
- Influences on the evolution of early anthropoids (man-like apes).
- The relationship between early religions and the development of agriculture.
- Characteristics of the Nile Valley and their influence on Egyptian society.
- The pharaoh's changing role in Egyptian politics.
- Ways in which art and architecture reflect Egyptian social and political life.
- The relationship between Egyptian politics and religion.

Unit Two

Episode 3. Mesopotamia
Episode 4. From Bronze to Iron

An examination of how western Europe, in many respects, owes more to Mesopotamian culture than to Egypt. The region geographically called Asia Minor now is widely regarded as the cradle of many civilizations that have produced far-reaching impact upon the birth of Mediterranean civilization which is ancestral to western civilization at large. Trade, commercial transactions, conquest of nature, human intellectual evolutions, technological progress (tools in particular), exchanges of different cultures and lifestyles eventually led human beings to a higher level of social and economic development.

Through or after this Unit, with the help of the class conductor and by reading relevant materials and viewing related video materials, it is expected that

Students should understand the following issues:
- Ways in which Mesopotamian civilizations were shaped by the dangers to which they were exposed as expressed in an antithetical pair Nature versus Man.
- Major technological and intellectual contributions of Mesopotamian civilizations.
- Roles of the great empires in spreading culture and technology.
- Methods used by peoples on the edge of the empires to resist more powerful states.
- Ways in which trade and economic issues led to important social and intellectual achievements.
- The impact of literacy on the spread and development of civilization.
- The continual mixing of peoples and cultures throughout the empires and their peripheries.

Unit Three *

Episode 5. The Rise of Greek Civilization
Episode 6. Greek Thought

An exploration of the growth of Greek civilization and the deep connection between its philosophy and political institutions is conducted in this unit so that the genetic nature of Greek civilization in relation to the whole western culture is deliberated and stressed. Human beings have started to appear more of a thinking animal than a mere biological creature whose meaning of life existence goes far beyond simple survival against odds of nature. It is with creative thinking ability that human beings have made a final departure from their barbarian past and embarked upon the journey toward a brighter future. (Please refer to Unit Five-2 of the Textbook)

Through or after this Unit, with the help of the class conductor and by reading relevant materials and viewing related video materials, it is expected that

Students should understand the following issues:
- The contrast between values of the Greek heroic age and those of the classical period.
- Some factors that united the Greeks despite the many problems that separated them.
- Problems that led to destructive rivalries among Greek cities.
- The most important questions addressed by Greek thinkers.
- The relationship of Greek art to Greek history, politics, and society.

Unit Four

Episode 7. Alexander the Great
Episode 8. The Hellenistic Age

Greek culture establishes its own dominant position throughout the eastern Mediterranean world as the successors of Alexander the Great establish empires of their own. Alexander III of Macedon (336—323 BC), student of Aristotle, better known as Alexander the Great, is remembered in history for his leadership role in the Eastward Expedition that spread the influence of Greek culture by extending his power to as far as present day India. He died very young at the age of 32 and his mysterious and sudden death changed history. Along with G. J. Gaius Julius Caesar, Hannibal Barca and Napoléon Bonaparte, Alexander the Great is deemed one of the four greatest military leaders in western history. Alexander's legacy includes the cultural diffusion his conquests engendered. He founded some twenty cities that bore his name, most notably Alexandria in Egypt. Alexander's settlement of Greek colonists and the resulting spread of Greek culture in the East resulted in a new Hellenistic civilization, aspects of which were still evident in the traditions of the Byzantine Empire in the mid-15th century. His role in connecting the East and West and in spreading western influence outside Europe is immense and unparelled. During his reign and after his death, Greece entered into the Hellenistic Age. The Hellenistic period or Hellenistic era of history in the West is the period which followed the expeditions and conquests of Alexander the Great who extended his influence of power through wars to Asia. It was so named by the historian J. G. Droysen. During this time, Greek cultural influence and power was at its zenith in Europe and Asia. It is often considered a period of transition, sometimes even of decline or decadence, between the brilliance of the Greek Classical era and the emergence of the Roman Empire. The lesson the Hellenistic Age revealed is that once a civilization reaches its apex, it has started to decline, a motif promulgated in Chinese traditional philosophy as represented by Taoism that things in natural as well as in social worlds will develop in the opposite direction when they become extreme. (Please refer to Unit Five-2 of the Textbook for more detailed information)

Through or after this Unit, with the help of the class conductor and by reading relevant materials and viewing related video materials, it is expected that

Students should understand the following issues:
- Reasons why various Greek states finally supported Alexander's campaigns in the East.
- Motives for Alexander and his successors to demand, in parts of their realms, to be worshiped as gods.
- Differences between Hellenistic and classical art and the causes of those differences.
- Ways in which Greek culture affected or failed to affect conquered peoples.
- Principal features of the philosophical movements of the Hellenistic period.
- Similarities and differences among various mystery religions.

Unit Five *

Episode 9. The Rise of Rome
Episode 10. The Roman Empire

A small city in Italy rises to become one of the greatest empires and most influential forces of the western tradition. What is the secret behind this is the question that interests so many historians for so long. Edward Gibbon once said that instead of looking into the reason why Roman Empire declined and eventually fell, people should pay more attention to why it could persist and remained so powerful for so long. The Roman Empire is the first human empire that has its territory span over three continents, providing a lot of historic materials for later generations to study its social structure, daily life and above all, its values that influenced the whole western civilization. (Please refer to Unit Five-1 of the Textbook for more detailed information in this aspect)

Through or after this Unit, with the help of the class conductor and by reading relevant materials and viewing related video materials, it is expected that

Students should understand the following issues:
- Cultural and economic strengths of the early Roman republic.
- Changes in Rome's policies toward conquered nations.
- The Roman state's successes and failures in adapting to new social conditions.
- Ways in which social forces shaped the Roman army.
- Ways in which the army affected Roman politics.
- Principal differences between the Roman republic and the new state established by Augustus.

Unit Six *

Episode 11. Early Christianity
Episode 12. The Rise of the Church

The growth and spread of Christianity influences in a hostile empire is a single most important event in the West. As one of the three origins of the western culture, Christianity as a dominant religion in the West has played an indisputable and irreplaceable role in shaping the orientation of western culture. Its influence is still strongly felt even today. Church as a strong social power, along with state power, governs the operation of society in the West while providing a substantial spiritual pillar for people to deal with various adverse elements of life. One of the biggest differences between the East and West lies in their different attitudes toward theological beliefs and religious faiths, which constitutes a typical feature of the western culture that has shaped basic mentality of westerners who attach great importance to the meaning of an after-world life. It is safe to say that without knowing something about Christianity, the study of western culture will have no sign-post for orientation as religion is a solid spiritual buttress of the West. (Please refer to Unit Three-1, 3 and 4 of the Textbook for more detailed information)

Through or after this Unit, with the help of the class conductor and by reading relevant materials and viewing related video materials, it is expected that

Students should understand the following issues:
- Important aspects of Roman humanism.
- Sources of long-term instability in the Roman Empire.
- Sources of instability and uncertainty that led many to seek consolation in religious creeds.

- Reasons for the rise of Christianity.
- Some of the continuities between Judaism and Christianity.
- Similarities and differences between Christianity and the mystery religions.
- Reasons behind Christian intolerance for other religions as well as dissension within the Church.
- The significance of a shift from God to Man in the West.
- Significance of spiritual belief in people's daily life.

Unit Seven

Episode 13. The Decline of Rome
Episode 14. The Fall of Rome

The Roman Empire is battered from without by a series of barbarian invasions and from within by moral decay. With the fall of Rome, the church and barbarian kingdoms become heir to the western empire. The fall of Rome has proved a rule of cultural transformation and replacement. One of the major themes of western culture is change, transition and replacement. Change is constant and the only thing that does not change is change itself. It is through constant change that society is advancing for good or ill. Change is natural law and nobody can stop it. The best thing people can do is to ride over the tide or keep pace with the times. The summary of the decline and eventual fall of Rome presents a hard lesson that nothing can remain unchanged. It is true that Rome is not built in a day, neither is it destroyed in a day. There is always a long and bumpy process of evolution for anything to change. The process of change is accumulative, but the result of it can be sudden and radical, which is expressed in a rule that quantitative change leads to eventual qualitative change. (Please refer to Unit Three-1 of the Textbook for more detailed and specific information)

Through or after this Unit, with the help of the class conductor and by reading relevant materials and viewing related video materials, it is expected that

Students should understand the following issues:
- Economic, administrative, and military causes of the fall of the western empire.
- The economic and political relationship between Roman cities and countryside.
- Causes that tempted or forced barbarians to invade the Roman Empire.
- Characteristics of various barbarian peoples and the tribes that were quickest to adopt the empire's customs in the process of civilization versus barbarism.
- Successes and failures of the Roman Empire's attempts to save itself in the third and fourth centuries.
- The beginnings of western Europe's manorial system.

Unit Eight *

Episode 15. The Byzantine Empire
Episode 16. The Fall of Byzantine

Following the fall of Rome, the Byzantine Empire based in Constantinople becomes the repository of culture from Egypt, Greece and Rome, thus preserving and enriching the ancient world throughout the Mediterranean. It is still a mystery for historians why the Byzantine Empire could persist so long amid a very adverse survival environment. The Byzantine Empire is a unique one in that it successfully combined many elements of both the West and East, forming a mixture of cultures that reflect the best of human civilization. The study of history of the Byzantine Empire remains a weak link in history study and a lot more is yet to be explored and discovered to provide useful lessons for current world to learn.

Through or after this Unit, with the help of the class conductor and by reading relevant materials and viewing related video materials, it is expected that

Students should understand the following issues:
- Principal differences among Islam, Orthodox Christianity, and Roman Catholicism.
- Political consequences that arose from these differences.
- Ways in which Byzantine and Islamic empires preserved and transmitted culture.
- Strengths and weaknesses of the Byzantine emperors.
- Military strengths and weaknesses of the Byzantine and Islamic empires.

Unit Nine

Episode 17. The Dark Ages
Episode 18. The Age of Charlemagne

A new political and economic order formed in the centuries after the fall of the western empire.

Through or after this Unit, with the help of the class conductor and by reading relevant materials and viewing related video materials, it is expected that

Students should understand the following issues:
- The impact of Christianity on barbarian cultures.
- Sources of the church's power within these cultures.
- Ways in which the church promoted learning and education, especially in the monasteries.
- The most important economic developments of the period.
- The Carolingians' attempts to create a new European empire.
- Effects of the ninth- and tenth-century barbarian invasions.

Unit Ten

Episode 19. The Middle Ages
Episode 20. The Feudal Order

A new society develops in the early Middle Ages, as Europe struggles to repel successive waves of invaders. The Middle Ages are also referred to as the Dark Ages during which time people are living in fetters, being unable to control their own destiny. However, a new age is going to dawn, pushing history forward by leaps and bounds and creating a brand-new social order.

Through or after this Unit, with the help of the class conductor and by reading relevant materials and viewing related video materials, it is expected that

Students should understand the following issues:
- Conditions in the European countryside that created feudal relations.
- Economic and military factors that affected feudal relations.
- Difficulties faced by medieval rulers who tried to maintain large states or empires.
- Changes that developed as Europe became more prosperous in the years after 1000.
- Goals and achievements of various crusades.
- The growth of increasingly secular culture.

Unit Eleven

Episode 21. Common Life in the Middle Ages
Episode 22. Cities and Cathedrals of the Middle Ages

An exploration into both the harsh realities of daily life in the Middle Ages and the blossoming of European trade and culture epitomized in the construction of some of the world's most magnificent churches will be presented here in this unit.

Through or after this Unit, with the help of the class conductor and by reading relevant materials and viewing related video materials, it is expected that

Students should understand the following issues:
- Sources of conflict between the church and secular powers in the Middle Ages.
- Limitations in food and shelter suffered during the Middle Ages.
- Health standards and disease patterns that struck western Europe during the Middle Ages.
- Cultural and economic forces at work in building the great medieval churches.
- The development of important trading patterns and techniques.
- Social and economic forces that affected the growth of European commerce.

Unit Twelve

Episode 23. The Late Middle Ages
Episode 24. The National Monarchies

An examination of the importance of religious and political thought and the expansion of great states in the late fifteenth century, a time during which many rulers were centralizing power within their own domains. (Please refer to Unit Seven-1 of the Textbook)

Through or after this Unit, with the help of the class conductor and by reading relevant materials and viewing related video materials, it is expected that

Students should understand the following issues:
- Major wars of the late Middle Ages.
- Economic recovery in Europe at the end of the Middle Ages.
- Some of the most influential religious leaders and thinkers of the High Middle Ages.
- The contributions of Thomas Aquinas to political thought.
- The expansion of France, Spain, and the empire.
- Successes and failures in the attempts to centralize power.
- The relationship between warfare and the development of the modern state.

Unit Thirteen *

Episode 25. The Renaissance and the Age of Discovery
Episode 26. The Renaissance and the New World

Great European explorers share the Renaissance spirit that appears in the works of artists, scholars, and writers of the period. Regarded as one of the three movements that shaped the history of western culture, the Renaissance has exerted tremendous influence upon the West, establishing a solid tradition of humanism in its cultural heritage. Since the Renaissance, the influence of the Church has started to decline and there has been a shift from God-dominated world to man-centered life in Europe. Man has been given more importance along with his emotions and feelings, artistic creativities, secular pursuits and material goals. (For more detailed information in this regard, please refer to Unit Six-1 and Unit Seven-1 of the Textbook)

Through or after this Unit, with the help of the class conductor and by reading relevant materials and viewing related video materials, it is expected that

Students should understand the following issues:
- Technical and scientific developments of the Middle Ages that paved and smoothed the way for and contributed to discoveries of the Renaissance.
- The relationship between the secular and the divine as it appears in Renaissance art.
- The contribution of the printing press to the development of intellectual life.
- The impact of the great explorers on intellectual life.
- The most important aspects of European humanism.
- Ways in which European intellectuals developed comparative habits of thought.
- European reaction to the inhabitants of newly discovered areas of the world.

Unit Fourteen *

Episode 27. The Reformation
Episode 28. The Rise of the Middle Class

The Protestant Reformation arises as many Europeans, particularly in cities, look for new forms of piety and worship. The significance of the Reformation is so tremendous that the whole history of the West would have been totally different without it. The Reformation provides a religious justification for the rise of capitalistic mode of production that in turn has led to the rise of the Middle Class. With the emergence of the Middle Class, the whole social structure of the West has fundamentally changed from a hierarchical one to a more egalitarian one with people's social position chiefly determined by their material properties rather than their status of births. The birth of the Middle Class has provided a stabilizer and buffer zone for the capitalistic society, which modifies if not invalidates Marxian theory about class struggle that eventually will lead to a revolution that destroys capitalistic social, political and economic system. The prospect of being able to become a middle class member through self-struggle offers a rosy vision for working class people to change their economic fate and political status.

Through or after this Unit, with the help of the class conductor and by reading relevant materials and viewing related video materials, it is expected that

Students should understand the following issues:
- The means by which rulers centralized power in the fifteenth and sixteenth centuries.
- Financial and economic bases of the new states.
- The changing economy of the sixteenth century.
- Ways in which Protestant reformers reacted to the Catholic church's popular, institutional piety.
- Ways in which Protestantism was suited to the urban bourgeoisie.
- Ways in which painters portrayed the relationship between everyday life and the sacred.
- Counter measures taken by the Catholic Church during the Counter-Reformation.

Unit Fifteen

Episode 29. The Wars of Religion
Episode 30. The Rise of Trading Cities

While, much of Europe is devastated by wars between Protestants and Catholics, trading begins to transform European politics and economics. (Please refers to Unit Three-1 and Unit Eight-1 of the Textbook)

Through or after this Unit, with the help of the class conductor and by reading relevant materials and viewing related video materials, it is expected that

Students should understand the following issues:
- Causes and results of sixteenth- and seventeenth-century religious civil wars.
- Ways in which international politics complicated the religious civil wars.
- Varying patterns of religious tolerance that appeared by the mid-seventeenth century.
- The importance of politiques as statesmen.
- The most important cities and trade routes to the European economy.
- The special qualities of art produced in trading cities.
- The development of the Dutch Republic into a new state.
- The major scientific discoveries of the period.
- Commercial spirit in changing common people's material well-being.
- westerners' idea about commercial mentality in the face of religion.

Unit Sixteen

Episode 31. The Age of Absolutism
Episode 32. Absolutism and the Social Contract

Some rulers, particularly in France, claim they are answerable to no earthly authority, while in England some political theorists argue that authority depends on the consent of the governed.

Through or after this Unit, with the help of the class conductor and by reading relevant materials and viewing related video materials, it is expected that

Students should understand the following issues:
- The major characteristics of political absolutism in the seventeenth century.
- Causes of political weakness in France during the first sixty years of the seventeenth century.
- Attempts by French statesmen to end political disorder.
- The changing status of French nobility during the seventeenth century.
- Ways in which art and architecture reflected political authority.
- Moral and political aspects of seventeenth-century French tragedy.
- The outcome of the conflicts between Parliament and the English crown.
- Ways in which Hobbes and Locke reflect the political events of their times.

Unit Seventeen *

Episode 33. The Enlightened Despots
Episode 34. The Enlightenment

During the Age of the Enlightenment, philosophers and social thinkers have become pioneering groups to challenge the status quo and to put forward new ideas that have changed people's mentality. In western Europe philosophers argue that the dignity of man can best be raised through practical knowledge and reforms. The Age of the Enlightenment is one of discoveries and explorations of new ideas and knowledge which have rendered great intellectual power to humankind who relying on their reason and wisdom have begun to reach for new frontiers. The Enlightenment is a great movement that has broadened people's vision and horizon, freeing them from any bondages imposed by the old feudal society and ignorance of the world around them. It is through the Enlightenment that people have begun to have more confidence in themselves and demonstrate more creative power in both natural and social scientific discoveries.

Through or after this Unit, with the help of the class conductor and by reading relevant materials and viewing related video materials, it is expected that

Students should understand the following issues:
- The relationship between warfare and economic growth.
- The rise and decline of major European powers.
- The relationship between the enlightened despots and the French philosophers.
- The relationship between the enlightened despots and their subjects.
- The ways in which the rococo style was a reaction against the more ponderous architectural and artistic style of Louis XIV of France.

Unit Eighteen *

Episode 35. The Enlightenment and Society
Episode 36. The Modern Philosophers

Many writers think of themselves as social reformers and work to change society and they have created a new age for common people to realize their own goals through self-struggle. (Please refer to Unit Seven-2 of the Textbook)

Through or after this Unit, with the help of the class conductor and by reading relevant materials and viewing related video materials, it is expected that

Students should understand the following issues:
- The relationship between economic growth on one hand, political and social ideas on the other.
- Causes of economic growth in the eighteenth century.
- The influence of science on religious ideas and the growth of intellectual relativism.
- The development of utilitarianism and the growth of laissez-faire economics.
- How did human beings in the West begin to pay more attention to individual benefits?

Unit Nineteen *

Episode 37. The American Revolution
Episode 38. The American Republic

The American Revolution is examined as a test case of Enlightenment ideals. Nobody can deny the significance of the birth of the USA for the development of the West. The single event that occurred on July 4, 1776 has changed the West as well as the human history once and for all. America is now indisputably viewed as the representative of the western tradition, amplified and glorified. American success story is a perfect version of the success story of the West, inheriting the best of the western traditions and improving them based upon its own fine features, which has facilitated the formation of an idea that American culture is the core of the western culture. In a sense, America has become the synonym of the West, invading and conquering the whole world with its products, material and cultural, ideas and values and institutions.

Through or after this Unit, with the help of the class conductor and by reading relevant materials and viewing related video materials, it is expected that

Students should understand the following issues:
- European myths about America and what they revel about European society.
- Patterns of European settlement throughout North and South America.
- Ways in which the American colonies became important factors in eighteenth century international politics and its impact upon future global political patterns.
- Ways in which England's imperialism created tensions with its North American colonies.
- Social and political divisions in the new republic.

- Tensions between political ideals and practice.
- The social and economic conditions that gave rise to the political ideals in the United States.
- The current position of the USA and its pop culture in the West as well as in the world.

Unit Twenty

Episode 39. The Death of the Old Regime and Birth of New Ideas/institutions
Episode 40. The French Revolution

As the kingdom of France collapses, the new revolutionary state becomes an ideal for some Europeans, a terror for others. The motto slogan of the French Revolution has become the universal value of human beings even though it appears too idealistic to realize in a class-based society when feudalistic elements linger on. However, its inspirational effect is mighty and significant, wakening many people from the passive acceptance of their unfair fate to aspire for a more free and fair society. A more enlightened and reasoned society is going to be established in the West, which has set a course for whole human beings. The French Revolution is a violent revolution that has destroyed the old social structure through fierce force as the old regime people were reluctant to adapt themselves to the new ideas and a new social structure aiming to promote common interest of mass people.

Through or after this Unit, with the help of the class conductor and by reading relevant materials and viewing related video materials, it is expected that

Students should understand the following issues:
- Stabilizing factors in the United States following the revolution.
- The fiscal weakness of the French crown.
- The factors working for and against French reform.
- The reforms of 1789.
- The transition from reform to revolution.
- New styles of warfare.
- Creation of the French Empire.
- The enduring legacy of the revolution.
- The impact of the French Revolution's logo ideals.

Unit Twenty-One *

Episode 41. The Industrial Revolution
Episode 42. The Industrial World

New sources of power and improved production techniques begin the age of industrial expansion. With the Industrial Revolution, human society has entered into a new age in which an unprecedented mode of production has arisen, greatly liberating the productive power of humankind. The Industrial Revolution is not a revolution in industrial field alone. Instead, it has produced tremendous effect on social structure and economic patterns. (Please refer to Unit Eight-2 of the Textbook for further information)

Through or after this Unit, with the help of the class conductor and by reading relevant materials and viewing related video materials, it is expected that

Students should understand the following issues:
- The relationship between revolutions in industry, commerce, communications, and agriculture.
- The network of markets and sources of raw materials created by the industrial revolution.

- Political and military effects of economic interdependence.
- The most significant improvements in the European standard of living.
- Effects of the popular press on social and political life.
- Ways in which nineteenth-century economic developments created a new kind of city.
- The significance of the Industrial Revolution in human civilization evolution.
- Different views concerning the aftermath of the Industrial Revolution.

Unit Twenty-Two

Episode 43. Revolution and the Romantics
Episode 44. The Age of the Nation-states

By the early nineteenth-century many central and eastern Europeans aspire to establish independent countries by freeing themselves from the bondages of colonialism. However, the role of colonialism in history should be viewed through dialectical perspectives just as many historical events that have produced dual effects upon the social development of human beings if observed in a long run. What has happened in history must have its own inherent logic of evolution. The rise of the nation-states has changed global pattern of politics and economy. (Please refer to Unit Nine-2 of the Textbook for more information)

Through or after this Unit, with the help of the class conductor and by reading relevant materials and viewing related video materials, it is expected that

Students should understand the following issues:
- Revolutionary aspirations that arose in many countries following the American and French revolutions.
- The outlines of romanticism in art, literature, and social thought.
- The relationship between romanticism and social reform.
- Similarities and differences among European movements and reforms.
- The development of a system of great powers during the nineteenth century.
- Patterns of European colonialism.
- Areas of greatest political instability.
- The hidden contradictions in European countries that paved the way for further reforms.
- Why did Europe first enter the age of modernization?

Unit Twenty-Three *

Episode 45. A New Public
Episode 46. Fin de Siècle

By the late nineteenth century the productivity of the Industrial Revolution is raising the standard of living throughout Europe and North America. The world has thus been divided into industrial nations and non-industrial nations, rich states and poor states and developed countries and under-developed countries, forming a global pattern of political and economic structure that has still persisted today. Development of mass communication becomes an increasingly important force in modern society. (Please consult Unit Nine-1 and 2 of the Textbook)

Through or after this Unit, with the help of the class conductor and by reading relevant materials and viewing related video materials, it is expected that

Students should understand the following issues:
- Ways in which the needs of the modern state affected social and economic legislation.
- Ways in which the working class and the peasantry began to get in the mainstream of social and economic life amid the process of mass democracy that eventually led to

representative democracy.
- Changing social and economic relations between the cities and countryside.
- Social and political consequences of widespread literacy.
- The development of large-scale organized sports.
- The rise of social Darwinism and its influence in Germany.
- The relationship between mass culture and the avant-garde.
- The social mentality toward the end of the century.
- The emergence of a new life-style as represented by leisure class.
- The global contradictions that led to two major world wars.
- Is there any other way to solve insolvable issues among nations than wars?

Unit Twenty-Four

Episode 47. The First World War and the Rise of Fascism
Episode 48. The Second World War

Wars and revolution arise from the unresolved conflicts of the previous century: class struggle, commercial and colonial rivalries, and struggles for national sovereignty.

Through or after this Unit, with the help of the class conductor and by reading relevant materials and viewing related video materials, it is expected that

Students should understand the following issues:
- Events that led to war in 1914 and factors preventing the establishment of a lasting peace in 1919.
- Why Russia, Italy, and Germany developed radically new kinds of states in the years between the wars.
- Reasons why England and France were unable to mount a more successful opposition to Germany and Italy before the outbreak of WW I.
- Ways in which the United States alternately intervened and stayed aloof from European affairs between 1914 and 1939.
- Ways in which Hitler's allies helped and hindered his ability to wage war.
- The United States' contribution to the Allied War effort.
- The motives and basic methods of Hitler's genocide policy.

Unit Twenty-Five *

Episode 49. The Cold War
Episode 50. Europe and the Third World

The United States and Soviet Union, the two great victors of World War II, dominate Europe while poor countries of the Third World try to develop in the midst of superpower rivalries and competition from industrialized nations. Through or after this Unit, with the help of the class conductor and by reading relevant materials and viewing related video materials, it is expected that

Students should understand the following issues:
- The division of Europe into Soviet and western spheres of influence.
- Ways in which Europe was affected by the changing relationship between Europe and the former Soviet Union against the background of Cold War.
- Relationships among military, political, and economic powers in Europe and the Third World.
- Distribution of wealth between the Third World and industrialized nations.

- The legacy of colonial imperialism in the Third World.
- Successes and failures of economic development in the Third World.
- The signs of the end of the Cold War.
- The legacy and aftermath of the Cold War.
- A new world order for political and economic development.

Unit Twenty-Six *

Episode 51. The Technological Revolution
Episode 52. Toward the Future

The concluding unit demonstrates the speed with which modern life has changed and considers the future of western civilization. With the coming of what is called "Post-industrial Society", human social structure and their daily life have been greatly transformed. The future of humankind in general and that of the West in particular is a big concern to everyone amid the age of economic globalization and knowledge economy. It remains yet to be seen if human future is rosy and gloomy given our current way of living which endangers our environment on the one hand and aggravates our climate on the other. Human beings must have a sound and thorough reflection upon themselves and their way of life based upon the excessive and constant acquisition of material wealth at the cost of losing spiritual souls and moral codes for a more simplistic and thrift life style, more specifically, a low-carbon life style.

Through or after this Unit, with the help of the class conductor and by reading relevant materials and viewing related video materials, it is expected that

Students should understand the following issues:
- The most important medical developments during this period.
- The development of atomic weapons.
- The dual role of science and technology in modern times.
- The interplay of inventions in transportation and communications.
- Improvements in the quality of daily life.
- Progress and setbacks in the emancipation of women.
- The nature of modern education.

Appendix Ⅱ

A Suggested Reading List for the Course of the Western Cultural Studies

1. Lawrence Cunningham/John Reich. *Culture and Values: A Survey of Humanities*. The Florida State University, 1990.
2. Marvin Perry. *western Civilization: A Brief History*. Cengage Learning, 2010.
3. Leften Stavrianos. *The World to 1500: a Global History*, 7th Edition. Random House Publisher, 2009.
4. L. S. Stavriano. *The World Since 1500: a Global History*, 8th Edition. Random House Publisher, 2009.
5. Philip J. Adler and Randall L. Pouwel. *World Civilizations, Volume Ⅱ: Since 1500*. New York, 2010.
6. McKay, Hill and Buckler. *A History of World Societies, Volume Ⅱ: Since 1500*. London, 2008.
7. Paul Levine and Harry Papasotiriou. *America Since 1945, The American Moment*, Second Edition. Palgrave Macmillan, 2011.
8. Zhang Xiaoli. *An Concise Anthology of Economics and Economy*, CFAU Edition. Beijing, 2012.
9. 张晓立. 美国文化变迁探索—从清教文化到消费文化的历史演变. 光明日报出版社, 2010年。
10. 张晓立. 解析美国高等教育. 中央编译出版社, 2011年。
11. 张晓立. 财富意识与文明演化：一个美国案例的诠释. 光明日报出版社, 2012年。

Postscript/Final Remarks for the Whole Textbook

　　An intellectual effort such as writing or compiling or editing a book is brain-raking and laborious. At the same time, it is also very interesting and rewarding. The process of having this concise textbook edited, compiled and eventually printed is a joyful one. It is sincerely hoped that readers will also find it is interesting and rewarding to read this book for the ideas contained in it are a result of classical and time-tested wisdom that can provide both useful information and inspiring vision. For non-native speakers of English, this concise textbook serves dual purpose. On the one hand, it is intended for non-native speakers of English to read something useful in English so that they can improve their English reading skill. On the other hand, and more importantly, this concise textbook is prepared for those who fully understand the fact that a basic understanding of western culture is of paramount importance to English language learning. It is well acknowledged that culture and language are closely intertwined. If one wants to learn a language well, he has to make some further effort in getting the culture well understood which the given language expresses. One can never fully and profoundly realize and appreciate the very essence of William Shakespeare's dramas and sonnets without being able to read them in the original language in which those masterpieces were produced. The best way to understand everlasting and profound values of German classical philosophy is to read Hegel and Nietzsche in Germany. Russian is the best vehicle to understand and appreciate Pushkin and Turgenev. Much has been lost in the translation of French literary works. Chinese ancient poems are untranslatable. The importance of language in understanding the culture in which this certain given language is used can never be over-stressed. And the value of culture in understanding the language of this culture is also beyond calculation. Culturally speaking, language is, in a sense, a philosophy, which expresses the core value of language in exhibiting the very ideas and ideals of human beings in their intellectual endeavor to bring a happy life to their physical and mental existence.

　　Learning should be viewed as a life time process of experiencing pleasure instead of accumulating pressure and sorrows. British philosopher and thinker Bertrand Russell's expression of equating accumulating knowledge to increasing of sorrows should be best understood as a philosophical reflection of his personal experience, which people of different social and intellectual backgrounds may agree or disagree for various reasons. As a compiler of this concise textbook, I personally hope it shall bring more pleasure to its readers than otherwise. Thus, I expect that if this concise textbook can bring some sort of mental pleasure and practical utility to the reader, my assiduous and pleasurable effort in getting this textbook published has not been spent in vain. Few books deserve the title of magnum opuses. Few writers deserve the title of great masters. There is only one Shakespeare and there is only one Newton and there is only one Plato. All writers want to leave readers with their Magnum Opuses, which is impossible. But it is possible, and can be expected that some readers will produce their own magnificent books with the academic influence they have achieved from Magnum Opuses of great minds in the past. That is the everlasting and insurmountable value of great books produced by past sagas and gurus. To their intellectual contributions, academic wisdom and life experience, the succeeding generations owe too much to their forefathers. It is along with this line of path that human beings keep making progress with an aspiration that tomorrow should, and will be better than today.